TERRORISM, 1996–2001

TERRORISM, 1996–2001

A CHRONOLOGY

VOLUME 1

Edward F. Mickolus

with Susan L. Simmons

GREENWOOD PRESS

Westport, Connecticut • London

Library of Congress Cataloging-in-Publication Data

Mickolus, Edward F.
     Terrorism, 1996–2001 : a chronology / Edward F. Mickolus with Susan L. Simmons.
         p. cm.
     Includes bibliographical references and index.
     ISBN 0-313-31785-2 (set : alk. paper) — ISBN 0-313-32464-6 (v. 1) — ISBN
0-313-32465-4 (v. 2)
     1. Terrorism—History—Chronology. I. Simmons, Susan L. II. Title.
HV6431.M4992 2003
909.82'9'0202—dc21   2002067759

British Library Cataloguing in Publication Data is available.

Library of Congress Catalog Card Number: 2002067759
ISBN: 0-313-31785-2 (set)
       0-313-32464-6 (v.1)
       0-313-32465-4 (v.2)

First published in 2002

Greenwood Press, 88 Post Road West, Westport, CT 06881
An imprint of Greenwood Publishing Group, Inc.
www.greenwood.com

Printed in the United States of America

The paper used in this book complies with the
Permanent Paper Standard issued by the National
Information Standards Organization (Z39.48-1984).

10 9 8 7 6 5 4 3 2

DEDICATION

SEVENTY-EIGHT STARS on the Memorial Wall at the Central Intelligence Agency display the names of American patriots who gave their lives for their country. In many cases, their names cannot be revealed even in death to ensure that the lives of others are not threatened. Many of these heroes perished at the hands of terrorists. This book is dedicated to the brave patriots of the CIA and to all men, women, and children who have been harmed or killed in terrorist attacks.

CONTENTS

INTRODUCTION

SINCE 1974, I HAVE WRITTEN six chronologies on international terrorism. With each volume, I hoped that we had reached the final volume in the series, or at least that its successor would be considerably smaller. Unfortunately, terrorists are not opting for retirement packages. With the events of 2001, it seems likely that this series will perforce continue.

Using a comprehensive definition, these books consider terrorism to be the use or threat of use of violence by any individual or group for political purposes. The perpetrators may be functioning for or in opposition to established governmental authority. A key component of terrorism is that its ramifications transcend national boundaries and, in doing so, create an extended atmosphere of fear and anxiety. The effects of terrorism reach national and worldwide cultures as well as the lives of the people directly hurt by the terrorist acts. Violence becomes terrorism when the intention is to influence the attitudes and behavior of a target group beyond the immediate victims. Violence becomes terrorism when its location, the nationality or foreign ties of its perpetrators, its choice of institutional or human victims, or the mechanics of its resolution result in consequences and implications beyond the act or threat itself.

The period from January 1996 to September 2001 saw the continuation of trends identified in previous years. Loosely knit bands of individuals, often linked to one particular religious zealot, continued to be viewed as the chief threat around the world. Even so, the number of attacks perpetrated by this type of terrorist was dwarfed by the number perpetrated by the traditional "political" terrorist and by the unknown miscreant.

The period also saw the further decline of "star" terrorists from previous years. Illich Ramirez (alias Carlos the Jackal) continued to languish in a French prison. Other terrorists who had engaged in one or two spectacular attacks, such as Theodore John Kaczynski (the Unabomber), Timothy McVeigh (the Oklahoma City bombing), Asahara (the Tokyo subway sarin poisoning), and Fhimah and Megrabi (the Pan Am 103 bombing), were jailed and awaiting trial or sentencing, were imprisoned, or had had a sentence of death fulfilled.

Along with the decline of star terrorists, this period witnessed an apparent decrease in patron state support to terrorists. International sanctions on Libya, previously the world's most unabashed supporter of terrorism, were relaxed. Libya appeared to have taken a new tack in its global diplomacy, turning over the suspects in the Pan Am 103 bombing to a Scottish court for trial and otherwise appearing more cooperative.

Replacing the terrorist stars and patrons in the headlines was a stateless Saudi-born multimillionaire named Osama bin Laden, who financed, trained, and armed numerous radical Islamic groups around the world. During this time period, bin Laden and his terrorist organization, al-Qaeda, were given sanctuary by Afghanistan's Taliban, and Western attempts to bring him to justice had largely failed.

The attacks of September 11, 2001, against four American airliners, the World Trade Center Towers, the Pentagon, and an unknown target, closely followed by what appears to have been a separate spate of bioterrorist attacks using anthrax, fundamentally changed the way in which professionals and the American public think about terrorism. The attacks challenged numerous assumptions about terrorist behavior that were based on the tens of thousands of attacks chronicled earlier in this series. Osama bin Laden, al-Qaeda, and the bioterrorist responsible for these attacks adopted a modus operandi that is very different from that of terrorists seen in the previous five decades. Even in the short time since September 11, however, identifying characteristics and patterns unique to the al-Qaeda attacks have begun to emerge.

Osama bin Laden's terrorist organization puts the lie to traditional wisdom that holds that terrorists want a lot of people watching, not a lot of people dead. Al-Qaeda wants a lot of people dead. Al-Qaeda is not only willing to cause mass casualties and mass damage, it seeks to accomplish just that. The scale of the September 11 attacks dwarfed anything seen in history. The death count surpassed the global total for the previous decade of international terrorist attacks. Although figures on dollar damage and secondary effects of most international attacks are sketchy, it could be easily argued that the September 11 attacks dwarfed previous damage totals as well. The World Trade Center site damage alone will amount to at least $10 billion. Secondary effects on the stock market (a $1.3 trillion loss soon after the attacks) and on the American and world economies (more than one hundred thousand jobs lost) are equally impressive. Al-Qaeda's *least* damaging attack to date involved the suicide bombing of a U.S. battleship. The bombing of the USS *Cole* resulted in 17 U.S. Navy deaths, the deaths of the terrorists, and the disabling of the ship.

Unlike previous terrorist groups, al-Qaeda does not use attacks as a means to publicize the group or its cause. Even though the size and audacity of al-Qaeda attacks ensure publicity, publicity seems to be a byproduct for al-Qaeda. Al-Qaeda does not send confessor letters, make calls taking responsibility for its attacks, or use code words to authenticate statements to the news media. Historically, terrorists have used publicity as a means to boost their negotiating status in their efforts to reach their true goal. For this reason, traditional terrorists planned a type of attack that would allow them to control the effects of their efforts. The ability to desist as their part of the bargain (e.g., release hostages, stop bombing, reveal the location of a bomb) gave traditional terrorists something to offer in a negotiation. The size and impact of al-Qaeda's spectacular attacks withhold no consequences as a bargaining chip. In addition, the attacks have ongoing consequences that are out of the group's hands. For example, the stock market shock continues to reverberate. Bioterrorism creates mounting casualties far beyond the time and place of the original attack. (If investigators discover that bin Laden was the architect of the anthrax attacks, that fact will underscore his willingness—even his preference—to resort to any means.) Al-Qaeda chooses types of attacks in which the genie cannot be put back in the bottle. The choice of an unmitigated method parallels the *fatwah* from the group's leaders calling for all Muslims to kill all Americans. Unlike traditional terrorist groups, al-Qaeda does not seem to be seeking negotiation leverage. Al-Qaeda's goals seem to obviate bargaining, negotiation, or resolution-seeking options. This makes dealing with them far more difficult than or at least very different from dealing with other terrorist groups that use historically traditional tactics.

Al-Qaeda's ability to coordinate simultaneous, complex attacks is unparalleled in the history of terrorism. This is due in part to the fact that al-Qaeda's recruitment potential is higher than that of other terrorist groups and in part to its ability to muster immense financial resources. However, the greatest difference is a difference in methodology. Al-Qaeda is enormously patient; terrorist operations are planned years in advance. Common terrorist attacks are relatively quick and simple, and employ relatively quick, simple, and inexpensive materials and techniques such as pipe bombs or snipers. Al-Qaeda conducts practice runs, places surveillance on sites for months, orchestrates elaborate timing of simultaneous attacks, and even places sleeper agents with families in target countries, where they may await orders for years. Suicide terrorists were in existence before September 11, but September 11 was the first time that groups of suicide terrorists operated in concert. In addition, rather than adhering to one type of attack methodology, such as bombing or assassination, al-Qaeda has diversified its type of attack, using unprecedented approaches, equipment, and scenarios. The signature of an al-Qaeda attack is its audacity and its complex, meticulously planned operation, rather than forensic similarities.

Bin Laden's inherited wealth, estimated at $250 million, creates another gulf between al-Qaeda and other terrorist groups. His wealth gives his organization access to resources that previous, traditional terrorists just could not secure. The conservative estimate of bin Laden's expenditure on the September 11 attacks was between $500,000 and $1 million. This included renting homes, funding pilot and martial arts training, buying tickets for at least 19 individuals, and financing a support network strewn throughout numerous countries. Some reports indicated that bin Laden maintains cells in 60 countries. No other single terrorist group can command this level of financing or type of resources.

As significant as $500,000 is to fund a terrorist venture, it pales in comparison to the amount of damage the attacks achieved. When not viewing al-Qaeda expenditures and losses as a *jihad* victory, bin Laden's view seems to reflect a type of demonic business profit-and-loss sheet in which al-Qaeda is currently in the black. Some observers have conjectured that al-Qaeda offset its losses by selling short on airline securities and other industries deemed likely to be affected by the attacks. The result might have been millions of dollars in paper profits for al-Qaeda.

In addition, bin Laden's wealth eliminates the need for a patron state to finance his terrorist organization. What he does need is turf. Bin Laden and his organization were given a home by his patron, Afghanistan's Taliban, in exchange for financial support. This unusual arrangement of patron state as beneficiary of a terrorist's largesse created a more mutually advantageous support dynamic between state and terrorist than other terrorist groups could rally. It was a dynamic that made state diplomatic intercession unpromising if not impossible.

The horror of the September 11 attacks has altered Americans' sense of security, trust, and a just world in ways that will not become clear for decades. The pain, grief, and confusion on every American face following the attacks heralded a transformation of some kind, in some direction. Some have said that Americans had been living a life of naïveté—or denial or ignorance or arrogance—and that the sense of safety that Americans held as a prerogative effaced the daily fear and loss in which many live their lives in other countries or, indeed, in the United States itself. Whether true or not, Americans proceeded to behave as Americans always behave during times of exigency. The nation's disbelief, confusion, fear, and outrage quickly turned to determination as Americans coalesced to comfort those who grieved and to supply the needs of strangers. Letters, editorials, poll results, and demonstrations of patriotism provided evidence of a new and growing respect for and appreciation of police officers, fire fighters, medical and rescue personnel, intelligence officers, military personnel, and politicians, especially President Bush and Mayor Giuliani of New York City. Americans' faith in their system was renewed as investigators released names, biographical information, and extensive details of the movements of the terrorists within hours of the attacks. The tremendous outpouring of shared grief and support from so many countries surprised Americans and gave a new sense of connection and solidarity with the nations of the world.

Finally, the September 11 attacks returned the importance of simple fellowship to the forefront of American daily life. Americans made time to renew and strengthen lost ties, made sure family and friends knew they were loved and valued, and made each casual encounter an opportunity to forge a brief connection. The fragility of life was suddenly palpable. While I am opposed to attributing good results to evil events, I find myself hoping that Americans will continue to cherish life and each other and nurture this newfound sense of fellowship.

These volumes follow the same format and method as the previous ones, except for two changes. Instead of beginning with information updating incidents initially reported in previous volumes, the updates have been placed after the Incidents section. In addition, these volumes include an index. As in earlier volumes, the international terrorist incidents and airline hijackings are identified by an eight-digit code. The first six digits identify the date on which the incident became known as a terrorist attack to someone other than the terrorists themselves (e.g., the date the letter bomb finally arrived at the recipient's office, even though terrorists had mailed it weeks earlier; or the date on which investigators determined that an anomalous situation was terrorist in nature). The final two digits ratchet the number of attacks that took place on that date. In instances in which either the day of the month or the month itself is unknown, "99" is used in that field. For further discussions of these conventions, please consult:

Mickolus, Edward F. *Transnational Terrorism: A Chronology of Events, 1968–1979.* Westport, CT: Greenwood Press, 1980. 967 pp.

Mickolus, Edward F., Todd Sandler, and Jean M. Murdock. *International Terrorism in the 1980s: A Chronology of Events, Volume I: 1980–1983.* Ames, IA: Iowa State University Press, 1989. 541 pp.

Mickolus, Edward F., Todd Sandler, and Jean M. Murdock. *International Terrorism in the 1980s: A Chronology of Events, Volume II: 1984–1987.* Ames, IA: Iowa State University Press, 1989. 776 pp.

Mickolus, Edward F. *Terrorism, 1988–1991: A Chronology of Events and A Selectively Annotated Bibliography.* Westport, CT: Greenwood Press, 1993. 917 pp.

Mickolus, Edward F., with Susan L. Simmons. *Terrorism, 1992–1995: A Chronology of Events and A Selectively Annotated Bibliography.* Westport, CT: Greenwood Press, 1993. 963 pp.

The current volumes are divided into three sections: Incidents, Updates, and Bibliography. The Incidents section provides a chronology and description of international terrorist activity for a given time period, based solely on publicly available sources. This series of chronologies is not intended to be analytical, but rather comprehensive in scope. As such, the Incidents section also includes descriptions of non-international attacks that provide the security and political context in which international attacks take place. In some cases, the international terrorists mimic the tactics of their non-international brethren. Often, these are the same terrorists working on their home soil against domestic targets, rather than foreign targets. Domestic attacks often serve as proving grounds for techniques later adopted for international use. I have therefore included material on major technological, philosophical, or security advances, such as: the use of letter bombs; food tampering; major assassinations; attempts to develop, acquire, smuggle, or use precursors for an actual chemical, biological, radiological, or nuclear weapon; key domestic and international legislation; key arrests and trials of major figures; and incidents involving mass casualties. Non-international entries do not receive an eight-digit code.

The Updates section included in these volumes provides follow-up material to incidents first reported prior to January 1, 1996. For example, updates include information about the outcome of trials for terrorist acts occurring prior to 1996 and "where are they now" information about terrorists and their victims. The update is identified by the original incident date, and I have included enough prefatory material to give some context and to identify the original incident in the earlier volumes.

The Bibliography section includes references drawn from the same public sources that provide the incidents, literature searches, and contributions sent by readers of the previous volumes. It does not purport to be comprehensive. The citations are grouped into six topical areas—General, Regional, Special (e.g., specific types of terrorist threats), Responses and Approaches, Fiction, and Bibliographies—that were chosen to make the bibliography more accessible. For the first time, I have included Web sites under Special Topics. The Bibliography section gives citations on key events and may be referenced for more detail on specific incidents described in the Incidents section.

For those who prefer to run textual searches for specific groups, individuals, or incidents, a computer version of the chronology and bibliography are available from Vinyard Software, Inc., 2305 Sandburg Street, Dunn Loring, Virginia 22027-1124; Greenwood also plans to offer an online version of this material in 2002. The data set comes in a WordPerfect textual version and looks remarkably like this volume. A numeric version offers circa 150 numeric variables describing the international attacks. Textual and numeric data sets for the previous volumes in this series are also available. The data sets can be purchased by specific year of interest.

Comments about this volume's utility and suggestions for improvements for its successors are welcome and can be sent to me via vinyardsoftware@hotmail.com. Please send your terrorism publication citations to me at Vinyard to ensure inclusion in the next edition of the bibliography.

Once again, there are many individuals who have contributed to this research effort. Of particular note are Susan Simmons, who once again edited this volume and incorporated additional material in the Bibliography section, and my family, who once again endured nights and weekends of clacking computer keys. I extend my thanks to Ciana Mickolus, Lilly Smith, and Scott Dutton of the Vinyard research department for their research on Web sites that provide September 11 information.

About the Authors

Dr. Edward F. Mickolus is a well-recognized lecturer, writer, and authority on terrorism. He is the author of seven previous volumes on international and transnational terrorism.

Susan L. Simmons, M.A., is a freelance writer and editor, who specializes in editing books and journal articles in the fields of international relations, psychology, art history, education, and medicine.

1996–2001 INCIDENTS

1996. *Israel.* U.S. District Judge Ronald R. Lagueux ruled in a 48-page decision released on July 27, 2001, that a $250 million lawsuit against the Palestinian Liberation Organization (PLO) and the Palestinian Authority could proceed in his Providence, Rhode Island, courtroom. The lawsuit concerned a shooting in 1996. Yaron and Efrat Ungar were shot to death by Hamas while riding in a car near the West Bank. Lagueux based his decision on the facts that Yaron Ungar was a U.S. citizen; that a Providence lawyer, David J. Strachman, was representing the couple's two surviving children; and that the PLO had offices, bank accounts, and promotional programs in the United States. The attorney sued the PLO for international terrorism, wrongful death, and emotional distress. He claimed the PLO was culpable by providing Hamas with support and a base of operations. Defense attorneys said the PLO could not receive due process so far away from home.

January–May 1996. *Turkey, Pakistan, Iraq.* Iranian government death squads were believed responsible for killing five Iranian exiles in early 1996. Three victims were members of the Mojahedin-e Khalq dissident exiles. Two people died in Turkey, two in Pakistan (one on February 20), and one in Baghdad, Iraq. 96999901-04

January 1996. *Lebanon.* Two Sudanese, Thabit 'Awad and Muhammad Ahmad, were arrested. On February 7, they were charged with gathering information on Sudanese oppositionists and Egyptians as well as with contacting terrorist networks. The duo faced three years in prison if convicted of engaging in banned activities. They confessed to receiving money from the Sudanese consul in return for information about security measures around the Egyptian Embassy. 96019901

January 1996. *Australia.* Attackers damaged the Australian-Chinese Community Center at Granville in the western suburbs of Sydney. 96019902

January 1996. *Cambodia.* Khmer Rouge guerrillas killed a U.S. tourist and her driver on the route from Angkor Wat to the Banteay Srei temple north of Siem Reap. 96019903

January 1996. *Colombia.* The Revolutionary Armed Forces of Colombia (FARC) threatened to kill a few of the South American distributors of Militec (based in Rosslyn, Virginia) if the company did not provide it with 15 free cases of Militec-1, a synthetic oil that reduces metal-on-metal friction and is particularly good for weapons. The firm refused to give up the $360-per-case lubricant, saying that the government, a $50,000-a-year client, did not want the guerrillas to have the oil. The firm's distributors hid the oil cases and fled. 96019904

January 1, 1996. *Costa Rica.* Ten masked kidnappers armed with AK-47 rifles took over a hotel in San Juan. They stole a vehicle and kidnapped German citizen Nicola Fleuchaus, 24, and Swiss citizen Regula Susana Sigfried, 50, owner of a local travel agency. The hotel vehicle was found along the San Juan River at the Nicaragua border. Police and troops from both countries searched the mountains for the kidnappers and victims. The kidnappers demanded $1 million ransom and freedom for Costa Ricans jailed for the 1993 takeover of San Jose's Supreme Court.

On January 4, the kidnappers threatened to blow up bridges and pylons and to attack a U.S. family if their demands were ignored.

On January 9, the kidnappers threatened to blow up the Arenal dam, the country's largest hydroelectric dam, if their demands were not met. The caller to Channel 7's Telenews had a Nicaraguan accent.

The two hostages were released on March 12. 96010101

January 1, 1996. *Iraq.* Three individuals attempted to leave a vehicle containing explosives near United Nations (UN) offices in Irbil. The driver abandoned the vehicle after a security guard ordered him to move it. 96010102

January 3, 1996. *United Kingdom.* The British government announced it would expel Saudi Arabian dissident Mohammed Masaari, 49, head of the Committee for Defense of Legitimate Rights. Masaari was to move on to Dominica. On March 5, Immigration Appeals Court Judge David Pearl said London had not proved that Masaari would be safe in Dominica and directed the government to reconsider Masaari's request for political asylum.

January 3, 1996. *India.* A bomb hidden in a motor scooter exploded in a New Delhi bazaar, killing 6 and injuring 35. A Kashmiri separatist group said it was protesting "atrocities" by Indian security forces in Jammu and Kashmir. The bomb set fire to a gas-lamp shop. Five gas cylinders exploded, setting nearby stores on fire.

January 4, 1996. *Sri Lanka.* The *Colombo Daily News* reported that the Liberation Tigers of Tamil Eelam (LTTE) might possess chemical weapons. The Colombo government had alerted the UN Center for Disarmament Affairs to that possibility, claiming that the LTTE had used phosgene gas against government troops in 1990. It charged that the LTTE was attempting to purchase chemical weapons from European-based arms dealers.

January 5, 1996. *Gaza Strip.* Yehiya Ayash (alias The Engineer), 32, Hamas's main bomb maker, was killed when a bomb hidden in his portable telephone exploded near his ear. He was in a private house in Beit Lahiya (variant Bayt Laliyah). Ayash was credited with at least seven major suicide bombings. He was suspected of involvement in the following attacks:

- April 6, 1994. Afula. A car bomb destroyed a school bus, killing 9 and injuring 45.
- April 13, 1994. Hadera. A bomb exploded in a bus station, killing 6 and injuring 28.
- October 19, 1994. Tel Aviv. A suicide bomber attacked a bus in Tel Aviv's shopping district, killing 22 and injuring 48.
- December 25, 1994. Jerusalem. A suicide bomber attacked a commuter bus, injuring 14, including a U.S. tourist.
- January 22, 1995. Beit Lid. Two suicide bombers attacked a snack stand, killing 21 and injuring 62.
- April 9, 1995. Gaza. A car bomb crashed into a bus near Kfar Darom, killing 7 Israeli soldiers and a U.S. tourist and injuring 34.
- July 24, 1995. Tel Aviv. A suicide bomber attacked a bus, killing 6 and injuring 28.
- August 21, 1995. Jerusalem. A suicide bomber attacked a bus, killing 4 and injuring 100.

Ayash (variant Ayyash) was born in Rafat, near Ramallah, on the West Bank. He obtained an electrical engineering education at Bir Zeit University, then joined the Izzedine al Qassam Brigades (variants Issadin Kassam Brigades, Izz-al-Din al-Qassam Battalions, 'Izz-al-Din al-Qassam Battalion) of Hamas, where he manufactured explosive belts used by suicide terrorists. He often was disguised as a woman or an Orthodox Jewish settler. *Qol Yisra'el* said Ayash was hiding in Beit Lahiya using the alias Abu Ahmad.

Hamas blamed Israeli intelligence for Ayash's death. Others claimed the PLO had worked with Shin Bet to kill him.

The media later reported that two ounces of explosives were hidden in a phone given to Ayash, whose voice print was confirmed by a computer. The bomb was set off by a radio in an airplane flying overhead. *Qol Yisra'el* reported that Ayash received the phone from Kamal Hammed, a building contractor who had recently declared bankruptcy. An estimated 100,000 people attended Ayash's funeral on January 6.

January 5, 1996. *United States.* A car bomb exploded at 4:45 A.M. outside the home of Cuban-American attorney Jose Pertierra, 43, on the 1200 block of Irving Street, N.E., in Washington, D.C. His black Acura Legend was destroyed. No one was hurt. He said the attack was meant to intimidate him and his client, attorney Jennifer Harbury. Harbury's husband, Guatemalan guerrilla Efraim Bamaca, was reportedly tortured to death by the Guatemalan military in 1992. Harbury was in Guatémala at the time of the bombing, attempting to enter an army base where she believes Bamaca's body is buried. Pertierra and neighbor Mercedes Johnson said a car pulled away from the street in front of Pertierra's house at midnight and suggested that the occupants could have set the bomb, which consisted of kerosene with a fire accelerant. Pertierra had received no threats. No group claimed credit. Harbury suggested that people hired by Guatemalan officials were responsible.

Five shots were fired at 1:00 A.M. the next morning at the Assisi Community, a home on Warder Street, N.W., Washington, D.C., inhabited by nuns, victims of foreign human rights abuses, and refugees. Harbury resides there when in Washington. Police found a bullet lodged in a living room wall. Ann Butwell, who lives in the home and is an activist in Central American human rights issues, said a bullet was found in the wall 4 feet from her bed and 12 feet from where a Salvadoran family slept. A shell casing found outside was fired from either a .38-caliber revolver or a 9-mm handgun. 96010601, 96010602

January 7, 1996. *Guatemala.* Lucinda Bousquet, 28 (or 50, according to AFP), and Ann Jahern, 25, both U.S. citizens, were shot dead near Atitlan Lake. Their bodies were found on Panajachel beach. Robbers were believed responsible.

January 8, 1996. *Corsica.* At least 37 bombs were set by the Resistenza separatist group, damaging public buildings and banks. In Ajaccio, bombs went off at the National Institute of Statistics and Information About the Economy, the Treasury, the general public revenue office, the Société Générale, and the Crédit Agricole. No one was injured by the bombs, all of which went off between 11:00 and 11:30 P.M. in Ajaccio, Bastia, Porticcio, Porto-Vecchio, Bonifaccio, Propriano, Haute-Corse, and Sartene in Corse-du-Sud. Eleven of the plastic explosives failed to go off; some of them were defused by bomb squads. Resistenza demanded that the state accept a "genuine political solution" in Corsica.

January 8, 1996. *Indonesia.* Some 200 Free Papua Movement (Organisasi Papua Merdeka; OPM) rebels kidnapped 26 people, including 13 wildlife researchers in the 1995–96 Lorentz expedition, in Mapunduma village in Irian Jaya. Seven hostages were Europeans. The rebels were armed with spears, bows and arrows, and firearms.

On January 12, nine Indonesian hostages were released (or rescued by the military—sources differ). These hostages included Mapunduma village chief Alex Musidi, village secretary Philipus Teseriat, village official Isak Weteirat, local chairman Jatiuh Ilupure, and four officials of the Public Health Center identified as Levi Nasariat, Martasina, Lasani Manibu, and Martin Lianga.

On January 14, the rebels asked for a plane and a pilot and demanded to hold talks with four Christian priests involved in local missionary work. German hostage Frank Momberg, 31, a Worldwide Fund for Nature worker, spoke on the radio, asking for food and medicine. He said the hostages were being well treated and their hands were no longer tied.

On January 15, the kidnappers released Momberg, who told a press conference that the kidnappers wore only *koteka* (penis sheaths). The kidnappers released him on condition that he publicize their cause, act as a mediator, and return.

On January 17, the kidnappers released two hostages—the wife of Yakobus Wendidi and her six-month-old child. Wendidi lived in Mapunduma village and provided food for workers of the Indonesian Institute of Sciences, who conduct research in the village. The government suspended military operations after the rebels threatened to kill the remaining hostages.

On January 22, the kidnappers released Yakobus Wendidi (variant Wandiba), an Indonesian.

The kidnappers released 13 people, but continued to hold Britons Daniel Start, 21, William Oates, 22, Annette van der Kolk, 21, and Anna McIvor, 20, along with Dutch citizens Mark van der Wal, an official with the Worldwide Fund for Nature, and Martha Klein, a UNESCO environmental official who was pregnant.

The kidnappers often requested medicine, food, and basic supplies. Indonesian armed forces dropped food on the village several times.

On January 20, Jose Ramos Horta, the East Timor National Council of Maubere Resistance Special Representative, offered to serve as a mediator. Later that day, the kidnappers extended their deadline to January 22.

Letters written by the hostages and dated January 10 arrived on January 21 at the embassies of the three countries in Jakarta and at the UN. Other letters were addressed to the hostages' families.

On January 23, Russel Betts, the Worldwide Fund for Nature representative in Jakarta, received a letter from Dutch hostage Mark van der Wal.

Missionaries met with the rebels, who were led by Kelly Kwalik of the Amungme tribe. The formal name of his group is the Security Disturbance Movement (GPK). Kwalik apparently took over from Daniel Yudas Kogoya of the Nduga tribe. Kwalik asked the missionaries to share documents with the British, Dutch, and German embassies in Jakarta. The missionaries were identified as Andreas van der Bijl, Paul Burkhardt, and Yohanes Gobay. Kwalik refused to hold direct talks with the government.

The army lost radio contact with the kidnappers on January 25, when the rebels left their radios behind as they moved to a new location. Kwalik met that day with Monsignor Herman M. F. Munninghoff, bishop of Jayapura; he had been Munninghoff's student 22 years earlier.

Authorities believed the kidnappers were on their way to the Papua New Guinea border.

Radio contact was restored on January 30.

On February 8, a team from the International Committee of the Red Cross (ICRC) went to the area to attempt to negotiate the hostages' release. They dropped thousands of leaflets asking Kwalik to contact them. The ICRC chief representative claimed that Kwalik's Amungme tribesmen gave him a pamphlet and that he agreed to meet with the organization. The ICRC finally made contact on February 15.

On February 14, Papuan couriers delivered two letters written on February 6 and 7 by hostages Mark van der Wal and Martha Klein, who said they were in good health, but weakened by the long march. However, Antara press service reported that the pregnant Klein was suffering from malaria. On February 29, an ICRC doctor who met with the hostages for six hours said they looked well and had no serious illnesses. The ICRC also gave the rebels clothes, food, and medicine for the hostages.

Army troops continued to search for the hostages and did not rule out a military rescue operation. They said they would continue to use clerics as mediators.

On February 27, *Kompas* reported that the hostages were being held seven meters above ground in a "Bat Cave" after being moved from Bakomdaum commune, Geselama Village, Tiom Subdistrict. An ICRC team met with the captors. Moses Weror, claiming to be chairman of the OPM Revolutionary Council, told Melbourne Radio he would not order the captors to free the hostages until the governments opened talks regarding the political status of Irian Jaya.

Kompas announced on March 2 that Kogoya and Kwalik had answered 22 written interview questions.

On March 5, Weror called for a government negotiating team to be composed of Foreign Minister Ali Alatas; Megawati Sukarnoputri, general chairwoman of the Indonesia Democratic Party Central Executive Council; Wahono, speaker of the House of Representatives and chairman of the People's Consultative Assembly; international organizations; and other unnamed leaders. He also wanted British, Dutch, ICRC, and UNESCO representatives on hand, along with Monsignor Munninghoff as the Vatican representative. He set a deadline of September, when the UN General Assembly was scheduled to reconvene. The ICRC and the Free Papua Movement Revolutionary Council agreed on March 8 to hold talks.

On March 11, Weror sent a "sacred letter" to Kelly Kwalik and Daniel Yudas Kogoya, telling them to free the hostages. The ICRC also resumed contact with the kidnappers. However, Weror also said that before the hostages could be released, the UN General Assembly—which was not due to meet until September—must state that the Papuans had the right to form an independent country.

The kidnappers released Abraham Wanggai, an Irian and local forestry official, on March 16. Wanggai was also identified as the dean of Irian Jaya's Cendrawasih University.

By April 2, the ICRC and the government were still in contact with the kidnappers. Doctors who examined the hostages said their health was deteriorating because of poor food and constant marching.

The Red Cross left Geselema in Irian Jaya and gave up as an intermediary on May 7 when the kidnappers reneged on their agreement to free the hostages after holding an elaborate six-hour farewell ceremony. Kelly Kwalik added the new demand of recognition of an independent West Papua, the exchange of ambassadors, and the supply of weapons. One ICRC representative remained behind to keep in touch with the seven-month-pregnant Martha Klein, her friend Mark van der Wal, and the other hostages.

On May 15, following a seven-day operation, the Indonesian armed forces freed nine hostages—four Britons, two Dutch, and three others. The rescue force battled 20 Free Papua Organization guerrillas and 200 tribesmen armed with spears, machetes, and arrows. Hostage Martha Klein was wounded in the hand by a spear. Nine hostages were then freed. Troops found McIvor, who had escaped, an hour later. At least eight rebels were killed in the fighting; two others were arrested. The troops had located the nine hostages using a pilotless plane.

The next day, the armed forces pursuing the kidnappers found two dead Indonesian hostages with stab wounds in their bodies. They were identified as Navy Panekenan, 28, and Yosias Mathias Lasamahu, 30.

The Indonesian government denied that the British had been involved with the rescue force. 96010801

January 9, 1996. *Russia.* Nearly 200 heavily armed Chechen separatists attacked the southern town of Kizlyar at dawn and seized a hospital and maternity ward, taking 2,000 civilians hostage. The attack began at 6:00 A.M., when rebels drove trucks and buses to a military base where they destroyed two helicopters before the Russians repulsed them. They then attacked the hospital.

The rebels demanded that the government withdraw military forces from Chechnya. The rebels released most of the hostages, but forced about 160 into buses and trucks, which they convoyed out of the area. At least 40 people were killed and 50 civilians wounded in the attack and subsequent firefights during the day. The dead included 17 Chechen guerrillas, 7 local policemen, 14 civilians, and 2 Russian soldiers. Russian television showed the bodies of two hostages. The rebels initially demanded the withdrawal of Russian troops from Chechnya. They then released many hostages and demanded safe passage to Chechnya on the buses, which was granted. The rebels also asked to speak to foreign journalists and for a meeting between Moscow officials and Chechen separatist leader Dzhokhar Dudayev.

The Russian special forces rolled 48 tanks and other armored vehicles into the town of 40,000. The rebels reportedly used the hostages as human shields while firing at the troops. They also claimed to have placed explosives inside the hospital. Salman Raduyev, leader of the Chechen militia unit Lone Wolf, spoke to Russian television from the hospital, saying, "We can easily turn this city to hell and ashes. We are not at all concerned for our own lives." The rebels took the bodies of seven dead colleagues on the buses with them. Eight local officials agreed to serve as surrogate hostages on the ride to the Chechen frontier.

Right after the last bus in the convoy, which had been stuck in mud, was pulled free, the Russians blew up a bridge six miles down the road, stalling the 11-bus convoy near Pervomayskaya in Dagestan, yards from Chechnya. The buses drove into a nearby field and 250 Chechens set up a defensive perimeter. The eight surrogate hostages were released unharmed. Russian troops surrounded the convoy, which included 50 women and children waving bed sheets, pleading with the troops not to shoot. The rebels demanded safe passage to Chechnya via a different route; the government demanded that the rebels first free the hostages.

The Chechens also took hostage 37 members of a Dagestani special forces unit that disarmed itself as the standoff began in Pervomayskoye (variant spelling). Many of the rebels moved into the village, away from the stalled convoy, and readied themselves for a confrontation with Russian helicopter gunships and tanks. Tass claimed that the rebels had dug trenches and deployed grenade launchers and antitank rockets. The Chechens told provincial officials, including the Dagestani deputy minister of interior affairs, that they wanted to talk to Russian Prime Minister Viktor Chernomyrdin. The government said President Boris Yeltsin had not delegated the authority to speak for the government. Rebel leader Salman Raduyev said this group wanted safe passage to be ensured by an escort of foreign journalists, Russian and Dagestani officials, members of the Russian Par-

liament, and officials of international organizations, including Doctors Without Borders.

On January 12, Interfax reported that the Chechens released four women and six children (Tass said it was three women and three children) and that four members of the Dagestani special forces unit escaped. The Chechens offered to release additional women and children, but they elected to stay because their husbands and fathers were also being held hostage. The hostages were dispersed throughout the village, whose 700 inhabitants had fled.

In a television interview, Salman Raduyev said, "We're here in a Dagestani village. Bring us to a Chechen village—in a Chechen village where we will leave all the women, leave all the children, all the prisoners, we'll hand over all our arms. We'll hand over everything. In any Chechen village!" He also demanded that four senior Russian officials volunteer to be surrogate hostages, naming former Prime Minister Yegor Gaidar, economist and reformist politician Grigory Yavlinsky, former General Alexander Lebed and General Boris Grimov.

Negotiations were being led by Internal Affairs Minister Muhamed Abdurazkov and Ramazan Abdulatipov, a Dagestani member of the Federation Council, the upper chamber of the Russian Parliament.

Russian government troops kept away Chechens and others who came to the area hoping to bolster the hostage takers. Still other local residents held protest demonstrations both against the troops and against the hostage takers.

On January 13, the head of the Federal Security Service, General Mikhail Barsukov, told the rebels that they had until 10:00 A.M. the next day to release the hostages. He said, "If even one hostage is killed, all of the [hostage takers] will be finished." He offered the Chechens safe passage home if they freed the hostages and surrendered their weapons. Moscow extended the deadline the next day and pulled back troops from some of their forward positions. Russian television reported that the rebels had fired on Russian ground forces, wounding four Russian servicemen. They also fired on two helicopter gunships in what

Moscow said it believed was an attempt to provoke an assault.

Russian forces launched a rescue mission at 9:00 A.M. on January 15 after the rebels ignored the army's second ultimatum ten minutes earlier. An artillery barrage set many buildings alight. At least 4 soldiers were killed and 18 wounded when the Chechens responded with rocket-propelled grenades, mortars, and machine guns. Three Russian armored personnel carriers were destroyed or damaged. The Internal Affairs Ministry claimed that 60 rebels were killed and another 8 taken prisoner. By January 16, only 20 hostages had been freed.

Later on January 16, another Chechen rebel group captured 30 hostages at an industrial facility in Grozny, the Chechen capital, and put them on buses to an unknown destination.

Russian forces gave up on freeing the hostages alive and conducted an artillery attack that leveled the town. Some reports claimed that the hostage takers escaped. Given that they were surrounded by a massive number of Russian troops, it is difficult to give credence to these reports. At least 153 Chechen rebels died in the attack; 28 were taken prisoner. Twenty-six Russian soldiers were killed, and 93 were wounded.

Follow-up articles by Moscow's Interfax reported that a Pakistani mercenary was involved in the Chechen attack.

January 11, 1996. *Philippines.* New Zealand Ambassador Colin Bell announced that although his name was found on a terrorist hit list, he had decided to stay in the country. The plot had been discovered two or three months earlier. Police were searching for six members of the radical Islamic Preaching Group (Hezbul Dawah Al Islamiah). This group was led by Bashar Habib, an Iraqi explosives expert trained in Libya. The hit list included Bell and the ambassadors of Australia, the United Kingdom, and Spain.

The next day, Philippine Radio-Television GMA-7 Network broadcast an interview with Javit Ali, 40, who had been a Hezbul Dawah Al Islamiah terrorist for 21 years and who planned to assassinate President Ramos. 96011101

January 12, 1996. *United States.* Cheryl Taylor sustained facial burns when a bomb exploded in Alvord, Texas. The bomb was wrapped inside two packages, which had been delivered by United Parcel Service. The next day, police arrested her estranged boyfriend, Roger Eugene Gresham, 50, of Searcy, Arkansas. He was found asleep in the cab of his truck at a Searcy truck stop. He faced a charge of aggravated assault in Wise County, where the sheriff had investigated mutual allegations of threats and theft filed by the duo in the previous four months.

January 14, 1996. *Palestine.* Palestine Authority police announced that two weeks earlier they had arrested members of the Abu Nidal Group who were planning an assassination and bombing campaign. The group was targeting senior Palestinian leaders and schools, hoping to derail the peace process. Police confiscated arms and explosives.

January 14, 1996. *Israel.* Israeli authorities expressed concern about the possibility of a terrorist attack by Hamas and Islamic Jihad against former President Jimmy Carter, who was visiting the country to monitor the local elections.

January 16, 1996. *Spain.* Justice and Interior Minister Juan Alberto Belloch announced that he would ask the Dominican Republic to extradite Basque Nation and Liberty ETA leader Eugenio Etxebeste (alias Antxon).

January 16, 1996. *Turkey.* Pro-Chechen gunmen took over the 3,800-ton Panama-registered *Avrasya*, a Sochi, Russia-bound ferryboat carrying 200 passengers and crew in Trabzon, threatening to sink it in the Bosporus Strait unless Russian troops stopped their attacks on the Chechen hostage takers in Pervomayskoye, Dagestan, Russia. A Turkish policeman was wounded in the takeover.

A Russian woman escaped before the ship left port. She claimed several passengers were beaten. Another woman also escaped. Nadezhda Naskova, a Russian woman, told the press that many people were wounded by the hijackers, who fired subma-chine guns indiscriminately.

ITAR-Tass reported that one hostage was killed and that the gunmen threatened to kill one hostage every ten minutes.

Interfax reported that the hijackers called themselves the Shamil Grandsons, named after a Chechen *imam* who fought against the czarists in the 19th century.

The leader of the hijackers told Turkish televi-sion that his name was Muhammed and that he led 50 armed pirates. He was later identified as Muhammed Tokcan, 28, a Turk of Abkhazian ancestry. The press claimed there were only eight hijackers. Television journalist Ugur Dundar used a helicopter to board the ferry. He noted that three hostages were suffering from rabies, diabetes, and influenza and needed medical attention. The hijackers attempted to release these three on Janu-ary 18, but the ferry could not get close enough to a smaller rescue boat in the heavy seas. Television footage showed the hijackers armed with AK-47s and daggers. Tokcan talked with Turkish officials, including the chief of Turkish intelligence, who reportedly agreed to permit the pirates to have a news conference. The deal was later quashed by the government, which said that reporters had confused Sonmez Koksal, the chief of intelligence, with Sonmez Baykan, a member of a Caucasian-Chechen friendship association.

Italian RAI Television reporters were also per-mitted to interview the pirates, who demanded that the Russians leave the Caucasus, halt the attack in Chechnya, and permit the Chechen voice to be heard.

Turkey sent a Coast Guard boat to monitor the ferry as it moved westward at 12 mph. Turkey announced that the ferry held 165 Russian tour-ists, several Turks, Kyrgyz, Ukrainians, and Geor-gians, a Jordanian, and 45 crewmen. Turkey refused to let the ferry anchor in Istanbul, fearing that it would sink and stall all shipping in the area.

On January 18, the pirates asked for a flight to Chechnya. The next day, they agreed to release the Ukrainian hostages and permit mediation by the Ukrainian National Assembly and Ukrainian National Self-Defense Forces. The press said they would surrender at Eregli port.

Chechen nationalist leader Dzhokhar Dudayev said it was possible that the ferry hijacking was a provocation by the Russian government.

Turkey assured the Russian government that the pirates would be tried as common criminals no matter what the outcome of the incident.

The pirates surrendered on January 19 in Riva Bay, after releasing 12 hostages.

On January 29, the Russian government de-manded that Turkey try the nine pirates as inter-national terrorists. (The *Washington Post* had reported that there were only four hijackers.) Moscow's *Trud* charged the next day that a tenth pirate, Abkhazian citizen Avit Sava, managed to escape. It also claimed that Sava and Raki Gisba, another Abkhazian pirate, had purchased ten pump-action shotguns to deliver to Trabzon. When the pirates surrendered near the Anadol lighthouse, they threw nine of the shotguns into the sea. 96011601

January 17, 1996. *Bahrain.* A homemade bomb exploded in a bathroom of the Meridien Hotel in Manama, where an international oil conference was taking place. No injuries were reported, but some damage was sustained. The Bahrain Free-men Movement denied involvement. 96011701

January 17, 1996. *Israel.* In an 8:30 P.M. drive-by shooting near Hebron, Palestinian gunmen in a Mercedes fired on an Israeli army car, killing two Israeli soldiers. The previously unknown Muja-heddin of Islam said the attack was in revenge for the murder of Yehiya Ayash, the Hamas bomb maker. Sergeant Yamit Shimel, 20, was the driver of the Israeli army car.

January 17, 1996. *Colombia.* U.S. citizen John M. McLay was kidnapped. He was later released. By March 20, 1996, he had been kidnapped a second time. 96011702, 96039901

January 18, 1996. *Ethiopia.* Four people were killed and 20 wounded when a bomb went off at

8:10 P.M. at the Ghion Hotel in Addis Ababa, where several diplomats from the Organization of African Unity (OAU) were dining. The hotel is located near the presidential palace. One man and two women, all Ethiopian waiters, were killed. The injured included citizens from France, India, Malawi, Mali, and the United Kingdom, and an Arab. In March, the al-Ittihaad al-Islami (Islamic Union), an ethnic Somali group, claimed credit. 96011801

January 18, 1996. *Germany.* Arsonists destroyed a four-story refugee hostel in Luebeck, killing 10 people, including 4 children, and injuring 50, 20 of them seriously. Four others were initially listed as missing, but were later found. The refugees came from Lebanon, Syria, Togo, and Zaire. Some residents were ethnic German immigrants from Poland. Four young neo-Nazi men, aged 17 to 36, from a nearby eastern German village, were detained as suspects. They had prior police records and burn marks in their hair. Police released them the next day for lack of evidence, accepting their claim that they were trying to set a dog on fire at a site some distance from the hostel.

On January 19 police arrested a Lebanese refugee, 21, for setting the fire where he and his family lived. A judge ordered him arrested on 10 counts of murder, 38 counts of attempted murder, and aggravated arson. His two brothers, arrested with him, were later released. Some residents said that the accused man had helped people escape the fire.

On June 30, 1997, in a Luebeck court, presiding Judge Rolf Wilcken dismissed all charges against Safwan Eid after prosecutors acknowledged they had no firm evidence that Eid had started the fire to end a quarrel with another resident of the building. 96011802

January 19, 1996. *Israel.* A Palestinian in a car fired at an Israeli checkpoint in Jenin, injuring a soldier. Other guards fired on the vehicle, killing three armed Palestinians.

January 19, 1996. *Colombia.* Six members of the Revolutionary Armed Forces of Colombia (FARC)

kidnapped a U.S. citizen and demanded a $1 million ransom. He was freed on May 22. 96011901

January 20, 1996. *Egypt.* The Islamic Group threatened to attack U.S. interests and citizens in revenge for the life sentence imposed on Shaykh Umar Abd-al-Raman on January 17 by the Federal District Court in Manhattan. 96012001

January 22, 1996. *Cabinda.* Local rebels took hostage three South Africans and another foreigner working for the Branch Energy Company, which mines gold in the north. The Front for the Liberation of the Cabinda Enclave (FLEC) wanted to trade the hostages for food, but released them a few hours later. 96012201

January 22, 1996. *Bosnia.* American media reported that Cleven Holt (alias Clevin Raphael Holt; alias Kevin Holt; alias Isa Abdullah Ali), 39, a U.S.-born suspected Hizballah terrorist, was in Bosnia working with local Islamic terrorists. The *Los Angeles Times* reported that fliers about Holt were handed out to U.S. guards in Bosnia earlier in the week. The posters said he was arrested earlier for posing as a U.S. serviceman. He had worked as a groundskeeper and janitor at Howard University. He claimed to have been a gunman with Hizballah in Beirut in the early 1980s. Those who recalled meeting him said that a six-foot three-inch black American gunman easily stood out in Beirut. He was interviewed by a *Washington Post* reporter in 1982, when he claimed he was a member of Amal, the Lebanese Shi'ite militia.

January 23, 1996. *United States.* Gouquiang Situ, a Chinese immigrant who had received his green card the previous week, was killed by a bomb planted at eye level in a bus shelter in North Bay Village, Florida. The bomb was triggered by a tripwire set above the sidewalk. Situ, a cook, was walking home from work at a nearby restaurant. He was married with no children. Police had no idea who planted the bomb.

January 23, 1996. *Gabon.* The Embassy of Equatorial Guinea was damaged when oppositionists broke windows and doors of the building. They assaulted some of the embassy staff, ransacked the building, destroyed furniture and archives, and damaged the ambassador's car. The staff had asked the oppositionists to produce identity documents so that they could be registered to vote. When they refused, they were not allowed to register, and violence ensued. Property loss in recent disturbances was put at 11 million CFA francs.

January 23, 1996. *Pakistan.* An arrested Afghan army brigadier, Mir Akbar Ansari, told officials that his government had planned to hijack an aircraft from Pakistan. His government was willing to pay 10 million rupees for the attack. He had entered Pakistan two years earlier to make contacts with local criminals and bureaucrats, including drug trafficker Barkat Shah of Achar Kale. Ansari was also linked to the assassination of General Abdol Hakim Katawaze and to prostitution dens in Peshawar. 96012301

January 24, 1996. *Yemen.* Four members of the Al-Aslam tribe stopped two tourist buses from a Yemeni travel agency returning to Sanaa after a trip to Marib's (variant Ma'rib) ruins. They forced the 2 drivers out and drove 18 kidnapped French tourists, a guide, and the 2 drivers to 'Ayn Hadi village in Shabwah Governorate. The kidnappers, led by 'Abdallah Dwman, demanded the release of his brother, Zabnallah Dwman, who was jailed three months earlier by a Yemeni court for kidnapping an American oilman in September 1996 during a monetary dispute. Dwman (variant Duman) was suspected of smuggling guns, cars, and electronic goods from Saudi Arabia.

The kidnappers freed a French hostage and a bus driver on January 27.

Nearly 1,000 Yemeni security officers surrounded the kidnappers later that day. They arrested 15 tribesmen to pressure the kidnappers.

Another hostage, released hours later, said the kidnappers took the elderly hostages on a tour of ancient Shabwah Governorate. One of the freed hostages, Jean-Jacques Abassin, 65, of Grenoble, France, returned to the kidnappers to be near his wife.

Tribal leaders leading the mediation efforts saw the tourists in good health, walking in orange groves. The kidnappers were also in direct contact with the French Embassy. French Ambassador Marcel Laugel, who had earlier demanded that one hostage be released to prove that they were in good health, was permitted to visit the 17 hostages.

The tribesmen freed the remaining hostages at 7:00 A.M. on January 29 after the government threatened to attack the village where they were being held. Some of the tourists were wearing *janibyas*—traditional daggers—given to them by their captors. Authorities immediately arrested four kidnappers.

The next day, the army attacked the tribesmen. One soldier was killed, and four were wounded.

Security officers arrested 14 members of the kidnap group on February 2 in the al-Ayn area of Shabwah Governorate. The head of the group was killed, and another was seriously wounded.

All 18 arrested members of the gang were handed over to judicial authorities. 96012401

January 25, 1996. *Lebanon.* Hizballah denied that it had kidnapped and then released three Swedish members of the SAEPO police in Beirut's southern suburbs the previous week.

January 29, 1996. *South Africa.* At 2:45 A.M., seven gunmen fired AK-47s into a crowd of 2,000 job seekers at a die-casting factory in Alrode, Alberton, killing 14 and injuring 26. Police said the gunmen had run to the front of the line. Authorities found a shotgun, two AK-47 rifles, and 9-mm cartridges.

January 30, 1996. *Bangladesh.* Gunshots were fired at the residence of the British deputy high commissioner at Gulshan, Shaka. The police constable serving as a sentry was injured. 96013001

January 30, 1996. *India.* Forty members of the Karnataka State Farmers Association destroyed furniture and utensils at the Kentucky Fried Chicken outlet in Bangalore. Some people were injured by glass splinters. The group was protesting against foreign fast-food restaurants. 96013002

January 30, 1996. *Nicaragua.* Three hundred armed students burst into the Foreign Ministry building at 3:20 P.M. and held hostage Pakistani Ambassador Manzar Shafiq, Philippine Ambassador Clemencio Montesa, the Canadian consul general, and more than 200 office workers. A German and a Bolivian diplomat escaped being seized. Some reports said the hostages also included Bolivian Ambassador Mario Cossio, a Canadian commercial attaché, and Philippine Consul Alfredo Lacayo. The students demanded more government money for higher education. The Managua police chief, Pedro Aguilar, entered the building to negotiate. Shafiq, Montesa, and several other hostages were released after four hours. Police later fired tear gas and rescued the 81 people who had not been released by the students. Some 107 students were arrested. Police confiscated 27 homemade mortars, numerous bombs, several slingshots, and an ax. One report said 520 bombs were found.

Montesa had been presenting her credentials as nonresident ambassador. She now lives in Mexico. 96013003

January 31, 1996. *Malaysia.* Police shot two Arabs brandishing iron rods who were believed to be involved in spreading "deviationist teachings." The pair resisted arrest and charged at the police near the Central Market in Kota Kinabalu at 2:00 P.M. Bullets hit one Arab in the leg, the other in the abdomen. Police were told that the two were threatening the public and shouting at passing motorists in a foreign language. A local passerby, 25, was hit in the right leg by a stray bullet.

January 31, 1996. *Ukraine.* The fire brigade at the Khmelnistkiy nuclear power plant received a morning phone call warning of a terrorist attack. The plant supplies power to Betishin.

January 31, 1996. *Liberia.* A UN convoy with five military observers was fired on by rebels in Tubmanburg, near Gomay Farm. No one was injured, but a windshield was broken. No one claimed credit. Roosevelt Johnson's faction of the United Liberation Movement for Democracy in Liberia blamed the rival Mandingo faction of Alhaji Koromah. 96013101

January 31, 1996. *Sudan.* The United States announced it was closing its embassy in Khartoum due to terrorist threats. The Sudanese government had refused to guarantee the safety of U.S. diplomats, who were ordered home. Sudan asked the United States to reconsider and pledged to provide full security for foreign embassies.

Meanwhile, the UN Security Council unanimously called on Sudan to comply with calls to extradite to Ethiopia three terrorists wanted for the attempted assassination of Egyptian President Hosni Mubarak on June 26, 1995.

January 31, 1996. *Saudi Arabia.* Americans were warned again of a possible terrorist attack by Islamic fundamentalists. Secretary of State Warren Christopher canceled a proposed trip to Riyadh to meet with caretaker ruler Crown Prince Abdullah.

January 31, 1996. *Sri Lanka.* At 11:00 A.M., a 400-kilogram Liberation Tigers of Tamil Eelam (LTTE) truck bomb exploded at the 11-story Central Bank of Sri Lanka building in Colombo, killing 90, including 9 foreigners (2 Americans) and wounding more than 1,400. Police reported that a second bomb was used. The bomb also damaged 400 cars, the 39-story World Trade Center, the Mercantile Building, Ceylon Hotels Corporation, ABN AMRO, Cargo Boat, George Steuarts, Air Lanka, Hotel Ceylon Inter-Continental, the Galadari Hotel, Reuters, and the Lighthouse Clock Tower. Huge reserves of Sri Lankan currency were buried under the rubble. Indian radio reported that some employees of the Indian Overseas Bank were injured and that more than 200 people were killed.

Three men in an Isuzu truck (license 42-6452) crashed into the security barricade at the front of the bank. Two gunmen fired automatic weapons at the guards, some of whom returned fire while others fled. The terrorists fired a grenade in front of a nearby office building. The driver attempted for several minutes to crash the truck through the security barriers and finally rammed his vehicle into the building, causing the first two floors to collapse. The gunmen then jumped into a three-wheeled taxi, fleeing to a Pettah bakery. They were grabbed by local citizens as they were fleeing the bakery after dropping off four grenades, a suicide kit, two bombs, and two walkie-talkies. By February 6, 34 people had been arrested.

Police later determined that the truck left Vavuniya, 155 miles away, the day before. The arrested gunmen, Rasu (or Raghu), 24, and Kittu, 26, said the driver was named Raju and they had entered the country on January 8. Two other three-wheeled vehicles were in the truck-bomb convoy, but apparently escaped unnoticed. 96013102

February 1, 1996. *Argentina. Noticias Argentinas* of Buenos Aires reported that police believed Ayman Zawahiri, an Egyptian member of the Islamic Jihad, may have sought refuge in Ciudad del Este, Paraguay, on the Brazilian border. He allegedly was involved in the assassination attempt against Egyptian President Hosni Mubarak in Ethiopia in June 1995.

February 2, 1996. *Kenya.* Two Ugandan robbers were injured and a third killed in a shootout with police following a botched robbery at a city market on Muindi Mbingu Street in Nairobi. The trio set off a hand grenade during the shootout, injuring ten workers and shoppers. Others were injured by stray bullets.

February 2, 1996. *Philippines.* The local Bureau of Immigration announced that the Liberation Tigers of Tamil Eelam (LTTE), a Sri Lanka separatist group, was conducting fundraising in the Philippines. Manila's *Philippine Daily* reported that the LTTE was also involved in human smuggling, forging foreign passports and visas, and counterfeiting dollars.

February 2, 1996. *Germany.* Unidentified individuals kidnapped a 28-year-old Iranian dissident near Bonn. The exiled National Resistance Council of Iran blamed Tehran's intelligence minister, Ali Fallahian. The group said the hostage freed himself after having been tortured for two days. They claimed he was a defector who had been trained to commit terrorist attacks. The Mojahedin-e Khalq claimed that four Iranian agents had been responsible for the kidnapping. 96020201

February 4, 1996. *Guatemala.* Pedro Haroldo Sac Sompij attempted to assassinate recently inaugurated Guatemalan President Alvaro Arzu Irigoyen as he was riding his horse along the Tanque de la Union Street near the ruins of Santa Clara in Antigua Guatemala, 45 kilometers south of the capital. Police killed the attacker with three gunshots after he crashed his pickup truck into the president's convoy, injuring Captain Byron Miguel Lima, a guard who was on horseback. Pope John Paul II was due to tour the country the next day.

At a news conference carried on Guatemala City's Cadena de Emisoras Unidas, Government Minister Rodolfo Mendoza said that, after the vehicle hit Lima, "The driver then tried to escape but was surrounded by vehicles of the president's security members. The vehicle collided head-on with one of these vehicles, and the driver immediately tried to back off, hitting one of the president's vehicles that was behind it. He collided with a pickup truck of the president's security staff. The driver again stepped on the gas pedal, hit a motorcycle driven by one of the president's security staff members, and then drove straight at the president—who had gotten off his horse to attend Captain Lima." The driver was grabbed by Captain Byron Rene Bohr, but drove again at the president. The guards then fired at the car's tires and subsequently at the driver.

February 6, 1996. *Russia.* Dzhokhar Dudayev, leader of Chechnya's separatist rebels, told a Russian television interviewer that his group might begin attacks against Western Europe in retaliation for its support for Moscow's attempts to crack down on Chechens. He claimed that "the entire Western world" had given the Kremlin $6 billion. He warned that "when the moment comes, we'll attack not Moscow but Western Europe." 96020601

February 6, 1996. *Colombia.* The National Liberation Army (ELN) kidnapped three cement industry engineers—a British citizen, a Dane, and a German—and their Colombian companion in San Luis. They were taken from their vehicle at a roadblock. They were later freed. 96020602

February 7, 1996. *Bahrain.* Police warned administrators of foreign schools to beware of possible attacks by local demonstrators and terrorists. Several cases of stoning and attacks on foreign cars had been reported in recent weeks.

February 8, 1996. *Venezuela.* The Colombian National Liberation Army (ELN), Domingo Lain Saenz Front, was believed responsible for the 11:30 P.M. attack on the Venezuelan naval post of Cararbo in Apure State. The group had attacked the same post on February 26, 1995. Eight Venezuelan marines were killed in the earlier incident. The rebels used light weapons with tracer bullets and machine guns in a 15-minute onslaught. 96020801

February 8, 1996. *Burma.* Unknown attackers armed with a 107-mm rocket launcher shelled the Kan Bauk field office of the French Total oil company, killing four local staffers and a French citizen and wounding five others. 96020802

February 9, 1996. *United Kingdom.* Breaking the ceasefire of Aug. 31, 1994, the Irish Republican Army (IRA) set off a 500-pound bomb at 7:02 P.M. in an underground parking garage in Canary Wharf, London's largest office and apartment development. Two news vendors were killed and 106 others injured, including two U.S. citizens. At least 36 people were hospitalized and another 70 received cuts and bruises from flying glass and debris. Windows were shattered and walls and ceilings damaged for miles. Insurance assessors set the damage at $127.5 million.

The blast was preceded by a coded IRA warning at 6:00 P.M. The IRA told Ireland's RTE Broadcasting Network that "the complete cessation of military operations will end at 6:00 P.M." An hour later, the bomb went off in the garage of the commuter light-rail station at the Docklands area along the Thames River in eastern London. On April 16, 1997, British police charged a man in connection with the bombing.

The Irish government rescinded a previous granting of early release to seven IRA prisoners. Irish Prime Minister John Bruton refused to meet with Sinn Fein leader Gerry Adams until the ceasefire was reinstated.

On February 16, police searching for the bombers raided 30 locations in London, Essex, Kent, and the West Midlands. Several people were arrested, but none were charged with the bombing. Local communities offered a $1.55 million reward. The main clue was the tracing of a long-bed truck that held the explosives in a parking garage at Docklands. It had been moved from Scotland to Northern Ireland to the mainland. 96020901

February 9, 1996. *Australia.* A Brisbane court sentenced Geoffrey Vernon Hughes, 61, a Queensland man, to two and a half years in jail after he pleaded guilty to planning to overthrow the government of Cameroon. He pleaded guilty to violating the Foreign Incursions and Recruitment Act by trying to buy weapons for the coup against a regime he believed had committed human rights violations. The judge recommended that he be released after eight months.

February 10, 1996. *Israel.* At a memorial rally at Al-Najah University in Nablus for Hamas bomber Yehiya Ayash, a speaker introduced a man he said was the next anti-Israeli suicide bomber.

February 11, 1996. *Bahrain.* A bomb injured a Sri Lankan and two Bahrainis in the lobby of the Diplomat Hotel in Manama. One of the Bahrainis was Khalil 'Abdallah Salman. The prime minister later visited him in the al-Salmaniyah Medical Center. None of the Americans, Britons, and Indians staying at the hotel was hurt. The Islamic Front for the Liberation of Bahrain claimed credit and called for a consumer boycott from February 15 to February 20 to protest government action. The London-based group later withdrew its claim of responsibility.

On February 19 Bahrain security forces arrested four people in connection with the Diplomat bombing and the bombing of Le Royal Meridien Hotel on January 17.

On June 26, 1996, the State Security Court sentenced seven defendants in the bombing of the Meridien Hotel, the Diplomat Hotel, and two branches of the Bahrain Corporation for International Shipping and Trade located in the Diplomatic Quarter. Al-'Adliyah 'Abdallah Nasir Muhammad Al-Tawq received a life sentence. 'Ali Hasan 'Abdallah Ghannam received 15 years. 'Abd-al-Husayn Ibrahim Salih and Husayn Ja'far Sadiq al-Najjar received ten years. Ahmad Haydar 'Abbas Haydar, an Iranian, received seven years in prison and was ordered deported after serving his sentence. 'Abbas 'Ali Ahmad Hubayl received seven years. Ja'far Khalil Ibrahim Hubayl received seven years and was fined 1,000 dinars. The court acquitted Sayyid 'Ali Ja'far Shabar 'Alawi, Mahdi Ibrahim Ja'far 'Ali, and 'Adil Hasan 'Abdallah Ghannam. 96021101

February 11, 1996. *Algeria.* Two car bombs in Algiers killed 21 and wounded 93. One bomb went off in the town hall in Bab El-Oued. The second exploded outside La Maison de la Presse. Pedestrians and passing motorists were among the victims. The Armed Islamic Group was blamed.

February 12, 1996. *Colombia.* Colombian police cracked a plot to attack the U.S. Embassy, the Government Ministry, the Defense Ministry, and the Office of the Prosecutor General. The National Liberation Army (ELN) also planned to attack the home of National Police Director General Rosso Jose Serrano and the Center of Higher Police Studies. In two raids on ELN safe houses in Bogota, police arrested two terrorists and confiscated 30 rifles, 73 fragmentation grenades, 4 rockets, an antitank mortar round, and propaganda. 96021201

February 14, 1996. *Philippines.* An M-209 (other reports said an M-203) grenade exploded at the Shell Building in Paseo de Roxas, Salcedo Village, Makati, Manila, 15 minutes after noon, injuring four people, including an engineer, and damaging the neighboring Citibank Towers. The injured were Jay Tagan, Ernesto Cabiz, Imelda Paredes, and Myrna Rosentoso.

Police later found two Armalite rifles, eight 40-mm grenade rounds, eight loaded M-16 Armalite magazines, five ski masks, and two crowbars in the Blanco Center residential building two blocks away. Police were searching for a silver, heavily tinted L300 car used in the escape.

Some observers suggested that they were bank robbers, not terrorists. Others compromised, suggesting that it was an Abu Sayyaf bank robbery attempt against either the China Bank or Citibank. 96021401

February 14, 1996. *Bahrain.* A car bomb exploded prematurely in a Manama marketplace. Police found a timing device, tubes, two gasoline containers, and explosives in the car.

February 14, 1996. *North Korea.* Junior Sergeant Cho Myong-kil, 25, a North Korean Army security guard, jumped the wall of the Russian Embassy's trade mission building in Pyongyang, killing three North Korean guards and wounding another in a gun battle. He threatened to kill himself if he was not given political asylum. Russian diplomats and North Korean authorities negotiated with him. He made no threats against the Russians, but demanded that a Russian stay with him at all times. Russia agreed to extradition. He died of a head wound the next day at 10:15 A.M., killed either by his own hand or by North Korean sharp-shooters (Russian press reports conflicted).

The attack came two days before North Korean leader Kim Chong-Il's birthday and the day after his first wife, Sung Hae-Rim, defected.

February 15, 1996. *United Kingdom.* An 11-pound IRA plastic explosive bomb placed in a phone booth was deactivated in London's Leicester Square during the lunch break. Police were alerted to the location by an IRA-coded phone message. The IRA phoned the BBC to claim credit. Police raids in more than 20 locations in the United Kingdom led to the arrests of several people for the two recent bombings. 96021501

February 15, 1996. *Bosnia.* Hundreds of NATO (North Atlantic Treaty Organization) peacekeepers raided a Fornica mountain chalet near Sarajevo, breaking up a "terrorist training school" led by Iranians working for the Bosnian government. Authorities found 60 weapons—including booby-trapped toys, AK-47 rifles, hand grenades, submachine guns, and blasting caps—camouflage uniforms, disguises, detonators, explosives, and books and pamphlets in Farsi. The Bosnian government said it was an antiterrorist training center. NATO detained two Iranians and eight Bosnians, who were later handed over to the Bosnian government. Another Iranian holding a diplomatic passport was released.

February 15, 1996. *Bahrain.* The Kuwaiti Embassy was warned that attacks would follow if Kuwait continued to support Bahrain in its antiterrorist efforts. 96021502

February 15, 1996. *Greece.* The November 17 group was believed to have fired a 3.5-inch rocket-propelled antitank grenade at a security wall of the U.S. Embassy, damaging three cars. The grenade landed 100 meters from the main building, causing no injuries in the midnight attack. The previously unknown National Struggle told Antenna Television that the attack would begin "the struggle against American and Turkish tar-

gets." A police spokesman said a launcher tube was found, a claim later denied by senior officials. 96021503

February 16, 1996. *Colombia.* Six members of the National Liberation Army (ELN) kidnapped a U.S. citizen in La Guajira Department. No ransom demand was made. The hostage was freed on November 15. 960210601

February 17, 1996. *Venezuela.* The Colombian National Liberation Army (ELN) was believed responsible for murdering two Venezuelan border guards at 3:45 P.M. Two civilian men at the La Llovizna gas station, on the outskirts of La Victoria, fired revolvers at two guards following an argument. They then stole the guards' rifles and escaped on a small boat on the Arauca River. The two guards were pronounced dead on arrival at a hospital. 96021701

February 18, 1996. *United Kingdom.* At 10:30 P.M. a bomb went off in a red No. 171 London Transport double-decker bus on Wellington Street near Trafalgar Square and Covent Garden. One person was killed and eight passengers and pedestrians were injured by flying metal and glass. The IRA claimed credit. No warning was sent. One of the injured people was put under police guard as a possible suspect. He was cleared following a raid on his Dublin home.

The IRA announced three days later that Edward O'Brien, 21, of Gorey, County Wexford, Ireland, was killed in the blast. They said he was an IRA operative "on active service." Police believed he was carrying the bomb to another location when it went off prematurely. Police found a weapon in the bus wreckage.

On February 19, police arrested two men under antiterrorist laws, but later released them. The next day, police seized explosives and bomb-making equipment in raids in London. 96021801

February 19, 1996. *France.* Police arrested 20 sympathizers of the Algerian Armed Islamic Group.

February 20, 1996. *Thailand.* Bangkok police arrested Keijiro Ota, 51, a member of the Japanese Aum Shin Rikyo cult, as he stepped off a bus from Chiang Rai. Police believed he was involved in a plot to attack leaders at the March 1–2 Asia-Europe Meeting (ASEM). Police confiscated his passport, his Sakura Bank passbook, a passport for a Japanese woman named Eiko Kawai, two credit cards in her name, Indian and Philippine currency, a pair of handcuffs, and ten pages of documents. Police believed a letter found on Ota included secret sect codes. Ota was also wanted for fraud and extortion. Japan reportedly was considering an extradition request.

Police announced that they were searching for 18 cult members, including Naoko Kikuchi, Kouichi Kitamura, Katsuya Takahashi, Makuto Hirata, Satoshi Matsushita, Tasuo Hayashi, and Zonji Yakisawa.

On February 22, immigration police in Trok Khao San arrested Hiroyuki Shiyama, 31, who reportedly worked for Ota, and another unnamed Japanese man, who was charged with possession of marijuana.

February 20, 1996. *Indonesia.* Rebels identified by the government as the Security Disturbance Movement (GPK) abducted Frederick Benti, a French researcher, and Gabriel Go, an Indonesian, in Okaitadi village in Western Paniai Subdistrict, Paniai District, at 7:00 P.M. They were freed the next day at 2:30 P.M. after the kidnappers fled at the sight of rescue helicopters bearing down on them. The duo worked for Nabire Delta Mining Company. 96022001

February 20, 1996. *Turkey.* Zahra Rajabi, a member of the Iranian dissident Mojahedin-e Khalq's National Council of Resistance in Paris, was shot to death while visiting Istanbul. 96022002

February 20, 1996. *Turkey.* Two members of the Iranian Mojahedin-e Khalq dissident group were found dead in their Istanbul apartment. In April, three Islamic militants and several Iranian and Turkish citizens were arrested for the murders.

The militants claimed they had received their orders from Iranian diplomats in Turkey. 96022003

February 22, 1996. *Australia.* A bomb went off at the Chinese Community Center at Granville in western Sydney, blowing off the front window. The device consisted of a large cardboard tube packed with gunpowder and ball bearings. 96022201

February 22, 1996. *Germany.* London's *Al-Hayat* reported that an assassination attempt had been made against Shaykh Rabah Kebir, the overseas leader of the Algerian Islamic Salvation Front. 96022202

February 24, 1996. *United States.* The Cuban Mission to the UN claimed it had received telephoned bomb threats against its building and assassination threats against its diplomats following the shooting down of two unarmed civilian planes by Havana. 96022401

February 24, 1996. *Israel.* A bomb exploded at 6:45 A.M. on the No. 18 Egged bus as it was stopped for a red light in Jerusalem, killing 23 people, including 2 American students, and injuring 49. Police believed that the bomb contained 10 to 20 kilograms of explosives and metal fragments. The bomb was hidden in an army kit bag. The bomber wore a disguise. The Americans were Matthew Mitchell Eisenfeld, 25, of West Hartford, Connecticut, and Sarah Duker, 22, of Teaneck, New Jersey. A No. 18 bus passing by was also damaged, as were numerous cars.

At 7:35 A.M., a bomb exploded at an Ashqelon soldiers' hitchhiking post, killing 2, including female soldier Hofit Ayash, 20, and injuring 31. The bomb was carried by a Palestinian wearing an Israeli army uniform and an earring.

Calls from the Izzedine al Qassam Brigades, the military wing of Hamas, said it was avenging the January 5 death of Yehiya Ayash, Hamas's chief bomb maker. The group claimed responsibility in the name of the Squads of the New Disciples of

Martyr Yehiya Ayash. Callers also cited the February 25, 1994, murder of 29 Muslims by a Jewish settler in Hebron and the death of Fathi al-Shaqaqi. A Hamas leaflet denied responsibility. On February 29, another Hamas leaflet credited Ibrahim Farhanah and Majdi Abu-Wardah, residents of the al-Fawwar refugee camp near Nablus, with the bombings. Palestinian police arrested 250 Hamas activists.

Ahmad Jibril, secretary general of the Popular Front for the Liberation of Palestine-General Command, sent a congratulatory telegram to Hamas.

The *Jerusalem Post* reported that Yasir (variant Yasser, Yassir) Arafat claimed that the Hamas "fanatics" were assisted by ex-Israel Defense Force members called the Secret Army Organization (OAS), which provided the bombs. 96022503

February 25, 1996. *Sri Lanka.* The Ellalah Force, alleged to be a front for the Liberation Tigers of Tamil Eelam (LTTE), made death threats against the staff of the Malaysian Embassy and the Japanese Embassy. The Japanese were told not to issue a visa to Neelam Thiruchelvam, a Tamil United Liberation Front member of parliament, who was to visit Japan for a seminar. Various human rights organizations faulted the Malaysians for announcing that Malaysia would revoke the permanent resident status of foreigners supporting LTTE activities.

LTTE used its *Tamil Eelam News* Web site to deny that it had made the threats. 96022601

February 25, 1996. *United States.* Dr. Haing Ngor, 45, a Cambodian refugee who won a Best Supporting Actor Oscar for the 1984 film *The Killing Fields*, was shot to death outside his car in front of his home in Los Angeles' Chinatown. He sustained a gunshot wound to the chest.

Ngor escaped from Cambodia in 1980. In *The Killing Fields*, he portrayed Dith Pran, the Cambodian translator and photographer for a *New York Times* reporter. The movie showed genocide and torture by the Khmer Rouge regime and many exile groups believed the Khmer Rouge had

ordered Ngor's murder. Ngor had also organized the Brussels-based Aid to Displaced Persons and the Paris-based Enfants d'Angkor.

On April 16, Tak Sun Tan, 19, Jason Chan, 18, and Indra Lim, 19, were charged with the murder and robbery of Ngor. The defendants were members of the Oriental Lazyboys, a Chinatown-based gang that engages in carjackings and residential burglaries. Chan and Lim had been arrested earlier on other robbery charges. They faced a death sentence if convicted. On October 11, 1996, Los Angeles Municipal Court Judge Stephen Marcus ordered the trio to stand trial for the killing. Defense lawyers contended that the police unfairly targeted their clients and that the star prosecution witness had recanted.

On April 9, 1998, one of the three juries—one for each defendant—reached a verdict. The decision regarding Jason Chan was kept secret while the other panels deliberated. On April 16, the three defendants were convicted of murder. None of the juries determined who was the triggerman, but they ruled that one of the defendants had the gun in the holdup in the alley behind Ngor's apartment. Chan faced a possible sentence of life in prison without parole; Tan and Lim faced sentences of 25 years to life. Prosecutors said the gang killed Ngor for money to buy crack. Ngor's $6,000 Rolex watch was missing, as was a gold locket he wore that contained a photo of his late wife, who died in childbirth. The defense pointed out that $3,000 in cash was left on the back seat of Ngor's car.

On May 19, 1998, Superior Court Judge J. D. Smith sentenced Chan to life without parole, Tan to 56 years to life, and Lim to 26 years to life. The list of charges against Chan and the list of prior convictions—dating back to when he was 13—brought him the longest sentence. 96022502

February 25, 1996. *Gaza Strip.* On May 14, 2000, Palestinian Authority police announced the arrest ten days earlier of Mohammed Deif (variants Dayf, Dief), 34. Deif, Israel's public enemy number one, was believed to be responsible for a series of Hamas Izzedine al Qassam Brigades bombings in early 1996 that killed 47 and wounded 96, including an attack on February 25 that destroyed a Jerusalem bus, killing 23. The son of a blanket maker, Deif grew up in Gaza's Khan Younis refugee camp, and took part in the *intifadah* clashes in the 1980s. He was an aide of Yehiya Ayash, Hamas's chief bomb maker who was killed in 1995 by a Shin Bet booby-trapped cell phone.

February 26, 1996. *United Kingdom.* The IRA reportedly threatened to attack the royal family. Security was increased at Buckingham Palace. 96022601

February 26, 1996. *Albania.* At 9:30 A.M., a car bomb consisting of 110 pounds of explosives stuffed in a Fiat Tipo went off in central Tirana next to a Vefa supermarket, killing 4 (some reports say 5) and wounding 30. The car had no license plates. Three former members of the Sigurimi secret police were arrested. Police denied a Reuters report that a member of the Italian Mafia was involved.

On March 1, a court ordered the arrest of *Populli Po* journalist Ylli Polovia for "public appeal for violent actions" under Article 223 of the Penal Code. He had written in newspaper articles that other terrorist attacks could occur. Six employees of *Koha Jone* were also detained.

Those who were killed in the blast—Vera Dume, Muhamet Karamani, Asim Karamani, and Vaid Osmani—were formally named "Martyrs of Democracy" by Tirana's municipal government.

The Albanian government offered a 5 million lek reward for the identities of the bombers.

February 27, 1996. *Colombia.* Police deactivated six remote-controlled bombs in Bogota. Bombs were found at a facility that houses the Defense Ministry and the new U.S. Embassy. 96022701

February 27, 1996. *Israel.* Ahmad 'Abd-al-Hamidah, 36, a naturalized U.S. citizen from California, killed an Israeli woman and injured 22 others when his Fiat crashed into a crowded bus stop at the French Hill junction. Some reports said two or three people were killed. Hamas claimed that 'Abd-al-Hamidah was a member of the Izzedine al Qassam Brigades, Hamas's military wing, and that he was marking the murder of Fathi al-Shaqaqi by Mossad agents in Malta in October. Armed civilians shot dead 'Abd-al-Hamidah when he got out of the car. Police found an Islamic Jihad leaflet in the car, which was rented in East Jerusalem. Police said he had recently become a devout Muslim and may have had links to Hamas. 96022702

February 28, 1996. *Bulgaria.* The government denied reports that Egyptian Jihad Group leader Dr. Ayman Zawahiri (variants Ayman al-Zawahiri, Ayman Zawahri, Iman Zowaheri) had been in the country since 1993.

February 28, 1996. *Guatemala.* Howard Turner Clark, 70, a U.S. businessman who owns part of a prestigious hotel in Guatemala City, was kidnapped. He was released on March 1 after his relatives paid a substantial ransom. Clark was a sponsor of the Miss Guatemala beauty pageant.

March 1, 1996. *Guatemala.* Kidnappers abducted Claire Phillips, 64, an American, in a southern Guatemala City neighborhood. They released her that night, telling her they had made a mistake. No ransom was demanded. 96030101

March 3, 1996. *Israel.* At 6:25 A.M., a bomb exploded on a No. 18 Egged bus on Jaffa Road and Rashbag Street between the central post office and police headquarters in Jerusalem, killing 19, including 5 Romanian migrant workers, a Romanian tourist, an Ethiopian tourist, 2 Palestinians, and the bomber, and wounding 10, 6 severely. Many shop fronts were damaged, including those of Helena Rubenstein beauty products and lingerie, Pizza Magic, Denis nail salon, and Diesenhaus Tours and Travel. A Hamas leaflet said the group was avenging the January 5 death of Yehiya Ayash. The leaflet was signed by the Students of Yahya Ayyash (variant spelling).

One of the Palestinians killed was Angel Siryani, 45, a nurse at Jerusalem's Hadassah Ein Kerem Hospital.

On March 8, Israeli soldiers blew up the two-room house of the family of Raed Shaghnoubi, who carried the bomb onto the bus.

One of the injured Romanian laborers died on March 9.

By March 10, Palestinian security forces had arrested the three members of Hamas suspected of involvement in the recent series of bombings. Abdel Fatah Satari, Salem Abu Marouf, and Kamal Khalifa were among the 11 the Israelis asked the Palestinians to arrest. 96030301

March 4, 1996. *Israel.* A Palestinian set off a bomb near a bus in Tel Aviv, killing 20, including 2 Americans, and wounding 150. He attempted to walk into the Dizengoff Center, an enclosed mall, but guards apparently scared him away. He triggered his bombs at an outdoor crosswalk at 4:01 P.M. when a red light halted numerous people. Several children, many of them wearing Purim costumes, were killed or injured. The Pupils of Ayash, a faction of the military wing of Hamas, claimed credit for this and two other blasts.

Sa'id Husayn Sulaymani, 45, an Israeli Arab from Manshiya-Zabda, had picked up the bomber in Gaza and driven him to Tel Aviv for $1,100. The bomber hid in a crate in a grocery truck, then walked to the mall. Sulaymani was arrested on March 4 and remanded into custody until March 20.

Palestinian security forces in Ramallah arrested Mohammed Abu Wardeh, 21, a student at an Islamic teachers college, believed to be the mastermind of three of the last four bombings. His chiefs were believed to be holed up in Damascus, Syria, although his recruiter was also arrested. Abu Wardeh was quickly convicted of recruiting three suicide bombers. Yasir Arafat approved a sentence of life at hard labor.

Iran denied involvement in the bombing campaign.

On March 9, an anonymous Arabic-speaking caller told Israel Television Channel 1 that the Islamic Jihad bomber was 'Ummar Siyam of Gaza's Sabra neighborhood. He had set off 17 kilograms of TNT, according to the caller.

On March 15, Palestinian sources were quoted by *Qol Yisra'el* as identifying the bomber as Ramiz 'Abd-al-Qadir Muhammad 'Abid, 22, an Islamic Jihad member from Khan Yunus.

Hamas and the Palestinian Islamic Jihad claimed credit.

Some time afterward, Israeli authorities prevented three would-be suicide bombers from entering the country. Later that night, they raided a Hamas safe house in Gaza, arresting Abdallah Yosef Abu Sakran, 21. 96030401

March 7, 1996. *South Korea.* A man in his 40s speaking fluent English called the British Embassy in Seoul at 2:35 P.M. to warn that two bombs had been planted in the compound. No bomb was found. 96030701

March 8, 1996. *Cyprus.* Ramazan Aydin, 20, a Turkish waiter sympathetic to Chechen rebels, hijacked a North Cyprus Turkish Airlines Boeing 727 flying from Ercan Airport in Turkish-controlled northern Cyprus to Istanbul, diverting it to Sofia, Bulgaria. The hijacker demanded fuel, then flew to Munich, Germany, where he freed the 101 passengers and 8 crew members and surrendered on March 9.

The hijacker had demanded to talk to the media and to a prominent human rights attorney; neither demand was met. Aydin initially released two men, three women, and several children, then an hour later freed the pilot and a flight attendant. Negotiations were conducted by telephone using a Turkish interpreter. Freed hostages said the hijacker was armed with an automatic weapon and a bomb; authorities later said the weapons were fake and that he carried only a replica pistol and a Russian passport. Police said they had arrested one hijacker; the media initially reported that four hijackers were involved. The hijacking lasted five and a half hours.

Among the passengers were 47 Turks, 33 Turkish Cypriots, 2 Russians, and 5 Belgians, as well as American, Japanese, Iranian, Danish, German, Ukrainian, and Sudanese travelers. The American was James Richard Walton.

The Turkish-Cypriot transportation minister named the hijackers, claiming they were Azerbaijanis. Vladimir Markov, deputy chief of Bulgaria's national security service, said they were Chechens carrying pistols. Other reports said they were Russians. 96030801

March 9, 1996. *United Kingdom.* A bomb exploded in a recycling bin outside Central London's Brompton Cemetery 38 minutes after midnight, causing no injuries. The bomb broke windows and damaged homes in Earl's Court and South Kensington. There was no advance warning, suggesting that it was not an IRA bombing. However, the IRA has set off bombs in trash cans.

March 10, 1996. *Egypt.* The Egyptian Islamic Jihad warned the Bulgarian government that if it extradited any wanted terrorists to Egypt, "Bulgaria would turn its own territory into an arena of confrontation. . . . What happened in Islamabad could be repeated anywhere." The group had bombed the Egyptian Embassy in Islamabad in November 1995. 96031001

March 13, 1996. *Bahrain.* Robert's Restaurant, a favorite of British and other European residents near Sanabis, was firebombed. No injuries were reported. 96031301

March 14, 1996. *Bahrain.* Five masked arsonists poured gasoline and threw Molotov cocktails at the al-Zaytun Restaurant in Sitrat Wadiyan, killing seven Bangladeshi workers.

On March 20, police announced that four suspects from Sutrah had confessed in front of an investigating judge. The four laborers were identified as 'Ali Ahmad 'Abadallah al-'Asfur, 31; Ahmad Khalil Ibrahim al-Kattab, 30; Qumbur Khamis 'Ali Qumbur, 22; and Khalil Ibrahim 'Abdallah Khamis, 21. Three other suspects were still being questioned. Exiled oppositionists

claimed 400 people were arrested and suggested that the government had staged the incident to obtain Western support. Shi'ite Muslims were suspected.

On July 1, the State Security Court passed sentence on charges of premeditated arson in connection with the case. Death sentences were given to 'Ali Ahmad 'Abdallah al-Asfur, 31, an Agriculture Ministry employee; Yusuf Husayn 'Abd-al-Baqi, 31, a teacher; and Ahmad Khalil Ibrahim Hubayl al-Kattab, 30, an employee at the Aluminum Bahrain Company (ALBA). Life sentences were imposed on Khalil Ibrahim 'Abdallah Khamis, 21; Qambar Khamis 'Ali Qambar, 23; 'Abdallah Ibrahim 'Abdallah Khamis, 27, all of whom are laborers; and Muhammad Rida Ya'qub Yusuf al-'Attar, 23, a fisherman. 'Abd-al-'Aziz Husayn 'Abd-al-Baqi, 18, a student, was to serve 15 years in prison. Bahrain opposition sources denounced the death sentences imposed on the three Shi'ite Muslims. 96031401

March 14, 1996. *Mexico.* Thirty peasants belonging to the Union of Organizations of Guerrero States Southern Mountain Range took over the Norwegian Embassy on Virreyes Boulevard, Number 1360, Lomas de Chapultepec, in Mexico City. They asked the Norwegians to ask Government Secretary Emilio Chuayffet about the murder of 17 peasants from Aguas Blancas. Pedro Navas Rodriguez, the group's spokesman, said that although the group had been in the facility for three days, it would not leave before the Coyuca de Benitez massacre was investigated.

Peasants belonging to the Sierra del Sur Peasants Organization occupied the embassies of Germany and Italy and the consulates of Germany, Italy, and Norway in Acapulco to make similar requests. The group believed that former Governor Ruben Figueroa Alcocer was behind the murders. The peasants requested the mediation of UN Secretary General Boutros-Ghali and the removal of the army from checkpoints.

March 14, 1996. *Belgium, Germany.* Munich police stepped up security precautions at Israeli facilities after Belgian police in Antwerp found explosives and mortars destined for Munich on the *Iran Kollahdooz*, an Iranian freighter. The mortar had a timer and a range of more than 700 yards. Its shell was equal to 275 pounds of TNT. Police arrested an Iranian owner of an import-export firm in connection with the seizure of explosives, which were hidden among garlic and cucumbers. The ship continued to Hamburg. Police later questioned two Iranian employees of the Iranian Ministry of Intelligence who were on the freighter. Two other Iranian residents of Munich to whom the container was addressed were also questioned. All four were later released. 96031402

March 17, 1996. *Bahrain.* The U.S. Embassy issued a security alert in the wake of a bombing campaign by Shi'ite Muslims against the Sunni Muslim Khalifa dynasty.

March 17, 1996. *Israel.* Hamas denied reports of an assassination plot against U.S. President Bill Clinton.

March 17, 1996. *Russia.* Moscow police defused a bomb found in a bus. The bomb had been set to go off 15 minutes later on Route 157.

March 18, 1996. *China.* South Korea claimed that North Korea was planning on conducting terrorist attacks and kidnappings of South Korean diplomats, businessmen, and students in China in revenge for the January defection of Sung Hae-Rim, former wife of Kim Chong-Il.

March 19, 1996. *Bahrain.* A bomb went off at 6:30 P.M. at the entrance to the health club on the lower ground floor of the three-star Baisan Hotel in Manama. Flying glass injured two Indians. The explosion cracked the walls and broke windows. 96031901

March 20, 1996. *Russia.* Moscow police found 2 unguided missiles, 108 firearms, 2 explosives, 1 antitank mine, and 4,300 rounds of ammunition during a check of vehicles on the streets.

Officers of the Moscow Regional Directorate

for the Struggle with Organized Crime and the Federal Security Service (FSB) detained three criminals who were carrying two bombs. Police pulled two men, identified as Aleksandr Gladkikh and Boris Kuzin, employees of Slovo i Delo, a private security firm, from their black Zhiguli. One of the suspects was carrying a forged militia identification card. The duo led police to the Polyany rest home, where they arrested Chechen Magomed Iznaurov and found another bomb hidden in an oven. *Kommersant-Daily* reported that his room had been rented by the American Orthodox Christian Foundation. The *Moscow Tribune* reported that they were ruled out as suspected terrorists.

March 20, 1996. *Colombia. El Tiempo* reported that there had been 103 kidnappings in January, 92 in February, and 22 through March 18. Of the 217 people kidnapped, 11 were foreigners and 26 were children. Forty-five foreigners were kidnapped in 1995.

March 21, 1996. *Russia.* Moscow officials found a 23-mm anti-aircraft shell in a schoolyard after a passerby told police that he found a 32-mm cannon shell on the Moscow circular highway.

March 21, 1996. *Colombia.* Police defused a 1-kg dynamite bomb that was placed at the door of the Venezuelan Consulate in Bogota. No one was injured and no damage was reported. The consulate had received earlier threats. 96032101

March 21, 1996. *Somalia.* Gunmen abducted five foreigners working for aid organizations at Balli Doogle Airport, 90 kilometers southwest of Mogadishu. One of the foreigners was the representative of the World Health Organization (WHO). The other four worked for the United Nations International Children's Emergency Fund (UNICEF). The five were on their way to Nairobi, Kenya, when they got into a dispute with Somali militiamen.

The next day, villagers traded gunfire with the kidnappers and released the hostages. A young boy was seriously wounded in the head during the evening shootout. 96032102

March 22, 1996. *Sri Lanka, United Kingdom.* *Colombo Radio* claimed that the Liberation Tigers of Tamil Eelam (LTTE) were forcing expatriates in London to pay 5 percent commissions when they sent money to their relatives back home.

March 23, 1996. *Somalia.* Gunmen kidnapped an American woman who worked for the U.S. branch of the French charity International Action Against Famine. The attack took place 250 kilometers south of Boosaaso, Bender Cassim, in northeastern Bari Province on the road between Soosaaso and Qardo. One of her Somali bodyguards died in a gun battle with the kidnappers. UN sources believe she was taken by car to an area south of Ceelaayo toward Qardo. Some observers suggested that she was kidnapped as part of a pay dispute on the part of former Somali employees of the organization. She was released on March 25. 96032301

March 23, 1996. *Venezuela.* Investigators blamed the Colombian National Liberation Army (ELN) for killing a policeman and injuring another policeman and a civilian in La Victoria.

March 24, 1996. *Sudan.* At 1:46 P.M., two Sudanese youths hijacked Sudanese Airways Flight 214, an Airbus 320 flying from Khartoum to Port Sudan and Jeddah, by pointing a pistol and forcing pilot Bashir 'Ali Bashir to land at Asmara, Eritrea, for refueling. The duo had threatened to set off explosives if they were not allowed to touch down. The 7 crew and 42 passengers, including 3 children and 7 women, were released unharmed and the hijackers surrendered. The hijackers wanted to go to Jeddah, Saudi Arabia. London's MBC Television reported that one hijacker was a former officer in the Sudan Army who had led a foiled coup attempt. One hijacker was 28 years old. Hijackers Jafar Ibrahim Hassan and Ezzedine Hassan, members of the Sudanese security services, requested political asylum. Sudan requested extradition.

Eritrean authorities detained three Iranians on the plane. Ten foreigners, including the Iranians, a Jordanian, and the manager of Shell in South Africa, were passengers. Tehran demanded their release, saying that they were working for the Iran Gas Company in Port Sudan. They were identified as manager 'Ali Rida (or Reza), engineer Muzaffar, and technician Abul Qasim Mahdian. Asmara authorities said they did not have proper documentation. Ethiopia released them on March 30. 96032401

March 26, 1996. *Cambodia.* At 9:00 A.M., 25 Khmer Rouge guerrillas kidnapped 26 Cambodian mine removers and their British supervisor, Christopher Malone Howes, 36, of Bristol, England, as they were clearing a road in Gradow village, Angkor Thom District, near the Angkor Wat temple. They were driven north to Varin District in Siem Reap Province. The kidnappers asked for a ransom of 10,000 baht ($400) for each Cambodian hostage (other reports said they asked for 100,000 baht for them all). The kidnappers were in radio contact with the government. The group worked for the British-based Mines Advisory Group and were making safe a German-funded road project. Another six people managed to avoid capture by running through a mined area.

Two policemen died searching for the hostages when one of them stepped on a landmine on March 27. At least five policemen would die from landmine explosions during the search.

On March 28, villagers contacted the Khmer Rouge and determined that they were still holding Howes and his Cambodian interpreter, Houn Hurth (variant Huon Hourth), some 50 kilometers from Siem Reap. The kidnappers released the landmine removers when Howes refused to act as a courier for the ransom. Authorities believed that the kidnappers were Khmer Rouge defectors who had joined the regular army, but then deserted near the Thai border. A Khmer Rouge radio broadcast on March 28 denied involvement.

On April 2, General Khan Savoeun, commander of the 4th Military Region, reported that three villagers sent to negotiate the release of Howes and his translator had been taken hostage by the kidnappers. Rit, one of the six landmine removers who escaped, said 30 Khmer Rouge wearing various uniforms and armed with, inter alia, four B-40s, forced the hostages to hand over their valuables. They then said that they "must be sent for reeducation." Prince Norodom Ranariddh ruled out the use of force to free Howes.

On April 9, Cambodian officials said the hostages were moved further north near the Thai border.

On June 26, Cambodian officials said Howes and Huon Hurth were still alive and being held in Anlung Veng.

On July 12, one of the kidnappers, Chiep Chet, 27, a former Khmer Rouge soldier who had surrendered in 1995, was sentenced by the Siem Reap provincial tribunal to five years for illegally detaining Howes and for serving Khmer Rouge policy. Chiep Chet was born in Chup village, Svay Chek commune, Angkor Thom District, Siem Reap Province. He was arrested at his home. He had received 500 baht from the Khmer Rouge and agreed to assist them in the kidnapping. He claimed he never received the money. Police said the kidnapping was ordered by Ta Mok, the notorious one-legged Khmer Rouge leader. 96032601

March 27, 1996. *Algeria.* At 1:00 P.M., rebels kidnapped seven French Trappist monks who were sleeping in the main building of the Notre Dame de l'Atlas monastery in Tibihirine municipality, Medea Province, in mountainous northern Algeria. The kidnappers were believed to be Muslim insurgents who claimed to be seeking a doctor. Monsignor Pierre Claverie, the Catholic bishop of Oran, told reporters that one of the hostages was the facility's doctor, Brother Luc Dochier, 83, who was in poor health.

On April 26, the Armed Islamic Group (GIA) threatened to "cut the throats" of the monks if their militants held in France were not freed. The GIA apparently had been in contact with French and Italian Catholic representatives. The GIA also claimed they had killed ten Algerian policemen searching for the monks near Medea.

France urged the remaining 8,370 French citizens to leave Algeria.

The exiled Islamic Salvation Front (FIS) condemned the kidnapping and called for the immediate release of the hostages.

On May 23, the GIA announced that it had murdered the hostages. The bodies of the seven monks were found a few kilometers from Medea on May 30. *Al-Hayat* attributed the murders to disagreements within the GIA. 960332701

March 27, 1996. *Egypt.* Three armed men hijacked an Egypt Air Airbus A-310 flying 145 passengers and 7 crew from Luxor to Cairo and diverted it toward Tobruk, Libya. The flight had originated in Jeddah, Saudi Arabia. Some reports said the passenger list included 17 Japanese, 59 Canadians, 35 French citizens, and 18 of other nationalities, all of whom were freed in Martubah, Libya. Other reports said the passengers included 54 Americans, 16 Egyptians, 30 Southeast Asians, 3 Dutch citizens, and 3 Saudi hijackers from the Qahtan family of the Bani Hilal tribe. Nine of the French were tourists from Club Med. Cairo's MENA later reported that the hijackers were Egyptians: Najib Muhammad Mahmud, owner of a Luxor restaurant, his son, 16, and his nephew, 14.

The pilot said the hijackers burst into the cockpit five minutes before the plane was due to arrive in Cairo. The leader threatened to explode a Molotov cocktail and case of gunpowder if the pilot did not fly to Libya. The pilot said he did not have enough fuel, whereupon the hijacker attempted to ignite the gunpowder with a lighter. The pilot then headed for Libya and landed at Martubah Airport, 90 kilometers from Tobruk. The hijackers' leader did not believe he was in Libya. According to the pilot, he had taken a "whole strip of sedative pills and was acting strangely."

The hijackers demanded a meeting with Egyptian President Hosni Mubarak, President Clinton, and Libyan leader Muammar Qadhafi. They surrendered to Libyan soldiers after five hours. Qadhafi spoke to one of them who claimed to be bringing a "message from God" to help the Palestinians reopen the West Bank and Gaza Strip, which the Israelis had sealed after a Hamas bombing campaign. They also wanted to discuss a solution to the Sudan issue. They claimed to be Mubarak supporters and to have information on the failed assassination attempt against him in 1995. The hijackers demanded that negotiations be held in Arabic.

Ahmad Qadhadhaf-al-Dam arrived to negotiate over the radio with the hijackers, who refused to let him board the plane. They surrendered an hour later.

The hijackers were remanded into custody for 15 days, pending investigation on charges that included the death penalty. MENA identified them as Muhammad Mahmud Humayd (alias Najib; AFP in Paris said he was Muhammad Mahmud Hamid Salim, a mentally ill Luxor restaurant owner), his son Khalid Mahmud, 17, and his cousin Ahmad Husayn Kamil (MENA also listed him as 'Ali Mahmud), 17, all of whom confessed they had hijacked the plane so that their leader could request political asylum and enhance the status of his Bani Hilal clan. Muhammad also told the pilot that he had dreamt of an assassination attempt against Qadhafi, and needed to warn him.

Egyptian authorities said Muhammad was mentally ill, an alcoholic, and a drug addict. He had lost his restaurant a year earlier for administrative irregularities. He was flying to Cairo to see his psychiatrist. His son was seeking treatment for a drug habit.

The hijackers had purchased explosives from a merchant on the Idfu mountains. The younger hijackers tied match cords around their waists. They then met Muhammad in the lavatory, where he transferred the cords to a Samsonite case lined with powder, explosives, three bottles of brandy, and a knife he had purchased in the duty-free shop. Returning to their first class seats, Muhammad then informed them that they were going to hijack the plane.

MENA reported that the crew included the pilot, Captain Amenhotob Nassar, copilot Khalid Samir, and flight attendants Hadir Salah-al-Din, Maysa Mahmud, Daliya Malak, Dina 'Adil 'Ali, and Hind Faruq.

Luxor Airport authorities reported that there had been no collusion between the hijackers and ground security.

Egypt's embassy in Libya announced that Libya would extradite the hijackers. Qadhafi ordered them to be handed over to the Egyptians on March 31. They arrived in Cairo that day. 96032702

March 28, 1996. *Germany.* Abdallah Ocalan, general secretary of the Kurdistan Workers Party (PKK), threatened attacks in Germany if Bonn continued to support "the Turkish genocide of Kurds." He also did not rule out attacks on German vacationers in Turkey. "Every Kurd will become a living bomb" in a potential suicide campaign in Germany.

March 29, 1996. *France.* Roubaix police raided a hideout of Algerian and Moroccan terrorists who had committed a series of bank, armored car, service station, and convenience store robberies during which bystanders were shot down. More than 1,000 shots were fired in the gun battle, which ended with four Algerians burning alive. Omar Zemiri, one of three gang members who escaped, said the robberies were to fund a *jihad.* They were associated with a mosque in Lille known for preaching radical theology to disaffected North African immigrants. Lionel Dumont, a Frenchman who converted to Islam in 1991, also escaped and turned up in Sarajevo, Bosnia, where he was arrested for armed robberies. He was sentenced to 20 years in prison, but escaped. He had trained with the Islamic rebels in Afghanistan, fought alongside Bosnian Muslims in the Bosnia war, and later joined the Algerian and Moroccan gang in Roubaix. 96032901

March 30, 1996. *Colombia.* The Colombian Armed Revolutionary Force (FARC) was believed responsible for kidnapping Italian engineer Renato Moretta, 64, who was constructing a bridge over the River Magdelena for a Milan building company. RAI Television said six "agents" were wounded in the abduction. 96033001

March 31, 1996. *Venezuela.* Four Colombian People's Liberation Army (EPL) rebels kidnapped a rancher from a store in La Gabarra. The rancher had been warned that he would be kidnapped if he did not pay $50,000. The four terrorists fired on security forces as they fled. The four were killed and the hostage escaped. 96033101

April 3, 1996. *Angola.* Two UN Angola Verification Mission-3 (UNAVEM-3) military observers, Major Al-Zahu Ziad from Jordan and Captain Murai Shakespeare from Zimbabwe, and Oxfam Director Chris Stewards from the United Kingdom were killed in a 10:00 A.M. attack along the Cubal–Benguela road. Major Singh from India was wounded in the attack. The National Union for the Total Independence of Angola (UNITA) condemned the action. 96040301

April 3, 1996. *United States.* The FBI announced the arrest of Theodore John Kaczynski, 53, in a one-room cabin in the hills near Lincoln, Montana. He was believed to be the Unabomber, who had sent 16 letter bombs that had killed 3 and injured 23 during the preceding 17 years. He had been under surveillance for several weeks. Bomb-making paraphernalia was found in the cabin, as was a typewriter that matched the fonts used in the Unabomber's 35,000-word manifesto that was printed in the *Washington Post* and *New York Times*. He was initially charged on one count of possession of bomb components.

A grand jury was scheduled to hear evidence on April 17. Kaczynski was represented by public defender Michael Donohoe.

Kaczynski's brother David contacted the FBI in February to say he believed that Theodore was the Unabomber. Texts he found in his mother's Chicago house when she was going to sell it were similar to the Unabomber's tract. He had hired teams of private investigators to check out his suspicions, and then had attorney Anthony Bisceglie serve as a go-between with the FBI.

The reclusive Harvard graduate received his doctorate from the University of Michigan before becoming a math professor at the University of California at Berkeley.

The *News* of Islamabad claimed on April 6 that Kaczynski might have lived in Peshawar from 1982 to 1987, during the height of the Afghan War. He had listed himself in the 1982 Harvard alumni directory as residing at 788 Banchat Peshawar and Khadarkhel in Afghanistan. There is no known Banchat in Peshawar, although Khadarkhel is a small village in Khugiani District, 50 kilometers southwest of Jalalabad, capital of Afghanistan's eastern Nangarhar Province.

Some of the Unabomber victims' names were found on handwritten notes and other documents in the cabin. The FBI found a live bomb apparently ready for shipment, a draft of the manifesto, and a secret number the bomber had used that had not been revealed to the public. In addition, Kaczynski's DNA matched DNA from saliva taken from stamps used on Unabomber packages. A bomb blew up at the cabin four days after his arrest. Ultimately, the FBI listed 700 items found in the cabin.

On June 18, 1996, Kaczynski was indicted for the killings of Gilbert B. Murray (the bomb was addressed to William Dennison) in 1995 and Hugh C. Scrutton in 1985, and the injuries of David Gelernter and Charles Epstein in 1993. He was charged with transporting an explosive device with intent to kill or injure and mailing the device. Conviction carried a sentence of death or life in prison. On June 21, U.S. District Court Judge Charles C. Lovell ordered his trial moved from Helena, Montana, to Sacramento, California. On June 25, Public Defender Quin Denvir pleaded not guilty to the charges read by U.S. Magistrate Peter A. Nowinski in Sacramento.

On June 28, 1996, Kaczynski was indicted for three more Unabomber attacks: the April 25, 1982, pipe bomb attack against Patrick C. Fischer in Nashville; the November 12, 1985, pipe bomb attack against James V. McConnell in Ann Arbor, Michigan; and the February 20, 1987, placing of a bomb in the parking lot behind CAAMS in Salt Lake City, Utah.

On September 20, Assistant U.S. Attorney Robert J. Cleary said in a pretrial hearing in Sacramento that Kaczynski kept detailed diaries in which he admitted to each of the 16 Unabomber bombings.

On October 1, 1996, a federal grand jury in New Jersey handed down a three-count indictment against Kaczynski, charging him in the December 10, 1994, bombing death of New Jersey advertising executive Thomas J. Mosser. He allegedly had mailed the parcel bomb seven days earlier. Kaczynski faced a death penalty. On December 10, Kaczynski pleaded not guilty to charges in Newark of killing Mosser. The plea was made via a live video hookup to California. Senior U.S. District Judge Dickinson R. Debevoise presided. On December 12, the court rejected Kaczynski's request that the case be heard in California instead of New Jersey.

On November 22, 1996, U.S. District Judge Garland E. Burrell, Jr., scheduled the trial on explosives charges to begin on November 12, 1997. Federal defenders Quin Denvir and Judy Clarke had asked for a lengthy period to prepare their case.

On May 15, 1997, Attorney General Janet Reno told reporters that prosecutors would seek the death penalty. The Kaczynski family asked that he be spared.

On October 3, 1997, Judge Burrell ordered that the names of the jurors be sealed to guard against the "kook factor." The names, ages, and occupations of the jurors were ordered withheld until the case was over. Judge Burrell also barred the news media from photographing or sketching prospective jurors. Jury selection was set for November 12.

Items from Kaczynski's diary were filed with the court on October 23. In 1985, he reportedly wrote "planted bomb disguised to look like scrap of lumber" behind a Sacramento computer store and that the store's owner was "blown to bits." His diary also referred to "nonbombing" acts of violence.

On October 24, Kaczynski refused to submit to a court-ordered psychiatric evaluation. His lawyers indicated they might use an insanity or diminished capacity defense.

The trial began on November 12, 1997, with the beginning of jury selection, which took five weeks to complete. Nine women and three men were chosen. Some 170 potential jurors were interviewed.

Kaczynski was agitated by suggestions that an insanity defense would be used by his attorney, Gary Sowards. He refused to be examined by government doctors, according to Prosecutor Robert Cleary. Judge Burrell said he would have to examine "the degree of willfulness" of Kaczynski's refusal. The defense claimed that Kaczynski was in denial of his paranoid schizophrenia. Defense lawyers Denvir and Clarke argued for the opportunity to bring in psychiatrists to testify. On December 23, the defense lawyers offered to withdraw the insanity defense if they could use schizophrenia as an argument to save his life if convicted. The government rejected the deal.

On November 19, the government released part of a journal in which Kaczynski had written "I intend to start killing people. If I am successful at this, it is possible that when I am caught (not alive, I fervently hope!) there will be some speculation in the news media as to my motives for killing people (as in the case of Charles Whitman, who killed some 13 people in Texas in the '60s). If such speculation occurs, they are bound to make me out to be a sickie, and to ascribe to me motives of a sordid or 'sick' type. My psychology will be misrepresented."

On December 5, 1997, his cabin arrived in Sacramento, brought from Montana by truck. It was stored at a former U.S. Air Force base as a defense exhibit.

The *New York Times* reported on December 29 that earlier in the month, federal trial prosecutors and the Justice Department rejected a defense offer to plead guilty in exchange for a promise that he would not be executed and would instead get life without parole. The defense also announced that it would not call expert witnesses to testify to Kaczynski's mental state during either the guilt or penalty phases of the trial. Plea bargaining resumed in mid-January.

Judge Burrell asked a local defense attorney, Kevin Clymo, to assist in the case.

Opening statements, scheduled for January 5, 1998, were halted by the judge when the defendant yelled that he had a "very important" statement to make about his attorneys. He was brought into the judge's chambers with his attorneys for four hours of discussions.

Kaczynski sought to dismiss his lawyers because they planned to introduce the issue of his mental health. The judge told him on January 7 that it was too late for him to change lawyers. Judge Burrell noted that he had received an offer from Tony Serra, an activist attorney from the San Francisco area, to represent Kaczynski for free and not use a "mental defect" defense. Kaczynski then said he would like to represent himself.

On January 8, Kaczynski agreed to a mental examination designed to determine his competence to stand trial and assist with his defense. Observers believed he might also be determining his competence to conduct his own defense. Authorities said he might have tried to commit suicide by hanging himself with his underwear in his jail cell the previous night. He was put under a 24-hour suicide watch. The psychiatric tests began on January 12 with Sally Johnson, chief of psychiatry at the Federal Correctional Institution (Butner, North Carolina) interviewing him in his cell. She spent 19 hours over four days interviewing him.

On January 20, prosecutors and defense attorneys agreed that Kaczynski was mentally competent to stand trial. Johnson had found him mentally fit, indicating that he understood the proceedings and could assist in his own defense. His diagnosis was sealed, although sources reported that she believed he suffered from paranoid schizophrenia. The judge indicated that he would not appoint a new attorney for Kaczynski. The trial was set to resume on January 22.

On January 21, attorneys for both sides agreed that Kaczynski had the right to represent himself in court. Meanwhile, a federal magistrate ordered the prosecution to give the defense any evidence they had about additional shacks that Kaczynski had used.

On January 22, Kaczynski pleaded guilty to all 13 federal charges (including the pending New Jersey case) as part of a plea bargain that spared him the death penalty. He was sentenced to serve life in prison without possibility of release. He also admitted that he placed or mailed another 11 bombs for which he was not yet charged. He agreed that he could not appeal any part of the sentence. Formal sentencing was scheduled for May. The judge warned that he would be forced to pay restitution if he received money for his writings, mementos, or interviews.

On April 28, federal prosecutors released parts of Kaczynski's diaries, in which he said he was seeking "personal revenge" and killed because he hated people, not because he loved nature. His bloodlust began when he was a graduate student in 1966.

On May 4, 1998, Kaczynski, still unrepentant, was sentenced to four life terms plus 30 years in prison. Many of the victims and their families called for the death sentence. He was sent to a maximum security cell in Colorado.

On August 20, 1998, the FBI gave David Kaczynski a $1 million reward for turning in his brother and solving the case. He had earlier said he would use most of the reward to ease the grief of the victims' families. He would use some of the money to pay off legal bills. A Justice Department spokesman said the reward, one of the largest antiterrorism rewards in history, would still be taxed at the highest bracket, although placing the money in trust could lessen the federal and state taxes.

On September 11, 1998, Johnson's 47-page forensic evaluation ordered by Judge Burrell was released. It indicated that Kaczynski considered having a sex change operation when he was in his 20s. His confusion over his gender identity led to the rage that contributed to his bombing campaign. He planned to kill a psychiatrist, but also would attempt to avoid detection.

David Kaczynski requested that the IRS not collect $300,000 in taxes on the $1 million reward so that he could donate all of the money to the victims and their families. Senator Daniel Patrick Moynihan introduced such a bill in the U.S. Senate; New York Representatives Amo Houghton and Michael R. McNulty, both members of the Ways and Means Committee, submitted similar legislation in the House of Representatives. The legislation fell through. David also said on November 22 that he and his wife planned to sell the book and movie rights to pay hundreds of thousands of dollars in legal fees. On January 12, 1999, David announced he would help people hurt by paranoid schizophrenics by establishing a fund with half of the reward. He said he would give $500,000 to the Albany branch of the Community Foundation; the other half would be used to pay taxes and legal fees.

On May 28, 1999, Judge Burrell in Sacramento denied Kaczynski's bid for a trial, rejecting his claim that he was forced into pleading guilty.

On June 16, 1999, Kaczynski asked the 9th U.S. Circuit Court of Appeals for a review of his case, saying the trial judge was unfair and his lawyers wrongly used a mental illness defense. On October 23, 1999, the court agreed to hear his case, which could result in the death penalty if he is convicted. The court said it found sufficient evidence to examine his contention that his guilty plea was coerced and that he was inappropriately denied the right to self-representation.

On February 12, 2001, the 9th U.S. Circuit Court of Appeals in San Francisco in a 2–1 decision rejected convicted Unabomber Theodore J. Kaczynski's request to be retried. The court ruled that he was not coerced into pleading guilty to three fatal mail bombings. He had entered his plea in January 1998. On August 17, 2001, he lost another appeal for a rehearing, although one judge wrote a dissent that a federal court had treated Kaczynski as less than human. Kaczynski can appeal to the U.S. Supreme Court.

April 4, 1996. *Croatia.* Zagreb's HTV Television reported that police arrested a group of Bosnian citizens planning to conduct a terrorist attack. 96040401

April 4, 1996. *Libya.* Travelers claimed that two Libyan police officers were killed when Muslim fundamentalists attacked the Egyptian Consulate in Benghazi. The travelers said the attackers were attempting to seize weapons. The Egyptian ambassador in Tripoli, Ahmad Wahdan, denied that an attack took place.

April 7, 1996. *Israel.* Two gasoline bombs thrown at an Israeli commuter bus at Beit Omar injured five people.

April 7, 1996. *Bahrain.* At 2:00 A.M., a time bomb caused a fire that damaged three stores in the Sheraton Hotel shopping center in Manama. Shi'ite Muslims were suspected in the attack on the center, which is popular with foreigners. Police arrested three suspects on April 10, thanks to a tip.

April 8, 1996. *Paraguay.* Police announced that new Islamic terrorist cells were under surveillance in Pedro Juan Caballero and Ciudad del Este.

April 11, 1996. *Liberia.* The home of the U.S. ambassador was attacked by one of the warring factions. Security guards repulsed the afternoon raiders. 96041101

April 11–12, 1996. *Italy.* The Yugoslav Consulate in Milan was attacked twice within 24 hours by individuals who threw Molotov cocktails in the early mornings. 96041101, 96041201

April 12, 1996. *Israel.* A Lebanese terrorist handling an explosive device in his east Jerusalem Lawrence Hotel room was seriously injured when it exploded prematurely that morning. One of his legs was blown off, and he sustained injuries to his face. Hussein Muhammad Hussein Mikdad, 33, of Faroun, Lebanon, lost the use of his other leg and an arm and was blinded. The explosion severely damaged several rooms in the hotel on Salah al-Din Street. Police found two pounds of RDX plastic explosive and a delay mechanism in his room. He had photographed several local mosques, perhaps planning a provocation against the Israelis.

Police later determined that the Hizballah terrorist had smuggled enough plastic explosives through Tel Aviv's airport on April 4 to blow up a plane. He had arrived on a Swissair flight from Zurich, carrying a British passport in the name of Andrew Jonathan Charles Newman, which had been stolen three years earlier. He had planned to set off the bomb on an El Al plane. He spent a few days in Tel Aviv, then moved to the Lawrence Hotel on April 9. *Qol Yisra'el* reported that he had obtained the explosives from the Iranian Embassy in Beirut. Israeli officials claimed that he had been sent by Imad Mughniyeh, who was involved in the planning of other major Hizballah bombings, kidnappings, and hijackings. Hizballah denied involvement. 96041202

April 17, 1996. *United Kingdom.* A bomb went off during the night in a house in The Boltons, a posh residential area in West London, causing no injuries. Windows were blown out in the house and neighboring buildings. The IRA made a coded warning phone call a half hour before the blast. 96041701

April 18, 1996. *Egypt.* At 7:00 A.M., three or four masked gunmen fired automatic pistols and Kalashnikov assault rifles at the Europa Hotel on al-Haram Street in Cairo, killing 18 Greek tourists, including 14 women, and wounding 21 others, including 12 Greeks and 2 Egyptians. All were waiting to board a tourist bus to the Pyramids, two miles away. One of those wounded was an Egyptian who guarded the hotel's vehicles. The killers escaped in a waiting white Volkswagen minivan of the al-Jizah Service. Among those injured was Marina Engliera, 45.

The Islamic Group claimed credit, saying it wanted to avenge Israel's raids on Lebanon. It said it would continue to attack Israeli interests in Egypt until the raids stopped. The group said, "The operation was meant to take place at a time when Jewish tourists were supposed to be going to Alexandria. But we were surprised to find the Jews had been replaced by Greeks as a result of security plans by the Egyptian police to safeguard the Jews only." Some 80 Israeli tourists were staying in the

hotel at the time of the attack. The tour operator, Mistakidis Tours of Athens, had taken the group to Jerusalem days earlier. Guests also included tourists from Australia, Brazil, Poland, Spain, and Switzerland.

On April 20, Interior Minister Hassan Alfi moved the tourism police chief, the Giza Province security chief, and his deputy to administrative positions. Thirteen other police officers responsible for the hotel's security were suspended.

Police rounded up 1,500 suspected militants, including one who may have been involved directly in the attack. Police were still searching for four gunmen and the getaway driver.

On April 23, a gun battle between hundreds of police and terrorists led to the deaths of six people. The gunmen, who were suspected of the Greek attack, shot to death police Major General Gamal Fayek; his brother, Lieutenant Colonel Magdi Fayek; Lieutenant Reda Wali; and another policeman in a battle in the fields near Ashmouneen in Minya Province. Islamic Group member Salama Abdel Hakeem Radwan and another gunman were killed. Two to four gunmen escaped.

On June 16, 1996, Australia deported from Melbourne an individual identified as Mohammed Hassanien, believed to have been implicated in the attack. He had arrived in Sydney on May 7. He was arrested on June 3, but was held in secret until his deportation to a location in Europe. Members of the Australian parliamentary opposition claimed that Danish authorities would soon free him, although the FBI wanted to question him.

On July 26, Egyptian Interior Minister Hasan al-Alfi announced the arrest of two of the attackers; two others were killed in a gun battle with police. 96041801

April 18, 1996. *Lebanon.* Israeli 155-mm artillery shelled a UN refugee compound near Tyre, killing 90 and wounding at least 100. The Israelis were retaliating for a rocket attack from Lebanon, but the gunners missed their targets.

April 18, 1996. *Colombia.* Bogota Television reported that authorities had foiled a National

Liberation Army (ELN) terrorist plot to attack the U.S. Embassy, the National Administrative Center, and the Presidential Guard Battalion. In an ELN safehouse, police found five cases, each filled with 20 kilograms of explosives, along with targeting maps, a rifle, and three grenades. 96041802

April 18, 1996. *Burundi.* A grenade was thrown at the Gitega headquarters of the International Committee of the Red Cross (ICRC), which announced it would leave the area. No injuries were reported. 96041803

April 18, 1996. *Mexico.* During the evening, 60 peasants from Oaxaca State took over the Spanish Embassy to demand solutions for their agrarian problems. They refused to meet a senior Oaxaca official, but peacefully left the embassy the next day.

April 19, 1996. *Israel.* Jerusalem Television reported that an anonymous caller phoned *Qol Yisra'el* to say that terrorists had kidnapped an American in the West Bank or Gaza territories. They would execute him the next morning unless Israel stopped its attacks in Lebanon. The U.S. Embassy warned its citizens to exercise caution, but said the report might have been a "cruel hoax." Palestinian Authority sources also had no information.

Shaykh Fadlallah, the spiritual leader of Hizballah, ruled out murdering a foreign national in retaliation for the Israeli shelling of a refugee camp.

The Islamic Group threatened to kill captured Israeli pilot Ron Arad in the next 48 hours in retaliation.

April 20, 1996. *Israel.* Palestinian Authority police arrested 'Adnan al-Ghul, the second-most-wanted Hamas (Islamic Resistance Movement) leader, considered a deputy of Muhammad Deif. Israel had placed him on a list of wanted fugitives. Palestinian authorities said he was involved in planning several bombings.

April 20, 1996. *Colombia.* Several people were killed when a bomb was thrown into the Hilton Bar, three blocks from the police post in Apartado, Uraba. There were nearly 250 people inside at the time. Eight were seriously injured. 96042001

April 20, 1996. *India.* A bomb exploded during the evening in a multi-story tourist guest house in Paharganj District of central Delhi during the night, killing 17, including 8 Nigerians, a Dutch tourist, and an unidentified woman. The injured included a Briton, a Dutch man, and a Nigerian. Muslim Kashmiri guerrillas were suspected. The Islami Harkat-ul-Momineen and the Khalistan Liberation Force claimed that the bomb had been detonated remotely. The groups said they were trying to stop elections in Jammu and Kashmir and to punish their rivals. Delhi Radio said 20 to 30 kilograms of RDX were in the bomb. 96042002

April 20, 1996. *Iraq.* Three Iraqi gunmen shot to death Jordanian citizen 'Awni Yusuf Ahmad 'Awad, 52, then threw him from the al-Taji Bridge in Gabhdad. They stole his car, watch, ring, and 500 dinars. His nephew, Rashad, said 'Awad was a taxi driver on the Amman–Baghdad–Damascus line. He left Amman for Baghdad on March 27, then disappeared for two weeks. His son, Muhammad, went to Baghdad to look for him. Four days later, Muhammad phoned Rashad to say he had determined that his father had been shot in the head three times.

Jordanian Ambassador Bassam Qaqish was recalled for consultation regarding the murder.

The Iraqi Embassy denied that Iraqi security services killed Jordanian citizens Muhammad Khayr Abu-Zayd, 'Izz-al-Din al-Duwayri, and Muhammad Salih 'Awadallah. The embassy personnel suggested they were killed by a gang of highway robbers and burglars.

April 21, 1996. *Egypt.* A spokesman for the Islamic Group, Mustafa Hamzah, said from exile in Afghanistan that his group was considering kidnapping Americans to win the freedom from jail of spiritual leader Sheik Omar Abdel Rahman (variants Umar Abd-al-Rahman, Omar Abd-al-Raman, Omar Abd-al Rahman), who was jailed for plotting to bomb New York City landmarks.

April 21, 1996. *Russia.* Authorities announced the death of Chechen separatist leader Dzhokhar Dudayev, 52, during a Russian missile attack in Gekhi-Chu, 18 miles southwest of Grozny. Several members of his entourage were also killed. His group vowed to continue fighting the Russian regime. Field commander Shamil Basayev announced that Zelimkhan Yandarbiyev would replace Dudayev.

April 21, 1996. *Pakistan.* The cause of an explosion at the USIS American Center in Lahore during the night was unclear. The blast destroyed windowpanes, but caused no injuries. Karachi *Dawn* said it was caused by two Russian-made hand grenades. Police claimed it was fireworks being used at a wedding ceremony.

April 21, 1996. *Lebanon.* The *Voice of Lebanon* reported that the Egyptian group Vanguards of Conquest (Tala'i' al-Fath) threatened to attack U.S. and Israeli interests "everywhere" to protest Israel's bombardment of Lebanon. The group said, "Blood, not cries, will be the response to the cowardly aggression in Lebanon. There can be nothing but *jihad* as a response and stance that must be taken toward the United States and Israel." 96042101

April 22, 1996. *Yugoslavia.* Claiming Albanian nationality, the Liberation Army of Kosovo claimed credit for shooting incidents in several locations in Kosovo in which an Albanian student and five Serbs, including a police officer, were killed and another five wounded. A child died and three people were injured when a bomb exploded in Velika Reka. The group had earlier told a Swiss-based, Albanian-language newspaper that it had bombed six Serb refugee camps in Kosovo on February 11. 96042201-03

April 24, 1996. *Uganda.* Ugandan rebels killed five Sudanese refugees and burned down a hospital run by the Dutch branch of Doctors Without Borders. 96042401

April 24, 1996. *United Kingdom.* At 11:00 P.M., a detonator failed to set off a powerful IRA bomb consisting of 30 pounds of Semtex that had been planted under the Hammersmith Bridge across the River Thames in London. 96042402

April 24, 1996. *Poland.* A bomb went off at a Shell station in Warsaw, killing a policeman who was attempting to defuse it. The GN 95 claimed responsibility and demanded $2 million from the Royal Dutch Shell Group. They said they opposed expansion of foreign investment. 96042403

April 25, 1996. *Colombia.* Colombian rebels kidnapped Eloy Quintero, the Colombian consul in Venezuela, and his wife on a road near Cucuta in the border area. Quintero was posted 800 kilometers west of Caracas in Maracaibo. He was released that day, but his wife was still held.

April 26, 1996. *United States.* Treasury agents arrested two members of the 112th Volunteer Battalion of the Militia at Large of the Republic of Georgia near Macon, Georgia, who were planning to make dozens of pipe bombs over the weekend in preparation for a "war" against the UN and the New World Order. William James McCranie, Jr., 30, a plumber from Crawford County, Georgia, and electrician Robert Starr, 34, were arraigned before federal magistrates in Columbus and Macon. Officials quickly dispelled the notion that they were planning to attack the Olympics in Atlanta.

On November 2, Assistant U.S. Attorney Sam Wilson told a jury in U.S. District Court that McCranie, Starr, and construction worker Troy Spain, 29, planned to bomb federal facilities. Each was indicted on two counts of conspiring to use a destructive device and one count of possession of such a device. Starr and McCranie were charged with threatening the life of the U.S. Bureau of Alcohol, Tobacco, and Firearms (ATF) supervisor in Macon. Starr was charged with possession of an assault rifle. The trio faced life sentences. Defense attorneys said that ATF undercover operatives Danny Barker and his brother Kevin, both disaffected militia members, had goaded the defendants to their actions.

After deliberating for 23 hours, a federal jury announced on November 6 that it found the trio guilty on two of the five counts of conspiracy to use a destructive weapon in a violent crime and possession of illegal explosives. They were acquitted of a second conspiracy count. Starr and McCranie were found not guilty of threatening the ATF supervisor; Starr was acquitted of possessing an assault rifle. Sentencing was expected to take place within two months. Observers believed they would receive a maximum of 17 to 22 years. Defense lawyers said they would appeal.

April 27, 1996. *Paraguay.* Israel announced that members of an Iranian-controlled Hizballah terrorist cell on their way to attack a Jewish institution were arrested at the tri-border area of Argentina, Brazil, and Paraguay. On April 29, *Noticias Argentinas* of Buenos Aires reported the release of two Lebanese citizens who were held for not presenting identity papers. Lebanese citizens Nasser Mahmud, 37, and Ali Mahmad, 48, claimed to be bakers from Foz do Iguacu, Brazil. They said their attorney, who was applying for their residency papers, was in possession of their identity papers.

Argentina had earlier denied reports that 20 Hizballah suicide commanders were in the area.

April 28, 1996. *Pakistan.* A bomb exploded on a passenger bus heading for Pattoki, 100 kilometers west of Lahore, killing 50 people and critically injuring 26. The passengers were going home to celebrate the three-day Muslim festival of Eid ul Azha. The bomb was planted just above the diesel gas tank. The bus had started from the Badami-bagh bus stand.

April 28, 1996. *Turkey.* During the evening, a bomb destroyed a door and blew out windows near the Istanbul office of Aeroflot-Russian International Airlines. The previously unknown Organization for Solidarity with the Chechen Resistance Fighters claimed credit. 96042801

April 29, 1996. *Russia.* Local media claimed that Chechen leader Zelimkhan Yandarbiyev, 44, died in a battle with a rival faction near Urus-Martan. On May 1, he held a news conference to say that he still ran the organization, which he took over from Dzhokhar Dudayev, who was killed by a Russian rocket blast.

April 30, 1996. *France.* Israeli Prime Minister Shimon Peres announced that a Hizballah commando was arrested in Paris as the commando was preparing an anti-Israel attack. 96043001

April 30, 1996. *Spain.* The Spanish Supreme Court said there was no evidence that departing Prime Minister Felipe Gonzalez had overseen a "dirty war" against Basque Nation and Liberty (ETA) rebels. Former security chiefs had claimed that Gonzalez and two other senior Socialist leaders approved a campaign of murder, kidnapping, and bombing from 1983 to 1987 that killed 27 people. The writ by Supreme Court Investigating Justice Eduardo Moner overturned the opinion of Judge Baltasar Garzon. Socialists claimed the charges against Gonzalez had led to his electoral defeat.

April 30, 1996. *South Africa.* President Nelson Mandela denied Israeli claims that Hizballah was training in local camps.

April 30, 1996. *Liberia.* U.S. Marines shot to death two Liberian rebels and injured a third during street fighting that had moved close to the U.S. Embassy. Two hours later, near the same Marine guard post, another six Liberians fired automatic weapons. Marines returned the fire, killing another rebel. 96043002-03

May 2, 1996. *Venezuela.* The Revolutionary Armed Forces of Colombia (FARC) attacked the Venezuelan Carabobo military post, where the group had killed eight soldiers in February 1995. Following a 15-minute gun battle, the rebels retreated without causing injuries. 96050201

May 4, 1996. *Afghanistan.* Several rockets were fired at Kabul. One hit the Iranian Embassy, causing slight damage.

May 5, 1996. *Bahrain.* Nine bombs hidden in booby-trapped cigarette packages exploded around 2:00 A.M. in Manama, destroying four shops and damaging five others. No injuries were reported. Police defused six other explosives at a nearby shopping center; a seventh exploded, but caused no damage. No one claimed credit, although Shi'ite Muslim activists were suspected. The government blamed Islamic terrorists for the explosions, which caused millions of dollars in damage.

At 1:00 A.M., a bomb started a fire that damaged the office of the British Norwich insurance firm, two other offices, a toy shop, and several stores. The fire raged for three hours. No injuries were reported at the building, which is owned by the Yussef ibn Ahmad Kanoo group, one of the Gulf's largest trading firms.

Two clothing stores in separate locations and owned by the Sana firm, an Indian company, were damaged.

A store selling Western, Arabic, and Indian music cassettes was destroyed in a blast.

The London-based Bahrain Freedom Movement blamed the blasts on the "collective punishment" that the government had used against the opposition. The group's spokesman, Mansur al-Jamri, also noted that the attacks coincided with the 40th day after the execution of Issa Qambar, a Shi'ite Muslim convicted of murdering a police officer in 1994. 96050501-03

May 5, 1996. *India.* Islamic separatists were believed to be responsible for murdering eight Nepalese Hindu migrant workers near Srinagar. 96050504

May 8, 1996. *Cambodia.* Armed Cambodians kidnapped one Cambodian and nine Thai quarry workers at Kompong Speu, south of Phnom Penh. The area is not controlled by the Khmer Rouge, who were suspected. The 40 to 80 armed Khmers fired on the quarry owned by the Aphiwatisla company (other reports said it was the Italian-Thai Construction Company) in a skirmish with authorities. Three Thais escaped capture. The Cambodian and two Thai women (Bunnam Pankhom, Suphaphon Kantabut, and Samak Atkophan) were later released with the kidnappers' demands. (AFP claimed that four people were released—two Thai women, whose husbands remained captives, the Cambodian, and a Thai man.) AFP reported that the remaining hostages included two employees of the Italian-Thai Construction Company, one who worked for the Sea Board Company, and four employees of the ASCO Quarry and Crushing Plant. The firms were supplying materials for the U.S.-sponsored reconstruction of National Route Four.

AFP said that according to Soeng Sambo, 18, the freed Cambodian, the kidnappers had demanded $100,000 from Italian Thai and Sea Board and $150,000 from ASCO. ASCO said it had paid ransom to the Khmer Rouge in 1993 to free ten Thais who had been held for four days. The firm was permitted to send food to the seven workers, identified as Wiwanchai Kantabut, Somnut Chaiyakhun, Thongsuk Pankhom, Sewoi Wongwan, Hatthaya, Thepkit, and Khomdi. The company paid $200,000 of the original $350,000 ransom demand, and the final hostages were released on May 9. Reports conflicted on whether the kidnappers had threatened the hostages' lives. 96050801

May 9, 1996. *Bosnia.* The previously unknown Islamic Group Military Branch told the *Europeana* that it would launch suicide missions against NATO-led Implementation Force (IFOR) troops in Bosnia. Salim al-Korshani, an Egyptian married to a Bosnian Muslim, told the journalist, "We are looking for ways to die so we can meet God in Heaven with dignity. I have a message for NATO forces in Bosnia. None of you will sleep peaceful-ly. We shall send suicide bombers to punish the U.S. and IFOR for their occupation of an Islamic land." Croatia was his second choice of target. 96050901

May 10, 1996. *Colombia.* The Movement for the Dignity of Colombia threatened to attack U.S. and Panamanian citizens and interests in Colom-bia. They asked Organization of American States (OAS) Secretary General Cesar Gavaria to reject the presence of U.S. troops at the border with Panama as a requirement to continuing negotia-tions to release his brother Juan Carlos, who was kidnapped in April in Pereira. The group rejected extradition of drug traffickers to the United States. 96051001

May 11, 1996. *Guatemala.* Yuriy Trushkin, a Russian diplomat, was hospitalized after he sus-tained gunshot injuries at kilometer 53 on the road to El Salvador. He died in Havana, Cuba. 96051101

May 13, 1996. *Israel.* In a drive-by shooting, two gunmen fired on Jewish settlers at a bus stop near Beit El, killing seminarian David Reuven Boim (or Baum), 17, who was born in the United States. He and his family had moved to Jerusalem from New York City 11 years earlier. Family friends claimed that he had retained U.S. citizenship. Three other people were injured in the spree, which was blamed on Hamas.

The gunmen began by firing at a bulletproofed bus carrying Jewish settlers. They dented the windshield. Two women were injured when the bus driver braked. One of them was Rivka David, 26, who was nine months pregnant and gave birth to a son.

The terrorists then moved on to the bus stop a mile away, firing at potential passengers. Boim was shot in the head; he died at Jerusalem's Hadassah Hospital. Yair (or Moshe) Greenberg, 17, another seminarian, was shot in the chest and lower back and was listed in serious condition.

The terrorists fled toward Jalazoun, a Palestin-ian refugee camp north of Ramallah. Their car overturned outside Beit El; they drove off in another vehicle.

U.S. Secretary of State Warren Christopher said the killers had been dispatched from Iran to disrupt Israeli elections.

On February 10, 1998, Amjad Hinawi, 26, a Palestinian charged in the shooting, pleaded not guilty at the start of his trial before a Palestinian court. Hinawi was driving near the settlement when his friend Khalil Sharif pulled out an auto-matic rifle and opened fire on the bus. 96051301

May 15, 1996. *Peru.* Police arrested Japanese Red Army terrorist suspect Kazue Yoshimura, 47, in Lince, Lima. Police found three identification cards for Kazuo Yoshihara, Yoko Okuyama, and Kazue Yoshimura, along with propaganda of the International Revolutionary Movement (MRI), which groups terrorists from various countries. Among them is the Peruvian Shining Path.

She was expelled from Peru on June 6, 1996, for violation of immigration laws. (The two coun-tries do not have an extradition treaty.) She was escorted by two Japanese police agents on a com-mercial plane bound for Amsterdam. There she was met by another group of Japanese policemen, who would join their colleagues in taking her to Tokyo. Peru also deported a boy taken into pro-tective custody who was with her at the time of her arrest.

Yoshimura was wanted for the armed attack on the French Embassy in The Hague in 1994 and the bombing of a Shell gas station in Singapore.

May 16, 1996. *Peru.* At 10:45 P.M., a car bomb destroyed a portion of Shell-Mobil's office and warehouse and injured four people in eastern Lima's La Victoria neighborhood. Five cars were destroyed; six Shell tankers filled with fuel were damaged. The blast weakened the infrastructure of several nearby buildings, shattered glass, and destroyed doors and walls of neighboring homes. A few hours later, Peru and the consortium were to sign a contract for the exploitation of the Camisea gas deposit in Cusco. The attack marked the 16th anniversary of the Shining Path's armed struggle in Chuschi, Ayachucho. Shining Path leaflets found in the area stated "Out with Fujimori's fascist government," "No to the sale of the country," and "Viva President Gonzalo." 96051601

May 16, 1996. *Saudi Arabia.* The U.S. Department of State warned Americans in the kingdom of the threat of another attack on U.S. institutions, following receipt of an anonymous telephone call threatening retaliation if four Saudis charged in the November 13, 1995, bombing in Riyadh were punished. 96051602

May 16, 1996. *Zambia.* The Black Mamba group claimed credit for setting off a 7:00 P.M. bomb in Lusaka's Kabulonga area, close to State House.

May 17, 1996. *Israel.* Police arrested Hasan Salamah, a Hamas leader, after a gun battle. He was believed to have planned three of four recent suicide bombings. He was caught during a vehicle search in which guns were found. He was taken to a Hebron hospital after being injured. The *Voice of Palestine* claimed that Israeli forces then raided the house of Rizq 'Abdallah Rujub that morning on charges of transporting Salamah in his car. The police arrested Rujub, his brother Hasan, and his nephew 'Awdah Misbah.

May 18, 1996. *Turkey.* A lone gunman failed to assassinate Turkish President Suleyman Demirel, 71, but wounded presidential bodyguard Sukru Cukurlu and *Milliyet* newspaper reporter Ihsan Yilmaz after Demirel opened a shopping mall in Izmit. The militant Muslim gunman, Ibrahim Gumrukcuoglu, 48, was angry about a recent military agreement with Israel. He was an Izmit pharmacist.

May 19, 1996. *South Africa.* Five men, two armed, attacked Lebanese Ambassador Charnel Stephan and his nephew Mansur Stephan during the night. Stephan said this was the second attack on the embassy that week and announced he was leaving

the country after four years because of the high crime rate. The ambassador required stitches. The gunmen stole a cell phone.

May 21, 1996. *Liberia.* During factional fighting, a rocket hit the U.S. Embassy compound where 20,000 refugees had huddled.

May 23, 1996. *Guinea.* Members of Charles Taylor's National Patriotic Front of Liberia killed two Guineans in Bounama locality in the southeast. The two were ordered by four rebels to help them carry a pump stolen from a Guinean diamond mine to their Liberian base. When they refused, the rebels shot them to death. 96052301

May 27, 1996. *Lebanon.* The Arabs' Eagles (Nusur al-'Arab) warned that the extradition of Yasir al-Shuraydi to Germany would lead to terrorist attacks. 96052701

May 28, 1996. *France.* Reza Mazlouman, an Iranian deputy education minister under the Shah who had lived in Paris since 1982, was found shot dead at his home in Créteil, east of Paris. 96052801

May 28, 1996. *Greece.* A bomb exploded at a building housing the main office of IBM in Athens, causing extensive structural damage, but no injuries. The Fraxia Midheniston (Nihilist Faction) claimed credit in a call to a local television station. 96052802

May 30, 1996. *Nicaragua.* Election observer Cynthia Gersony (also identified as Sandy Garzon), 41, of New York, was kidnapped with her Nicaraguan driver, Antonio Moncada, while on a field trip near the border with Honduras. The armed Contras captors demanded a greater voter registration effort in the remote areas of the country. She was released after two days, reporting that she had been well treated. The kidnappers met with a four-member team from the Organization of American States. The elections were scheduled for October 20. 96053001

June 1996. *Germany.* A 49-year-old male Slovak engineer was arrested in Ulm on suspicion of smuggling 6.1 pounds of radioactive uranium into the country. The uranium was found in a bank safety deposit box in Ulm. The engineer was detained as he entered the bank. The material was partly low-grade natural uranium and partly more fissile enriched uranium. Austrian police said he was trying to sell the material. Bavarian Radio reported that the uranium originated in the former Soviet Union.

June 1996. *Colombia.* Colombian architect Juan Carlos Gaviria Trujillo, brother of former President Cesar Gaviria (now serving as secretary general of the OAS), was kidnapped. The Cuban government, at the family's request, interceded. Twelve people—two Cuban envoys, two children, and eight members of the Movement for the Dignity of Colombia—were permitted to travel to Havana on June 13. The next day, Marco Tulio Gutierrez, director of the Administrative Department of Security (DAS), resigned. Although the kidnappers had been arrested, they were given safe passage to Cuba. Colombia's delegate to the OAS voted against the Helms-Burton law, which attempts to block foreign investment in Cuba. 96069901

June 1996. *Bahrain.* The government arrested 44 Iranian-trained Shi'ite members of Hizballah Bahrain, which it claimed were plotting to overthrow the ruling Khalifa family. Six appeared on television to back the government's charges, saying that Iranian intelligence had recruited them while they were undergoing religious studies in Qom. Fifteen plotters were found guilty and sentenced to jail terms of up to 15 years on March 26, 1997. Ringleaders Ali Ahmad Kadhem Mutaqawwi and Jassim Hassan Ali Khayyat received 14- and 12-year sentences, respectively. Thirteen received three to eight years. Eleven were acquitted. Iran denied involvement.

On March 29, the government sentenced another 21 Muslim militants to jail terms of up to seven years. A dozen others were acquitted.

June 3, 1996. *United States.* Federal prosecutors announced the arrest in a New York federal prison of Julian Salazar Calero, 46, who was named in five arrest warrants in Peru for membership in the Shining Path. He had been detained pending deportation. The Peruvians said he had been involved in numerous attacks that had resulted in the deaths of police officers and civilians.

June 4, 1996. *Burundi.* Two Swiss workers and one Italian employee with the International Committee of the Red Cross (ICRC) were shot in an ambush near Mugina, Cibitoke Province, as they were delivering food and water to hospitals in the north. An ICRC chase car managed to escape. Hutus were suspected. The dead were identified as Reto Neuenschwander, 39, Juan Ruffino, 36, and Cedric Martin, 32. The Red Cross suspended operations in the country. 96060401

June 4, 1996. *United States.* Kevin Foster, 18, and Christopher Black, 18, were charged with conspiracy to commit murder by plotting to dress as Disney characters and kill black visitors to Walt Disney World in Orlando, Florida. The duo, both white, were also charged with racketeering and arson against a historic Coca-Cola bottling plant. They planned to ambush Disney employees, steal their costumes, sneak into the park, and murder black tourists. Foster led a teen militia called the Lords of Chaos. Along with Derek Shields, 18, and a 17-year-old, the two pleaded not guilty in May to first-degree murder in the April 30 death of Mark Schwebes, Riverdale High School band director. The four and another 17-year-old were charged with other lesser crimes. A 16-year-old had also been charged in the Coca-Cola case.

June 4, 1996. *Bahrain.* Authorities announced the arrest of 44 Bahrainis involved in a plot to overthrow the government. At least 34 of them confessed to an investigating judge. Six of the suspects were shown on state television. One said Iranian officials supported the plotters, and that one—Wahidi, who claimed to report directly to Iranian leader Ayatollah Ali Khameni—asked them to gather information on U.S. forces in Bahrain, where the U.S. Fifth Fleet is based. One suspect said the group had been trained by Hizballah in Lebanon. Hussain Youssef Ibrahim Mohammed, a Bahrain University student, said the training included work with "light, medium, and heavy weapons . . . using explosives, and techniques of making bombs." Ali Ahmed al-Mutaqawi said the Iranian Revolutionary Guard trained them in Qom, Iran, in May 1994. The group claimed to be the military wing of Hizballah Bahrain.

June 4, 1996. *Tajikistan.* Gunmen shot and killed two Russian servicemen's wives in a Dushanbe cemetery. The Tajikistan Internal Affairs Ministry blamed Muzlokandov's Gang, an Islamic extremist group. 96060402

June 6, 1996. *Zambia.* At 9:00 P.M., the Black Mamba set off a bomb at Lusaka International Airport. The group made a warning phone call, leading police to the bomb. When two bomb experts began to defuse the device, it exploded, killing one technician and injuring the other, Paul Ngoma, 48, on the face. The group opposes the government's recent laws that prevent former President Kenneth Kaunda from running for his previous office.

June 7, 1996. *Jordan. Al-Bilad* reported that Iraqi diplomat Sa'd Muhammad Rida mysteriously disappeared after he refused to return to Baghdad. He had prepared to leave with consular officer Salim 'Abd-al-Husayn al-Rabi'i and intelligence officer Husayn Faraj. The paper claimed he had been helping Iraqi refugees by renewing and stamping their passports without charging them fees.

June 7, 1996. *Ivory Coast.* Liberian rebels belonging to Charles Taylor's National Patriotic Front of Liberia crossed the border to attack the village of Basobli, Giuglo District, and killed 14 people. They wounded four others before taking five women hostage. The dead included six Ivorian women, six Liberian women, a child, and an 18-year-old Ivorian. The terrorists torched a dozen homes before fleeing. 96060701

June 8, 1996. *Colombia.* Ten Colombian National Liberation Army (ELN) gunmen killed a Venezuelan man they believed was an informant for Venezuela's National Guard in Apure State, on the border. 96060801

June 9, 1996. *Nicaragua.* Mariana Marling de Pulido, wife of Mauricio Antonio Pulido Leon, the commercial attaché of the Venezuelan Embassy, and Third Secretary Horalia Pachuca received anonymous telephoned death threats. 96060901

June 9, 1996. *Israel.* Gunmen fired on a car near Zekharya, killing a U.S.-Israeli citizen. The Popular Front for the Liberation of Palestine (PFLP) was suspected. 96060902

June 13, 1996. *United States.* John Ford, 47, of Bellport, Long Island, and Joseph Mazzachelli, 42, of Manorville, New York, were charged with conspiracy to commit murder by seeking to assassinate Long Island Republican Party officials with radium. Ford apparently intended to kill Suffolk County GOP leader Jon Powell by spreading radium on the seat of his car or in his food. Republican county legislator Fred Towle and Brookhaven Public Safety Director Anthony Gazzola were also to be killed. Police found five canisters of radium in the home of Ford, a former court officer who once led a UFO group. Police also confiscated weapons, ammunition, a mine detector, a gas mask, and militia literature.

June 15, 1996. *United Kingdom.* The IRA claimed credit for setting off a huge truck bomb that destroyed a Manchester shopping district and injured 206 people, including two German tourists. A caller, who used an IRA code word, said, "An active service unit placed a device which detonated in central Manchester Saturday. We sincerely regret the injuries to civilians which occurred." 96061501

June 18, 1996. *Morocco.* Two gunmen seriously wounded Babi Azinkoff, vice-president of the Jewish community in Casablanca. The duo escaped.

June 18, 1996. *Angola.* Three members of a UN mine-removing team were wounded in Mailing Province. The Uruguayan, Pakistani, and Angolan were evacuated to Luanda. 96061801

June 18, 1996. *Honduras.* Nicaraguans kidnapped 28 people working for the Nicaraguan Supreme Electoral Council (CASE) and three people working on a stalk-borer program and held them in rural Honduras. The attack came when the voting board members were delivering elections materials by canoe in the Coco River.

A negotiations team was composed of Monsignor Abelardo Mata and members of the Peace and Justice Commission of the diocese of Esteli, Nicaragua, and Dr. Sergio Caramana and eight officials of the OAS International Support and Verification Commission (CIAV). The kidnappers demanded that the army withdraw as a precondition to holding talks. The kidnappers said they were members of El Licenciado and Pajarillo and wanted the army to withdraw from the area adjacent to the Coco River on the Nicaraguan side. Authorities believed they were Contra rebels.

On June 21, Nicaraguan television reported that there were 33 hostages and only 7 of them worked for CASE. One of the leaders of the kidnappers was seeking medical assistance; several of his men were injured in a battle with government troops the previous day.

Yet another media report stated that there were 51 hostages, but that 18 escaped. The largest reported number of hostages was 56 Miskito indigenous people. The remaining hostages were released later that day, after the army had withdrawn from the banks of the river. 96062001

June 21, 1996. *Ethiopia.* Police were investigating reports that the Ethiopian Unity Patriot Front,

later named the Ethiopian National Patriot Front, led by Dr. Taye Woldesemayat and Seleshi Berhane, planned to throw grenades at the USAID office near Bole Road. The group was also believed responsible for a 1993 murder attempt against an American working for AID.

June 25, 1996. *Saudi Arabia.* At 10:28 P.M., a tanker truck bomb exploded at the U.S. military's compound at Khobar Towers (variant al-Khubar), near Dhahran, killing 19 U.S. airmen and wounding 547 others, including nearly 250 Americans, 147 Saudis, 150 Bangladeshis, 4 Egyptians, 2 Jordanians, 2 Indonesians, and 2 Filipinas. Investigators found a detonator like those used by Hizballah. Many suspected local Saudi Islamic radicals, perhaps aided by Iran. Scores of people were rounded up for questioning, and a Palestinian magazine in London claimed that six people belonging to the Movement for Islamic Reform, a Saudi dissident group, had confessed. It claimed the group included two Kuwaitis and two Lebanese, all of whom had been tortured.

Those killed included:

- Master Sergeant Michael George Heiser of Palm Coast, Florida
- Master Sergeant Kendall K. J. Kitson of Yukon, Oklahoma
- Technical Sergeant Thanh V. Nguyen of Panama City, Florida
- Technical Sergeant Patrick P. Fennig of Greendale, Wisconsin
- Staff Sergeant Daniel B. Cafourek
- Staff Sergeant Kevin J. Johnson of Shreveport, Louisiana
- Staff Sergeant Donald L. Kling
- Sergeant Millard D. Campbell of Angleton, Texas
- Senior Airman Paul A. Blais
- Senior Airman Earl F. Cartrette, Jr.
- Senior Airman Jeremy A. Taylor
- Airman First Class Brian W. McVeigh
- Airman First Class Brent E. Marthaler of Cambridge, Minnesota

- Airman First Class Peter J. Morgera of Stratham, New Hampshire
- Airman First Class Joseph E. Rimkus
- Airman First Class Justin R. Wood of Modesto, California
- Airman First Class Joshua E. Woody
- Airman First Class Christopher B. Lester, 19, of Pineville, West Virginia
- Captain Christopher J. Adams of Massapequa Park, New York (initially listed as killed, later as injured)
- Captain Leland T. Haun

The United States offered a $2 million reward for apprehension of the bombers, supplementing a $3 million Saudi reward.

Three groups initially claimed credit: the Combatant Partisans of God Organization (Munazzamat Ansar Allah al-Muqatilah), the Tigers of the Gulf, and the Islamic Movement for Change. The Legions of the Martyr Abdullah Hudhaif later claimed responsibility. Hudhaif was an Afghan War veteran who threw acid on an Interior Ministry security official, Saud Sibreen, after accusing him of torturing his jailed brother. An Islamic court had sentenced him to 20 years in jail, but a state court later sentenced him to death. The previously unknown Hizballah Gulf (Hizballahl-al-Khalij) claimed credit on June 27. On July 19, the Movement for Islamic Change claimed credit for the bombing.

Saudi police announced on July 14 that they had found the stolen white Chevrolet Caprice getaway car in Dammam, six miles from the scene of the bombing. It had been repainted from its original gray. The truck used in the bombing had been stolen from a building company. Two people had been seen running from the truck to the car minutes before the truck exploded. Saudi and U.S. officials were just beginning an evacuation when the blast occurred.

American intelligence, military, press, and congressional players became embroiled in disputes regarding whether there was adequate intelligence warning of the attack, and what protective steps should have been taken after receipt of the warning.

The focus later shifted to individuals who kept surveillance on the area and crashed a truck against the facility's fence some weeks earlier, who may have traveled through Syria. The Saudi government denied that Syria was involved.

The Defense Special Weapons Agency estimated the blast as equivalent to 20,000 pounds of dynamite, a figure supported by the Institute for Defense Analysis. A Defense Department investigation team had estimated the bomb at 5,000 pounds, based upon physical evidence.

The *Washington Post* reported on November 1, 1996, that the Saudi government had arrested 40 Saudi citizens, including the truck's driver, believed involved in the bombing. The Saudis believed that Iran and Syria were behind the attack. All detainees were Shi'ite members of Saudi Hizballah, possibly a wing of the Lebanese-based Hizballah. The Saudis were seeking a Lebanese man who built the bomb and the Saudi leader of Saudi Hizballah. A third man was arrested in Syria at Saudi request, but the Syrians claimed that Gaffer al-Marduk Cached committed suicide on September 17, shortly after being arrested by the Syrian Mukhabarat security service in the Yarmouk Palestinian refugee camp in Damascus. Saudi sources told the press that the Iranian Embassy in Damascus, Syria, had provided fake Kuwaiti passports to some of those involved in the attack.

On November 23–25, Riyadh provided an FBI team with its evidence of Hizballah and Iranian complicity. Hizballah members visited Tehran before and after the explosion, meeting with Iranian intelligence. Hizballah trained the Saudi Shi'ite extremists in Lebanon, according to the Saudis.

On November 27, renegade Saudi financier Osama bin Laden, 40, told London's *Al-Quds* during an interview in Afghanistan that his followers were responsible for the bombing. He warned that further bombings would occur if the West did not withdraw its troops from the Middle East. He said he did not plan to return to Sudan—which he left in May—but might move to Yemen if forced out of Afghanistan. He also claimed that "Afghan

Arabs" were involved in the fighting against U.S. forces in Somalia and were involved in killing several U.S. soldiers there.

On December 11, the U.S. Air Force exonerated the officers who were responsible for the security at the bombed facility. Several congressmen observed that the decision contradicted the findings of an assessment conducted by retired U.S. Army General Wayne Downing for Defense Secretary William J. Perry three months earlier.

On December 23, Iranian President Ali Akbar Hashemi Rafsanjani told London's *Asharq Al-Awsat*, "What we have heard officially is that those involved are Saudi citizens and that some escaped from the Kingdom and possibly came to Iran. We searched for them carefully and have found no trace of them in Iran. One was called Maarouf and was said to be in Iran; then it was discovered that he had died in a Syrian jail."

On December 26, Mohammad Hussein Fadlallah, the spiritual leader of Hizballah, told the Kuwaiti *As-Siyassa* that his group had no links with Saudi Shi'ites and that his group was not involved in the bombing.

On January 22, 1997, FBI Director Louis J. Freeh publicly criticized the Saudis for lack of cooperation in the investigation, complaining that Riyadh had withheld important evidence. Attorney General Janet Reno echoed his complaints. The Saudis did not permit the Americans to interview suspects.

On March 18, Ottawa immigration officials detained Hani Abdel-Rahim Hussein al-Sayegh, 28, a Saudi, as a "security risk to Canada." The FBI announced that it wished to question him regarding the bombing. Sayegh said he did not want to return to Saudi Arabia because he was the subject of a manhunt there. U.S. officials believed he was a Shi'ite Muslim, possibly the driver of the truck or the getaway car. One U.S. official said Sayegh had been in Canada since August, arriving from Saudi Arabia after a brief layover in Boston. Shi'ite activists said the Sayegh family comes from Tarut, 25 miles northwest of the Khobar Towers. Sayegh told authorities that he was in Syria at the time of the bombing and that he had come to

Canada as a refugee. He claimed he had lived in Syria for the previous two years to avoid government harassment for his dissident views. He had studied Islam in Qom, Iran, in 1987. He claimed that his wife wanted to visit her family in Tarut and was to meet him in Kuwait. However, after the bombing, she was placed under house arrest.

Sayegh reportedly had surveyed the area of the bombing and was the driver of the car that signaled the truck bomber where to park, according to Canadian court documents. The court also identified the mastermind as Ahmed Ibrahim Ahmad Mughassil (variants Ahmed Ibrahim Mughassil, Ahmed Mughassil). On March 30, the Saudis requested his extradition. Washington said he could be deported to the United States, from which he had entered Canada.

Sayegh was carrying an international driving permit issued in Syria on August 3, 1994. It listed a Damascus address as his permanent residence.

Canadian immigration officials also arrested Fahad Shehri, a Saudi who arrived in Canada in December and claimed refugee status. He said he was wanted for questioning in Saudi Arabia for the bombing and feared for his life. The United States disavowed interest in him; Riyadh said he was not a suspect. Shi'ites said he was probably a Sunni from the Hijaz area. The Canadian government charged him with being a terrorist on March 26. Some reports indicated he had bought weapons for Central Asian Muslim fighters.

The two were held in the Ottawa Detention Center.

On April 4, the Saudis claimed that the Syrians refused to help them capture Mughassil, who was with Hizballah in Lebanon, because they did not wish to risk a clash with Hizballah. Mughassil may have fled to Iran. The Saudis also linked him to a November 1995 bombing in Riyadh in which seven persons, including five Americans, were killed.

On April 10, an Afghan official announced that Osama bin Laden, who was stripped of his Saudi nationality in 1994, was now living in the Jalalabad headquarters of the Taliban militia. Bin Laden was wanted in connection with the

November 1995 Riyadh car bombing and the Khobar Towers bombing.

On April 13, the *Washington Post* claimed that U.S. and Saudi intelligence officials linked Sayegh to a 1994 meeting with Iranian intelligence officer Brigadier Ahmad Sherifi, a top official in the Iranian Revolutionary Guards. Evidence included phone calls made by Sayegh and bank checks signed by Sherifi. Sherifi was implicated in the 1996 trial in Bahrain of 14 Bahraini Shi'ite dissidents. These dissidents were convicted of several hotel and restaurant bombings in 1994 to 1995 that killed 20. Six of those convicted said they were recruited by Sherifi in 1993 while studying at the religious school in Qom.

Meanwhile, a second Air Force investigation exonerated all officers responsible for Khobar security.

The *New York Times* reported on May 1 that Iran was harboring at least one of the bombers, Ahmed Mughassil.

On May 5, Canadian Federal Judge Donna McGillis ruled that there was conclusive evidence that Sayegh participated in the bombing, clearing the way for deportation. Sayegh declined to take the stand in his own defense. Canadian intelligence officials, according to the *Los Angeles Times*, claimed that Sayegh kept surveillance on the target, was at the wheel of the car that signaled the driver of the truck bomb, and assisted in the terrorists' escape. Three vehicles were involved in the attack. Canada issued a conditional deportation order on May 14. On May 16, Sayegh expressed interest in cooperating with U.S. authorities. Sayegh told Canadian authorities he had studied in Shi'ite Muslim schools in Iran for ten years and that he was a member of Hizballah in Saudi Arabia. He claimed to have close contacts with Iranian intelligence.

On May 29, Sayegh dismissed his Canadian attorney, Douglas Baum, saying he did not want to cooperate with the United States. Sayegh reiterated that he feared returning to Saudi Arabia, where he would face the death penalty.

In a letter sent to a London-based human rights group and released on June 5, Sayegh said he wanted the U.S. "forces of evil" to leave Saudi Arabia and that he was angry over Riyadh's crackdown on Shi'ites in the early 1980s. He claimed he was tortured as a youth by the Saudis.

The FBI took custody of Sayegh on June 17. Sayegh had agreed to cooperate in the investigations and to enter a guilty plea to surveying U.S. installations for a planned 1995 attack that never took place. He was represented by New York City immigration attorney Michael Wildes when indicted on one count of conspiracy on June 18. The charge carried a ten-year prison term. Sayegh's anxiety-produced asthma attack on June 20 postponed the plea hearing. On June 26, Judge Emmet Sullivan delayed the case until July 10 to give new court-appointed attorney Francis Carter time to prepare a plea. Carter had defended Fawas Younis, the Lebanese Shi'ite who hijacked a Jordanian airliner in 1985.

On June 28, 1997, the *Washington Post* reported that Sayegh told U.S. authorities that Sherifi was involved in a 1994 to 1995 conspiracy to attack U.S. targets in Saudi Arabia. He said Sherifi ordered him to keep surveillance on U.S. military installations in Saudi Arabia. In December 1995, Sayegh traveled to Jizan in the southwest to determine the availability of weapons and explosives for use against U.S. targets, according to the grand jury indictment of Sayegh. He denied involvement in the Khobar bombing.

On June 30, 1997, Saudi Arabia asked Lebanon and Afghanistan to extradite a dozen Shi'ite Muslims suspected in the case. Riyadh suggested that Mughassil was hiding in Lebanon.

On July 7, Sayegh said that an airline manifest and his passport indicated that he was in Iran and then flew to Kuwait and that he had not been in Saudi Arabia at the time of the bombing. He earlier had said he was in Syria at the time of the bombing. He also denied involvement in Sherifi's plot or knowing the location of Khobar. On July 9, he decided he wanted to explore political asylum in Cuba. He had not taken a polygraph test that he had agreed to take when setting up the plea bargain in Canada.

On July 10, the *Washington Times* suggested

involvement on the part of Seyed Hadi Khosrow-shahi, an Iranian who served as the late Ayatollah Khomeini's representative at the Ministry of National Guidance.

Sayegh derailed the plea bargain on July 30, pleading not guilty to the conspiracy charge and saying he had no information about the Khobar attack. Federal Prosecutor Eric Dubelier said the government now planned to try him on the conspiracy charge. The judge set a November 3 trial date. The court appointed Francis D. Carter as Sayegh's attorney. Immigration attorney Wilde said Sayegh would seek political asylum in the United States. Some believed that Sayegh's tergiversation was due to concern about the fate of his wife and two children in Saudi Arabia if he confided terrorist details.

Also on July 30, Secretary of Defense William Cohen announced he would block the promotion of Brigadier General Terryl J. "Terry" Schwalier, USAF, who commanded the air wing in Dhahran, Saudi Arabia, saying that Schwalier should have conducted evacuation drills and installed alert systems. Two Air Force reports had exonerated Schwalier. General Ronald R. Fogleman, U.S. Air Force chief of staff, resigned earlier in the week in protest of the decision. Schwalier requested retirement.

On September 8, the Justice Department announced it was dropping charges against Sayegh because it lacked sufficient evidence to prosecute. The department said U.S. immigration authorities would seek to deport Sayegh to Saudi Arabia. FBI Director Louis Freeh said Saudi Arabia had prevented the United States from interviewing dozens of other suspects who could have provided evidence in the case. U.S. officials were expected to block an expected application for asylum. On October 21, 1997, U.S. District Judge Emmet Sullivan formally dropped the bomb plot charges against Sayegh. On December 16, 1997, a three-judge panel of the U.S. Court of Appeals for the D.C. Circuit said Judge Sullivan erred by refusing to let Sayegh withdraw the bargain from the court docket. The court ruled that the public has no right of access to the plea agreement.

On December 11, 1997, the *Washington Times* reported that Saudi exile and terrorist financier Osama bin Laden was involved in the Riyadh and Dhahran bombings and that he appeared to have had advance knowledge of both attacks. He apparently had arranged to ship large amounts of C-4 explosive from Eastern Europe to Persian Gulf states, including Saudi Arabia.

Also on December 11, 1997, Attorney General Janet Reno, FBI Director Freeh, and other officials met with families of the victims to say that they had not solved the case.

On January 22, 1998, the Immigration and Naturalization Service ordered Sayegh deported from the United States. The Saudis noted on March 30 that they had yet to hear from the United States regarding their request for his extradition. His appeals exhausted, Sayegh was deported to Saudi Arabia on a U.S. government plane on October 11, 1999.

The Saudis announced on March 30, 1998, that they had completed their investigation of the case, but would hold off releasing the results until the appropriate time.

On May 22, 1998, Interior Minister Prince Nayef bin Abdul-Aziz publicly stated that there was no foreign involvement, absolved Iran of responsibility in the case, and blamed local dissidents. He did not indicate whether the government knew the bombers' whereabouts. The United States continued its investigation of possible foreign links. On July 10, cabinet member Prince Abdul Aziz bin Fahd, 24, the king's youngest son, insisted that the investigation was continuing and that Saudi Arabia was cooperating with the Americans, who had complained of a breakdown in the investigation and cooperation.

On July 16, Ahmad Rezaei, 21, who was seeking U.S. asylum, told *Al-Watan al-Arabi* that the Iran-backed Hizballah Gulf was responsible, having received funding from Tehran. The defector is the eldest son of Major General Mohsen Rezaei, secretary of Iran's Expediency Council and former Revolutionary Guards commander.

On November 4, 1998, Saudi Interior Minister Prince Nayef said Osama bin Laden was not directly responsible for this bombing or the 1995 blast in Riyadh that killed five American servicemen and two Indians. However, he said, it was possible that the attacks were carried out by individuals who "adopted his ideas."

In August 1999, Bruce Reidel, the senior Middle East specialist on the president's National Security Council, sent the Iranians a request for information via an emissary from Oman in Paris. The Iranians rejected President Clinton's request on October 6, 1999.

On October 7, 1999, two three-judge federal appeals court panels in Washington and Atlanta refused to block the Justice Department's proposed deportation of Sayegh to Saudi Arabia.

On March 24, 2001, FBI Director Freeh reassigned the investigation of the Khobar Towers bombing from the Washington U.S. Attorney's Office to federal prosecutors in Richmond, Virginia.

On May 14, 2001, the *New Yorker* magazine reported that outgoing FBI Director Freeh had given the Bush administration a list of people—possibly including Iranian officials—who should be indicted for the Khobar Towers bombing. On June 12, 2001, federal prosecutors said they would seek grand jury indictments of several suspects the next week. CBS News reported that 13 men, mostly Saudi citizens, and a Lebanese chemist who allegedly built the bomb, would be indicted. *Al-Hayat* had reported earlier that the three main suspects—two Saudis and a Lebanese—had disappeared. 96062501

June 26, 1996. *Israel.* Three Israel Defense Force (IDF) soldiers were shot and killed by terrorists in an ambush on their morning patrol near the Jordan River, not far from the settlement of Na'aran in the Jordan Valley. The terrorists attacked the patrol vehicle, killing two soldiers. A third later died of his wounds. Two soldiers in the command car jumped out and ran for cover. The terrorists dismantled the vehicle's machine gun. Another IDF patrol reached the area, but was fired on by the terrorists. Two more soldiers were wounded. The terrorists fled to Jordan. 96062601

June 26, 1996. *El Salvador.* The Major Roberto d'Aubuisson National Force (FURODA) sent a note to Notimex in which it threatened to kill Salvadoran leaders, local journalists, and foreign correspondents, calling them "maggots and ill-bred." 96062602

June 27, 1996. *United States.* Police in Herndon, Virginia, arrested Basheer Nafi, 43, a Palestinian. He was deported to London on July 1 on charges of violating his immigration status. Some believed he was a leader of Islamic Jihad. He worked as a researcher and editor at the International Institute of Islamic Thought (IIIT) in Herndon. His Irish wife, Imelda Ryan, said he was going to leave the United States permanently anyway, having resigned from the IIIT and booked a flight to London. Nafi had last entered the United States in August 1994. He admitted knowing Fathi Shiqaqi, the assassinated leader of Islamic Jihad. The two attended a university in Cairo in the 1970s. Nafi had earlier worked for the Tampa-based World and Islam Studies Enterprise, whose former administrator, Ramadan Abdullah Shallah, 37, succeeded Shiqaqi as the Islamic Jihad leader.

June 27, 1996. *United States.* Police arrested seven people and charged them with conspiracy to make pipe bombs. They pleaded not guilty in a Seattle court on August 15. The defendants were Richard F. Burton, 37, of Seattle; Frederick B. Fisher, 61, of Bellingham, Washington; Judy C. Kirk, 54, and her husband, John Kirk, 55, both of Tukwila, Washington; Gary Marvin Keuhnoel, 47, of Bellingham; Marlin L. Mack, 23, of Bellingham; and Tracy Brown (alias William R. Smith) of Seattle. The FBI accused them of preparing for an "eventual confrontation" with the U.S. government and the UN. 96062701

June 27, 1996. *Bosnia.* A bomb went off at a Zvornik building, causing major damage but no injuries. The building housed the Socialist Party of the Serb Republic, the International Police Task Force, the Organization for Security and Cooperation in Europe, and the Europe Community Monitoring Mission. 96062702

June 28, 1996. *Germany.* The Irish Republican Army took credit for firing three mortars at the British army base near Osnabrueck. Only one mortar round exploded. No one was injured. The IRA claimant used the name P. O'Neill, the name usually given in IRA statements. The IRA had attacked the barracks in 1989, setting off a 330-pound Semtex bomb that destroyed a dormitory. 96062801

July 1, 1996. *Rwanda.* The *Standaard* in Groot-Bijgaarden reported in Dutch that a new group of Hutu extremists named PALIR had announced it would "pay $1,000 for every American killed in Rwanda." U.S. Ambassador Robert Gribbin, chief of mission in Kigali, would be worth $1,500. The group might have a base in south Cyangugu and also operate from Nairobi, Kenya. 96070101

July 1, 1996. *United States.* Federal authorities arrested a dozen members of the Viper Militia in Arizona who were planning to attack government buildings in Phoenix, including the Internal Revenue Service, the U.S. Secret Service, and the Bureau of Alcohol, Tobacco, and Firearms. For two years, the group had practiced firing illegal fully automatic weapons and constructed and detonated ammonium nitrate bombs and rockets, according to a seven-count indictment. Authorities seized more than 70 unregistered assault rifles fitted for fully automatic fire, hundreds of blasting caps, 8 grenades, and 650 pounds of ammonium nitrate fertilizer, along with other ingredients to produce ANFO explosive. The ten men and two women were charged with conspiracy to manufacture and possess unregistered destructive devices. Six were charged with conspiracy to illegally instruct persons in the use of explosive devices to create civil disorder. Three were charged with illegal possession of machine guns.

The FBI was investigating whether the group was involved in the October 1995 derailment of an Amtrak train.

Members of the group vowed to kill infiltrators and suggested killing a juror and retaliating against a Treasury agent's family. Authorities showed a videotape made in 1994 of the group's training and discussions.

On December 19, Viper leader Gary Bauer, 50, pleaded guilty to 11 federal felony charges, including conspiracy to unlawfully make and possess unregistered destructive devices, unlawful possession of unregistered machine guns, unlawful possession of other unregistered destructive devices, and furnishing instruction in the use of explosive devices, in an appearance before a U.S. magistrate in Phoenix. Bauer faced five years in prison and a $250,000 fine for each charge. Sentencing was scheduled for March 3, 1997. On March 20, 1997, he was sentenced to nine years in prison and fined $16,100. He was given 36 months' probation.

Colleague Randy Nelson was also expected to plead guilty.

On December 27, Scott Shero, 30, and Henry Overturf, 37, changed their not guilty pleas to guilty on one count each of conspiring to illegally make and possess unregistered destructive devices. Walter Sanville, 37, changed his plea to guilty to the same conspiracy charge and to two counts of unlawful possession of machine-gun parts. The plea bargain stated that Shero would be sentenced to 24 to 30 months in jail; Overturf would receive 12 to 18 months; Sanville would receive 37 to 46 months.

December 31 plea bargains saw four other Vipers changing their pleas to guilty. Finis Walker, 42, and David Belliveau, 28, each pleaded guilty to three felony counts. Ellen Belliveau, 27, pleaded guilty to two counts. Donna Williams, 44, pleaded guilty to one count. Dean Pleasant, 28, decided to stay out of the plea bargain, but also pleaded guilty to three felony charges.

The remaining two Vipers were scheduled to go on trial on January 27 or 28, 1997.

On March 19, 1997, the judge sentenced six Vipers to terms of up to 57 months.

On March 20, 1997, Finis Walker and Randy Nelson were given 70-month sentences and fined.

On November 18, 1997, jurors acquitted Christopher Floyd, 22, on an explosives posses-sion charge. They said they were hopelessly dead-locked on a related conspiracy charge. U.S. District Judge Earl Carroll declared a mistrial on the conspiracy charge. Government attorneys were not certain whether they would retry him. Floyd had faced 15 years in prison; he was the only Viper who was not sentenced to prison.

July 4, 1996. *Sri Lanka.* A Tamil Tiger with explo-sives hidden on her body jumped at the motorcade of a government minister in Jaffna, killing 21 peo-ple, including Brigadier Ananda Hamangoda, and injuring 50 others, including Housing Minister Nimal Siripala de Silva.

July 4, 1996. *Colombia.* The Revolutionary Armed Forces of Colombia (FARC) fired at the helicopter carrying Swiss Prosecutor Carla del Ponte and local counter-narcotics police. No injuries were reported. 96070402

July 7, 1996. *Pakistan.* The U.S. Embassy received "a specific threat" against U.S. interests. 96070701

July 7, 1996. *Cuba.* Retired Cuban Lieutenant Colonel Jose Leonardo Fernandez Pupo, armed with two .22-caliber pistols, hijacked a Cuban Aerotaxi AN-2, registration CUT1183, flying from Bayamo and Santiago de Cuba to Guan-tanamo, Baracoa, and Moa with 17 other peo-ple—including 2 children—and forced it to land at the U.S. naval base in Guantanamo. During the flight, Fernandez fired a shot through an open cockpit window. Fernandez requested political asylum. Havana demanded repatriation. The United States condemned the act as air piracy. All the rest of those on board returned to Cuba. In May 1997, a jury in Washington acquitted him on grounds that his alternative had been imminent arrest as an anti-Castro rebel leader of the 1,000-strong Fifth of August 2000. In late November 1997, Immigration Judge John Bryant refused his request for asylum. Bryant recommended that he

not be returned to Cuba because of the probabili-ty that he would be tortured. Defense attorney Wilfredo Allen said deportation was the most like-ly outcome, although he knew of no country will-ing to accept Fernandez. 96070702

July 8, 1996. *India.* The Muslim group Jammu Kashmir Ikhwan took hostage 19 journalists at Anantnag, 55 kilometers south of Srinagar. They demanded that editors of all newspapers in the summer capital meet the group that evening. The journalists included AFP correspondent Surinder Oberoi and photographer Tauseef Mustafa, Reuters correspondent Seikh Mustaq and photog-rapher Fayaz Kablil, Associated Press Television's Mehrajuddin, Bilal Bhat of Asian News Interna-tional, and a journalist from the *Uqab (Falcon)* newspaper. The kidnappers set a deadline of 4:00 P.M. They released all 19 hostages after eight hours. 96070801

July 8, 1996. *Uruguay.* A homemade firebomb failed to explode after it was planted at the Mon-tevideo office door of former Uruguayan Interior Minister Angel Maria Gianola. An employee from a neighboring office saw smoke coming from the package and doused it with water. Gianola was interior minister in August 1994, when his coun-try handed over to Spain three alleged members of the Basque Nation and Liberty (ETA). 96070802

July 8, 1996. *Ethiopia.* Two Somali gunmen fired on the minister of transport and communication as he arrived at his office in Addis Ababa, wound-ing him and killing two guards and two passersby. Al-Ittihaad al-Islami claimed credit. 96070803

July 11, 1996. *Russia.* At 8:53 A.M., a bomb exploded on Moscow's Route 12 trolley bus as it was cruising on Strastnoy Boulevard, injuring driver Aleksandr Koktev, 38, and four passengers. A woman found a suspicious bag filled with veg-etables, which she handed to Koktev. It exploded when he opened it. The bomb contained 100 grams of trotyl.

July 12, 1996. *Russia.* At 8:20 A.M., a TNT bomb exploded in a Route 48 trolley bus near Moscow's Alekseyevskaya subway station, injuring 27. The bomb was planted by the central door of the bus.

July 12, 1996. *Russia.* Three more explosive devices were found in the Suschevskiy Val area of Moscow.

July 12, 1996. *Guatemala.* One thousand peasants led by the National Settlers Movement took over the Costa Rican Embassy. Guatemalan National Police rescued Consul Diogenes Amador and other officials. The peasants were demanding homes from Guatemalan President Alvaro Arzu. 96071201

July 12, 1996. *Bosnia.* A bomb placed under a truck badly damaged a UN police station in Vlasenica, northeast of Sarajevo. The truck was parked in front of the residence of three UN cease-fire monitors—two Nepalese and one Senegalese—injuring two of them. The blast also damaged two cars and broke 30 windows. 96071202

July 12, 1996. *Bosnia.* During the night, an American woman working for the U.S. Embassy was shot twice in the back in a drive-by shooting while she and her husband were driving between Kiseljak and Sarajevo. She underwent surgery at a NATO military hospital. The attack occurred in a Muslim/Croat-controlled area at a roadblock. She was driving in a car with local registration plates. Police believed it was a carjacking/robbery attempt. The U.S. Embassy said she was working for a U.S. government agency and was attached to the engineering unit of NATO's headquarters in Bosnia.
    On July 22, Bosnian authorities arrested nine Croat men in the case. 96071203

July 12, 1996. *Austria.* Four individuals suspected of membership in the Kurdistan Workers Party (PKK) occupied a Reuters office in Vienna, holding two employees hostage for several hours before surrendering. 96071204

July 13, 1996. *Yemen.* A bomb went off during the night near the Egyptian Embassy, shattering windows in nearby buildings. Police blamed "separatist elements." 96071301

July 14, 1996. *Uganda.* Kony rebels attacked the Acholi Pii refugee camp in Kitgum and kidnapped Godfrey Lutwana, a driver with the Uganda-Australia Foundation, and Rasa Lakaka, the group's architect. Their truck was ambushed and burned at the Achwa bridge, 27 miles from Lira. The truck was carrying books for five schools in the Kitgum District, including the primary schools at Kachoko, Kilak, Agoro, Pajule, and Lunyir. 96071401

July 14, 1996. *Colombia.* Armed men forced an Italian engineer out of his vehicle, taking him hostage in Antioquia Province. No ransom demand was made. Police suspected the Revolutionary Armed Forces of Colombia (FARC) or the National Liberation Army (ELN). 96071402

July 15, 1996. *United Kingdom.* Police raided a suspected IRA bomb factory in London, seizing a large quantity of bomb-making material and arresting several men. 96071501

July 15, 1996. *Bosnia.* Serb gunmen led by Malko Koroman, police chief in Pale, threatened to take UN staff hostage and use them as shields to prevent the NATO-led peace force from arresting Radovan Karadzic, leader of the ruling Serbian Democratic Party. 96071502

July 15, 1996. *Russia.* Moscow police received 118 bomb threats; only one was real. Two students and the chief of a ministry's security service were arrested on suspicion of setting off a bomb under a decommissioned tank in Poklonnaya Gora.

July 15, 1996. *Egypt.* At 9:30 P.M., Judith Irish Goldenberg, 56, an analyst with the U.S. Defense Intelligence Agency, was stabbed to death outside Cairo's Semiramis International Hotel by Omar Mohammad Noaman, 28, a mentally disturbed Egyptian diagnosed with schizophrenia. The government said there was no political motive in the attack on the Jewish woman who was on temporary duty (TDY) for four days. Noaman had been released from a psychiatric hospital on June 10.

July 16, 1996. *Ukraine.* A remotely detonated bomb planted at the shoulder of a Kiev road exploded under the limousine of Prime Minister Pavlo Lazarenko. No serious injuries were reported and Lazarenko continued on to the airport. The bomb left a crater three feet deep and six feet across and seriously damaged the car. Some observers blamed Lazarenko's political opponents. He later blamed "forces" within the country's coal industry and fired several security officials in the Donbass mining area.

July 16, 1996. *Saudi Arabia.* The Movement for Islamic Change, the Jihad wing in the Arabian Peninsula, threatened U.S. troops in the country. The group said, "The blasphemous Al Sa'ud regime continues its injustice by detaining preachers and reformers, combating Islam and Muslims, and allowing invading enemy crusaders to control the land of the two holy shrines and the Arabian peninsula. It seems that the Americans have not gotten the message from the blowing up of the main command center of the infidel U.S. Army in al-'Ulya neighborhood of Riyadh, which killed 80 Crusaders, and left. Instead, their Defense Secretary has come to threaten the mujahidin that he will fight them if necessary. The reply was harsh and suitable to the challenge of the invaders' Secretary, the insolent William Perry. Once again the Movement for Islamic Change has proven that it has long and capable arms by targeting the pilots' complex in al-Khobar. The blast destroyed six buildings, including two entirely. According to our information, their number of their dead exceeds three hundred and the wounded six hundred. The targets were absolutely all Americans; what has been carried in the Saudi and U.S. media are misleading and untrue reports. The mujahidin will give their harshest reply to the threats of the foolish U.S. president. Everybody will be surprised by the magnitude of the reply, the date and time of which will be determined by the mujahidin. The invaders must be prepared to leave, either dead or alive. Their time is at the dawn. Is not dawn near?" 96071601

July 18, 1996. *Spain.* Badadi Omar, the leader of the Popular Front for the Liberation of Saquia El Hamra and Rio de Oro (POLISARIO) in Morocco, applied for political asylum.

July 20, 1996. *Spain.* Minutes after a Basque Nation and Liberty (ETA) phone caller warned that the group had planted four bombs at tourist locations, a bomb went off at 7:40 P.M. in the airport of Reus, injuring 35, 4 seriously. British and Irish tourists were among those injured. Two other bombs went off at beach resort hotels in Cambrils and Salou, but caused no injuries. No fourth bomb was found. 96072001

July 20, 1996. *Algeria.* Islamic radicals attacked a bus carrying employees of a state-owned vehicle company at Keddara, killing 12 and injuring 14.

Elsewhere, 7 people died and 38 were injured when a bomb exploded in a café in Kolea, Blida.

July 21, 1996. *Philippines.* Police reported that they had discovered a communist terrorist plot to attack the Asia-Pacific Economic Cooperation (APEC) summit. The faction, led by Filemon Lagman, former leader of the Alex Boncayao Brigade, was planning bombings, murders, and hostage taking. 96072101

July 22, 1996. *Pakistan.* A bomb hidden in a briefcase exploded in Lahore's international airport, killing 9, injuring 68, and damaging four airline ticket booths. The bomb was placed near a telephone booth by the main departure lounge.

July 24, 1996. *Morocco.* The Darl al-Islam (House of Islam) Western Front threatened to attack the Russian Embassy in Rabat. It also threatened to attack Russians considered to be "participants in the Judeo-Christian plot against Muslims in the Caucasus." 96072401

July 24, 1996. *Germany.* Leftist Turks seized a German Social Democratic Party (SPD) office in Frankfurt, holding it and four party officers for several hours. The Turks demanded improved conditions for political prisoners in Turkey and SPD support. Police stormed the office and arrested the Turks. 96072402

July 25, 1996. *Algeria.* A lone Algerian hijacker seized an Air Algérie Boeing 767 with 232 passengers aboard, including an Italian Embassy employee, Elena Conocchiali Infavale, another Italian, a Russian, a Spaniard, and six Moroccans. Some 80 women were on the plane. Four hours later, he was arrested before the plane could take off from Oran's Es-Senia Airport. 96072501

July 26, 1996. *United States.* A bomb exploded at the Miami office of the Sandinist National Liberation Front, causing some damage, but no injuries. 96072601

July 26, 1996. *Israel.* Terrorists conducted a drive-by Kalashnikov shooting at Tirosh village near Bet Shemesh. An Israeli, Uri, 53, and his daughter-in-law, Rachel, 24, were killed. Rachel's husband, Zeev Monk, 28, was critically wounded and died two days later. Zeev's mother, Aliza, survived. Police said the attackers might belong to the Halhul gang, which is affiliated with George Habash's Popular Front for the Liberation of Palestine (PFLP).

July 26, 1996. *Spain.* Sa'du Muhammad Ibrahim (variant Saado Mohamed Ibrahim Intissar), 28, a Lebanese-Palestinian barber, hijacked Iberia flight 6621, a DC-10 flying 218 passengers and 14 crew from Madrid to Havana, and forced it to land in the United States. He surrendered peacefully to FBI authorities. None of the crew and passengers, mostly European and Cuban tourists, was injured. European passengers included Italian, Swiss, French, and Andorran citizens.

The flight began in Beirut, with stops in Zurich and Madrid. Ibrahim did not explain how a barber making $120 a month could purchase a tourist-class ticket, nor where his $1,374 in cash came from.

At 1:50 P.M., Ibrahim, seated in Row 8, went into the plane's lavatory and assembled a fake bomb consisting of two large batteries and loose wires. He forced his way into the cockpit using half of a pair of scissors, telling Captain Javier Echabe, 53, that he wanted to go to the United States. Echabe agreed, suggesting Miami.

Ibrahim appeared before a U.S. magistrate in Miami on July 29. Magistrate William Turnoff set a bond hearing for August 1 and an arraignment for August 8. Ibrahim claimed to have been a soldier in the Lebanese Army and a barber in southern Lebanon. He faced a 20-year minimum sentence on air piracy charges. During the bond hearing, he was declared a fugitive risk and danger to the community and ordered held without bond.

Lebanese authorities announced that the hijacker was a Palestinian, not a Lebanese. He was born in the 'Ayn al-Hulwah camp in Lebanon in 1968. He was registered with the UN Relief and Works Agency on the card of his father, Muhammad Hashim Ibrahim, under number 33016240. He carried a card bearing number 15960 and left Lebanon with travel document 088415. The Lebanese authorities denied that he had ever worked for a government agency.

On April 25, 1997, a Miami jury deliberated for four hours before declaring him guilty. Sentencing was scheduled for August 11. 96072602

July 26, 1996. *Germany.* Gunmen occupied a Turkish Consulate office in Berlin. They tied up four staffers and painted leftist slogans on the walls. Police suspected the Turkish Communist Party Marxist/Leninist (TKP-ML). 96072603

July 26, 1996. *Tajikistan.* Two gunmen arrived at a Dushanbe airport in a taxi, shot the driver, and went to the airport's military section where they shot two Russian soldiers and injured several other people. Russian soldiers arrested the gunmen. 96072604

July 27, 1996. *United States.* A bomb hidden in a green knapsack exploded at 1:26 A.M. in the Centennial Olympic Park in Atlanta, Georgia. Two people were killed and 111 wounded. Alice Hawthorne, 44, was killed by the blast and Turkish cameraman Melih Uzunyol, 40, had a heart attack while running to film the devastation. Among those injured were six state troopers, one Georgia Bureau of Investigation agent, and Fallon Stubbs, 24, of Albany, Georgia, daughter of Hawthorne.

Bomb experts said the crudely made device was filled with masonry nails that served as shrapnel and was designed to kill. The bomb contained wire, a nine-volt battery, a clock, blasting caps, plumber's pipe, and two types of powder.

Initial suspicions centered around Richard Jewell, 33, a contract guard with AT&T, who brought the bomb to the attention of authorities. Some believed he could have made the warning phone call to police 18 minutes before the bomb went off. (The caller said the bomb would go off in 30 minutes.) Jewell's attorneys announced that he had successfully passed a polygraph examination and that his voice differed from that on the tape of the phone call. The Justice Department formally declared that he was not a "target" of investigation on October 26. On December 9, NBC agreed to make a monetary out-of-court settlement with Jewell. On December 19, FBI Director Louis J. Freeh told the Senate that the Justice Department had yet to determine who leaked Jewell's name as the leading suspect. On January 16, 1997, the Georgia State House of Representatives declared Jewell a hero. On May 20, 1997, three FBI agents were disciplined for their handling of the case. Woody Johnson, head of the Atlanta office, and David Tubbs, head of the Kansas City office, were censured; Don Johnson was suspended for five days without pay. On December 2, 1998, Jewell quit his job with the Lutherville, Georgia, police department because he was tired of the 40-mile commute.

On December 9, the FBI asked for any photographs or videotapes taken in the park on the night of the bombing, and offered a $500,000 reward.

The agency also released a tape of the 911 call warning of the bomb.

On January 26, 1997, three men arrested on October 8, 1996, near Yakima, Washington, for several bank robberies were being investigated for links to the Olympics blast. Justice and FBI spokesmen said the Sandpoint, Idaho, residents—Charles Barbee, 42, Robert S. Berry, 42, and Verne Jay Merrell, 51—were held without bail on charges of robbing banks and bombing one of the banks, an abortion clinic, and a newspaper office. They were believed to be members of white separatist sects based in northern Idaho. The bomb went off in the AT&T Global Village; Barbee worked for AT&T in Georgia, Florida, and Idaho. In a 1995 interview with the *Spokesman-Review*, he called AT&T an immoral corporation that mistreated Christian white men. "Half the people I worked with were women. They were working instead of being helpmates to their husbands, as God requires." On April 2, 1997, a federal jury deadlocked on the bombing and robbery charges, but convicted them of conspiracy, interstate transportation of stolen vehicles, and possession of hand grenades during their October 8 trip to Portland, Oregon. The sentences carried 35-year terms.

On January 28, 1997, Jewell sued the *Atlanta Journal-Constitution* and Piedmont College, where he once was a security guard, saying that they had libeled him. CNN and NBC settled out of court earlier.

On February 21, 1997, a dynamite bomb exploded at 9:45 P.M. at the Otherside Lounge, a gay/lesbian bar in Atlanta's Piedmont Road neighborhood, spewing nails and injuring five people. A second bomb was found in the parking lot and detonated the next morning. Police believed the second bomb was designed to kill police and rescuers. In addition to being similar to the Olympics bomb, this bomb resembled one used at the Atlanta Northside Family Planning Services clinic, a suburban abortion clinic in Sandy Springs, on January 16. Federal officials suggested that a serial bomber could be involved. A letter postmarked February 22 claimed that the Christian militant

"Army of God" would fight the "new world order" and called for "total war" against the federal government, homosexuals, and those involved in abortion. The letter also mentioned April 19, the fourth anniversary of the Waco, Texas, standoff with the Branch Davidians and the second anniversary of the Oklahoma City bombing. The letter mentioned details of the construction of the bombs and offered ways authorities would be able to identify the group's further attacks by a five-digit number in confessor letters. The Gay Community Yellow Pages received a voicemail claiming that the attack was carried out by the "Sons of the Confederate Klan, SOCK, a new neo-Nazi KKK organization from Los Angeles."

On June 10, the FBI said it had received hundreds of clues via its tipster hotline (1-888-ATF-BOMB) regarding the Atlanta abortion clinic, gay nightclub, and Olympics bombings. Federal agents believed they had discovered links between the cases.

On July 25, 1997, attorneys for 17 people injured in the Olympics bombing filed a $100 million lawsuit against Olympics organizers, claiming that the attack could have been foreseen and prevented. The suit was filed in Fulton County State Court against the Atlanta Committee for the Olympic Games (ACOG), AT&T, and two security firms. Meanwhile, investigators released a new sketch of an individual who was seen sitting on the bench under which the bomb was placed.

On July 28, senior Justice Department officials told the Senate that the FBI had acted in a "constitutionally suspect" manner in interrogating Jewell.

On October 13, 1997, the task force investigating the series of Atlanta bombings found bomb components at the home of Gregory Paul Lawler, 45, who was accused of murder and aggravated assault in the death of officer John Sowa, 28, and the wounding of officer Patricia Cocciolone, 35. Police also found militia manuals and stockpiled weapons in Lawler's apartment.

On November 18, 1997, the FBI task force made public some of the key physical evidence in hopes that someone would recognize the work of an acquaintance. The FBI displayed the ingredients of the pipe bombs used in three attacks in Atlanta.

On November 25, Richard Jewell started a new job as a police officer in Luthersville, a town of 750 people 40 miles southwest of Atlanta.

On May 5, 1998, the FBI offered a $1 million reward for help in arresting Eric Robert Rudolph, 31, who was charged in the January 29, 1998, fatal bombing of a Birmingham, Alabama, abortion clinic. For the first time, the FBI linked him to the Olympics bombing (although he was not officially a suspect), saying that the bombs were similar. The FBI increased the earlier $100,000 reward and placed Rudolph on the 10 Most Wanted Fugitives list. Rudolph was last seen on January 30, 1998, near his home in the mountains of western North Carolina. He abandoned his pickup truck and disappeared. Hundreds of federal and local agents searched the area for what FBI Director Freeh called "an accomplished hiker, a backwoods person, a survivalist."

On October 14, 1998, Attorney General Janet Reno and FBI Director Freeh announced that Rudolph was charged with three unsolved bombings—the Olympics attack and the 1997 bombings of a gay bar in Atlanta and an abortion clinic in Sandy Springs. They described Rudolph as a terrorist inspired not by politics or religion, but by indiscriminate hate.

On November 12, 1998, at 8:00 P.M., an FBI agent's head was grazed by a bullet fired into an Andrews, North Carolina, warehouse serving as the FBI command post coordinating the search for Rudolph.

On March 22, 1999, the Southeast Bomb Task Force announced it was scaling back its search for Rudolph. The Task Force reduced the use of helicopters. By June 25, 2000, authorities had significantly scaled down their search for Rudolph. 96082701

July 29, 1996. *Tajikistan.* Doctor Mohammad Assemi Khojandi, a Tajik scholar and director of the Central Asian project of UNESCO, was shot to death. Iran condemned the killing.

July 29, 1996. *Russia.* Slovak citizen Stefan Hajdin, who worked for a Czech firm, was kidnapped in Grozny. As of August 7, he had not been found. Chechen separatists were suspected. 96072901

August 1996. *United States.* Immigration and Naturalization agents detained Yahia Meddah, 27, an Algerian asylum-seeker suspected of involvement in terrorism. Meddah had settled in West Virginia after entering the United States on a false French passport ten months earlier. He requested political asylum, claiming he faced persecution from Algerian opposition forces, whom he claimed had kidnapped his father and sister and killed many of his relatives.

Human Rights Watch used his case to criticize U.S. treatment of immigration detainees, citing two suicide attempts on his part.

In 1997, an immigration judge denied his asylum request and attempt to stop a deportation order. The judge based his decision in part on secret evidence that he said showed Meddah's "connection with international terrorism."

On October 2, 1998, Meddah climbed over an eight-foot fence in a recreation area of Miami's Windmoor psychiatric hospital and fled to Canada. 98089901

August 1, 1996. *Algeria.* Islamic fundamentalists killed Pierre Chaviere (or Claverie), 85 (or 58), the Roman Catholic bishop of Oran, and his driver by setting off a remotely detonated bomb as his car was entering his residence. The explosive was linked to a gas canister. Hours earlier, the French bishop had met with French Foreign Minister Hervé de Charette. He was the 40th French citizen murdered in Algeria since 1993, when the Armed Islamic Group (GIA) began its attacks on foreigners.

The Islamic Salvation Front condemned the attack.

On August 14, police killed six terrorists in a shootout near Oran. The six were believed to be involved in the attack on the bishop. Police confiscated several automatic weapons and explosives from the hideout. 96080101

August 3, 1996. *Italy.* Two bombs were hidden inside beach umbrellas at the Adriatic coastal resorts of Lignano and Bibione. The first injured a sunbather's leg. The Bibione bomb was disarmed. Some observers believed the Mafia was attempting to scare off foreign tourists.

August 5, 1996. *Bosnia.* Following a phoned bomb threat, authorities evacuated two Sarajevo buildings that house the offices of the Organization for Security and Cooperation in Europe. The bomb was found and defused. No one claimed credit. 96080501

August 5, 1996. *Ethiopia.* A bomb exploded in the lobby of the Wabbe Shebelle Hotel in Addis Ababa, killing 2 and injuring 17, including a Belgian. No one claimed credit. 96080502

August 8, 1996. *South Africa.* Police dismissed as a hoax media reports that three foreign men were kidnapped during the hijacking of a minibus near Sandton, Johannesburg. The minibus, license PSG222T, was found and three people were arrested for its theft. Two firearms were confiscated.

August 9, 1996. *Colombia.* Leftist guerrillas kidnapped an Italian restaurateur and longtime Colombian resident. 96080901

August 10, 1996. *Mexico.* Following a Saturday afternoon baseball game in the Tijuana suburbs, Sanyo executive Mamoru Konno, 57, and two cheerleaders were abducted when two cars filled with gunmen swerved in front of his Cadillac sedan. Witnesses said a car had been driving around the field before the kidnapping. The occupants had asked several people for a description of Konno. Hours later, Konno phoned his secretary to say the kidnappers demanded a $2 million ransom and had set a deadline of August 17. The next morning, the two Mexican women were released near the Sanyo assembly plant.

Konno lived in the southern California town of Chula Vista, south of San Diego, and commuted to Tijuana. He was the president of Sanyo Video Component Corporation USA, the San Diego subsidiary of Sanyo Electric Company.

A Sanyo executive told an Osaka press conference that the money would be paid.

Konno was released on August 19 after Sanyo paid the $2 million ransom. A Sanyo official delivered the money to two gunmen, who then ran off. A few hours later, the kidnappers contacted the company with instructions on where to find Konno. He was in the basement of an abandoned building in the city.

Sanyo officials said they had no plans to scale down their operations in Mexico.

Police said they were not involved in the resolution of the kidnapping because they had never been contacted by Sanyo or family members. No official kidnapping report was filed. 96081001

August 10, 1996. *Panama.* Fifty Colombian guerrillas kidnapped the former representative for the Democratic Revolutionary Party in Boca de Cupe. The Revolutionary Armed Forces of Colombia (FARC) and National Liberation Army (ELN) were prime suspects. 96081002

August 11, 1996. *Somalia.* The al-Ittihaad al-Islami was suspected of killing two Ethiopian businessmen in Beledweyne to avenge Ethiopia's two-day military incursion into Somalia earlier in August. 96081101

August 13, 1996. *Mexico.* The Sanyo assembly plant in Tijuana was evacuated after a bomb threat. No bomb was found. 96081301

August 13, 1996. *Bosnia.* U.S. troops were placed on high alert when civilians were arrested while photographing and videotaping U.S. bases in the area. Observers suggested that it was part of terrorist planning.

August 14, 1996. *Colombia.* The National Liberation Army (ELN) was suspected of kidnapping two Brazilian engineers working on a highway in Meta Department. 96081401

August 14, 1996. *Sri Lanka.* The Liberation Tigers of Tamil Eelam (LTTE) bombed offices and residences belonging to two South Korean firms, Korea Telecom International and Samsung Electronics, causing serious damage but no injuries. This was the first LTTE attack against foreign investors in Sri Lanka. 96081402

August 15, 1996. *Tajikistan.* A one-kilogram homemade TNT mine exploded during the morning in Dushanbe, killing the Russian driver of a ZIL-130 truck and wounding two Russian soldiers serving with the border guard. The remotely detonated mine was placed in a section of the water supply pipeline under Borbad Street, near where air force regiment pilots reside. Nine other soldiers in the truck were unharmed. 96081501

August 15, 1996. *Sri Lanka.* The Liberation Tigers of Tamil Eelam (LTTE) set off grenades at the (South) Korean Telecommunications International office in Trincomalee, 150 miles northeast of Colombo, causing no injuries. The bombing came on the day that Sri Lankan President Chandrika Kumaratunga returned home from a visit to Seoul, South Korea. 96081502

August 16, 1996. *Cuba.* Three Cubans armed with a knife hijacked a small Cuban plane flying out of Guanabacoa, diverting it to the west coast of Florida. The plane crashed into the Gulf of Mexico. All four Cubans on board were rescued by the lifeboat team of the *Irbenskiy Proliv*, a Russian freighter. The three hijackers requested political asylum; the pilot wanted to return home. U.S. Customs agents said they had been pursuing the plane on suspicions it was operated by drug smugglers when it appeared on radar at 9:10 A.M. After tailing the single-engine, six-seater Polish Wilga for an hour, Customs agents reported that the craft jettisoned its two doors and then crashed.

The hijackers claimed they had earlier dropped leaflets protesting the February 24 Cuban shooting down of two planes flown by the exile group Brothers to the Rescue. 96081601

August 16, 1996. *China.* Pak Pyong-hyon, 55, an executive of the Kia Business Group supervising the Kia Training Institute in Yanji, was assaulted and killed by two attackers five meters from his office at 5:30 P.M. He was stabbed in the waist by a needle that was shaped like a ballpoint pen. He was on his way to a restaurant with two visitors from South Korea. The Kia Institute, with its staff of two South Koreans and eight Chinese, conducts automobile-related vocational training. 96081602

August 17, 1996. *Sudan.* Sudan People's Liberation Army (SPLA) rebels kidnapped six Roman Catholic missionaries, believing they were spying for the government. The rebels said the missionaries were "agents of Islam" after the rebels found a quotation from the Koran on a bookmark in a Bible belonging to two nuns who were hostages. On August 27, the rebels freed four hostages at the Roman Catholic mission in Mapourdit, 650 miles south of Khartoum. The rebels said the former hostages could not leave that area until they "finished their investigation" into the allegations. Those released were identified as Australian nuns Moira Lynch, 73, and Mary Batchelor, 68; American priest Rev. Michael Barton, 48; and Sudanese priest Rev. Raphael Riel, 48.

The next day, the rebels released Australian nun Maureen Carey, 52, and Italian brother Raniero Iacomella, 28. 96081701

August 17, 1996. *France.* A bomb exploded at the construction site for a McDonald's restaurant in Saint-Jean-de-Luz, causing extensive structural damage. Basque separatists were suspected. 96081702

August 21, 1996. *Colombia.* Gunmen kidnapped an Italian engineer working on an oil pipeline in northern Colombia. 96082101

August 22, 1996. *Germany.* Gary Rex (alias Gerhard) Lauck, 43, a Lincoln, Nebraska, right-wing extremist known as the Farm Belt Fuehrer, was found guilty in a German court of distributing neo-Nazi propaganda materials and inciting racial hatred. He was sentenced to four years in prison after a four-month trial in Hamburg. He claimed he was wrongfully arrested in Denmark in March 1995 and extradited to Germany in August 1995. He also claimed he was merely conducting a mail-order business from the United States, where his actions were legal. He published the newspaper *NS-Kampfruf (National Socialist-Battle Cry)*, produced by his National Socialist German Workers' Party-Overseas Organization. His attorney said he would appeal.

August 25, 1996. *Bahrain.* Three Bahrainis shot and wounded a Pakistani policeman guarding the Russian Consulate. No one claimed credit. 96082501

August 26, 1996. *Sudan.* Seven Iraqi hijackers claiming to have TNT and a grenade hijacked Sudan Airways Flight 150, an Airbus 310 carrying 186 passengers and 13 crew from Khartoum to Amman, Jordan. They diverted it to Larnaca, Cyprus, where they demanded political asylum in London. Some 25 minutes after takeoff, the pilot notified ground control that there was a hijacker on board and asked to fly to Rome. He later said he did not have enough fuel and landed at Larnaca. Reports were initially unclear regarding how many hijackers there were. After seven hours of negotiations, the hijackers surrendered at London's Stansted Airport. Police had agreed to bring Iraqi Community Association leader Saddiq Saddah, who works with refugees and exiles, to the control tower to witness the peaceful surrender. Police also detained six female relatives of the male hijackers and were caring for two children traveling with them as well. No injuries were reported. Police found knives and fake explosives. Iraqi oppositionists said the hijackers were defecting military advisers. 96082601

August 26, 1996. *Macedonia.* The Communist Party of Macedonia in Gostivar faxed a threatening letter to the South Korean Embassy in Belgrade. The group protested "the unprecedented terror against young communists and students" during clashes with police in Seoul in which 400 students were arrested. The fax said Korean interests in Macedonia would be "most strongly, ferociously, and mercilessly attacked." 96082602

August 27, 1996. *Germany.* Turkish leftists shot at a vehicle carrying two members of a rival leftist exile group, killing one of the occupants and injuring the other. 96082701

August 28, 1996. *Indonesia.* At 10:00 A.M., a Molotov cocktail was thrown at the U.S. Consulate in Surabaya. The attacker was identified as a person of Arab descent who had visited the consulate three days earlier. The bomb was thrown by a person who exited a taxi, threw the bomb, then re-entered the taxi and escaped. No one was injured, but the guard shack and fence were burned. Police called the attack a criminal act. 96082801

August 29, 1996. *Afghanistan.* The London-based *Al-Quds Al-Arabi* reported it had received a 12-page letter from exiled Saudi dissident Osama bin Laden calling for Saudis to strike at American military personnel in Saudi Arabia. The letter noted that "the infidels must be thrown out of the Arabian Peninsula" even though they had been invited in by the Saudi government. He said his followers should use "fighting tactics using light and quick-moving troops. . . . In other words, launching guerrilla war in which the sons of the nation take part but not the armed forces." Bin Laden was known to be one of the major financiers of Islamic extremists.

August 31, 1996. *United States.* Police stopped Roman Regman, 21, a Romanian seminarian, as he was boarding a flight at Tampa International Airport. They found explosives and weapons in his luggage. Among his stash were 5 handmade explosive devices, 2 hand grenades, bomb-making materials, a 9-mm pistol, 180 rounds of ammuni-

tion, and 6 military-style knives. He was charged with seven counts of carrying explosive devices, six counts of carrying weapons, and one count of carrying a concealed firearm. He was held without bail at the Hillsborough County Jail.

Regman had entered the United States four years earlier and was a legal resident, living with his mother in Brooksville, Florida. He had a round-trip ticket to Wilkes Barre/Scranton via Pittsburgh. He claimed he was returning to St. Tikhons Seminary in South Canaan near Scranton. 96083101

September 1996. *Turkey.* Christopher N. Mrozowski, 34, of Bethesda, Maryland, a Polish woman, and an Iranian man were arrested by the Turkish government on charges of aiding Kurdish rebels. Mrozowski was hiking in Turkey after finishing a summer job teaching Peace Corps volunteers in Warsaw. The three were taken off a bus in eastern Turkey. They denied the charges and were released on October 10, 1996, pending trial for assisting the rebels. No trial date was set.

September 3, 1996. *Lebanon.* A Palestinian, Nazir Abdullah, claiming to have a bomb, diverted a Bulgarian Hemus Air Tupolev 154 after taking off from Lebanon. He released the 150 passengers in Bulgaria, then forced the crew to fly to Norway, where he surrendered at an airport 60 miles from Oslo. He asked for a lawyer and political asylum. 96090301

September 8, 1996. *Bosnia.* A Ukrainian soldier serving with the NATO peace mission was fatally shot as he was guarding a Sarajevo warehouse filled with balloting materials. Gunmen fired on him and his party. Two other Ukrainian soldiers returned fire. The terrorists escaped. 96090801

September 11, 1996. *Iraq.* Kurdish refugees took hostage nine UN employees near Sairanbar. Among the hostages were a World Food Program official, a UNICEF official, and a UNHCR (United Nations High Commissioner for Refugees) employee. A crowd of refugees demonstrating near the UN offices seized the workers as thousands chanted anti-U.S. slogans and threw rocks at UN employees. The refugees later released all the hostages. 96091101

September 13, 1996. *Iraq.* The Patriotic Union of Kurdistan (PUK) kidnapped four French workers for Pharmacists Without Borders, a Canadian UNHCR official, and two Iraqis. 96091301

September 14, 1996. *Bahrain.* Three assailants threw a flammable liquid into an An Nuwaydirat parts shop, setting it on fire. The attackers then pulled down a rolling metal door, preventing an Indian employee from escaping. He died from his burns the next day. 96091401

September 14, 1996. *Venezuela.* National Liberation Army (ELN) guerrillas fired on a military post in Los Bancos, killing one soldier and wounding two civilians. 96091402

September 17, 1996. *Somalia.* Daniel Suther, a USAID worker, was kidnapped by eight Somali gunmen, who freed him in Giohar the next day, claiming mistaken identity. They took him and his Somali driver from a four-wheel-drive vehicle on the Sanaa road in northern Mogadishu after disarming his two Somali guards. Ali Mahdi Mohamed, a Somali militia leader with whom Suther met shortly before his abduction, noted that a group of businessmen, who claimed that the World Food Program owed them money, had hired the kidnappers. Suther was seized because they thought he was with that organization. Mohamed, the Abgal subclan chief, ordered an Islamic court to seize the kidnappers and sent two pickup trucks with mounted machine guns to the area to rescue Suther. 96091701

September 23, 1996. *United Kingdom.* Police in West London conducted dawn raids of IRA hideouts, seizing ten tons of explosives and arresting five men. One IRA gunman was fatally shot. Police found Semtex, fertilizer-based explosives, three Kalashnikov assault rifles, two handguns, trucks, and other vehicles to be used in bombings.

One of those arrested was an employee of British Airways. 96092301

October 1996. *United States.* Twelve lab workers were hospitalized after eating tainted doughnuts and muffins that had been left in a break room at St. Paul Medical Center in Dallas, Texas. Someone had swabbed the pastries with *Shigella dysenteriae* type 2, which came from a lab culture freezer in the medical center.

October 1996. *Austria.* The Eurobomber, using the name Bavarian Liberation Army on behalf of Germanic tribes, threatened to send another wave of letter bombs on the eve of European Parliament elections. A small bomb went off in a Graz post office. There were no casualties. 96109901

October 1, 1996. *Russia.* Choi Duk Keun, 54, a South Korean cultural attaché assigned to the consulate in Vladivostok, was bludgeoned to death in the stairwell of his apartment building. He was hit on the head at least eight times. Blood was discovered on the staircase from the third to the sixth floors. He was also stabbed twice, possibly by a poisoned knife. Police ruled out theft because they found the equivalent of $1,200 in cash and his passport in his pockets. A witness saw two Asian men running from the scene.

Choi was believed to have been collecting intelligence on the thousands of North Korean expatriates in the area. North Korea was suspected, although Pyongyang denied involvement. 96100101

October 2, 1996. *Bulgaria.* Andrei Lukanov, 58, the country's first post-Communist prime minister, was shot to death outside his home. His second government had been ousted by strikes in November 1990, although he retained a leadership position in the Socialist Party's parliamentary delegation. He had been under the protection of the National Bodyguard Service from February 1 to April 14 because of death threats.

October 4, 1996. *Honduras.* A five-pound dynamite time bomb exploded in the Honduran Legislative Palace shortly after midnight. There were no injuries, but windows were shattered in the palace and in the neighboring Central Bank, a private local bank, and an office building. No one claimed credit, although unions and other groups had conducted protest marches and strikes regarding rising food and fuel prices.

October 5, 1996. *France.* A dynamite bomb exploded at 11:41 P.M. in the Bordeaux mayoral offices of French Prime Minister Alain Juppé, breaking windows and doors in the reception hall, but causing no casualties. Corsican separatists claimed credit; they had threatened to conduct attacks on the mainland. The attackers had managed to scale a ten-foot wall, cross a police-patrolled garden, and set the bomb under the steps leading to Juppé's ceremonial chambers.

October 5, 1996. *Zaire.* Gunmen attacked a Swedish Free Pentecostal Church hospital in Lemera, killing 38, most of them patients who were shot or stabbed. An attack at a neighboring Roman Catholic mission led to the deaths of 12 others, including 2 priests. The violence was attributed to Tutsis angered by medical care being given to rival Hutus. 96100501-02

October 5, 1996. *Ethiopia.* Gunmen shot and killed a German botanist near the Taiwan Market shopping area in Dire Dawa. No one claimed credit. 96100501

October 7, 1996. *Northern Ireland.* Two IRA car bombs wounded 31 people outside British Army headquarters at Lisburn, outside Belfast. The first blast, a 500-pound car bomb, went off at 4:30 P.M. The second, smaller bomb exploded at 4:43 P.M. at a nearby medical station that was receiving casualties. Several medical workers were injured. Five victims were critically injured. The army reported that 21 soldiers and 10 civilians were hurt. Two children were injured. No warning call was reported.

The IRA claimed credit on October 8 in a call to the Irish broadcasting network RTE, using a code word.

On October 11, Warrant Officer James Bradwell, 43, died of his wounds. Burns covered 60 percent of his body.

October 10, 1996. *Venezuela.* The National Liberation Army (ELN) of Colombia was suspected of kidnapping a Venezuelan cattleman at the Colombian border. The victim was found dead a few hours later in Libertador. 96101001

October 11, 1996. *United States.* The FBI arrested seven members of the Virginia Mountaineer Militia, charging them with attempting to collect and transport explosives and planning to destroy the FBI's $200 million Criminal Justice Information Services Division, a fingerprint installation in Clarksburg, West Virginia. Those arrested included a member of the Clarksburg Fire Department, who provided photos of the center's blueprints, which were sold for $50,000 to an undercover agent. Militia members thought this agent was a member of a Middle Eastern terrorist group. The FBI said the group's leader, Floyd Raymond Looker, had collected the explosives. The arrests were made in West Virginia, Ohio, and Pennsylvania.

Those arrested were the fire department lieutenant, James R. Rogers, 41 (or 56), of Jan Lew, West Virginia; chemical engineer Jack Arland Phillips, 57, of Fairmont, West Virginia; Edward F. Moore, 52, of Lavalette, West Virginia; James M. Johnson, 48, of Maple Heights, Ohio; Terrell P. Coon, 46, of Waynesburg, Pennsylvania; and Imam A. Lewis, 26, of Cleveland, Ohio.

The FBI had learned about the plot 16 months earlier, when O. Marshall Richards, a member of the militia, became disenchanted with its bomb making. Richards had served as the group's intelligence and security leader and made more than 200 tapes of conversations by militia members.

On October 16, a federal judge in Cleveland ordered two of the men extradited to West Virginia. An attorney for one of the suspects appealed.

On October 17, federal magistrates ordered four of the men held without bond.

On November 8, the seven men were indicted

by a federal grand jury in Wheeling, West Virginia. They were charged with conspiracy to manufacture explosives, to transport them across state lines, and to target the FBI center. Conviction on the individual counts entailed a maximum sentence of ten years in prison and a $250,000 fine.

On May 29, 1997, Edward Moore pleaded guilty to possession of a bomb he made during a March 24, 1996, militia training session. He made the bomb using ammonium nitrate and nitromethane racing fuel. Prosecutors dropped the charge of conspiracy to manufacture explosives.

During the trial in U.S. District Court in Wheeling on June 12, 1997, Larry Martz, an Ohio militia member not charged in the plot, was quoted in FBI affidavits as indicating that the militia considered killing Senator John D. "Jay" Rockefeller IV, Federal Reserve Chairman Alan Greenspan, and their families in a "holy war" against the federal government.

On August 8, 1997, following a four-day federal trial, Looker was convicted of conspiracy to engage in manufacturing and dealing in explosives without a license. The charge carries a maximum sentence of five years in jail and a $250,000 fine. Jack Phillips had entered a guilty plea. On August 13, Looker pleaded guilty to selling blueprints of the FBI's fingerprint complex in Clarksburg to what he believed was a terrorist group.

On August 25, jurors completed three days of deliberations before declaring guilty Lieutenant James "Rich" Rogers, who had taken 34 photos of the blueprints of the FBI facility and stored them in the fire hall basement. He faced a ten-year sentence. He was acquitted of a conspiracy charge. Rogers was the first to be convicted under the 1994 antiterrorism law that makes it a crime to knowingly provide resources to someone planning a terrorist attack. Attorney Gary Zimmerman said he would appeal the verdict.

October 16, 1996. *Ethiopia.* Unknown gunmen shot and killed a French citizen and a Yemeni citizen near the Taiwan Market in Dire Dawa. 96101601-02

October 20, 1996. *Cambodia.* Forty Khmer Rouge kidnapped three Frenchmen and five Cambodians who were traveling by motorcycle in Kampong Chhnang Province. They were released unharmed 24 hours later. 96102001

October 21, 1996. *Yemen.* Toaiman tribesmen kidnapped Serge Lefevre, first secretary of the French Embassy, in Sanaa. The government arrested 18 tribesmen and gave the group until midnight on October 22 before it would conduct a rescue operation. The tribe had wanted government compensation for losses sustained by June floods. They also called for more jobs. Marib Province Governor Abdul-Wali Shumairi said, "The government will look into these demands, but only after the release of the hostages . . . and the surrender of the captors." On October 26, Lefevre was handed over to tribal chiefs who had acted as mediators; they were expected to turn him over to the authorities. The kidnappers had dropped their original demands and just asked for a guarantee against prosecution.

On October 27, however, Lefevre was again kidnapped by members of the same tribe. He was grabbed while on his way back to the capital. He appears to have been freed on November 1, when the government agreed to the kidnappers' conditions. 96102101, 96102701

October 24, 1996. *Uganda.* Gunmen attacked a Sudanese refugee camp in Palorinya, western Moyo, killing 16 Sudanese refugees and injuring 5 others. No one claimed credit. 96102401

October 26, 1996. *Colombia.* Leftist rebels kidnapped a French geologist and a Colombian engineer in Meta Department after attacking their convoy. Suspects included the National Liberation Army (ELN) and the Revolutionary Armed Forces of Colombia (FARC). 96102601

October 26, 1996. *France.* Gunmen killed the international treasurer of the Liberation Tigers of Tamil Eelam (LTTE) and a companion in Paris. Authorities suspected that the LTTE killed him for misappropriating funds for personal use. 96102602

October 27–28, 1996. *Zaire.* Gunmen twice attacked the Katale refugee camp near Gisenyi, which was crowded with 220,000 Rwandan Hutu refugees. Zairian armed forces repelled the attackers. The attackers torched the hospital where the wounded refugees were housed. At least 6 people were killed and 60 injured in the second incident. Tutsi tribesmen, possibly aided by the Rwandan and Burundian armies, were suspected.

November 1, 1996. *Sudan.* Rebels led by Kerubino Kwanyin Bol kidnapped a Red Cross worker from New Mexico, an Australian nurse, and a Kenyan Red Cross worker in southern Sudan. An ICRC (International Committee of the Red Cross) effort to offer goods for the hostages failed.

At the behest of the ICRC, on December 8, U.S. Rep. William Richardson (D–N.M.) flew into the area in a World War II cargo plane to rescue the hostages, who had been beaten and held in a reed hut shrouded with vultures. Following a five-hour negotiating session at Gogrial, Richardson talked rebel leader Bol into reducing the $2.5 million ransom demand to five tons of rice, four jeeps, nine radios, a health survey, and a personal pledge to help solve the unrest in Sudan. U.S. Ambassador Tim Carney printed out the agreement on his laptop computer. Former hostages Moshen Raza, Red Cross pilot John Early, and Mary Worthington flew to freedom with Richardson, who had earlier negotiated for the release of captives in North Korea, Iraq, Bangladesh, Burma, and Cuba.

Several aid groups expressed concern that hostage takers had been rewarded. Richardson later said intercepts of rebel radio communications suggested that the group would step up hostage taking.

President Clinton named Richardson his UN ambassador in December 1996. 96110101

November 5, 1996. *Paraguay.* A threat was made against the U.S. Embassy and diplomats in Asuncion on the eve of U.S. elections. Israeli officials reported being targets of a similar threat by an organization believed to be connected to Hizballah. 96110501

November 7, 1996. *Paraguay.* Local authorities arrested Marwan al-Sadafi (or Safadi; alias Marwan Adib Adam Kadi; alias Ibrahim Mahmood Awethe), 40, a Lebanese suspected of involvement with Hizballah. He was extradited to New York the next day. He was placed in a Chicago jail on November 9 on charges of passport fraud. He was later extradited to Canada, where he had escaped while serving a nine-year prison sentence for drug trafficking.

He was linked to an alleged plan to bomb the U.S. Embassy on the anniversary of the November 1995 bombing of a U.S. military facility in Saudi Arabia. He apparently had conducted surveillance of the area. Argentine officials apparently told the Paraguayans about his Hizballah connections. Sadafi was arrested along with another Arab man (who was later released) at a hotel (or apartment house) in Ciudad del Este, on the Argentine–Brazil–Paraguay border. He was picked up in a raid against smugglers during which police discovered double-barreled shotguns, revolvers, pistols, and Canadian passports.

U.S. officials later said Sadafi's nationality was unclear. He had obtained a valid U.S. passport in Chicago by using a fake driver's license and birth certificate for Ibrahim Mahmood Awethe. 96110701

November 12, 1996. *Bahrain.* Two propane gas cylinders exploded behind a strip mall near the Shia village of Wattyan, damaging the Gulf Motor Agency Hyundai dealership and injuring a security guard. 96111201

November 15, 1996. *Switzerland.* A letter bomb killed a 13-year-old girl and wounded her mother in their Buchs apartment. The girl was opening the parcel. Police suspected that the Bavarian Liberation Army, which had conducted a letter bomb campaign throughout Europe for the preceding two years, could have been responsible.

November 15, 1996. *Algeria.* Assailants beheaded a Bulgarian businessman who had once been Bulgaria's defense attaché in Algeria. The body was found at the entrance to Bainem Forest, west of Algiers. No one claimed credit, but the Algerian Armed Islamic Group (GIA) was suspected. 96111501

November 16, 1996. *West Bank.* Hamas bomb maker Mohammad Assaf was killed while assembling a bomb in Qabatya, near Jenin. PLO military intelligence arrested five Qabatya Hamas members who were his associates. Assaf had been released from an Israeli prison two months earlier. He had served numerous six-month jail terms.

November 16, 1996. *Russia.* Two bombs went off at a military residence in Kaspiysk, Dagestan, near Chechnya, killing at least seven. The nine-story facility collapsed, and 50 people were missing and feared trapped. The bombs contained 55 pounds of TNT and were hidden in the basement. Suspects included Chechen activists, individuals opposed to the Chechen peace agreements, smugglers, and the local mafia.

November 17, 1996. *Colombia.* Medellin Airport police arrested Werner Mauss, 54, a former German intelligence agent and private investigator, and a 36-year-old woman (who used the alias Michaela Moellner) claiming to be his wife, as the duo was boarding a private plane. They were accompanied by Brigitte Schoene, a German they had ransomed from the National Liberation Army (ELN). Mauss was carrying 14 passports, a satellite telephone with a global positioning system, a satellite fax, a computer with encryption, and letters from the German Embassy saying the two were on an "official mission."

The police claimed that Mauss, who had acted as an intermediary in peace talks between narco-terrorists and the government, had helped the rebels select kidnap targets and increase their ransoms. He would then offer his services as an intermediary and obtain multimillion-dollar commissions. He arranged for the release in 1995 of three Ital-

ians who were kidnapped by the ELN. Schoene was kidnapped in September 1996, after which family members nearly closed a deal to pay a $200,000 ransom. After Mauss entered the picture, the ransom demand increased to $1.5 million, according to the family.

Mauss also tried to get the Cali cartel to close up shop in return for the government permitting its members to keep 20 percent of its drug profits.

On July 26, 1997, Mauss was freed. His lawyer, Abraham Casallas, said the Mausses would stay in the country to clear their name. Germany pressured Colombia to deport Mauss. The regional head of Colombian intelligence in Medellin, Emilio Rojas, told reporters that as soon as legal issues were cleared up, Mauss and Moellner would be deported for entering the country on false passports.

November 17, 1996. *Turkey.* A fire broke out at the Tozbey Hotel in Istanbul, killing 17 Ukrainians and injuring 40 others. On November 22, the Turkish Islamic Jihad said it had started the fire. Authorities believed that faulty wiring and negligence on the part of hotel guests might have been the cause.

November 20, 1996. *Philippines.* Bombs were found at Manila's Ninoy Aquino International Airport and Subic Bay, the former U.S. military base, where President Clinton and seven other Pacific Rim leaders were scheduled to meet on November 25 for the Asia-Pacific Economic Cooperation summit. One bomb was found in a bag in the airport's arrival area. It was detonated outside the terminal. The Subic Bay Freeport bomb was found near the main gate by a janitor. It was defused. No one claimed responsibility. Some police sources said the bombs were part of an exercise, but many other security sources disputed the claim.

On November 22, the U.S. State Department warned Americans that they could be under threat of terrorist attack at the summit. 96112001

November 23, 1996. *Ethiopia.* Ethiopian Airlines Flight ET961, a Boeing 767 carrying 163 passengers and 12 crew, was hijacked at 11:20 A.M. after takeoff from Addis Ababa. It was scheduled to fly to Nairobi, Kenya; Brazzaville, Congo; Lagos, Nigeria; and Abidjan, Ivory Coast. The hijackers demanded to go to Australia, where they would seek political asylum. They were armed with an ax, a fire extinguisher, and a device they claimed was a bomb. At one point, a drunken hijacker forced copilot Yonas Mekuria away from his seat and then played with the joystick controls, putting the plane into steep turns and banks. The hijackers refused to believe that the plane was running out of fuel, claiming that the plane could fly for 11 hours without stopovers. Rekha Mirchandani, 29, an Indian passenger, said crewmen told her that the hijackers had responded, "If we die, we want others to die with us. We want to make history." The plane crashed at 3:20 P.M. into the Indian Ocean near the Grand Comore Mitsamiuti tourist beach in the Comoros Islands, killing 127 people, most of them Africans and Asians. The pilot, Captain Leul Abate, tried to minimize casualties by landing in the sea near the shore, where rescuers would quickly find survivors. However, the plane bounced and flipped before breaking apart. This was the third hijacking Abate had survived.

Among the survivors were U.S. Consul General Franklin Huddle, his wife, Chanya, another American named McFarland, and three Italians. Eight Israelis were on the flight. A Nigerian passenger, Alphonso Dala, survived.

Police initially arrested two men for the hijacking, but determined that they were innocent when the copilot said he did not recognize them.

Survivors were unclear whether explosives were used and about how many hijackers (2, 3, or 11) were on board. Authorities later settled on three, all of whom died in the crash. The hijackers were ultimately identified as Ethiopians who had lived in Djibouti for years. They had arrived in Addis Ababa five weeks before the hijacking. Authorities were unable to determine the motives of Alamayhu Bekele, Mateias Solomon, and Sultan Hussein, who did not belong to any political party. Kenyan survivor Kanaidza Abwao, a young hotel executive whose hand was broken in the crash, said the

hijackers used the plane's public address system to read a statement in Amharic, French, and English: "There is a problem with the government. We were prisoners, and now we have changed the destination. If anyone tries to attack us, we are going to blow the plane up. I have a grenade." Ethiopian survivor Bisrat Alemu remembered similar statements.

Among the dead was Mohamed Amin, 53, a Reuters Television cameraman whose 1984 photos alerted the world about the Ethiopian famine. He was returning home to Nairobi with Brian Tetley, who wrote the text for Amin's photo books. Also killed was Leslianne Shedd, 28, a commercial officer with the U.S. Embassy, who was headed for Kenya to meet friends for Thanksgiving. Missing was Ron Farris, 46, a missionary doctor returning from India to Abidjan.

Four injured passengers died of their wounds on November 25, bringing the total dead to 127. 96112301

November 25, 1996. *Dubai.* The Movement for Islamic Change, a radical underground Saudi Islamic group, threatened to attack U.S. forces in Saudi Arabia unless jailed Muslims were freed. Oppositionists had claimed that Riyadh had jailed hundreds of people for questioning in the June 26 bombing of a U.S. military barracks near Dhahran. The group set the end of Ramadan (mid-February) as its deadline and specifically called for the release of Salman Awdah, a Muslim cleric jailed in September 1994 for his sermons against the presence of Western troops.

On November 28, Defense Secretary William Perry said U.S. and Saudi intelligence efforts, including preventative arrests, may have forestalled new attacks. 96112501

December 1996. *Lebanon.* Gunmen fired on a Syrian-registered minibus near Tabarja, 15 miles north of Beirut, killing a Syrian driver and injuring a passenger.

A bomb exploded near a Syrian intelligence post in Tripoli, injuring two Syrian intelligence officers. A Syrian military spokesman claimed that it was an accident—a detonator was burned in a pile of trash. 96129901-02

December 3, 1996. *France.* A bomb went off at 6:05 P.M. in the Paris underground RER Metro station at Port Royal, killing a Canadian woman and a Frenchman and seriously injuring 86 others, including an American and a Canadian. Seven were listed in grave condition. The 13-kilogram bomb destroyed the fourth car of a southbound train, throwing several passengers out of the car and onto the platform. The Algerian Armed Islamic Group (GIA) was suspected because it had used the same bomb type—a butane gas canister packed with explosives and nails—in earlier incidents.

The next day, extra police and 1,800 soldiers were posted in major cities and border crossings in Opération Vigipirate.

On December 5, a third victim, a 25-year-old Moroccan man, died. Another Moroccan man died on December 8.

On December 9, the trial opened of 34 Muslim men accused of violent crimes in support of Moroccan Islamic militants. Thirteen were in prison on separate charges in other countries or were still at large. The terrorists were charged, inter alia, with the 1994 robbery of a Marrakesh hotel in which two Spanish tourists were shot dead. The prosecution claimed that the defendants were trained abroad in the use of weapons and carried out holdups in France. The 21 who appeared in court were some of the 200 Arab men detained for a 1995 wave of bombings.

On December 10, Paris police arrested 15 suspected Muslim militants, then freed all but 4 later that day. Police were investigating a similar series of 1995 bombings by Algerians that killed 8 and injured more than 160. 96120301

December 6, 1996. *United States.* The Immigration and Naturalization Service (INS) detained Anwar Haddam, U.S.-based spokesman for Algeria's Islamic Salvation Front (FIS), at his home in northern Virginia. He was in the United States on "advance parole," which ended on December 5.

Haddam's party had won 188 seats in Algeria's 430-member legislature in the December 1991 elections; the regime canceled runoff elections the next month, preventing an FIS victory and sending many FIS leaders into exile. Haddam, who traveled to France and then to the United States in 1992, faced a civil lawsuit charging him with human rights violations. Seven anonymous Algerian and French plaintiffs served him with a class-action suit seeking damages for "crimes against humanity, war crimes, and other gross human rights and humanitarian law violations," accusing him of involvement in assassinations, torture, hijacking, sexual violence against women, and "sex-based apartheid."

Haddam's 1993 request for political asylum in the United States was denied. He moved in and out of the United States with INS approval until his arrest.

On December 7, 2000, Haddam, 45, who had been in Rappahannock Regional Jail in Stafford, Virginia, for four years under a secret evidence law, was conditionally released after the Board of Immigration Appeals determined that the evidence did not indicate that he was a terrorist. On November 30, the immigration judges had issued an opinion granting him political asylum. The INS had sought his deportation on the grounds that he had ordered, incited, assisted, or otherwise participated in the persecution of others in Algeria. The INS asked Attorney General Janet Reno to set aside the asylum grant.

December 8, 1996. *Tajikistan.* Gunmen attacked a Tajik-British gold mine in Darvaz, kidnapping four employees, including a British citizen and a South African. The terrorists occupied the mine for five days, negotiating with the UN, the Red Cross, British diplomats, and an inter-Tajik joint commission monitoring the current peace accord. The hostages were released on December 28 in Childara village. 96120801

December 10, 1996. *Colombia.* Five Revolutionary Armed Forces of Colombia (FARC) gunmen kidnapped Frank Pescatori, 40, a New Jersey geologist working at a coal mine and methane gas exploration site at Hato Nuevo, La Guajira Department. Pescatori worked for Geomet of Bessemer, Alabama. His body was found on February 25, 1997, in San Juan del Cesar, 25 miles south of where he was seized. The rural area is a guerrilla stronghold. 96121001

December 11, 1996. *West Bank.* Palestinian gunmen ambushed and killed a 12-year-old Israeli and his mother and injured four other passengers (three girls, aged four to ten, and their father) in their Volkswagen Golf station wagon while they were driving on a new bypass road near Surda. Two gunmen, armed with automatic weapons, and a driver sped off to Ramallah, 12 miles north of Jerusalem. The victims of the evening killing were among the founding families of the Jewish settlement of Bet El. Survivor Yoel Tsur is director of the settlers' pirate radio station Channel 7. The Popular Front for the Liberation of Palestine (PFLP) took credit.

On December 18, the State Security Court of the Palestine Liberation Organization (PLO) convicted three 20-year-old Palestinian PFLP members for the murders. Abdel Nasser Qaisi and Ibrahim Qam were sentenced to life in prison at hard labor for killing Etta Tsur and Ephraim Tsur. Ibrahim Massad, the driver, was jailed for 15 years. The PLO said the trio would not be extradited to Israel.

December 17, 1996. *Russia.* Gunmen armed with silenced weapons killed six Red Cross workers, five of them women, in their beds at a hospital at Novye Atagi at 4:00 A.M. The terrorists broke down doors to the rooms and shot each worker in the head. Christophe Hench, a Swiss citizen who ran the project, survived his gunshot wound. The gunmen fled.

The victims were identified as:

- Nancy Malloy of Vancouver, British Columbia, a medical administrator who had worked with the Red Cross in Belgrade, Kuwait, and Ethiopia. She came to

the region in September on a six-month contract.
- Johan Joost Elkerbout, 47, a Dutch construction technician.
- Fernanda Calado, 49, the Spanish head nurse.
- Sheryl Thayer, 40, a New Zealand nurse who had worked with the Red Cross in Afghanistan and Thailand.
- Ingeborg Foss, 42, a Norwegian nurse who had worked with the Red Cross in Pakistan and who was beginning a three-month tour.
- Gunnhild Myklebust, 50, a Norwegian nurse who had worked at a Norwegian Red Cross hospital in Bosnia and who had come to the region the previous month.

Tobias Bredland, 48, a Norwegian surgeon, said he was saved only because his door was locked.

The International Committee of the Red Cross (ICRC) suspended operations in the region. The 14 survivors were evacuated to Geneva.

The next day, Chechen rebel field commander Salman Raduyev released 21 Russian police who had been taken hostage on December 14. 96121701

December 17, 1996. *Peru.* Two dozen Tupac Amaru Revolutionary Movement (MRTA) gunmen blew a hole in a concrete wall at 8:20 P.M. and stormed a birthday party for Japanese Emperor Akihito, 63, at the residence of the Japanese ambassador, seizing 700 diplomats, business leaders, and government officials. After an explosion was heard, the gunmen told the hostages to lie on the ground, not to look up, and to keep silent. One hostage said she saw six or seven guerrillas dressed in green army fatigue pants. They covered their faces with red and white bandannas and carried small arms. Some barricaded the doors and windows with furniture. They calmly put on gas masks hidden in small backpacks when the Peruvian police fired tear gas into the residence. The gunmen joined comrades who were disguised as waiters for the cocktail reception. Cartridges had been smuggled inside flowers and the Christmas cake. *La Republica* reported that the rebels had rented an adjacent house three months earlier and tunneled into the grounds.

The rebels included two young women and appeared to have automatic weapons and night-vision equipment. They told hostages the garden was mined and the back door booby-trapped.

A rebel was injured in the initial firefight with police.

The rebels said they were protesting the Japanese government's support of the Peruvian regime. The hostages included at least 60 Japanese, including 17 Japanese Embassy staff members and representatives of 17 Japanese firms doing business in Peru, as well as guests from at least 28 countries.

The terrorists threatened to kill the hostages one by one, starting with Peruvian Foreign Minister Francisco Tudela, unless the government freed 400 to 500 jailed insurgents, including their leader Victor Polay and Lori Helene Berenson, 27. Polay was captured in 1992, and Berenson, a New Yorker, was serving a life sentence in Yanamayo Prison. She was arrested in November 1995. The Marxist rebels also called on the government to change its economic policies "to benefit the poor" and to provide a monetary "war tax" ransom and safe passage to the Amazon jungle, where their last hostage would be released. A spokesman in Germany relayed the MRTA demands. A deadline was passed without bloodshed.

The government said the rebels would have to free all the hostages and surrender their weapons to a commission of guarantors before the regime would consider "an exit" for the gunmen. The government rejected the demand for release of the prisoners.

Among the hostages were the president of the Peruvian Supreme Court; President Alberto Fujimori's brother; the Speaker of Parliament; Agriculture Minister Rodolfo Munante Sanguineti; the current and past chiefs of the antiterrorism police; an admiral; generals; senior intelligence officials; several congressmen; 19 foreign ambassadors, including those from Japan, Cuba, South

Korea, Panama, Austria, and Spain; and other senior diplomats from Argentina, Brazil, Bulgaria, Egypt, Spain, Guatemala, Honduras, Poland, the United Kingdom, and Venezuela. During the event, the rebels released scores of women, including Peruvian President Fujimori's mother and sister. They also freed the ambassadors from Germany, Greece, and Canada, and the French cultural attaché. They reported that the rebels were "polite and courteous." The Europeans had been kept from the other hostages in a separate room on the second floor and were able to provide limited information. U.S. Ambassador Dennis Jett and his deputy chief left the reception shortly before the attack began, although seven other Americans were taken hostage, including four officials of the Agency for International Development.

Also held were executives from Mitsui, Marubeni, Kanematsu, Fujita, Japan Water Works, Japan Airlines, Nissho Iwai, Ajinomoto, Matsushita Electric Industrial, NGS Consultants, Toyota, Nissan, NEC, Asahi Chemical Industry, and Tomen, plus employees of several Japanese trade associations and Japanese teachers. Representatives from Malaysia, the Dominican Republic, the European Union, and Uruguay were also held. Manuel Torrado, general director of the polling firm Datu, was among the hostages.

The rebels permitted all female hostages and four elderly Japanese guests to leave on December 17.

Fernando Andrade, the mayor of Miraflores, Lima, escaped by sneaking out a bathroom window.

The rebels' first communiqué, from the Edgar Sanchez Special Forces commanded by comrade Edigiro Huerta, issued the group's demands to end the "military occupation." The group contacted radio and television stations throughout the day. They asked to see Jorge Santistevan, Peru's human rights ombudsman, and Rev. Hubert Lanssiers, another human rights advocate. These two were turned back from the residence by Peruvian authorities.

The Peruvian government refused to negotiate,

although the Japanese government announced that the hostages' safety was its first priority. Japan sent Foreign Minister Yukihiko Ikeda to help mediate. The United States also sent a team of security advisers. Fujimori appointed Education Minister Domingo Palermo Cabrejos to begin talks. Fujimori ignored a December 18 ultimatum for his presence.

Peru's stock exchange dropped 3.58 percent before trading was stopped.

The gunmen, who included at least three non-Peruvians, permitted family members to send in fresh clothing to the hostages via the Red Cross. Maria Isabel Eda, previously a hostage, sent in shirts and clean underwear to her husband, Luis. The guerrillas asked for cell phones from a specific company, toothbrushes, toilet paper, sutures, bandages, and an x-ray machine. Supreme Court President Moises Pantoja Rodulfo needed a pill for high blood pressure. Captives were permitted to make brief phone calls. Hubert Zandstra, Canadian director general of the nonprofit International Potato Center, told his colleagues that he was "okay." He was released on December 23 and reported that the hostages were not being maltreated. A fax signed by the hostages and sent to family members said there were 490 hostages.

Michael Minnig, a Swiss Red Cross official, led the negotiations. Four ambassadors were released on December 18 to serve as "hostages on parole" and were to "act as a link for communications," according to Canadian Ambassador Anthony Vincent, who often shuttled between the residence and the outside world during the negotiations.

On December 19, two shots were fired inside the compound at 4:30 P.M. At 6:00 P.M., four men—two Japanese businessmen and two Peruvians, one of them a businessman—were freed for medical reasons.

Japanese NHK Television conducted two interviews, in Spanish, with hostage Japanese Ambassador Morihisa Aoki, who reported that six gunmen were guarding him and the other second-floor hostages.

Among the second-floor hostages was Gilbert Siura Cespedes, president of the parliamentary defense committee. He was one of five members of Fujimori's Cambio 90 ruling party who were taken hostage. The rebels threatened him for his role in the earlier pardon of military commanders convicted for their role in an anti-rebel massacre.

The other members of Fujimori's party included his brother, Pedro, and the brother-in-law of the president's sister. Her husband is Peru's ambassador to Japan.

Apoyo pollster Alfredo Torres, one of 38 hostages released at 7:20 P.M. on December 20, reported that the terrorists "classified" the hostages by their "value," sending the more valuable 180 upstairs. Torres released the results of a poll of the first-floor hostages, indicating that 78 percent thought their treatment was favorable; 83 percent said the worst thing was uncertainty; and 87 percent said the attack revealed a serious security lapse. He also reported that a Japanese restaurant owner gave a lecture on Andean food, while another discussed insurance. Some hostages watched soccer and sitcoms on television.

Also freed were the ambassadors of Brazil, Egypt, and South Korea, who were chosen by the remaining diplomats to "establish channels of communication." The rebels also freed businessmen, two adult Boy Scouts, a former presidential candidate, an economist, the director of an anthropology museum, and Japanese and Japanese-Peruvians. The rebels also sent out a 12-point communiqué. A hostage letter indicated that the government had cut off water, electricity, and communication, putting the hostages "in a difficult situation," according to freed Congressman Javier Diez Canseco. An English-language sign read, "No Food. No Water.—The Hostages." Another hostage asked for a Japanese NHK Television crew. The rebels also asked to talk to imprisoned colleagues and offered to release "a significant quantity" of nonpolitical hostages. The UN began daily delivery of full meals and bottled water.

The rebel leader was identified as Nestor Cerpa Carolini (alias Comrade Evaristo; alias Commandante Huertas), a Marxist ideologue and the only MRTA leader at large. A former textile union official, he was one of the group's founders in 1984 and served as its military commander. He was a highly successful tactical commander and obsessed with the treatment of imprisoned comrades. He demanded to talk to the prisoners and the media, but a speech by President Fujimori seemed to rule out both options. Cerpa said he was surprised that his van, which was painted to look like an ambulance, was not stopped by police.

On December 21, Cerpa said over a walkie-talkie that he would release more hostages. He also permitted broadcasts by Peruvian Foreign Minister Tudela and Japanese Ambassador Aoki, who urged the government to begin talks. Aoki said several Japanese hostages were ill.

On December 22, in a "Christmas gesture," the MRTA released 225 hostages, among them all of the Americans, including political counselor Jim Wagner; economic counselor John Riddle; Don Boyd, deputy director of the local Agency for International Development (AID); John Crowe, director of the narcotics assistance section; AID officials David Bayer and Michael Maxey; American citizen Kris Merchrod; and Pedro Carrillo, a Peruvian who worked at the U.S. Embassy. Among those released were the ambassadors of Panama, Cuba, and Venezuela, along with Elmer Escobar, the representative to Lima of the Washington-based Pan-American Health Organization. Until his release, he had served as the principal coordinator for health care inside the residence. Also freed was the Austrian ambassador, who reported that each terrorist had 15 kilograms of explosives strapped to his body. Released Britons included Roger Church, deputy head of mission at the British Embassy, and David Griffiths, a hotel manager.

Meanwhile, hundreds of Peruvians conducted a March for Peace in Lima and other cities to underscore their concern for the safety of the hostages. The Red Cross was able to alleviate conditions for the hostages, providing chess sets, dominoes, and mail from relatives. Special envoy Ikeda flew back to Tokyo after conferring for three days with Peruvian officials, who still had not ruled out a military rescue.

By December 23, Fujimori had not restored basic services to the residence, suggesting that he would continue to take a hard line in negotiations.

On December 24, the rebels freed Uruguayan Ambassador Tabare Bocalandro Yapeyu. Uruguay later confirmed that a Uruguayan appeals court had released Sonia Silvia Gora Rivera and Luis Alberto Miguel Samaniego, two MRTA members imprisoned in December for entering the country with false passports, but denied that it had arranged for the ambassador's release. The Peruvian and Bolivian governments were not convinced. Peru recalled its chief of mission in Montevideo after the Uruguayan court finished its seven-month review of Peru's request for extradition of the duo. Peru claimed that Gora had rented safe houses where the MRTA had kept several captives, and that Samaniego was a senior member of the MRTA executive committee. Meanwhile, Bolivia continued to hold MRTA members accused of kidnapping former Economics Minister Samuel Doria Medina in 1995. That kidnapping led to the payment of a ransom (variously reported as worth from $100,000 to $2 million).

Lima permitted the delivery of a Christmas cake to the residence, where a hostage priest celebrated midnight Mass.

On Christmas Day, the rebels freed Kenji Hirata, 34, a Japanese Embassy first secretary, who was led out in a wheelchair. The hostages were given ten turkeys by the family of Fujimori; they were delivered by the president's daughter, Keiko Sofia. A friend of the president, Juan Luis Cipriani, bishop of Ayacucho, was permitted inside the residence for seven hours; he spent two of them hearing confessions.

The Red Cross noted that 4 of the 225 released had not been identified, suggesting that some were rebels.

On December 26 at 1:45 A.M., an explosion was heard inside the residence. No hostages were released; the hostage takers had earlier released injured and ill hostages, so authorities believed no one was hurt. Observers suggested that an animal had set off a mine.

The Peruvian government suspended a March

1993 accord that permitted the Red Cross to visit 4,000 accused or convicted terrorists, including the 404 MRTA prisoners. Police also detained 28 people, including 6 women, on suspicion of being involved in the siege. On December 27, the government revealed that the state of emergency that had existed in parts of Lima had been extended to the rest of the capital and to neighboring Callao on December 18.

Guatemalan Ambassador Jose Maria Argueta was released, reducing the number of hostages to 103. He said the MRTA move was in "recognition" of the peace treaty to be signed by his government and Guatemalan rebels on December 29.

On December 27, Russia and the Group of Seven leading industrialized nations announced that they supported Lima's efforts to resolve the crisis peacefully.

The rebels freed another 20 hostages on December 28 after having their first direct talks—which lasted three and a half hours—in the residence with Education Minister Palermo. He was accompanied by Bishop Cipriani and Red Cross representative Minnig. The freed hostages included the ambassadors of Malaysia and the Dominican Republic and a Peruvian businessman. After they were released, Minnig used a bullhorn to read a rebel communiqué in which the MRTA criticized the rival Shining Path terrorists and complained that they were being mislabeled as terrorists. The other 17 hostages, many of them Japanese businessmen, filed out of the building. The freed hostages said the guerrillas had strapped explosives to their bodies and had booby-trapped the entrances. The MRTA appeared to be softening its demands and might have been looking for a face-saving solution for both sides, in which a peace process would permit the MRTA to form a political party and the conditions of MRTA prisoners would improve.

The next day, Isaac Velazco, an MRTA representative, told Reuters in Hamburg, Germany, that the group was willing to accept an "intermediate solution" rather than immediate release of the prisoners. Fujimori told EFE and Associated Press reporters on December 31 that he was will-ing to consider safe passage out of the country if the rebels freed all of their hostages and laid down their weapons. Singing was heard in the residence.

On December 31, the guerrillas permitted Foreign Minister Tudela, Japanese Ambassador Aoki, and Peruvian Congressman Gilberto Siura to address an impromptu two-hour news conference with 23 journalists. The rebels reiterated their demand that the 404 prisoners be freed, shifting their focus from their prison conditions. The guerrillas freed Honduran Ambassador Eduardo Martel and Argentine Consul Juan Antonio Ibanez.

Seven more hostages were freed on New Year's Day. They were identified as a Peruvian and four Japanese businessmen and two Peruvian officials.

In a surprise move the next day, Fujimori relieved the chief of national security, the president of the Supreme Court, and the head of the antiterrorist police of their government posts. All were being held hostage.

Fujimori ordered his government to resume normal operations on January 5.

On January 7, at 4:00 A.M., a rebel fired his gun; no injuries were reported. Negotiations had been suspended for the previous five days. Later that day, a Japanese NHK Television journalist and his Peruvian assistant sneaked into the residence for an interview. The Peruvian police detained them when they exited.

Four shots rang out inside the residence on January 10 at 3:00 A.M.

Later that day, Fujimori said in an interview that his government had conducted only three direct conversations with the rebels and none for a week. One country—not Cuba—had offered asylum; others might be contacted. The government had proposed that an independent commission might find an "exit" for surrendering rebels. The "commission of guarantors," to be named by the government and rebels, would include three to five people, possibly including foreigners. He noted that no other country or international organization was involved in mediating the crisis. He ruled out Cuba as a safe haven, charging that Cuba had trained MRTA members eight years before.

Several pundits suggested that negotiations could drag out, as Cerpa was a union negotiator.

The government softened its position somewhat on January 12, saying that it was willing to consider "all subjects" raised by the MRTA. It also suggested forming a special commission to mediate. The Vatican approved the participation of Bishop Cipriani on the commission. Education Minister Domingo Palermo also offered to include the International Committee of the Red Cross (ICRC) on the commission. Palermo also complained about media coverage, noting that the government had had to cut off radio communications with the rebels because a newspaper had intercepted and published one conversation.

Three bursts of gunfire were heard from the residence on January 13 at 11:20 A.M. Police believed they were shooing away helicopters that ventured too close.

The rebels agreed to the mediation offer on January 15, accepting Cipriani and Minnig as commission members. Cerpa also requested representatives from Guatemala and a European country. Peru rejected Guatemala the next day. Lima suggested Canada as an observer on January 17; Canada said the representative would be Ambassador Anthony Vincent, himself a former hostage. Cerpa accepted a Canadian role the next day.

Second-floor hostage Luis Valencia was released for medical reasons on January 17. He had served as a commander of an antiterrorist unit. He was the lowest-ranking antiterrorist hostage.

On January 26, the rebels released police General Jose Rivas Rodriguez. He was wheeled out on a stretcher and taken to a local hospital.

The next day, during a police show of force that included armored vehicles, a volley of shots fired into the air rang out from the compound. No injuries were reported. Red Cross representatives cut down the number of hours that they spent onsite monitoring the condition of the hostages.

On January 29, President Fujimori and Japanese Prime Minister Ryutaro Hashimoto agreed to a summit meeting set for February 1 in Toronto, Canada. Japan twice called for the Peruvians to cease hostile activities in the area of the residence.

After the two-hour meeting, Fujimori announced that as long as the hostages were unharmed, he would not use force to rescue them and end the incident. Fujimori announced that Cerpa had given up on the demand for prisoner release; Cerpa angrily denied the claim. Following a meeting in Washington with President Clinton on February 3, Fujimori said the rebels' public and private positions differed.

On February 6, the special commission began facilitating negotiations by hosting a meeting that lasted two and a half hours.

On February 10, the rebels said they were willing to restart face-to-face talks with the government, but would not drop their prisoner release demand. The next day, the government and rebels discussed terms of the talks for four hours. Fujimori, in London for an investment conference, said he would be willing to contact Cuban President Fidel Castro regarding asylum for the rebels.

The second round of talks was held on February 14 in a house across the street from the residence. A white sedan drove Roli Rojas Fernandez, a sociologist serving as Cerpa's deputy, across the street, where he met with four international mediators and Palermo. Meanwhile, the rebels permitted the Red Cross to bring Valentine's Day gifts of boxes of chocolate bars and CDs of romantic songs to the hostages. Archbishop Cipriani celebrated Mass. A third round of talks was held the following day. Cerpa joined the talks personally on February 20.

On February 18, Reuters reported that the Peruvian government's antiterrorist police had warned in October that MRTA terrorists were planning high-profile hostage-taking attacks around November 30, the first anniversary of a shootout between police and the MRTA in Lima's La Molina district. Police also said the Japanese residence operation was financed by a kidnapping in Bolivia.

On February 23, Fujimori publicly admitted that the police and intelligence services were negligent in not preventing the attack. Intelligence had indicated that terrorists were moving weapons into the city for a major operation.

Talks resumed on February 24.

By March 1, the government and rebels had held seven talks, which usually took place once every three days, for three hours apiece. Fujimori announced that the next day he would visit the Dominican Republic, leading many to believe he was arranging for asylum for the rebels. Fujimori had earlier acknowledged receiving one offer in private, but did not identify the country. Meanwhile, the Red Cross announced that by March 1, it had delivered more than 5,700 messages between the hostages and their family members.

Following Fujimori's visit to Havana, Cuban President Fidel Castro offered asylum to the rebels on March 3; the next day, the rebels rejected asylum in the Dominican Republic. Cerpa said the rebels wanted to stay in Peru. Talks between the rebels and government resumed on March 3, but were suspended by the rebels on March 6 when they claimed they had heard tunneling by security forces. Japanese Deputy Foreign Minister Masahiko Komura visited Lima for two days, then met with Fidel Castro in Havana on March 19 to formalize a request for granting asylum.

On April 19, Interior Minister Juan Briones and Police Chief Ketin Vidal resigned under mounting criticism.

The government conducted a surprise raid at 3:17 P.M. on April 22, freeing 71 of the hostages. The 140 rescuers from the army, air force, and navy killed all 14 terrorists after setting off explosives under a rebel soccer game. One hostage, Peruvian Supreme Court Justice Carlos Giusti Acuna, died from a heart attack; 25 others, including Japanese Ambassador Morihita Aoki, Foreign Minister Francisco Tudela, and Supreme Court Judge Luis Serpa Segura, were slightly injured. Two soldiers—Captain Raul Jimenez Chavez and Lieutenant Colonel Juan Valer Sandoval, 38— died in the gunfire that ended the 126-day standoff. (They were promoted posthumously.) President Fujimori was at the scene to give the orders to attack. The soldiers swarmed through tunnels secretly dug by local miners. Hours after the hostages had been taken, Fujimori had ordered the military to begin training for the rescue operation

at a secluded naval base on Fronton Island, off the port of Callao.

The news media reported that the Peruvians used several methods to gather information about the whereabouts and intentions of the terrorists. *Aviation Week and Space Technology* reported that a CIA-operated Air Force Schweizer RG-8A aircraft took forward-looking infrared photos at night, spotting mines and booby traps. An RU-38A Twin Condor surveillance plane was also used. A transmitter was smuggled in for the hostages to use to keep in touch with the government. The Associated Press claimed that microphones were hidden in a chess piece, crutches used by terrorist Eduardo Cruz, a thermos, a guitar, and a Bible. Red Cross workers denied knowingly bringing in the microphones. The rescuers used periscopes to keep tabs on the terrorists. The rescuers tipped off some of the hostages ten minutes ahead of time that they would swarm in via a network of tunnels.

Family members and conspiracy theorists charged that some of the terrorists were executed on the spot by the rescuers. Fujimori said five died in the initial explosion; Cerpa and four others died going up a staircase; and the other four died in a gun battle on the second floor.

Foreign governments were not told ahead of time of the Peruvian government's plans for the rescue.

Peru asked Germany to cancel the political asylum granted in 1993 to Isaac Velazco, spokesman for the rebels. On April 28, the German government asked Hamburg to ban his political activity.

The following list of hostages was constructed by the media after the rescue:

High-Profile Captives
- Morihisa Aoki, Japanese ambassador to Peru
- Jorge Gumucio Granier, Bolivian ambassador
- Pedro Fujimori, the president's brother
- Francisco Tudela, Peru's foreign minister
- Rodolfo Munante, Peru's agriculture minister

Peruvian Congressmen
- Samuel Matsuda

- Eduardo Pando
- Carlos Blanco
- Luis Chang
- Gilberto Siura

Peruvian Supreme Court
- Moises Pantoja Rodulfo, Supreme Court president
- Hugo Sivina, justice
- Mario Urrelo, justice
- Luis Serpa, justice
- Alpino Montes, magistrate

Cabinet and Sub-Cabinet Level
- Ricardo Kamiya, Peruvian Presidency secretary general
- Carlos Tsuboyana, Presidency deputy minister
- Juan Mendoza, deputy mines minister
- Felipe Ramirez, Presidency Ministry official
- Salvador Romero, Energy and Mines Ministry secretary
- Rudolfo Masuda, deputy minister of agriculture
- Dante Cordova, former prime minister

Peruvian Security Forces
- Navy Vice Admiral Luis Giampetri, president of National Institute of the Peruvian Sea
- General Maximo Rivera, head of the antiterrorism police
- General Alfonso Villaneuva, head of police intelligence
- Guillermo Bobio, chief of state security
- Navy Captain Alberto Heredia
- Army Lieutenant Colonel Roberto Fernandez
- Army General Arturo Lopez Pardo
- Air Force Colonel Julio Rivera
- Air Force Colonel Orlando Denegri
- Police General Carlos Dominguez
- Police General Julio Pinto, secretary of the National Police Directorate
- Police General Hugo Vera, police economy director
- Police Colonel Alberto Castillo

- Police Colonel Jorge Villacort
- Police Colonel Jaime Valencia, head of the kidnapping division
- Police Colonel Marco Miyashiro, former head of DINCOTE Intelligence
- Police Colonel Romulo Zevallo
- Police Colonel Rowel Rivas
- Police Lieutenant Colonel Gerardo Haro
- Police Major Oscar Pajares

Other Peruvians
- Pedro Jaritomi, the president's brother-in-law
- Rev. Juan Julio Wicht, Roman Catholic priest and professor of economics at Lima's Pacific University
- Miguel Takahasi, adviser to Pescaperu (Peruvian state fishing firm)
- Jose Ishiki, accountant for Cogorno (food firm)
- Juan Gibu
- Tokeshi Gusukuda, researcher for the Center for Development Promotion
- Pedro Inomoto
- Francisco Salinas
- Alfonso Yamakawua
- Jaime Bisso, manager of Peruvian Banco Regional del Norte
- Marco Molina

Japanese Business Executives
- Shiguero Taki, director general of Panasonic
- Kosabe Shoji, engineer for NOYS
- Masao Nakashi
- Jorge Hasawara, executive at Ajinomoto

Japanese Embassy Staff
- Kazumi Ono, diplomat
- Sinichi Takeda, diplomat
- Shigeru Yamakasi, diplomat
- Fumio Sunami, first secretary
- Hajime Nakae, first secretary
- Ghiroyuki Kimoto, counselor minister
- Shinji Yakamoto, cultural attaché
- Hirio Nakamura, second secretary
- Nasahiro Nakai, first secretary

- Hiroto Morozumi, second secretary
- Hirofumi Sueyoshi
- Hidekata Ogura, first secretary
- Katsumi Itagaki, second secretary
- Tsutomu Taka, consul general

96121702

December 20, 1996. *Northern Ireland.* Two IRA gunmen fired at a Protestant politician who was visiting his sick son at a children's hospital. A policeman was wounded.

December 20, 1996. *Tajikistan.* Gunmen stopped a convoy between Fayzabad and Gharm, seizing 23 hostages, including 7 foreign national UN military observers and Tajik government officials. The group claimed loyalty to Rezvon Sodirov, leader of an armed gang, and demanded that several of their supporters be returned to them. The hostages were eventually released. 96122001

December 21, 1996. *Northern Ireland.* A Sinn Fein activist was injured when his booby-trapped car exploded. Protestant loyalists were suspected, although no one claimed credit.

December 22, 1996. *Nigeria.* Nigerian workers demanding pay raises took hostage 30 foreigners on the *Tabang Cora*, barge WB-82, near Lagos. They freed 28 of the hostages at 8:15 P.M. on December 27, but another group of workers kept two Frenchmen prisoners on another vessel, the *American Pride*, according to the Filipino barge captain. The freed hostages were ten Filipinos, nine Frenchmen, five Indians, two Britons, one Lebanese, and one Belgian.

December 23, 1996. *Algeria.* A car bomb exploded in Algiers, killing 3 and injuring 70.

December 24, 1996. *Germany.* A bomb exploded at 11:15 P.M. during a Christmas Eve service in a Lutheran church in Sindlingen, a Frankfurt suburb, killing three women and badly wounding six others, including a 12-year-old girl. Police believed a masked female suicide bomber was responsible, but they could not initially determine whether the explosives were strapped to her or planted by her. Police suggested that a personal vendetta was involved.

December 24, 1996. *United States.* A package bomb exploded in the face of Jordan Reardon, 10, as she was opening the package at 10:00 P.M. in the Clifton Park, New York, home of her parents, Jude and Mary. The girl was scheduled to undergo plastic surgery for second-degree burns and cuts to 27 percent of her body. The home was severely damaged. On January 7, 1997, investigators said the bomb came from a family acquaintance, Christopher P. Gilson, 58, who lived two miles away. He had worked for Jude Reardon's twin brother, John, until he was fired in 1991 from his sales job. A police raid on Gilson's home on January 3 matched bomb fragments. Gilson had committed suicide on December 29.

December 24, 1996. *Lebanon.* A roadside bomb exploded as Israeli soldiers walked in the Israeli-occupied zone on a road between Marqaba and Odeissi. Two died and two were seriously injured by the bomb, which was claimed by Hizballah. 96122401

December 24, 1996. *South Africa.* A homemade time bomb and two hand grenades went off in a Worcester grocery store and outside a pharmacy a few blocks away, killing 3 and injuring 67 others. Two children died during treatment at the Eben Donges Hospital; an adult died at the scene. A fourth person died later from the suburban Cape Town blast. Pharmacist Harish Narotam, whose shop was damaged, reported, "I just heard a massive bang, and then there was something dripping out of my ear. It was blood." Three men sped off in a red car. On January 3, the previously unknown Boer Attack Force claimed credit and threatened new attacks unless all Afrikaner "freedom fighters" were freed from prison and prosecutions were suspended.

December 24, 1996. *France.* Suggesting that it was responsible for the December 3 bombing of the Paris Metro, the Algerian Armed Islamic Group (GIA) sent a letter to French President Jacques Chirac in which it threatened to "destroy" France if prisoners were not released. The letter apparently had been sent earlier in the month. It said GIA would "destroy your country whatever it costs us" if Chirac did not release GIA members, including Abdelhaq Layda, who was on Algeria's death row. 96122402

December 26, 1996. *Algeria.* A car bomb exploded in an Algiers suburb, killing 20 and injuring 86, 50 of them seriously. Most of the casualties were motorists and pedestrians.

December 27, 1996. *Yemen.* Yemeni tribesmen took hostage five European tourists, wounding several villagers in the attack. They fired rocket-propelled grenades at a military rescue team that had surrounded them, killing three soldiers and wounding five others. Mediators from other tribes assisted in the negotiations. 96122701

December 27, 1996. *Eritrea.* Gunmen ambushed and killed five Belgian tourists and their Eritrean driver as they returned to Asmara from a field trip. No one claimed credit. 96122702

December 28, 1996. *Corsica.* At 10:15 P.M., a bomb blew up the empty car of an Agriculture Department agent in a Bastia suburb.

At 10:30 P.M., another bomb destroyed the car of a second Agriculture agent.

At 11:10 P.M., a bomb destroyed a three-story building that housed the local agricultural headquarters in Village Di Pietrapugno, north of Bastia.

A fourth bomb tore off the front door of the city hall of Ghisoni, a mountain village 62 miles south of Bastia.

No one claimed responsibility.

December 29, 1996. *Guatemala.* Rebels and the government formally ended 36 years of fighting with the signing of a peace agreement. More than 100,000 people were killed and another 40,000 disappeared during the fighting, which had also affected the country's economy. The rebels were represented by Rolando Moran, Pablo Monsanto, Carlos Gonzalez, and Jorge Rosal, who were joined by chief government negotiator Gustavo Porras and President Alvaro Arzu. The accord included, inter alia, an amnesty for the guerrillas and government soldiers, formation of a truth commission to investigate human rights violations, demobilization of the 2,000 rebels and of the government-supported civil defense militias, redefinition of the army's mission, commitments by the government to increasing spending on health and education and to increase taxation to finance these programs, and a commitment to end discrimination.

December 30, 1996. *India.* Two bombs exploded on the Gauhati–New Delhi Brahmaputra Express train in Assam, throwing the train off the tracks. Dozens of the 1,200 passengers and crew were killed; railway workers initially put the number of dead at 300. No one claimed credit. Police suspected Bodo tribal insurgents. Rescuers found 26 bodies in the wreckage. Another 42 people were hospitalized. The next day, the toll had risen to 38 dead, including 7 children, and 80 hospitalized.

The bombs were hidden in a culvert and set off remotely from 800 yards away. Strands of wire were found near the blast.

December 30, 1996. *Chile.* Four members of the leftist Manuel Rodriguez Patriotic Front escaped a high-security prison via helicopter. Ricardo Palma, Mauricio Hernandez, Pablo Munoz, and Patriocio Ortiz jumped into a basket dangling from the helicopter during a gun battle between guards and the helicopter's team. Palma and Hernandez were serving life sentences for the 1991 assassination of rightist Senator Jaime Guzman. The helicopter was rented at a Santiago airfield by three women who appeared to be from the United States and two Argentine-accented men. Prison director Claudio Martinez resigned. Police later found the helicopter and a getaway car with two M-16 rifles in a park in southern Santiago.

December 31, 1996. *Bahrain.* Eight attackers surrounded a building in a Shia village, set several tires on fire, and threw Molotov cocktails inside, killing an Asian man and injuring two others. 96123101

December 31, 1996. *Northern Ireland.* A man using the IRA code word told the media that there was a landmine in a truck the group had parked near a Belfast hotel. He claimed that the group had abandoned the truck because of the high level of British security in the area. Police discovered that the vehicle contained 1,000 pounds of homemade explosives, detonating cord, and other bomb-making equipment. British authorities evacuated the parkland around Belfast Castle, a 19th-century former private mansion, where a wedding reception with 400 guests was being held.

December 31, 1996. *Syria.* At noon, a bomb exploded in a bus after it had left the Intilak Center bus terminal in Damascus, killing 11 and injuring 42 who were on their way to Aleppo for New Year's celebrations. Syria blamed Israel, which denied the accusation. The United States condemned the bombing, but doubted Syria's charges.

On January 9, 1997, the Islamic Movement for Change claimed credit, saying it was retaliating for Syria's "execution" of Jaafar Shweikhat, one of its members who took part in an attack on U.S. soldiers in Saudi Arabia in June 1996. The group also claimed credit for a November 1995 attack against American forces in Saudi Arabia. The Arabic-language statement was faxed to an international news agency in Nicosia, Cyprus; Syrians claimed it was a fake sent by the Israelis.

1996. *Colombia.* On January 8, 1997, the Colombian armed forces announced that 780 leftist rebels and more than 500 members of the armed forces were killed in the guerrilla war during 1996. The Revolutionary Armed Forces of Colombia (FARC) lost 462 members. The National Liberation Army (ELN), second in size to the FARC, lost 248 members. The Maoist People's Liberation Army and a dissident faction of the defunct M-19 lost more than 60 members. At least 133 police were killed; 360 soldiers also died. Another 80 were listed as missing.

1997. *Russia.* An Italian journalist was kidnapped by Chechen rebels and freed in the spring after a ransom was paid. 97999901

1997. *United States.* The Justice Department and Immigration and Naturalization Service (INS) claimed that Mazen A. al-Najjar, 43, a former professor of Arabic at the University of South Florida in Tampa (a Palestinian born in Gaza and raised in Saudi Arabia) had ties to the Syrian-based Palestinian Islamic Jihad (PIJ), which conducted terrorist attacks. He was linked to two groups that laundered PIJ money. The now-defunct World and Islam Studies Enterprise, based in Tampa, employed Ramadan Abdullah Shallah, who became the PIJ leader in 1995. He was ordered deported when his visa expired in 1997. He was jailed after the INS presented secret evidence under the 1996 Anti-Terrorism and Effective Death Penalty Act.

U.S. District Judge Joan Lenard ruled in Miami in May 2000 that al-Najjar must be told enough about the evidence to have a fair chance of responding. Al-Najjar's defense team was led by David D. Cole, a Georgetown University professor of law. If freed, al-Najjar and his wife, Fedaa, faced deportation hearings. Their three daughters were U.S. citizens. On December 12, 2000, Attorney General Janet Reno blocked the release of al-Najjar, who had been jailed for more than three years without criminal charges on secret evidence. Reno said she would review the evidence. The previous week, Immigration Judge R. Kevin McHugh ordered al-Najjar freed on $8,000 bond. Reno released him on December 15, 2000. Deportation hearings were set for January 9, 2001. He sought political asylum as a stateless Palestinian; the INS wanted to send him to the United Arab Emirates, where he resided for two years before entering the United States in 1981.

January 1997. *Kazakhstan.* Chris Gehring, 28, Central Asian director of Internews Network, was killed in his Almaty apartment. His hands and feet were tied and his throat was slit. He was overseeing a journalism training program.

On June 25, the government announced that three men were convicted and sentenced to 15 years in prison. They were drug addicts seeking money. They had confessed during interrogations, but claimed to be innocent in court.

January 1, 1997. *West Bank.* At 10:00 A.M., Noam Friedman, 22, an off-duty Israeli soldier, fired ten rounds from his M-16 assault rifle into an Arab marketplace in Hebron, injuring seven Palestinians. The mentally unbalanced Orthodox Jew from the Maale Adumim settlement said he was attempting to kill "Israel-haters" and stop the peace process that would transfer Hebron to Palestinian self-rule. He failed on both counts. He sat on the ground and held the pistol grip with both hands. A poor shot, he injured only one victim directly; the other six were hit with shrapnel. Israeli Lieutenant Avi Buskila, a platoon commander, jumped onto Friedman and disarmed him. Meanwhile, Yasir Arafat and Prime Minister Benjamin Netanyahu worked together to defuse possible violence.

Among the injured were Salman Abu Obeid, 55, who was hit in both arms while walking to a doctor's appointment, and twin brothers Akram and Abd-al-Karim Atrash, 16, who were hit in the legs as they sold fruit at the family's stand.

The following day, Israeli police arrested Yuval Jibli of Jerusalem, also a soldier, for being an accomplice.

Many commentators wondered how a former psychiatric patient was permitted to join the army and given an automatic weapon.

On August 12, Friedman was indicted by a military court on a charge of attempted murder. The court had decided that he was fit to stand trial after he had been confined to a psychiatric hospital for treatment of schizophrenia in February.

January 2, 1997. *United States.* Seven letter bombs were found and disabled in Washington, D.C. and Fort Leavenworth, Kansas. An eighth was found in the Kansas postal system the next day. Five of the letter bombs were mailed to the *Al-Hayat* newspaper offices in Washington. The paper, owned by Saudi Prince Khaled bin Sultan, son of the defense minister, is headquartered in London. Two other bombs were addressed to a nonexistent parole office of the federal penitentiary where Mohammed Salameh, 29, one of the World Trade Center bombers, was held. (There has not been a parole for federal prisoners for a decade.) Victor Alvarez and Mohammed Saleh, convicted in the plot to blow up UN headquarters for blind Sheik Omar Abdel Rahman, also were incarcerated there. Four of the letter bombs made it to the *Al-Hayat* offices in the National Press Building; the fifth was found at the Brentwood regional mail distribution center in northeast Washington. Two hundred people were evacuated from the National Press Building.

All the bombs had Alexandria, Egypt, postmarks but were mailed on different dates: December 21 and 23. They were made with Semtex hidden inside musical Christmas cards on heavy stock paper and had pins for shrapnel. The address labels were computer generated and pasted on white envelopes. They had no return addresses.

An FBI team went to Cairo and Alexandria to investigate.

Al-Hayat's Washington office on January 4 received a phone call, originating in Europe, from the Islamic Group that denied involvement and claimed that Libya was behind the attack. The caller said Tripoli was sending a message to the United States in retaliation for alleged CIA efforts to recruit Libyan military officials. The caller also observed that it would have been easier to send letter bombs to *Al-Hayat*'s London or Cairo offices. Libya denied involvement. 97010201-08

January 2, 1997. *Tajikistan.* Unidentified gunmen shot to death a Russian medical service major and a Tajik senior medical nurse in a Dushanbe apartment. Some believed the killers were Islamic oppositionists. 97010209

January 4, 1997. *Saudi Arabia.* Explosives experts defused a letter bomb sent to the *Al-Hayat* office in Riyadh. 97010401

January 4, 1997. *United States.* Agriculture officials announced that someone had tainted animal feed with the pesticide chlordane. The Purina Mills feed was recalled in Wisconsin, Minnesota, and Michigan. Chlordane, an anti-termite agent, was outlawed in Wisconsin 20 years earlier for being carcinogenic. Police had received a letter warning of the contamination.

January 4, 1997. *Tajikistan.* A car bomb exploded near a major Dushanbe market, killing a Russian soldier and wounding three others, along with a Tajik driver employed by the Commonwealth of Independent States joint peacekeeping forces. Islamic oppositionists were suspected.

January 5, 1997. *South Africa.* Bombs went off around midnight at a mosque, a post office, and a store in Rustenburg. A Sudanese citizen and a South African were injured. Two white mine workers were arrested at a roadblock outside the mining town of Mooi Nooi and charged with the blast. Christiaan Harmse, 26, and Pierre Jacobs, 32, were held for court action after explosives were found in their car and in the home of one of the men. The Boere Aanvals Troepe claimed credit. 97010501

January 6, 1997. *Northern Ireland.* A police guard and a passerby were hurt when the Irish Republican Army (IRA) fired a rocket at midday from a car driving past the Northern Ireland High Court in Belfast. The rocket hit a security building outside the courthouse and broke windows, knocking the pedestrian down. The blast injured a guard's eardrums. He avoided more serious injuries because he ducked down when he saw the terrorist aiming the rocket. The IRA promised that more attacks were pending. It was the seventh

attempted terrorist attack by the IRA in the last month; five had been thwarted by authorities.

Police held two men for questioning about the attacks. Two others were released after questioning.

January 7, 1997. *Northern Ireland.* The IRA took credit for setting off a bomb in an ambush against a two-vehicle police patrol in the Shantallow area of Londonderry. No one was injured in the attack on the armored cars.

Belfast police carried out a controlled explosion on a car suspected of containing a bomb. They also evacuated the Europe Hotel after a telephone hoax warning of a bomb.

January 7, 1997. *Algeria.* A car bomb exploded in an Algiers shopping area, killing 13 people and wounding 100. Two men were seen leaving the vehicle just before it exploded, blowing out storefronts and sending glass into a passing bus. The two men died.

January 7, 1997. *Germany.* A 39-year-old male Bosnian refugee facing deportation used a knife to hijack an Austrian Airlines plane. He was disarmed by Berlin police who secretly entered the plane and pushed him out of an open door. The hijacker fell 21 feet to the tarmac at Tegel Airport. He was overpowered and detained. His residence permit was scheduled to expire on January 14. None of the passengers or crew was hurt; 21 passengers flew to Vienna hours later. The hijacker was to appear in court the next day on charges of kidnapping and air piracy. He faced 15 years in jail. 97010701

January 7, 1997. *Spain.* A Basque Nation and Liberty (ETA) gunwoman shot and killed Spanish army Lieutenant Colonel Jesus Cuesta, 60. The young woman and a man approached Cuesta as he was exiting his car to go to his house. She fired twice, hitting Cuesta in the head and jaw. The man fired at Cuesta's driver, but missed. Cuesta was dead on arrival at the hospital.

Shortly afterward, a car exploded near a shopping center in the same Madrid neighborhood, slightly injuring a member of the Royal Guard who was passing by. Police said the woman and a male partner may have used the car and destroyed it afterward, a common ETA technique.

January 9, 1997. *Israel.* Two crudely designed, nail-encased pipe bombs went off minutes before 8:30 P.M. in a lightly populated Tel Aviv commercial center, injuring 13. Arab terrorists were suspected of placing the bombs in garbage cans near the old central bus station, near a pornographic movie theater. The second bomb was timed to catch rescuers.

Islamic Jihad, Hamas, and the Islamic Resistance Movement had distributed leaflets threatening to retaliate for Noam Friedman's massacre of seven Palestinians on January 1.

January 13, 1997. *United States/United Kingdom.* One of four letter bombs exploded at the London *Al-Hayat* office, injuring two mail-security specialists. Barry Roach, 46, was seriously injured in the eye and abdomen. Andy McKenzie, 35, suffered shock and hearing damage. They were hurt when they pulled one of the bombs from a security scanner. Police blew up the three other bombs without injury. London police believed the explosive to be Semtex.

Two more letter bombs were found during business hours at the UN and another two in the late evening. UN guards found one bomb in a mail distribution center; a second was in the basement mailroom. Three floors of the 38-story building were evacuated while the New York bomb squad disposed of the bombs. The other bombs were found as UN mail and security personnel searched all unopened, undelivered mail. The bombs were identical and came in greeting-card-sized envelopes with a December 21, Alexandria, Egypt, postmark. Egypt said the stamps and postmarks were counterfeit. They were addressed to the UN bureau of *Al-Hayat* and had no return addresses.

Arab newspapers in London suspected Saudi dissidents, Algerian and Egyptian fundamentalists, Israeli intelligence, and Libya and Iraq. 9701301-08

January 16, 1997. *United States.* Minutes after a young couple parked their Nissan Pulsar at a women's health clinic, a bomb exploded. Some 45 minutes later, after police had arrived, a second bomb exploded just a few feet away, shooting shrapnel at the investigators and rescue workers, injuring seven people. The hulk of the Nissan absorbed most of the blast. The Army of God, a militia group, claimed credit for this bombing and one in February against a gay bar in Atlanta.

January 17, 1997. *Denmark.* Police arrested seven Danish neo-Nazis who apparently were planning to send letter bombs overseas. Police linked them to three packages of explosive detonators seized from a mailbox in Malmo, Sweden, that were to be sent to the United Kingdom. Police also seized a dozen detonators, black powder, and several shotguns. Thomas Derry Nakaba, 26, was charged with shooting a policeman during the arrests. Nakaba had placed the packages in the mailbox. 97011701

January 18, 1997. *Rwanda.* Three Spanish aid workers affiliated with Doctors of the World were killed in an attack by Hutu militants. An injured U.S. citizen had to have his leg amputated. 97011801

January 18, 1997. *Pakistan.* A bomb exploded at the Lahore Sessions Court where leaders of a militant Sunni Muslim group called Guardians of the Friends of the Prophet were on trial, killing 25, including 1 of the Sunni leaders, and wounding more than 100 others. Shi'ite Muslims were blamed. Zia-ul (variant Zia-ur) Rehman and Azim Tariq had stepped out of their prison van when the 11-pound remote-controlled bomb exploded in a motorcycle. Rehman was killed; Tariq, a parliamentary candidate, was seriously wounded.

January 19, 1997. *Algeria.* A car bomb exploded at 8:00 P.M. outside a café in downtown Algiers, killing 21 and wounding 60 others, at least 30 of them seriously.

An armed group attacked the village of Beni-

Slimane, 45 miles south of Algiers, killing 36. Some of the victims were decapitated.

A bomb exploded near Reghaia, 20 miles east of Algiers, injuring several people.

Police dismantled six other car bombs in Algiers.

Islamic radicals were suspected.

January 19, 1997. *Pakistan.* Sunni Muslim militants set fire to an Iranian cultural center in Lahore, accusing Tehran of inciting Pakistani Shi'ite Muslims to violence. The Guardians of the Friends of the Prophet were incensed over a bombing that killed their leader, Zia-ul Rehman, and 24 others on January 18. There were no injuries in the fire, which gutted the building. The 500 rioters demanded that the government break diplomatic ties with Iran. 97011901

January 19, 1997. *Russia.* Near Sasmashki village in Chechnya, Chechen rebels kidnapped two Russian journalists who were traveling to the Ingush region's capital, Nazran. A $500,000 ransom was demanded. The hostages were freed on February 18. No ransom was paid. A Jordanian militant was believed to be the kidnappers' leader. 97010902

January 20, 1997. *Japan.* A man wielding a knife was prevented from hijacking a plane in southern Japan. 97012001

January 20, 1997. *Bosnia-Hercegovina.* A Bosnian-Croatian businessman was killed after setting off a booby-trapped explosive attached to his apartment's front door.

January 21, 1997. *Iraq.* Some 400 militants took 1,500 Turkish male refugees hostage at the Atrush refugee camp. They took the hostages to the nearby Garo mountain after the UN High Commission for Refugees closed the camp. The Kurdistan Workers Party (PKK) was suspected. 97012101

January 21, 1997. *Algeria.* Two car bombs exploded in Algiers, killing 16. The first went off at 4:40 P.M. near a cultural center and an apartment block housing hundreds of people. Four hours later, another car bomb went off at the Ryad el Feth trade center, injuring ten.

January 23, 1997. *Tajikistan.* Gunmen in Dushanbe shot and killed a retired Cossack military commander, his mother, and his fiancee.

January 25, 1997. *United States.* Two children found a backpack containing 3 detonators and 30 sticks of dynamite outside a Vallejo public library in California. The device was not set to explode.

January 26, 1997. *United States.* A dynamite bomb exploded outside a Wells Fargo Bank's automated teller machines (ATMs), causing no injuries, but damaging three ATMs. Police released a photo of a man crouching in front of the ATMs.

January 27, 1997. *United States.* A bomb threat was received at the Solano County Courthouse in Vallejo, California. The building was evacuated, but no bomb was found.

January 28, 1997. *Saudi Arabia.* The U.S. Embassy alerted American citizens that it had received reports that U.S. interests were targeted by terrorists.

January 30, 1997. *United States.* A bomb blew a three-foot crater in the wall of the Solano County Courthouse in Vallejo, California. No injuries were reported, but 22 windows were broken in neighboring buildings. Police found a wire leading from the device to an alley, where the bomber set off the charge.

On February 2, police arrested a man at an apartment complex. Outside, they seized a car that contained 60 sticks of wired dynamite.

January 30, 1997. *United States.* After Mousa Abu Marzook, the financial chief of Hamas, announced he was ending his 19-month battle against extradition to Israel, the U.S. State Department warned that the militant Islamic group could turn to bombings in Israel and possibly go after American targets. The Islamic Resistance Movement (Hamas) issued threats against Israel and "all the Americans who have interests in the Arab and Muslim world." 97013001

January 30, 1997. *United States.* Authorities detonated a mail bomb sent to the Kearny Mesa, California, FBI office. (Kearny Mesa is a suburb of San Diego.) The building's 200 employees were evacuated while a robot removed the package. The bomb was inside a brown cardboard box. Handwritten in the upper left corner were the French words "Je suis prest" or "Je suis preste," meaning "I'm quick" or "I'm ready." The package also had six canceled 32-cent stamps. Two pipe bombs were in the package.

January 31, 1997. *United States.* Less than 24 hours after discovery of the FBI bomb, an identical bomb was discovered and disarmed at Laidlaw Waste Systems, a waste management company located in nearby Chula Vista. No injuries were reported. It had the same French phrase.

January 31, 1997. *Croatia.* Belgian Corporal Olivier Gossye was killed and two other UN personnel were wounded in the Serb-held town of Vukovar. A young Serbian man with a criminal record opened fire with an automatic weapon from his car on the main road near the headquarters of the UN Transitional Administration of Eastern Slavonia. The United States said it believed it was the work of a lone individual, but the Croatian government blamed local Serb leaders trying to slow reintegration. 97013101

February 1, 1997. *United States.* Dave McGruer, 45, a federal employee in Chula Vista, California, received a package containing two pipe bombs. McGruer opened the package, saw what it contained, threw it on the bed, and called 911. The bombs did not explode. Bomb squad members said the "fairly sophisticated" devices were similar to the ones sent to the FBI and a waste manage-

ment company earlier in the week. This package, however, did not contain French phrases. FBI agents removed armloads of rifles and cases of ammunition from his house the next day.

February 1, 1997. *Algeria.* Knife- and ax-wielding men forced 31 people from their Medea homes before decapitating them. Muslim militants were suspected.

February 2, 1997. *United States.* Vallejo, California, police evacuated a five-block area after discovering 500 pounds of dynamite in a house. They continued to search for two suspects thought to be responsible for a series of bombings.

Following a phone call from an intermediary to police, Kevin Lee Robinson, 29, surrendered to police in the case. It was believed that he was trying to derail a drug trial that could imprison him for life. He allegedly hired several men to carry out the bombings. Robinson had earlier been convicted of drug and weapons charges and faced California's third-strike rule that exposed him to a prison sentence of 25 years to life.

Police also arrested Oston Osotonu, 24, at a Vallejo motel, his brother Army Osotonu, 34, and Francis Ernestburg, 40, at a nearby residence. The next day, police arrested Orlando Johnson, 30, and Jason Pascual, 22. The group faced conspiracy, explosives, and weapons charges. Police said these bombings apparently were not tied to the recent letter bomb cases in San Diego.

February 2, 1997. *Corsica.* Separatists set off 61 bombs, damaging post offices, tax offices, and other symbols of French authority, mostly in the rural north. No injuries were reported and no one was arrested. Four bombs failed to explode. The Corsican National Liberation Front's Historic Wing claimed credit. Three of its political leaders had been arrested earlier. The group warned, "We will have multiple struggles, both in Corsica and in Europe."

February 2, 1997. *Rwanda.* A Canadian priest was shot to death by gunmen. 97020201

February 4, 1997. *Rwanda.* Gunmen ambushed a UN human rights team in the southwest, killing a British citizen, a Cambodian, and three Rwandan employees. A driver was shot in the stomach and died after surgery. The victims were carrying out a human rights investigation near Karengera, 180 miles southwest of Kigali. Rwandan security forces arrested five suspects in Cyangugu on February 17; two other suspects were shot dead by Rwandan troops. Rwandan officials claimed that the suspects confessed.

On June 2, 1998, a Rwanda court convicted six Hutu rebels of killing the UN human rights monitors and sentenced them to death. 97020401

February 4, 1997. *Tajikistan.* Four Russian journalists were taken hostage near Obigarm by Bakhran (or Bakhram) Sadirov, the brother of Rezvon Sadirov, a renegade warlord. They worked for two Russian TV stations, Tass and Interfax. The rebels ultimately seized 16 people, including 8 UN personnel—a Ukrainian, a Nigerian, 2 Swiss, and 4 Tajiks.

The Red Cross evacuated most of its foreign staff and suspended activities in the country when two of its employees—a Briton and a Tajik—were taken hostage. The Red Cross said it would resume operations when all the hostages were released unharmed.

On February 7, the rebels took hostage the Tajik security minister, who was negotiating with them. They released the two Red Cross officials.

On February 8, the journalists said the rebels had agreed to release them, their Tajik driver, nine UN workers, and the Tajik security minister. The journalists claimed that the Tajik government had agreed to send helicopters to Afghanistan to bring home 40 followers of Rezvon. Sadirov had split with the main armed opposition in 1996.

On February 11, they released an ill Austrian hostage.

On February 13, the journalists claimed that one of the three UN military observer hostages had been killed. It was unclear whether the journalists had been forced to make the statement to pressure the government. The next day, Russian

Deputy Prime Minister Vitaly Ignatenko, who negotiated by phone with the rebels, said no one was killed. He claimed that the rebels promised that no one would be harmed.

On February 14, Bakhran freed three captives. Two Russian journalists and their driver were permitted to leave the rebels' base in Kalainav, 50 miles east of Dushanbe, for a meeting with the guerrillas. Six hours later, the guerrillas went back to the base, accompanied by a Russian diplomat, who was guaranteeing their safe passage.

The deal to swap the hostages for the guerrillas hit a snag the next day. The government permitted 28 guerrillas to rejoin Bakhran, but he cut off radio contact without freeing the hostages.

On February 16, Bakhran released five hostages—two Russian journalists and three UN workers—after President Emomali Rakhmonov agreed to meet directly with him in Obigarm. To date, the government had delivered 33 of the rebels.

On February 17, Bakhran released the final six hostages after meeting with President Emomali Rakhmonov at an eastern mountain village. 97020402

February 7, 1997. *Canada.* A deranged man screaming "devil worshipers" drove a vehicle up several flights of stairs to the front door of the Parliament building, just missing a maintenance worker. He ran into the lobby of Parliament, then battled with 30 officers for several minutes before being overpowered.

February 7, 1997. *Colombia.* The Revolutionary Armed Forces of Colombia (FARC) kidnapped two German and two Austrian tourists in Los Katios National Park, demanding $15 million. On March 4, Colombian soldiers patrolling an area in Choco Department spotted the group. The rebels killed two hostages when the troops discovered the hideout. The army killed four guerrillas and rescued the two surviving hostages. 97020701

February 8, 1997. *Angola.* The Cabinda Liberation Front-Cabindan Armed Forces (FLEC-FAC) kidnapped a Malaysian and a Filipino forest engineer. The kidnappers charged the two with spying for the Angolan government and said they would be punished by expulsion or death. The group warned Western companies to leave the enclave of Cabinda or become targets in the independence struggle. 97020801

February 10, 1997. *Spain.* The Basque Nation and Liberty (ETA), in two attacks aimed at avenging the jailing of leaders of its political wing, shot to death a Supreme Court judge outside his Madrid home and set off a car bomb in Granada, killing a civilian air base worker and wounding seven others.

Eugenio Aranburu, 41, leader of ETA's political wing, was found hanged at his family home in northern Spain hours before he was due to appear before the Supreme Court.

February 11, 1997. *Yemen.* Murad tribesmen kidnapped Joe Dell'Aria, 50, an American oil engineer with Houston-based Haliburton Energy Services, as he was working in oil fields east of Sanaa. The desert tribesmen were battling the government regarding a plot of land in the capital. They permitted him to call his wife three times on a satellite phone, took him on escorted walking tours, and let him be visited by a Yemeni colleague, who brought him canned food and reading material. He was released after 17 days. 97021101

February 11, 1997. *Ethiopia.* Two Ethiopian gunmen tried to sneak past security guards at the Belaneh Hotel in Harer, killing a guard and wounding another person. The gunmen threw grenades into the hotel lounge, wounding three Britons, a German, a Dutchman, and a Frenchman. 97021102

February 12, 1997. *Iran.* The 15th Khordad Foundation, a religious foundation, upped by $500,000 the eight-year bounty on British author Salman Rushdie, bringing the total to $2.5 million.

February 12, 1997. *Egypt.* Gunmen attacked a youth meeting held at a Coptic Christian church near Abu Qurqas in Minya Province, killing ten. The Islamic Group was suspected. One Islamic Group spokesman claimed credit, but another denied the claim. Some observers suggested that the group was splintering.

February 12, 1997. *Northern Ireland.* An IRA sniper was suspected of shooting to death Stephen Restorick, a British soldier, at a checkpoint at Bessbrook, site of a helicopter base for security forces patrolling the area. A civilian was wounded.

On February 15, London deemed as "inappropriate" further contact with Sinn Fein, the IRA's political wing.

February 12, 1997. *Venezuela.* Two oil engineers were kidnapped from Apure oilfields by presumed Colombian guerrillas. 97021201

February 13, 1997. *United States.* A bomb threat was phoned in before former Israeli Prime Minister Shimon Peres was due to address an audience at the Jacksonville, Florida, Jewish Center. On February 22, three children tried to open a pipe bomb they found in a hallway behind the temple's sanctuary. An adult grabbed the device and turned it over to police. Harry Shapiro of Jacksonville, a Jewish man working as a gas station cashier, was charged on February 25 with placing a destructive device and making a bomb threat. The former kosher butcher was taken to the hospital because he was having "some physical or emotional difficulty," according to police. 97021301, 97022201

February 14, 1997. *Venezuela.* Six Rebel Armed Forces of Colombia (FARC) guerrillas kidnapped a U.S. oil engineer and his Venezuelan pilot in Apure. The pilot was released on February 22. 97021401

February 15, 1997. *Ecuador.* Achuar Indians kidnapped a U.S. geologist, a British technical assistant, and two Ecuadoran scientists in Shimi. The hostages worked for an Argentine firm, conducting environmental research in an area being explored for oil.

The American was identified as Mark Thurber, 34, an expert climber, guidebook author, and geologist. He and his colleagues were held for $3 million ransom by an anti-development splinter group of the Cuban-trained Achuar Indians. His parents did not have private insurance to pay the $2,500 daily fee of private hostage negotiators. While dealing with the State Department, they also brought in the FBI, according to *Wall Street Journal* reporter Ann Hagedorn Auerbach, author of *Ransom: The Untold Story of International Kidnapping.* Since the 1984 passage of the Hostage Taking Statute, the FBI has been responsible for negotiating for U.S. hostages anywhere in the world for free. The Thurbers also persuaded their friends in the Washington media not to report on the case.

The Ecuadoran military issued a stern warning to the kidnappers.

The kidnappers released the two Ecuadorans on February 16 and the two others on February 22. 97021501

February 17, 1997. *Lebanon.* Lebanese security forces arrested Iraqi citizen Bassam Ya'qub Yusuf (also spelled Yaaqoub Youssef), 28, who was hiding in a convent. He was suspected of involvement in political assassinations of Iraqi opposition figures in London, Morocco, Kuwait, and Albania for the Iraqi intelligence services. Judge Khalid Hammud, the government assistant commissioner at the military court, said the Iraqi intelligence agent was born in 1969. His last entry into Lebanon was on October 15, 1996. He resided at a monastery in Mount Lebanon. He was found in possession of documents showing that he was involved in operations in four countries and reported to Abu Ahmad in Jordan in 1996, where he received instructions on his next operations. The duo allegedly traveled to Morocco, where Yusuf killed an Iraqi opposition figure on September 15, 1996. Yusuf allegedly also worked as a veterinarian for Iraqi intelligence and had an affair with a Lebanese girl.

February 18, 1997. *Tajikistan.* Gunmen shot to death seven people, including two ethnic Russian security guards at the U.S. Embassy in Dushanbe. The United States announced it was temporarily evacuating embassy staff dependents. 97021801

February 19, 1997. *Germany.* The trial began of Harry Dahl, 68, Guenter Jaeckel, 63, Hans Petzold, 53, and Gerd Zaumseil, 49, former senior officers at the counterterrorism department in East Berlin's Ministry for State Security (Stasi). The four were charged with helping West German Red Army Faction (RAF) terrorists start new lives in East Germany and escape Western justice. Among their clients were:

- Susanne Albrecht, wanted for the 1977 murder of Juergen Ponto, the chairman of Dresdner Bank in Frankfurt. The Stasi gave her a false identity in 1980 and a job in a Cottbus laboratory. She married an East German scientist and had a child. After she was identified in a photo on West German television, the Stasi had her still-oblivious husband posted to Russia for two years.
- Silke Maier-Witt and Inge Viett, wanted for the 1977 kidnap/murder of Hanns-Martin Schleyer, chief of the Employers' Federation. They were wanted for other attacks as well. Maier-Witt worked in Erfurt as a nurse until 1986, when an East German defector reported her to West German police. The Stasi destroyed all evidence of her identity, even wiping fingerprints at her apartment. They gave her a nose operation in Berlin in 1987, and she was given a new identity and job in Neubrandenburg.

To throw off West German intelligence, the East Germans had planted photos showing the RAF terrorists in Middle Eastern settings.

After the fall of the Berlin Wall, ten of the retired terrorists were arrested in summer 1990. Eight of them were convicted and sentenced to 6 to 13 years; the statute of limitations had run out for the other two.

The four did not dispute that they helped the

terrorists, but claimed that by taking them out of circulation and keeping an eye on them, they prevented more terrorist attacks and the development of a terrorist "scene" in East Germany. The prevention of justice charges carry a five-year jail term.

The charges were dropped against Petzold on March 5.

On March 7, a Berlin court sentenced Dahl, Jaeckel, and Zaumseil to two years' probation for preventing the course of justice. The court issued formal reprimands to the trio and said they would be fined between 2,400 marks ($1,400) and 5,000 marks ($2,800) if they violated the terms of their probation. Defense lawyers said they would appeal the verdict.

February 20, 1997. *Pakistan.* Twelve gunmen shot and killed seven workers at an Iranian cultural center in Multan. The attackers fired automatic weapons while storming the center after spraying guards with chili powder. Once inside, they shot the Iranian head of the center and six other employees. They then torched the building and escaped by car and motorcycle. The Sunni Muslim Warriors of Jhangvi claimed credit, naming Riaz Basara, wanted in the 1990 assassination of a former head of the Iranian cultural center in Lahore, as a key organizer. Authorities arrested three suspects. 97022001

February 20, 1997. *Colombia.* National Liberation Army guerrillas kidnapped a Norwegian employee of a Swedish-owned construction company in Urra. 97022002

February 21, 1997. *Bosnia.* A 64-mm antitank rocket was fired at a vehicle carrying five Spanish soldiers; none was hurt when their vehicle was hit in the Croat sector of Sarajevo.

February 21, 1997. *Azerbaijan.* Gunmen killed a prominent member of Parliament in the lobby of his Baku apartment building.

February 22, 1997. *Georgia.* A landmine exploded in Gali, Abkhazia, when a Russian armored personnel carrier passed by, killing three Russian soldiers and wounding another. A responding ambulance hit a second mine, killing three Russian medics. Both blasts caused major damage. The White Legion and other Georgian partisans were suspected. The White Legion denied responsibility. 97022201

February 22, 1997. *Bosnia.* A grenade was thrown at an Italian peacekeeping vehicle patrolling Mostar. None of the four Italian soldiers was hurt and their vehicle was not damaged. The attackers escaped by car.

February 23, 1997. *United States.* Ali Hassan Abu Kamal, 69, a Palestinian, fired a 14-shot .38-caliber Beretta at tourists on the observatory deck of the Empire State Building's 86th floor. Kamal killed one person and wounded five others before shooting himself to death. He was described as a nonpolitical, deranged man by his West Bank family, who explained that he had lost his $500,000 life savings in a few weeks in an American business scheme. Police were not able to verify the claim. Police said he had no links to Middle East terrorism and his family in Gaza claimed he was not political. Two neatly handwritten two-page notes—one in English and one in Arabic—were found. The notes blamed the United States for using Israel as "an instrument" against Palestine and also expressed anger at France and the United Kingdom. Other enemies he named included individuals from the Gaza Strip, Egypt, and the Ukraine.

Abu Kamal had arrived in New York on a tourist visit. Born in Jaffa on September 19, 1927, to a refugee family, he was a Ramallah resident who taught high school and college English. He stayed at a New York YMCA and a modest motel in Florida, where he purchased the gun on January 30.

The dead man was Christoffer Burmeister, 27, a musician from Denmark who was visiting the building with fellow Bushpilots band member

Matthew Gross, 27, of Montclair, New Jersey (other reports have Gross hailing from Connecticut), who was wounded. Abu Kamal also wounded a French couple, Patrick, 44, and Virginie Demange, 36 (their daughter, Amandine, 16, was not harmed); Jacob Schaad, 32, of Maur, Switzerland; Mario Carmona, 52, of Mendoza, Argentina; and Hector Mendez, 35, from the Bronx. Several people, including two small children, were knocked down and trampled in the panic.

Kamal had gone to the building on the previous day, perhaps to evaluate security procedures.

February 23, 1997. *Russia.* Four gunmen kidnapped an Italian photojournalist traveling between Chernorechye village and Grozny. In late March, they demanded $1 million. Russian and Chechen authorities and the humanitarian agency Intersos helped bring about the hostage's release. Chechen militants were suspected of attempting to undermine talks between Moscow and the recently elected Chechen government.
97022301

February 24, 1997. *United States.* The FBI announced it was searching for a U-Haul truck that could be carrying bomb components similar to those used in the Oklahoma City bombing. The truck pulled into a Texaco station in Haltom City, Texas, on February 22; its two occupants purchased 30 gallons of diesel fuel. A station employee spotted three large blue plastic containers that could contain ammonium nitrate fertilizer. The fuel and fertilizer were used in the Oklahoma bomb. The FBI noted that February 28 is the anniversary of the beginning of the Waco, Texas, standoff with the Branch Davidians. On February 25, the FBI rescinded the advisory after the truck was discovered in Atlanta carrying baking soda.

February 24, 1997. *Colombia.* National Liberation Army (ELN) guerrillas kidnapped a U.S. citizen employed by a Las Vegas gold corporation who was scouting a gold mining operation. The ELN demanded $2.5 million. 97022401

February 25, 1997. *China.* Three bombs exploded in Urumqi, the provincial capital of Xinjiang Province. The bombs blew up within minutes of each other, killing 9 and wounding 74. A fourth bomb failed to explode. Seven suspects were arrested. Separatists were suspected.

February 25, 1997. *Saudi Arabia.* The U.S. Embassy issued a strong warning of a potential terrorist attack against U.S. personnel in the kingdom, noting televised threats by Osama bin Laden in Afghanistan. The embassy also cited reports of suspicious figures conducting surveillance of U.S. facilities. Bin Laden told London's Channel 4-TV on February 20 that "if someone can kill an American soldier, it is better than wasting his energy on other matters."

February 28, 1997. *United States.* Police found 16 bombs in the home of Aubrey Mark Turner after he was wounded in a gun battle with sheriff's deputies. Turner had stolen some propane tanks from a Roopville, Georgia, grocery store at 5:00 A.M. Police found his truck at a nearby home and discovered Turner hiding in the bushes. He fired at the police, who returned fire, hitting him in the arm, and then arrested him. He was charged with aggravated assault on police officers and theft. Police found a metal pipe bomb, two large bombs in plastic PVC pipe, eight smaller PVC pipe bombs, and four other bombs in carbon-dioxide canisters, along with bomb-making materials.

March 1997. *United States.* On February 9, 1998, Peter Howard, 44, pleaded guilty to attempted arson and use of an explosive device and was sentenced to 15 years in prison for trying to blow up the Family Planning Associates abortion clinic in Bakersfield, California. He intended to set off a truck filled with tanks of propane and cans of gasoline. A small fire started, but there were no reports of an explosion or injuries.

March 3, 1997. *China.* A bomb went off in Zinjiang Province. Turkic-speaking Muslim separatists were suspected.

March 4, 1997. *Yemen.* In early March, seven German motorcyclists were taken hostage by tribesmen in Wadi al-Dabaat in the Hadramut region. The group demanded $12 million from the government. A tribal sheik was seeking the government's intervention in a dispute with a car dealer. The hostages were released on March 12. 97030401

March 5, 1997. *United States.* Police in Roanoke, Virginia, arrested nine men and were seeking a tenth suspect—Ahmad Thiab, an Iraqi who holds a doctorate in political science—suspected of laundering hundreds of thousands of dollars for Middle Eastern terrorist front organizations during the previous seven years. The suspects were held on federal murder, racketeering, narcotics, and extortion charges and were believed to have built a fortune via narcotics distribution and insurance scams involving arson, burglary, robbery, and fraud. The group owned or had a financial interest in 33 restaurants, convenience stores, and other shops. One of the front organizations was SAAR (expansion unknown), an investment-management agency that reportedly supported Hamas and had ties to Osama bin Laden.

The U.S. Attorney's Office for the Western District of Virginia identified the group as the Abed family, named after the two brothers who controlled it, Joseph Abed and Abed Jamil Abdeljalil, both born in El Bireh, Palestinian Authority. They and four sons born in northern Virginia, along with a Jordanian, a Saudi, an Iraqi, and an American employee of the Postal Service, faced charges that could lead to life in prison. 97030501

March 7, 1997. *China.* A bomb exploded on public bus No. 22 in a Beijing shopping area during the evening rush hour, injuring 30. Some sources said two people were killed. (Reports in January 2000 said there were two dead and eight wounded.) The bus was heading south on Xidan, a shopping area less than a mile west of Tiananmen Square. The bomb went off as the vehicle stopped near a McDonald's north of Chang An Street. Police suspected Uighur Muslim separatists trying to create an independent East Turkestan out of Xinjiang Province. The attack was believed to be the first terrorist incident in Beijing since the 1949 revolution.

The Istanbul-based Eastern Turkestan Freedom Organization, made up of Uighur exiles, claimed credit. Chinese officials at the time claimed that separatists were not involved.

Chinese officials asked Israeli forensic scientists for assistance in analyzing the explosives, which were export-grade goods made in China. The explosives had been exported to Pakistan and then on to Afghanistan, where the Uighurs may have obtained them.

March 7, 1997. *France.* A member of the Church of Scientology defused a bomb found in the church in Angers in the early morning. The device was concealed in a sports bag. The church member defused the bomb in a nearby park. It had been primed to explode minutes later. No one claimed credit.

March 7, 1997. *Colombia.* The Rebel Armed Forces of Colombia (FARC) kidnapped a U.S. mining employee and his Colombian colleague who were searching for gold. On November 16, FARC released the hostages after receiving a $50,000 ransom. 97030701

March 10, 1997. *Taiwan.* A disgruntled Taiwanese journalist forced a Far East Air Transport Boeing 757 flying 150 passengers and 8 crew members on a domestic flight to land in Xiamen, China. He doused himself with gasoline and threatened to set himself on fire. Chinese police arrested him. No injuries were reported. The hijacker had recently been fired from a job in Hualien, Taiwan. He said his colleagues had harassed him because he was born in China and could not speak the Taiwanese dialect. On May 14, China permitted 15 Taiwanese officials and policemen into Xiamen to take custody of Liu Shang-chun, after having first refused to repatriate the hijacker. 97031001

March 13, 1997. *Egypt.* Muslim militants were suspected of firing assault rifles at passersby in Nag Dawoud, a Christian village in southern Egypt, killing nine Coptic Christians and four Muslims. The four gunmen were dressed in masks and military fatigues when they ran out of sugar cane fields at 6:30 P.M. Among the dead were Jadala Mansour, 46, a Coptic tailor, and Fadel Hanafi, a Muslim father of 11.

An hour later, gunmen—possibly those responsible for the Nag Dawoud attack—fired on a Cairo-bound train 12 miles south of the village, killing a woman, 40, and wounding six men.

The Islamic Group denied responsibility, claiming that the Egyptian security forces were responsible and were trying to discredit the militants. Egyptian police were searching for three militants.

March 13, 1997. *Jordan.* At 11:20 A.M., a Jordanian military driver grabbed a colleague's M-16 rifle and fired at a group of 51 eighth-grade Amit Fierst School schoolgirls, ages 12 and 13, touring the Baqura (Israelis call it Naharayim) border outpost, killing 7 and wounding 6. He chased the screaming children, who resided in Beit Shemesh, down a hill, firing on automatic as he ran. He then used single shots when he was one meter from the girls, firing at their heads. As he was loading another clip, he was overpowered by Jordanian soldiers. He was identified as Corporal Ahmad Mousa Daqamseh, 28. His mother claimed the high school dropout from Ibdir, who had been drafted 12 years earlier, was mentally ill and not affiliated with a political group. Among the dead were Yaela Meiri, Nurit Fatihi, and Keren Cohen. One of the girls had signed for her deaf mother. The only wounded adult was Yaffa Shukroun, 37, an Israeli teacher.

On March 16, Jordan's King Hussein visited the seven bereaved families in their homes, often getting on his knees to ask their forgiveness.

On March 27, Daqamseh was quoted by his attorney, Ahmad Najdawi, as saying, "I heard laughter and jeers and girls mocking me when I ended my prayers. . . . I was outraged by one girl

taking pictures and other girls laughing at me." He claimed he fired "on the spur of the moment."

On July 19, a military court in Naour, Jordan, convicted him of killing the seven girls and sentenced him to life in prison. He faced the death penalty, but the five-judge court gave him life because he was mentally unstable, according to Brigadier Maamoun Khassawneh, the presiding judge. The court also convicted him of plotting to kill Israelis since 1993, threatening to shoot his fellow soldiers on the day of the attack, and disobeying army orders. He was demoted to private and dismissed from the army. Jordanian law interprets a life sentence as 25 years in prison. The verdict cannot be appealed, but King Hussein can reduce or cancel the sentence. Hussein had said that Daqamseh should have been shot on the spot for the "heinous crime." Daqamseh had a 92-member defense team.

March 21, 1997. *Israel.* A young Palestinian male wearing faded jeans and a yellow coat draped on his arm set off a bag of explosives and nails, killing himself and 3 Israeli soldiers (other reports said 3 women) and injuring 47 others in Apropo, a Tel Aviv café. The attack came during the holiday of Purim, when children dress in costumes. Hamas claimed credit, saying it was protesting construction of a Jewish housing project in East Jerusalem. Israeli Prime Minister Benjamin Netanyahu blamed Yasir Arafat for tacitly giving terrorists a green light to protest the Har Homa (Jabal Abu Ghneim in Arabic) construction.

The terrorist carried an identity card for a 28-year-old Palestinian from Tsurif, near Hebron. Israeli soldiers kicked down the doors of the house where the bomber's family lived. The Israelis arrested all close male relatives of Mousa Abdel Khader Ghneimat, including his 68-year-old father and his wife, before sealing the house and preparing to demolish it. The Israeli army said it had arrested 13 people and that the search was conducted under a legal warrant.

Among those wounded were Mark Roitman, 8, and Ruth Shany, 73.

Jewish-Arab clashes the next day in Hebron left 102 injured.

Palestinian officials announced that they had arrested Ibrahim Muqadmeh, a senior Hamas military leader who was released earlier in March from a Gaza City cell. Palestinian Attorney General Khaled Kidrah said a warrant had been issued, but that Muqadmeh was not there when police went to his home.

On April 10, Israeli and Palestinian Authority security services announced they had broken up the Hamas cell responsible for the attack and several others. Israeli troops went back to Tsurif, where Rayed Salah Abu Hamadia, 21, a Hamas suspect, led them to the grave of Israeli army Sergeant Sharon Edri, 19, missing since September. Hamas gunmen disguised as Israeli Jews picked up the hitchhiking soldier; Hamadia shot him in the head. Two Hebron men were also arrested. The Israeli army determined that the bomber did not intend to commit suicide; a delayed-action detonator malfunctioned.

On September 10 at 2:30 P.M., 100 Israeli troops burst into a remote farmhouse west of Hebron and killed Imad, 29, and Adel Awadallah, 31, two brothers suspected as masterminds of several Hamas attacks, including the café bombing. The farmhouse, from which gunshots and an explosion had been heard two days earlier, was owned by Akram Maswadeh, a wealthy Hebron businessman. The brothers were planning another terrorist attack. Soldiers seized nine grenades, two pistols, an Uzi, a Kalashnikov, and several wigs. Hamas vowed revenge. Adel was a senior commander of Hamas's military wing in the West Bank; Imad was his chief assistant. They were responsible for five attacks that killed 5 Israelis and injured 51. They were also suspected of involvement in the March killing of Muhyideen Sharif, Hamas's chief bomb maker. Imad had been arrested for the bombing, but escaped from a Palestinian jail in Jericho in August.

March 21, 1997. *Germany.* Suspected members of the Kurdistan Workers Party (PKK) set off an improvised explosive device next to propane/butane gas tanks outside a Turkish-owned fast-food restaurant in Bad Vilbel, injuring one person and causing extensive damage. 97032101

March 22, 1997. *Nigeria.* Ijaw villagers held Royal Dutch/Shell oil workers hostage. The hostage takers were armed with cutlasses, automatic rifles, cudgels, and crude implements when they attacked the Egwa flow station and disarmed a lone policeman. The Ijaw villagers occupied the Shell buildings to protest the redrawing of regional boundaries. The 40 tribesmen made political demands and beat their 127 Nigerian captives, threatening to kill them. The Delta State natives released 76 captives on March 26 and the remainder on March 27. Three of the hostages had been injured. The incident was part of the rivalry between the Ijaw, the Itsekiri, and the Urhoboh tribes. 97032201

March 25, 1997. *Netherlands.* Suspected members or sympathizers of the Turkish Grey Wolves or the PKK set fire to a home in a predominantly Turkish neighborhood in The Hague, killing a mother and her five children and causing extensive damage. 97032501

March 26, 1997. *United Kingdom.* The IRA claimed credit for planting two bombs and making a bomb threat, disrupting rail services on the line south of Manchester near Wilmslow Station. Authorities at Doncaster Station received a telephoned 90-minute warning. The bombs tore up track and destroyed signaling equipment. 97032601-02

March 27, 1997. *Algeria.* A bomb exploded in a restaurant in El Marsa port, 12 miles east of Algiers, killing 4 and injuring 27. The Jihad Islamic League Front, a new faction, was responsible.

March 27, 1997. *Yemen.* Two elderly German couples returning to Sanaa from Marib were taken hostage by local tribesmen. The local military commander insulted the tribal sheik, who had ordered the kidnapping. In a gun battle, three Yemeni soldiers died. A letter sent to the German Embassy threatened to kill the hostages if the Yemeni government did not pay a $3 million ransom. The hostages were released on April 6 without a ransom payment. 97032701

March 29, 1997. *India.* Two bombs destroyed a bus station in Kashmir, killing 18 and injuring between 53 and 60. The first bomb torched a bus. A second bomb went off a few minutes later on a motor scooter parked outside the bus station. No one was injured in that blast. Two bombs were defused outside the station. The government blamed Muslim rebels fighting for Jammu and Kashmir's independence.

March 29, 1997. *Colombia.* In Zulia municipality, five uniformed and heavily armed Colombian Simon Bolivar Guerrilla Coordinating Board members kidnapped a Venezuelan cattle rancher who is the godfather of Venezuela's president. 97032901

March 30, 1997. *Cambodia.* Terrorists threw grenades at the National Assembly building during an Easter Sunday protest march, injuring Ron Abney, an American whose leg caught a pellet of metal shrapnel. Abney was an official of the International Republican Institute, which helped organize the party that sponsored the march. Three other grenades blew off the arms or legs of dozens of other onlookers, killing 20 and injuring 150. Surprisingly, soldiers surrounding the protest let the terrorists escape through their cordon and blocked the protestors from pursuing. They also prevented ambulances and taxis from carrying away the wounded and discouraged passersby from offering assistance. The FBI tentatively determined that the personal bodyguard forces of Hun Sen, 46, one of the country's two prime ministers, were responsible, according to the *Washington Post.* Sam Rainsy, 48, leader of the opposition Khmer National Party and organizer of the march, called for an international investigation.

April 1, 1997. *Gaza Strip.* A bomb exploded where a school bus was scheduled to leave the Jewish settlement of Nezarim; the bus had been delayed.

Another blast occurred near Kfar Darom when a cart loaded with explosives exploded near an Israeli bus, injuring seven Palestinians but no Israelis.

Police seized 30 people, most of them supporters of Islamic Jihad. Thirteen were released after questioning.

April 1, 1997. *Venezuela.* Thirty Colombian National Liberation Army (ELN) guerrillas killed two Venezuelan naval officers in El Ripial, Apure State. The officers were part of a patrol group sailing on a river along the Venezuelan shore. 97040101

April 2, 1997. *West Bank.* At 1:40 P.M., the driver of a truck carrying Israeli soldiers lost control when a firebomb was thrown through the windshield. The bus crashed down a slope near the Palestinian Jelazoun refugee camp, injuring 13. The driver suffered a broken leg. Tracks of two assailants led to the center of the camp.

April 3, 1997. *United Kingdom.* IRA-coded telephone warnings to police led to the closure of key stretches of expressways in central England between London and Birmingham. Two bombs were found. 97040301

April 3, 1997. *Ethiopia.* A Danish nurse who had worked in Ethiopia for the Danish Ethiopian Mission since 1993 was found murdered in the southern region of Bale. She had been missing since her car was stopped by armed men in late March. 97040302

April 3–5, 1997. *Algeria.* Islamic fundamentalists used knives, axes, and guns to kill 90 people in two days in attacks within a 60-mile radius of Algiers. Attackers slit the throats of 52 people near Medea, then burned their homes. The previous night, 15 people in Amroussa had their throats slit. Their bodies were soaked in gasoline and burned. Another eight died in Kabylie. Four members of the same family were killed in M'Ridja. Another dozen people were killed overnight south of Algiers. Their throats were slit and their bodies left by a road.

April 4, 1997. *United Kingdom.* Police closed the Waterloo and Euston rail stations in London after IRA bomb threats. Police conducted a controlled detonation of a suspect package found at the King's Cross train station in London. The device was not a bomb. 93040401-03

April 5, 1997. *United Kingdom.* The IRA claimed credit for two telephoned bomb threats that disrupted the Grand National steeplechase at Aintree race course near Liverpool. The claiming call was made to Dublin's RTE broadcasting network. The warning said the bombs would explode at 3:50 P.M., when the race would be ending. Police detonated three suspicious packages, none of which turned out to be bombs. Some 60,000 spectators, including Princess Anne and Gregory Peck, 81, who was there celebrating his birthday, were evacuated. 97040501

April 6, 1997. *Burma.* A parcel bomb exploded at the home of Lieutenant General Tin Oo, a secretary of the ruling State Law and Order Restoration Council and army chief of staff, killing his eldest daughter, Cho Lei Oo, 34.

April 7, 1997. *Bahrain.* The United States announced it had discovered a plot by Bahraini dissidents to attack U.S. troops stationed in the country. The navy canceled shore leave for 12,000 sailors in the Persian Gulf. One plan called for members of Bahrain's Shi'ite Hizballah to attack U.S. servicemen from the Fifth Fleet. The U.S. Embassy also recommended that civilians avoid certain locations and advised against travel outside the capital. 97040701

April 8, 1997. *Colombia.* The Revolutionary Armed Forces of Colombia (FARC) bombed a rail line at a mining complex in El Cerrejon, derailing 27 railcars, spilling 2,700 tons of coal and 3,700 gallons of diesel fuel, and damaging 550 yards of rail line. The mine is operated under concession by Intercor, an Exxon subsidiary. 97040801

April 12, 1997. *Bosnia.* Some 23 antitank mines and 50 pounds of plastic explosives with a remote-control detonator were found planted under a bridge on the route that was to be taken by Pope John Paul II's motorcade. The Pope continued his trip. No one claimed credit. 97041201

April 12, 1997. *Ethiopia.* Grenades were thrown during the night at the Tigray Hotel and an Italian restaurant in Addis Ababa, killing a waitress and injuring 42, including 4 Britons and a French couple. Two of the Britons wounded at the restaurant were training police officers. At least 33 people were wounded at the restaurant. The government blamed Islamic radicals. 97041202

April 16, 1997. *Italy.* Italian security forces went on alert after receipt of information indicating that Islamic extremists were planning to attack Pope John Paul II. 97041601

April 18, 1997. *United Kingdom.* A bomb went off in a cabinet containing signaling equipment near a parking lot at Leeds railway station.

Another bomb went off on a road over a railway bridge north of Doncaster, 30 miles southwest of Leeds.

The IRA was suspected in both incidents. 97041801-02

April 18, 1997. *Iran.* Hossein Allah-Karam, head of the Ansar'e Hizballah, an extremist Shi'ite fundamentalist group, threatened Germany with suicide bombings if Berlin did not apologize for a court ruling that blamed Tehran for ordering the assassination of Kurdish dissidents in September 1992. The court had convicted an Iranian grocer and three Lebanese of killing the Kurds at a Berlin restaurant. Demonstrations against Germany continued in Tehran. 97041803

April 21, 1997. *United Kingdom.* Callers using IRA code words threatened bomb attacks throughout London that would tie up road, rail, and air traffic. Four rail stations and two airports were evacuated. No bombs were found.

A simple bomb went off in the Sinn Fein office in Londonderry, causing damage but no injuries. 97042101-06

April 22, 1997. *United States.* The Dallas Joint Terrorism Task Force raided a safe house in rural Wise County, arresting four would-be terrorists who planned to stage attacks and rob an armored car of $2 million in Chico on May 1. Local and federal officials held the suspects without bond. They were charged with conspiracy to commit a robbery affecting interstate commerce, which carries a maximum 20-year sentence. Edward Taylor, Jr., 34, was an artist from Boyd. His wife, Catherine Dee Adams, 35, was also held. Carl J. Wascom, Jr., 34, of Boyd, a plumber's helper, was arrested at a work site in Fort Worth. Taylor was a member of the True Knights of the Ku Klux Klan in north Texas, according to Klanwatch.

The terrorists' plan was to blow up a gas refinery owned by Mitchell Energy and Development Corporation in Bridgeport. Two to four pipe bombs were to be planted at the refinery, one in a visible location. The foursome believed the blast would release a deadly cloud of hydrogen sulfide gas, killing policemen who would be responding to a bomb threat to be phoned in by Catherine Adams. After police found the visible bomb, the others would detonate 45 minutes later. The bombing would give them the diversion they needed to rob the truck and use the money to finance other terrorist excursions. They provided gas masks to their family members. They had tested small pipe bombs twice in previous weeks in the Lyndon B. Johnson National Grasslands, a 20,000-acre preserve in Montague and Wise Counties.

Things did not go as planned. Thanks to an informant in the group, the terrorists were arrested. A gas firm spokesman said hydrogen sulfide would not have been released, because the company produces only "sweet gas."

April 22, 1997. *Algeria.* Muslim militants used sabers, axes, and knives to kill 47 people in two villages south of Algiers. Three babies were mutilated and a pregnant woman was hacked open.

Thirty insurgents attacked Omaria, killing 42. In nearby Ouzera, ambushers set up a roadblock, stopped a bus, and killed five passengers.

Just before dawn, attackers took three hours to kill 93 villagers in Haouch Mokhfi.

April 22, 1997. *Cambodia.* Khmer Rouge guerrillas attacked two trucks in the Barkeo District of Ratanakkiri Province, killing three Vietnamese citizens, wounding six others, and destroying the trucks. 97042201

April 24, 1997. *United States.* On Take Our Daughters to Work Day, a package containing an unidentified substance in a petri dish was sent to the B'nai B'rith Building in Washington, D.C., along with a threatening note that said, "The only good Jew is an Orthodox Jew." A variant of the word "anthrax" was written on the side of the petri dish. Initial radio reports said that Rusty Mason, a mailroom employee who discovered the oozing package, and security chief Carmen Fontana were hospitalized with headaches and shortness of breath. Several blocks of the city were sealed off for eight hours and 108 employees in the building were quarantined. Rescue workers in decontamination gear hosed down Fontana, Mason, two other employees, and a dozen firefighters and other emergency personnel with water and chlorine. One elderly employee was so humiliated by being sprayed in the open (the District of Columbia government does not have a decontamination tent) that he announced he would retire.

The Naval Medical Research Institute in Bethesda, Maryland, determined that the unidentified red gelatin was not toxic. Four days later, it was determined that the dish contained agar, a readily available material derived from algae that is used as a medium for growing bacteria. A common household bacterium, *B. cereus*, was growing on it.

The FBI sent alerts to other Jewish groups, saying that the rambling two-page letter was from the previously unknown Counter Holocaust Lobbyists of Hillel. The typed, unsigned letter called the brownish, bubble-lined envelope (five inches wide and ten inches long) a "chemical weapon" and derided Jewish liberalism and the Jewish community in general. The obscured postmark began with "MA."

Local organizations, including the McLean Post Office, had similar scares the next day. The McLean site was evacuated after employees reported suspicious liquid seeping from a package; it was identified later as strawberry juice.

April 25, 1997. *Algeria.* A bomb hidden under railway tracks exploded under two passenger cars on a train south of Algiers, killing 21 and injuring 20. Terrorists had killed at least 440 people over the previous month.

April 25, 1997. *West Bank.* Palestinian guerrillas were believed to be responsible for stabbing to death two teenage girls in a West Bank nature reserve near Jerusalem. Police said the murder occurred two or three days earlier.

April 27, 1997. *Cambodia.* Khmer Rouge guerrillas attacked Vietnamese fishermen and wood cutters in Barkeo District in Ratanakkiri, killing nine and wounding ten others. 97042701

April 28, 1997. *Russia.* In Grozny, Chechnya, assailants kidnapped the son of the late Georgian President Zviad Gamsakhurdia. The kidnappers threw the hostages out of their vehicle when police approached them.

April 29, 1997. *United Kingdom.* Police closed five highways, evacuated parts of Heathrow and Gatwick Airports, and suspended incoming flights at Southampton Airport after receiving telephoned bomb threats that included IRA code words. 97042901-08

April 30, 1997. *Tajikistan.* Firdavs Dustboboyev, 21, an anti-government activist, was arrested after

he threw a hand grenade at President Imamali Rakhmonov as he was getting out of his car in Khudjand. The president was wounded in the legs. Two people were killed and another 60 injured. The country was in the midst of a civil war involving Islamic militants, although the armed Islamic opposition denied involvement.

May 4, 1997. *Egypt.* The al-Gamaat al-Islamiya threatened to kill American officials if Sheik Omar Abdel Rahman, 58, died in the federal prison hospital in Springfield, Missouri. He had been sentenced to life in prison in 1995 for conspiring to blow up New York City landmarks. "If harm comes to the sheik, al-Gamaat al-Islamiya will target—with the help of God and his strength—all of those Americans who participated in subjecting his life to danger. Al-Gamaat al-Islamiya considers every American official, starting with the American president to the despicable jailer, partners in endangering the sheik's life." 97050401

May 4, 1997. *Cyprus.* *O Agon* reported that U.S. officials had warned local authorities that Hizballah was going to attack U.S. interests in Cyprus.

May 5, 1997. *Colombia.* National Liberation Army (ELN) rebels kidnapped a Brazilian construction worker, releasing him on October 15 in Santa Marta. The Red Cross helped the construction company negotiate. The firm did not disclose whether ransom was paid. 97050501

May 9, 1997. *Italy.* Eight Venetian separatists, ages 20 to 45, drove a makeshift armored vehicle to the Venice bell tower, which they seized to publicize their independence demands. The Venetian Serenissima Army attackers, dressed in camouflage, conducted their evening raid nearly 200 years to the day of the fall of the Republic of Venice. Shortly after midnight on the Tronchetto lagoon island, they took over a public ferryboat, loaded on their vehicle and a white camper, and ordered the captain to take them to St. Mark's Square. They then climbed the tower, which is under restoration, and unfurled a banner with the words "Serenissima Repubblica," the name of the former Venetian republic. Seven hours of negotiations ended when carabinieri commandos stormed the 325-foot bell tower. The separatists surrendered without a fight. Six men were arrested in the tower; two others were arrested in the vehicle. Police recovered food, water, wine, sleeping bags, and a submachine gun in the bell tower. The separatists were charged with kidnapping, belonging to an armed gang, subversion, and lesser charges relating to disturbing public order. The separatist Northern League denied involvement.

May 13, 1997. *United States.* FBI Director Louis Freeh and acting Director of Central Intelligence George Tenet told a Senate hearing that two American embassies had been targets of bomb plots within the last six months. Freeh also noted that Hamas and Hizballah had support networks inside the United States.

May 13, 1997. *China.* At 5:00 P.M., a bomb exploded in Zhongshan Park, northwest of Tiananmen Gate and east of the Zhongnanhai leadership compound, killing one person. Uighur nationalists were suspected.

May 16, 1997. *United Kingdom.* Newly elected British Prime Minister Tony Blair lifted the ban on official contact with Sinn Fein, the IRA's political arm.

May 16, 1997. *Venezuela.* In Urena municipality, four armed men kidnapped a Venezuelan politician, forced him into a vehicle, and took him to Colombia, where he was shot and killed by his captors as he attempted to escape. ELN and FARC both operate in the area in which he was kidnapped. 97051601

June 1, 1997. *Algeria.* Two bombs exploded on buses in Algiers, killing 7 and wounding 77. The bombings occurred four days before the scheduled general election. The first bomb went off at 4:00 P.M., blasting a bus about to leave the Martyr's Square station, killing 6, including a baby, and

wounding 48. Less than an hour later, a bomb exploded inside a bus on Gharmoul Street, killing 1 person and wounding 29, 4 seriously. Muslim radicals were suspected.

June 9, 1997. *Malta.* Two Turks, one with a fake bomb strapped to his chest, hijacked an Istanbul-bound Air Malta Boeing 737 after it took off from Valetta with 81 people aboard. The hijackers diverted the plane to Cologne, Germany. They demanded the release of Mehmet Ali Agca, who was serving a life sentence in Italy for the attempted assassination of the Pope in 1981. They demanded the reading of a manifesto calling for his release. Police, via a Turkish interpreter, talked one hijacker into giving the pilot what they claimed was a fuse to the explosives. The hijackers then freed their hostages after three hours and surrendered to police. No one was injured. 97060901

June 11, 1997. *United States.* A JFK Airport maintenance worker discovered that wires in a Pan Am plane were cut overnight. Pan Am suspected vandalism. The severed wires were in the electronic compartment beneath the cockpit of the A300 Airbus that was to fly to Miami.

June 13, 1997. *Bahrain.* Arsonists torched a Manama upholstery shop, killing four Indians who were trapped in their home above the shop. Shia extremists were suspected. 97061301

June 17, 1997. *Tajikistan.* A gunman fired on two Russian CIS Collective Peacekeeping Force officers in Dushanbe, killing one and wounding the other. 97061701

June 19, 1997. *Algeria.* Muslim terrorists killed 26 people, including 6 children and a pregnant woman, in two attacks. Eleven people died in the first attack.

June 22, 1997. *Algeria.* The Armed Islamic Group was suspected of killing a French woman in Bouzeguene and dumping her body in a well. 97062201

June 27, 1997. *Russia.* A bomb exploded on a train traveling from Moscow to St. Petersburg, killing three people—possibly including an unidentified suicide bomber—and injuring seven others. A 13-year-old boy and another man died when the bomb, planted in a toilet, exploded when the train was near Torbino station in the Novgorod region northwest of Moscow. The train arrived four hours after the explosion.

June 27, 1997. *Colombia.* In San Pablo, 60 National Liberation Army (ELN) guerrillas kidnapped three employees of a Brazilian company contracted to repair rail track in Cesar and Magdalena departments. They released two workers unharmed on July 1. The rebels demanded a $9,000 ransom of food "for the people" in exchange for a Spanish engineer. 97062701

June 30, 1997. *Germany.* Police in Dresden announced that someone threw a firebomb through a window of an asylum seeker's home, setting a small fire, but causing no injuries. Neo-Nazis were suspected. In previous weeks, neo-Nazis had twice torched a Protestant church in Luebeck, painted swastikas on the walls, and threatened the pastor, who had offered shelter to an Algerian family that was seeking asylum. 97063001, 97069901-02

July 1997. *Lebanon.* A court sentenced to three years in jail four men and one woman who were members of the Japanese Red Army on charges related to their illegal stay in the country. On June 3, 1998, a court rejected a retrial appeal.

July 1, 1997. *Russia.* Christophe Andre, a worker for the French medical aid group Doctors Without Borders, was kidnapped in Ingushetia. The organization had kept his kidnapping secret in hopes of gaining his release quietly, but the media reported the kidnapping on July 8. No ransom demands were made. 97070101

July 1, 1997. *Sri Lanka.* Liberation Tigers of Tamil Eelam rebels captured an Indonesian-flag passenger ferry, taking two Indonesian and seven Sri Lankan crew members hostage before torching the ship. The terrorists released the Indonesians. 97070102

July 2, 1997. *Russia.* Masked Chechen gunmen kidnapped two British aid workers, John James and Camilla Carr, a married couple who worked for the Center for Peacemaking and Community Development, in the late night or early morning in Grozny. Their bodyguards were knocked unconscious. Three people were held for questioning, including the couple's two bodyguards and Adnan Adayev, the deputy director of the Quaker aid group. As of July 8, no ransom demands had been made.

The duo was freed unharmed on September 20, 1998. They flew to the United Kingdom after a brief stopover in Moscow. 97070201

July 6, 1997. *Bahrain.* Arsonists torched a Sitra store, killing a Bangladeshi and injuring another. Shia extremists were suspected. 97070601

July 7, 1997. *Sri Lanka.* Liberation Tigers of Tamil Eelam (LTTE) guerrillas hijacked a North Korean food ship, killing a North Korean crew member and holding 37 others hostage. On July 12, LTTE released them to the International Committee of the Red Cross. 97070701

July 10, 1997. *Spain.* Basque Nation and Liberty (ETA) gunmen kidnapped Ermua town councilman Miguel Angel Blanco, 29, and threatened to kill him if the government did not move 500 ETA inmates to prisons in the Basque region. Prime Minister Jose Maria Aznar led a rally of 500,000 people in Bilbao protesting the death threat. ETA shot Blanco after the rally. He was found by a hunter who heard a shot in a wooded area near San Sebastian. Blanco died in a coma the morning of July 13, with two bullets lodged in his brain. The next day, 1.5 million Spaniards, including all four of Spain's prime ministers during its 20-year democracy, marched in Madrid to protest the killing. Another million marched in Barcelona. On July 15, ETA threatened to kill a second low-ranking politician from Spain's ruling Popular Party. On July 19, the Basque government called on ETA to declare a truce, following the announcement of an IRA truce.

July 12, 1997. *Cuba.* A bomb exploded in Havana's Hotel Nacional, injuring three people, including a Jamaican man and a Cuban woman, and causing minor damage to the five-star hotel. It is 200 meters from a hotel that was bombed ten minutes earlier. The Cuban government said, "The people responsible for the bombings and also the material used in them came from the United States." The Military Liberation Union claimed credit and said it was composed of disenchanted Cuban soldiers. A former Cuban Air Force colonel said dissident soldiers were stealing explosives from military arsenals. On September 10, the Ministry of the Interior announced the arrest of a Salvadoran who had confessed. 97071201

July 14, 1997. *Algeria.* A bomb exploded in Cite Baraka, an Algiers market, killing 21 and wounding 40. The bombing followed a weekend during which Islamic militants killed 44 people, including 14 women and 4 adolescents. Islamic terrorists had killed 400 people since the June 5 election, when a pro-government party won.

July 17, 1997. *Bosnia.* Several explosive devices were thrown at a British base in the early morning. The terrorists apparently were retaliating for a NATO raid on Serbs indicted for war crimes. The hand grenades were thrown into the base's parking lot in the Serb-controlled northwestern city of Banja Luka. British soldiers fired warning shots and detained four suspects. No one was seriously injured. During the previous four days, three other bombs had gone off in the presence of international monitors working in Bosnia's Serb Republic for the UN or the Organization for Security and Cooperation in Europe. No one was hurt. The NATO peace force also received anonymous threats after British special forces arrested a war crimes suspect and killed another who resisted

arrest on July 10 in Prijedor, near Banja Luka. 97071701, 97079901-04

July 18, 1997. *Bosnia.* A bomb was thrown from a passing car at the office of an American soldier, slightly wounding him with flying glass. The bomb destroyed a vehicle in front of the office where he and several other military observers worked. He did not need medical attention. The attack took place in the Serb-controlled town of Doboj, 50 miles east of Banja Luka.

Later that night, bombs damaged vehicles outside a British base in the Serb-controlled town of Mrkonjic Grad and at private homes accommodating UN police monitors in Prijedor. The attacks raised to ten the number of bomb and grenade attacks against NATO and other international organizations' personnel since the crackdown on war criminals. 97071801-04, 97079905

July 19, 1997. *Colombia.* National Liberation Army (ELN) guerrillas kidnapped a dual Canadian-Colombian citizen and a Colombian in El Bagre. The dual citizen may have been hired by a U.S. mining company to negotiate the release of its U.S. employee who was being held captive by the Revolutionary Armed Forces of Colombia (FARC). 97071901

July 22, 1997. *Algeria.* Algerian army troops killed Antar Zouabri, 27, and 100 of his followers in a gun battle in the ancient tunnels where Armed Islamic Group terrorists were hiding near Tipasa. At least 300 others surrendered. Zouabri, son of a shoemaker, had succeeded Jamal Zitouni, who died in late 1996 under mysterious circumstances.

July 22, 1997. *Israel.* A 32-year-old Hamas supporter from Nazareth attacked foreign tourists in Tel Aviv. Nine people suffered minor injuries when he drove his car into a group of 20 visiting British Jewish teenagers in the Jaffa quarter. He then stabbed a Toronto woman and her daughter, who were sitting at a sidewalk restaurant. He was overpowered by police officer Daniel Konson, who said, "The driver got out holding a sword and a commando knife and went toward the civilians and tried to stab a number and succeeded." Konson tied up the terrorist and took him to a police station. The terrorist said he could not remember anything. 97072201

July 22, 1997. *Colombia.* Rebels kidnapped six people who were flying to a remote area in Antioquia to work on electrical lines and seized their helicopter. The Guevarista Revolutionary Army demanded $500,000 and said they had mined the jungle site where the six were taken and had loaded the helicopter with explosives. The helicopter engineer was a Nicaraguan. On July 30, Colombian troops found three of the hostages unharmed and recovered the helicopter. 97072201

July 26, 1997. *Yemen.* Gunmen kidnapped two Italian tourists and their Yemeni driver near Kohlan. Security forces freed them the next day. 97072601

July 30, 1997. *Israel.* Two suicide bombers set off their bombs yards and seconds from each other at 1:18 P.M., killing 15 and wounding 170 in the Mahane Yehuda bazaar, a Jerusalem landmark. The bombs, packed with screws and nails, were hidden in the briefcases carried by men dressed in black suits, white shirts, and dark ties, disguised as businessmen or ultra-Orthodox Jews. A flier outside Red Cross offices in Ramallah claimed credit for the Issadin Kassam military wing of Hamas. The group threatened further attacks if Israel did not release all prisoners "in occupied Palestine" by 9:00 P.M. on August 3. Abdel Aziz Rantissi, a Hamas leader released in the spring, said in a telephone interview from Gaza that the leaflet was bogus. Among the dead were two Arab laborers, along with Lili Zelezniak, 45, Sami Malka, and David Nasko, 42. The injured included legal secretary Orly Ohayon and Ella Dubchikov, 48, a recent Russian immigrant.

Israeli authorities arrested 37 Palestinians on August 3 after receiving more threats.

Israeli Prime Minister Benjamin Netanyahu demanded that Yasir Arafat round up terrorists. Netanyahu stopped payment of $25 million in taxes and customs fees that Israel owes the Palestinian Authority, leaving Arafat unable to meet the $40 million payroll due to his 80,000 civil servants and police. Israel also threatened to jam Palestinian broadcasts and dispatch special forces into Palestinian-ruled cities. Soldiers and border police closed West Bank towns and villages. Israeli warships blockaded the coast.

On August 13, following a four-day trip to the region by U.S. envoy Dennis Ross, the Israelis and Palestinians agreed to a three-way panel on security issues to be assisted by the local CIA station chief, who would determine the degree of Palestinian cooperation in finding terrorists.

For 13 days, the Israelis were unable to identify the bombers. Their upper torsos, heads, and faces were all that remained of them. No match was found for their fingerprints. Labels in their clothes had been torn out. They had carried Jordanian money, suggesting a foreign connection, although many Palestinians travel. Hizballah was suspected. No families claimed the bodies.

On January 12, Palestinian intelligence uncovered 1,500 pounds of explosive materials in Nablus. Two days later, Jasser Samara and Nassim Abu Rous were arrested. Following a three-hour trial, the Hamas duo were sentenced to 15 years in prison at hard labor for building the bombs and recruiting the five suicide bombers who killed 26 people on July 30 and September 4.

July 30, 1997. *Algeria.* Between 40 and 60 Muslim terrorists armed with swords and guns killed 41 people in Metmata village in Ain Defla Province, 76 miles southwest of Algiers. The terrorists killed elderly men, 7 women—two of them pregnant—and 11 children. One man, Ahmed Menal, lost 25 family members and relatives in the raid. The terrorists shot him in the face and cut his throat. Four girls were kidnapped; two of them were later found dead with their throats slashed. The Armed Islamic Group was suspected.

July 30, 1997. *Algeria.* A car bomb exploded outside an Algiers restaurant, killing 8 and wounding 25. The Armed Islamic Group was blamed.

July 30, 1997. *Colombia.* The National Liberation Army (ELN) bombed the Cano Limon-Covenas oil pipeline in Norte de Santander. The rebels wrapped sticks of dynamite around the pipes of the pump, causing a major oil spill and suspending pumping operations for more than a week, resulting in several million dollars in lost revenue.

July 31, 1997. *United States.* New York police and federal agents arrested Gazi Ibrahim Abu Mezer (variant Gazhi Ibrahim Abu Maizar), 23, Lafi Khalil, 22, and another person and seized five powerful bombs after a dawn shootout in a Brooklyn apartment at 248 Fourth Avenue. Police had been tipped off by one of the men that his colleagues intended to blow up transportation facilities in New York City, including the subway system. Investigators discovered papers in which Abu Mezer identified himself in an application for political asylum, claiming that he was arrested in Israel for "being a member of a known terrorist organization." The unidentified man expressed support for the Jerusalem suicide bombers.

The Arabic-speaking tipster, initially identified as Pakistani Mohamed Shindli, tried to tell two Long Island Rail Road police officers through sign language that a bomb was going to go off. They brought him to the New York Police Department's 88th Precinct station house, where the FBI was summoned. As police entered the apartment, one man ran toward the bomb. Although police fired, he threw one of several detonating switches. A second man was shot while moving toward the bomb.

Abu Mezer told police how to render the bombs harmless and how they were to be used against the subway system's Atlantic Avenue station and a commuter bus. One of the bombs lacked a timer and was constructed of four separate pipe bombs, each loaded with black powder and wired to a single power source. Police said it could have been a suicide bomb. A separate pipe

bomb wrapped with nails was also found. A note taped to one of the bombs threatened violence against U.S. and Jewish targets around the world.

The two would-be terrorists were hospitalized.

One of the men claimed to be Pakistani; the other two had Jordanian passports. One man had obtained a visa from the U.S. Consulate in Jerusalem in November 1996.

The FBI interviewed the duo's families in Israel.

Abu Mezer's relatives in Hebron, West Bank, said he had been arrested once during the 1987 to 1993 *intifada* after a clash between teenage stone throwers and Israeli soldiers. He was released without charges after a few days. His brother claimed that he had served on the Palestinian negotiating team that reached the last major accord with Israel in September 1995. He claimed that his brother supported the peace process and admired the United States.

Khalil's parents lived near Aqaba, Jordan, after expulsion from Kuwait. Khalil stayed for four years with an uncle in Ajjul, a village north of Ramallah. In November, he obtained a visa at the U.S. Consulate in Jerusalem, moved to Brooklyn, then to California, and then back to Brooklyn. His tourist visa expired in December 1996.

Hamas denied any connection with the duo, saying its only battlefield was on Israeli soil.

The duo did not fit the standard profile of the suicide bomber—poverty, hopelessness, religious zeal, and a close relative killed in clashes with the Israelis. The Abu Mezers are middle class; their home has a fax and a satellite dish. The suspect's four sisters and two brothers are employed; most of them are teachers and one is a tax attorney.

Gazi Abu Mezer finished at the top of his high school class and went to the United States to seek his fortune. He never went to mosque and was not religiously observant or political. He told his family of an American Christian girlfriend. He had also lived in Canada and Florida. The family did not provide details about where he worked or lived. In September 1993 he moved to Canada and obtained refugee status after claiming harassment by the Israeli authorities for "being a Palestinian Muslim." He was arrested in Toronto the next year for using a stolen credit card. He was later picked up for assault. Twice in June 1996 he was picked up in Washington trying to cross the border. Each time he returned voluntarily to Canada. Abu Mezer entered the United States illegally on January 14, 1997, at Bellingham, Washington. He was arrested by U.S. Border Patrol agents and held on a $15,000 bond. He was released from a Seattle jail on a reduced $5,000 bond on February 6 and given an April court date by a judge attached to the Justice Department's Office of Immigration Review. Canada refused to accept him back. The Immigration and Naturalization Service (INS) began deportation proceedings. He twice applied for political asylum in the United States, saying the Israelis believed he was a Hamas member. He claimed he had been arrested several times by the Israelis, who beat and tortured him and shot off the top of his right-hand middle finger. His older brother denied the story, saying he lost the fingertip at age six when a neighborhood girl slammed his hand in a door. The INS said it had received only one of the applications. The court set a day of January 20, 1998, for a hearing on the asylum application; they are usually scheduled within 120 days of the time of application. He withdrew his application on June 23 and agreed to a judge's order that gave him 60 days to get out of the United States.

The duo then showed up in early July in North Carolina. Walid Museituf, owner of the IGA grocery store in Ayden, hired them but soon fired Abu Mezer when he could not produce papers. He stayed in Ayden while Khalil worked in the store for three weeks. Those who knew them said they talked about women and money, not religion and politics.

Police later said the tipster was the suspects' roommate, Abdul Rahman Mossabah, an Egyptian who had arrived in New York in the previous two weeks. He was held on federal immigration charges. After tipping off police, he returned to his apartment for a nap. Neighbors said he spoke several languages and had graduated from a Cairo college. He wanted to be a language teacher. Terror-

ists do not usually manufacture bombs in plain sight of unwitting roommates.

FBI investigators suggested on August 12 that the duo was setting up a hoax designed to extort money from the U.S. State Department's Heroes antiterrorism rewards program. The State Department received a rambling communiqué—a copy of which was found in the apartment—on August 1. This document threatened suicide attacks and demanded the release of Sheik Omar Abdel Rahman, Ramzi Yousef, and Sheik Ahmed Yassin, known terrorist leaders. The communiqué's author claimed to have blown up TWA Flight 800, although authorities had determined that a bomb did not bring down the plane.

A New York judge issued a permanent order of detention and scheduled a court hearing for August 14. Defense lawyers did not request bail.

On August 15, the U.S. Department of State confirmed that its reward program had received a letter about planned bombings in New York, but would not confirm that it was related to this case.

On August 29, the two were indicted by a federal grand jury in New York for plotting to set off a pipe bomb in the subway. They faced life in prison if convicted of conspiracy to use a weapon of mass destruction. Arraignment was expected within the fortnight.

The trial began on July 6, 1998. Police Officer David Martinez testified that he fired his gun after one of the accused attempted to grab his weapon.

On July 20, Abu Mezer told the jury in the Federal District Court in Brooklyn that before he came to New York, "I failed to assassinate President Clinton in Seattle, Washington." He claimed that he intended to kill as many Jews as possible in a suicide bomb attack, but not in the planned subway bombing. He had also left a note in his apartment claiming responsibility for the crash of TWA flight 800 in July 1996, which CIA analysts had established was not caused by a missile and which the FBI said was not the result of a criminal act. His lawyers had claimed that the defendant had not intended to set off the pipe bomb, but rather was using it to collect reward money from the U.S. antiterrorism program. He claimed that co-defendant Lafi Khalil was not involved in the bombing plan. He said a roommate named Abdel Rahman Mosabbah was involved, a claim investigators denied. He claimed he was a supporter, but not a member, of Hamas. He had testified against the counsel of his attorneys, who rejected his testimony.

On July 21, Prosecutor John F. Curran said the defendants were motivated by a "warped view of Palestinian nationalism."

On July 23, the jury found Abu Mezer guilty of plotting to blow up the subway station. The jury acquitted Lafi Khalil of the plot, but found him guilty of having a fake immigration card. Abu Mezer faced life in prison. 97073101

August 1997. *Yemen.* Tribesmen kidnapped Italian Giorgio Bonanami and held him for a week, during which they "treated him royally." They passed letters to his girlfriend in her hotel. Upon his release, he said, "They ought to make this a tourist package." 97089901

August 1997. *Sri Lanka.* The Internet Black Tigers, a faction of the Liberation Tigers of Tamil Eelam (LTTE), conducted what it called "suicide e-mail bombings" and swamped Sri Lanka embassies with junk e-mail, possibly a first for terrorists.

August 1, 1997. *Algeria.* Muslim terrorists armed with swords and guns killed 38 villagers in Sidi el Madani in Blida Province.

August 3, 1997. *Bahamas.* A bomb exploded at the Havanatur tourist office in Nassau, shattering windows and damaging four other businesses. No injuries were reported. 97080301

August 4, 1997. *Cuba.* A bomb went off in the early morning at the Mehia (or Melia) Cohiba Hotel in Havana. No injuries were reported. Three weeks earlier, similar bombs damaged the lobbies of two other Havana tourist hotels—the Nacional and the Capri. The Cohiba was bombed in April. On April 1, 1999, Otto Rene Rodriguez Llerena,

after confessing to setting off the bomb in the lobby, became the second man convicted of the series of tourist hotel bombings. He was sentenced to death. His sentence would be appealed automatically to the Supreme Court.

August 5, 1997. *Israel.* Hamas and Hizballah threatened more terrorist attacks.

August 6, 1997. *Yemen.* Tribesmen kidnapped an Italian tourist they randomly picked out among six others traveling between Rada and Aman. They wanted to pressure the government to recover a car confiscated in 1994. They released the tourist on August 10. 97080601

August 7, 1997. *Pakistan.* The U.S. Information Service center in Islamabad received a telephoned bomb threat. No bomb was found. 97080701

August 7, 1997. *Colombia.* In Yopal municipality, gunmen attacked the installations of a Colombian firm that works for British Petroleum, harassing workers, torching machinery, and causing $2 million damage. 97080702

August 13, 1997. *Yemen.* Tribesmen kidnapped six Italian tourists traveling to Aden from Mukallah. They released them on August 15. 97081301

August 14, 1997. *Yemen.* Tribesmen kidnapped four Italian tourists in Khami, freeing them the next day. 97081401

August 15, 1997. *Peru.* The Maoist Shining Path kidnapped 29 Peruvians working for a French oil company and Peru's Compania General de Geofisica. The rebels forced the men to listen to ideological talks before releasing them after four hours. The 50 or 60 rebels stole food, medicine, and communication equipment from the oil workers' camp in Junin Department. 97081501

August 15, 1997. *Venezuela.* Fifteen Colombian guerrillas kidnapped a Venezuelan army lieutenant and a resident in Chorrosquero. Three other army officers escaped capture by jumping into a nearby river. Authorities believed the victims were taken to Colombia. The National Liberation Army (ELN) and Revolutionary Armed Forces of Colombia (FARC) operate in the area. 97081502

August 16, 1997. *Kenya.* About 40 youths armed with spears and machetes attacked the village of Mtwapa, six miles north of Mombasa, killing three Kenyans whom they had beaten. The terrorists set alight two houses, including a holiday villa where several foreign tourists were staying. The tourists escaped unharmed.

The next day, armed gangs attacked and set fire to 100 roadside vending stands and dozens of houses in Shauri Yako. Terrorists had also attacked a coastal police station near Mombasa on August 13, killing 15, including 7 policemen. 97081601

August 25, 1997. *Sweden.* We Who Built Sweden, a group opposed to Stockholm's 2004 Olympics bid, claimed credit for setting off a bomb at Sweden's largest stadium, the New Ullevi in Goteborg. The group sent a confessor letter to the Associated Press in London. The group also claimed credit for the August 8 bombing of Stockholm's Olympic Stadium. It threatened to turn Stockholm into a "war zone" if it won the September 5 vote by the International Olympic Committee over finalists Rome, Athens, Cape Town, and Buenos Aires. Eight fires had also been set at sports facilities in protest of the Olympics bid. 97082501

August 25, 1997. *Mexico.* A Mexican drug trafficking organization issued a death threat against U.S. White House drug policy director Barry R. McCaffrey during his tour of the southwestern border area. A caller said he had been contracted to carry out the assassination. The caller knew the timing and itinerary of McCaffrey's travels, which had not been made public. He said the attack would occur between Ciudad Juarez and Tijuana. He said a missile would be used.

August 27, 1997. *Kuwait.* An anonymous caller warned of an attack on an "American location" in Kuwait. 97082701

August 28, 1997. *Algeria.* During a nighttime attack, Islamic terrorists were believed to be responsible for killing 514 civilians in three villages in Blida Province in the single bloodiest attack of the five-year insurgency. The terrorists decapitated many victims and placed their heads on walls and doorsteps in Sidi Rais. One attacker cut the throat of a two-year-old boy, then burned his body in a bread oven. An infant's throat was cut. A mentally retarded man was burned alive. Fetuses were ripped from the wombs of two pregnant women. Survivors said their attackers were "Afghans," which refers to Islamic mujahidin who battled the Soviet occupation of Afghanistan in the 1980s. Soldiers did not respond during the bloodshed.

September 4, 1997. *Cuba.* Bombs went off within 20 minutes of each other in the lobbies of three ocean hotels in Havana, killing an Italian visitor and spewing glass. The bombs went off at the Copacabana, Chateau, and Triton Hotels in the Playa district of Havana. Fabio di Celmo, an Italian-Canadian, was hit in the throat by rubble at the Copacabana. He died on the spot. No other casualties were reported in the morning bombings. Three bombs had gone off between July and August in other Havana hotels; the Cuban government had blamed Cuban exiles staging the attacks from U.S. soil. Alpha 66, a Miami-based Cuban exile organization, denied responsibility, but said it was in contact with clandestine cells in Cuba that were involved in the bombings.

On September 10, Havana announced that it had arrested a Salvadoran, Raul Ernesto Cruz Leon, 26, who confessed to taking $4,500 for each of the four recent bombings. Havana said the bombings were "carried out from Miami . . . by a subversive structure under the direction of the Cuban American National Foundation." The exile group denied the claim. The *Miami Herald* reported on September 12 that Cruz Leon may have been in contact with Luis Posada Carriles (alias Bambi), a Cuban exile bomber. Cruz had told relatives that he was going to Havana on vacation, claiming that his trips were set up by Orlando Ramos Blanco, a Cuban who ran the San Cristobal Travel Agency in San Salvador. Cruz left El Salvador for Costa Rica on July 9 and returned from Los Angeles on July 14. Havana said he had confessed to two bombings on July 12, as well as the September 4 bombings. Cruz had worked for a Salvadoran man in the entertainment business. He dropped out of a military high school after six to eight months. 97090401-03

September 4, 1997. *Israel.* At 3:00 P.M., three Palestinians set off bombs in Ben Yehuda Street in Jerusalem, killing themselves, 5 others, and wounding 190 shoppers, including many foreign visitors, among them Americans. Greg Salzman, a chiropractor from East Brunswick, New Jersey, had just moved to Israel and was dining with friends at the Village Green vegetarian café when the bombs went off. He received minor shrapnel wounds and burns. Abie Mendelsohn, 17, a religious student from Los Angeles, was also wounded. Hamas took credit, warning that it would carry out more bombings unless Israel released Hamas prisoners by 9:00 P.M. on September 14.

The next day, a reprisal commando raid by the Israelis went awry, and 11 Israelis were killed in fighting with Lebanese army troops and Shi'ite Muslim gunmen in Lebanon.

On September 23, Israel announced that four Palestinians living in the West Bank village of Asirah Shamaliya, north of Nablus, were responsible for this attack and an attack on July 30. The government identified the four men as Mouaia Jarara, 23, Bashar Zoualha, 24, Touwafik Yassin, 25, and Yosef Shouli, 23.

As of January 4, 1998, Daniella Birman, 13, was still horribly injured with second-degree burns on half of her body.

On January 12, Palestinian intelligence uncovered 1,500 pounds of explosive materials in Nablus. Two days later, Hamas members Jasser Samara and Nassim Abu Rous were arrested. Fol-

lowing a three-hour trial, they were sentenced to 15 years in prison at hard labor for building the bombs and recruiting the 5 suicide bombers who killed 26 people on July 30 and September 4. 97090404

September 5, 1997. *Algeria.* At 10:00 P.M., 50 Muslim fundamentalists armed with hatchets attacked the secluded Beni Messous neighborhood, 12 miles west of Algiers, slitting the throats of families and killing at least 80 in a three-hour attack.

At Blida, 30 miles south of Algiers, a bomb exploded under a seat on a bus, killing 4 and wounding 27.

September 9, 1997. *United Kingdom.* Sinn Fein, the political arm of the Irish Republican Army, announced it was renouncing violence and committing itself to "exclusively peaceful means" to end the conflict.

September 9, 1997. *Philippines.* Suspected members of the Abu Sayyaf Group kidnapped a German business executive in Zamboanga City and released him on December 26. 97090901

September 9, 1997. *Sri Lanka.* The Liberation Tigers of Tamil Eelam (LTTE) attacked a merchant ship with rocket-propelled grenades, causing major damage to the ship. Approximately 20 people were killed, wounded, or reported missing, including 5 Chinese crew. The ship was owned by the China Ocean Shipping Company, registered in Panama, and chartered by the U.S. firm ACI Chemicals. 97090902

September 12, 1997. *Lebanon.* Hadi Nasrallah, 18, the son of Hizballah Secretary General Said Hassan Nasrallah, was killed in a gun battle with Israeli troops in the Jabal al-Rafei area of southern Lebanon. The Hizballah leader declared his son's death a victory over Israel.

September 15, 1997. *Egypt.* A military court sentenced four Muslim extremists to death and

another eight to life in prison. The court convicted 50 others.

September 16, 1997. *Georgia.* Three men carrying
AK-47s kidnapped an Egyptian and a Jordanian
UNOMIG military observer and their local interpreter near the Georgian side of the Injuri River.
The kidnappers released the Egyptian and
demanded $50,000 for the Jordanian. The kid-
nappers released the Jordanian after the UN paid
them $7,000. 97091601

September 17, 1997. *Pakistan.* Three gunmen on
a motorcycle fired on a van carrying five Iranian
air force technicians to an air base near Rawalpindi, killing all five and their Pakistani driver. The
van was stopped at a red light in the center of
town. 97091701

September 18, 1997. *Egypt.* Five Islamic gunmen
shouting "God is great" opened fire on and threw
firebombs at a busload of tourists in front of the
Egyptian Museum at Tahrir Square in Cairo,
killing 10, including 6 Germans, and wounding
12 others. Some tourists escaped by breaking windows or jumping from the rear exit. Three attackers were arrested after a gunfight with authorities.
No group claimed credit. The Interior Ministry
said the leader of the gunmen was Saber Mohammed Farahat Abu Ele, an escaped mental patient.
He had been held in a psychiatric hospital since he
shot three foreigners in a Cairo hotel's coffee shop
in 1993. His brother was also arrested. A third
gunman was in critical condition with a gunshot
wound to the head.

The group of 33 German tourists had earlier
visited the Pyramids.

The government announced on October 13
that the duo accused of the attack would stand trial
in a military court. The announcement came the
same day that bands of gunmen killed 11 policemen in rural Minya Province at several roadblocks
set up by the terrorists. The gunmen pulled passengers out of cars if they were carrying police
documents, tied their hands, read a statement

accusing them of crimes against rebels and their
families, and then shot them.

On October 30, Abu Ele and his brother were
sentenced to death for killing nine German
tourists and their Egyptian driver. The Egyptian
judge called the attack the work of "Satan reincar-
nated." Abu Ele yelled, "Jews, Jews! The army of
Mohammed is coming back!" He called the sentence a Day of Feasts, as he believed he would die
as a martyr for Islam and go straight to Heaven.
97091801

September 19, 1997. *Bosnia.* A car bomb exploded at 11:30 P.M. at an apartment complex in
Mostar, injuring 50. No one claimed responsibility for planting the 70 pounds of explosives in the
Volkswagen Golf that was parked at the complex,
which housed senior Croatian military and police
officials and their families. The explosion took out
the first two floors of the building and shattered
windows 100 yards away.

September 22, 1997. *Jordan.* Gunmen fired on
two Israeli Embassy security guards as they drove
through the Deir Ghbar neighborhood on their
way to work in Amman. They returned fire, injuring one of the terrorists. Yaakov Levine and
Amikam Hadar were slightly wounded. King
Hussein visited them in the hospital. Several people were arrested. The Jordanian Resistance
claimed credit and demanded the release of a Jordanian soldier serving a life sentence for killing
seven Israeli schoolchildren. The group threatened
further attacks if Israeli diplomats did not leave
within a month. 97092201

September 23, 1997. *Algeria.* Terrorists killed 214
Algerian civilians in an attack at Bentalha in which
the terrorists slit throats, disemboweled pregnant
women, beheaded children, shot the survivors and
burned their bodies, plundered and torched
homes, and kidnapped young women. They used
homemade bombs to open doors. Islamic militants were blamed. The gunfire could be heard
two miles away in Baraki, where hundreds of sol-

diers occupy a fortified compound. The soldiers did not leave the compound. Some observers said the government was not responding to these attacks in an effort to discredit the militants.

September 24, 1997. *Algeria.* Madani Mezerag, the commander of the Islamic Salvation Army, said in Paris that his followers would suspend military operations on October 1. The group is the military wing of the Islamic Salvation Front. Mezerag denounced recent terrorist actions by the Armed Islamic Group.

September 25, 1997. *Jordan.* Israeli Mossad agents failed to assassinate Khaled Meshal, 41, a Jordanian citizen who served as political chief of Hamas, in Amman. The two agents were captured on an Amman street after trying to jab poison into Meshal's left ear as he entered his office. Meshal was treated with a medicine obtained after King Hussein asked American assistance in dealing with the nerve toxin that generated uncontrollable vomiting and respiratory arrest. Meshal's bodyguards ran down the duo—one was dark and muscular and the other bearded and blond—who had fled in a Hyundai and on foot. Mohammed Abu Saif and members of a crowd subdued the attackers in a bloody fistfight about a mile away from the attack. The arrested agents were thrown into a taxi and brought to a police station, where they identified themselves as Shawn Kendall, 28, and Barry Beads, 36, but refused the aid of the Canadian Embassy. Police later determined that their Canadian passports had been stolen and doctored. Another man, Guy Eris, 30, who may have been involved in the attack, was believed to have fled the country. On October 2, Canada recalled its ambassador to Israel in protest.

The real Kendall, of Toronto, works for a Jerusalem charity.

The two agents were released into Israeli custody after the Israelis released Hamas's founder and spiritual leader, Sheik Ahmed Yassin, 61, a quadriplegic who was nearly blind, and pledged to free 40 to 50 other Palestinian and Jordanian activists on October 1. Yassin had served eight years of a life sentence for ordering the killings of Palestinian collaborators with Israel. Yassin issued a call for moderation, saying he was ready to coexist with Israelis as long as Palestinian rights are respected.

On October 10, Israel apologized to Canada for using forged Canadian passports in the attack.

By November 4, two Israeli investigating committees had determined that Prime Minister Benjamin Netanyahu had played a direct role in selecting the target. However, on February 16, 1998, an official government inquiry concluded that Netanyahu bore no personal responsibility. It concluded that Danny Yatom, the head of Mossad, and other senior agents bungled the affair. It did not recommend that anyone be fired. Yatom resigned on February 24.

September 27, 1997. *Algeria.* Armed men attacked the Ain Adden School in Sfisef, 260 miles south of Algiers, shooting or hacking to death 11 female teachers and 1 male instructor. Authorities blamed the Armed Islamic Group.

September 30, 1997. *Algeria.* Fifteen men armed with knives and guns slit throats and decapitated 52 members of an extended family in Cerbil, 30 miles south of Algiers. Among the victims was an infant. The bodies of most of the victims were mutilated and then burned. The group then kidnapped five women. North of Algiers, another group killed 32 people in two other attacks. Sword-wielding men killed four construction workers. Others disguised as policemen slit the throats of a couple and their two daughters. The Armed Islamic Group was suspected.

October 1, 1997. *India.* Three bombs exploded on a passenger train as it approached Ghaziabad in Uttar Pradesh, killing 2 and injuring 38, including 1 Japanese and 4 Australian passengers. 97100101

October 3, 1997. *Algeria.* Islamic terrorists were blamed for firing rockets on Blida, killing 10 and injuring 20. Terrorists killed 20 members of a nighttime wedding party at Kharrouba near Oran,

220 miles west of Algiers. The victims were aged 15 to 20. Another 30 people were injured. The Armed Islamic Group was suspected.

October 4, 1997. *Algeria.* In the morning, men armed with guns and sharp weapons killed 75 people, including 34 children, in two attacks. In Mahelma, outside Blida, terrorists slit the throats of or beheaded 26 adults and 12 children in a pre-dawn attack. They then burned the bodies and homes. The attackers injured dozens and kidnapped two young women. They also stole food, money, and jewelry. Meanwhile, other armed men killed 37 people, including 22 children, in a dawn raid at Ouled Benaissa, 30 miles south of Blida. The Armed Islamic Group was suspected.

October 4, 1997. *Iraq.* Four men fired guns and threw four hand grenades at a UN building housing the World Health Organization's headquarters during the night, destroying one vehicle and damaging two others. One attacker was wounded and captured by the Iraqi army. The others escaped. The Baghdad building housed an office for UN officials who monitor the oil-for-food program. Iraq blamed Iran. The Iraqi News Agency quoted the detainee as saying that he was sent by Iran's intelligence service. It claimed he was an Iraqi of Iranian origin who was deported in 1983. 97100401

October 5, 1997. *Algeria.* Gunmen attacked a school bus in Bouinan, near Blida, 30 miles south of Algiers, killing 16 children and their driver. The bus crashed and rolled onto its side when the driver tried to run the terrorists' roadblock. Some of the children died of gunshot wounds to the head. The Armed Islamic Group is active in the area.

October 8, 1997. *United States.* The State Department designated 30 groups as foreign terrorist organizations by adding 18 groups to a list of 12 issued by President Clinton in 1995 via executive order. Under the 1996 Antiterrorism Act, providing funds or other material support to these groups is illegal and visas for members must be denied.

American financial institutions are required to block funds that belong to these groups. Missing from the list was the Irish Republican Army, which had declared an "unequivocal ceasefire" to permit its political wing, Sinn Fein, to conduct peace talks. The State Department's list included:

- Abu Nidal Group (Palestine)
- Abu Sayyaf Group (Philippines)
- Armed Islamic Group (Algeria)
- Aum Shin Rikyo (Japan)
- Basque Nation and Liberty (ETA; Spain)
- Democratic Front for the Liberation of Palestine–Hawatmeh Faction (Palestine)
- Al-Gamaat al-Islamiya (Egypt)
- Hamas (Islamic Resistance Movement; Palestine)
- Harakat ull-Ansar (Supporters Movement; Pakistan)
- Hizballah (Party of God; Palestine)
- Islamic Group (Iran)
- Japanese Red Army (Japan)
- Kach (Israel)
- Kahane Lives (Israel)
- Khmer Rouge (Cambodia)
- Kurdistan Workers Party (Turkey)
- Liberation Tigers of Tamil Eelam (LTTE; Sri Lanka)
- Manuel Rodriguez Patriotic Front Dissidents (Chile)
- Mujahedeen e-Khalq (Holy Warriors of the World; Iran)
- National Liberation Army (Colombia)
- Palestine Islamic Holy War-Shaqaqi Faction (Palestine)
- Palestine Liberation Front-Abu Abbas Faction (Palestine)
- Popular Front for the Liberation of Palestine (Palestine)
- Popular Front for the Liberation of Palestine–General Command (Palestine)
- Revolutionary Armed Forces of Colombia (Colombia)
- Revolutionary Organization of November 17 (Greece)

- Revolutionary People's Liberation Party–Front (Turkey)
- Revolutionary People's Struggle (Greece)
- Shining Path (Peru)
- Tupac Amaru Revolutionary Movement (Peru)

October 13, 1997. *Spain.* Police approached a suspicious van parked near the new Guggenheim Museum in Bilbao. Three Basque separatists posing as gardeners had been unloading flowerpots from the van for a giant plant sculpture in front of the museum. The guerrillas opened fire, wounding officer Jose Maria Agirre, 35, in the chest. He died of his injuries the next day. Police arrested three suspects later that day and seized explosives at a farmhouse. They also found 12 grenades in the flowerpots. Spain's king and queen were scheduled to open the museum on October 18. 97101301

October 13, 1997. *Turkey.* Nine Kurdistan Workers Party (PKK) terrorists kidnapped two Bulgarian engineers and one Turkish engineer from a coal mine. The Turk was found dead. The Bulgarians were freed unharmed on October 16. 97101302

October 14, 1997. *Philippines.* Two Arab gunmen attacked Philippine Army Camp Siongco with grenades and automatic rifles, killing three soldiers and wounding ten people, including five civilians who were enlisting in the army. Authorities returned fire, killing the two terrorists after a 30-minute battle. The camp is three miles from Cotabato on Mindanao Island. One terrorist carried an Egyptian passport; the other carried a Saudi passport. 97101401

October 15, 1997. *Sri Lanka.* Liberation Tigers of Tamil Eelam (LTTE) rebels were blamed for setting off a truck bomb outside a luxury hotel, seizing a newspaper office, and engaging in gun battles that killed 18 and injured 110 others, including 7 Americans and 33 other foreigners. The LTTE denied involvement. The truck bomb damaged two hotels and the World Trade Center, which opened on October 12. Two other bombs went off before the attackers fled toward Lake House, headquarters of the government-run newspapers. Soldiers killed three of the attackers before they could enter the building. The other 3 terrorists ran inside, where 25 people were working. The soldiers fired grenades into the building, then stormed it, killing one gunman. The other two swallowed poison capsules, a standard LTTE modus operandi. A soldier died in the gun battle, in which all 25 civilians were rescued. 97101501

October 15, 1997. *Yemen.* Bani Dabian tribesmen kidnapped one British businessman and two Yemenis near Sumayr. They demanded financial aid for their tribes and completion of electricity and water projects in the region. The hostages were freed on October 30. 97101502

October 15, 1997. *Yemen.* Tribesmen kidnapped four French tourists in Saada, demanding the return of a car they claimed the government confiscated because of lack of proper documentation. Authorities freed the hostages the next day. 97101503

October 15, 1997. *Egypt.* A military court sentenced to death 3 Muslim militants and ordered 53 others imprisoned for plotting assassinations, bombings, and other subversive acts. The terrorists were members of Jihad. Another 31 people were acquitted. Among those sentenced to death was Adel Ali Bayoumi Sudani, 41, the head of the group's military wing. The other two sentenced to death remained at large. Two men were sentenced to life in prison; the others received 2 to 15 years of hard labor.

October 16, 1997. *Tajikistan.* More than 70 gunmen attacked the headquarters of the Presidential Guards in Dushanbe, killing 14 servicemen. Five soldiers were shot to death in their sleep. More than 20 were wounded in the ensuing gun battle, in which some attackers were killed.

October 18, 1997. *Sri Lanka.* The navy of the Liberation Tigers of Tamil Eelam (LTTE) and the Sri

Lankan navy battled for five hours off the country's east coast near Pulmoddai, killing at least 100 terrorists and 2 navy sailors and wounding 3 other sailors. Seven rebel boats were sunk in the evening battle. The battle began when the guerrillas attacked a government Dvora fast-attack craft on patrol. The Dvora was hit by gunfire, then sank after being rammed by two LTTE suicide boats. The crew of 14 jumped overboard; 5 were rescued.

October 20, 1997. *Lebanon.* Two gunmen shot to death Omar Banna, 39, a grandnephew of Abu Nidal and wounded Omar's brother, Nasseredine, 36, as their car was stopped at a Beirut traffic light. Nasserdine's seven-year-old daughter was in the car, but was unharmed. Authorities blamed Palestinian factional violence. 97102001

October 22, 1997. *Egypt.* The government hanged four terrorists found guilty in January of killing policemen and attacking tourist buses in 1993 and 1994. Yasser Fawaz, Irfan Kholi, Yasser Suleiman, and Ali Mohammed Farahat were among 19 members of the outlawed Islamic Group who were tried for several offenses, including the murder of a police colonel. Farahat was convicted for grenade attacks on two Cairo movie theaters in which a police guard died and six civilians were wounded and for an attack on a tourist bus that wounded eight Austrians and eight Egyptians. The four were convicted of plotting to kill senior state officials and tourists.

October 22, 1997. *Yemen.* Al-Hadda tribesmen kidnapped two Russian doctors and their wives in Zamar to pressure the government into handing down death sentences for four residents who raped a boy from their tribe. They released the four hostages on November 10. 97102201

October 23, 1997. *Colombia.* The National Liberation Army (ELN) kidnapped a Colombian human rights official and a Chilean and a Guatemalan who worked for the Organization of American States (OAS). The hostages were taken at a roadblock. The ELN wanted "to show the

international community that the elections in Colombia are a farce." The ELN said it would release the hostages after the election and that a nationwide "armed strike" would aim at preventing the elections from being held. On October 28, the rebels demanded that the army lift its checkpoints on the highway between Bogota and Medellin, clear La Pinuela base, clear Granada municipality, and halt operations for eight consecutive days from the time of the release. On November 1, masked ELN rebels dressed in Colombian national police uniforms turned the hostages over to representatives of the Red Cross, the Catholic Church, national and local peace commission members, and other witnesses in front of a parish church in Santa Ana. The hostages had been transferred by helicopter to the village. 97102301

October 23, 1997. *Russia.* Chechen rebels kidnapped two Hungarian aid workers in Chechnya. Istvan Olah and Gabor Dunajszky worked for the Hungarian Ecumenical Charity. They were distributing food relief in Grozny when gunmen kidnapped them from their office, blindfolded them, and took them to a house possibly on the outskirts on the city. They were held for 48 hours in a pit in which they could neither stand nor lie down. They were barely fed; each lost 30 pounds. They were chained in a dark room.

Hungarian, Russian, and Chechen authorities, other governments, and the ecumenical charity worked jointly for their release.

On July 25, 1998, Olah and Dunajszky were released. They told the media that they had been held in inhuman conditions during the first five months of their captivity. They said they did not know why they had been freed. Dozens of hostages, including several foreigners, remained in rebel hands. A charity spokesman said no ransom was paid. 97102302

October 27, 1997. *Lebanon.* Dynamite was thrown over a wall at the American University of Beirut, wrecking two cars, but causing no injuries. Observers noted that the bombing could have been a warning to John Waterbury, the school's new president and the first to live in Beirut since the 1984 assassination of then-President Malcolm Kerr. 97102701

October 27, 1997. *Philippines.* Suspected Moro Islamic Liberation Front (MILF) rebels kidnapped an Irish Roman Catholic priest in Marawi, demanding $192,000 and the release of livelihood funds promised under the amnesty program. The priest was released on November 4. 97102701

October 27, 1997. *Puerto Rico.* U.S. authorities stopped a boat off the west coast of Puerto Rico and arrested four Cuban exiles apparently planning to assassinate Cuban President Fidel Castro. The agents seized two rifles, ammunition, and other military supplies. One of the men said the weapons would be used to kill Castro during an Ibero-American summit in November on Isla Margarita off the coast of Venezuela. One of the weapons was a high-powered rifle belonging to Francisco "Pepe" Hernandez, president of the Cuban American National Foundation. The boat was owned by Jose Antonio Llama, a member of the group's executive board. The two were summoned to testify before the U.S. grand jury in San Juan. They were charged with violations of the U.S. Neutrality Act, illegal weapons possession, and attempting to bring those weapons into U.S. territory. On August 26, 1998, a federal grand jury in San Juan, Puerto Rico, indicted Llama and six other Cuban Americans on charges of conspiring to assassinate Castro. The indictment stated that the seven, with others, began plotting to kill Castro in 1995. They obtained two .50-caliber semiautomatic rifles, a 46-foot yacht modified for long-distance cruising, night-vision goggles, and satellite positioning devices. The indictment said Llama obtained one of the sniper rifles and purchased the yacht. He accompanied his colleagues to Isla Margarita on October 17, 1997, where they identified a hill-point stakeout that overlooked the airport. He noted its location and an offshore spot using satellite location devices. The team intended to use the hand-held positioning devices to land

at night in a dinghy and fire at Castro. Llama was represented by attorney Jose Quinon.

On December 8, 1999, the jury found the five Cuban exiles not guilty of plotting to assassinate Castro. This was the first time the U.S. Department of Justice had charged anyone with plotting to kill Castro. The U.S. District Court jury deliberated for eight hours over two days before declaring not guilty on all charges Angel Alfonso, 59, Angel Hernandez Rojo, 62, Francisco Secundino Cordova, 51, Jose Rodriguez Sosa, 59, and Jose Antonio Llama, 67. Charges against another defendant were dismissed the previous week; a seventh defendant was too ill to stand trial. 98102702

October 29, 1997. *Yemen.* Gunmen fired on the Qatari ambassador's car in Sanaa. He escaped the attack. Militants opposed to the mid-November Middle East and North Africa economic conference in Qatar may have been responsible. 97102901

October 30, 1997. *Northern Ireland.* The Continuity Army Council (alias Continuity IRA), a dissident group of IRA guerrillas, set off a bomb on the eve of a visit by American First Lady Hillary Rodham Clinton.

October 30, 1997. *Yemen.* Steve Carpenter, the American director of a Yemeni company that subcontracts to the U.S.-based Hunt Oil, was abducted by Al-Sha'if tribesmen near Sanaa. He was held at a desert site 100 miles to the north. The tribesmen demanded the release of two fellow tribesmen who were arrested on smuggling charges and the implementation of several public works projects they claimed the government had promised them. Carpenter was freed unharmed on November 27. Authorities could not determine the reasons for his release. 97103001

October 31, 1997. *Uganda.* Two hand grenades were thrown into a backpackers' hotel in Kampala, injuring a South Africa, a Briton, and another foreign tourist. 97103101

November 1997. *France.* Police arrested Yacine Anthamnia, a member of the Hassan Hattab network, which is linked to the Algerian Armed Islamic Group (GIA). Anthamnia carried several Belgian passports and visa stamps. About 30, he was a rival of Antar Zouabri, the GIA chief operating in the Kabylia Mountains east of Algiers. Hattab wanted to extend the Algerian conflict to European targets. 97119901

November 7, 1997. *India.* A bomb exploded at Raishyabari as two truckloads of Border Security Forces soldiers traveled near the Bangladesh border, killing 20, including 10 villagers, and wounding 2 other border guards. Authorities believed the attackers used an antitank landmine.

November 9, 1997. *United States.* A small bomb broke windows in Wall Street offices right when authorities were starting a terrorist safety drill. The bomb caused minor property damage, but no injuries at the 222 Broadway offices of the Swiss Bank Corporation and Merrill Lynch Swiss Security Bank. 97110901

November 9, 1997. *Syria.* An anonymous caller warned the U.S. Embassy of attacks if the United States moved against Iraq in its showdown with the UN over inclusion of American inspectors at Iraqi weapons sites. 97110902

November 11, 1997. *Colombia.* Gunmen kidnapped a German industrialist in Cundinamarca. No one claimed credit. 97111101

November 11, 1997. *Pakistan.* Mir Aimal Kasi was convicted in the January 23, 1995, murder of two CIA staffers. The U.S. State Department issued a warning to Americans in Pakistan and elsewhere in the region to be on alert.

November 12, 1997. *Pakistan.* Four American auditors for Union Texas Petroleum Holdings and their local driver were shot to death on a bridge by Kalashnikov automatic weapons fired from a red car that had tailed them in Karachi on N. T. Khan Street. The gunmen forced the Nissan station wagon off the road, then walked up to it and fired long enough to ensure that everyone in the Americans' car had died. The gunmen later abandoned their Toyota Corolla a half mile away near the city's central post office and escaped. (Other witnesses said it was a white Honda.) Police determined that the license plate was registered in Islamabad to a different vehicle. No arrests were announced. Witnesses disagreed as to whether there were two, three, or four gunmen. Police were searching for clean-shaven men in their mid-20s. They had hijacked the car from a textile factory owner in Karachi. The previously unknown Islami Inqilabi Council (Islamic Revolutionary Council) telephoned the U.S. Consulate in Karachi to take credit. The Aimal Secret Committee and Aimal Khufia Action Committee also claimed credit in a letter to Pakistani newspapers.

The victims were senior auditor Ephraim Ebgu, 42, manager of audit projects; Joel Brian Enlow, 40, audit manager; Larry W. Jennings, 49; and senior audit supervisor Tracy Lane Ritchie, 41; all of Houston. They had arrived in Pakistan less than three weeks earlier and were staying at the Pearl-Continental Hotel. Anwar Murza (or Mirza), 51, was a Union Texas driver from Karachi. They were driving from their Sheraton hotel to their office at 8:10 A.M.

Observers noted that a day earlier, a jury in Fairfax, Virginia, had announced a guilty verdict against Mir Aimal Kasi, killer of two CIA employees in January 25, 1993. Kasi had told relatives that he expected that sympathizers would retaliate. Police speculated that the Harakat ul-Ansar terrorist group had harbored Kasi while he was at large and conducted the attack. The previously unknown Aimal Secret Committee claimed credit and warned that more Americans would die in Pakistan if Kasi was sentenced to death. The letter, signed by Ajab Gul, said, "If Aimal Kasi is martyred then we will not spare any American Jes [*sic*] on Pakistani soil and we will destroy the American Embassy in Pakistan. Clinton will die" if Kasi remains in prison.

The FBI sent agents to investigate. UPI reported on December 18 that U.S. and Pakistani investigators were looking at a possible Iranian link. Police arrested more than a dozen Iranians; as of December 18, six were still being held as possible participants in a carjacking ring that could have provided the getaway car.

On June 5, 1998, the United States offered a $2 million reward for information leading to the arrest and conviction of the killers.

On February 28, 1999, Pakistani police announced the arrest of two men who had confessed to involvement in the killing. Saleem Fanja and Saeed Bharam said they were among several people involved.

On August 21, 1999, a special antiterrorist court imposed the death sentence on Ahmed Saeed, 29, and Mohammed Salim, 39, for the killings. They were also sentenced to seven years in prison for possession of illegal weapons. They had been charged in January 1999 with the murders. They were members of the Muttahida Qami Movement, which represents Urdu-speaking people who migrated from India in 1947. They appealed the verdict. 97111201

November 12, 1997. *Colombia.* The Revolutionary Armed Forces of Colombia (FARC) kidnapped a Mexican and a Colombian engineer from a hydroelectric plant and stole dynamite and two getaway vehicles. 97111202

November 17, 1997. *Egypt.* At 9:30 A.M., six Muslim militants dressed in black sweaters similar to the winter uniforms of the Egyptian police got out of a car and fired on foreign tourists at Luxor, killing 58 foreigners and 4 Egyptians (including 2 policemen). The terrorists were armed with six machine guns, two handguns, and police-issue ammunition. They also had two bags of homemade explosives. Witnesses differed as to whether they arrived by taxi or on foot. Some wore red bandannas with black lettering that said, "We will fight until death."

Ahmed Ghassan, 40, a police guard at the ticket booth, said he stopped the six men and asked for their tickets. The last man pulled out a gun and said, "This is the ticket." He then shot Ghassan in the elbow and leg. Ghassan said several other guards were also shot and fell on top of him. The terrorists later slit the throats of wounded tourists.

An early tally of the dead included 14 Japanese, 34 Swiss, 3 Egyptians, 5 Germans, and 6 Britons, and included a child, a Bulgarian, a Colombian, and several French tourists. (There was some confusion about nationalities and duplication in the count.) Eight of the 24 wounded were in critical condition. A doctor removed a bloody Islamic Group pamphlet from a wound in the abdomen of a dead Japanese man. A Japanese woman was missing an ear. A European man's nose had been cut off. Robyn Du Plessis, 22, of Durban, South Africa, said the tourists hid in the tombs for three hours.

After an hour-long gun battle in which one terrorist died, the five surviving terrorists hijacked the tour bus of Hagag Nahas, 36, who had dropped off 30 Swiss visitors an hour earlier. The terrorists forced him to drive "to another place so they could shoot more people." He drove for an hour before stopping near the access road to the Valley of the Queens, half a mile away from the temple. A terrorist clubbed Nahas in the chest with the butt of his rifle. Police fired on the gunmen, killing a terrorist. The rest fled into nearby mountains. Police said they had caught up to the bus and killed all five gunmen, who had fired into the crowds along the plaza facing the 3,400-year-old Hatshepsut temple.

One of the dead terrorists was identified as Midhat Abd-al-Rahman, who had left Egypt in 1993 for Pakistan and Sudan, where he received military training and was involved with Islamic Group leaders.

In a November 20 fax to foreign news agencies, the Islamic Group said it would quit its attacks if its leader was released from a U.S. jail, several of its members were released from prison, and the government severed relations with Israel. One leaflet said the attack was a gesture to Mustafa Hamza, an exiled mastermind of the June 1995 assassination attempt against Egyptian President Hosni Mubarak.

The Islamic Group said it had not intended to kill the victims, but had planned to take them hostage to force the United States to release its leader, Sheik Omar Abdel Rahman, from a New York federal prison. However, witnesses said there was no evidence that the terrorists attempted to take hostages. Rather, they chased the tourists, made them get down on their knees, and systematically shot them. Rosemarie Dousse, who was wounded in the arm and leg, told Swiss television, "A man who was very heavy fell on top of me, and the lady behind me also covered me. And then they started again shooting those who were still alive, in the head." Other Swiss survivors said the gunmen beat children with guns, raped and mutilated women, and danced for joy as they slaughtered the tourists.

Mubarak deemed Luxor security "a joke" and fired his Interior Minister, the Luxor police chief, and several other security officials. On November 22, new Interior Minister Major General Habib Adli told Parliament that the armed forces would join police in protecting tourist sites. Mubarak ruled out a dialogue with the Islamic Group.

On November 24, Tala'eh Al-Fath (the Vanguards of Conquest) told *USA Today* that orders "have already been given for attacks against Americans and Zionists not only in Egypt but elsewhere." They claimed to be the successors of the Jihad group that assassinated Egyptian President Anwar Sadat in 1981. Meanwhile, Sheik Salah Hashem, 44, of the Islamic Group (al-Gamaat al-Islamiya), said the government should be prepared for more attacks.

Within a week, tourism in Egypt had halved and had dropped 90 percent in Luxor.

On June 28, 1998, in the first trial of its kind, a police disciplinary tribunal fired former Luxor police chief Major General Medhat Shanawani and his deputy, Major General Abul-Atta Youssef Abul-Atta, for ignoring security warnings that the sites in Luxor could be targeted. Their police pensions were also reduced.

In February 1999, Uruguay arrested Said Hazan Mohammed while he was trying to enter the country from Brazil with a fake Malaysian passport. On February 24, it appeared that Uruguay would extradite him to Egypt to stand trial for the Luxor attack. 97111701

November 18, 1997. *Tajikistan.* Karine Mane, a Frenchwoman who worked at the UN High Commissioner for Refugees office, was kidnapped at her Dushanbe apartment along with a male companion. Authorities believed the abduction was ordered by separatist leader Rezvon Sadirov to obtain the freedom of his brother, Bakhrom, who was awaiting trial for another kidnapping. A grenade exploded during a government rescue operation; it was unclear whether the government forces or the terrorists had thrown it. The male hostage was released on November 29. Mane and 5 kidnappers (some reports said 20) died in the failed rescue attempt on November 30. On December 2, Tajik forces killed Rezvon Sadirov. 97111801

November 18, 1997. *Philippines.* Two suspected former members of the Moro National Liberation Front (MNLF) kidnapped a Belgian Roman Catholic priest in Ozamis as he returned home from a farewell party for the Irish priest who had been kidnapped ten days earlier. The Belgian priest was released on November 19. 97111802

November 19, 1997. *Taiwan.* Chen Chin-hsing, who was wanted by police in an April kidnapping and murder of a popular entertainer's teenage daughter and the murder of a plastic surgeon and two nurses, surrendered to police after taking hostage the family of South African defense attaché E. G. M. Alexander. He released Anne Alexander, the attaché's wife, and then was driven by a police motorcade to an undisclosed location. 97111901

November 19, 1997. *India.* A remotely detonated car bomb exploded outside the D. Rama Naidu film studio in Hyderabad during a gathering of actors, fans, and journalists for the filming of a movie. The bomb killed 23 and injured 20 others, including actor Mohan Babu. No one claimed credit. Police suspected rivals of Paritala Ravi, a former People's War Group Maoist separatist guerrilla leader and producer. Ravi was injured in the attack.

November 20, 1997. *Israel.* Shortly after midnight, an unidentified gunman fired an assault rifle from close range at two Jewish religious students in Jerusalem's Old City. Gabriel Hirshberg, 26, Ateret Cohanim Yeshiva student and Hungarian immigrant, was killed in a narrow alley near Damascus Gate. His Israeli colleague was injured. 97112001

November 21, 1997. *Somalia.* Some 20 Wasangeli subclan gunmen kidnapped five aid workers from the UN and the European Union in Elayo village in the self-proclaimed Republic of Somaliland in northern Somalia. The five were an Indian, a Canadian, a Briton and two Kenyans. Two of the five were employees of the UN Children's Fund (UNICEF), one was from UN Habitat, one from the UN Office for Project Services, and one was a British citizen from the European Union. The five were kidnapped in retaliation for the seizure by the Marjeteen of a Palestinian partner of two Somali charcoal dealers. On November 23, clan elders negotiated for the hostages' release in return for the release of the Palestinian, according to a source in El Ayo, a town on the Gulf of Aden coast. The five were freed on November 24 in good health. They arrived safely at the UNICEF office in Bossasso. 97112101

November 21, 1997. *Tajikistan.* Rebels attempted to kidnap a UN aid worker. 97112102

November 22, 1997. *Israel.* A Palestinian chemistry teacher, Badran Abdo, 23, died when a bomb he was building exploded in his residence in Rafat, near Nablus.

November 22, 1997. *Algeria.* Hooded attackers killed a German-born man in his Ain el-Hajar home in Saida Province. He had lived in Algeria since 1952, had converted to Islam, and was married to an Algerian woman. 97112201

November 24, 1997. *Somalia.* Militiamen killed nine people south of Mogadishu in a dispute over farmland. They briefly took hostage two Italian aid workers and looted their offices. A driver for CARE International was wounded. 97112401

November 25, 1997. *Yemen.* Tribesmen kidnapped one U.S. citizen, two Italians, and two other Westerners near Aden to protest the eviction of a tribesman from his home. The hostages were released on November 27. 97112501

November 27, 1997. *Algeria.* Attackers disguised as policemen at roadblocks near Souhane slit the throats of 18 men, 3 women, and 4 children.

November 28, 1997. *Algeria.* Gunmen disguised as policemen tied up four construction workers, slit their throats, and set the corpses on fire near El Afroun. Seven others were wounded.

November 28, 1997. *Israel.* Israeli authorities arrested Stefan Josef Smirk, 26, at an Israeli airport. Smirk, a German Christian who converted to Islam, was charged with planning to carry out a suicide attack on behalf of Hizballah. He was in Lebanon between August and November 1997. 97112801

December 1997. *United States.* In mid-December, a Little Rock federal grand jury indicted three men from Idaho, Washington, and Oklahoma on murder, kidnapping, and conspiracy charges related to their plan to overthrow the federal government and create an Aryan People's Republic that would foster polygamy.

December 3, 1997. *Turkey.* A homemade grenade or bomb was thrown over a wall of Istanbul's Phener Patriarchate, a leading center of the Greek Orthodox faith, injuring a deacon in the shoulder. The site, seat of Ecumenical Patriarch Bartholomeos I, spiritual head of 250 million Orthodox Christians worldwide, had been the scene of grenade attacks by Turkish Muslim militants in 1994 and 1996. 97120301

December 5, 1997. *Spain.* Basque separatists were blamed for shooting a politician's bodyguard in San Sebastian, then blowing up their getaway car after their escape. Police believed this was a reprisal for convictions on December 1 of 23 leaders of the Herri Batasuna independence party. They had been sentenced to seven years in jail for collaboration with the Basque Nation and Liberty (ETA) terrorist group.

December 6, 1997. *Czech Republic.* A bomb exploded at 4:00 A.M. outside the home of Finance Minister Ivan Pilip, 34, who had called for the resignation of outgoing Prime Minister Vaclav Klaus over a funding scandal. Klaus had announced he was quitting several hours after the call for resignation.

December 6, 1997. *India.* Bombs exploded on three passenger trains, killing 11 people and injuring 58 others. Police believed the attacks were related to the destruction by Hindus of the Babri Mosque in Ayodhya on December 6, 1992.

December 8, 1997. *Egypt.* The Islamic Group announced that it would stop attacking foreign tourists as part of its drive to weaken President Hosni Mubarak's government.

December 9, 1997. *Mexico.* Ten heavily armed black-clad gunmen posing as federal police kidnapped Vincent Carrosa, the U.S. manager of Princess, one of Acapulco's leading hotels. The kidnappers took Carrosa from his car near the hotel in the morning and forced him into their truck. A passing police squad chased them, opening fire. The gunmen returned fire, fatally wounding Deputy Commander Jose Martinez Manriquez in the head and neck. Another officer, who was shot in the lungs, was in serious condition. 97120901

December 10, 1997. *Russia.* A hijacker took over a Swiss plane flying from Magadan to Moscow with 140 passengers. He threatened to set off what he claimed was a bomb if he was not paid $10 million. He rambled on about political issues. Commandos arrested the hijacker at Sheremeteyevo Airport in Moscow. 97121001

December 10, 1997. *Turkey.* Authorities defused a powerful time bomb found inside a gas cylinder at a Turkish facility adjoining the international ATAS oil refinery in Mersin. The refinery was a joint venture of Royal Dutch/Shell group, Mobil Oil, British Petroleum, and Turkey's Marmara Petrol. 97120102

December 11, 1997. *Rwanda.* Hundreds of former Rwanda Army soldiers and Hutu militiamen killed 327 Congolese Tutsi refugees and wounded another 227 in the Mudende refugee camp, 80 miles northwest of Kigali. Some 90 percent of the refugees were killed with machetes and hoes in the 10:00 P.M. raid; others were shot. Other raiders freed 900 Hutu prisoners arrested for the 1994 genocide. Still others attacked Cyangugu, a town across the river from Bukavu, Congo. 97121101

December 11, 1997. *Iran.* In a meeting in Tehran, the 55 members of the Organization of the Islamic Conference summit condemned terrorism committed in the name of Islam. The joint declaration said, "The killing of innocent people is forbidden in Islam," and urged states to deny asylum to terrorists. However, it also distinguished "terrorism from the struggle of peoples against colonial or alien domination or foreign occupation and their right of self-determination."

December 11, 1997. *United Kingdom.* Sinn Fein leader Gerry Adams joined British Prime Minister Tony Blair for talks at 10 Downing Street in London, the first visit of an Irish Republican leader to the residence since Michael Collins met David Lloyd George in 1921. The 1921 visit led to the partition of Ireland into the 6 counties of Northern Ireland and the 26 counties of the Irish Republic.

December 13, 1997. *Nigeria.* Employees and villagers kidnapped one U.S. citizen, one Australian, two British oil workers, and at least nine Nigerian staff members of Western Geophysical, a U.S.-owned oil exploration company off the coast of Nigeria. The victims were released on December 17 and 18. 97121301

December 17, 1997. *Russia.* Fifteen armed men kidnapped five Polish nationals working for the Catholic charity Caritas in Chechnya. 97121701

December 18, 1997. *Colombia.* The National Liberation Army (ELN) kidnapped four Colombian Coca-Cola employees at a roadblock in Norte de Santander. They sought individual ransoms and a payoff from Coca-Cola to prevent further kidnappings. They approached other Coca-Cola officials, demanding protection money. 97121801

December 19, 1997. *Algeria.* Islamic insurgents used explosives to blow out doors of homes in Larba, 15 miles south of Algiers, then killed 31 people, including 13 children, and injured another 17. They kidnapped two young women after slitting several throats.

Men posing as security forces killed 30 people at a false roadblock near Lakhdaria, 35 miles southeast of Algiers.

Gunmen slit the throats of ten nomads and stole their cattle in Aflou, 200 miles south of Algiers.

Two bombs exploded at a Blida market, killing 4 and injuring 20. The Armed Islamic Group was held responsible.

December 21, 1997. *Colombia.* Nearly 400 Revolutionary Armed Forces of Colombia (FARC) guerrillas staged a dawn raid at a military outpost in Narino province, killing 22 soldiers, wounding 3, and taking 7 prisoners. Two privates and a junior officer, one of whom had shrapnel wounds to the head, hiked for two days down the 12,500-foot Cerro de Patascoy mountain through dense fog and freezing temperatures to safety.

December 22, 1997. *Mexico.* One hundred masked (other reports say unmasked) gunmen wearing blue uniforms gunned down Acteal villagers using .22-caliber rifles and AK-47s in a nine-hour slaughter that began after a 9:00 A.M. church service. The victims included 14 children, 1 infant, 9 men, and 21 women, 4 of whom were pregnant. Some were hacked to death. Most of the victims were members of the peasant group Las Abejas (The Bees), who support the goals, but not the violence, of the Zapatista National Liberation Army. The Zapatista National Liberation Army had rebelled in January 1994 to demand rights for Chiapas State's impoverished Tzotzil Indians. State police visited the town once, perhaps twice, during the incident, but apparently did nothing to stop it, saying they heard no gunshots.

On December 26, police arrested and charged 16 people in the case. Two minors were not arrested, but were turned over to a juvenile facility.

On December 27, authorities charged Jacinto Arias Cruz, the mayor of Acteal, with providing the weapons used to kill the 45 people in his Mayan village. He and 23 supporters from nearby villages were charged with homicide, causing injuries, and illegal association. They were imprisoned in Tuxtla Gutierrez, the Chiapas State capital. Many of them were members of the ruling PRI.

Villagers claimed the attackers were Catholics and PRI members; the victims were principally Protestants.

On January 3, 1998, Interior Secretary Emilio Chuayffet Chemor resigned, accused of not doing enough to prevent the attack.

On January 7, Julio Cesar Ruiz Ferro, governor of the region, resigned, accused of ignoring warnings of the attack and then trying to cover it up.

On January 12, federal prosecutors charged Felipe Vazquez Espinoza, commander of the state police in Los Chorros, with assembling the weapons stockpile used in the attack and ordering police trucks to collect the arms from surrounding villages.

On January 16, the Mexican Attorney General's Office said the attack might have been to avenge a son's death. Antonio Vazquez Secum, 70, confessed to being enraged by his son's death in a December 17 ambush; he held Acteal residents responsible.

On January 18, the government said it would open its files regarding the massacre to opposition leaders. To date, 49 people had been charged in the case.

On March 13, investigators announced that the attack was planned in October 1997 in Canolal and that state police had helped the gunmen to obtain high-caliber weapons. The government had accused 124 people of involvement; 52 remained at large.

On April 2, the Mexican army arrested Mariano Perez Ruiz, 23, a Mexican soldier suspected of training the paramilitary group responsible for the attack, and turned him over to civilian prosecutors. Meanwhile, police arrested Julio Cesar Santiago Diaz, a retired army general serving as chief of staff of the Chiapas State Police and head of the state's auxiliary police force. The Attorney General's Office said that by standing by and doing nothing, he contributed to the slaughter. He was in the area with other police officers for five hours during the massacre. The Attorney General's Office said, "He heard sporadic gunshots and machine-gun bursts, but he did not intervene or ask for help from a nearby police detachment." Instead, he hid inside the Acteal schoolhouse and told his superiors that nothing unusual was happening.

On July 19, 1999, 20 government supporters were sentenced to 35 years in prison.

December 23, 1997. *Pakistan.* Gunmen fired at the teachers' residential compound of the Karachi American School, wounding a Frontier Constabulary guard. The compound houses nine U.S. and six Canadian teachers and is a block from the school compound in a neighborhood with seven other consulate residences. 97122301

December 24, 1997. *Algeria.* Islamic gunmen killed 11 people at Bainem, north of Algiers, and another 48 near Tiaret, 140 miles to the southwest.

December 27, 1997. *Northern Ireland.* Prisoners of the Irish National Liberation Army assassinated Billy Wright (alias King Rat), 37, jailed leader of the Protestant Loyalist Volunteer Force. Wright was a notorious thug who ran a Protestant hit squad opposed to peace talks. The group had conducted numerous drive-by shootings. He had apparently financed his activities by trafficking in the drug known as "ecstasy." He was expelled from the Ulster Volunteer Force, in part for the abduction and murder of a Catholic taxi driver in 1995 in violation of a Protestant cease-fire. Fellow Protestant paramilitary groups delivered a death threat against him on television news; he had lived underground for some time before his arrest. He was serving eight years for threatening to shoot a Protestant woman who was to testify against him. The guns were smuggled into Belfast's Maze Prison for the 10:00 A.M. attack, which occurred as he was being driven in a van to the visitors' center. Three Catholic men agreed to surrender to guards only after a priest was called in.

December 27, 1997. *Algeria.* Some 40 hooded men armed with guns and axes attacked a tiny white mosque at the end of prayers in Safsaf, shooting and hacking to death 30 peasants. The mosque's government-paid *imam* was shot several times and seriously injured.

December 31, 1997. *Algeria.* Another 412 Algerian civilians were murdered on the first day of Ramadan. Terrorists attacked Khourba, Sahnoun, El Abadel, and Ouled Taieb in Relizane Province at sundown and stayed till dawn, slitting throats wherever they went. The government denied that 412 had died, noting that the official numbers were 78 killed and 73 wounded. The Armed Islamic Group was blamed.

January 1998. *Russia.* On December 12, 1998, Russian commandos rescued Vincent Cochetel, 37, a French UN official held for nearly 11 months in Russia's southern region of North Ossetia. Three kidnappers died in the five-minute raid. Cochetel headed the office of the UN High Commissioner for Refugees in North Ossetia. He said he knew who his captors were and demanded that they be seized and put on trial. 98019901

January 1, 1998. *Burundi.* At 4:00 A.M., at least 1,000 Hutu rebels killed 200 people and injured others in an attack on Rukaramu village and military camp near Bujumbura. The National Council for the Defense of Democracy rebels battled the army for an hour near the airport. At least 100 rebels and 4 soldiers died in the fighting.

January 1, 1998. *Russia.* A bag containing a small bomb exploded at 9:37 A.M. at a Moscow subway station, injuring three female subway workers. A worker told the media, "A driver found a package resembling a woman's handbag in one of the connecting tunnels. He looked in there and saw batteries and wires so he gave it to the station master." The bomb exploded near the station's duty office while the station master was calling police.

January 1, 1998. *Israel.* At 1:30 A.M., gunmen shot and critically wounded in the head and neck Yael Lieber, 25, an Israeli woman who was traveling near the Jewish settlement of Alei Zahav, southeast of the Palestinian-ruled Qalqilyah in the West Bank. The male driver, Yoman Doctori, was unhurt. Israeli officials blamed Palestinian terrorists.

January 2, 1998. *Iraq.* A rocket-propelled grenade carrying no explosives slammed into a UN building in Baghdad during the night, causing no injuries, but slightly damaging the walls of the cafeteria. The building houses UN weapons inspection team offices. 98010201

January 3, 1998. *Jordan.* A gunman fired at Rahim Taher, a commercial adviser at the Iraqi Embassy, hitting his car, but leaving him unharmed near his home in Amman. 98010301

January 4, 1998. *Israel.* A magistrates court in Acre lifted an order that had banned reports about an American electrical engineer of Lebanese extraction, who was being held on suspicion of being sent to Israel "by a Lebanese terrorist group" and carrying out "a mission at its behest." The court extended its detention order for ten days. His Israeli wife said the pair lived in the United States and came to Israel to visit her family. Their date of arrival and names were not released. 98010401

January 4, 1998. *Algeria.* Terrorists killed 117 people during the night in Remka in Relizane Province.

January 5, 1998. *Yemen.* Two Yemeni tribesmen kidnapped three South Koreans, including the wife and daughter of the first secretary of the South Korean Embassy in Sanaa. They were released on January 9. 98010501

January 5, 1998. *Algeria.* Muslim terrorists killed 12 and wounded another 12 in Kalaat Ouled Bounif. Another 21 were killed and 9 wounded in Ihdjaidia.

During the weekend, 35 people died in a bombing attack and scattered shootings.

January 5, 1998. *Algeria.* Muslim terrorists killed 29 and wounded 27 in Relizane Province.

January 6, 1998. *Algeria.* Muslim terrorists massacred 170 men, women, and children in villages south and west of Algiers. Several hundred people were burned alive by 30 Muslim terrorists in Had Chekala, in the Ammi Moussa area of Relizane Province. A survivor said, "The bodies were mutilated, and many were disfigured by axes." An Algerian academic said, "Every Ramadan is like this in Algeria. For them, Ramadan is the month of *jihad* because in the history of Islam all the conquests happened in Ramadan."

January 8, 1998. *Russia.* Dagestanis claimed credit for kidnapping two Swedish missionaries in Makhackala. A caller claimed that the hostages were moved to Chechnya. They were released on June 24. 98010801

January 8–9, 1998. *Algeria.* Terrorists killed 35 people in attacks during the night and early morning. Fifteen men attacked Saida, 200 miles southwest of Algiers, slashing their victims and shooting those trying to escape. Another group attacked the garrison town of Sour el Ghozlane, 50 miles southeast of Algiers.

January 9, 1998. *Spain.* Jose Ignacio Iruretagoyena, a Basque politician from Spain's ruling party serving as a town councilman, was killed in a car bombing by the Basque Nation and Liberty (ETA).

January 10, 1998. *Spain.* An ETA letter bomb sent to the coastal Vitoria home of a Spanish army officer injured two women when it exploded in a mailbox.

January 11, 1998. *Pakistan.* Gunmen shot to death 24 Shi'ite Muslims and wounded 30 at a morning religious service in Lahore.

January 11, 1998. *Northern Ireland.* Two gunmen from the Loyalist Volunteer Force shot to death Terence Enwright, 28, a Catholic who worked as a Belfast doorman. In the early morning, the terrorists opened fire on staff at the entrance to a Belfast nightclub. Enwright was the father of two children and married to a niece of Gerry Adams, head of Sinn Fein, the political wing of the Irish Republican Army. The group said the attack was in response to the December 27 Maze Prison murder of Billy Wright, the group's leader.

January 11, 1998. *Algeria.* Muslim terrorists attacked a movie theater and a mosque in two villages south of Algiers, killing more than 120 and injuring 70. In Sidi Hamed, a bomb exploded inside a room where many people were watching a video. As the survivors ran into the open air, they were hacked to death by waiting attackers with spades and axes. Others were shot or had their throats cut. In Haouche Sahraoui, people were killed as they were leaving a mosque.

January 12, 1998. *Rwanda.* Hutu rebels killed nine Roman Catholic nuns—three Rwandan Tutsis, three Rwandan Hutus, and three Congolese—with guns, machetes, and axes at a convent in Rwerere on the Congo-Rwanda border.

January 14, 1998. *Israel.* A booby-trapped videocassette exploded at the Israel-Lebanon border crossing near Metulla, injuring three Israelis and three Lebanese, including the man who carried the bomb. Amal said the intended target was a senior Israeli intelligence officer. 98011401

January 16, 1998. *Guatemala.* Five students from St. Mary's College of Maryland were attacked by four gunmen in a pickup truck near Santa Lucia Cotzumalaguapa—a center of Indian art and culture—as the students were returning to Guatemala City. At 3:30 P.M., the gunmen forced their study-tour bus off the road, hijacked the bus, and drove it deep into a sugar cane field. After holding the passengers at gunpoint for more than an hour, they robbed them and raped the five students. The tour guide may also have been raped. The group was part of a 16-member troupe (13 students, 3 professors, along with a Guatemalan driver and tour guide) from the southern Maryland college. Two gunmen were arrested; one was identified by three of the victims. There was no indication that the attack had political overtones.

On February 8, 1999, a tribunal in Escuintla found the three men guilty in the rapes and robbery and sentenced each to 28 years in prison. Only Cosbi Gamaliel Urias Ortiz, 38, a construction worker, was identified by a rape victim. Rony Leonel Polanco Sil, 29, a seller of firewood, and Reyes Guch Ventura, 25, a seller of wool hats, were convicted as "authors" of the rapes because they were present, carried guns, and helped intimidate the victims. Guatemalan law views a crime's author as a person without whom the crime could not have been committed. Guatemalan police announced the previous week that they had arrested a fourth suspect and were searching for two other attackers.

January 17, 1998. *Jordan.* Unidentified killers slit the throats of eight people in a hilltop village, including Iraqi diplomat Hikmet Hajou, the deputy at the embassy, and Iraqi billionaire businessman Namir Ochi, who ran a company for Saddam Hussein that imported food into Iraq. He reportedly was involved in illegal arms imports and owed the Iraqi leadership millions of dollars. The four or five masked men, speaking with Iraqi accents, broke into the Amman home of Iraqi businessman Sami George Thomas, who had hosted a banquet breaking the daily Ramadan fast. The lone survivor, Thomas's cook, told police that the terrorists slit throats and stabbed the victims. Thomas was believed to have been involved in private business deals with Saddam and his eldest son, Uday, for the last ten years. The other victims were Hajou's wife, Leila Shaaban, two other wealthy Iraqi businessmen, and an Egyptian night watchman and his friend. 98011701

January 17, 1998. *United Kingdom.* Raymond G. H. Seitz, former U.S. ambassador to the United Kingdom, charged in his book that current U.S. Ambassador to Ireland Jean Kennedy Smith is an "ardent IRA apologist" who leaked British intelligence on Northern Ireland to the Irish Republican Army (IRA). On January 31, the British army announced that it was investigating how secret intelligence documents on the IRA had been leaked to IRA supporters. Some of the documents were published the previous week in a Dublin newspaper; others were published later that week in the *Republican News* (the IRA-Sinn Fein weekly) and described Operation Vengeful, a joint army-police operation that monitored movements of IRA suspects.

January 20, 1998. *Cambodia.* Military police arrested one of its second lieutenants and two privates for shooting at a U.S. Embassy Jeep Cherokee that was carrying a suspected criminal. One passenger was injured and a tire was damaged when the two shots were fired at the diplomatic-plated vehicle during a car chase through Phnom Penh.

January 21, 1998. *Algeria.* A bomb exploded in Algiers, killing the man attempting to plant it and wounding another. Two other bombs exploded without causing injuries.

In other attacks, 43 people, including 21 rebels and 7 members of one family, were killed.

January 21, 1998. *Yemen.* Armed tribesmen kidnapped a Chinese engineer and a German engineer in two separate incidents. The two engineers were released the next day. 98012101-02

January 23, 1998. *Algeria.* A bomb exploded in an Algiers hilltop neighborhood, killing the two people carrying it.

Passengers on an Algiers bus threw a bomb out the window before it exploded in an Algiers mountainous suburb.

Four other hidden bombs exploded near the city in the previous four days.

January 24, 1998. *Algeria.* A bomb exploded at night in a café south of Algiers, killing three people. Four other bombs near the capital killed seven people. A fifth bomb exploded as it was being transported to a mosque outside Algiers, killing the two terrorists. In two other attacks, armed groups killed seven people in one village and ten people from a single family in a second village. Both villages were located west of Algiers.

January 25, 1998. *Algeria.* Muslim terrorists slashed the throats of 20 villagers in Frenda, 190 miles southwest of Algiers.

Other attacks in the previous three days claimed 45 victims.

January 25, 1998. *Sri Lanka.* Three suicide bombers drove their truck bomb through the gates of the Buddhist Temple of the Tooth in Kandy and blew themselves up, killing 13 people besides themselves and wounding 23 more. The temple houses what is believed to be a tooth of Buddha. General Anurudha Ratawatte, who was leading the war against the Tamil Tiger rebels, resigned.

The attack occurred ten days before a scheduled visit from Prince Charles of Britain.

January 26, 1998. *India.* Masked Muslim separatists killed 23 Hindu men, women, and children and set fire to parts of Wandhama, a Himalayan village 13 miles north of Srinagar, Kashmir. Police said the killers were "Afghans," non-Kashmiris who come from Pakistan. The lone survivor said the heavily armed gunmen were Urdu-speaking foreigners who first took tea with the four Hindu families before opening fire. The killers also set fire to a Hindu temple and some homes.

January 28, 1998. *Algeria.* Islamic terrorists killed 34 people in three separate attacks. Eighteen Muslim rebels, including "The Throat Slasher," were also killed.

January 29, 1998. *United States.* A bomb killed Robert Sanderson, an off-duty police officer at the New Woman All Women Health Care Center in Birmingham, Alabama. Nurse Emily Lyons, 41, lost her left eye and suffered injuries to her legs and abdomen. On February 2, the Army of God claimed credit; it had earlier said it had set off two bombs in Georgia in 1997. The group threatened bombings against manufacturers and distributors of RU-486, a morning-after pill that causes a woman's body to reject fetal tissue in the days immediately after conception. RU-486 is manufactured by Roussel Uclaf, a French firm.

On February 4, federal investigators launched a manhunt for Eric Robert Rudolph, 31, of Murphy, North Carolina, who was believed to be a material witness. By February 9, they were still searching the mountainous woodlands. Rudolph's gray 1989 Nissan pickup truck, which was seen leaving the scene of the blast, was found near Murphy over the weekend. Rudolph had been living in a trailer five miles from where the pickup was discovered. Bomb-sniffing dogs detected possible explosive residue in the truck and in a mini-warehouse that Rudolph once rented. On February 11, the Army of God, which had claimed credit for similar blasts in Atlanta, sent a letter with an Asheville, North Carolina, postmark to Murphy's weekly newspaper, the *Cherokee Scout.* The letter said, "Be advised, the Army of God is more than one."

On February 14, U.S. Attorney G. Douglas Jones announced in Birmingham that an arrest warrant had been posted with a $100,000 reward for Rudolph's capture. In May, the reward reached $1 million, and Rudolph was on the 10 Most Wanted Fugitives List. The Southern Poverty Law Center reported that Rudolph is a disciple of the late Nord Davis, founder of Northpoint Tactical Teams, an anti-government clan based in the mountains. Rudolph also followed the Christian identity movement, whose pastors promote anti-Semitic, racist, anti-government ideologies. Rudolph had also frequented Hayden Lake, Idaho, the headquarters of the Aryan Nation and other white supremacists. He also visited the Church of Israel congregation in Schell City, Missouri, whose leader, Dan Gayman, argued that the white race is the true nation of Israel. On July 7, Rudolph approached former neighbor George Nordmann, giving him a list of needed provisions, including batteries and beans. Nordmann refused a second request for help. On July 14, authorities announced that Rudolph had helped himself to 100 pounds of canned goods and Nordmann's 1977 Datsun pickup truck, which was later found abandoned at the Bob Allison Campground in North Carolina. As of July 21, Rudolph was still at large.

On March 8, Rudolph's brother, Daniel, a self-employed carpenter, videotaped himself intentionally cutting off his hand with a circular saw. 98012901

January 31, 1998. *Algeria.* Government forces killed 30 suspected Muslim rebels in Algiers and two nearby provinces in a massive search operation.

January 31, 1998. *Israel.* An Arab woman stabbed and wounded a 15-year-old Jewish seminary student at an entrance to the Old City of Jerusalem as he was walking toward the Wailing Wall for Sabbath prayers.

February 1998. *Colombia.* On April 6, the Cuban-oriented National Liberation Army (ELN) said its leader, Manuel Perez, 54, had died from hepatitis in northeast Santander Province in February. The Spanish-born former Catholic priest joined the group in 1969 and became the group's leader in the late 1970s. The group had grown to 5,000 members since its inception in 1964.

February 1998. *Switzerland.* Local authorities arrested five Israeli Mossad agents attempting to bug an apartment in the Bern suburb of Liebefeld. The group believed it was bugging a Hamas agent. Four of them were released after questioning. On April 29, one of the Mossad agents was released on $2 million bail. Israel guaranteed that he would appear for trial in Switzerland.

February 1998. *United States.* Dr. Abdelhaleem Ashqar, 39, began a hunger strike after being imprisoned for refusing to testify during a grand jury investigation into U.S. money laundering. Investigation suspect Mousa Abu Marzook was the political leader of the Gaza-based Islamic Resistance Movement (Hamas). Ashqar said he would rather die than betray "long-held and unshakable religious, political, and personal beliefs . . . and commitments to freedom and democracy for Palestine." He was kept alive by forced feeding that began in June 1998 in the Westchester Medical Center in New York. His hands were shackled to the bed to prevent him from removing feeding tubes. U.S. District Court Judge Denise Cote issued a sealed order on August 21 for his release after hearing testimony indicating that further imprisonment would have no effect in compelling his testimony.

February 2, 1998. *Japan.* At 9:00 P.M., the Revolutionary Workers Association fired three homemade rockets from a parking lot at Tokyo's Narita Airport, slightly injuring a male airport employee in the cargo-handling area. The group told news organizations that "we defeated the heavy, counterrevolutionary security for the Olympics." It said it opposed construction of a second runway at Narita (which has been opposed by local farmers) and the U.S.-Japanese military agreement.

February 3, 1998. *Chad.* Five armed members of the oppositionist Democratic Union kidnapped four French nationals in Manda National Park in Moyen-Chari Prefecture. They were released unharmed on February 8. 98020301

February 3, 1998. *Greece.* Bombs caused extensive damage at two McDonald's restaurants in the Halandri and Vrilissia suburbs of Athens. Anarchists were believed to be retaliating for the arrest of the alleged leader of the Fighting Guerrilla Formation (MAS). 98020302-03

February 5, 1998. *Algeria.* Three bombs exploded in and around Algiers, killing 2 and injuring 28.

February 5, 1998. *Algeria.* Terrorists slit the throats of nine civilians in Tlemcen.

February 6, 1998. *Corsica.* Two gunmen assassinated Claude Erignac, 60, Paris-appointed prefect of Corsica, as he was walking to a classical music concert after parking his car in Ajaccio. He had dropped his wife off at Le Kallyste theater. He was hit three times in the head with 9-mm bullets at 9:15 P.M. Three suspects were arrested. The murder pistol was recovered at the scene and identified as having been stolen from police during a hostage incident in September 1997. The Historic Wing of the National Front for the Liberation of Corsica had announced 12 days earlier that it was ending its cease-fire, but condemned the killing. A militant separatist group later claimed responsibility.

February 6, 1998. *Sri Lanka.* A suicide bomber set off explosives in her handbag when she was at a checkpoint 300 yards from the gates of Sri Lanka's air force headquarters, causing 13 casualties in Colombo hours after Prince Charles had left the island following a four-day visit. Nine people, including the bomber, three air force guards, and two soldiers, died in the attack.

February 6, 1998. *Algeria.* A bomb killed two Algerians and wounded four others in a Birtouta market, south of Algiers. Another bomb went off in Douera, southwest of Algiers.

February 7, 1998. *Algeria.* A homemade bomb exploded in a café in central Algiers, killing three and injuring eight. Later that day, a bomb exploded in Blida, 30 miles south, killing a mother and father of three in their sleep and injuring 12. A neighbor, Redha, followed the detonation wires to two other unexploded bombs and surprised an attacker, who fled. No one claimed responsibility. The bombings came as European lawmakers were preparing for a fact-finding mission to the area.

February 9, 1998. *Georgia.* Antitank grenades, machine guns, and antitank shells were fired shortly before noon (other reports say late at night) at the seven-car motorcade of President Eduard Shevardnadze, 70, who survived because his Mercedes Benz was armored. Two bodyguards and one attacker died in an ensuing ten-minute gun battle in central Tbilisi. Four other bodyguards were seriously wounded. The dead attacker was identified in the news media as an ethnic Chechen from the Russian republic of Dagestan, which borders the separatist republic of Chechnya in southern Russia.

Shevardnadze charged on television that the 18 assailants were supporters of former President Zviad Gamsakhurdia. Others fingered Igor Giorgadze, a former Georgian security chief, who was accused of organizing the August 29, 1995, bombing of Shevardnadze's car as he left to sign a new constitution for Georgia. Giorgadze was believed to reside in Moscow, which had not acted on an extradition request. Still others said the attackers were trying to derail a Caspian Sea oil pipeline deal that would bypass Russia.

Six FBI investigators were sent to assist the police.

On February 11, investigators reported finding a car containing automatic weapons and camouflage clothing used in the attack.

Russian Internal Affairs Minister Anatoly Kulikov denied that Russians were involved.

On February 15, investigators arrested four or five suspects. Two days later, they released a videotape of the attack that had been filmed by the attackers. Apparently the tapes were made to prove to their financiers that they had succeeded. Police also released details of the interrogation of six suspects, one of whom claimed that each would be paid $200,000. They had tracked Shevardnadze for months. They rented 11 apartments and several vehicles, which were used by Georgians, Chechens, and members of other nationalities, some of whom had combat experience in the 1995–96 Chechen war with Russia. Chechen commander Salman Raduyev took credit, but investigators said he often exaggerated.

Police arrested a number of suspects on May 23, 1999.

February 9, 1998. *Yemen.* Yemeni tribesmen kidnapped a Dutch tourist in Sanaa and demanded the release of three clan members who had been arrested for stealing a UN vehicle. The hostage was released on February 25. 98020901

February 11, 1998. *Israel.* A French national ultra-Orthodox Jew, who had immigrated to Israel, was stabbed to death on his way to morning prayers in a Jewish enclave in an Arab sector of Jerusalem, apparently by a Palestinian. 98021101

February 12, 1998. *United States.* A gunshot hit a passenger window of a Delta Air Lines jet taxiing for takeoff at Hartsfield Atlanta International Airport. No one was hurt. The Mobile, Alabama-bound Boeing 727 returned to the gate. The outer shell of the triple-pane window was broken. Police believed the shot was fired from outside the boundaries of the airport.

February 13, 1998. *Iran.* Morteze Moqtadaie, Iran's chief prosecutor, renewed the death sentence against British author Salman Rushdie, who wrote *The Satanic Verses.* The late Ayatollah

Khomeini claimed the book insulted the prophet Muhammad.

February 14, 1998. *Algeria.* Armed men killed 32 people in three weekend attacks. They slit the throats of 17 people. No one claimed credit.

February 14, 1998. *People's Republic of China.* A bomb went off in a bus that was approaching the Yangtze Bridge in Wuhan in Hubei Province, killing 16 and injuring 30. Two taxis and three other buses were damaged. Islamic separatists were suspected.

February 14, 1998. *Sierra Leone.* Gunmen loyal to ousted junta leader Johnny Paul Koromah took hostage three Spaniards, one Austrian, and one Italian who were working on an emergency aid mission. The Spanish Foreign Ministry said it believed its nationals were captured because the rebels needed medical assistance. Koromah had been ousted by a Nigerian-led West African military intervention force the previous week. On February 24, Ercole Marcellini, a Catholic official, said the rebels held at least 25 Western missionaries, including 10 Italians, 3 Irish nationals, 1 Australian, 1 German, 1 Spaniard, and 6 members of the late Mother Teresa's Sisters of Mercy order. Five men and four nuns who escaped from the area earlier in February said three other foreign church workers with the St. John of God order at Lunsar, north of Freetown, were missing. On February 28, the rebels released seven Western hostages. On March 3, Nigerian-led peacekeepers seized the town of Makeni from the rebels and freed 50 church workers.

February 16, 1998. *United States.* Federal investigators said 1,800 pounds of an ammonium nitrate fuel oil mix and other blasting supplies were apparently stolen from a locked bunker at C&K Coal Company in Sligo, Pennsylvania. Two men were seen near a green pickup truck in the area. The FBI said it was possible that terrorists or criminals were involved.

February 17, 1998. *Israel.* Hamas said it would attack Israel if the United States attacked Iraq.

February 18, 1998. *Algeria.* Terrorists killed 23 people in Sidi Djilali, near the Algeria-Morocco border.

February 19, 1998. *United States.* Larry Wayne Harris, 46, a Lancaster, Ohio, microbiologist, and William Leavitt, 47, a microbiologist and former Mormon bishop, were arrested in Las Vegas on charges of possessing anthrax for use as a weapon. Many speculated that Harris intended to attack the New York subway system. The army's biological lab at Fort Detrick later determined that he carried a harmless anthrax-based veterinary medicine instead; charges were dropped. Harris contended that biological weapons go virtually unregulated in the United States and overseas and wrote a manual on how to defend against an Iraqi biological attack. Police said Harris had inoculated Ohioans with an unknown substance. He had also looked into the Ebola virus. Harris was a sometime member of the white supremacist Aryan Nation and Christian Identity groups. He was charged on February 23 with violating probation for his 1995 conviction on federal charges of fraudulently buying bubonic plague bacteria by mail. He faced five years in prison. Harris said he had worked for the CIA in the 1980s; CIA denied his claim.

On February 22, Leavitt said he would fast and pray until his name was cleared. The former Mormon bishop was released from a Las Vegas jail after being held for three days. He was a successful businessman who had taken in indigent children and was searching for cures for various diseases. His lawyer said he was searching for an anthrax vaccine.

An informant had told police that Harris and Leavitt had bragged that they had enough "military grade" anthrax hidden in their Mercedes trunk to "wipe out the city."

February 19, 1998. *Greece.* A time bomb went off at a General Motors car dealership in Athens, causing no injuries. The independent dealership was closed at the time. 98021901

February 19, 1998. *Georgia.* Rebels kidnapped four UN military observers from the Abkhazia mission and four members of a family and demanded the release of suspects held in the February 9 assassination attempt on Georgian President Eduard Shevardnadze. UN and Georgian officials negotiated with the gunmen who were barricaded in a remote farmhouse. The gunmen had surrounded themselves with the hostages, including two Uruguayans, one Czech, and one Swede. On February 22, one of the Uruguayan military observers was released. The other hostages were released after Shevardnadze met with the Gamsakhurdia opposition on February 25. Eight of the kidnappers were captured. On February 26, 20 gunmen loyal to the late Georgian leader Zviad Gamsakhurdia surrendered. The last of the hostages sneaked away from his captors while they were having a party in a nearby room. Czech Lieutenant Colonel Jaroslav Kulisek was found in the woods near the western village of Dzhikhaskari after he radioed for help, saying he was lost. The group's leader, Gocha Esebua, 30, escaped with two comrades. Esebua, a key figure in the February 9 assault on Shevardnadze's motorcade, was tracked to western Georgia and killed in a police shootout on March 31.

On April 5, five mourners were killed and eight wounded when gunmen fired on a funeral procession for the leader of the kidnappers. 98021902

February 19, 1998. *Yemen.* Al-Hadda tribesmen kidnapped a Dutch agricultural expert in Dhamar. The kidnappers demanded development projects in their area. They released him on February 20. 98021903

February 20, 1998. *Algeria.* Suspected Muslim terrorists ambushed a truck in a deserted mountain road near Gijel, 180 miles east of Algiers, killing 19 people riding in the vehicle. Terrorists conducted a separate ambush elsewhere.

February 20, 1998. *Algeria.* Muslim terrorists ambushed soldiers near Boghni in the Kabylie region, 60 miles east of Algiers, setting off explosives buried in a road under a transport truck. The terrorists then fired on the soldiers and seized their weapons before fleeing. They killed 27 soldiers and injured 4 others; 2 terrorists died.

February 20, 1998. *Algeria.* Terrorists set off a bomb in a market outside Algiers, killing 2 and wounding 32.

February 21, 1998. *Pakistan.* Two Iranian construction workers were shot to death near the Iranian Cultural Center in Karachi. The shooting came a year after the February 20, 1997, attack on the Iranian Cultural Center in Multan. 98022101

February 22, 1998. *Sri Lanka.* Tamil Tiger terrorists attacked a Sri Lanka naval landing craft carrying more than 50 soldiers. After being torched, the craft sank.

February 23, 1998. *Algeria.* A bomb exploded at 4:45 P.M. on a commuter train traveling between Algiers and Afroun, killing 18 and wounding 25 others.

February 24, 1998. *Mideast.* Reuters quoted U.S. intelligence officials as saying that Muslim radical clerics had issued *fatwahs* calling for attacks on American civilians and allied interests worldwide. The London-based *Al Quds al-Arabi* said an edict had been published by a group headed by Osama bin Laden, a stateless Saudi financier of terrorists who lives in Afghanistan. The paper said, "The ruling to kill the Americans and their allies—civilians and military—is an individual duty for every Muslim who can do it in any country in which it is possible to do it in order to liberate Al Aqsa mosque and the holy mosque (in Mecca) from their grip." The Senate Judiciary Subcommittee on Terrorism released a translation of the bin Laden text, along with the text of a declaration of holy war against the United States and United Kingdom, issued by a coalition of Muslim groups on February 10. It called for attacks until economic sanctions against Iraq were lifted and the United States retreated from Saudi Arabia and Jerusalem. 98022401

February 24, 1998. *Turkey.* Passengers on a Turkish Airlines plane overpowered Mehmet Dal, 31, a Turkish hijacker who wielded a teddy bear that he claimed concealed a bomb. The plane, carrying 73 passengers and 5 crew, was hijacked shortly after it took off from Adana on a flight to Ankara and was diverted to Diyarbakir. Dal released 20 hostages, including 8 who were ill. He demanded another plane to take him to Tehran with several hostages. The passengers grabbed him just as special forces were entering the RJ-100 from the front and back doors. He was driven away in a military ambulance. 98022402

February 25, 1998. *Algeria.* A bomb exploded on a bus in central Algiers, wounding 13 people, 2 of them critically.

February 25, 1998. *Ethiopia.* Ogaden National Liberation Front (ONLF) gunmen kidnapped an Austrian as she traveled from Gode to Denan. They freed her on March 23 after announcing their intention to release her during a radio broadcast. 98022501

February 28, 1998. *Pakistan.* Two bombs exploded 20 minutes apart in a Karachi apartment complex, killing eight people and wounding dozens.

March 1998. *United States.* Immigration and Naturalization (INS) officers arrested Hany Mahmoud Kaireldeen, 30, a Palestinian who worked as a manager of an electronics store in Passaic, New Jersey, and who had lived in the United States since 1990, when he entered from Israel on a student visa. While he was not charged with any crime, INS accused him of overstaying his student visas and held him at the Mercer County Jail. On June 26, INS officials said they wanted to deport him because the FBI believed he was plotting to kill Attorney General Janet Reno and that he was

familiar with the World Trade Center bombing conspiracy. He was a suspected member of an unnamed terrorist organization and had made a "credible threat" against Reno for her role in the conviction of the bombers. He had also met with other suspected individuals at his then-home in Nutley, New Jersey, including Nidal Ayyad, who was convicted in the bombing. Family and friends said his ex-wife lied to the FBI. (He married in 1994 and had a daughter. Following a bitter divorce, he remarried and petitioned to become a permanent resident. He was in a custody dispute with his ex-wife.) His attorney, Regis Fernandez, said he denied everything in the legal summaries. Immigration court hearings were adjourned until July 31.

In a landmark ruling on October 20, 1999, U.S. District Judge William Walls (Newark, New Jersey) held unconstitutional the use of classified terrorism evidence in court against immigrants who were not permitted to see the evidence against them. He ordered Kaireldeen released. The use of classified evidence in some two dozen immigration cases was first authorized in 1996 by an antiterrorism bill that followed the Oklahoma City bombing. All of the cases were against Arab or Muslim immigrants.

March 1, 1998. *Israel.* Palestinian officials denied Israeli accusations that they were involved in an attempt to smuggle two boatloads of weapons from Jordan across the Dead Sea. 98030101

March 1, 1998. *Algeria.* Terrorists killed eight people in Ouled Salem; hours earlier, President Liamine Zeroual had vowed to end the country's insurgency.

March 5, 1998. *Belgium.* Police arrested seven Algerians after a shootout and a 12-hour standoff. The detainees belonged to the European-based support network for Algeria's Armed Islamic Group. One of them was identified as Farid Mellouk, a French national of Algerian extraction. 98030501

March 7, 1998. *Algeria.* Muslim rebels conducted two attacks, killing 13 people. Elsewhere, a bomb went off in a bus station, wounding 12.

March 8, 1998. *Algeria.* Suspected Muslim terrorists slit the throats of six people, including four blind women, in Haouch Mena, a village south of Algiers.

March 9, 1998. *Pakistan.* A bomb went off outside a court in Sindh Province, injuring 13, including 6 policemen. Later that day, a bomb went off on a Chiltan Express train in Punjab Province, killing 7 and wounding 35.

March 10, 1998. *Algeria.* Terrorists killed 19 civilians. A military operation in the west killed six rebels.

March 12, 1998. *United States.* The Pentagon announced it had gone to Threatcon Alpha, which entailed tightened security and suspended public tours. The action was taken following FBI notification of a threat of possible terrorist activity.

March 13, 1998. *Israel.* A bomb went off near Jerusalem's Old City, wounding four Palestinians. National police chief Yehuda Wilk said, "We're talking about a bomb with the characteristics of a terrorist bomb that was apparently (carried by someone) on his way to the western part of the city to attack Jews." Palestinian officials blamed the bombing on radical Jewish settlers.

March 14, 1998. *Colombia.* The Revolutionary Armed Forces of Colombia (FARC) kidnapped two French brothers who run a hotel in Meta Department. One hostage was released shortly after the kidnapping to deliver a huge ransom demand. 98031401

March 16, 1998. *Colombia.* Fabian Ramirez, chief of the Revolutionary Armed Forces of Colombia (FARC), told Reuters that his group, in "combative mood," would soon attack U.S. military advisers. Ramirez believed the advisers were heading

covert counterinsurgency operations. "The claim that the U.S. is combating drugs in Colombia is a sophism. All the military and economic aid it is giving to the army is to fight the guerrillas." Two weeks earlier, 300 members of the FARC Southern Bloc attacked the U.S. Army Third Mobile Brigade, killing 83 soldiers and capturing 43 others. 98031601

March 18, 1998. *Russia.* Mormon missionaries Andrew Lee Propst, 20, of Lebanon, Oregon, and Travis Robert Tuttle, 20, of Gilbert, Arizona, were kidnapped during the night in Saratov, 450 miles southeast of Moscow. A $300,000 ransom was demanded. The kidnappers drove the duo to the countryside, where they were released unharmed on March 22. The missionaries walked back to Saratov, where they contacted their local mission leader. 98031301

March 19, 1998. *Spain.* Police arrested ten people and seized 265 pounds of explosives in a raid against the Basque Nation and Liberty (ETA) group.

March 21, 1998. *Colombia.* The Revolutionary Armed Forces of Colombia (FARC) kidnapped an American in Sabaneta. He was released to the International Red Cross on September 6. 98032101

March 22, 1998. *Chad.* The National Front for the Renewal of Chad (FNTR) claimed credit for kidnapping six French nationals and two Italians in the Tibesti region. Chadian forces freed all but one hostage within hours. The FNTR said it would release the remaining hostage if French troops withdrew from Chad and Western oil companies halted exploration and exploitation of all resources in the country. On March 27, Chadian security forces freed the last hostage. 98032201

March 23, 1998. *Colombia.* Four Americans and one Italian were taken hostage by 50 Revolutionary Armed Forces of Colombia (FARC) guerrillas 35 miles south of Bogota. The Colombian military said 32 people were kidnapped at a roadblock that stopped the tourists, who were returning from a hummingbird-watching trip. At least 3 people were killed and another 14 wounded in the attack. Among the hostages were the acting president of the National Electoral Council (CNE) and his wife, who were freed on March 25. The FARC commander threatened to kill the Americans if they were determined to be spies for the CIA or DEA (Drug Enforcement Administration). The Colombian media identified the Americans as Peter Chen (or Shell, or Shen), of New York, Todd Mark of Houston, Thomas Fiore (or Fiori), 43, of New York, and former nun Louise Augustine, 63, of Chillicothe, Illinois; the Italian was Vito Candela. The U.S. Department of State said they were on a bird-watching trip. The Clinton administration said the four never worked for U.S. intelligence agencies. Colombian President Ernesto Samper asked other governments to suspend peace negotiations with FARC's international delegates. Costa Rica, Spain, Mexico, and Germany had been assisting the peace talks between the government and the rebels.

On March 27, the rebels freed nine kidnapped Colombians. The guerrillas said they were determining how much ransom to ask for the foreigners. They indicated that they were prepared to hold the tourists for a year.

On April 2, Fiore arrived in Bogota; local television journalists had found him wandering in the mountains. Some media, citing Chen and Fiore, reported that he escaped; others said he was set free to deliver a message to the U.S. government. U.S. Ambassador Curtis W. Kamman referred to Fiore's "liberation" in a news conference.

On April 15, Candela was released. The United States said the Colombian Army's ground offensive against the rebels could endanger the hostages.

The Colombian media agreed, in return for the hostages' freedom, to broadcast a rebel communiqué denouncing longstanding U.S. intervention in the Colombian guerrilla war.

On April 24, 30 rebels armed with Galil and AK-47 automatic assault rifles and heavy mortars released Augustine to a Red Cross delegation 1.5 miles from Los Alpes. She told Reuters that two weeks into her captivity she had almost died when she fell 130 feet into a ravine and was knocked unconscious. She was held with ten other hostages, including Colombians, Americans, and a German. She said they were well treated and never threatened. A rebel leader, Marco Aurelio, apologized for her injuries. Romana, commander of FARC's 53rd Front, said the other two American hostages would be released that weekend.

On April 25, Chen and Mark were handed over to Red Cross officials in Los Alpes. Chen, a research scientist, said they were handcuffed at night. They had been told they would be shot if they tried to escape and had feared for their lives after Fiore escaped. They had been relieved of their bird-watching equipment after being taken hostage. Chen and Mark believed they had heard the call of the rare *Cundinamarca antitta* hummingbird during their captivity.

Army mortars blasted away at guerrilla positions in the mountains. 98032301

March 23, 1998. *Angola/Cabinda.* Rebels from the Front for the Liberation of the Cabinda Enclave-Cabinda Armed Forces (FLEC-FAC) kidnapped two Portuguese citizens in Cabinda who worked for Mota and Company, a Portuguese construction firm. The FLEC-FAC demanded $500,000 ransom, the intervention of Portuguese authorities, and negotiations for the withdrawal of Portugal from Angola. On June 24, the hostages were freed. It was not known whether a ransom was paid. 98032302

March 25, 1998. *Colombia.* A bomb blast injured one American and two British workers at the British Petroleum oil field in Cupiagua. At least one bomb was planted near the oil workers' sleeping trailer and set off at midnight. Police blamed the National Liberation Army (ELN). 98032501

March 26, 1998. *Algeria.* Muslim rebels were blamed in two nighttime massacres. Attackers killed 47 people in Djelfa; another 11 were killed in Saida Province.

March 27, 1998. *Pakistan.* Security was tightened at the U.S. Embassy after receipt of "credible information" of terrorist threats. Authorities erected cement barriers. In recent weeks, Afghan-based former Saudi citizen and multimillionaire terrorist financier Osama bin Laden, 41, had faxed threats against U.S. interests. Islamabad's *Al-Akhbar* reported that bin Laden was targeting the U.S. Consulate in Peshawar and U.S. Embassy in Islamabad. 98032702

March 28, 1998. *Gaza.* Palestinian police uncovered seven large Hamas explosives factories in Gaza. Ten Hamas activists were arrested.

March 29, 1998. *West Bank.* A car time bomb containing more than 100 pounds of explosives went off in Bituniya, a suburb of Palestinian-ruled Ramallah, during the night. The body of Mohia-din Sharif, 32, a Hamas bomb maker, was found nearby. Pathologists determined that he had been killed by gunfire three hours earlier, shot twice in the chest and once in the leg. Israeli officials denied Shin Bet involvement. Palestinian Authority police later determined that he was killed in an inter-Hamas dispute and detained 30 Hamas members. Following questioning, they arrested five Hamas members who had helped set up the plot and announced that a sixth man, still at large, had shot "The Engineer II" (named after Yahya Ayyash, an earlier Hamas bomber apparently killed by the Israelis) in a remote area and then driven the body to the white Peugeot that contained the bomb. Hamas nonetheless blamed the Israelis and threatened retaliatory attacks around the world.

On April 11, 1998, Palestinian police arrested Imad Awadallah, suspected triggerman, at a Ramallah café. A Hamas fax said its own investigation showed Palestinian security chief Jibril Rajoub cooperated with Israel in killing Sharif. Hamas claimed the body was blown up so that traces of torture could not be detected.

April 1998. *Colombia.* On September 6, 1998, the Revolutionary Armed Forces of Colombia (FARC) freed captive Donald Lee Cary, a retired Exxon executive, on his 64th birthday, more than five months after they had kidnapped him from his ranch near Bogota. They dropped him off at the Red Cross facility outside Medina, southeast of Bogota. A government official said he had no information whether a ransom was paid. Cary was born and raised in Texas and had lived in Colombia for 19 years. He spent most of his captivity walking through rugged mountains to and from six rebel camps. He believed he had broken a rib in a fall. 98049901

April 1998. *Morocco.* An armed Islamic group killed ten Moroccans near the border town of Oujda.

April 1998. *Angola.* Late in the month, the National Union for the Total Independence of Angola (UNITA) was suspected of abducting a Portuguese couple involved in trading. The attack took place after 150 armed men occupied the Ebanga commune. 98049902

April 2, 1998. *Ireland.* Police intercepted a huge bomb hidden in a car at Dublin's main ferry port. The Irish Republican Army (IRA) was blamed for hiding the bomb in a car waiting to board a ferry to Holyhead, a Welsh port. 98040201

April 3, 1998. *Egypt.* The U.S. State Department warned Americans that the government had received "information of undetermined reliability that extremist groups may be planning terrorist attacks against U.S. interests in the near future. U.S. citizens traveling to or residing in Cairo are advised to exercise greater caution than usual."

April 4, 1998. *Uganda.* Bombs exploded at the Nile Grill and the Speke Hotel's café in Kampala, killing five people, including a Swede and a Rwandan. The restaurants are within walking distance of the U.S. Embassy and the Sheraton Hotel. A Ugandan official suggested that the Allied Democratic Forces were responsible. 98040401-02

April 6, 1998. *Latvia.* An antipersonnel mine exploded at 2:00 A.M. outside the Russian Embassy. The blast followed international controversy over a reunion of Latvian SS veterans and the April 2 predawn bombing of a synagogue. The bomb contained plastic explosives and was detonated in a concrete trash bin outside the facility. No injuries were reported. 98040601

April 8, 1998. *Greece.* The November 17 Movement fired an antitank missile at the Citibank branch in Athens. The group said it was "aimed against American imperialism-nationalism." 98040801

April 9, 1998. *Algeria.* Nearly 100 civilians and Muslim terrorists were killed during the week as the country celebrated the Feast of Sacrifice. More than half the dead were civilians, mostly women and children.

April 10, 1998. *Turkey.* Nine people were wounded when two Kurdistan Workers Party (PKK) members on a motorcycle threw a bomb into a park in Sultanahment near Istanbul's Blue Mosque, the center of Istanbul's tourist district. The explosion injured two Indian tourists, one New Zealander, four Turkish civilians, and two Turkish soldiers. Authorities arrested the two PKK terrorists on April 12. 98041001

April 13, 1998. *Albania.* A masked gunman opened fire on the car of two British diplomats, causing minor injuries. Deputy Ambassador Catherine Jones and Vice-Consul Dave Bicker were released from the hospital. A third diplomat, Jim Warren, was unhurt. It was unclear what the attacker wanted. 98041301

April 14, 1998. *Algeria.* Several local officials and commanders of pro-government militia groups were arrested on charges of carrying out massacres of civilians. Authorities found two mass graves of civilians alleged to have been killed by western Algerian militias. Militias were suspected of killing 17 civilians and dumping their bodies in a well in the Sidi M'Hamed Benaouda area, 150 miles southwest of Algiers. Another mass grave was dis-

covered in Relizane, where 62 bodies, many of them buried alive, were found.

April 15, 1998. *Somalia.* Unidentified gunmen kidnapped ten Red Cross and Red Crescent workers, including Ibrahim Ahmad, a naturalized American of Somali origin. The other hostages were a German, a Belgian, a French nurse, a Norwegian, two Swiss, a Somali, a Kenyan pilot, and a South African pilot. The gunmen took them after their airplane landed at an airstrip in north Mogadishu. Diplomats and UN officials suspected the abductions were part of an intra-clan power struggle; the gunmen were members of a subclan loyal to Ali Mahdi Mohammed, who controlled the northern section of the capital. Somali elders, faction leaders, and the Red Cross initiated negotiations for their release. The next day, three Somali warlords flew home to help negotiate. The group was released unharmed on April 24. They were put into a car and driven to a Red Cross hospital in northern Mogadishu. They then flew back to their headquarters in Nairobi, Kenya. No ransom was paid. 98041501

April 17, 1998. *Cambodia.* Some 60 Khmer Rouge terrorists attacked two fishing villages on the Tonle Sap Lake in Kampong Chhnang Province, killing 21 and wounding 9 others. At least 12 victims were Vietnamese. The attack came in the early morning when the victims were asleep. 98041701

April 17, 1998. *Yemen.* Tribesmen kidnapped a British Council official and his wife and son as they traveled from Aden to Sanaa. They were released on May 3. 98041702

April 18, 1998. *India.* Lashkar-i-Taiba Muslim militants attacked Barankot village in Udhampur District, Kashmir, killing 29.

April 19, 1998. *Venezuela.* Colombian guerrillas kidnapped a Venezuelan cattleman in a Los Flores hacienda. The Venezuelan Directorate of Intelligence and Prevention Services rescued him on April 23. 98041901

April 20, 1998. *Peru.* Police arrested Pedro Domingo Quintero, 56, the deputy to Shining Path leader Oscar Ramirez Durand (alias Feliciano), in a Lima restaurant. Quintero was a founder of the Shining Path. Four days later, police arrested Alberto Ramirez, the group's military leader; Maximo Anosa, its operations planner; and Rodolfo Condori, its chief car bomb maker.

April 20, 1998. *Cambodia.* The Khmer Rouge killed 22 ethnic Vietnamese in Chhanok Tru, during the run-up to July 26 national elections. Khmer Rouge leader Pol Pot had died the week before. 98042001

April 20, 1998. *Germany.* The leftist Red Army Faction announced in an eight-page document that it had formally disbanded and would no longer bomb, kidnap, and assassinate. It told news organizations that "we are stuck in a dead end. . . . It was a strategic error not to build up a social-political organization next to the illegal, armed one. . . . The RAF emerged from a liberation action nearly 28 years ago on May 14, 1970. Today we are ending this project. The urban guerrilla group in the form of the RAF is now history." The group, founded by Andreas Baader and Ulrike Meinhof, had been credited with more than 50 murders.

April 21, 1998. *Colombia.* Carl Hood, 44, an American Southern Baptist missionary, was shot to death as he walked in western Bogota. He had worked in Bogota since 1987. He was shot once in the head. 98042101

April 22, 1998. *Angola.* The Front for the Liberation of the Cabinda Enclave was blamed for kidnapping a Portuguese citizen and nine Angolans. The victims were employed by Mota and Company, a Portuguese construction company. The Portuguese hostage was freed unharmed on June 24. 98042201

April 22, 1998. *Iraq.* A gunman shot and killed an Iranian clergyman and injured his two companions in An Najaf. No one claimed credit. 98042202

April 23, 1998. *Yemen.* A police officer from the Al-Marakesha tribe kidnapped a Ukrainian on his way to Sanaa and handed him over to the tribe, who released the hostage the next day. 98042301

April 24, 1998. *Yemen.* A bomb exploded in the courtyard of Sanaa's Al-Kheir mosque after midday prayers, killing 2 and wounding 26 others, including 2 Americans, 1 Canadian, 1 Libyan, and several Somalis. 98042401

April 25, 1998. *Colombia.* The Revolutionary Armed Forces of Colombia (FARC) kidnapped a Palestinian connected to the Palestine Liberation Organization in Bogota. The kidnap victim was a Colombian citizen who had resided in Colombia for 20 years. FARC released him on July 17 at the request of the International Red Cross and a special envoy of the Palestinian Authority. 98042501

April 28, 1998. *Algeria.* Some 43 villagers were killed in a Muslim New Year massacre in Medea Province.

April 29, 1998. *Colombia.* The Central Staff of the Revolutionary Armed Forces of Colombia (FARC) released a communiqué (dated April 20) declaring U.S. Embassy official Joseph McBryan a military target "because he is meddling in the country's affairs with the pretext of fighting drugs." 98042901

May 1, 1998. *India.* Muslim militants were suspected of setting off a bomb under a crowded bus in Shupiyan, injuring six.

May 2, 1998. *Russia.* Four neo-Nazi skinheads badly beat a black U.S. Marine at an outdoor market during the afternoon. Another U.S. Embassy employee ran for help. A leader of a skinhead group was detained after the attack. Russian neo-

Nazis had threatened to attack people of African and Asian descent to mark Hitler's birthday in April. 98050201

May 4, 1998. *United States.* The Clinton administration named Richard Clarke, 47, the government's first national "terrorism czar," overseeing a $7 billion antiterrorism budget. The Office of Management and Budget said the money would be spread across 17 federal agencies; the congressional Government Accounting Office said 43 agencies were involved in antiterrorism efforts.

May 4, 1998. *India.* Police blamed Muslim militants for killing four members of a Manchar village defense committee, four other villagers, and one police officer east of Jammu, Kashmir.

May 5, 1998. *India.* Armed Islamic militants entered a home in Surankote, north of Jammu, and killed four people.

May 6, 1998. *Germany.* The government announced that racist and anti-Semitic attacks by right-wing extremists had increased by 27 percent in the past year to 790, including 13 cases of attempted manslaughter and 677 assaults. There were 11,000 other offenses by such groups, which claimed 48,400 members; hardcore extremists believed capable of violence numbered 7,600.

May 6, 1998. *Spain.* The Basque Nation and Liberty (ETA) was believed responsible for killing Tomas Caballero, 63, a member of the ruling Popular Party in Pamplona. A gunman shot him twice in the head as Caballero, an outspoken opponent of ETA, left his home by car in the morning.

Minutes before the killing, Interior Minister Jaime Mayor-Oreja told the media that authorities had discovered that ETA planned to assassinate the king on his visit to the Basque country in August.

May 6, 1998. *India.* Muslim militants killed five Hindu family members during a funeral procession outside Punch, Kashmir.

May 8, 1998. *United States.* Three members of the racist neo-Nazi National Alliance were arrested on charges of having fully assembled 14 pipe bombs that they planned to plant across Orlando, Florida, as diversions for two bank robberies. The bombs would be planted along Interstate 4, the major access road to Disney World, and U.S. Highway 441. Brian Pickett, 38, a Tampa bank security guard, was charged with bank robbery and conspiracy. Deena Wanzie, 46, of Orlando was charged with conspiracy and destruction of property. Christopher Norris, 25, was charged with conspiracy and possessing and making pipe bombs. The three were accused of working with white supremacist Todd Vanbiber, 29, who was injured in 1997 as he was assembling a pipe bomb. Vanbiber was serving six and a half years in federal prison on a guilty plea to possession of explosives. Vanbiber planned the robberies for April 19, 1997, the second anniversary of the Oklahoma City bombing, but changed his mind.

The National Alliance was led by William Pierce of Hillsboro, West Virginia, author of *The Turner Diaries*, which inspired Timothy McVeigh in the Oklahoma City bombing.

May 12, 1998. *Algeria.* Muslim rebels slit the throats of 22 people in Oran. Only a baby survived; three children between the ages of 2 and 14 were killed.

May 12, 1998. *United Kingdom.* British, French, and Belgian security services arrested eight suspected Algerian Armed Islamic Group members in London. 98051201

May 14, 1998. *Russia.* At 11:00 P.M., a half kilogram of TNT exploded in central Moscow's Lubavitch Maryina Roshcha Synagogue, only minutes after 70 children and teachers had left the building. The bomb ripped a hole in the side of the building and damaged nearby cars, but caused no serious injuries. Several construction workers at a nearby Jewish community center suffered minor injuries. The synagogue had burned down in 1993 in an arson attack. It was bombed two months after it reopened in August 1996. The visitors were celebrating the Jewish holiday of Lag b'Omer. Neo-Nazi skinheads had earlier threatened Asians and beaten up a black U.S. Marine. President Boris Yeltsin deemed the bombing an act of barbarism.

May 16, 1998. *Colombia.* Dozens of heavily armed paramilitary troops believed to be members of a right-wing death squad attacked the Twentieth of August neighborhood in northeast Barrancabermeja, a leftist rebel stronghold. The attackers killed 7 people and kidnapped 25 others. The next month, the killers announced they had killed all the hostages and burned their bodies after determining that the victims had leftist links. Despite two communiqués from the country's intelligence agency, no policemen or soldiers responded to the attack. Investigators said at least one soldier participated in the attack and that soldiers had waved the attackers through a checkpoint. The Self-Defense Force of Santander and Southern Cesar claimed credit.

May 16, 1998. *Colombia.* Six heavily armed men kidnapped an Italian engineer near Medellin. The engineer had been overseeing tunnel construction. He was taken from his car and forced to enter a taxi with the gunmen. Leftist guerrillas may have been responsible. 98051601

May 16, 1998. *India.* Militants killed at least seven former militants who had become police informants or members of village defense groups opposed to the militants in Binola Chuora village, Kashmir.

May 17, 1998. *Tanzania.* Seth Sendashonga, 47, a former Rwandan government minister, was shot dead during the weekend. Attorney Pascal Besnier said the victim had agreed to testify on behalf of two suspects in the 1994 Rwandan genocide "despite threats against him." He would have been the most senior Rwandan official to appear for the defense. Sendashonga and other Hutus were sacked from the Tutsi-led government in 1995. 98051701

May 19, 1998. *Angola.* The National Union for the Total Independence of Angola (UNITA) was blamed for attacking a marked UN vehicle at Calandula, killing an Angolan UN interpreter and an Angolan police officer. 98051901

May 22, 1998. *Sudan.* The Sudan People's Liberation Army (SPLA) kidnapped a British contractor working for the World Food Program (WFP) and demanded $58,000 and 125 drums of diesel fuel. He was employed by Terra Firma and was on a survey mission for the WFP. He was freed on June 19. 98052201

May 22, 1998. *Algeria.* A bomb went off in the crowded Boumaati outdoor market in El-Harrach, an Algiers suburb, killing 17 and wounding 61. Muslim fundamentalists were blamed.

May 23, 1998. *India.* Pakistani-supported Muslims were suspected of setting off a bomb beneath an armored car on the outskirts of Srinagar, destroying the vehicle and seriously injuring a provincial legislator, his driver, a bodyguard, and three other people.

May 25, 1998. *Colombia.* Ninety members of the Revolutionary Armed Forces of Colombia (FARC) attacked Popayan's San Isidro Prison, 230 miles southwest of Bogota, freeing 324 inmates in the country's largest prison escape. FARC set off three dynamite charges, blowing down a wall near the main gate and destroying a portal opening onto the prison's four cell blocks. After the three-hour firefight, two prisoners and one guard died. A third of the inmate population escaped; 46 were recaptured. Police believed the escape was planned by inmate El Rojo, a FARC leader.

The group had recently orchestrated similar successful prison breaks, including the April 4 Santander de Ouilichao Prison break that freed 54 inmates, including a rebel leader. In the February 23 Blancas de Calarca Penitentiary break, 18 prisoners, most of them rebels convicted of murder, tunneled out of Penas.

May 26, 1998. *Algeria.* A bomb hidden in a cow carcass exploded in a market in Khemis-Miliana, 70 miles south of Algiers, killing seven people. Islamic militants were suspected.

May 26, 1998. *Europe.* Police arrested 88 Muslim guerrillas in France, Belgium, Italy, Germany, and Switzerland and claimed that there was information that Algerian rebel support networks contemplated attacks against the World Cup soccer games, which began on June 10. Paris police later said that Islamic militants arrested there might have been planning to kill a moderate Muslim leader. 98052601-05

May 26, 1998. *India.* Activists allied with the ruling Hindu nationalist Bharatiya Janata Party torched a Baskin-Robbins ice cream shop in Ahmedabad. 98052606

May 26, 1998. *Venezuela.* Three armed Revolutionary Armed Forces of Colombia (FARC) rebels kidnapped a Venezuelan engineer in La Victoria. They freed him on June 18, giving him money to travel home. FARC told him that they intended to kidnap a businessman from the area and had abducted him by mistake. 98052607

May 27, 1998. *Colombia.* Twenty National Liberation Army (ELN) rebels bombed the Santa Marta offices of a subsidiary of the U.S.-owned Dole company. They overpowered guards, gagged employees, and destroyed files before setting off four bombs that partially destroyed the headquarters. They painted graffiti accusing the firm's owners of assisting paramilitary groups in the region. They fired at police during their escape. 98052701

June 1998. *India.* Young men riding on three motor scooters pulled up alongside a Pepsi truck, drawing a crowd that stole the truck's contents. The next day, six young men intercepted another Pepsi truck, breaking bottles and setting fire to the truck. A few days later, a Coca-Cola truck driver was robbed and his vehicle stoned. The youths were

believed to be members of the Bajrang Dal, a militant youth group affiliated with a Hindu nationalist brotherhood. Police arrested 16 people on robbery charges in connection with the Pepsi attacks, which came on the heels of U.S. imposition of sanctions against India for its nuclear bomb tests.

June 1998. *Colombia.* Members of the Revolutionary Armed Forces of Colombia (FARC) took hostage Edward Leonard, who worked for a Canadian drilling company, and demanded a $500,000 ransom. After three months of negotiations, the rebels refused to release Leonard to his wife and three children. The owner of the firm, Norbert Reinhart, offered himself in exchange for the hostage. Some 106 days after Leonard was taken hostage, he was freed and Reinhart took his place, to the consternation of the Canadian government and Reinhart's wife. The rebels demanded $2 million for his release. As of November 9, 1998, he had not been released. 98069901

June 1, 1998. *Dominican Republic.* Drug traffickers took credit for bombing a drug intelligence center. On May 28, retired U.S. General Barry McCaffrey, director of the Office of National Drug Control Policy in the White House, had visited the Dominican National Drug Control Directorate intelligence and counterdrug operation in Santo Domingo. The 3:00 A.M. bombing left a bucket-size crater in the ground and broke windows, but no one was hurt. 98060101

June 1, 1998. *Libya.* Would-be assassins attacked the convoy of Muammar Qadhafi on a coastal road near Benghazi in eastern Libya as his convoy was en route to Egypt for an official visit. Qadhafi was slightly wounded in the elbow. One of his female bodyguards was killed. Libya denied the attack took place. The Islamic Martyrs Movement opposition group claimed to have carried out the unsuccessful assassination attempt. On July 7, 1998, Qadhafi told Idriss Deby of Chad and Ibrahim Bare Mainassara of Nigeria, two African heads of state who had ignored the UN embargo on flights to Libya, that he had merely broken his hip in a fall.

June 1, 1998. *India.* A bomb went off at a busy market in Jammu, Kashmir, killing a child, injuring 19 other people, and damaging ten shops. Muslim militants were suspected.

June 1, 1998. *India.* Muslim militants were blamed for setting off a bomb at an army base in Jammu, Kashmir, killing two civilians and damaging the army's intelligence wing.

June 2, 1998. *Iran.* Iran said it had foiled an attack by Iraq-based Mujaheddin e-Khalq rebels, who fled after they left explosives and ammunition at the Tehran headquarters of the Revolutionary Guards. The group had set off two explosions, one of which killed three people at a court building. The second nighttime bomb at a military-industrial building in Tehran caused no casualties.

June 3, 1998. *Turkey.* Armed Kurdish Workers Party (PKK) militants kidnapped a German tourist and a Turkish truck driver at a roadblock in Agri. The German was found unharmed the next morning near the kidnapping site, but the truck driver was still missing as of April 1999. 989060301

June 3, 1998. *Turkey.* Kurdish Workers Party (PKK) rebels killed eight civilians in a wave of attacks in Tunceli.

June 6, 1998. *Turkey.* An AOM French Airlines MD-83 plane carrying 163 passengers and crew made an emergency landing on its fuselage in Antalya in southern Turkey after an explosion damaged its landing gear. The plane departed for Paris, then circled the Turkish airport for more than two hours to burn off fuel. No further details about the explosion were released.

June 7, 1998. *Pakistan.* A bomb exploded at 4:00 A.M. on a crowded 18-car Khyber Mail train near Kairpur in southern Sindh Province on the Karachi-Peshawar route, wounding 45 and killing 26, including 4 women and 2 children. The bomb was hidden under a seat in the middle of an economy-class passenger car. Pakistan immediately blamed India's Research and Analysis Wing (RAW) intelligence service. Pakistani Information Minister Mushahid Hussain said the government had arrested an Indian agent near the border. Hussain reported that the agent had confessed to similar terrorist attacks, including ten bombings in nine weeks in 1998 that led to 16 deaths and 93 injured people. Hussain also identified the bombing of a Lahore movie theater that had occurred earlier in the week as another Indian attack. That bombing killed three. The main suspect was an Indian citizen. Both countries had recently conducted publicly acknowledged nuclear bomb tests.

June 7, 1998. *Mexico.* Popular Revolutionary Army gunmen fired on an army anti-narcotics patrol at dawn outside Acapulco; the resulting six-hour firefight led to 11 rebel deaths.

June 9, 1998. *Uganda.* Rebels attacked a technical school near Kabarole, 195 miles west of Kampala, killing at least 60 students and kidnapping 8 others. Some rebels were former members of armies or groups defeated by the current President Yoweri Museveni's National Resistance Movement in 1986.

June 9, 1998. *United States.* Federal authorities in Chicago seized $1.4 million in cash and property that was believed part of a Hamas money-laundering operation that had begun in 1989. The money was moved from Europe and the Middle East to a U.S. network of Hamas supporters who aided the group in Israel and Palestine. Some $1.2 million in cash was seized from Mohammad Salah and his wife, Azita, in Bridgeview, a Chicago suburb. The government also moved to claim their home and a Quranic Literacy Institute van. Salah, a U.S. citizen, was convicted in Israel of sending money to Hamas. He returned to the United States in November after serving nearly five years in prison. The FBI affidavit said he gave money to

Hamas, and Hamas used the funds to buy weapons used in attacks that killed Israeli soldiers. U.S. attorney Scott Lassar said it was the first time that civil asset forfeiture had been used to seize money in U.S. banks to prevent it from being used for terrorism abroad. 98060901

June 10, 1998. *Sudan.* Gunmen fired on a UN relief convoy in southern Sudan, killing two workers with the UN World Food Program and one person with the Red Cross. Four others were wounded. 98061001

June 18, 1998. *Iraq.* Gunmen shot and killed an Iranian Shi'ite cleric, two of his relatives, and his driver. The victims were driving back to An Najaf after a pilgrimage to a shrine in Karbala'. 98061801

June 18, 1998. *Yemen.* Tribesmen kidnapped nine Italian tourists and their Yemeni driver in Husn al-Ghurab in the Bir Ali area of Mayfaah District and demanded that the government pay them the 800,000 riyals that were pledged to them in a previous agreement, pay compensation for a car lost in the 1994 civil war, and implement construction of a school and health facility in their region. The kidnappers released two elderly women and the driver on June 19. They released the remaining hostages on June 21. 98061802

June 19, 1998. *India.* Five gunmen fired automatic rifles at a newlywed couple and their wedding guests as they walked back to their village after the ceremony in Champnari village in Jammu's Doda District in Kashmir. Twenty-five people were killed, including the groom, and another six injured. Pakistan-backed Muslim separatists were accused of attacking the Hindus.

June 21, 1998. *Lebanon.* Bombs exploded near the U.S. Embassy, causing no casualties and minor damage to a contractor's business. No one claimed credit. The three rocket-propelled grenades were attached to a detonator half a mile from the embas-

sy compound. The grenades were found in the Christian suburb of Aukar. Police believed the embassy was not the target. No one claimed credit.

June 23, 1998. *Spain.* A mentally disturbed man hijacked an Iberia jet carrying 131 people from Seville to Barcelona and demanded to be flown to Tel Aviv. He was carrying a television remote control device, which he claimed was a bomb. The plane touched down in Valencia, where he demanded to talk to his psychiatrist, who was brought in from Seville and talked to the man for four hours by cell phone before the hijacker surrendered. No one was injured and no bomb was found. Earlier reports said three hijackers were involved. 98062301

June 23, 1998. *India.* A remotely detonated bomb exploded under the Delhi-bound Shalimar Express in Kashmir, injuring 35 of the 2,000 passengers and derailing seven cars. Muslim militants were suspected.

June 25, 1998. *Egypt.* Police uncovered a plot by 17 suspected Islamic militants to kidnap Americans in Egypt and swap them with jailed terrorists, including Aboud el-Zomoor, who was serving a 40-year sentence for taking part in the assassination of Anwar Sadat, and Sheik Omar Abdel Rahman, who was serving a life sentence for his part in the World Trade Center bombing and a similar plot involving the New York subway system. The militants were trying to revive Islamic Jihad. 98062501

June 25, 1998. *Algeria.* The Armed Islamic Group claimed credit for killing popular Berber singer Matoub Lounes, 42, who was driving from Tizi Ouzou to his village at midday when his car was fired on at a roadblock. He was a critic of Muslim extremists and the government, promoting secular democracy and Berber identity. A law making Arabic the country's official language went into effect the day of Lounes's funeral; Berbers do not speak Arabic as their first language.

The Armed Islamic Group had kidnapped Lounes in 1994, calling him "an enemy of God," but released him 15 days later after 100,000 people demonstrated for his release.

Rioters took to the streets in several towns in Algeria to protest his killing.

June 25, 1998. *Algeria.* Terrorists slit the throats of 17 villagers.

June 25, 1998. *Ethiopia.* Six staffers of the International Committee of the Red Cross (ICRC) were kidnapped while traveling from Gode to Degeh Bur in three marked vehicles. They included one Swiss and five Somalis. The Islamic group al-Ittihad al-Islami claimed credit on July 3, indicating that the hostages were being investigated for spying. They were released on July 10. 98062502

June 25, 1998. *Colombia.* The Revolutionary Armed Forces of Colombia (FARC) kidnapped a Canadian, a Bolivian, and a Colombian in Santander Department while the three were driving on a rural road. The Bolivian worked for a Colombian-German firm; the other two worked for a Canadian mining company. 98062503

June 28, 1998. *Colombia.* The National Liberation Army (ELN), the country's second-largest rebel group, agreed to meet with the new government of President Andres Pastrana. The group had met for three days in Mainz, near Frankfurt, Germany, with representatives from the government, business, and clergy. One of the two ELN negotiators was Pablo Beltran, a member of ELN's high command, who said, "A cease-fire is a possibility we have not ruled out." (However, the ELN's top commander, Nicolas Rodriguez Bautista, had recently stated that ELN would "never demobilize.") The government and rebels agreed to a new round of talks on July 12. The National Council for Peace, representing a cross-section of Colombian society, would seek to arrive at terms for a national convention. However, the largest rebel group, the Revolutionary Armed Forces of Colombia (FARC), did not participate.

June 28, 1998. *Colombia.* The Revolutionary Armed Forces of Colombia (FARC) declared that foreign oil companies and the Cano Limon-Covenas petroleum pipeline—the country's second-largest pipeline—were now military targets. 98062801

June 28, 1998. *India.* A bomb hidden in a lunchbox went off in Achaval Gardens, a popular picnic site in Anantnag, Kashmir, killing 2 and injuring 15.

June 29, 1998. *Albania.* Police arrested Maget Mustafa, 36, and Muhamet Houda, 39, two Egyptians accused of attempting to organize an Islamic fundamentalist network throughout the country. They led the Renaissance of the Islamic Heritage, which had been active in charitable work for a year. Such groups were also suspected of being covers for terrorist groups. The duo rented an apartment in the Tirana suburbs. The apartment contained forged documents, two automatic pistols, two rifles, and ammunition.

On July 4, the Albanian newspaper *Tirana Koha Jone* claimed that the two were arrested in Elbasan, escorted to Rians Airport, put onto a military plane, and handed over to the CIA. The paper said they were wanted for two murders committed in France and Algiers and were thought to belong to a Saudi terrorist group. The *Tirana Shekulli* paper the previous day had claimed that CIA and FBI commanders had taken the two terrorists away on July 2 with the support of the National Intelligence Service. A judge had allegedly freed them, but the police helped to spirit them out of the country after they were declared persona non grata.

On July 14, the *Tirana Gazeta Shqiptare* claimed that the two would set up a training camp in Elbasan for young Muslims who, upon graduation, would infiltrate the Kosovo Liberation Army. They were alleged to be members of the Selephist sect. 98062901

June 29, 1998. *Guatemala.* Eight heavily armed gunmen kidnapped four U.S. missionaries, identified as Barbara and Anita Stolfus and Otto and Jane Glick, from a remote ranch in the north. They were freed after a gun battle with troops and police along the Usumacinta River near the Mexican border in Peten region. Authorities had first said that 13 missionaries were taken. The four were members of a Christian group called Nueva Vida (New Life). 98062902

July 1998. *Japan.* Four people died and 60 others were sickened when they ate a pot of curry laced with arsenic at a Tokyo festival. On October 4, Masumi Hayashi, 37, a former insurance saleswoman, was arrested. Police believed she had tainted the food. She and her husband Kenji, a former pest exterminator, were held on a separate case of arsenic poisoning and insurance fraud. She was also held on suspicion of attempting to murder a visitor to her home by feeding him arsenic-laced curry.

July 1, 1998. *United States.* The FBI arrested three Texas men—Johnnie Wise, 72, Jack Abbott Grebe, Jr., 43, and Oliver Dean Emigh, 63—on charges of threatening via e-mail to use biological weapons against federal agents, including the directors of the FBI and the Internal Revenue Service, and of conspiracy to use weapons of mass destruction. The three were arrested at a mobile home in Olmito, five miles south of Brownsville, and were held in the Cameron County Jail. They were ordered held in custody on July 2 by U.S. Magistrate John Black, who refused to release them on bond. It was unclear whether they belonged to the separatist Republic of Texas group.

July 2, 1998. *Hungary.* A car bomb exploded shortly before noon in downtown Budapest, killing 3 men and 1 woman and injuring 25. Police believed the bombing was part of a turf battle involving Russian, Ukrainian, Romanian, Turkish, and Arab criminal gangs.

July 8, 1998. *Algeria.* The government announced that Khalifi Athmane (alias Hossein Flicha), 24, leader of the Armed Islamic Group, was shot dead along with ten others in the forested heights of the La Vigie District of Algiers. Also killed was Abderrahmani Redouane (alias Riad Le Blond), a leading rebel activist in the city.

July 8, 1998. *Uganda.* A UN World Food Program (WFP) worker was killed when guerrillas from the Uganda National Rescue Front II fired a rocket-propelled grenade at his WFP truck. 98070801

July 9, 1998. *Algeria.* A bomb exploded in a flea market in a poor Algiers neighborhood, killing 10 and wounding 21. At least 1,000 people were in the market at the time of the mid-morning bombing, which occurred just before a march by the Front of Socialist Forces to protest a law making Arabic the official language.

July 9, 1998. *Lebanon.* Lebanon's military prosecutor charged 18 members of the outlawed Lebanese Forces, a Christian militia group, with bombings and other attacks over the previous two years, trying to assassinate leading politicians, and collaborating with Israel. Eleven of the group were arrested in late June; seven remained at large. The next day, they were charged with bombing a bus in Syria in 1996 that killed 11.

July 10, 1998. *United Kingdom.* London police arrested seven suspected Irish terrorists minutes before they planned to detonate a bomb in central London. Five of their colleagues were arrested in Ireland. The group had a number of homemade bombs. Scotland Yard said the arrests came after an investigation of "dissident criminal Irish Republican terrorist groups." Police charged three men aged 19, 21, and 25 and one woman aged 21 with conspiracy to cause explosions. The two younger men and the woman were also charged with possession of explosives. Police called them IRA (Irish Republican Army) dissidents. Three of them were sentenced on May 21, 1999, to more than 20 years in prison for conspiracy. 98071001

July 14, 1998. *Georgia.* Maria-Magdalena Wewiorska, 31, a Polish member of the UN military observer team in Georgia, was shot to death outside her Tbilisi home. She had begun working as the secretary to the head of the UN mission three weeks earlier. 98071401

July 14, 1998. *Kuwait.* The U.S. Embassy was evacuated after receiving a bomb threat, the third in three weeks. A telephone operator in Canada received and relayed the threat. 98071402

July 14, 1998. *Colombia.* The Revolutionary Armed Forces of Colombia (FARC) kidnapped an Ecuadoran near Medellin. The victim, a U.S. resident, was en route to visit his family in Ecuador when he was abducted. FARC demanded a $1 million ransom. 98071403

July 17, 1998. *India.* An individual believed to be associated with Muslim militants threw a grenade in the Jehangir Chowk area in Srinagar, Kashmir, injuring 13. Police claimed that the grenade was thrown at a Border Security Force post, but exploded in the road instead.

July 18, 1998. *Ecuador.* The Indigenous Defense Front for Pastaza Province (FDIP) kidnapped three employees of an Ecuadoran pipeline maker subcontracted by a U.S. oil firm in Pastaza Province. The group accused the company of causing environmental damage in its oilfield developments. The FDIP released one hostage on July 28 and the other two the next day. 98071801

July 19, 1998. *Israel.* Jalal Rumaneh, 30, a Palestinian member of Hamas, was severely injured when he prematurely ignited a car bomb in his Fiat van on Jerusalem's Jaffa Road at 8:30 A.M. The bomb contained 160 gallons of flammable liquid and a large quantity of nails. The mixture caught fire, but failed to explode. The terrorist

lived in the Amari refugee camp near Ramallah. He was hospitalized with extensive burns and was reported in serious condition.

July 20, 1998. *Tajikistan.* Four UN Mission of Observers employees were shot to death in an ambush on the road from Tavildara to Labidzhar, 125 miles east of Dushanbe. In response, the head of the UN mission in the country then ordered all personnel to return to Dushanbe. Their bodies were found the next day. Local officials initially said they had died in a road accident. The dead were identified as Major Ryszard Szewczyk of Poland and Major Adolfo Sharpegue of Uruguay, both military observers; Akino Yutaka of Japan, a civil affairs officer; and Dzhourazhon Makhramov, the Tajik interpreter. Tajik President Imomali Rakhmonov termed the killings "a terrorist act carried out for political motives," according to presidential spokesman Zafar Saidov. 98072001

July 20, 1998. *Guatemala.* Sebastiano Crestani, 66, an Italian-born priest, was shot four times by unidentified gunmen during the afternoon in the parking lot of the San Juan de Borromeo Church in a southern neighborhood of Guatemala City. He was reported in serious condition. 98072002

July 21, 1998. *Rwanda.* Some 150 suspected rebel Hutu gunmen kidnapped Belgian missionaries Mark François, 51, and Jean Lefevre, 65, from the Ruhondo commune in the northern Ruhengeri District, 44 miles north of Kigali, during the evening. The Belgian Embassy sent two senior diplomats and two soldiers to the area. 98072101

July 21, 1998. *Macedonia.* Three 3:00 A.M. explosions went off in Skopje and two locations near the Yugoslav border. One blast shattered windows at a publishing company in Skopje. Another occurred near a high school in Kumanovo, on the border. A third damaged a locomotive parked along the border between Macedonia and Serbia. Some observers believed it was the work of the Kosovo Liberation Army, which had claimed credit for a series of explosions in January in three Macedonian towns populated by ethnic Albanians.

July 22, 1998. *Yemen.* An individual possibly associated with the Abu Nidal Organization murdered Muhammad Salah Sha'ban, an Egyptian citizen who was the *imam* of al-Husayni Mosque in Sanaa and a member of the Egyptian al-Gamaat al-Islamiya. 98072201

July 24, 1998. *United States.* At 3:40 P.M., Russell Eugene "Rusty" Weston, Jr., 41, a deranged gunman, opened fire with a .38 caliber revolver on guards at a security checkpoint in the U.S. Capitol Building, killing two Capitol police officers and seriously wounding a tourist, Angela Dickerson, 24, of Chantilly, Virginia.

Weston shot Officer Jacob J. Chestnut, 58, an 18-year veteran within months of retiring, in the back of the head at the Document Room metal detector, then ran down a corridor, exchanging fire with Officer Douglas B. McMillan. Weston chased a woman down the hall. She opened a door that led to the office of House Majority Whip Tom DeLay, where Weston exchanged gunfire with and killed Special Agent John Gibson, 42, an eight-year veteran. An arriving officer also shot Weston, who was captured in DeLay's office complex. Weston sustained bullet wounds in both legs and his stomach and was reported in stable condition. Dickerson, the injured tourist, sustained gunshot wounds to the shoulder and face. She was released from the hospital the following day.

Weston, a loner, believed that the government was using a satellite dish to spy on his Montana shack. The U.S. Secret Service had twice visited him in 1996 after he had made threatening statements about President Clinton. A judge committed him to a Montana state mental institution on October 11, 1996, after Weston threatened a Helena resident. A medical team released him 52 days later.

Weston was charged with murdering the two policemen. The District of Columbia Superior Court ordered him held without bond.

Weston had stolen the Smith and Wesson revolver from his father, shot his father's cats, and then driven his red 1983 Chevy S-10 pickup to Washington.

The funerals for the two slain officers included a 14-mile procession of police cars that wound from northern Virginia to Washington.

On September 23, 1998, Weston first appeared in U.S. District Court in a wheelchair and wearing casts on his left foot and right arm. Magistrate Judge John M. Facciola ordered him held without bond and set a follow-up hearing for October 14.

On October 9, a federal grand jury indicted Weston on two counts of murder and other charges. He was charged with killing officers Chestnut and Gibson and attempting to kill McMillan. He was also charged with three counts of weapons violations. He was not charged with wounding Dickerson; she may have been hit by McMillan in the firefight.

On December 4, 1998, psychiatrist Sally Johnson told the judge that the defendant was mentally incapable of standing trial and, even with treatment, might not be ready for several months. On January 28, 1999, Judge Emmet G. Sullivan ordered two more psychiatric exams for Weston. Weston would be hospitalized for 30 days, forcing a rescheduling of a February 22 competency hearing.

On April 13, 1999, federal prosecutors decided not to challenge a psychiatric determination that Weston was not competent to stand trial, thereby delaying a trial indefinitely. Judge Sullivan ordered both sides to return to court on April 22 for a formal ruling and said he would reevaluate the situation after Weston received 120 days of treatment in a federal psychiatric facility. Sullivan also said he might release Johnson's report.

On July 9, 1999, Judge Sullivan ruled that Weston could be forced to take medication to control his illness, thereby making him competent to stand trial. Sullivan delayed enactment of his ruling until September 9 to give defense attorneys A. J. Kramer and L. Barrett Boss time for an appeal. Doctors said the medication was also needed to reduce the threat Weston posed to himself and to other prisoners.

On March 24, 2000, Judge David S. Tatel, writing for the District of Columbia Circuit Court of Appeals, overturned the ruling by Judge Sullivan in September and held that several legal issues must be considered before forcing psychiatric medication on Weston. Prosecutors argued during the next four days of hearings that the government's rights to bring Weston to trial outweighed the defendant's arguments to remain drug-free.

On March 6, 2001, Judge Sullivan ruled that prison officials could forcibly medicate Weston so that he could stand trial, noting that medication is "essential to control and treat Weston's dangerousness to others."

On July 27, 2001, the three-judge panel of the U.S. Court of Appeals agreed with the forcible medication of Weston.

On December 10, 2001, the U.S. Supreme Court declined to hear the case, permitting Weston to be forcibly medicated.

July 24, 1998. *India.* A bomb exploded near the railroad tracks moments after the Shalimar Express passed by in Jammu and Kashmir, killing one soldier and injuring two civilians. Muslim militants were suspected.

July 25, 1998. *Yemen.* A Yemeni shot and killed three Catholic nuns, one Filipino, and two Indians in the Red Sea port city of Al Hudaydah. The killer considered himself a Muslim fundamentalist and claimed to have trained in Bosnia as a fighter. Yemeni officials deemed him "deranged." 98072501

July 25, 1998. *Japan.* Dozens of people ate poisoned curry at a summer festival in Wakayama in the west. By August 11, at least 4 people had died and another 60 had taken ill. On August 10, another ten workers at a company in Niigata on the Sea of Japan were hospitalized after drinking green tea and coffee made with poisoned hot water. On August 14, sisters Michiko, Wakako, and Natsue Nishimoto were hospitalized after complaining of numbness and trembling after eating cakes from a Kyoto pastry shop.

July 26, 1998. *India.* A bomb went off on an empty bus parked at the interstate bus terminal in New Delhi, killing two people and injuring eight others while destroying the bus and causing major damage to six other buses.

July 27, 1998. *Yemen.* Abdullah Nasheri, 22, a suspected Islamic extremist from Sanaa, shot to death three Roman Catholic medical nuns in Hodeidah, 140 miles west of Sanaa. The nuns worked as nurses for a charity organization affiliated with an international order founded by the late Mother Teresa. They were on their way from home to work when the killer fired on them with a Kalashnikov assault rifle. The killer confessed and said he would go to heaven. He said he killed the nurses because they were "preaching Christianity." The gunman said he had fought in Bosnia as a volunteer in 1992. He had lived there since 1992 and had acquired Bosnian nationality. He married a Bosnian woman.

The dead were identified as Sister Zilia, 35, from India, Sister Elita, 40, from India, and Sister Michaela, 36, from the Philippines. 98072701

July 28, 1998. *India.* Suspected Muslim militants killed ten villagers in a predawn attack northwest of Doda, Kashmir. Five persons were reported missing.

July 28, 1998. *India.* Suspected Muslim militants killed at least eight members of two Hindu families and wounded three others in Doda. The killers lined up the victims and shot them at point-blank range.

July 29, 1998. *Spain.* By a 7–4 vote, the Supreme Court sentenced former Socialist Interior Minister Jose Barrionuevo, former Secretary of State for Security Rafael Vera, and former Vizcaya Civil Governor Julian Sancristobal to ten years in jail for their involvement in the GAL "dirty war" against the Basque Nation and Liberty (ETA) terrorist group in the 1980s and for misuse of public funds and kidnapping. It was the first time in Spanish history that a minister or former minister had been sentenced to prison. The three were also barred from holding public office for 12 years. Barrionuevo was currently a Socialist member of parliament.

The crimes were related to the 1983 mistaken-identity kidnapping of Basque businessman Segundo Marey, which started the covert campaign against the ETA. Marey was held for ten days before being released, even after his captors realized they had grabbed the wrong man. The GAL was a front for security forces and hired assassins paid with secret government funds.

Nine other former officials and police were sentenced to two- to nine-year terms.

July 30, 1998. *St. Kitts.* Drug trafficker Charles Miller (alias Little Nutt), 37, threatened to murder at random American veterinary students if the United States obtained his extradition to the United States. Some 250 American students were at Ross Veterinary University, along with 50 American faculty members. At least 50 students left following the warning.

July 30, 1998. *Lebanon.* Hizballah gunmen ambushed Israeli soldiers on an operational firing exercise near Rihane post. Terrorist machine guns and mortars killed one Israeli soldier and injured five others. 98073001

August 1998. *Philippines.* On August 18, local police arrested the two main suspects in a shooting rampage that killed ten people, including Robert Bock, 33, of New York, a Peace Corps volunteer working as a fishery consultant in Concepcion, near Sara. Suspects Ricky Braga and his cousin Feliciano Braga were found in the town of Sara, about 300 miles from Manila. 98089901

August 1, 1998. *Northern Ireland.* A 500-pound car bomb exploded outside a shoe store in Banbridge, injuring 35 people and damaging 200 homes. Police had received a warning telephone call and were evacuating the area when the bomb went off. The Real IRA, the Republic of Ireland-based military wing of the 32 County Sovereignty Council, claimed credit.

August 3–4, 1998. *Colombia.* Marxist rebels conducted at least 42 attacks throughout the country, leaving 275 dead and scores wounded in a "farewell to the current government." The Revolutionary Armed Forces of Colombia (FARC) and the National Liberation Army (ELN) wrecked oil installations, attacked the main port city, blasted a major anti-drug base, and blocked highways. They set off car bombs in city centers, attacked villages, and fired rockets and mortar shells at military bases in 16 provinces. Seven rebels died in the fighting. Nearly 30 soldiers and police were missing and believed kidnapped. Pumps and storage tanks at three oil fields operated by U.S.-based Argosy Energy International were destroyed. 98080301-02

August 4, 1998. *India.* Separatist guerrillas in Kashmir killed 19 people from three families as they slept in Salina, 27 miles from the district town of Poonch. The Pakistan-based Lashkar-e-Tioba blamed India for the killings. More than 80 people had been killed since July 30 in heavy cross-border shelling.

Another 24 people were wounded when separatists threw a grenade into a crowded marketplace in Lal Chowk in Srinagar, Kashmir.

Militants from the Harakat ul-Muhajidin gunned down 19 people near Surankot, Kashmir. Two survivors traveled six hours on foot to report the attack. The victims were family members of a rival group that reportedly had been collaborating with Indian security forces.

Gunmen fired automatic rifles on a group of sleeping laborers at a remote construction site in Himachal Pradesh, killing 26 and wounding 8 others. The militants attacked a second group of workers, killing eight and wounding another three. Authorities blamed Pakistani-backed militants.

August 4, 1998. *Israel.* Gunmen shot to death two Jewish settlers on a routine security patrol near Yitzhar in the West Bank. Shlomo Liebman, 24, and Harel Binun, 18, were shot in their Toyota pickup and then dragged from their vehicle. The terrorists shot them again, then stole the victims' lone weapon before fleeing.

August 7, 1998. *Kenya and Tanzania.* Approximately 247 people, including 12 Americans, were killed and more than 5,500 wounded, including 80 non-Africans, when a car bomb went off in the Ufundi Cooperative Building in Nairobi, Kenya, next door to the U.S. Embassy, at 10:35 A.M. Five minutes later, a truck bomb exploded at the U.S. Embassy in Dar es Salaam, Tanzania, killing 10 Tanzanians and injuring at least 70 people, including an American who was medically evacuated to London. Former U.S. Ambassador Robert Oakley said embassy guards had prevented the terrorists from driving their car bombs into the embassy garages. (Six more people died on August 20 in Kenya, raising the count to 253 dead.)

Several groups claimed responsibility. The previously unknown Islamic Army for the Liberation of Holy Places (variant Liberation Army of the Islamic Sanctuaries, usually meaning Mecca and Medina; variant Islamic Army for the Liberation of Holy Shrines) claimed credit, saying it opposed the U.S. military presence in Muslim countries. The group told Qatar Television that "Islamic holy warriors from all countries of the world" would drive U.S. troops out of Saudi Arabia and other Muslim countries. It would "strike at American interests in all places until all its objectives are met." It claimed that the Nairobi attack was carried out by two men from Mecca; the attack in Dar was conducted by an Egyptian. The group demanded that the U.S. military leave Saudi Arabia and that the United States end support to Israel. It demanded the release of detained Islamic militants and denounced economic sanctions against Muslim nations. It said Osama bin Laden and Sheik Omar Abdel Rahman served as their inspiration. In late July, Egypt's al-Gamaat al-Islamiya's exiled leader, Sheik Abu Yasser Rifai Taha, had announced that al-Gamaat was not a member of the Islamic Front for Holy War Against the Jews and Crusaders, which it had joined in February. A communiqué sent to Agence France Press claimed credit for the Dar bombing

for the Abdallah Azzam Battalion. Azzam died in 1989 fighting against the Soviets in Afghanistan. He was close to Osama bin Laden.

Most observers believed that terrorists from outside the countries were responsible. Many suspected exiled Saudi terrorist financier Osama bin Laden of being behind the attacks. Others suggested Ayman Zawahiri (variants Ayman al-Zawahiri, Ayman Zawahri, Iman Zowaheri), the exiled leader of the Egyptian Islamic Jihad organization. The previous week, the group had threatened to attack the United States for the June 28 capture in Albania and extradition to Egypt of three Islamic militants connected to the ethnic Albanian separatist movement in Kosovo, Yugoslavia. One of the captured individuals was Ahmed Ibrahim Najjar, who was under sentence of death in Egypt for his role in the attack on Cairo's Khan el Khalili bazaar. Both suspects were believed to be hiding out in Afghanistan.

Still others believed hard-liners in Iran were responsible. Iran condemned the bombing.

Early reports said that one man had been taken into custody.

In an address to the nation, President Clinton vowed, "No matter how long it takes, or where it takes us, we will pursue terrorists until the cases are solved and justice is done. The bombs that kill innocent Americans are aimed . . . at the very spirit of our country and the spirit of freedom, for terrorists are the enemies of everything we believe in and fight for: peace and democracy, tolerance and security. As long as we continue to believe in those values and continue to fight for them, their enemies will not prevail. Our responsibility is great, but the opportunities it brings are even greater. Let us never fear to embrace them."

Kenya bombing. The bomb went off in a parking lot at one of the city's busiest intersections. It flattened the Cooperative Building and seriously damaged the U.S. Embassy. Numerous cars were destroyed and windows one and a half miles away were broken. Damaged buildings included the Cooperative Bank House, the Extelcoms telecommunications headquarters, the Kenya Railways Headquarters, and the Pioneer House. Passengers in a bus were incinerated where they sat. At least 12 U.S. citizens were killed, along with 14 Kenyans who worked at the U.S. Embassy. Some 153 Kenyans were blinded. The remaining dead were Kenyans. Among those injured was Kenyan Trade Minister Joseph Kamotho. Five Americans and 109 Kenyan employees of the U.S. Embassy were missing. Several witnesses said they had heard a small explosion—perhaps an exploding grenade—before the main blast. Others claimed to have heard gunfire minutes before the bombing. Nairobi hospitals were overburdened. U.S. Ambassador Prudence Bushnell was hospitalized and later released.

An embassy guard said that someone got out of a truck and threatened him with a grenade. The guard ran away, but the terrorist threw the grenade. There apparently were some shots before the vehicle exploded.

The next day, numerous rescue teams dug through the rubble, finding remains and the occasional survivor. The State and Defense Departments and FBI sent emergency response teams, including doctors, disaster relief experts, military protection units, and counterterrorism investigators. The 175 FBI agents were led by Sheila Horan, a career counterintelligence agent, who heads an FBI counterterrorism unit in Washington. An Israeli urban rescue team used Homatro hydraulic pliers, Husqvarna saws, listening devices, and dogs trained to find corpses. One group of 12 girls and a man was found, but the concrete shifted, crushing them.

Included among the dead were:

- Marine Sergeant Jesse Nathanael Aliganga, 21, of Tallahassee, a member of the Marine Security Guard detachment. He had made sergeant on his first four-year tour. He had been posted to Okinawa, Japan, and Camp Pendleton, California.
- Consul General Julian Bartley, Sr., 55.
- Jay Bartley, son of Consul General Bartley. Jay Bartley had lived in Bowie, Maryland, before going overseas.

- Jean Dalizu, of the defense attaché's office. She had a daughter in Washington, D.C.
- Molly Huckaby Hardy, 51, of Centreville, Virginia, and Valdosta, Georgia. She was due to be replaced in the administrative division of the embassy. Hardy, a divorced mother who had raised a daughter alone, had served on three continents during her 20-year career with the State Department.
- Army Sergeant Kenneth Hobson, II, 27, of Nevada, Missouri, who worked in the defense attaché's office as an administrative specialist. He had been in the U.S. Army for seven years, following graduation from Nevada High School in Missouri. He was a Gulf War veteran.
- Prabhi Guptara Kavaler, 46, who had left her Balsam Drive, McLean, Virginia, home with Howard Kavaler, her State Department husband, and their two daughters ten days earlier to start a new assignment in the administrative division of the General Services Office. She was born in India to a university professor. After receiving a master's degree in sociology from the University of New Delhi, she became a U.S. citizen and foreign service officer. The couple had served in Pakistan, the Philippines, Israel, France, and earlier in Nairobi.
- Arlene Kirk, 50, of South Bend, Indiana, a U.S. Air Force budget and fiscal officer in the Military Assistance Office. She was on her first day back at work after a six-week vacation.
- Louise Martin, 45, of Atlanta, an employee of the Centers for Disease Control and Prevention.
- Air Force Senior Master Sergeant Sherry Lynn Olds, 40, of Panama City, Florida, who worked in the Military Assistance Office. She had served in the U.S. Air Force for 20 years after graduating from junior college. She had also earned a degree from the University of South Carolina.
- Michelle O'Connor, who worked in the General Services Office.

- Tom Shah, of Vienna, Virginia, who worked in the Political Section.

Some press reports claimed that a CIA officer was among those killed.

British Captain Rhyl Jones of the Royal Engineers estimated that the bomb consisted of 400 to 500 pounds of commercial explosives.

Tel Aviv's *Ha'aretz* claimed that a man in contact with Mossad had warned that the U.S. Embassy in Kenya might be a target just before the bombing. However, Mossad said that he had been unreliable in the past.

On August 11, the State Department said that it was temporarily closing six embassies—including those in Uganda, Malaysia, and Swaziland—to update security. The department had received two dozen threats since the bombings.

On August 12, the press reported that U.S. intelligence agencies had foiled at least two attacks on embassies in the past two years and that 40 terrorists had been apprehended. These included the November 1996 arrest of a Lebanese who had been suspected of trying to plant a car bomb at the embassy in Paraguay.

The same day, investigators believed that they had found the remains of the truck used as the bomb carrier.

The bodies of 11 dead Americans were brought home to U.S. soil on August 14, accompanied by Secretary of State Madeleine Albright, who had announced a $2 million reward for information leading to the capture and conviction of the killers. Ten of the Americans arrived at Andrews Air Force Base in Maryland. Another woman, married to a Kenyan, was buried in Kenya. Olds was flown directly to Florida.

Israeli investigators said the bomb was triggered by Semtex; it was later determined to be TNT.

Iranian exiles blamed Iran; Tehran denied the charges.

Tanzania bombing. Most of the dead had been working at the guard post at the embassy entrance near where the bomb exploded. All either worked at the embassy or for a security company that guarded the gate. The bomb apparently was attached to an embassy-owned tanker truck delivering water. After it was waved through the security gates, it exploded several feet from the embassy's southeastern edge, tearing a large crater in Laibon Street. The blast destroyed the guardhouse and killed the driver, Yusuf Shamte Ndange. It was unclear whether the bomb was remotely detonated or had exploded when it was discovered by guards, including Paul Elisha, 32. Nearby cars were badly damaged. The home of the British high commissioner (ambassador) two blocks away had broken windows and damage from debris. Other nearby homes were similarly damaged. The home of an electric company official, Bariuany Luhanga, was damaged. He, his wife, and three children, all of whom were in the home at the time the bomb exploded, were hospitalized for cuts and shock. A multi-car pileup ensued when cars were hit by debris. The nearby French and German embassies were damaged, but no injuries were reported there. At least 22 cars were destroyed.

On August 11, the Tanzanian police announced that they had arrested 30 foreigners in connection with the blast. They included six Iraqis, six Sudanese, one Somali, and one Turk. The Sudanese included a teenager and a man who claimed to work for the Saudi Embassy. The Iraqis included a teacher, a civil servant, a telecommunications technician, an engineer, and an agricultural engineer. FBI agents were permitted to question them. Fourteen lacked passports and could not give a reason for being in the country.

A surveillance camera atop the embassy survived the blast, but did not record the attack.

As of August 14, authorities were searching for Saidi Rogati, 49, a missing embassy employee who had regular access to the water truck. Under normal circumstances, he would have been sitting next to the driver when the bomb exploded at 10:39 A.M. The driver's body was found. Later investigation suggested that the bomb was not in the water truck.

Epilogue. Pakistani officials arrested a Jordanian-born Palestinian, Mohammed Saddiq Odeh (variant Howeida), 32 (or 34), an engineer, at

Karachi Airport the day of the bombings and returned him to Kenya on August 14 for traveling on a false Yemeni passport with a fake visa in the name of Abdull Bast Awadah. An immigration official noted that the photograph in his passport was not of Odeh. He had flown to Pakistan on August 6 on Pakistan International Airways flight 943, departing Nairobi at 10:00 P.M. and arriving in Karachi at 8:25 A.M., the day of the blast. He said his spiritual guide was bin Laden and that he was attempting to seek refuge with him in Afghanistan. He claimed that the bomb contained 1,760 pounds of TNT and was assembled over several days at the hotel under his direction. Kenyan television claimed that he was married to a Kenyan. Police held three other people in connection with the attack. Two were identified as Mohammed Saleh and Abdullah. Odeh also claimed that his group had taken part in the October 3–4, 1993, attack on U.S. forces in Mogadishu, Somalia, in which 18 Americans were killed. Former Ambassador Robert Oakley and several journalists who had covered the attack said they were unaware of any foreign involvement in the Somalia killings. Islamabad's *News* claimed Odeh had confessed to conducting other missions for bin Laden in the Philippines, Cairo, and Jordan.

Odeh's Yemeni passport (No. 0011061) was stamped for entry into Mombasa, Kenya, on August 3. He apparently took a ten-hour bus ride to the capital.

On August 14, Benson Okuku Bwaku, a Kenyan security guard at the U.S. Embassy in Nairobi, picked a bin Laden operative out of FBI photos. He claimed he had seen the man near the embassy.

On August 15, Pakistan arrested a Saudi and a Sudanese carrying fake Yemeni passports at Torkham, in the Khyber Pass on the Afghan border. Odeh had identified them as his accomplices. They appeared to be between 25 and 35 years old. They entered Pakistan on August 6, on the same flight from Kenya as Odeh.

On August 17, Pakistani authorities arrested Mohammad Abdullah Madni, 22, a Saudi who was attempting to enter Afghanistan at the Towr

Kham border post in the North West Frontier Province. He claimed he was a bin Laden associate, but authorities said he was not involved with the bombings. He was to be handed over to Saudi security agents. Pakistani officials stopped a second foreigner at the border, but did not arrest him. They announced that no foreigners would be permitted to cross into Afghanistan. Odeh had by then identified six accomplices.

The *East African*, a Kenyan newspaper, reported that a Pakistani suspect was arrested in the United Arab Emirates and shipped back to Kenya. Some 20 suspects, most of whom were freed for lack of evidence, had been detained in Kenya and Tanzania.

On August 18, 15 FBI agents and 6 Kenyan detectives raided the seedy Hilltop Hotel, located one mile from the U.S. Embassy, and carried away several cartons of evidence. They were acting on information provided by Odeh. They arrested the hotel manager, James Mnuri Nnanga, a Christian, and seized the hotel register. They concentrated on rooms A107, a two-bedroom suite on the first floor, and B102, a single room on the second floor, which had been occupied by four men—two Palestinians, one Saudi, and one Egyptian—from August 3 to 7. None of the hotel staff recalled seeing anything suspicious. The hotel was owned by the Yemeni-Lebanese family of Arafad Said Abdalla. Odeh said the bomb was made between August 4 and August 6 in the rooms, then moved for final assembly to the back of the covered 3.5-ton Mitsubishi pickup truck used in the bombing. The Nairobi *Nation* reported that all three bombers in the truck died in the blast.

On August 19, the Afghan Taliban refused to turn Osama bin Laden over to the West, even if the West had proof that he was behind the bombings. Secretary of State Madeleine K. Albright said the Taliban would not receive diplomatic recognition if it continued to harbor terrorists. The Taliban said bin Laden would be punished in Afghanistan because "it is not right to give a Muslim to an infidel country." The United States ordered the evacuation of Americans from Pakistan, which arrested two men who were trying to cross into Afghanistan.

On August 20, FBI Director Louis Freeh and senior FBI agents visited Nairobi for an update on the investigation. FBI and local police officers raided the local headquarters of the Mercy International Relief Agency, a Muslim group, carting away files, computer equipment, a fax machine, audio and video tapes, $3,500 in cash, and three glass bookshelves. They also took into custody Shaban Hassan Ismail, the group's education coordinator. The group's attorney, Abdikadir Hussein Mohamed, said the agency is registered in Ireland and that the local chapter was founded by Kenyans of Somali extraction. It operates orphanages and other charities in Kenya, Ethiopia, Uganda, and Somalia and has no association with Osama bin Laden, who often uses charities as covers for his overseas operations. The group's bank accounts were frozen after the raid.

The *Nawa-i-Waqt* of Rawalpindi, Pakistan, claimed that U.S. military commandos and FBI agents were planning to kidnap or kill bin Laden. The United States urged all non-Muslim foreigners to leave Afghanistan.

Later that evening, the United States fired 79 Tomahawk cruise missiles at the Zhawar Kili Al-Badr paramilitary training camps in Afghanistan and at Sudan's Shifa pharmaceutical plant that was used to develop EMPTA, a VX chemical weapons precursor. All facilities were suspected of being used in planning new anti-U.S. attacks. Bin Laden's terrorist training complex in Khost, Afghanistan, 94 miles southeast of Kabul and just inside the border with Pakistan, was deemed by President Clinton to be "one of the most active terrorist bases in the world." The United States said it was attacking to preempt several other attacks, based upon excellent evidence, and was not designed to deflect attention from President Clinton's admission of having had an affair with Monica Lewinsky, a White House intern. The bin Laden training center was the site of a meeting of major international terrorists. Taliban sources said bin Laden was not harmed. Senior officials warned that "this is not a one-shot deal" in the war against terrorism, but that terrorist retaliatory attacks

could be expected. Initial damage was reported to be moderate to heavy. Afghanistan said 21 people were killed and more than 50 wounded in the camps around Khost, near the Pakistan border. The Taliban reported destruction of six camps, including Salman Farcy, Al-Badar, and Tajik camps. An unconfirmed Pakistani report said bin Laden was killed. Sudan said ten people were hospitalized.

One of the camps was run by Harkat Ansar as a site where Pakistani guerrillas were armed and trained to fight in Kashmir. Another camp was run by Pakistanis belonging to Jamit Mujaheddin guerrillas. Harkat ul-Jihad al-Islami, bin Laden's main camp, trained various Arabs. Pakistan claimed and then denied that a missile hit Pakistani territory, killing 11 Pakistanis. Numerous Islamic leaders condemned the raids; radical terrorist leaders threatened revenge.

President Clinton froze bin Laden's U.S. assets and those of his two senior lieutenants and their Islamic Army organization. The order also prohibited U.S. firms and individuals from doing business with them.

Bin Laden was at one of the camps. He apparently left before the missiles arrived.

On August 21, the Nairobi *Daily News* reported that Khalid Mohammed was identified as the man who threw the grenade at the guards before escaping. He was picked out of a police lineup by witnesses.

On August 24, a federal grand jury in New York handed up a sealed indictment against bin Laden for terrorist acts against the United States that preceded the Africa bombings.

On August 25, National Public Radio reported that bin Laden had twice attempted to assassinate President Clinton. In one instance, the president changed his travel plans. In the other, Ramzi Ahmed Yusuf, the World Trade Center bombing mastermind, was to be the killer.

On August 27, Pakistan claimed that its scientists and weapons experts were studying ways to reverse-engineer components from a Tomahawk cruise missile that crashed into Pakistani territory near Kharan, 370 miles south of the Afghan terrorist camps. They said it would assist Pakistan's missile program's guide systems, onboard computers, and propulsion systems. Some suggested that Pakistan would share the information with the Chinese. Pentagon officials declined comment although many privately doubted Pakistan's claims.

Mohamed Rashed Daoud al-Owhali (alias Khalid Salim Saleh bin Rashed), a Yemeni who rode on the truck in Nairobi, was flown to the United States on August 26. He was arraigned the next day in a Manhattan courthouse on 12 counts of murder—1 for each American killed in the attack—1 count of conspiracy, and 1 count of using weapons of mass destruction. FBI Director Freeh told a news conference that al-Owhali had admitted that he was trained in Afghan camps affiliated with bin Laden, that he had attended meetings with bin Laden, and that he had expected to die in the bombing. Al-Owhali traveled to Nairobi on July 31 from Lahore, Pakistan. A week later, he threw the grenade at the guard. He was hospitalized in Nairobi with lacerations on his hands and face and a large wound on his back. He was questioned by Kenyan police two days later, then arrested. At the hospital, he discarded two keys that fit a padlock on the rear of the truck, and three bullets from a gun he had in the truck. Hospital employees later found the evidence. On August 12, he initially told the FBI that he had been standing in a bank near the embassy when the bomb went off and claimed he was wearing the same clothing as on August 7. The affidavit doubted this claim, because "his clothes bore no traces of blood." He later admitted lying. On August 20, al-Owhali confessed to the FBI, saying he had been trained in explosives, hijacking, and kidnapping in Afghan camps. Some were affiliated with al-Qaeda, which, according to the affidavit, was "an international terrorist group led by Osama bin Laden, dedicated to opposing non-Islamic governments with force and violence." He was aware that bin Laden had issued a *fatwah* calling for the killing of Americans. He was ordered held without bail pending a September 28 court appearance. Al-Owhali applied for free legal services, saying he

was single, unemployed, and had received $12,000 from his father in the past year. His only asset was a 1992 Chevrolet Caprice.

Freeh noted that 550 people had been interviewed in the case and more than three tons of debris had been sent to the FBI lab in Washington for testing.

On August 27, Mohammed Saddiq Odeh, 33, the Palestinian engineer, was brought out of Nairobi and arrived in New York City the next day to be arraigned on similar charges. In the affidavit, federal prosecutors accused bin Laden's al-Qaeda group of bombing the embassy in Kenya. Odeh was charged with 12 counts of murder, 1 count of murder conspiracy, and 1 count of conspiracy to use weapons of mass destruction. Jack Sachs, Odeh's court-appointed attorney, said Odeh lived in Jordan with his wife and one daughter and was last employed making and selling furniture. The affidavit said Odeh joined al-Qaeda in 1992 and received explosives training at bin Laden's camps. Odeh later trained other Islamic radicals opposed to the UN humanitarian mission in Somalia. In 1994, he moved to Mombasa, Kenya, where he used al-Qaeda money to establish a fishing business, whose profits supported al-Qaeda members in Kenya. He met with senior al-Qaeda commanders. On August 2, he met with al-Qaeda members, including an explosives expert who ran the Kenyan cell. On August 4, the group, minus Odeh, surveilled the U.S. Embassy. On August 6, all but one member of the group left Nairobi. Odeh was told that al-Qaeda members in Afghanistan were also moving "to avoid retaliation from the U.S."

On September 2, the Yemeni government newspaper *Al-Wihdah* said authorities had no record in the country's population registry of Khalid Salim, reportedly a Yemeni national who threw grenades at the U.S. Embassy in Kenya.

Odeh claimed on September 3 that the Pakistanis had coerced him into a confession, which Pakistan denied.

On September 5, Tanzania arrested two suspects—one Tanzanian and one foreigner. The FBI filed an arrest warrant for a third man wanted in

Nairobi. The three were all Islamic extremists with ties to bin Laden. The Nairobi suspect, Haroun Fazil (alias Abdallah Mohammed Fadhul), an explosives expert, was a citizen of the Comoros who had been living in Sudan. On September 2, the FBI and Comoran police raided homes belonging to his wife and parents in Moroni, Comoros, but he eluded capture. The Comoros agreed to extradite Fazil to Kenya if he was found. Investigators believed the explosives for the bombs came from the Middle East and were shipped to the Comoros. From there, they went via small boat to a landing north of Dar and were trucked to Nairobi and a truck repair plant. Police believed that Fazil rented the villa outside Nairobi that was used to build the bomb, helped plan the assault, then drove a white pickup truck that led the truck bomb to the embassy. Fazil was charged with 12 counts of murder, 1 count of conspiracy to commit murder, and 1 count of conspiracy to use weapons of mass destruction. He faced the death penalty if convicted in the United States.

Tanzanian and American investigators were looking into the activities of the Tommy Spades Manufacturing Company plant in Kimara, Tanzania, the possible site of the bomb's manufacture and where the bomb was welded to the chassis of the water truck. The truck was reportedly at the plant for repairs shortly before the explosion. Thomas A. Lyimo, the plant's owner, was jailed along with four others. Investigators found some of the same chemicals at the plant that were found in the bomb crater.

On September 16, 1998, German police arrested Mamduh Mahmud Salim, 40, an al-Qaeda member who was described as a major financial operative who also procured weapons. A sealed warrant seeking his arrest had recently been filed in Manhattan. He carried a Sudanese passport and claimed to have been born in Khartoum. Some believed he was of Iraqi descent. He was arrested while visiting a friend near Freising in Bavaria. His plane ticket would have taken him to Turkey. He told investigators that he planned to purchase 20 used cars in Germany, but was not carrying a large amount of money. On November 30, a Munich court approved Salim's extradition to the United States to face charges in U.S. District Court in New York. Germany's highest court approved the extradition on December 11, 1998. By December 19, Bavarian regional justice authorities and the Foreign Ministry had agreed to hand him over to the United States. He was turned over to U.S. officials the next day, flying from Munich Airport to the United States on a U.S. government plane. He was held without bail after appearing in a New York City court and charged with murder, conspiracy, and use of weapons of mass destruction in an international plot to kill U.S. citizens. His court-appointed lawyer, Paul J. McAllister, said the charges were vague.

Later that night, the FBI arrested U.S. citizen Wadih el-Hage, 38, a Lebanese Christian who converted to Islam and married an American and who once served as bin Laden's personal secretary. The Arlington, Texas, resident lived in a three-bedroom apartment with his wife and seven children at the South Campus Apartments in Arlington. He drove a 1981 Honda Prelude and 1984 Chevrolet Caprice and had $150 in a checking account. He was earning $1,600 a month as a manager at Lone Star Wheels and Tires. He was held without bail on charges of lying to the FBI about not knowing Odeh and Abu Ubaidah al Banshiri, a former military commander for bin Laden. He was well known to bin Laden's top military commanders, al Banshiri and Abu Hafs el Masry. He had told the FBI that he did not know that al Banshiri had drowned in a Tanzanian ferry accident in Lake Victoria in May 1996, even though he traveled to the scene with Haroun Fazil. He was bin Laden's secretary while living in Sudan until 1994. He had lived and worked with Fazil while employed in the Kenya gem business until 1997. He helped Odeh obtain an identity card and sent him to Somalia in 1997 for bin Laden. The U.S. State Department announced a $2 million reward for the capture of Fazil, who was charged in the Kenya attack. On September 21, el-Hage was indicted with eight counts of perjury. During el-Hage's September 23 bail hearing in Manhattan, federal prosecutors said that he once purchased guns in Texas for Mahmud Abouhalima, one of the 1993 World Trade Center bombers, and that he had contacts with El Sayyid Nosair, who helped plan the World Trade Center bombing and who killed Jewish Defense League leader Meir Kahane in 1990. Magistrate Judge Leonard Bernikow ordered el-Hage held without bail. Prosecutor Patrick Fitzgerald suggested that additional charges could be filed against him. Prosecutors believed that el-Hage was associated with the suspected murder of a radical Islamic preacher in Texas in the late 1980s. Bruce McIntyre was named el-Hage's court-appointed attorney.

The indictment of el-Hage indicated that al-Qaeda operated in Sudan, Saudi Arabia, Egypt, Yemen, Somalia, Eritrea, Afghanistan, Pakistan, Bosnia, Croatia, Algeria, Tunisia, Lebanon, the Philippines, Tajikistan, Chechnya, Kashmir, Azerbaijan, Kenya, and the United States.

On September 17, federal prosecutors unsealed a criminal complaint against an at large bin Laden associate who helped carry out the Nairobi attack. Prosecutors also announced that 18 people were detained in Uganda after an alleged plot against U.S. interests led to the closure of the U.S. Embassy in Kampala.

The FBI backed away from the water truck theory, saying that the truck carrying the bomb drove up behind the water truck.

The United States froze the Bank America accounts of Salaheldin Idris, the Sudanese-born businessman whose pharmaceuticals plant was bombed. He claimed he did not know bin Laden or his associates. Idris hired the law firm of Akin, Gump, Strauss, Hauer, and Feld, whose senior partner was Vernon Jordan, President Clinton's friend. The bank also froze the accounts of Bashir Hassan Bashir, the plant's original majority owner, following the August 21 order by the Treasury Department blocking financial transactions by bin Laden and his associates. On October 3, the *New York Times* reported that the United States had discovered that Idris had had financial dealings with members of the Egyptian Islamic Jihad, which received money from bin Laden.

On September 21, Egyptian Mustafa Mah-

moud Said Ahmed (alias Said Ahmed; alias Saleh Aben Alahales) and Tanzanian Rashid Saleh Hemed, a Zanzibar native, were charged in a Dar courtroom with 11 counts of murder. Resident Magistrate Amiri Maneto disallowed bail. October 5 was set as the trial date. Traces of chemicals that could have been used to make the bomb were found in Saleh's home and car. Ahmed, heavyset and bearded, said that he was in Arusha, in northern Tanzania, on the day of the bombing. Police were also seeking two men who had often visited Saleh. Another suspect arrested in Germany was to be held in Munich until he could be extradited to the United States. Tanzania released three other suspects the next day. The suspects were local garage owner Thomas Lyimo, another Tanzanian, and an Algerian.

On September 21, another bombing victim, a woman, died in Kenya, bringing the tally to 254.

Federal prosecutors in New York unsealed the criminal complaint against Mamdouh Mahmud Salim on September 25. The complaint charged Salim with conspiracy to commit murder and use weapons of mass destruction. It said that Salim helped bin Laden to found al-Qaeda and that Salim sat on the group's *majlis al shura*, the advisory council that approves military attacks, and on the *fatwah* committee, which issued Islamic edicts promoting attacks on Americans. It noted that Salim had worked for al-Qaeda in Sudan, Afghanistan, Malaysia, the Philippines, and Pakistan. He obtained communications equipment and "electronic items necessary for the detonation of explosives." It indicated that bin Laden, in conjunction with the governments of Iran and Sudan, sent individuals around the world in the early 1990s to obtain nuclear weapons. The prosecutors charged that Salim met with Iranian officials in Tehran and Khartoum to arrange for al-Qaeda members to receive explosives training in Lebanon from Hizballah. The complaint mentioned attempts in 1993 to purchase enriched uranium to fabricate a nuclear bomb. On September 29, federal prosecutors in Manhattan expanded the charges against him, saying that between 1992 and 1998 he had taken part in a conspiracy to attack

U.S. military sites abroad and had conspired to transport explosives. They said they would seek his extradition from Germany. On October 6, the Delhi, India *Pioneer* reported that Indian intelligence was investigating Salim.

On September 27, London police rearrested Saudi national Khalid 'Abd-al-Rahman Hamad al-Fawwaz, 36, and arrested six other fundamentalists in Operation Challenge. London police said the U.S. request for al-Fawwaz's deportation to the United States was for "conspiring with bin Laden and others against U.S. citizens during January 1993 through September 27, 1998." In al-Fawwaz's house, police found copies of statements issued by the World Islamic Front for Fighting Jews and Crusaders, bin Laden and Zawahiri's group. Scotland Yard also found a forged passport in his home. He had been released on September 26; no charges had been made up till then. Others arrested with him included 'Adil 'Abd-al-Majid 'Abd-al Bari, sentenced to death in absentia in Egypt in connection with the Khan al-Khalili bombings. He was released on bail after being charged with possessing firearms without a license, provided that he returned to appear before the Bow Street District Court on October 12. The other fundamentalists held under the immigration law were Hani al-Siba'i Abu-Karim, Sayyid 'Ajami, Ibrahim al-'Aydarus, Sayyid 'Abd-al-Maqsud, and Osama Ahmad Hasan, the latter a member of the Armed Islamic Group in Egypt and brother of Sharif Hasan, a leader of the Returnees from Afghanistan who was executed in Egypt years earlier. On September 8, 1999, Fawwaz's lawyer, Edward Fitzgerald, claimed his client was regularly in touch with MI5 before and after the attacks. The next day, a British magistrate ordered Fawwaz held for extradition to the United States on conspiracy charges. His lawyers said they would appeal to London's high court. The final extradition decision rested with Home Secretary Jack Straw.

On September 29, investigators identified the Tanzanian bombing vehicle, which was destroyed except for the chassis.

On September 30, two FBI agents were slight-ly injured in a Nairobi road accident involving a public service vehicle and their rental car. A minivan ran a red light and rammed their car. They were robbed of their firearms and a radio transceiver in the aftermath. FBI Special Agent Bryant Ling was treated at the hospital for bruises; FBI Special Agent Mark Allan was treated and released.

On October 1, Tanzanian Home Affairs Minister Ali Ameir Mohamed said that Mustafa Mahmoud Said Ahmed, one of two men charged in the bombing, had confessed to having links with bin Laden and said that he knew the two men charged in New York with the Nairobi bombing. He claimed, "Mustafa is either the mastermind behind the bombing or is a key person in the bombing conspiracy." Ahmed, an Egyptian with passports from Yemen, Congo, and Iraq, claimed to have warned Kenyan intelligence officials about the plot to bomb the U.S. embassies.

On October 2, Italian police arrested on weapons possession charges two Egyptians and a Yemeni man detained on suspicion of links with bin Laden. One of them, linked to Egypt's Al-Jihad, had been involved in guerrilla activity in Albania before fleeing to Turin, where he created a base. Police seized arms, gold ingots, cash, forged documents, and propaganda material from a Turin garage.

On October 7, the Taliban reportedly told the Saudis that it would put bin Laden on trial for a 1996 bomb attack on U.S. airmen in Saudi Arabia if the victims' families made a request.

On October 5, Ugandan Minister of State for Foreign Affairs Amama Mbabazi said that terrorists initially intended to simultaneously bomb the U.S. Embassy in Kampala.

On October 7, a federal grand jury in New York handed down a 238-count indictment, charging several of bin Laden's disciples with planning to kill Americans. The plot included the Tanzania and Kenya bombings and the training of militias that attacked U.S. soldiers in Somalia in 1993. The plot named U.S. citizen Wadih el-Hage, Mohammed Rashed Daoud al Owhali, Azzam (who apparently died in the Nairobi blast),

Mohammed Saddiq Odeh, and Abdallah Mohammed Fazil, and Mahdouh Mahmud Salim.
Unindicted co-conspirators included Ayman al
Zawahiri, Islamic Jihad leader; Ahmed Refai
Taha, al-Gamaat leader; and former al-Gamaat
leader Sheik Omar Abdel Rahman. Owhali and
Azzam made a video before the blast and claimed
credit for a fictitious organization. Prosecutors
also sought the extradition of Khaled al Fawaz, a
bin Laden spokesman who was arrested in September in London. Mohammed, Odeh, and al
Owhali were charged with 224 counts of murder.
Odeh and Mohammed were charged with training
the Somalis. On October 8, el-Hage, Odeh, and
Owhali pleaded not guilty.

On October 20, Abdul Hakeem Muhajid, the
Taliban's chief representative in the United States,
said the militia would put bin Laden on trial if the
United States provided convincing evidence.

On October 22, the *New York Times* reported
that nine months before the attack, U.S. intelligence officials had received a detailed warning
from a man who walked into the Nairobi embassy
in November 1997. The man said Islamic radicals
were planning to blow up the U.S. Embassy in
Kenya. The warning came from Mustafa Mahmoud Said Ahmed, charged with the Tanzania
bombing. American officials said that a cooperating intelligence service labeled him a fabricator at
the time. Kenyan officials interrogated and then
deported him. His attorney in the Dar case, Abdul
Mwengela, said his client's information came from
an overheard conversation at a Nairobi hotel. A
Tanzanian court refused bail and ruled that the
FBI could question him. The United States did
not request extradition. He told a court that he
had contacted the British Embassy in Dar the day
after the bombings and offered investigators his
help.

On October 30, the *New York Times* reported
that on September 11 federal prosecutors had filed
sealed charges against former army sergeant Ali A.
Mohamed (alias Abu Omar), 46, a native of
Egypt, who was in custody at the Metropolitan
Correctional Center in New York. Mohamed
served for three years at the U.S. Army's Special

Forces base in Fort Bragg, North Carolina. A witness at the 1995 New York subway trial testified
that he traveled to New York while on active duty
to provide military training to Muslims preparing
to fight Soviets in Afghanistan. Students included
El Sayyid A. Nosair, who killed Meir Kahane.
Sometime in the 1990s, he became involved with
the al-Qaeda group. On May 19, 1999, federal
officials indicted Mohamed on charges of training
bin Laden's terrorists and Islamic militants who
were implicated in the World Trade Center
bombing. Mohamed was a former major in the
Egyptian Army. He was granted a visa to the United States in 1985 and eventually became a U.S.
citizen. He joined the U.S. Army in 1986 and
traveled frequently to New York, where he trained
Islamic militants in basic military techniques.
Some members of the group were later convicted
of the New York subway bombing conspiracy and
the World Trade Center bombing. He also made
at least two trips to Afghanistan to train rebel commanders in military tactics. He established ties
with bin Laden's organization in 1991 and obtained false documents for the group. He assisted
with logistical tasks, including bin Laden's 1991
move to Sudan. He was honorably discharged in
1989 and lived for much of the 1990s in California. He was represented by attorney James Roth.

On November 5, the U.S. State Department
offered a $5 million reward for bin Laden's arrest.
Bin Laden and Muhammed Atef, bin Laden's top
military commander, were indicted by a New
York federal grand jury in U.S. District Court on
238 counts for the August 7 bombings and for
conspiracy to kill Americans overseas. The Taliban vowed to protect bin Laden "at any cost"
because there was no evidence against him. On
November 9, the Taliban's chief justice, Noor
Mohammed Saqid, set a November 20 deadline
for the United States to provide evidence.

A Pakistani group, the Sunni Muslim Sipah-e-
Sahaba (Guardians of the Friends of the Prophet)
also threatened the United States.

On November 8, Egyptian fundamentalist and
bin Laden associate Tariq 'Ali Mursi, who was
extradited the previous month by South Africa,

refused to make any statements before the State Security High Court. Two other Egyptian fundamentalists extradited by South Africa in the same case, Jamal Shu'ayb and 'Id 'Abd-al-Mun'im, were also interrogated. The authorities were searching for information about Muhammad 'Atif Mustafa (alias Abu-Hafs al-Misri), a bin Laden aide.

On November 14, the U.S. Embassy in Nairobi resumed limited consular services, accepting only student applications.

On November 17, 49 Kenyans received compensation for injuries. The National Disaster Emergency Fund Committee had $4 million in donations and was reviewing 2,514 claims ranging from $500 for those who were badly cut and bruised to $5,000 for those who were blinded or lost limbs.

The Taliban cleared bin Laden of the bombings on November 20.

On December 3, federal prosecutors in New York released a copy of a 1997 letter written by Haroun Fazul Mohammed to his al-Qaeda superiors in which he warned that U.S. intelligence was closing in on them all. The same day, an unnamed bin Laden aide listed as "C-1" entered a guilty plea to terrorism charges in a secret hearing.

On December 16, 1998, the U.S. District Court in Manhattan issued a 238-count indictment against fugitives Mustafa Mohammed Fadhil, an Egyptian in his early 20s; Khalfan Khamis Mohamed, a Tanzanian, 24; Ahmed Khalfan Ghailani, a Tanzanian, 24; Fahid Mohammed Ally Msalam, a Kenyan, 22; and Sheik Ahmed Salim Swedan, a Kenyan, 29, on charges of bringing the vehicles used in the attacks, including the 1987 Nissan Atlas truck that carried the bomb, and the oxygen and acetylene tanks used in the Dar attack. Mohammed took photos of the embassy from a nearby Suzuki Samurai after the bombing. The charges carried the death penalty. The State Department announced a $5 million reward for their capture, similar to the $5 million reward for bin Laden's arrest. The department circulated posters printed in English, Arabic, French, Dhari, and Baluchi at all its diplomatic facilities and announced that it would advertise the reward on

the Internet. Fadhil, Mohamed, and Msalam met with a co-conspirator in a Dar house in late July and the first week of August to plan the bombing. According to the indictment, the explosion was detonated by "Ahmed the German."

On December 24, bin Laden told an ABC News interviewer in Afghanistan that while he was not responsible for the bombings, he supported them and knew some of the people involved. He did not deny trying to develop chemical and nuclear weapons.

On February 4, 1999, the *Washington Post* reported that Saleh Idris, owner of the El Shifa plant, had demanded compensation from the Clinton administration and called for the release of $23 million in assets frozen by U.S. officials in a U.K. Bank of America account on grounds that he was linked to bin Laden. The Treasury Department's Office of Foreign Assets Control had frozen the account under an executive order issued in August freezing any U.S. assets owned by bin Laden or his associates. He hired the Washington law firm of Akin, Gump, Strauss, Hauer, and Feld to pursue his legal interests with the White House. He claimed he paid $12 million for El Shifa and agreed to assume $18 million in debt.

On February 8, 1999, Kenyan police and FBI agents reportedly questioned Ali Mohfoudh Salim, who may have worked on the Toyota truck that was used to transport the bomb. He had not been implicated, but had been taken into custody briefly the previous week after denying knowing Owhali and Odeh, two of the men arrested in the case, despite evidence to the contrary. He was released over the weekend. Salim owned a commercial garage in Mombasa.

On February 10, 1999, the Taliban ruled out extradition of bin Laden. The Taliban said it would control his political and military activities. It claimed that it had deprived him of communication with the outside world (taking away his cell phone), banned him from talking to the media, and limited whom he could meet. The Taliban said it would soon ask bin Laden to leave the country. As of February 14, bin Laden reportedly was either in another country or hiding somewhere in

Afghanistan; the Taliban said it had no idea where he was. Meanwhile, state-run Algerian radio quoted repentant rebel Mohammed Berrached as claiming that bin Laden had telephoned orders to Hassan Hattab, one of the main leaders of the Armed Islamic Group of Algeria.

On March 4, 1999, the Taliban claimed that it had played an important role in helping bin Laden reach "a safe place," and that at the time of his departure on February 10, it had provided him with a group of soldiers for his protection. Meanwhile, the Western press reported that he had had a violent falling out with the Taliban on February 10, when ten Taliban officers tried to replace bin Laden's guards and the two groups exchanged automatic weapons fire.

On April 7, 1999, the United States announced it would give Tanzania $9.2 million to help it recover from the bombing.

On April 15, 1999, the *Washington Times* reported that three U.S. law firms planned to sue the U.S. government on behalf of the Kenyan victims, claiming negligence because the embassy was deemed unsafe. The attorneys included Kenyan lawyer Caesar Ngige Wanjao, California lawyer George Sterns, Wynne Herron, Philip Musolino of Washington, and John Burris, who had represented Rodney King and Tupac Shakur. Ambassador Prudence Bushnell had signed a $37 million compensation agreement for the Kenyans the previous day.

On May 4, the Clinton administration decided not to challenge Saleh Idris's lawsuit filed on February 26 and agreed to release the $24 million in assets that he had deposited in U.S. banks. An administration official said the El Shifa plant was bombed based on "physical and circumstantial evidence" and those involved were "totally confident" that the information was correct. However, the administration was concerned that classified information and methods used to gather it would have been compromised in a court proceeding. Idris's attorney, George Salem, a partner at the Washington law firm of Akin, Gump, Strauss, Hauer, and Feld, said the government could not prove its case. Idris had filed suit in U.S. District

Court in Washington, demanding the release of the $24 million that had been frozen by the Treasury Department's Office of Foreign Assets Control. He filed a similar suit in U.S. District Court in San Francisco against the Bank of America. Salem said both actions would be dismissed. Idris was also represented by attorney Steven R. Ross.

On June 16, 1999, Khaled Al-Fawwaz and Ayman Zawahiri, leader of the terrorists who killed Egyptian President Anwar Sadat, were charged with conspiracy in the African bombings and with conspiracy to kill Americans in an effort to secure the "Nuclear Bomb of Islam." The indictment superseded a previous indictment and alleged that, three days before the bombings, Al-Zawahiri threatened to retaliate against the United States for capturing Al-Jihad members. The indictment said that by February 1998, Al-Zawahiri had merged his group with bin Laden's al-Qaeda. The duo then endorsed a *fatwah* stating that Muslims should kill Americans, including civilians, anywhere.

On June 22, 1999, Wadih el-Hage sprang from his chair in the courtroom and rushed U.S. District Judge Leonard Sand, who had refused to publicly read a letter from el-Hage. El-Hage was subdued and handcuffed by U.S. marshals. He was one of 15 men charged with conspiracy in the bombings. Fellow defendant Mohamed Rashed Daoud Owhali yelled, "God is great," in Arabic. The other defendants—Mamdouh Mahnmud Salim, Mohamed Sadeek Odeh, and Ali Mohamed—were also handcuffed. El-Hage railed against the restrictions placed on him in prison. Each of the defendants had been held in solitary confinement. Sam Schmidt, his attorney, asked that the letter be made a part of the public record. Sand refused, saying that it could contain codes to fugitives. Sand reaffirmed his decision on June 29, but said the letter could be paraphrased and released by el-Hage's lawyer after federal prosecutors reviewed it.

On June 24, 1999, a prosecutor in London said that several faxes had been found at the London offices of Khalid Fawwaz linking him to the bombings and to bin Laden.

On July 5, President Clinton signed an executive order that banned all commercial and financial dealings between the United States and Afghanistan's ruling Taliban militia, which was providing refuge to bin Laden. The order froze all Taliban assets in the United States, barred the import of products from Afghanistan, and made it illegal for U.S. firms to sell goods and services to the Taliban. The order made exception for food and other humanitarian supplies. Trade between the United States and Taliban came to $24 million in 1998. The Taliban representative to the UN, speaking of bin Laden, said, "We do not know his whereabouts." However, on July 7, Taliban spokesman Wakil Ahmed Muttawakil said that bin Laden was in Afghanistan "under the protection of a special commission." Sources in Washington said bin Laden had a close relationship with Taliban leader Mullah Omar, who was married to one of bin Laden's daughters.

On July 7, federal agents arrested Mustafa Elnore (alias Mustafa Saif), 39, and announced that Mary Jo White, U.S. attorney for the Southern District in Manhattan, had filed a ten-count indictment against him for committing perjury during a grand jury investigation into the 1993 World Trade Center bombing and other terrorist activity in the United States. The New Jersey man faced up to five years in prison. He was tied to Sheik Omar Abdel Rahman, El Sayyid Nosair, and Wadih el-Hage. The indictment mentioned that a poster in a New York mosque advertising military training listed Elnore's name and phone number. The indictment said that Elnore, who worshiped at the Salaam Mosque on Kennedy Boulevard in New York City, lied about his role in recruiting and training Muslims to undergo weapons training in Connecticut, Long Island, and upstate New York. It did not charge him with involvement in a specific terrorist act.

London police arrested Ibrahim Hussein Abd-al-Hadi Eidarous, 42, and Adel Meguid Abd-al-Bary, 39, on extradition warrants on July 11, 1999, on a request from the United States. On July 12, they appeared in Bow Street Magistrates Court where Arvinder Sambi of the Crown Pros-

ecution Service said that their fingerprints appeared on originals of faxes that claimed credit for the bombings. One fax was received at a shop in London; another was sent after the bombings from a post office. The originals were found at the London offices of the Advice and Reform Council, believed to be an al-Qaeda front. Chief Magistrate Graham Parkinson ordered the duo held for a week, pending receipt of more evidence from the United States. Gareth Peirce served as Eidarous's attorney. He claimed his client had been released on July 9 after being held by immigration authorities for ten months.

The New York Times reported on July 30, 1999, that Sudan had detained two men immediately after the Africa bombings, but released them two weeks later after the U.S. air attacks. They were detained after arriving from Nairobi and were discovered by Khartoum police to be carrying false Pakistani passports.

On August 9, 1999, Salah Idris filed a $30 million lawsuit for damages to al Shifa. The United States was expected to plead sovereign immunity.

On October 6, 1999, the United States and Russia introduced a UN Security Council resolution that would impose an air embargo and financial sanctions on Afghanistan unless it surrendered bin Laden.

On October 8, Khalfan Khamis Mohamed, 26, a Tanzanian whose house was used as a bomb factory and who was arrested in South Africa on October 5, was arraigned in New York federal court on charges of murder and conspiracy in the two bombings. He pleaded not guilty. He had been living in Cape Town since a few days after the bombs went off. Mary Jo White, U.S. attorney for the Southern District of New York, said he was the first person in custody believed to have had "direct operational responsibility" in the Tanzanian bombing. He had rented a house in Dar es Salaam that was used as the bomb factory and base of operations. He was also charged with purchasing the white Suzuki Samurai that was used as a utility vehicle by the killers. Mohamed's South Africa alias of Zahran Nassor Maulid was the same alias he used to apply for a Tanzanian passport in May 1998.

On February 3, 2000, the U.S. Embassy in Nairobi announced that the bombing site would be turned into a memorial park dedicated to those who were killed in the explosion.

On March 16, 2000, Tanzania dropped charges against Egyptian Mustafa Mahmoud Ahmed and deported him. He had been charged with Tanzanian Rashid Salehe Hemed with murdering 11 people and injuring 70 people in the bombing. Hemed was to stand trial in Tanzania. On April 4, 2000, prosecutors reduced charges against Hemed, who now faced a maximum penalty of 14 years in prison on one count of conspiracy to commit murder. But on April 14, 2000, Tanzania's High Court ordered a trial for Hemed on a charge of conspiracy to murder.

On May 2, 2000, the Bow Street Magistrate's Court ordered the extradition from the United Kingdom to the United States of Ibrahim Hussein Abdelhadi Eidarous and Adel Mohammed Abdul Almagid Bary, both Egyptians suspected of membership in the Egyptian Islamic Jihad, ten months after they were arrested in London in connection with the case. Federal prosecutors in New York indicted the Londoners, along with Khalid Al-Fawwaz, on charges of involvement in the bombing. The United States demonstrated in U.K. courts that the fingerprints of Eidarous and Adel Abdul Bary were on an al-Qaeda fax to Fawwaz in London from an al-Qaeda official telling how the group would claim credit for the attacks. Al-Fawwaz once ran al-Qaeda's U.K. cell from a North London storefront. As of November 28, 2001, the trio had successfully avoided extradition. The United Kingdom's Law Lords approved extradition on December 17, 2001. However, the trio could appeal to the European Court of Human Rights in Strasbourg, France, which could take another year to decide.

On July 18, 2000, the Tanzanian High Court released on $25,000 bail Rashid Salehe Hemed, who also put up three surety bonds worth $62,500. The Tanzanian from Zanzibar was told to remain in Dar es Salaam. Police had found samples of substances used to prepare the bomb on his clothes. He was also accused of housing some of the suspects.

On October 20, 2000, former U.S. Army Sergeant Ali Mohamed, 48, pleaded guilty in a New York federal court to conspiring with bin Laden in the bombings. He pleaded guilty to five criminal felony counts, including conspiracy to murder, kidnap, and maim Americans in connection with terrorist acts, and to conspiracy to destroy U.S. defense facilities. He had been scheduled to go on trial in January with five other defendants jailed in New York.

The naturalized American, Egyptian-born terrorist told U.S. District Judge Leonard B. Sand that in 1993 he had briefed bin Laden after scouting possible U.S., U.K., French, and Israeli terrorist targets in Kenya. He put together a study replete with sketches and photos. The U.S. Embassy in Nairobi was included. "Bin Laden looked at the picture of the American Embassy and pointed to where the truck could go as a suicide bomber." Mohammed, honorably discharged in 1989 after serving for three years, trained members of al-Qaeda in the early 1990s. He also arranged a meeting in Sudan between bin Laden and the head of Hizballah. He said he was involved with the Egyptian Islamic Jihad before joining the army. He taught Muslim culture at Fort Bragg, North Carolina.

He faced a life sentence, but could get substantial time off for his cooperation.

On November 2, 2000, detainees Khalfan Khamis Mohamed and Mamdouh Mahmud Salim stabbed a 43-year-old guard's eye with a sharp object at the Metropolitan Correctional Facility in New York. The guard lost his eye and the implement penetrated the guard's brain. The guard underwent surgery for 12 hours at Bellevue Hospital and was in a coma. The attack took place after the duo had met with their attorneys.

On December 12, 2000, Mohamed Resahed Daoud al-'Owhali alleged in an affidavit that FBI agents threatened violence against him and his family if he did not cooperate during interrogations. He said he did not understand that he had a right to an attorney during the questioning. The FBI presented investigators with a detailed account of the interview, denying his claims. He faced a January 2001 trial. Meanwhile, al-'Owhali and co-defendant Khalfan Khamis Mohamed were denied their motion to dismiss their death penalty notices based on an internal Department of Justice study. U.S. District Judge Leonard Sand of the U.S. District Court for the Southern District of New York rejected their claim that the application of the federal death penalty is influenced by geography and the defendants' race, noting that the duo had shown "absolutely no evidence" that they were "treated differently from persons of other races who are comparably situated."

On December 15, 2000, Judge Sand ruled that Wadih el-Hage, 40, was fit to go on trial on January 3, 2001, despite defense attorney Sam Schmidt's claims that his client had suffered a mental breakdown in November when harsh security measures were implemented at the Metropolitan Correctional Facility after two co-defendants of el-Hage were accused of stabbing a guard in the eye. Schmidt claimed that el-Hage believed he was an 18-year-old college student living in 1978. In a November 21 letter to his wife, whom he now claims not to know, the defendant said that he was kidnapped after being in an accident in Louisiana.

El-Hage, the father of seven, was charged with lying to a federal grand jury. On December 5 (the ruling was unsealed on December 19), Judge Sand ruled that evidence taken from illegally tapped phones may be used in el-Hage's trial because he was believed to be an agent of a foreign power—the al-Qaeda terrorist group. According to the Associated Press, "U.S. intelligence in Kenya began monitoring el-Hage's cell phone in 1996."

On December 19, the UN Security Council, by a vote of 13–0 with 2 abstentions (China, Malaysia), adopted a resolution cosponsored by the United States and Russia that imposed an arms embargo on Afghanistan's ruling Taliban and increased financial, diplomatic, and travel sanctions on the militia for harboring terrorists, including bin Laden.

On December 20, a federal grand jury in New York indicted four fugitives—Saif al Adel, Muhsin Musa Matwalli Atwah, Ahmed Mohamed Hamed Ali, and Anas Al Liby—who faced life in prison without parole on various conspiracy charges. A fifth fugitive, Abdullah Ahmed Abdullah, faced a death penalty for playing a direct role in the Nairobi bombing, sitting next to bin Laden and others on the al-Qaeda consultation council that "discussed and approved major undertakings, including terrorist operations." In separate charges, Mamdouh Mahmud Salim, 41, already in prison, was indicted on charges including conspiracy to escape, possession of dangerous weapons in a prison, hostage taking, conspiracy to murder, and attempted murder for the November 1 attack in New York on the prison guard who was stabbed in the eye with a comb filed down to a point. Salim and Khalfan Khamis Mohamed attacked the guard after meeting with their attorneys. The guard remained hospitalized in critical condition. The first trial in the case was scheduled to begin on January 3 against four incarcerated suspects. Ali Mohamed had pleaded guilty in October to conspiracy with bin Laden and was expected to serve as a prosecution witness.

On January 2, 2001, U.S. District Judge Leonard B. Sand barred the public and press from jury selection in the trial in New York. He said questions asked of the jurors would be "so personal and required the divulgence of intimate family facts and circumstances." He also said that if the four defendants did not behave properly, they would be forced to watch the trial on video from their jail cells.

On January 29, 2001, Judge Sand reversed an earlier decision and refused to suppress incriminating statements made by Owhali, Odeh, and Mohamed. Sand had earlier made legal history by ruling that wiretaps conducted without a warrant in Kenya could be used against el-Hage, a U.S. citizen.

The trial opened in New York on February 5, 2001, with a jury of six men and six women. Owhali and Mohamed were accused of directly participating in the bombings and could receive the death penalty. Odeh and el-Hage faced life in prison if found guilty of helping to plan the bombings or training terrorists. Samuel Schmidt, attorney for el-Hage, said his client had legitimate business associations with bin Laden. Jeremy Schneider, Mohamed's attorney, said his client took part in the plot, but was simply following orders. Anthony Ricco, Odeh's attorney, deemed him merely a "soldier" for Islam and joined al-Qaeda because it was "helping people who were poor and down and, in some instances, fighting." Fredrick Cohn, Owhali's attorney, waived the right to present an opening argument. Assistant U.S. Attorney Paul Butler led off the prosecution of the 4, who were the first of 21 people indicted to stand trial.

On February 6, Jamal Ahmed Fadl, 38, a Sudanese Muslim defector from bin Laden's organization who had been a U.S. informant since 1996, was the first government witness. He joined the group in 1989 in Afghanistan. He defected after he was caught stealing money from bin Laden. He pleaded guilty to an unspecified charge and cooperated with the government under a plea agreement. He lived and studied in the United States in the mid-1980s and attended a Brooklyn mosque where he was recruited to fight in Afghanistan against the Soviets. He met bin Laden in Afghanistan. He testified that al-Qaeda received military and political support from Hizballah and from Sudan's ruling Islamic party. He said the group received extensive training in explosives and disguises. In 1991, he managed bin Laden's businesses, purchasing a farm north of Khartoum and a salt flat near Port Sudan for $430,000. The facilities were used to train terrorists in the use of light weapons and explosives. He said the Sudanese intelligence agency provided information on suspicious Afghan travelers who entered the country. Sudan Airlines transported weapons from Afghanistan. Sudan's president provided a handwritten letter that permitted a bin Laden firm to bring goods into the country without being subject to search or tax.

In his second day of testimony, Fadl said that al-Qaeda tried to buy uranium in late 1993 from a former Sudanese military officer, Salah Abdel Mobruk. A Mobruk associate had offered to sell uranium for $1.5 million plus commission. The individual showed al-Qaeda negotiators a bag containing a two- to three-foot cylinder, along with documents saying it came from South Africa. Fadl was withdrawn from negotiations soon after and was paid $10,000 for arranging the deal. He did not know if the deal was consummated. Fadl said he warned U.S. officials in 1996 that the group planned to attack U.S. targets. He helped transfer money and weapons to like-minded terrorist groups in Yemen, Pakistan, the Philippines, and Tajikistan, and used camels to smuggle Kalashnikov automatic weapons into Egypt. Fadl handled the group's payroll, and chafed at being paid only $500 per month while colleagues received $1,500 per month. So he took $110,000 in kickbacks from the sale of oil and sugar from one of bin Laden's companies. He was soon found out and bin Laden demanded repayment. He fled Sudan for an undisclosed country. Between May and July 1996, he walked into the visa line of a U.S. Embassy and offered to provide intelligence. He said he was brought to the United States and put under the witness protection program after two years. The United States brought his family from Sudan and lent him $20,000. He pleaded guilty to weapons and explosives charges, which carried a maximum of 15 years in prison. Defense attorneys questioned the witness's reliability, noting that he had cost federal authorities $945,000 in subsidies since agreeing to testify five years earlier.

Back in Washington on the same day, Director of Central Intelligence George Tenet told the Senate Select Committee on Intelligence that bin Laden's global network was the "most immediate and serious" terrorist threat to the United States.

On February 14, 2001, Texas-based commercial pilot Essam Ridi, a naturalized U.S. citizen born in Egypt, testified that he purchased a used T-39 jet in 1993 for bin Laden, who wanted to transport U.S.-made Stinger missiles from Pakistan to Sudan. Ridi said the request came from el-Hage, who specified that the jet needed to have a 2,000-mile range. The duo had met in the early 1980s as foreign students in Louisiana. At the time of the purchase, Ridi was living in Arlington, Texas. Ridi found the jet in Tucson and refurbished it before flying it to Khartoum; el-Hage wired him $200,000. Ridi said he gave the keys to bin Laden, but never transported the Stingers himself. Ridi returned to fly commercial flights, but found the plane in terrible condition and wrecked it after a test flight when the brakes failed.

On February 20, 2001, Fadl claimed that two Saudi intelligence officers asked for his assistance in 1996 to assassinate bin Laden in Sudan.

On March 7, 2001, a dozen U.S. and Kenyan survivors described the bombing in Nairobi.

On March 22, 2001, FBI agents arrested Mohamed Suleiman Nalfi, a Sudanese who was lured from his home with a false job offer in Amsterdam, as he changed planes. He was indicted in New York for having links to bin Laden and charged in federal court with forming and leading a Sudanese *jihad* group, following bin Laden's al-Qaeda organization, and helping bin Laden start an investment business in Sudan. Nalfi was added to the list of 22 defendants in the bin Laden conspiracy, which included the Africa bombings.

On April 12, 2001, U.S. District Judge Sand told prosecutors to pare down the indictment so that the jury could better understand it. He earlier dismissed several charges against two defendants; none of the charges were significant enough to affect potential penalties.

The defense began its case on April 16 by calling John Lloyd, a former British government forensic scientist, who testified that the FBI had failed to quantify explosive residue collected on clothing belonging to Odeh. He said he would have expected larger amounts of the residue if Odeh had been making bombs. The defense ended its case on April 30.

The prosecution began its closing arguments on May 2, when U.S. Attorney Kenneth Karas walked the jury minute-by-minute through the bombing. At 4:53 A.M. on August 7, a bin Laden operative in Baku, Azerbaijan, faxed a London media outlet claiming credit for the attacks. Four hours later, shortly before the bombs exploded, a call was placed to the Baku phone number from a satellite phone in Afghanistan used by bin Laden and other al-Qaeda members. The satellite phone was also used to call a Yemeni outpost. The

Yemeni phone had received frequent calls from residences in Dar es Salaam and Nairobi where the bombs were built. A few minutes before 9:00 A.M. on August 7, a suicide truck bomber in Tanzania called his family in Egypt on a cell phone to say goodbye. At 10:30 A.M., he drove the white Nissan Atlas to the U.S. Embassy.

The defense lawyers said their defendants were bit players in the bombing, part of a much larger conspiracy.

The case went to the jury on May 10, 2001, when Judge Sand read 140 pages of instructions to them.

On May 29, 2001, the jury found the defendants guilty of all 302 counts. Khalfan Khamis Mohamed, 27, and Mohamed Rashed Daoud Owhali, 24, were found guilty of conspiracy and murder and faced the death penalty. Mohammed Saddiq Odeh, 35, and Wadih el-Hage, 40, were found guilty of conspiracy and could face life in prison. The next day, prosecutors urged the jury to impose the death penalty on Owhali, who drove the truck and threw grenades at embassy guards. A separate hearing was scheduled for Mohamed, who helped grind the explosives in the Tanzania attack.

Also on May 29, the Constitutional Court of South Africa ruled that authorities had violated the local constitution by handing Mohamed over to the United States without a formal extradition procedure for trial on a charge that carries a possible death penalty.

On June 1, the jury sentenced Owhali to life in prison without parole, having deadlocked on the death penalty.

On June 28, Hidaya Juna, the mother of Khalfan Khamis Mohamed, told the court that "it [would] hurt" her if he was executed for the crime. Witnesses from South Africa said he was a devout Muslim who taught the Koran to children. Assistant U.S. Attorney Michael Garcia told the jury that the defendant had shown no remorse. On July 10, a federal jury of seven women and five men, after deliberating for three days, rejected the death penalty for Mohamed, who faced an automatic sentence of life in prison without parole.

Three years to the hour after the bombing, Kenyan and U.S. officials opened a park dedicated to the memory of those killed in the bombing. Protestors scrambling over turnstiles in protest of the 25-cent admission fee, called it an insult to the everyday Kenyans who were hurt in the bombing. Trustees claimed it would cost $1,500 a month in upkeep. 98080701-02

August 8, 1998. *Afghanistan.* Taliban militia were accused of taking hostage 47 Iranians, including 11 diplomats and a journalist who worked for the government-controlled IRNA news agency, from their compound in the northern city of Mazar-e Sharif. They were taken. Tehran accused the Taliban of seizing and plundering an Iranian consulate and cultural center in its capture of Bamiyan. Iran requested UN and Red Cross assistance in securing their release. The Taliban denied holding the diplomats, but said they had arrested 35 Iranian truck drivers whom they claimed were transporting food and ammunition to anti-Taliban factional fighters. Five of the truck drivers were reported released by September 5. Iran state radio said the hostages had been transported to Kandahar. Although the Taliban was holding Kabul, the capital city, few governments recognized the group as the country's legitimate government. On September 3, the Taliban suggested that the missing Iranians had died, a view echoed by Pakistani officials. Meanwhile, Iran conducted large-scale military maneuvers, involving 70,000 troops supported by tanks, artillery, and aircraft, on the common border. Ayatollah Ali Khamenei ruled out military strikes.

The Taliban announced that its militia, acting without their commanders' orders, had killed nine Iranian diplomats. The Taliban rejected Iran's demand to turn over the killers, calling it an internal affair. The Taliban said it would punish the killers and launched an investigation, questioning three people in the killing. Iran vowed revenge; more than 200,000 Iranian soldiers conducted more exercises on the border. Hundreds of thousands of Iranians joined a funeral procession for six of the murdered diplomats on September 18.

On September 19, following Pakistani mediation, the Taliban freed five surviving Iranians and asked Tehran to free Taliban militia from Iranian jails. The five, described by the Taliban as "military drivers," were flown to a military base outside Islamabad, Pakistan. The last of the Iranian hostages were freed on November 26. 98080801

August 8, 1998. *Egypt, Malaysia, Eritrea.* Threats were made against the U.S. embassies. 98080802-04

August 9, 1998. *Russia.* The crew in the business section of an East Line TU-154 commercial aircraft en route to Moscow from Tyumen, Siberia, found an anonymous note demanding the equivalent of $100,000 and threatening to blow up the plane. The plane landed safely in Moscow. No money was paid; no bomb was found; no one was arrested. The note read, "There is a bomb on board. We will detonate it if we are not given 621,000 rubles. We need the money in Moscow." 98080901

August 9, 1998. *Dominican Republic.* The *Miami Herald* reported that Luis Posada Carriles, 71, a Cuban exile leader, had planned to assassinate President Fidel Castro on a visit during August 20–26 to the Dominican Republic. He reportedly had met three other Miami-based exiles in the Holiday Inn in Guatemala City in July to discuss smuggling guns and explosives into the Dominican Republic. Posada had claimed that his attacks had been funded by Jorge Mas Canosa, the late founder of the Cuban American National Foundation (CANF), which the group had denied. Posada had spent nine years in a Venezuelan prison awaiting trial for planting a bomb that blew up a Cubana airliner off Barbados in 1976, killing all 73 on board. The plot reportedly fizzled after it was leaked to the FBI. 98080902

August 10, 1998. *India.* Gunmen threw a grenade and fired automatic weapons into a crowded bus in Anantnag, Kashmir, killing four and injuring seven. Pakistani-backed separatists were blamed.

August 11, 1998. *Swaziland.* The U.S. Embassy in Mbabane was evacuated for several hours after receipt of a bomb threat.
98081101

August 12, 1998. *Democratic Republic of the Congo.* Suspected former Rwandan soldiers abducted six tourists—one Canadian, two Swedes, and three New Zealanders—after the tourists crossed into the Congo from Uganda. Two of the New Zealanders escaped a week later. The Canadian was released on August 19 with a statement from the previously unknown People in Action for the Liberation of Rwanda, which said that the remaining captives would be freed if a message was read on BBC broadcasts in Africa. The remaining hostages were sighted in the forests in eastern Congo.
98081201

August 14, 1998. *Algeria.* Rebels killed 16 Algerians in overnight attacks south of Algiers.

August 14, 1998. *Turkey.* A homemade bomb wounded four people, including a policeman, at an Istanbul University building known as a center of Islamic activism.

August 14, 1998. *Albania.* The U.S. Embassy suspended normal activities and ordered most employees to leave the country after receiving a threat of an attack by Islamic terrorists. The State Department encouraged other Americans to leave the country and warned "against all travel to Albania." The United States sent 150 Marines and Navy commandos to secure the compound. The warnings followed several arrests of suspected Islamic militants. Raids in June and July led to the arrest of four suspects, believed to be Egyptians, who worked for Islamic organizations and who were also involved with terrorist activities sponsored by terrorist financier Osama bin Laden. The London-based Islamic Observation Center claimed that on August 13 Tirana officials had arrested an Egyptian who had been sentenced to death for the plot against Egyptian Prime Minister Atef Sedki in 1993. 98081401

August 14, 1998. *Colombia.* Colombian authorities said that at least 40 soldiers were killed and 130 missing in a three-day battle in the Uraba jungle pitting 300 counterinsurgency troops against 600 members of the Revolutionary Armed Forces of Colombia (FARC). There was no word on guerrilla losses.

August 14, 1998. *Sri Lanka.* The Liberation Tigers of Tamil Eelam (LTTE) seized a Dubai-owned cargo ship and abducted 21 crew members, including 17 Indians. The LTTE evacuated the crew before the Sri Lankan Air Force bombed and destroyed the ship on suspicion that the vessel was transporting supplies to the LTTE. The 17 Indian hostages were released to the International Committee of the Red Cross on August 19. As of April 1999, the LTTE still held four Sri Lankans.
98081402

August 15, 1998. *West Bank.* Imad Awadallah, a leader of Hamas, escaped a Palestinian jail where he had been held since April on suspicion of killing Hamas bomb maker Muhyideen Sharif, who was found dead on March 29 beside a car that blew up in Ramallah. Palestinian Authority police conducted a house-to-house search in Jericho and established the first curfew for Palestinians.

August 15, 1998. *Northern Ireland.* The Real IRA, a splinter group, set off a 500-pound car bomb in the Omagh town square during the afternoon, killing 28 (ultimately 29) people—including babies, grandfathers, and a pregnant woman—and wounding more than 350 others. The bombing was the bloodiest single incident in three decades of sectarian violence. The group said it was "part of an ongoing war against the Brits," but that "it was not our intention . . . to kill any civilians." The group claimed it had given a 40-minute warning. However, according to police, the warning said that the bomb had been placed near the courthouse, near the west end of town. Shoppers were directed to move east down Market Street, where the bomb was actually located. Police believed the bomb might have been placed by a young terrorist who did not know the town's layout. Several thousand people representing Catholics and Protestants conducted an outdoor memorial service. Among the dead were Avril Monaghan, 30 (who was pregnant with twins), her 18-month-old daughter, Maura, and her 65-year-old mother. Nine children were killed. A pregnant woman lost both legs.

The maroon Vauxhall sedan used for the bomb was stolen in Ireland the previous week.

On August 17, police arrested five suspected Real IRA members. Among the suspects was Shane Mackey, son of Francis Mackey, an Omagh city council member and chairman of the 32-County Sovereignty Committee, a group opposed to the peace plan and believed to be the political arm of the Real IRA. The group was headed by Mickey McKevitt, 49, a former senior IRA member. He had served as the IRA's quartermaster. He had been shot in both legs by the IRA in 1975 for breaking rules. However, he never revealed the names of his attackers.

The United Kingdom and Ireland vowed to institute a severe crackdown on terrorists.

The United States refused a visa to Bernadette Sands-McKevitt, a spokeswoman for the Real IRA's political front. She was the sister of the late Bobby Sands, an IRA member who died during a prison hunger strike in 1981. Store owners demanded that she be evicted from her print shop in a local mall.

On August 21, Nicola Emery, 21, who sustained minor injuries in the bombing (her mother received serious leg wounds), gave birth to a girl.

On September 3, the British and Irish parliaments approved emergency legislation making it easier to arrest suspected terrorists and hold them without bail. Judges were authorized to order that suspects be jailed without bail if a police official testified that they were believed to be terrorists; corroborating evidence was no longer needed. The statutes also permitted courts to consider an accused's refusal to answer questions as evidence of guilt.

On September 5, the 29th victim, Sean McGrath, 61, died.

On September 7, the Real IRA declared "a complete cessation of all military activity," although it did not apologize for the bombing.

On September 21, police arrested nine people in dawn raids on both sides of the Irish border. Irish police grabbed three men aged 19 to 34; Northern Ireland authorities detained another six. Northern Ireland authorities released the six on September 27.

Sinead O'Connor, U2, Liam Neeson, Boyzone, and Van Morrison joined several other rock stars in releasing an album entitled "Across the Bridge of Hope" on November 30, the profits of which would be given to the victims. Neeson read a poem written by Shaun McLaughlin, 12, who was killed in the bombing.

On December 5, Karen Armstrong, who suffered head injuries and burns in the attack, gave birth to a healthy Lucy Jean Armstrong.

On February 22, 1999, Belfast police began interrogating nine men on suspicion of involvement in the bombing. The Royal Ulster Constabulary said they were questioning six men in a crackdown on the IRA. Irish Republic police released two of five men they had arrested on February 21 in a related operation. On February 23, a spokesman for the Garda Siochana, Ireland's national police, said it would charge a man with two offenses in Dublin's three-judge no-injury Special Criminal Court, which hears terrorist offenses. He would be accused of being a member of an illegal paramilitary group that broke away from the IRA and one other unnamed charge. The Real IRA was believed responsible for the bombing.

On February 27, 1999, Irish police questioned two more male unnamed suspects, who were detained in Dundalk. Another man was arrested in connection with the inquiry in another border town. The next day, Dublin police arrested a woman in connection with the case. She was held and questioned under Section 30 of Ireland's Offenses Against the State Act, which allows suspects to be held for up to 72 hours.

On February 24, 1999, Irish authorities charged their first suspect in the case, Colm Murphy, 46, a building contractor and pub owner. He appeared in Dublin's Special Criminal Court three days after police arrested him at his Dundalk farmhouse, 50 miles north of Dublin.

Police in both parts of Ireland arrested ten suspected IRA dissidents on June 20, 1999. They had arrested, then freed without charge nearly 100 people in the case. The next day, Irish police arrested two women in Cavan and Monaghan counties and a man in his 20s in Dundalk. On June 23, Irish police detained two more men in Dundalk under the Offences Against the State Act.

As of August 14, 1999, no one was in jail for the crime. Two dozen people had been arrested, some more than once, but all but one had been released without charges. Colm Murphy was charged with conspiracy, but was free on bail; no trial had been scheduled.

On October 9, 2000, the BBC documentary show "Panorama" identified four men it claimed were involving in building and delivering the Real IRA bomb that exploded in Omagh. Only one man had been charged in the bombing, and his trial had been delayed. The show claimed that the two men who delivered the bomb had been using cell phones that had been intercepted. On October 17, 2000, police arrested three men in connection with the bombing. On April 29, 2001, Irish National Police announced the arrest of Michael "Mickey" McKevitt of Dundalk, Ireland, on charges of "directing terrorism," based on a law enacted after the Omagh bombing. The charges grew out of a series of car bombs planted by the Real IRA in recent months. He and his colleagues had been arrested before, but were released for lack of evidence. However, McKevitt's bail request was rejected, suggesting the police had a winnable case, based on a Real IRA informant, an American who ferried cash from U.S. supporters. His wife, Bernadette Sands-McKevitt, traveled often to the United States to raise funds. She was arrested under the new law, but released without charge. A hearing was scheduled for April 24.

On August 17, 2001, Northern Ireland's police ombudsman Nuala O'Loan launched an investigation into a report that the Royal Ulster Constabulary (RUC) had two days' warning of the Omagh bomb. A former RUC double agent said he had tipped off police that the bomb was being made by a senior member of the Real IRA. The RUC denied the report. 98081501

August 15, 1998. *Albania.* The *Washington Post* reported on December 19, 2001, that a week after the Africa bombings, U.S. intelligence foiled a truck bomb plot against the U.S. Embassy in Tirana. U.S. intelligence tipped off Albanian authorities to five Egyptian Islamic Jihad members. "The Americans flew the five men to Egypt, where they were executed after a military trial."

August 18, 1998. *Egypt.* Egyptian authorities denied rumors that they had arrested Palestinian terrorist Abu Nidal (alias Sabri al-Banna), 61, whose group was credited with killing 300 people and wounding 650 in 20 countries since 1973. However, on August 25, U.S. officials confirmed that Egypt had apprehended him earlier in the month and was holding him in a Cairo hospital. He was grabbed when he crossed into Egypt from his base in Libya. He was undergoing treatment for cancer. He was never indicted under U.S. law, although his organization was responsible for the deaths of several Americans. He was also sought by the United Kingdom, France, Italy, Greece, and the Palestinian Authority. Dissidents in his group apparently had tipped off the Egyptians, who detained him for entering the country illegally.

August 19, 1998. *Albania.* The U.S. Embassy in Tirana received another terrorist threat. Local officials said Albania was the locus of Muslim terrorist groups because of its poverty and social chaos, which left immigration, law enforcement, and the judiciary in tatters. In 1997, criminals stole 100,000 Albanian passports, which were for sale on the black market. 98081901

August 20, 1998. *West Bank.* A Jewish settler was stabbed to death by a Palestinian in a Jewish enclave in Hebron. The assailant also wounded the man's wife in their home in an isolated Jewish compound. He entered the home through a window, carrying a knife and a Molotov cocktail. The victim momentarily broke free of his attacker, who then stabbed the man outside the home before torching the structure.

August 20, 1998. *West Bank.* At 10:30 P.M., Shlomo Raanan, 63, a rabbi, was stabbed to death in his bedroom in Hebron by an Arab assailant who fled to the Palestinian section of town. He was the grandson of a venerated chief rabbi of Palestine during the British mandate. The killer climbed a ten-foot wall, entered via a window, and stabbed Raanan in the neck.

August 20, 1998. *Worldwide.* The World Islamic Front for Jihad Against Jews and Crusaders, founded by Osama bin Laden, told the London-based *al-Hayat* that the "strikes will continue from everywhere." The statement was accompanied by similar threats from the Islamic Army for the Liberation of Holy Shrines, which claimed credit for the Nairobi and Dar es Salaam bombings. 98082001

August 21, 1998. *Lebanon.* Two Israelis contracted by the Israeli army—a soldier and a civilian—were killed during the night by a roadside bomb detonated by Hizballah. The next day, two Israeli planes fired two rockets on Iqlim al-Toufah, a Hizballah stronghold north of Israel's southern Lebanon occupation zone. A second raid sent another two Israeli rockets into the town. 98082101

August 21, 1998. *Albania.* Police raided several terrorist safe houses and arrested ten foreigners, including several Arabs. The manhunt had begun two days earlier, when authorities received word that terrorists planned to use a car bomb to blow up the U.S. Embassy in Tirana. 98082102

August 22, 1998. *Northern Ireland.* The Irish National Liberation Army declared a cease-fire. The Real IRA had earlier announced that it was suspending attacks. The Continuity IRA had yet to call a truce.

August 23, 1998. *Iran.* Unknown gunmen shot to death Assadollah Lajevardi, a former Iranian chief prosecutor and head of Iran's prison system.

August 23, 1998. *Albania.* At 11:45 A.M., security guards shot and killed Shkelqim Shehu, 35, an Albanian policeman who climbed the seven-foot wall of the U.S. diplomatic compound in Tirana. They shot in the air to warn him back, but when he ignored them, they shot him in the chest. He was armed with a pistol. His motive was unknown. He was from the village of Ndroq, ten miles west of the capital. He was a member of a police unit in charge of security at a Tirana bank. 98082301

August 23, 1998. *United States.* Police arrested Kathryn Schoonover, 50, a homeless cancer patient, outside the Marina del Rey post office and seized a box containing 100 envelopes addressed to doctors and lawyers containing cyanide packaged to look like free samples of a nutritional supplement. Police believed she had already sent similar packages. A passerby saw her at the post office counter wearing protective gloves and taking a powder from a container labeled "poison" and placing it into envelopes. A teaspoon of sodium cyanide was placed in clear plastic pouches attached to brochures for health and diet products. Most of the letters were addressed to people she had known or dealt with earlier. Some could not recall her. She was booked for investigation of attempted murder. Four people in New York State had received unsolicited letters from her in the past two months. She claimed to have a chemistry background. Intended victims included members of the police force in West Covina, east of Los Angeles. She was charged with mailing the packets on August 26. She faced up to 20 years in prison on each of two federal counts of using the mail in an attempt to injure and kill. The federal affidavit accused her of mailing cyanide packets to at least eight people, including a New York nurse who tasted the substance and got an immediate severe headache.

August 25, 1998. *Uganda.* Grenades and bombs exploded on three buses, killing 21 people, including a child. No one claimed credit.

August 25, 1998. *South Africa.* The previously unknown Muslims Against Global Oppression (MAGO) set off a bomb at the South African-owned Planet Hollywood restaurant in Cape Town's most popular tourist district at 7:20 P.M., killing Fanie Schoeman, 50, a South African bank employee, and injuring 27, including a child and 9 British citizens. The restaurant was heavily damaged. No American casualties were reported. Local radio said a second person died of a heart attack. The group said it was retaliating for the U.S. missile attacks against terrorist facilities in Sudan and Afghanistan. The pipe bomb was hidden under the bar. Local radio commentators said the group had 2,000 members and had protested President Clinton's visit to South Africa in March. A spokesman for the group later denied the claims of the telephone caller, saying the individual was attempting to discredit Muslims. Police noted that pipe bombs are often used by the local Muslim vigilante organization People Against Gangsterism and Drugs (PAGAD).

On August 27, South African police stopped one man and two women who were boarding a flight at Cape Town airport and questioned them about the bombing. A local Muslim vigilante group said its members had been taken off a flight to Egypt. The three were released without charges the next day.

On September 3, Brian Duddy, 55, a South African who had lost a leg in the blast, died at a Cape Town hospital, becoming the second death from the blast.

On October 23, police confirmed that there was no connection between this blast and the explosions at the U.S. embassies in Kenya and Tanzania.

By November 30, 1999, another 80 pipe bombs had exploded in Cape Town. No one had credibly claimed credit for the attacks. Among them was a blast on November 28 at a pizzeria that injured 43 customers and workers, including several who lost limbs. 98082501

August 25, 1998. *India.* Militants threw a grenade in downtown Srinagar, killing a civilian and injuring 11 others.

August 26, 1998. *Yugoslavia.* An unidentified attacker threw a gasoline bomb at the U.S. Information Center in Pristina, Kosovo during the evening, setting off a fire that scorched the entrance to the two-story building. No injuries were reported. 98082601

August 27, 1998. *Israel.* A two-pound bomb loaded with nails and hidden in a trash can exploded in a Tel Aviv market area near the Great Synagogue at 8:40 A.M., injuring more than 20 people, one seriously, and blowing out windows. Hamas denied involvement.

August 29, 1998. *Belgium.* The Animal Liberation Front (ALF) firebombed a McDonald's restaurant in Puurs, destroying the restaurant and causing up to $1.4 million in damage. 98082901

August 31, 1998. *Togo, Ghana.* The United States closed its embassies in Ghana and Togo following receipt of threats against the facilities. The State Department advised people to avoid U.S. facilities in Ghana. 98083101-02

August 31, 1998. *Algeria.* A bomb in Algiers killed 17 people. The bomb went off hours after the government announced it would open 48 offices to investigate those missing in the Islamic insurgency.

September 1, 1998. *France.* The trial of 138 individuals charged with selling arms to Algerian terrorists began in Fleury-Merogis, with the defendants and their lawyers boycotting the proceedings. Twenty-seven of the suspects were arrested between November 1994 and June 1995. Many of the defendants were captured with weapons, explosives, caches of money, false identity papers, and forged documents. Among the defendants was Farouk Haddad, who said he was asked to keep the weapons.

September 2, 1998. *Kuwait/Philippines/Yemen.* The U.S. Embassy in Kuwait said a possible attack was being planned against the embassy.

A note found on a plane warned of a bombing at the U.S. Embassy in the Philippines. Police tightened security on the eve of a planned protest march by Islamic militants.

A Coca-Cola factory in Yemen received a warning to shut down before militants bombed it. 98090201-03

September 2, 1998. *India.* Muslim militants detonated a land mine under a bus carrying troops from Jammu to Punch, killing the civilian driver and seriously injuring 15 soldiers.

September 8, 1998. *Netherlands.* Shortly before 1:00 P.M., a masked man set off three or four bombs at a ferry terminal in Hoek Van Holland, injuring nine people, including two British children. Police believed it was an attempted robbery of a bank at a rail station linked to the terminal that is used by Stena Line passengers traveling between Harwich, England, and the Netherlands.

September 8, 1998. *Philippines.* Thirty suspected Muslim militants armed with rifles and grenade launchers abducted an Italian priest and 12 Filipinos from a cooperative store in the parish church. The Filipinos were released the next day; as of April 1999, the Italian was still a hostage. No ransom was demanded. Police suspected either the Abu Sayyaf Group (ASG) or the Moro Islamic Liberation Front (MILF).

September 9, 1998. *Philippines.* The Abu Sayyaf Group was suspected of kidnapping three Hong Kong businessmen in Mindanao. The three worked for the Jackaphil Company. No ransom was demanded. They were freed unharmed on December 23. 98090901

September 9, 1998. *Lebanon.* The U.S. Embassy warned all Americans in the country to take the "highest level of caution" after receiving information that the embassy could come under an attack

similar to the African blasts. 98090902

September 14, 1998. *Turkey.* An Islamic militant armed with a toy gun hijacked a Turkish Airlines plane bound for Istanbul from Ankara and diverted it to a Black Sea port, where he freed his hostages and surrendered. 98091401

September 15, 1998. *Uganda.* The Ugandan government detained 20 suspects, including two ringleaders, who were attempting to enter the country from Kenya. The *Washington Post* claimed that the police had been tipped off by the CIA that the Islamic extremists planned to bomb the U.S. Embassy in Kampala. The two men were believed to be associates of Osama bin Laden. The other suspects included Sheikh Abduwel Abdullah Amin, the *imam* of Kampala's Tawheed Mosque; Ahmed Mandela, treasurer of the SC Villa soccer team; a few local businessmen; a 15-year-old boy; and Mohamed Gulam Kabba, a Ugandan aid worker who had assisted southern Sudanese refugees and had visited Somalia in 1997 on an official invitation from UNESCO. They had no overt links to bin Laden, but supported his anti-Americanism. The FBI and Ugandan police seized documents in raids on their homes and businesses. Amnesty International claimed that the 20 suspects were Muslims. An unnamed American source said that the Tawheed Islamic Association in Kampala was a "holding pen" for terrorists. All but four of the suspects were released on October 5. The foursome had not been charged as of October 5, although Ugandan law required that charges be made within 48 hours of arrest. 98091501

September 16, 1998. *Algeria.* A UN observer team led by former Portuguese President Mario Soares gave its qualified support to Algeria's antiterrorist initiative.

September 16, 1998. *Spain.* The Basque Nation and Liberty (ETA) announced a cease-fire after a 30-year terrorist campaign for an independent homeland. The truce was sent to the Basque daily

Euskadi Informacion. However, the Spanish government said it would continue its crackdown on the ETA, which had killed 800 people in its campaign. On September 21, the government demanded that the ETA agree to disarm and disband as a condition for beginning the peace process.

September 16, 1998. *Germany.* Police arrested Mamdouh Mahmud Salim, 40, who was visiting a friend near Freising. The United States said he was a top financial accountant and weapons procurer for Osama bin Laden. Germany asked the United States to accelerate its extradition request. There was a sealed warrant for his arrest in New York.

September 18, 1998. *United Kingdom.* The first five Northern Irish terrorists serving life sentences for murder were released from prison under the terms of the province's peace agreement. Two murderers from the Ulster Defense Association, two from the Ulster Volunteer Force, and one from the Irish Republican Army (IRA) were freed from the Maze Prison. They had served from 10 to 14 years each.

September 20, 1998. *Russia.* Sergeant Vitaly Pryakhin, Russian deputy commander of the guards at a sensitive nuclear reprocessing plant of the Mayak Production Association near Chelyabinsk in the Ural Mountains, opened fire on three other servicemen, killing two before he fled.

September 21, 1998. *Georgia.* Gunmen fired on a bus in Sukhumi, wounding three UN military observers and another UN mission employee, including two Bangladeshis and one Nigerian. 98092101

September 22, 1998. *Colombia.* The Revolutionary Armed Forces of Colombia (FARC) kidnapped Shoro Shimura, a Japanese farmer, in central Cundinamarca Province. The ailing man was released on February 25, 1999. 98092201

September 22, 1998. *India.* Two gunmen shot and wounded a French tourist near the Jama Masjid mosque in Srinagar. Muslim terrorists were blamed. 98092202

September 23, 1998. *United Kingdom.* Police arrested seven Middle Eastern men on terrorism charges. They were identified as Adel Abdul-Mageed Abdul-Bari, an Egyptian who was sentenced to death in absentia in 1997 for conspiring to blow up a Cairo marketplace; Khaled al Fawaz, a Saudi dissident who had served as a London spokesman for Osama bin Laden and for Advice and Consent, a group dedicated to ousting the Saudi monarchy; and five other Egyptians.

September 24, 1998. *Germany.* German police said they had received information that terrorists planned to bomb the U.S. Consulate in Hamburg over the weekend. They said it was probable that there were links to the bombings in Africa on August 7.

September 24, 1998. *Cambodia.* Cambodian leader Hun Sen survived an assassination attempt when a rocket tore through a gap in his motorcade as he was driving to a swearing-in ceremony at Angkor Wat. The rocket missed the politicians, but struck a home and killed a 12-year-old boy. Eight people were arrested. Leaders of the major opposition parties condemned the attack.

September 27, 1998. *Algeria.* A bomb went off in Khemis, killing 4 and injuring 15.

September 29, 1998. *West Bank.* A Palestinian was killed and two others wounded when a bomb exploded in their car. They were suspected to be Hamas terrorists who had collected a bag they believed to contain weapons. The bag went off in the trunk as the trio drove from Beitounia, near Ramallah.

September 29, 1998. *Ecuador.* A bomb exploded at the Ecuadoran Bishops Conference, injuring a Spanish missionary and causing major damage. The explosion released leaflets calling for improved cost of living and utility services. Police believed the bombing was linked to a national strike protesting the economic package implemented by the country's president. 98092901

September 30, 1998. *West Bank.* A man threw two grenades at Israeli troops in Hebron, injuring 11 soldiers and 11 Palestinians. The grenade thrower was shot in the leg, but managed to escape into the Palestinian-controlled section of town.

October 3, 1998. *Russia.* Chechen rebels kidnapped three Britons and one New Zealander who had been installing a cell phone network for the British firm Granger Telecom in Chechnya. The rebels conducted a shootout with the bodyguards before the abduction. The Britons were Darren Hickey, Rudolf Petschi, and Peter Kennedy; the New Zealander was Stanley Shaw.

On December 8, 1998, authorities found the severed heads of the hostages in a sack two miles outside Dovydenko village, near the town of Ahkhoi Martan in western Chechnya. The Chechen president had told reporters that his security officers had launched a rescue attempt the previous night. The beheaded bodies were found on the outskirts of Grozny on December 25.

On December 10, the Chechen government showed a videotape of Peter Kennedy admitting to being a British spy who had been sent to monitor telephone conversations aimed at stopping the spread of Islamic fundamentalism.

On December 11, Chechen gunmen abducted Mansur Tagirov, Chechnya's top prosecutor, who was investigating the killings. He was grabbed during the evening while returning to Grozny from a small village nearby. 98100301

October 5, 1998. *Ecuador.* Kidnappers abducted two American and one Ecuadoran employee of the Santa Fe Oil Company. One American escaped the next day. 98100501

October 6, 1998. *India.* Suspected Muslim militants threw a bomb at a vehicle carrying a prominent former militant in Tral, Kashmir, killing him and ten others.

October 7, 1998. *Egypt.* The U.S. Embassy was evacuated after an anonymous caller claimed a bomb was inside. No bomb was found. 98100701

October 7, 1998. *Saudi Arabia.* All U.S. diplomatic missions in the kingdom were closed to review security following information that the Riyadh embassy was targeted for terrorist attack. 98100702

October 8, 1998. *Nigeria.* Protesting their alleged exclusion from the political process, mobs seized two Shell Oil helicopters and an oil rig. Days earlier, anti-regime demonstrators seized nine other oil pumping stations, halting the daily transfer of 250,000 barrels of oil. Groups in the delta region claimed they were shut out of registering to vote in the 1999 presidential elections.

October 8, 1998. *India.* Muslim militants threw a grenade at a police post in Srinagar, Kashmir, injuring five civilians, four police officers, and four soldiers.

October 8, 1998. *India.* Militants set off a bomb near the state secretariat building in Srinagar, Kashmir, injuring 13 and causing minor damage.

October 9, 1998. *Pakistan.* Unidentified gunmen fired on the Iranian Cultural Center in Multan, killing a Pakistani security guard and wounding another. 98100901

October 12, 1998. *Colombia.* The People's Liberation Army (EPL) kidnapped 20 people, including 4 foreigners, at a roadblock on the Northeastern Highway. They burned three cars and released two hostages to report the situation to the media. 98101201

October 17, 1998. *Russia.* Two Mormon missionaries were stabbed after the duo left the home of a Mormon family in Ufa, 750 miles east of Moscow. Jose Manuel Mackintosh, 20, died; Bradley Alan Borden, 20, was wounded in the liver and pancreas. One suspect was arrested. Borden, of Mesa, Arizona, gave evidence about a second suspect. 98101701

October 17, 1998. *Colombia.* On October 21, the government arrested and deported to Ecuador Mohamed Abid Abdel Ebld, a senior member of the Egyptian al-Gamaat al-Islamiya. He had entered Colombia illegally on October 17. No extradition warrants had been filed against him. 98101702

October 18, 1998. *Colombia.* At 2:00 A.M., National Liberation Army (ELN) rebels bombed the 480-mile Ocensa crude oil pipeline, killing at least 741 and injuring 100 others. The bombing occurred six days after the ELN had agreed to participate in exploratory peace talks. The powerful bomb caused major damage when the spill caught fire and burned houses and part of the conduit in Machuca, near Segovia in Antioquia Province. Wounded civilians included a six-month-old and a ten-month-old, along with other children. British Petroleum Exploration of Colombia provided some of the crude oil used in the line. The pipeline was jointly owned by the Colombia State Oil Company Ecopetrol and a consortium including U.S., French, British, and Canadian companies. Between 20,000 and 40,000 barrels of crude were spilled in the attack. 98101801

October 18, 1998. *Algeria.* Muslim rebels slashed the throats of nine people in an overnight attack at Hamma Bouziane village in Constantine Province, 212 miles east of Algiers.

October 18, 1998. *United States.* The Earth Liberation Front claimed credit for setting a series of fires that caused $12 million in damage at Vail, Colorado, the nation's busiest ski resort. The group was protesting a planned 885-acre ski resort expansion. Environmentalists claimed that the terrain is vital to the reintroduction of lynx into Colorado. Environmentalists had lost a court battle the previous week. The blast destroyed five buildings and four ski lifts.

October 19, 1998. *Israel.* The armed wing of Hamas claimed credit for a grenade attack that injured 64 Israelis, including 20 soldiers, at the central bus station in Beersheba. The attack came while Yasir Arafat and Israeli Prime Minister Benjamin Netanyahu were negotiating a U.S.-mediated peace settlement at Wye Plantation in Wye Mills, Maryland. At 8:00 A.M., a young Palestinian man threw two grenades into the terminal. The blast blew out windows in nearby restaurants and shops. Bystanders tackled and beat the assailant, who later confessed to police.

October 23, 1998. *United States.* At 10:00 P.M., a sniper shot and killed prominent obstetrician-gynecologist Barnett Slepian, 52, in his home in Amherst, New York, as he stood in front of his kitchen window. He had just returned from a synagogue with his wife and four sons. U.S. and Canadian police had warned of such an attack, noting that there were four previous shootings against abortion doctors (three Canadian doctors and one Rochester physician) at this time of year during the previous four years in Canada and upstate New York. Hours before the killing, his wife had faxed to local police a warning from the National Abortion Federation of possible violence. He was the seventh person killed in the United States by anti-abortion extremists since 1993. The shootings all took place near November 11, Canadian Remembrance Day, the equivalent of the U.S. Veterans Day. The holiday is used by anti-abortion activists as the day to "remember the unborn children." The FBI offered a $100,000 reward (increased to $500,000 by Attorney General Janet Reno on November 9) for the arrest and conviction of the sniper; the Canadian Medical Association added $150,000. In early November, police announced that they were searching for James Charles Kopp (alias Atomic Dog), 44, who had spent time in jails in New York, Georgia, West Virginia, and Vermont for blockading abortion clinics. Reno announced the creation of the National Task Force on Violence Against Health Care Providers to coordinate investigations and prosecutions.

On November 21, the FBI announced that the search had widened and it was looking for Ronald Stauber and Michael Gingrich, who might have information about the sniper. Authorities believed that Kopp might have gone to Mexico or Central America.

On December 18, law enforcement officials stumbled across Kopp's black 1987 Chevrolet Cavalier at Newark Airport. It was left in a large parking lot on November 4, the day the Justice Department issued a warrant for Kopp as a material witness. Police used the car to track Kopp's whereabouts—he was in the Buffalo area from October 18 to 21.

October 24–25, 1998. *Kenya.* Attackers hit Bagala, 125 miles west of Wajir in northeast Kenya, killing 142 villagers. Another 59 people were missing and 7 others were hospitalized with serious injuries. The authorities blamed the Oromo Liberation Front from Ethiopia, although others believed that clan-based banditry was involved. The Front faxed news services, denying the charges.

October 25, 1998. *Russia.* A car bomb killed Shadid Bagishev, Chechnya's top anti-kidnapping official, on the day that he was scheduled to launch an anti-kidnapping initiative. His two bodyguards and several passersby were also injured. At least 100 people were being held hostage in the breakaway republic.

October 26, 1998. *Colombia.* The Peasant Self-Defense Force of Cordoba and Uraba, a paramilitary right-wing death squad, killed between 31 and 36 people in attacks during the weekend.

October 26, 1998. *Colombia.* Rebels kidnapped a Danish engineer and two Colombians at a roadblock in San Juan. Police believed the Revolutionary Armed Forces of Colombia (FARC) or National Liberation Army (ELN) was responsible. However, the People's Liberation Army (EPL) released the Danish hostage on January 21, 1999.

As of April 1999, there had been no reports on the fate of the two Colombians. 98102601

October 28, 1998. *Yemen.* Armed tribesmen in the Mahfad Region kidnapped two Belgian citizens, demanding the release of a tribesman sentenced to death by a Yemeni court. The hostages were released on October 29. 98102801

October 28, 1998. *Colombia.* The Revolutionary Armed Forces of Colombia (FARC) fired homemade missiles, destroying a police station in Hacari, in Norte de Santander Province. At least 16 people were killed. Two police agents died trying to defend their barracks as gas cylinders packed with explosives rained down. Six soldiers and eight guerrillas were killed.

October 28, 1998. *Taiwan.* Yuan Bin, 30, the captain of an Air China jet, hijacked his flight, carrying 104 people. He claimed he was frustrated over pay and working conditions. The plane landed safely in Taiwan. No one was injured. He was taken into custody without incident. 98102801

October 28, 1998. *Turkey.* London's *Al-Hayat* reported that the Kurdistan Workers Party (PKK) claimed that PKK leader Abdallah Ocalan had departed for Russia because Mossad had pinpointed his location and Turkey planned to shell his position.

October 29, 1998. *Turkey.* The government detained 23 militant Muslims who planned to crash an explosives-laden plane onto the Ankara mausoleum of Mustafa Kemal Ataturk, the founder of the secular state. The suicide attack was planned for the 75th anniversary of the republic. A second operation would entail the takeover of a major Istanbul mosque the next day. Police found sticks of dynamite, rifles, revolvers, ammunition, and Islamic green flags.

October 29, 1998. *Turkey.* Mursel Peker hijacked a Turkish Airlines Boeing 737 shortly after it left

Adana Airport on a domestic flight. He issued a statement saying he was protesting Turkish military actions against Kurdish rebels who were fighting for self-rule in the mainly Kurdish southeast region of Turkey. He demanded that the plane fly to Lausanne, Switzerland. The pilot claimed he needed to refuel and landed in Ankara. Negotiations with Turkish officials in the control tower lasted for more than six hours. Turkish special forces then stormed the plane, killing the hijacker and freeing 6 crew members and 34 passengers, none of whom were hurt. 98102901

October 29, 1998. *Israel.* A Palestinian suicide bomber drove his explosives-packed car at two school buses carrying Jewish children in the Gaza Strip, but was stopped by an Israeli Army jeep escorting the buses. The jeep absorbed most of the blast, which killed the bomber and Israeli Army Sergeant Alexei Neykov, 19, a recent Ukrainian immigrant, who was riding in the jeep. Two soldiers were injured. The 40 children on the armored bus, aged 6 to 14, were not harmed. Hamas took credit for the attack against Jewish settlers in Gaza. Yasir Arafat blamed Hamas. The Palestinian Authority cracked down on Hamas, arresting several hundred individuals and putting Sheik Ahmed Yassin, 62, the Hamas founder and spiritual leader, under house arrest. Three other senior Hamas figures—spokesman Mahmoud Zahar, Ismail abu Shanab, and Ismail Hania—were called in for questioning. The attack was the first following the Wye Accord. Hamas threatened retaliation against the Palestinian Authority.

October 30, 1998. *United States.* Eight abortion clinics in New Albany, Indiana; Knoxville, Tennessee; Louisville, Tennessee; and Kansas received letters that were postmarked in Cincinnati and claimed to contain anthrax.

The Indianapolis Planned Parenthood clinic was evacuated and 33 people were sent to hospitals. They were stripped and scrubbed down by emergency crews after one of them opened a small powder-filled letter.

In Louisville, the postal worker and an employee of the Women's Health Services Clinic were treated with antibiotics.

The Knoxville Reproductive Health Center received a letter saying that anyone who opened the letter had been exposed to anthrax.

On November 1, federal authorities said they intended to find and prosecute the individual who sent letters to the eight Midwestern abortion clinics that received the hoax anthrax letters.

November 1998. *Yugoslavia.* Kosovo Liberation Army rebels kidnapped several people. On November 27, following the November 24 release of a Serbian policeman, the rebels, in what they claimed was a goodwill gesture, freed two Serbian reporters and two ethnic Albanian politicians, handing them over to an international liaison team in Dragobili in Western Kosovo Province.

November 1998. *Yemen.* In late November, Jahm tribesmen bombed the U.S.-owned Hunt Oil Company pipeline. 98119901

November 1, 1998. *Colombia.* Some 600 Revolutionary Armed Forces of Colombia (FARC) rebels fired homemade missiles at dawn at a police base in a remote jungle in the east, killing at least 150. At least 120 police agents were stationed at the base near Mitu in Vaupes Province. Troops took back control of the town on November 4.

November 2, 1998. *Russia.* Leftist extremists were blamed for blowing up a statue of Czar Nicholas II in a small town outside Moscow.

November 4, 1998. *Russia.* A car bomb exploded near a main gate to the Kremlin during the evening, injuring three guards and the driver, Irvan Orlov, 65, a retiree and writer for the nationalist *Russkaya Pravda* magazine, who jumped out of the Moskvich car. The driver apparently planned to drive through the Kremlin's Spassky Gate, which was damaged. Federal Security Service agents were interrogating him at the hospital.

November 4, 1998. *Germany.* Police raided several locations near Bonn after receiving word of a terrorist threat against the U.S. Embassy. No evidence of a planned attack was found, although police questioned several suspects in an industrial zone and other sites. No arrests were made.

November 6, 1998. *United States.* A federal judge sentenced three members of the anti-government Montana Freemen in Billings. They had been accused of organizing an assault on the U.S. banking system, partly through the circulation of falsified financial instruments. The trio had been arrested after an 81-day standoff in 1996. Russell Dean Landers received 11 years and 3 months for conspiracy, bank fraud, threatening a federal judge, and being a fugitive in possession of a firearm. Emmett Clark was sentenced to time served plus three years under supervision after pleading guilty to threatening to kidnap and murder U.S. District Judge Jack Shanstrom of Billings and using the U.S. mail to send the threat. Dana Dudley, after pleading guilty to interstate transportation of stolen property, received one year and nine months, with credit for two years and three months already served. The extra six months served were to be applied toward a sentence imposed in Colorado for other convictions.

November 6, 1998. *Israel.* Tel Aviv unilaterally suspended the Wye peace accords after two terrorists set off a car bomb in Jerusalem's Mahane Yehuda central street market, killing themselves and wounding 21 Israelis. The bomb apparently went off prematurely. Islamic Jihad took credit and threatened more attacks to derail the Wye accords. At least half a dozen activists were detained. Palestinian Authority officials said the terrorists came from Anata and Silat Harithiya. The duo met in an Israeli jail and were identified as Yusef Ali Mohammed Zughayar, 22, and Seleiman Musa Dahayneh, 24, who had been married for three months to Zughayar's sister, Basma. Dahayneh lost part of his leg after he was shot during a clash with Israeli troops when he was 13 years old.

November 8, 1998. *Martinique.* Striking workers held 373 Club Med tourists hostage. The resort was ordered closed until the labor dispute could be resolved. Police in riot gear raided the resort during the night to free the guests. Four employees were injured; others were treated for tear gas inhalation. None of the French, German, and Italian guests were hurt. 98110801

November 8, 1998. *Angola.* Some 50 gunmen in Lunde Norte Province attacked a Canadian-owned diamond mine, killing 1 Portuguese, 2 Britons, and 3 Angolans, and wounding 18 others. They also took hostage four workers, including one South African, one Briton, and two Filipinos. Angolan officials blamed the National Union for the Total Independence of Angola (UNITA), whose secretary general took credit for the attack, but denied taking hostages. 98110802

November 9, 1998. *Iran.* The Fedayeen for Islam (variant Volunteers for Martyrdom for Islam) told the *Qods* newspaper that it would carry out suicide attacks against Bruce Laingen and Barry Rosen, former U.S. hostages who planned to travel to Iran. The press had reported that the duo had applied for visas after receiving invitations from the radical-now-moderate student group responsible for the seizure of the embassy. Laingen was the chargé d'affaires; Rosen was the press secretary for the embassy. The previous July, Rosen met Abbas Abdi at UNESCO headquarters in Paris. Abdi was one of the leaders of the hostage takers and a supporter of President Mohammad Khatami. 98110901

November 10, 1998. *United States.* Schoolchildren were sent home after receipt of a threat to distribute anthrax at a school in Indianapolis, another school, and an anti-abortion facility. Six of the school's workers were given antibiotics. The threats were similar to recent threats against abortion clinics.

November 11, 1998. *Russia.* Four male kidnappers abducted Herbert Gregg, 51, an American teacher and Christian missionary, during the night in Makhachkala, the capital of Dagestan, a Muslim area that borders breakaway Chechnya. He was dragged into a car and taken to Chechnya. He was freed by Russian security forces on June 29, 1999. No ransom was paid, although his captors had chopped off one of his fingers to press their ransom demands. He said that except for the finger incident, he had been well treated much of the time. He said on arrival in London after a flight from Moscow that "a lot of the time it was good. There were some good people there." He did not confirm that Russian security forces had freed him. 98111101

November 12, 1998. *Italy.* Police at Rome's Leonardo da Vinci Airport arrested Abdullah Ocalan, 49, founder and head of the Kurdistan Workers Party (PKK), on the basis of international warrants from Germany and Turkey. He was flying from Russia to Italy, where he requested political asylum. He was arrested carrying a false passport. *Corriere della Sera* said the Russians had tipped off the Italians. Turkey requested extradition for Ocalan, who was on trial for a terrorist campaign that had led to the deaths of 30,000 people. Hundreds of Kurds entered Italy for a vigil calling for Ocalan's asylum; many began hunger strikes. He was held in the Celio military hospital.

On November 20, an Italian appeals court dismissed Turkey's extradition request. The Italian constitution forbids extradition for political crimes or to countries with the death penalty. Ocalan was on trial in absentia in Turkey on charges punishable with a death sentence, including leading a terrorist organization, threatening the country's territorial integrity, and ordering killings. Turkey said Italy would be an accomplice to mass murder.

Italy freed Ocalan in Rome on November 21. Ocalan told thousands of Kurdish supporters who had come from throughout Europe to "go back to your towns and your jobs and continue supporting the Kurdish cause." The court order that freed him said that Ocalan had to stay in Rome, but the order could be lifted in December.

The Turkish *Hurriyet* claimed that Libya might offer Ocalan asylum if he had to leave Italy.

Turkish businesses announced a boycott of Italian products. Italian firms were barred from obtaining Turkish defense contracts; an Italian firm was a candidate for a $3.5 billion contract to build 145 attack helicopters. Turkey pulled the plug on two Italian state-run cable television channels.

The Italian Foreign Ministry advised Italians to avoid travel to Turkey.

Germany renewed a 1990 warrant for Ocalan, but said it would not seek extradition. The warrant accused Ocalan of killing PKK dissidents and staging a series of arson attacks in Germany. Chancellor Gerhard Schroeder said an international court should try Ocalan.

On November 28, National Liberation Army of Kurdistan (ARGK; the military wing of Ocalan's PKK) guerrillas claimed they had shot down a Turkish Army Sikorsky helicopter, killing 17 troops. The army initially claimed that a technical fault had brought down the helicopter, but later said the ARGK was responsible. The next day, Turkey rejected German and Italian plans for European mediation. Ocalan's lawyer, Giuliano Pisapia, said Ocalan was willing to face an international court. Turkey initiated a massive crackdown against the PKK.

Ocalan claimed on December 13, 1998, that he had cut ties with the PKK. Italian Prime Minister Massimo D'Alema said on December 16 that Ocalan would be kept under police surveillance and could not leave Italy, despite Rome's Court of Appeals statement that Ocalan was freed because Germany had withdrawn its international arrest warrant and possible extradition request. Turkey's extradition request was sent by Italy's Justice Ministry to Rome magistrates for consideration.

Turkish Prime Minister Suleyman Demirel said on December 26 that he did not support a government attempt to abolish the death penalty to gain Ocalan's extradition.

On January 18, 1999, Russia said it had no information on Ocalan's whereabouts, but was checking reports that he had traveled to Russia after leaving Italy on January 16. Turkey claimed that he was stranded for two weeks at Nizhny Novgorod, a Russian military airfield in the Volga region. Ocalan had unsuccessfully sought landing permission in the Netherlands, Belgium, and Switzerland. Italy denied that he had returned to Italy via Milan Airport. Turkey said he had spent some time in Serbia after being expelled from Syria.

On February 1, the Turks charged that Ocalan had landed at Athens Airport or the island of Corfu in a private Falcon-20 jet leased from Estonian Airlines and was hiding in Greece. Turkey demanded his arrest and extradition. Greece denied that he was in the country.

November 13, 1998. *Belgium.* Hansje Boonstra, 62, wife of Philips Electronics President Cor Boonstra, was forced into her car by unidentified kidnappers near Antwerp. She was found several hours later wounded and handcuffed by a road in the Netherlands. 98111301

November 14, 1998. *India.* Militants threw a grenade near a telephone booth near Srinagar, Kashmir, seriously injuring one person.

Meanwhile a bomb went off at a taxi stand near Srinagar, injuring four people and damaging four vehicles.

November 15, 1998. *Colombia.* Gunmen followed an American businessman and his family home in Cundinamarca Department and kidnapped his 11-year-old son after stealing money, jewelry, a car, and two cell phones. They demanded a $1 million ransom. On January 21, 1999, the kidnappers released the boy to his mother and uncle in Tolima Department. It was not known if a ransom was paid to the kidnappers, who claimed membership in the Leftist Revolutionary Armed Commandos for Peace in Colombia. 98111501

November 15, 1998. *Sierra Leone.* Rebels from a faction of the Armed Forces Revolutionary Council led by Sierra Leone's ousted junta leader, Solomon Musa, kidnapped an Italian Catholic missionary from his residence. Musa demanded a satellite telephone, medical supplies, and radio contact with his wife for release of the priest. His wife, Tina Musa, was arrested in September and was being detained in Freetown. 98111502

November 17, 1998. *Greece.* A bomb exploded outside a Citibank branch in Athens, causing major damage. A phone caller to a local newspaper said the attack was protesting against arrests made during a student march. 98111701

November 17, 1998. *India.* Muslim militants were suspected of setting off a bomb near the Madana Bridge in Surankot, Kashmir, killing four persons and injuring several others.

A bomb detonated near a crowded bus stand in Anantnag, killing 3 and injuring 38 others.

November 19, 1998. *Thailand.* The U.S. Embassy was closed for three days because of security concerns. The State Department had issued a public warning on November 12 following the military buildup against Iraq, observing that "the potential for retaliatory acts against Americans and American interests overseas continues to exist."

November 20, 1998. *Swaziland.* A bomb went off in the office of Deputy Prime Minister Arthur Khoza, killing one person and injuring six. It was the second bomb attack in the country in less than a month and followed recent protests against a ban on political parties.

November 20, 1998. *Austria.* The U.S. Embassy received information on a possible terrorist threat against U.S. affiliated facilities in the country. Austrian police enhanced security.

November 20, 1998. *Colombia.* National Liberation Army (ELN) rebels bombed seven branches of Colombia's top bank in Bogota. Police said leftists were protesting foreign investment and a government economic plan. The early morning blasts caused extensive damage, but no injuries.

November 21, 1998. *Iran.* During the morning, a gang attacked a bus carrying U.S. tourists as it arrived at the Esteglal Hotel in northern Tehran.

A hard-line newspaper had accused the visitors of belonging to the CIA. The assailants used stones and iron rods to break windows, but did not hurt any of the tourists. 98112101

November 22, 1998. *Colombia.* U.S. Drug Enforcement Administration (DEA) agent Frank Arnold Moreno, 37, was shot and killed outside Bogota's El Divino bar. The Edinburg, Texas, native was shot once in the back after a bar brawl; the incident did not appear to be drug related. Moreno, a male friend, and the gunman were thrown out of the bar because of their exchange of insults and other aggressive behavior. Police were pursuing a suspect, who also wounded a bystander. On November 27, Jorge Figueroa Monroy surrendered to police in Tolima Province, where he had been hiding. He confessed to the killing. He was the son of a wealthy leather goods manufacturer.

November 23, 1998. *Colombia.* The National Liberation Army (ELN) kidnapped a French citizen who died of natural causes some time in March 1999. 99112301

November 24, 1998. *Yemen.* A car bomb exploded near the German Embassy in Sanaa, killing two and injuring several others. No Germans were hurt. 98112401

November 25, 1998. *India.* Muslim militants threw a grenade at a wedding party in Handwara, Kashmir, injuring 11 people.

November 27, 1998. *Uganda.* Thirty Lord's Resistance Army rebels attacked a World Food Program (WFP) convoy, killing 7 and wounding 28. The rebels abducted five WFP officials and one other person. 98112701

December 1998. *Colombia.* Midlevel U.S. State Department officials traveled to San Jose, Costa Rica, to meet with senior leaders of the Revolutionary Armed Forces of Colombia (FARC). Their goal was to discuss the status of three American missionaries kidnapped five years earlier and resurrect peace talks with the government. For the

first time, the FARC acknowledged some involvement in the narcotics trade. The talks took place at the home of Alvaro Leyva, a former leftist leader who fled Colombia after he was ordered arrested on charges of corruption. He obtained political asylum in Costa Rica. The U.S. delegation was led by Phil Chicola. The rebels were led by Raul Reyes, a senior commander and diplomatic representative. Colombian President Andres Pastrana, 44, also sent representatives to the two meetings, which each lasted four to five hours.

On January 7, 1999, the Colombian government began talks with the FARC high command in San Vicente del Caguan. Manuel "Sureshot" Marulanda Velez, 68, the FARC leader, and Jorge Briceno, his closest aide and FARC's top military strategist, did not attend because of threats from right-wing paramilitary death squads. With 15,000 members, the 34-year-old FARC is the hemisphere's oldest and largest insurgency.

December 1, 1998. *Australia.* Canberra authorities found 21 letter bombs at the city's main mail processing center after a bomb exploded there earlier in the day, injuring a postal worker. The next day, police detonated a second bomb. The following day, they arrested a disgruntled tax worker.

December 2, 1998. *Yemen.* At dawn, Jahm tribesmen in Marib blew up a U.S.-owned Hunt Oil Company pipeline, which carries oil out of the Safer field. The pipeline caught fire, but there were no injuries. 98120201

December 2, 1998. *Algeria.* Attackers killed a dozen villagers in their sleep in the Sidi Rached region, 60 miles west of Algiers.

December 3, 1998. *Algeria.* A bomb exploded at a market in Ein Delfa, 80 miles west of Algiers, killing 14 and injuring 23.

December 3, 1998. *Colombia.* Rebels kidnapped one German and two Colombians from a bus at a roadblock in Cauca Department. They set the bus on fire and dynamited a tollbooth after stealing the money. Authorities suspected the Revolutionary

Armed Forces of Colombia (FARC) or the National Liberation Army (ELN). On January 8, 1999, ELN released the German unharmed. 98120301

December 5, 1998. *Algeria.* Muslim rebels slashed the throats of eight villagers at Les Eucalyptus, 55 miles east of Algiers, in a nighttime raid.

December 6, 1998. *Yemen.* Bani Dhabiane tribesmen kidnapped four German tourists—including one woman—and demanded $500,000 and public works to develop health and educational facilities in their part of the country. The hostages were freed by their captors on December 30, according to a tribal chief who took part in the negotiations. 98120601

December 7, 1998. *Italy.* During the week, the ALF sent panettone cakes laced with rat poison to two branches of the Italian news agency ANSA. Two Italian subsidiaries of Swiss Nestlé were forced to halt production, costing the firm $30 million. According to Italy's ALF founder, the poisoned cakes were sent to protest Nestlé's genetic manipulation of food. 98120701

December 8, 1998. *Colombia.* The Revolutionary Armed Forces of Colombia (FARC) kidnapped one Spaniard and three Colombians, but made no ransom demands. 98120801

December 9, 1998. *Algeria.* Armed terrorists killed 45 people in a predawn attack in the mountain town of Tadjena, 125 miles west of Algiers.

Elsewhere, authorities pulled 46 bodies from a 180-foot-deep well used as a mass grave, which could be as much as two years old. By December 13, authorities had found the remains of 110 people.

December 9, 1998. *India.* A bomb went off in a shop in the Punch District of Kashmir, wounding the shopkeeper. Muslim militants were suspected.

Muslim militants threw a grenade at a group near a bus station in Bandipura, Kashmir, killing 3 people and injuring 20.

December 9, 1998. *Yemen.* In Sanaa, Yemeni passengers on a chartered Egyptian airliner demanded to be flown to Libya. The Egyptian pilot landed the plane in Tunisia and told the 150 passengers that he could not fly the plane to Libya due to UN sanctions. The plane and passengers remained on the ground for 15 hours before returning to Yemen. 98120901

December 10, 1998. *Armenia.* An unknown gunman shot and killed Deputy Minister of Defense Bagram Khorkhourni, 48, outside his apartment as he left for work.

December 11, 1998. *Algeria.* Muslim militants slashed the throats of four villagers in Ahmer el Ain, 35 miles west of Algiers.

December 13, 1998. *United Kingdom.* The Irish Republican Army (IRA) announced it had appointed Brian Keenan, 56, as overall leader of the IRA at a General Army Convention in Ireland the previous week. He had masterminded bombing campaigns in the United Kingdom as its chief of staff. He replaced Thomas "Slab" Murphy, 49, the South Armagh commander. Murphy remained on the Army Council, along with Gerry Adams, Martin McGuinness, Pat Doherty, and Martin Ferris. Keenan had served 14 years in prison for planning 18 attacks, including a bomb blast that killed nine servicemen, one woman, and two children. He conducted relations with Libya beginning in 1972, to obtain arms. Murphy took over the Libyan connection when Keenan was jailed. Keenan and Murphy had never held Sinn Fein posts.

December 13, 1998. *Algeria.* A bomb exploded at a weekly market in Aflou, 180 miles south of Algiers, killing a man, 25.

December 13, 1998. *Persian Gulf.* The U.S. Embassies in Kuwait, Saudi Arabia, Bahrain, and the United Arab Emirates warned Americans of a "strong possibility" of terrorist attacks during the next month. Americans were also warned in Yemen, Qatar, and Oman.

December 16, 1998. *Africa.* The United States announced it was closing all but three of its embassies in Africa because of security concerns in the wake of the August 7 bombings in Nairobi and Dar es Salaam. The State Department had earlier said it would close the embassy in Nairobi on December 18 (the day before Ramadan) and December 24.

December 18, 1998. *Brazil.* Jurandir dos Santos, 26, and Roberto Oliveiro, 22, disappeared near Sao Jose dos Campos, 62 miles northeast of Sao Paulo. They were leaders of the radical Landless Movement and worked with landless peasants who in September invaded the Santa Rita ranch in Vale do Paraiba. They were ambushed and shot execution-style in Sao Paulo State.

December 19, 1998. *Syria.* Demonstrators angered at the U.S. bombing of Iraq stormed the U.S. Embassy in Damascus, causing $500,000 damage to the embassy and the ambassador's residence. The protestors threw rocks and ripped down the U.S. flag. No one was injured. On February 17, 1999, Syria apologized and agreed to pay the $500,000.

December 21, 1998. *Kuwait.* Kuwait stepped up security measures in Kuwait City and at its foreign missions after receiving a terrorist threat following the U.S. and U.K. bombings of Iraqi CW and BW facilities. 98122101

December 22, 1998. *Ireland.* Ireland freed three Irish Republican Army (IRA) members, including Peter Rogers, from their 40-year prison terms for killing three policemen in the 1980s. Policemen and relatives of the victims, including those of Seamus Quaid, who was shot dead by Rogers in 1980, protested the decision.

December 22, 1998. *Canada.* Pierre Vallieres, 60, a leftist journalist who led the Quebec Liberation Front, died at a Montreal hospital after a heart attack. The Front conducted numerous bombings and kidnappings in the 1960s. When his col-

leagues were arrested, he fled to New York, but was arrested and deported. He spent his four years in prison writing a book about the downtrodden French Canadians. In 1971, he renounced violence. In 1980, he abandoned support for Quebec independence, saying that Quebec was doomed to remain within Canada.

December 23, 1998. *India.* Muslim militants forced their way into three homes in three separate villages in Kulham District, Kashmir, killing nine people. The victims were close relatives of former militants who now supported the pro-Indian government militia. Authorities blamed the Hizbul Mujahidin.

December 24, 1998. *Algeria.* Muslim terrorists ambushed two military vehicles patrolling the Zaccar Mountains, 90 miles west of Algiers, killing 8 soldiers, wounding 15, and stealing weapons.

December 24, 1998. *Turkey.* A female Kurdistan Workers Party (PKK) rebel set off a bomb outside an army barracks in Van, injuring 14 soldiers and 8 others and killing herself and a passerby in the third suicide attack against security forces since mid-November.

December 25, 1998. *Worldwide.* Osama bin Laden called for Muslims around the world to attack U.S. and U.K. citizens and interests to avenge their bombing of Iraq. Bin Laden also threatened Israelis and called for a fight against "the Jews and the crusaders, especially the Americans and British, who did not care about the rights of any child, elderly man, or woman in Iraq." 98122501

December 26, 1998. *Angola.* UNITA (the National Union for the Total Independence of Angola) was blamed for shooting down a UN-chartered C-130 transport plane carrying 14 people, 10 passengers and 4 crew. The UN called for a 48-hour cease-fire between the government and rebels to search for survivors in the central highlands near Huambo, 310 miles southeast of Luanda. UNITA would neither confirm nor deny the charge. The ten passengers included three Angolans, two Russians, one Egyptian, one Cameroonian, one Zambian, and one Namibian. Eight were members of the UN Observer Mission in Angola; two were employed by a communications company, Dinacom, that worked with the UN. The plane crashed 25 miles away from Huambo in Vila Nova, a rebel-held area. The plane was painted with UN colors and both sides had been informed of the flight before takeoff. On January 8, 1999, a UN rescue team found 14 burned bodies in the wreckage. The plane disintegrated as it hit the ground and burst into flames, killing everyone on board. 98122601

December 26, 1998. *Ireland.* Cathal Goulding, 75, a Marxist who had been chief of staff of the Irish Republican Army (IRA), died in a Dublin hospital. His poorly armed and organized IRA decided against insurrection in Northern Ireland in the late 1960s, leading younger Catholic militants to break away and form the Provisional IRA and Sinn Fein. Goulding's Official IRA called a cease-fire in 1972.

December 28, 1998. *Yemen.* Islamic militants kidnapped 16 tourists—12 Britons, 2 Americans, and 2 Australians—in the early afternoon on the main road from Habban to Aden in the southern province of Abyan. A Yemeni guide and a British man escaped in one of the tourists' five vehicles and told embassies of the kidnappings. The others were believed to have been driven to al-Wadeaa, an area 250 miles south of Sanaa. The next day, authorities tried to free the hostages, but four of the British travelers were killed and an American woman and an Australian were wounded in the battle with the Islamic Jihad. (British Foreign Secretary Robin Cook said three Britons and one Australian were killed.) The Aden-Abyan Islamic Army also claimed credit. The others were rescued from the 15 kidnappers, 3 of whom were killed. One policeman died. The kidnappers were hoping to free a group leader recently jailed by Yemeni

authorities. Yemeni officials said police were negotiating with the kidnappers and took action only after two hostages were killed. The tourists were on a visit sponsored by the London-based Explore Worldwide.

Female survivors of the kidnapping included Claire Marston of the United Kingdom and Mary Quin of Rochester, New York.

After the fact, reporters learned that the kidnappers were demanding the freedom of one of their members and the end to UN sanctions against Iraq. Osama bin Laden had urged Muslims to kill Americans and Britons to avenge the four nights of air strikes against Iraq that ended on December 19.

London's *Al-Hayat* reported that two of the dead kidnappers were 'Ali all-Khadr al-Haj and Ahmad 'Abdallah Barsha from the Shabwah area. The third, an Egyptian, went by the alias Usamah al-Masri, had lived in Aden for several years, and was a member of the Islamic Army of Aden.

Yemeni authorities said that the three detained were Abu-al-Hasan al-Mihdar, the group's leader, and two brothers, Ahmad and 'Abadallah Muhammad 'Atrif.

On January 4, 1999, London's *Sunday Telegraph* reported that the FBI had evidence that the kidnappers had trained at camps run by Osama bin Laden. Some authorities believed the attacks were in retaliation for the U.S. bombing of Iraqi weapons of mass destruction. The kidnappers were armed with rocket-propelled grenades and automatic weapons and equipped with a laptop computer and a satellite phone. They were funded by bin Laden.

On May 5, 1999, Judge Najib Mohammed Qaderi announced that his court in Abyan had sentenced three Islamic militants to death for the kidnapping and murder. A fourth defendant was sentenced to 20 years in jail. A fifth was acquitted, as were nine other men tried in absentia. Other charges included highway robbery, sabotage, and forming an armed group aimed at destabilizing the government. On October 17, 1999, a Yemeni firing squad in Sanaa executed Zein Abidine Mihdar, an Islamic fundamentalist leader who was convicted of abducting the Western tourists. He was the first person executed on kidnapping charges under a law passed in August 1998. 98122801

December 29, 1998. *Yemen.* Yemeni tribesmen seized four German tourists and held them for 24 hours before freeing them. Among those held was Roswitha Adlung, 49, who said they might have been released unharmed because of the previous day's tragedy. 98122901

December 31, 1998. *Israel.* The U.S. ambassador closed the embassy in Tel Aviv after receiving a "direct and credible" threat the previous evening. The embassy was reopened on January 4, 1999. 98123001

December 31, 1998. *United States.* San Francisco police found hundreds of pounds of bomb-making materials and bomb-making handbooks in a Pacific Gas and Electric Company (PG&E) storage facility. Paul Joseph Madronich, Jr., 44, a 19-year employee of PG&E, led investigators to more materials at a second company facility. Police speculated that the materials were to be used for fireworks rather than bombs. Among the items found in Madronich's locker were five 50-pound bags of ammonium nitrate, the same substance used by Timothy McVeigh in the Oklahoma City bombing. PG&E does not use the material. Police also found a 33-gallon drum of calcium nitrate, broken flares, electronic devices, blasting caps, gunpowder, and fuses. Madronich, nicknamed "The Unabomber," used the explosives to make cherry bombs and M-80s that he sold to coworkers. PG&E said he was a loner; authorities said he did not have a political agenda. He was held in lieu of $1 million bail on three counts of possessing an explosive device. On February 18, 1999, Madronich pleaded guilty to possession and faced three years in prison. His attorney, Jerry Ladar, said Madronich had no intention of harming anyone.

1999. *United States.* On September 27, 2000, U.S. Federal Judge Wilkie Ferguson sentenced Conor Claxtron, 27, to a 56-month prison sentence for buying and shipping weapons in an Irish Republican Army (IRA) gun-running operation. The weapons in the 1999 plot were to be disguised as toys, VCRs, and computers going from Florida to Northern Ireland via the U.S. mail. Anthony Smyth, 43, and Martin Mullan, 30, received three-year sentences in the Fort Lauderdale court.

January 1999. *Uruguay.* Montevideo police arrested El Said Hassan Ali Mohamed Mukhlis, an Egyptian living in Ciudad del Este who was tied to Egypt's Islamic Group. He was en route to Europe to meet an al-Qaeda cell.

January 2, 1999. *Angola.* A UN-chartered aircraft carrying seven UN workers from Huambo to Luanda was shot down in the central region of the country, presumably by the National Union for the Total Independence of Angola (UNITA), which denied involvement. No casualties were reported. One American citizen was on the plane. 99010201

January 2, 1999. *Algeria.* Rebels slashed the throats of 22 people in an overnight attack at Oued al Aatchaane, 240 miles southwest of Algiers.

January 3, 1999. *Pakistan.* At 4:50 A.M., a bomb went off at a bridge near the Raiwind residence of Prime Minister Nawaz Sharif outside Lahore, killing three civilians and a policeman, injuring several others (including three policemen), and ripping apart the bridge he was scheduled to cross on the Lahore–Raiwind road. A mechanic working on a gas pipeline under the bridge was killed on the spot and two other workmen died later. A police traffic inspector was among the wounded.

January 3, 1999. *Israel.* Police arrested 14 members of the Denver-based Concerned Christians and accused them of coming to Jerusalem to plan their own violent deaths to mark the millennium. The three adult couples, two single men, and six children are members of a cult led by Monte Kim

Miller, 44, who disappeared from Denver with 56 followers in October. Miller, a former Procter and Gamble Company executive, had told a television interviewer two years earlier that "Jesus Christ died on the cross and we have a duty to die. The Lord's judgment has been with the Earth for 2000 years and now judgment is ready to begin." Oddly, Miller had worked in the mid-1980s as a lecturer on the dangers of cults and the New Age movement. Miller was apparently in London at the time of the arrests of the 14, who included Karen (or Corrine) Stevens and Eric Malesic. (Five of Malesic's siblings—Mark, Steve, Joe, Matthew, and Kevin—had also joined the cult.) Police said, "They intended to carry out extreme acts of violence in the streets of Jerusalem towards the end of 1999 with the aim of beginning a process that would bring about the second coming of Jesus." Miller saw himself as Christ's contemporary reincarnation and believed he could channel the word of God. Miller based his beliefs on the Book of Revelations and planned to die a violent death in Jerusalem, but be resurrected three days later. He said Denver would be destroyed on October 10. Police said that those detained had arrived in Israel "a few months ago." None were employed in Israel. They were living in two Jerusalem suburbs. They did not resist arrest; no weapons were found. The 14 were deported to the United States on January 8. They arrived via Air Canada in Denver the next day, but were escorted by police to an undisclosed destination and did not meet with relatives waiting for them at the airport.

January 4, 1999. *Pakistan.* Eight gunmen riding four motorcycles killed 17 Shi'ites and wounded 24 in a mosque at Quereshi More, 20 miles east of the southern Punjab city of Multan. Scores of people had died in a yearlong feud between the Sunni Muslim group Sipah-e-Sahabah (variant Sipah-e-Sahaba; Guardians of the Friends of the Prophet) and the Shi'ite group Tehrik-e-Jaffria (Group for Shi'ite Muslim Law).

January 4, 1999. *West Bank.* Gunmen hiding in an alley in Hebron fired two dozen bullets at a passing van, wounding two Jewish female settlers,

one seriously. The attack occurred on a winding road connecting Kiryat Arba and Hebron. Palestinian militants were blamed.

January 6, 1999. *Angola.* Thirty National Union for the Total Independence of Angola (UNITA) gunmen fired on a vehicle, killing one Briton, one Brazilian, and two Angolan security guards. The vehicle apparently belonged to the Australian-owned Cuango mine. 99010601

January 6, 1999. *Sierra Leone.* Armed Forces Revolutionary Council rebels kidnapped two Italian missionaries, who were rescued on January 13 by government-sponsored forces. 99010602

January 7–10, 1999. *Colombia.* Right-wing death squads killed more than 100 people in five northern provinces. In Playon de Orozco in Magdalena Province, 70 members of the United Self-Defense Forces of Colombia broke into a church, consulted lists of intended victims, dragged them out, and shot them dead as parishioners and priest Giovanni San Juan watched helplessly. Gunmen killed eight people at dawn in Toluviejo, in northern Sucre Province. Gunmen killed 15 suspected rebel sympathizers in Antioquia Province. Paramilitary gangs killed 23 people in Putumayo Province.

January 8, 1999. *Albania.* Authorities in Tirana arrested Maksim Ciciku, 34, an Albanian who headed a private security firm, for spying on American diplomats in preparation for an attack by a group with links to Osama bin Laden. The interior minister was quoted as saying that Ciciku was monitoring U.S. Ambassador Marisa Lino. He was released without charge on January 11. He told a television reporter that police had confiscated a weapon and radio equipment that he used in his work. He said he was educated in Saudi Arabia and had provided bodyguards for Arabs in Albania. The local media claimed that the CIA had tipped off police. 99010801

January 8, 1999. *South Africa.* Five youths firebombed a Kentucky Fried Chicken restaurant in

Cape Town, causing major damage, but no injuries. No one claimed credit. 99010802

January 9, 1999. *Yemen.* Armed tribesmen abducted John Brooke, 46, a British oil worker stationed at an oilfield operated by the U.S.-based Halliburton oil company in Marib Province, 105 miles southeast of Sanaa. He was freed unharmed on January 13. 99010901

January 9, 1999. *Colombia.* The right-wing United Self-Defense Forces of Colombia killed 20 people in Playon de Orozco, a remote village in Magdalena Province. During the previous three days, more than 80 people had been killed.

Meanwhile, Jorge Briceno (alias Mono Jojoy), the military leader of the Revolutionary Armed Forces of Colombia (FARC), said the group would not disarm and threatened to step up attacks if peace talks bogged down.

January 11, 1999. *Colombia.* The National Liberation Army (ELN) kidnapped two vacationing Italians and one Colombian at a roadblock in Chinacota. The ELN freed an Italian hostage in Norte de Santander on March 9. 99011101

January 12, 1999. *Pakistan.* Gunmen broke into the Peshawar home of Afghan moderate Abdul Haq and murdered his wife, his 11-year-old son, and a guard. Haq was not at home at the time. The victims were sleeping when the attack took place. No one claimed credit. 99011201

January 12, 1999. *Sierra Leone.* Revolutionary United Front (RUF) rebels kidnapped a Spanish missionary who belonged to the Xaverian Monastic Order. He was rescued on January 22 by soldiers of the Economic Community of West African States Cease-Fire Monitoring Group (ECOMOG). 99011202

January 17, 1999. *Yemen.* Gunmen kidnapped an elderly British couple and four Dutch citizens who were traveling on a road in the north. They freed the hostages on February 2. Hans Koolstra, a Dutch national who was taken hostage along with

his wife and two children, said the kidnappers had treated the hostages "generally well." They were freed after mediation by a senior Yemeni tribal leader. The tribesmen apparently were hoping to kidnap the U.S. ambassador in Sanaa or any U.S. Embassy staff member. Other tribesmen had attempted to kidnap two U.S. Embassy employees as they drove to work, but the would-be victims drove around them and escaped. 99011701-02

January 18, 1999. *France.* On February 15, the government announced the arrest of Ahmed Loudaini, 30, a French citizen of Algerian extraction and suspected associate of Osama bin Laden. Loudaini had been picked up at Paris's Gare du Nord rail station the month before by DST officers investigating a forgery ring. He was about to board the Eurostar cross-Channel train for London. Police found a coded document they were attempting to decipher. Loudaini, who lives in Montfermeil in the northeastern Paris suburbs, was indicted for "criminal association with the aim of preparing terrorist acts." The Europe 1 radio station claimed that the CIA had tipped off the French and that a four-man terrorist team had been sent to France by bin Laden. The arrest was carried out under the aegis of France's top antiterrorist judge, Jean-Louis Bruguiere. 99011801

January 19, 1999. *India.* Indian police arrested four people, including a Bangladeshi man accused of working for Pakistan's Inter-Services Intelligence Agency (ISI), and charged them with involvement in a plot by Osama bin Laden to bomb the U.S. Embassy and two consular offices in Madras and Calcutta. The attacks were to have taken place before the January 26 anniversary of the Indian constitution. The ringleader was identified as Sayed Abu Nasir, 27, of Bangladesh, who was arrested the previous week. Police recovered two kilograms of RDX explosives and five detonators when they arrested him and three Indians at New Delhi's rail station. (Other reports said that he had been detained in December or on January 7.) His Indian accomplices were identified as Mohammed Gulab, Mohammed Nawab, and Aga Khan, who were picked up in Siliguri, in West

Bengal State. Other members of the terrorist group still at large included four Egyptians, a Sudanese, and a Myanmar (Burma) national. Police said Abu Nasir and his gang crossed the border between Bangladesh and West Bengal in October. They then traveled to Madras and Calcutta to surveil targets. Abu Nasir claimed he had met bin Laden at a terrorist training camp in Kunsar, Afghanistan, in 1995. 99011901

January 19, 1999. *Colombia.* The Revolutionary Armed Forces of Colombia (FARC) suspended peace talks pending government action against right-wing death squads. Paramilitary gunmen had killed 140 people in five provinces.

January 19, 1999. *Bangladesh.* Three members of the previously unknown Harkat-ul-Jihad attempted to kill Shamshur Rahman, 70, one of the country's leading poets, with an ax. Rahman's wife, daughter-in-law, and maid warded off the trio, two of them teens. Besides the ax, the attackers also carried a homemade single-shot rifle. Two attackers were arrested at the victim's home. They said they planned to kill Rahman and three other intellectuals because of their liberal beliefs. Police detained 16 more suspects in Dhaka, a suburb, and Chittagong. The group's two top leaders fled the country. Some suspects said that one of the fugitives, Abdul Hye, a Muslim cleric from Chittagong, received funds directly from Osama bin Laden. A local newspaper said bin Laden sent $1 million to the group through four bank accounts in Dhaka. Police confiscated $1,650 in local currency during a January 19 raid on the small Dhaka apartment where Hye had lived for three years. Another detainee, Ahmed Sidiq Ahmed, a South African of Indian descent, was a personal friend of bin Laden. A Pakistani was also detained. Police ultimately arrested 47 members of the Harakat ul-Jihad Islami (HUJI) and Harakat ul-Mujahidin (HUM).

It appeared that Hye and fellow cleric Sheik Farid created the group circa 1995 in an Islamic seminary in Chittagong. The group trained seminary students on the use of light arms at two small camps in southeastern Bangladesh. They then sent them to fight alongside the Taliban against other factions in Afghanistan. The group had between 2,000 and 3,000 activists and perhaps 10,000 members. The group publishes a monthly magazine called *Wake Up, Freedom Fighter*. 99011902

January 22, 1999. *Sierra Leone.* Nigerian ECO-MOG (Economic Community of West African States Cease-Fire Monitoring Group) intervention troops rescued the Roman Catholic archbishop of Freetown, Joseph Henry Ganda, and five European priests. Rebel kidnappers escaped Freetown with several other foreigners. The Nigerian troops rescued the hostages from the outskirts of Freetown after a heavy gun battle. 99012201

January 22, 1999. *France.* A court in Fleury-Merogis convened in a prison gymnasium and convicted 107 people on charges of supporting Islamic insurgents in Algeria. The court acquitted 31 others. The 138 people were arrested in 1994–95 and charged with engaging in "a terrorist enterprise." The enterprise involved three overlapping networks. 99012201

January 22, 1999. *Worldwide.* Richard A. Clarke, national coordinator for counterterrorism and computer security programs, announced that U.S. intelligence and law enforcement agencies had prevented two truck bombings of U.S. embassies by Osama bin Laden's terrorists since the August bombings. Some officials indicated that one of the embassies was in Uganda. The Clinton administration announced a $10 billion budget proposal for fighting terrorism and protecting the nation's computer infrastructure from attack.

January 23, 1999. *India.* Hindu right-wing activists were suspected of setting alight an off-road vehicle, killing the people who were sleeping inside it. The three victims were Graham Stewart Staine (or Staines), 58, an Australian-born Baptist missionary, and his two sons, Philip, 10, and Timothy, 8. They had traveled from neighboring Baripada to attend a meeting at a church in Bhubaneswar in Orissa State's remote Kheonjar District, 660 miles southeast of New Delhi. They had also attended a Bible study session in Manoharpur village. His wife and daughter stayed home. Staine had been working among tribal peoples and lepers in Orissa for 30 years. In recent weeks, Hindu terrorists had attacked Christians, burning churches and attacking clergy in Gujarat State. No one claimed credit. Hundreds attended the funeral.

On February 1, 2000, Dara Singh, the suspected Hindu militant in the case, was arrested while he negotiated to buy a gun. 99012301

January 23, 1999. *South Africa.* Opposition politician Sifiso Nkabinde, secretary general of the United Democratic Front, was ambushed and assassinated in rural Richmond, his home base. Many observers had blamed him for a wave of political violence in KwaZulu-Natal. Hours later, 11 people were killed and 8 wounded in an apparent revenge attack against the ruling African National Congress in Richmond.

The next day, two gunmen shot to death Vulindlela Matiyase, deputy chairman of a local branch of the United Democratic Movement. He was hit four times in the chest and back as he opened his front door.

The violence continued on January 28, when a bomb exploded in a trash can outside Cape Town's main police station during lunch hour, injuring another 11. Police detained two suspects believed involved in Muslim battles against drug traffickers as well as those angry at Western attacks on Iraq.

January 24, 1999. *Sierra Leone.* Revolutionary United Front (RUF) rebels in Freetown kidnapped 11 Indian businessmen, including Japan's honorary consul, Kishoie Shakandas. He was freed on January 29. 99012401

January 25, 1999. *Sierra Leone.* Revolutionary United Front (RUF) rebels kidnapped two European journalists in a Freetown suburb. They freed Frenchman Patrick Saint Paul so he could deliver demands to the authorities. 99012501

January 26, 1999. *Venezuela.* The Colombian National Liberation Army (ELN) kidnapped five Venezuelan engineers working for the Venezuelan Petroleum Company. The ELN released one hostage on February 15 and the other four on February 17. 99012601

January 27, 1999. *Yemen.* Local tribesmen kidnapped a German aid worker (or midwife), her visiting mother, brother, Yemeni husband, three Yemeni children, and the family's Yemeni driver. They were taken to Al-Jawf in the north, where a group of two Britons and a Dutch family of four had been held since January 17. The tribesmen released the Yemenis on January 28. On January 30, the tribesmen released one of the women, but hours later demanded that she be returned to them, claiming that the 30-year-old aid worker was to deliver their demands to the German Embassy, but then return. They threatened her mother and brother if she did not return. The German foreign minister asked Yemeni officials to avoid any rescue attempts that could endanger the hostages. 99012701

January 28, 1999. *China.* A homemade nail bomb exploded in a farmers market in rural Hunan Province, killing 8 and injuring more than 65. It was the fourth bombing in the province during January.

January 29, 1999. *Uruguay.* Authorities led by Luis Saldias, intelligence head of the Uruguayan police, arrested Sa'id Muhklis, an Egyptian man linked to Osama bin Laden. He was believed to be a member of an Egyptian militant group seeking to establish a Muslim state in Egypt. Muhklis was picked up attempting to enter the country from Brazil on a false Malaysian passport. London's *Sunday Times* claimed that, based upon intercepted phone calls, authorities believed he was about to fly to London to form a terrorist cell that would conduct attacks against the British embassies in Paris and Brussels. He was suspected of involvement in the 1997 al-Gamaat massacre of 58 tourists in Luxor. He faced extradition to Cairo on murder charges.

Muhklis had lived in Brazil for five years. He took his wife and their three children, all under age five, to the border. They were all carrying false Malaysian passports. They arrived in Chui, a border town on the Atlantic coast, and checked into a hotel. He told neighbors he had lived in Brazil for ten years, yet he knew no Portuguese. 99012901

January 30, 1999. *South Africa.* A bomb exploded at a Cape Town police station, wounding a woman.

January 31, 1999. *Algeria.* Muslim rebels slashed the throats of 34 villagers in three separate attacks on Sunday night. They killed 19 people in el-Merdja, 9 in Sahariidji, and 6 in Telassa, all in western Algeria. Most of the dead were women and children.

January 31, 1999. *Yemen.* Tribesmen kidnapped a British oil worker employed by the U.S. firm Hunt Oil. He was released six hours later. 99013101

February 1999. *Uzbekistan.* Salai Madaminov (alias Mukhammed Salikh), poet and a leader of the banned Erk (Freedom) Party was connected with a series of bombings in which 16 people died. Madaminov had lost the 1991 election to Uzbek President Islam Karimov. He went into exile in 1993, and was sentenced in absentia in 2000 to fifteen and a half years in prison by a Tashkent court. President Karimov had narrowly escaped being killed in the bombings.

On November 28, 2001, Prague Airport border police detained the poet when he arrived from Amsterdam.

February 1, 1999. *Egypt.* A military tribunal in Haekstep began the trial of 107 members of the outlawed Jihad movement on charges including forgery, criminal conspiracy, subversion, membership in an outlawed group, plotting to carry out attacks on officials and police, attempting to prevent security forces from carrying out their jobs, and conspiracy to overthrow the government.

Some 62 defendants were tried in absentia.

They included Ayman Zawahiri, Jihad's leader and aide to Osama bin Laden, believed to be hiding in Afghanistan. Also at large were Yasser Tawfik Sirri and Adel Abd-al-Meguid, leaders of the Islamic Observation Center in London, and Adel Abd-al-Quddous, another London-based Islamic activist.

The defendants also included 13 Jihad members who were extradited from Albania in 1998.

Seven defendants were locked in a steel cage in the courtroom. They claimed they had not seen their families during their four years in custody. Others complained of police torture.

February 2, 1999. *China.* A time bomb exploded in a central Chinese province, blinding a policeman, who also lost both arms.

In southeastern Fujian Province, police arrested two men for detonating a remote control bomb outside a bank in an attempted robbery, killing two and injuring five.

February 3–4, 1999. *United States.* Hoax letters claiming to contain anthrax arrived at an NBC News office in Atlanta and a U.S. Post Office in Columbus, Georgia. The next day, two letters containing an unidentified substance were sent to the *Washington Post* building and the Old Executive Office Building. Since late 1998, two dozen similar letters and packages purporting to contain anthrax had been delivered to courthouses, abortion clinics, and office buildings across the country. Law enforcement officials said the Georgia incidents did not appear to be the work of the same individual.

February 4, 1999. *Northern Ireland.* The Irish Republican Army (IRA) admitted that dissidents had stolen some of its arsenal of guns and bomb-making equipment.

February 8, 1999. *Greece.* A bomb exploded near the Turkish Consulate in Komotini, wounding a member of the bomb squad and causing minor damage. A caller to local authorities warned of and later claimed credit for the bomb on behalf of the group Support of Ocalan—The Hawks of Thrace. 99020801

February 9, 1999. *India.* Muslim militants threw a grenade at a security patrol in Pulwama Chowk, injuring 12 civilians and 2 security officers.

February 9, 1999. *Nigeria.* One British and one Italian employee of an unidentified oil company were kidnapped. The Italian was released shortly after. No demands were made, and no group claimed credit. 99020901

February 10, 1999. *Angola.* The National Union for the Total Independence of Angola (UNITA) kidnapped two Portuguese nationals and two Spaniards who worked for Navacong, a firm renovating M'Banza Congo's public infrastructure. They were kidnapped from a church where they had sought shelter from fighting between UNITA and the government. 99021001

February 11, 1999. *Angola.* UNITA rebels attacked the scout vehicle for a convoy of SDM/ Aston diamond mine vehicles, killing three Angolan security guards and wounding five others. Angolan and Australian mining companies jointly owned SDM/Aston Mining. 99021101

February 12, 1999. *Sierra Leone.* The Revolutionary United Front (RUF) kidnapped an Italian missionary from a church, but made no demands. The hostage was released unharmed on April 8. 99021201

February 14, 1999. *Uganda.* A pipe bomb at a popular Kampala night spot killed 4 Ugandans and 1 Ethiopian and wounded 35 others, including a U.S. citizen working for USAID, 2 Swiss, 1 Pakistani, 1 Ethiopian, and 27 Ugandans. The bar was damaged extensively. Witnesses said two Asians and a Ugandan police officer also were wounded. No one claimed credit, but the authorities blamed the Allied Democratic Forces (ADF). 99021401

February 14, 1999. *Nigeria.* Three armed youths kidnapped a British employee of Shell Oil and his young son. The two were freed unharmed the next day. No ransom was paid, and no one claimed credit. 99021402

February 15, 1999. *Kenya.* Turkish authorities arrested Abdullah Ocalan (alias Apo), 50, leader of the Kurdistan Workers Party (PKK), after he left the Greek ambassador's residence in Nairobi, where he had stayed for two weeks. Ocalan was wanted for leading a 14-year separatist war in which 37,000 people died. Stories conflicted as to whether he left in his own motorcade that was then stopped by Kenyan government vehicles or whether he was dragged out of the Greek Embassy. Turkish officials said he would be held on the island of Imrali in the Sea of Marmara, south of Istanbul. He faced six counts of promoting separatism and at least one count of treason, which carries a death penalty. The Turkish press said the trial by a military-civilian state security court would probably begin in early April and have a verdict in May.

Kenyan officials claimed that when they learned that Greek diplomats were sheltering Ocalan, they demanded that he be expelled. Some reports said that Ocalan was on his way to the airport when his car lost its Greek chase cars in traffic. The Ocalan car was then intercepted by Turkish commandos. A Kenyan official said Ocalan apparently intended to go to the Seychelles. Other reports said he was on his way to Amsterdam, the Netherlands, or to an African country. He reportedly was flown out of Kenya on a private jet owned by a Turkish textile executive. The plane's markings had been painted over.

Kenya also asked that Greek Ambassador George Kostoulas leave the country. Kenya charged that Kostoulas had permitted Ocalan to fly in on a private jet, then bypass immigration controls using his diplomatic privilege. Kostoulas gave the Kenyans false names for Ocalan and his party and denied that Ocalan was in the country when the Kenyans confronted him. Reporters were shown photocopies of a passport issued in the name of Mavros Lazaros, a Greek Cypriot journalist with PKK ties. The passport was stamped with a Kenyan visa.

Ocalan apparently had failed to use proper precautions in hiding out, frequently using an unsecured cell phone.

Ocalan had been living in exile since 1980 when he founded the PKK. The PKK began its terrorist attacks in 1984. He was expelled from Syria in November 1998. He had been on the run since leaving Italy on January 16. A Rome court was scheduled to hold a first hearing on February 24 on his request for asylum, which he had made after arriving in Italy on November 12, 1998. His private plane was permitted to refuel in Greece on February 2. The Associated Press reported that Greece had attempted to find an African country that would grant him asylum. On February 21, Greece reportedly had decided to grant asylum to one of the three women who were escorting Ocalan when he was arrested. (The three were being sheltered in the Greek ambassador's residence in Nairobi.) Greek media speculated that this woman was Melsa Deniz, a Turkish national. The other two were believed to be a Dutch woman and a Belgian. One of the women, Semsi Kilc (alias Dylan), told the press the PKK would officially open an office in Athens. The Greek government denied the report.

Turkey sent home three Dutch lawyers who flew in to Istanbul hoping to represent Ocalan. Under Turkish law, foreign nationals cannot defend Turkish citizens in Turkish courts.

Ocalan was formally arrested and charged with treason on February 23. Prosecutors sought the death penalty. The hearing was closed to the media and the public and was presided over by a judge from a special state security court in which one of the three judges is a military officer. Ocalan also faced five additional charges of "seeking to undermine the indivisible unity of the Turkish state."

On February 26, Ahmet Zeki Okcuoglu, one of Ocalan's attorneys, said he was resigning because he feared for his life. Meanwhile, Istanbul police detained Osman Baydemir, a second member of the 15-member volunteer legal team, for suspected PKK ties.

On April 28, Turkish prosecutors formally requested the death penalty in a 139-page indictment that accused Ocalan of ordering killings of children and teachers.

The treason trial began on May 31 in front of a special state security court led by Judge Turgut Okyay. Ocalan said he was willing "to work for peace" and asked that his life be spared so that he could "serve the Turkish state." He also warned that his death would plunge the country into further violence by his followers. He apologized to the families of the 5,000 Turkish soldiers killed in the insurgency. The next day, he claimed that the government had negotiated with his group for several years, despite claims that it would never deal with them. He also confirmed charges that his group trained in Greece and the Netherlands with the full knowledge of local officials.

On June 8, chief prosecutor Cevdet Volkan dismissed Ocalan's calls for peace and demanded the death penalty. The trial was adjourned until June 23.

On June 18, the Turkish Parliament voted to withdraw a military judge from the panel hearing the case, an attempt to deflect international criticism that the trial was unfair. (The Strasbourg-based Council of Europe threatened to suspend Turkey's membership if Ocalan were to be executed. The trial could also derail Turkey's efforts to host a summit on human rights of the 55-nation Organization for Security and Cooperation in Europe, due to take place in Istanbul in November.) Legislators voted 423–40 to amend two constitutional articles and withdraw military judges from all state security courts.

The defense wrapped up its case on June 24, warning of further attacks if Ocalan were to be hanged. A judge ordered a recess until June 29, when a guilty verdict was expected to be announced. Ocalan blamed the Turkish state for 14 years of violence, but also declared his guilt in thousands of deaths. His attorneys called on the judges to invoke a legal article permitting them to favor life imprisonment in recognition for good behavior since capture. He could appeal a death sentence. Parliament must approve an execution. He could appeal a parliamentary vote to the European Court of Human Rights, which could take from six months to a year to decide the case.

On June 29, the Turkish court sentenced Ocalan to death by hanging. The PKK's new leader, Cemil Bayik, warned of violence if Ocalan were executed. On July 1, two PKK guerrillas opened fire with automatic weapons, killing three men in an Elazig coffeehouse and injuring three others. One attacker was killed by security forces in a subsequent gun battle.

Ocalan's lawyers said they would appeal the sentence within ten days. On June 30, they asked the European Court of Human Rights in Strasbourg for a stay of execution. The lawyers appealed the sentence on July 5. Ocalan ordered his followers not to carry out any violent attacks that could provoke Turkey into executing him.

Ocalan formally called upon the PKK to end its armed struggle on August 3, 1999. He did not call upon the group to disarm and surrender. He urged the PKK's members to flee Turkey before September 1.

On November 25, the five-judge Turkish appeals court unanimously upheld Ocalan's death sentence. The 550-person parliament would have to approve the death sentence before it could be carried out. Ocalan's defense team said it would take his case to the European Court of Human Rights.

On December 30, 1999, a chief prosecutor refused to overturn the death sentence. The appeal was the last legal move before the sentence went to parliament and later the president for approval. The European Court for Human Rights had asked Turkey not to execute Ocalan until it reviewed the case.

On January 12, 2000, Turkish leaders announced the postponement of the execution until the European Court of Human Rights ruled on Ocalan's appeal. Following protests, they announced they would execute Ocalan if he attempted to run the terrorist group from prison.

February 15, 1999. *India.* Muslim militants shot and critically injured the owner of a video shop in Srinagar, Kashmir.

In an attempt to ban Western broadcasts, Muslim militants shot in the legs and wounded three cable television operators in Srinagar. They ordered the victims to broadcast only news and current affairs.

Muslim militants were also believed to be responsible for setting off a bomb in a crowded Srinagar marketplace, injuring six.

February 16, 1999. *Europe.* Kurdish demonstrators across Europe protested Ocalan's arrest.

More than 100 Kurds took over the Greek Embassy in Bonn while another 500 watched from outside. Kurds also occupied the Kenyan Embassy, 1,000 meters away.

Some 150 Kurds stormed the Greek ambassador's residence in The Hague, the Netherlands, taking the ambassador's wife and eight-year-old son hostage for most of the day before freeing them. The boy was reportedly threatened with hand grenades.

Forty protestors held a clerk hostage inside the Greek Embassy in London, then announced a hunger strike.

Kurds occupied Greek and Kenyan facilities in Vancouver, British Columbia, Canada; Russia; Italy; Sweden; Denmark; Sydney, Australia; Norway; the United Kingdom; France; Austria; Bern and Zurich, Switzerland; Belgium; and the German cities of Hamburg, Hanover, Stuttgart, and Cologne. Demonstrators also attacked the UN buildings in Geneva and Yerevan, Armenia. They took hostages in Greece's missions in the Netherlands and Switzerland. Others threatened mass suicides at the Greek embassies in Brussels and London. Three demonstrators set themselves on fire. A one-day standoff ended in Hamburg on February 18 when the Kurds released a hostage and departed; several were arrested.

Kurds also seized the offices of the ruling parties in Sweden and Austria. The protestors held several hostages in the Stockholm office.

A Kurdish prisoner in a Turkish jail burned

himself to death to protest. Another protestor in Turkey set himself on fire, but lived.

February 16, 1999. *Worldwide.* U.S. and Israeli embassies were placed on a heightened security alert following the storming of Greek embassies throughout Europe to protest Ocalan's arrest. Some media reports claimed that the United States had played a role in his capture. Washington denied direct involvement although unnamed U.S. officials said that the United States had worked for months via diplomatic channels to help Turkey arrest Ocalan. The Israeli Mossad also refused comment on reports that it had aided Turkey in finding and capturing Ocalan.

February 16, 1999. *Uzbekistan.* President Islam Karimov declared a day of national mourning after eight car bombs killed 13 and wounded 80 in Tashkent in an apparent attempt to assassinate him. Karimov was being driven to a cabinet meeting at government headquarters. Two attackers were gunned down in a shootout with police as they drove into Independence Square, where four of the bombs went off. Karimov was unharmed. The explosions blew out windows at the National Bank and a regional office of the Interior Ministry. Muslim militants were blamed. On June 28, 1999, Uzbekistan sentenced 6 men to death and imprisoned 16 others for their involvement in a series of bombings in February that killed 16.

February 17, 1999. *Germany.* Israeli security guards fired on 200 Kurds who stormed the Israeli Consulate in Wilmersdorf, a suburb of Berlin, at 2:00 P.M., killing 3 and wounding 16. The Kurds were protesting Ocalan's capture. The protestors broke through a security cordon of German police and ran at the four-story building. Armed with sticks, two dozen protestors climbed fences and crawled through windows on the first and second floors. One protestor tried to wrestle a pistol away from an Israeli security guard, who shot and killed the attacker. Two of the dead—a man and a woman—were shot in the foyer; another man was shot on the stairwell. Other Kurds inside the

building took an Israeli staff member captive, but quickly released her. Israeli guards fired for ten minutes before the battle ended. No Israelis were injured, but at least 43 others were injured—the 16 demonstrators and 27 police officers. Police arrested 220 Kurds, 45 at the consulate and the others at demonstrations. Israeli Prime Minister Benjamin Netanyahu denied that Israel had a hand in the arrest, but ordered the temporary closure of all Israeli diplomatic missions in Europe.

February 17, 1999. *Germany.* A Turkish cultural center in Hamburg was firebombed during the night. Several Turkish fast-food stands were also firebombed. 99021701-03

February 18, 1999. *Sudan.* Gunmen in southern Sudan abducted seven people, including two Swiss citizens working for the International Committee of the Red Cross (ICRC). The group was visiting a village near Bentiu in an area controlled by the Sudanese government. They were assessing the need for seed distribution. As of March 6, negotiations were under way. The government blamed the Sudan People's Liberation Front (SPLA). On March 12, the rebels released the two Swiss, but killed the five Sudanese hostages on April 1. 99021801

February 18, 1999. *Colombia.* The Revolutionary Armed Forces of Colombia (FARC) kidnapped two Spaniards, one Algerian, and two Colombians. On November 2, FARC released the foreigners unharmed. 99021802

February 18–19, 1999. *United States.* Another 14 hoax letters claiming to contain anthrax were mailed to abortion clinics and Planned Parenthood centers. Postal inspectors determined that they were postmarked in Lexington, Kentucky. Authorities believed that the February threats, as well as similar ones in October 1998, were connected. The letters were received on February 18 at centers in Asheville, North Carolina; Charleston, South Carolina; Cincinnati, Ohio; the District of Columbia; Manchester, New Hampshire;

Milwaukee, Wisconsin; and Rapid City and South Falls, South Dakota. The next day, letters were received in Birmingham, Alabama; Des Moines, Iowa; and several cities in Vermont.

February 21, 1999. *Colombia.* The Revolutionary Armed Forces of Colombia (FARC) kidnapped two Spaniards and seven Colombians. They released one Spanish hostage and two Colombians and demanded 300 million pesetas for the release of the second Spanish hostage. The rebels released the Spaniard on February 28 without receipt of a ransom. 99022101

February 24, 1999. *Nigeria.* Armed youths kidnapped a U.S. citizen for ransom. A local militant group rescued the hostage, but then demanded ransom for his release. Bristow Helicopters, the victim's employer, paid the demanded $53,000. The hostage was released unharmed on March 4. 99022401

February 25, 1999. *Colombia.* The 45th Front of the Revolutionary Armed Forces of Colombia (FARC) kidnapped three Americans who had been helping an Indian group in a land dispute with a U.S. oil company. Terence Freitas, 24, an environmentalist from Los Angeles; Ingrid Inawatuk (or Washinawatok), 41, a member of the Menominee Nation of Wisconsin; and Gay Laheenae (variant Lahe'ena'e Gay), 39, a Sioux who headed the Hawaii-based Pacific Cultural Conservancy International, were grabbed during the morning near Royota village in Arauca Province. The three were studying the U'wa culture, which is in conflict with the Colombian government.

The bodies of the three Americans were found on March 5 amid signs that they had been tortured. The blindfolded and bound bodies were on the Venezuelan side of the Arauca River in the Venezuelan hamlet of Los Pajaros. The two women had been shot four times each in the face and chest with 9-mm weapons; Freitas had been shot six times. Colombian and U.S. officials said the killings were on the orders of senior insurgent commanders, citing eyewitness accounts and elec-

tronic intercepts of two rebel conversations, including a recording of the order to execute them. One of the intercepted cell phone conversations was between the 45th Front and German Briceno, the front commander and brother of Jorge Briceno, FARC's leading military strategist. The 45th Front was one of the groups most closely tied to drug trafficking. German Briceno protected large cocaine laboratories in the jungle.

Raul Reyes, a member of FARC's seven-man ruling junta, said on March 8 that FARC would investigate, but said he had seen no sign of any rebel role.

FARC admitted to the murders on March 10, but refused to extradite the suspects to the United States, saying that they would be "sanctioned" by their code of revolutionary justice. The killers believed the activists worked for the CIA. The killers were identified as German Briceno (alias Grannobles) and El Marrano (alias Rafael; alias Marrano; alias Alveiro; alias Reynaldo). Inawatuk had been bitten by a snake and taken to a clinic in Arauca Department for first aid. The doctors told FARC she would have to stay there, but the kidnappers took her away. When she became seriously ill with life-threatening complications, El Marrano called Briceno, who gave the order to kill the Americans. The group received a second radio communication revoking the kill order, but it arrived too late. Senior FARC leaders apparently were unaware of the killings and did not support them.

On March 25, authorities ordered the arrest of German Briceno, who on July 16, 1999, was charged with ordering the killings. Gustavo Bogota, a member of the U'wa tribe, was charged as an accomplice. The duo remained at large. FARC claimed that Briceno was not responsible and that a lower-ranking squad leader and two fighters under his command were involved.

On February 11, 2000, Colombian President Andres Pastrana refused to extradite to the United States German Briceno. Pastrana said Briceno would be tried in Colombia. U.S. diplomats had broken off exploratory contacts with the rebels after the murders. On September 10, 2001,

Colombia sentenced German Briceno in absentia to 40 years in prison for the murders. The verdict came the day before U.S. Secretary of State Colin Powell was to begin a visit to Colombia. The Colombians also convicted Gustavo Bocota, a suspected low-level FARC member.

On March 23, 2000, police arrested Nelson Vargas, a guerrilla commander suspected of ordering the killings of the Americans. Police also detained an unnamed Argentine man. 99022501

February 26, 1999. *Colombia.* A powerful bomb caused major damage, but no injuries at the headquarters of the Colombian Daily Company, a subsidiary of the Swiss-owned Nestlé Multinational. 99022601

February 28, 1999. *Zambia.* A bomb went off at the Angolan Embassy in Lusaka, killing a security guard and extensively damaging the building. Bombs exploded in 15 other locations in the capital, including near major water pipes, power lines, parks, and residential districts. Two people were injured. Bomb experts detonated five more bombs and defused two others. No one claimed credit. The government blamed Angolan agents. 99022801

February 28, 1999. *Uganda.* Congo-based Rwandan Hutu rebels, firing AK-47s and other automatic weapons, killed 3 people and kidnapped 13 (some reports said 31) foreign tourists, including 3 Americans, 6 Britons, 3 New Zealanders, and an Australian, from the Buhoma campsite on the northern edge of the Bwindi National Park—known as the Impenetrable Forest—in southwestern Uganda. The camp was the main starting point for trips to see the 320 mountain gorillas that live along the border. (French diplomats said March 1 that 150 armed Hutu rebels attacked three tourist camps, killing four Ugandans and kidnapping three Americans, six Britons, three New Zealanders, two Danes, one Australian, and one Canadian.) Private tour operators said the dead included a foreign tourist and two Ugandans, including a wildlife authority employee. (The Ugandan government later said four Ugandans—game warden Paul Wagaba and three park rangers—were killed in the initial assault.) France's deputy ambassador to Uganda, Anne Peltier, escaped abduction, as did Elizabeth Garland, 29, a student at the University of Chicago. Garland's father reported, "She said she was awakened by gunfire all around her and apparently a raid of 100 to 150 Hutu rebels came in armed and started taking hostages. She said they were looking specifically for Americans and would release hostages if they were not American or British." Linda Adams of Alamo, California, said the assailants demanded money and valuables, then segregated the captives by nationality, keeping the Americans and Britons. Others escaped into the forest; Adams was released after faking an asthma attack.

The attackers called themselves the Interahamwe, Kinyarwanda for "those who work together." Other officials said it was the Army for the Liberation of Rwanda, which is closely associated with the Interahamwe.

The battered bodies of eight foreign tourists—four men, four women—were found in the jungle above their camp. There were two Americans—Hillsboro, Oregon-based Rob Haubner, 48, and his wife, Susan Miller, 42, who worked for Intel Corporation—four Britons and two New Zealanders. The British victims were Mark Lindgren, 23, Steven Roberts, Martin Friend, and Joanne Cotton. The dead New Zealanders were Rhonda Avis, 27, and Michelle Strathern, 26. Mark Avis, Rhonda's husband, escaped the attack. At least three of the victims were fatally beaten and hacked by their Hutu captors. The rebels freed six hostages, including Mark Ross, 43, an American, who said they were force-marched into Congo. Ugandan officials said five of the victims might have perished in crossfire between the kidnappers and a Ugandan rescue force. Ross said he knew of no rescue attempt, a view echoed by the State Department. Some of the victims were killed because they could not walk fast enough to suit the kidnappers.

Ross said the captives had been split into several groups and frequently warned to stay together.

The smaller groups were rejoined twice during the day. His group of six captives—himself, one Canadian, one Swiss, one New Zealander, and two Britons—reached the Congo border at 4:00 P.M. on March 1. Some two and a half hours later, they were released. Retracing their route, they found the bodies of three tourists who had been hacked to death; a woman appeared to have been raped. Ross reported, "The ones I saw had their heads crushed in and then deep slashes with machetes." Ross was born in Arkansas, but had spent most of his life in Kenya. His captors told him in Swahili that their aim was to destabilize Uganda. Others spoke Kinyarwanda and French. They attached notes to the corpses that said, "Americans and British, we don't want you on our land. You support our enemy."

The Ugandan government said on March 2 that its soldiers had killed four of the attackers in a jungle pursuit. Ugandan President Yoweri Museveni promised to hunt down and kill the murderers. A Ugandan commander said soldiers had tracked the rebels to a base in Congo's Virunga National Park, killing some of them.

On March 4, hundreds of Uganda Army troops entered Congo, digging through dense tropical rain forests to find the killers. National Public Radio quoted the Ugandan army as claiming that it had killed two dozen rebels. Four days later, Uganda said it had killed another 10 Rwandan rebels responsible for the attack, bringing the tally to 25.

The rebels had sent letters to Ugandan officials two weeks earlier warning that Americans and Britons would be attacked, but the warnings were not passed on to British tour operators or diplomats.

On March 29, Uganda announced that its army had killed another 18 Hutus who had killed the tourists. Another four were captured in the clash in neighboring Congo. 99022802

March 2, 1999. *France.* A former Italian police officer hijacked an Air France jetliner carrying 76 passengers and forced it to detour to a different Paris airport, where he held a dozen hostages for three hours. He threatened to blow up the plane, but surrendered to Roissy police after freeing the hostages. 99030201

March 2, 1999. *Nigeria.* Twenty gunmen attacked a compound housing a large Italian construction company and its workers, injuring six people. No one claimed credit. 99030202

March 6, 1999. *Pakistan.* Three Muslim militant groups, angered because some of their comrades were killed in August in U.S. missile attacks against six of Osama bin Laden's terrorist training camps in Afghanistan, threatened to carry out revenge killings against Americans.

Harkat Ansar said at least seven of its members were killed and two dozen wounded in the attacks. A senior Harkat leader said, "The veterans of the Khost bombing form the nucleus of Osama bin Laden loyalists whose sole mission in life is to settle the score with the U.S. For each of us killed or wounded in the cowardly U.S. attack, at least 100 Americans will be killed. . . . I may not be alive, but you will remember my words." Pakistani intelligence officials said that Harkat had at least 500 well-trained militants.

Eight members of the Lakshar-e Taiba and Hizb-ul-Muhajideen were killed in the bombings. 99030601

March 7, 1999. *Algeria.* Muslim militants killed 16 soldiers and wounded 21 others in a dawn ambush on a highway near Bouira, 75 miles east of Algiers.

March 7, 1999. *Colombia.* The National Liberation Army (ELN) or Revolutionary Armed Forces of Colombia (FARC) were believed to be behind the kidnapping of an Argentine citizen at a checkpoint. No demands were made. 99030701

March 7, 1999. *Colombia.* The ELN and FARC were believed to be responsible for abducting one Swiss citizen and seven Colombians from another checkpoint. No one claimed credit. 99030702

March 9, 1999. *France.* Police arrested the Spanish Basque Nation and Liberty (ETA) military chief. 99030901

March 9, 1999. *Nigeria.* Unidentified assailants kidnapped an American from his office. No demands were made; no one claimed credit. 99030902

March 9, 1999. *Venezuela.* The National Liberation Army (ELN) or Revolutionary Armed Forces of Colombia (FARC) were believed to have attacked a Venezuelan patrol unit, injuring one civilian and kidnapping three others. 99030903

March 10, 1999. *Spain.* Police arrested nine suspected Basque Nation and Liberty (ETA) members.

March 10, 1999. *Angola.* An unidentified group, possibly the Front for the Liberation of Cabinda (FLEC), kidnapped two French citizens, two Portuguese citizens, and one Angolan. The hostages were freed unharmed on July 7. 99031001

March 12, 1999. *Colombia.* Army troops outside Bogota killed Vladimir Gonzalez Obregon (alias Miller Perdomo), the top regional commander of the Revolutionary Armed Forces of Colombia (FARC) rebels operating around the capital. He was known for his role in major kidnappings, including the 1998 abduction of four Americans.

March 13, 1999. *Turkey.* A firebomb went off in a crowded Istanbul department store, killing 13 and wounding 3. No one claimed credit, although the radical Maoist group TIKKO, which had links to Abdullah Ocalan's Kurdistan Workers Party (PKK), had claimed credit for a similar bombing in Istanbul the previous week. Three people in a car threw the devices onto the ground floor of the five-story Mavi Carsi department store building in the Goztepe District on the Asian side of Istanbul. The attackers fled on foot, pursued by a policeman. Prime Minister Bulent Ecevit said the attackers were attempting to disrupt the April 18 elections.

March 13, 1999. *United States.* The People's Mojahedin Organization of Iran and Sri Lanka's Liberation Tigers of Tamil Eelam (LTTE) hired prominent lawyers to ask the District of Columbia Court of the U.S. Court of Appeals to challenge the Clinton administration's designation of them as terrorist groups. They said that Secretary of State Madeleine K. Albright named them terrorists in October 1997 based on mostly secret evidence with no advance notice or opportunity to respond. The cases attack the constitutionality of the Antiterrorism and Effective Death Penalty Act of 1996. The 2 groups are among the 30 on the State Department's list, which freezes the groups' assets in the United States, makes it a crime punishable by up to ten years in prison for Americans to provide them money, and denies U.S. visas to group members. The Mojahedin were represented by attorney Jacob A. Stein; the LTTE by former Attorney General Ramsey Clark. The cases were heard by judges A. Raymond Randolph, Stephen F. Williams, and James L. Buckley.

March 15, 1999. *Turkey.* Kurdish rebels warned foreign tourists against visiting Turkey, saying they could be hurt in an "all-out war" against the government to win freedom for Abdullah Ocalan, leader of the Kurdistan Workers Party (PKK). Hours after a rebel spokesman issued the threat from Brussels, a firebomb exploded under a car parked across the street from the European Union office in Ankara, injuring a pedestrian and shattering windows. The U.S. Department of State issued a travel advisory. Several bombings had killed nearly 20 people during the previous three weeks. 99031501

March 17, 1999. *Somalia.* About 50 gunmen in speedboats hijacked a Taiwanese fishing boat near Eil, some 500 miles northeast of Mogadishu, capturing more than 30 Taiwanese, Ugandan, Tanzanian, and Indian nationals. Other gunmen hijacked a Ukrainian fishing boat, taking 1 Somali and 20 Ukrainian crewmen hostage. 99031701-02

March 17, 1999. *Pakistan.* Karachi Airport police arrested Shibli Mustafa, an alleged associate of Osama bin Laden, and four of his associates from Turbat, Balochistan. Following an Interpol report, they were picked up as they arrived at the Jinnah terminal after being deported from Dubai. Mustafa was returning from London after having served five years in prison for arms smuggling. 99031703

March 19, 1999. *Algeria.* Muslim rebels slashed the throats of ten villagers in an overnight attack southwest of Algiers.

March 19, 1999. *Russia.* Shortly before noon, a powerful time bomb containing 15 pounds of dynamite went off in the southern city of Vladikavkaz, the capital of the North Ossetia region of southern Russia, killing 63 and wounding 107 in a central food market. The explosion destroyed a 50-foot-high wall in the market's main trading hall, spraying shrapnel all around. An anonymous "diversionary group" claimed credit. Police were searching for a man and a woman and said the message suggested that the motive was "religious fanaticism." Russian Interior Minister Sergei Stepashin called the attack an "act of sabotage aimed at destabilizing the situation in the North Caucasus and throughout Russia, at instigating a clash between the peoples." The bomb was planted in a sack of potatoes by a man and a woman who left it in a section of the market crowded with people. Police showed composite sketches of the duo on national television.

March 20, 1999. *Somalia.* Deena Umbarger, an American consultant for the United Methodist Committee on Relief, was shot and killed at a restaurant on the Somali side of the Kenyan border. Umbarger, from Sumner, Washington, would have turned 36 years old later in the week. An unknown gunman apparently began shooting wildly. 99032001

March 21, 1999. *Turkey.* A bomb exploded on the southeast Turkey pipeline that brings Iraqi crude oil into the country. The attack stopped the oil flow on the Kurdish New Year's festival. The bomb caused a large fire, but limited damage. The pipeline was closed for inspection after the blast. The pipeline runs through remote uplands that are strongholds for the Kurdistan Workers Party (PKK), which had sabotaged the pipeline in November 1998.

March 21, 1999. *Russia.* One person was killed and eight injured when a radio-controlled mine exploded near Chechen President Aslan Maskhadov's motorcade as he was returning to his Grozny home from a meeting. He was not injured. The mine was hidden 220 yards from his residence in a sewage drain on the main street. It was the fourth assassination attempt against him in three years.

March 23, 1999. *Paraguay.* Four gunmen dressed in camouflage assassinated Vice-President Luis Maria Argana, 64, when they blocked his sport utility vehicle and fired automatic weapons at him. He was hit by ten bullets. His driver was killed and a bodyguard gravely wounded. He had been driving to his office in Asuncion in the morning.

President Raul Cubas condemned the attack and closed the country's borders to prevent the assassins' escape. Cubas was a political enemy of Argana and had battled him for control of the ruling Colorado Party. Congressional leaders blamed the attack on former army chief General Lino Cesar Oviedo, the president's political ally. The National Congress had voted two months earlier to begin impeachment proceedings against Cubas for illegally freeing Oviedo, leader of a failed 1996 coup. The president had refused to follow the Supreme Court's order to reimprison Oviedo. On March 24, the Chamber of Deputies, the legislature's lower house, voted to impeach the president.

On March 26, snipers shot and killed 4 young protestors and wounded more than 150.

After a week of political violence, Cubas resigned on March 28. Senate President Luis Gonzalez Macchi, the constitutionally designated replacement, was sworn in as president. Cubas had been president for just 7 months and 13 days and was only the second freely elected civilian chief of state in Paraguay's 188 years of independence.

Oviedo reportedly left in a private plane for Buenos Aires, where he received asylum.

Cubas was granted political asylum at the Brazilian Embassy. Brazil dispatched an air force jet to retrieve him. Gonzalez Macchi declared Cubas immune from arrest for the deaths of six protestors. Cubas automatically became a senator for life upon stepping down. Former Paraguayan dictator Alfredo Stroessner, who ruled for 35 years until a 1989 coup, also lived in Brazil. Brazil formally granted political asylum to Cubas and his family on May 10.

Gonzalez Macchi named Nelson Argana, son of the slain vice-president, as defense minister.

On May 5, 1999, police detained three suspects—army Colonel Wladimior Woroniecki and civilians Walter Gamarra and Maximo Osioro—all of whom had links to Oviedo. Cubas was declared immune from arrest by the new Paraguayan government.

In August, following Argentina's refusal to extradite Oviedo, Paraguay recalled its ambassador.

By September 22, 1999, Oviedo had caused local friction and told a newspaper that he wanted to return to Paraguay, face the courts, and run for president. The new Paraguayan government wanted to extradite him on murder charges. On October 2, Argentine Interior Minister Carlos Corach said Argentina might expel Oviedo, who was saying he would return to Paraguay to stage "coups through votes" and comparing himself to Jesus Christ.

On December 10, 1999, Oviedo eluded his Argentine police guards and disappeared. Some Paraguayan news services claimed he had flown back to Paraguay in a private plane. His wife said he had left the country so that the newly elected Alliance government of Fernando de la Rua would not have to live with the diplomatic problem he had caused. The Alliance had said that once it came into power, it would expel him from the country. Corach said that by fleeing the country, Oviedo's asylum automatically expired.

On January 10, 2000, Oviedo emerged from hiding in Paraguay and said he was protected by "peasants, police, and soldiers."

On June 11, 2000, Brazilian police arrested Oviedo, who was wanted in connection with the assassination of Paraguayan Vice-President Luis Maria Argana. He was detained at a friend's apartment in Foz do Iguacu, on the southwestern border with Paraguay and Argentina. Police found him by tracking his phone calls; he had ten cell phones when he was located. He was brought to Brasilia the next day pending extradition. He was officially sought for his role in a 1996 attempted coup; he had never completed his jail term. Support for Oviedo had waned since a failed coup attempt on May 18, 2000. On December 17, 2001, Brazil's Supreme Court rejected Paraguay's request for extradition, deeming it "politically motivated."

March 23, 1999. *Colombia.* National Liberation Army (ELN) guerrillas kidnapped a U.S. citizen in Boyaca and demanded a $400,000 ransom. On July 20, the victim was freed unharmed in exchange for $48,000. 99032301

March 23, 1999. *Colombia.* The Revolutionary Armed Forces of Colombia (FARC) kidnapped a German engineer and a Swiss engineer from the El Cairo Cement Works in Antioquia. No demands were made. 99032302

March 24, 1999. *Algeria.* Muslim rebels slashed the throats of nine villagers, including two children, and kidnapped two women during the night near Blida.

March 25, 1999. *Macedonia.* Firebomb-throwing Serbs attacked the U.S. Embassy in Skopje, using a flagpole to shatter windows. They were protesting North Atlantic Treaty Organization (NATO) air strikes on Yugoslavia. No Americans were injured. Ambassador Christopher Hill and his staff hid in a basement vault. The attackers burned vehicles, destroyed air conditioners, and tried to penetrate the building's armored doors. Local riot police used tear gas to disperse the crowd. Some of its members had been bused in.

The rioters moved on to the French, German, and British embassies. German Embassy guards fired two percussion grenades to break up the crowd, which had broken windows and ransacked the ground floor.

March 26, 1999. *Greece.* Some 500 Greek and Serbian protestors broke down the gates at the British Embassy, entered the British ambassador's residence, injured three local guards, and caused major damage.

March 26, 1999. *Serbia.* Demonstrators burned down the U.S. Information Service (USIS) American Center. 99032601

March 27, 1999. *Pakistan.* Unidentified assassins killed Mohammed Jehanzeb, an Afghan secretary to Taliban opponent Haji Qadir, in Peshawar. Qadir was the brother of Afghan moderate Abdul Haq, whose wife and son were murdered in Peshawar on January 12. 99032701

March 27, 1999. *Uganda.* In Kisoro, suspected Rwandan rebels armed with machetes attacked a village, killing three. The military reported that the gang crossed into Uganda from the Democratic Republic of the Congo. 99032702

March 28, 1999. *Russia.* Police traded gunfire with an unidentified attacker protesting the NATO bombing campaign against Yugoslavia. The individual tried to fire a grenade at the U.S. Embassy in Moscow from a crowded boulevard that had been the scene of other anti-U.S. protests. No one was injured. One or more men had stolen a white police jeep at 1:30 P.M. on a street near the embassy, then parked it nearby. A passerby videotaped a man wearing a black ski mask and camouflage taking a grenade launcher from the car and failing to fire it. He threw two launchers to the ground, then fired a semiautomatic rifle, putting 11 bullet holes in the side of the building. Police opened fire, forcing the vehicle to speed away. The vehicle was later discovered not far from where it was stolen. Police were hunting for three suspects

seen running away. No one claimed credit. 99033101

March 28, 1999. *Australia.* Demonstrators threw stones through windows of the U.S. Consulate in Melbourne. Similar protests were reported in Europe.

March 28, 1999. *India.* Suspected Muslim militants threw a grenade into a crowd in Anantnag, injuring 28 people.

March 31, 1999. *Belgium.* Hackers in Belgrade conducted a low-level cyber attack against a NATO Web site, sending thousands of "pings" (i.e., "identify yourself" computer instructions) against the site and overloading its ability to respond. Another Belgrade computer sent more than 2,500 e-mails to the site, freezing its e-mail capabilities. Some of the e-mails contained viruses. The computers were not entered and no programs were corrupted.

April 1999. *Libya.* The regime closed down training camps used by the Abu Nidal Organization.

April 1, 1999. *Zambia.* Three shots were fired from a white Toyota Minibus at a Toyota Landcruiser belonging to former President Kenneth Kaunda during the night. He was not in the car at the time, and none of his three bodyguards in the car was harmed in the attack at the gate of Kaunda's home. Earlier in the week, Zambia's high court had declared Kaunda stateless because he was born in Zambia of Malawian missionary parents. Kaunda ruled Zambia from its day of independence in 1964 until 1991.

April 3, 1999. *Bosnia-Herzegovina.* The press reported that gunmen fired on a Stabilization Force (SFOR) vehicle carrying two Bosnian employees, injuring one. No one claimed credit, although authorities believed SFOR was the target.

April 3, 1999. *Ethiopia.* The Ogaden National Liberation Front kidnapped one French aid worker, two Ethiopian staffers, and four Somalis. The French diplomat was freed on May 4. 99040301

April 4, 1999. *Russia.* A bomb exploded outside a Federal Security Service building in Moscow, blasting a hole in the wall, shattering windows, and slightly injuring three people. No one claimed credit.

April 5, 1999. *Algeria.* Muslim rebels ambushed a military convoy, shooting dead 22 soldiers.

April 7, 1999. *Algeria.* Algerian troops shot to death the top aide to the leader of the Armed Islamic Group (GIA), along with 18 other GIA members.

April 9, 1999. *Niger.* Members of the Presidential Guard wielding machine guns shot to death Niger's president, Ibrahim Bare Mainassara. Four other people were killed. Major Daouda Malam Wanke, head of the Presidential Guard, gave the order to kill Mainassara after greeting him at Niamey Airport. The president was preparing to travel to Inates, 125 miles northwest. Unnamed military sources blamed individuals close to Colonel Moussa Djermakoye, the armed forces chief, who was out of the country. Prime Minister Ibrahim Assane Mayaka disbanded the National Assembly and temporarily suspended all political parties. The military met to name a new chief of state.

Mainassara, a former army colonel, had come to power in a January 1996 military coup, ousting the country's first democratically elected government. He released then-President Mahamane Ousmane from house arrest after three months.

On April 11, Wanke was named president and head of the National Council for Reconciliation, which would head the country during a nine-month transition period.

April 9, 1999. *Colombia.* The National Liberation Army (ELN) kidnapped two Swiss, one Israeli, and one Briton in Cauca Department. The British hostage escaped on May 8. The ELN released the Israeli and one Swiss hostage on May 15. 99040901

April 12, 1999. *Colombia.* The National Liberation Army (ELN) and Revolutionary Armed Forces of Colombia (FARC) were suspected of hijacking Avianca Flight 9463, a Fokker-50 turboprop with 46 people on board as it was flying from Bucaramanga to Bogota in the morning. The five men in dark suits were armed with pistols and hand grenades that they had hidden in their briefcases. Two other men, including one disguised as a Roman Catholic priest who had earlier blessed a passenger, jumped up and joined the hijackers. One hijacker entered the cockpit and forced the pilot to land on a remote airstrip at 11:00 A.M. The hijackers, aided by a waiting band of guerrillas, made the 39 passengers and crew trek through dense jungle to canoes on a nearby river in northern Colombia. From there they were transported upstream. Pilots flying overhead saw people in green combat fatigues accompanying the hostages. The hostages then were forced on another five-hour trek along dirt roads, arriving at a secluded farm secured by another 100 rebels.

Searchers found an empty plane showing no signs of a violent struggle. The airstrip had earlier been dynamited by the authorities because it was used by drug traffickers.

The following day, the rebels freed five elderly hostages and a three-month-old baby, handing them over to a regional Red Cross official in southern Bolivar Province. One of them was Luis Flores, 72, a diabetic without enough medication for an extended ordeal. His wife was also freed. They were taken to San Pablo and flown to Bucaramanga. Hundreds of elite army and police units searched the swamp and jungle region where the plane landed. That day, President Andres Pastrana blamed the ELN alone for the hijacking. A day later, the rebels freed six more hostages, including infirm and elderly passengers and several women.

Observers believed the ELN was attempting to get a role in the negotiations that FARC had established with the government. But President Pastrana temporarily cut off communication with the ELN.

On April 15, Colombian Special Forces found the mountain redoubt where 32 hostages were being held. One was believed to be an American living in Mexico, despite earlier reports that no foreigners or senior government officials were involved. The U.S. Embassy refused to comment.

In addition to the military, another 1,000 special police were sent in as a rescue squad. Two soldiers and five ELN guerrillas were killed in a gun battle. ELN commander Alonso told RCN radio that "the kidnap victims are in good health, and they are out of the way (of the combat area)."

The ELN freed three hostages on April 16.

On April 26, an ELN communiqué indicated that the group was planning to free more of the hostages and was preparing a proposal to end the guerrilla war. The ELN's five-man ruling Central Command signed a note stating, "This week we hope to liberate another group of passengers from the Avianca plane. . . . In the presence of national and international personalities, we will issue our proposal." The group said it would release the hostages only if the government pulled security forces out of the rural area around Simiti town. It also demanded that Pastrana return to jailed ELN leaders Francisco Galan and Felipe Torres radiotelephones that were confiscated after the hijacking. The government rejected the proposal and said it would meet no demands.

The *New York Times* reported on May 2 that the ELN was demanding that the government cede territory to the organization, as it had done to FARC.

On May 7 (or 17), the rebels freed another 7 hostages, but kept 25 others, including an American.

On June 18, the rebels freed another eight passengers to Colombian and international observers in the northern state of Bolivar. They kept 16 hostages, including the 5 crew members.

ELN freed seven more hostages on September 5 and the American on October 2.

On February 13, 2001, Venezuelan police arrested Jose Maria Ballestas, a member of the ELN, at a Caracas shopping mall. He was wanted for the hijacking of the Avianca airliner.

The last of the passengers were released after ransom payments in November 2000. Interior Minister Luis Miquilena, one of Venezuelan President Hugo Chavez's closest advisers, released Ballestas soon after the arrest. Government officials denied the guerrilla had been captured, calling Colombian magazine *Cambio*'s report on the arrest "magic realism." However, Colombian officials on March 8, 2001, produced a videotape of the arrest. On March 16, 2001, Venezuelan authorities reordered the provisional arrest of Ballestas, who was charged with car theft and weapons possession pending a decision on his request for political asylum. Colombia requested his extradition. The arrest revived charges that the Chavez government was secretly supporting Colombia's leftist insurgent groups. 99041201

April 12, 1999. *Venezuela.* The Revolutionary Armed Forces of Colombia (FARC) kidnapped a rancher in Cunaviche, Apure State. He said he was released in Caracolito, Norte de Santander Department on April 18. 99041202

April 14, 1999. *Angola.* The National Union for the Total Independence of Angola (UNITA) was suspected of attacking a Save the Children vehicle in Salina, killing six Angolans. 99041401

April 15, 1999. *Greece.* Two bombs exploded at the Detroit Motors car dealership in Athens, causing extensive damage but no injuries. Enraged Anarchists claimed credit. 99041501

April 16, 1999. *Argentina.* A small homemade bomb packed with pamphlets exploded outside the Argentine branch of BankBoston in Buenos Aires, causing minor damage and no injuries. The pamphlets read, "Assassin NATO out of Yugoslavia," and were signed by the Anti-Imperialist Commando. 99041601

April 16, 1999. *Italy.* The Fighting Communist Party (NTA) claimed credit for two nighttime attacks against the Verona headquarters of the Italian Democrats of the Left. The male caller warned of upcoming attacks "against NATO and against the imperialist state."

April 18, 1999. *United Kingdom.* A bomb packed with six-inch nails exploded at a south London street market at Brixton Road and Electric Avenue at 5:25 P.M., injuring 48 people, 4 of them seriously. No one claimed credit, and police suggested the explosion was the work of criminals, not terrorists. Shopkeeper George Jones, 42, said the bomb was in a gym bag turned over to him by someone who thought a shopper had forgotten it. Jones said, "I unzipped it and opened it wide, and I could see what it was. I picked it up and moved it 10 to 15 yards and put it by a brick wall to stop people getting hurt. Then it went off. I was blown across the road, and a couple of nails lodged in my leg." At least 37 people were hospitalized with shrapnel wounds. A 23-month-old boy suffered a nail embedded in his skull. Other victims were Ijeona Nwokolo, 17, Neall Whatley, 36, and Metin Saglam, 34.

The neo-Nazi group Combat 18 claimed credit a week later. The "18" stands for the first and eighth letters of the alphabet—the initials of Adolf Hitler. Three other far-right organizations claimed credit.

April 18, 1999. *Egypt.* Ahmed Salama Mabruk, the jailed head of the Islamic Jihad's military operations, told *Al-Hayat* that the group had chemical and biological weapons that it intended to use in "one hundred attacks against U.S. and Israeli targets and public figures in different parts of the world." He was sentenced to hard labor for life in a mass trial of Jihad members. He claimed the plan was on a computer disk that was taken from him during his arrest in Azerbaijan.

An Egyptian military court in Huckstep, north of Cairo, sentenced nine people to death for membership in an outlawed group seeking to topple the government. Eleven more Jihad defendants received life at hard labor. Some 67 others received

sentences ranging from 1 to 16 years in prison. Another 20 were acquitted. Jihad chief Ayman Zawahiri, among the 59 defendants tried in absentia, was sentenced to death. Jihad Secretary General Abdallah al-Mansour, still at large, issued a statement saying, "We will pursue the path of Jihad until victory or martyrdom . . . the unjust verdicts from the regime in power will only bolster the belief of the mujahedeen."

April 20, 1999. *Corsica.* A firebomb exploded in Chez Francis, a Corsican beach restaurant south of Ajaccio, the capital. Four members of the elite antiterrorist squad, including the chief of the national police (Gendarmes) on the island, were placed under investigation and imprisoned in Paris in early May on charges of "voluntary destruction" caused by "an organized gang." Local residents found a ski mask and a police-issued walkie-talkie and combat knife amid the rubble. The police officers said three of the men had been at the scene on routine patrol, but could not explain burns suffered by one of them.

The trio belong to a group of 85 men known as the Security Squad, whom politicians had demanded be disbanded.

On May 3, Bernard Bonnet, France's top official in Corsica, and his top aide were taken into custody.

On May 4, Prime Minister Lionel Jospin disbanded the antiterror squad.

April 20, 1999. *Colombia.* Revolutionary Armed Forces of Colombia (FARC) guerrillas stopped four vehicles at a roadblock on the Pamplona–Bucaramanga road, kidnapping four prison guards and two truck drivers. They also stole a cargo truck and three tractor-trailers transporting 27 vehicles from Venezuela. They later freed the two drivers. 99042001

April 20, 1999. *India.* In Rajauri, Kashmir, a bomb exploded in a goldsmith's shop, killing 5, injuring 47, and causing major damage. Police suspected Muslim militants.

April 21, 1999. *Tajikistan.* A Tajik plane was hijacked to Russia, where the hijackers released 90 passengers, but kept 46 hostage. Initial media reports said the hijackers were Kurdish rebels who wanted to go to Iran, but authorities said the hijackers' nationalities and demands were unknown. 99042101

April 21, 1999. *Liberia.* Gunmen from Guinea crossed the border and attacked Voinjama town, kidnapping the visiting Dutch ambassador, the Norwegian first secretary, a European Union representative, and 17 aid workers. The hostages were released later that day. Witnesses said the attackers were members of the militia groups ULIMO-K and ULIMO-J. 99042102

April 24, 1999. *United Kingdom.* A bomb exploded at 5:45 P.M. on Brick Lane in east London, injuring seven people. A man found the bag and took it to the Bricktown police station, which was closed. So he stuffed the vinyl bag in the trunk of his car for safety. Two minutes later, as he was telephoning police, the bomb exploded in his Ford sedan. The neo-Nazi group Combat 18 claimed credit for the attack in Bricktown, one of the United Kingdom's largest Bangladeshi communities.

April 24, 1999. *Russia.* A homemade bomb hidden under a car in a parking lot exploded in Yekaterinburg outside a building housing the U.S. and U.K. consulates, causing no injuries. 99042401

April 24, 1999. *Canada.* Montreal police discovered and disarmed five bombs that had been planted outside police stations. No one claimed credit. A letter found in a phone booth after a tip from an anonymous caller warned of the bombs.

April 26, 1999. *Russia.* In mid-afternoon, a bomb hidden in an elevator exploded on the 20th floor of Moscow's Intourist Hotel, showering glass on the main street near the Kremlin and injuring ten people, who suffered burns, cuts, and contusions.

The bomb destroyed windows and part of the exterior walls on both the 19th and 20th floors.

April 27, 1999. *Macedonia.* Passengers in two passing vehicles lobbed two hand grenades at a NATO (North Atlantic Treaty Organization) facility. 99042701

April 27, 1999. *Greece.* A bomb exploded at the Intercontinental Hotel, killing one person and injuring another.

April 30, 1999. *United Kingdom.* At 6:30 P.M., a nail bomb exploded at the crowded Admiral Duncan Pub, a well-known gay hangout in Soho, central London, killing two people (another died on May 1) and hospitalizing 27. Many suffered severed limbs, serious burns, and major lacerations. At least two victims had limbs sliced off by flying glass. Some 60 were categorized as "walking wounded." More than 100 were injured. This was the third homemade nail bomb to explode in the city in a fortnight. Police blamed right-wing extremists targeting minority groups. Only the third bomb involved injuries.

The dead were identified as Andrea Dykes, 27, who was pregnant, and John Light, 32, the best man at Dykes's 1997 wedding. Her husband, Julian Dykes, 26, was seriously injured.

Scotland Yard's antiterrorist units arrested a white man in his early 20s in connection with the bombings. He resembled a man wearing a tan baseball cap who was seen on a security video of the street scene where the first bomb went off. He might have been carrying a black vinyl sports bag like the one that held the bomb. Police had earlier arrested, but later released, three others.

The White Wolves claimed credit.

On May 2, David Copeland, 22, an engineer from a London suburb, was charged with acting alone in committing the three murders. Copeland was also charged with three counts of causing an explosion—the Admiral Duncan bomb, the April 17 Brixton bombing, and the April 24 Brick Lane bombing. Police said he was not linked to extreme right-wing groups that had claimed credit for the blasts. Police found explosives at his suburban home and said he was the man seen on the April 17 videotape carrying a vinyl bag. He appeared at a five-minute hearing at West London Magistrates Court the next day, but did not enter a plea, only confirming his address. He was slated for a return court appearance on May 8.

May 1, 1999. *Russia.* Two bombs went off near Moscow's most prominent synagogues during the night, causing light damage to nearby structures, but no injuries. One bomb, containing 400 grams of explosives, went off at 9:15 P.M. 50 meters away from the Choral Synagogue. A religious service attended by 50 people was taking place inside. Glass hit a nearby medical building and an Interior Ministry pharmacy. A second bomb went off at 9:53 P.M. near the Marina Roshcha Synagogue in northern Moscow. Neo-Nazis were suspected.

May 13, 1999. *Angola.* The National Union for the Total Independence of Angola (UNITA) downed a privately owned plane with surface-to-air missiles, then abducted the three Russian crew and three Angolan passengers. 99051301

May 13, 1999. *Colombia.* Four gunmen kidnapped a U.S. helicopter technician in Yopal. The Revolutionary Armed Forces of Colombia (FARC) and National Liberation Army (ELN) were suspected. 990501302

May 15, 1999. *Russia.* Gunmen abducted two employees of the International Committee of the Red Cross (ICRC)—a New Zealander and a Russian; the latter was released the same day. No one claimed credit, no demands were made, and the New Zealander was freed on July 19. 99051501

May 16, 1999. *Greece.* A rocket-propelled grenade exploded on the second floor of the residence of German Ambassador Heinz Kuhna, who was seated next door in his study.

The previous week, a similar attack was made against the Dutch ambassador. The November 17 terrorist group was suspected. 99051601, 99069901

May 20, 1999. *Italy.* At 8:30 A.M., Massimo D'Antona, 51, a top consultant to Italy's minister of labor, was shot three times and killed as he walked to his northern Rome office. The two gunmen were waiting beside a van parked on Via Salaria. The duo may have escaped on a motorcycle. Three groups, including the Red Brigades, took credit. A 28-page letter from the Red Brigades to two newspapers denounced U.S. imperialism, NATO, cuts in social spending, and the evolution of Italy's leftist parties away from their traditional foundations. The letter said D'Antona was killed because of his role as one of the chief authors of a government plan regarding employment, development, and the relations between labor and industry. The group signed the letter "Red Brigades for the Construction of the Communist Combatants Party."

D'Antona was professor of law at Rome's La Sapienza University. He had also served as an undersecretary in the Transport Ministry in the government of Foreign Minister Lamberto Dini and as a consultant in the government of Romano Prodi, now president of the European Commission.

Politicians and labor leaders pledged a united front against terrorism.

May 28, 1999. *United States.* Fuad K. Taima, 63, founder of American-Iraqi Finance and Trade and of the American Iraqi Foundation, his wife Dorothy, 54, and their son Leith, 16, were found shot to death in their home on Broyhill Street in McLean, Virginia. They were apparently killed in an execution-style slaying—two bullets to each chest. No gun was found at the scene. Police suggested that his ties with Iraqi President Saddam Hussein made him a target, either of oppositionists or of Saddam because of a failed business deal. He had returned home from a business trip to Baghdad ten days before the killings. Police ruled out a domestic dispute or robbery attempt. Neighbors said they had heard what sounded like gunfire at 10:45 P.M. two evenings earlier, but no one called police, thinking it was fireworks.

Taima had claimed that his car had been fire-bombed in front of their home in 1990, around the time that he created the foundation, although police had no record of the attack. He was part of a seven-person delegation that met with Saddam Hussein in 1991 and returned with 14 former hostages. He had migrated to the United States 30 years earlier.

The FBI assigned Special Agent Brad Garrett to work with local officials. He had spent four years chasing Mir Aimal Kasi, who killed two CIA employees.

Fuad Taima had attended a board meeting of the local soccer organization. His wife was at home with a stocky white male of Middle Eastern descent. She paged her son to come home when she decided that she was uncomfortable being alone with the visitor. The visitor was a suspect in the killings. Police e-mailed an artist's rendering of the man to Fuad's e-mail contacts. 99052801

May 30, 1999. *Colombia.* Thirty National Liberation Army (ELN) rebels dressed in military garb drove up in two canvas-covered trucks and kidnapped 143 churchgoers, including the parish priest and 15 children, at the end of the 10:00 A.M. Mass at La Maria Church in Ciudad Jardin, an exclusive Cali neighborhood. The rebels shot to death the bodyguard of a hostage. The kidnappers abandoned 79 hostages, who were found by pursuing soldiers in nearby mountains above the town of Jamundi. Some 43 of them were taken by helicopter to a military base. Army and police commandos killed at least two guerrillas; one rebel and two soldiers were wounded in subsequent firefights.

On June 5, the rebels freed 5 hostages, but more than 50 hostages remained in their hands. Two women, both 52, two elderly men, and a teenage boy were handed to the Red Cross. Some were in poor health. President Andres Pastrana had earlier agreed to demands that he suspend the military rescue operation. Thirty-three more hostages were released to a 12-member commission of Colombian and international politicians

on June 15 in front of live television cameras in the mountains south of Cali. The commission included Venezuela's ambassador and German legislator Bernd Schmidbauer, a member of the opposition Christian Democratic Union. The guerrillas had requested Schmidbauer's participation in the negotiations; the Colombian government then invited him to join.

Among those released were three minors and parish priest Rev. Humberto Cadavid. Colombian television credited Werner and Isabel (also known as Michaela) Mauss, a middle-aged married couple, with arranging the transfer and claimed they were German intelligence agents. The German Embassy dissociated the Social Democratic-led German government from Schmidbauer and the couple. In the 1980s, Schmidbauer and the Mauss couple had arranged for the release of four employees of the German engineering company Mannesmann. They had also been instrumental in the release of another German hostage in 1996. Some of the female hostages turned and kissed the masked guerrillas before being freed. A few days later, hostage families said they had been forced to pay ransom to the guerrillas for the release, counter to the ELN–government agreement. President Pastrana denounced the "extortion" and said he would not talk with the ELN until all hostages were freed unconditionally.

On October 13, 1999, the rebels freed Roy Howard Saykay, 56, of Long Island, who said he was in good health although he had lost 45 pounds. It was not clear if a ransom had been paid. Another 30 (or 25) people remained in captivity.

The rebels freed the last three hostages on December 10, 1999, according to hostage spokesman Julian Otoya. 99053001

May 31, 1999. *Democratic Republic of the Congo.* Rebels backed by Rwanda and Uganda claimed to have shot down two Zimbabwean MiGs that were flying in support of the Congolese government. 99053101

June 1999. *United States.* The FBI placed Osama bin Laden on its 10 Most Wanted List. Bin Laden told a Qatar television station later in the month that his mission was to incite Muslims against the U.S. "occupation" of Saudi Arabia.

June 1, 1999. *Philippines.* U.S. Ambassador Thomas Hubbard said a communist rebel threat to "punish" U.S. soldiers who committed "crimes" while on exercises in the country would not deter the United States from carrying out joint military exercises with Philippine troops. 99060101

June 4, 1999. *Turkey.* The leftist Revolutionary People's Salvation Party-Front claimed credit for a foiled attack on the U.S. Consulate in Istanbul. Police shot and killed two attackers who were armed with guns and a shoulder-mounted rocket launcher before they could fire it. 99060401

June 6, 1999. *Iraq.* Two bombs exploded near the Baghdad headquarters of the Iranian exile group Mojahedin-e Khalq, causing no injuries. 99060601

June 6, 1999. *Colombia.* The National Liberation Army (ELN) kidnapped nine people, including an American, near Barranquilla. The American was released on September 24. 99060602

June 7, 1999. *Spain.* A bomb squad safely defused a letter bomb sent to an Italian diplomat in Burgos. The Italian Red Brigades were suspected. 99060701

June 7, 1999. *Spain.* Authorities safely defused a letter bomb sent to the Italian Consulate in Barcelona. Authorities suspected the Italian Red Brigades. 99060702

June 8, 1999. *Spain.* A bomb squad safely defused a letter bomb sent to the Italian Consulate in Zaragoza. Authorities suspected the Italian Red Brigades. 99060801

June 9, 1999. *Iraq.* A pickup truck bomb killed 7 people, including 1 Iraqi, and wounded 23 others, including 15 Iraqi civilians, in an attack against

the Iranian exile group Mojahedin-e Khalq. The group said four of its members died immediately and two more were hospitalized; they blamed the Iranian government. The victims were riding in a bus that was passing when the bomb exploded. 99060901

June 12, 1999. *Philippines.* The Abu Sayyaf Group and the separatist Moro Islamic Liberation Front (MILF) were suspected of kidnapping two Belgians in Zamboanga. One Belgian was released on June 18; the other was freed on June 23. 99061201

June 13, 1999. *Serbia.* Serbian gunmen were suspected in the shooting death of two German journalists. No one claimed credit. 99061301

June 15, 1999. *Iran.* The Iranian government claimed that armed assailants kidnapped three Italian steel experts in Bam. The hostages were freed unharmed on June 20. 99061501

June 16, 1999. *United Kingdom.* A gunman shot and wounded a former special branch agent in Whitely Bay, Tyneside. The Irish Republican Army's Belfast Brigade was suspected. 99061601

June 22, 1999. *India.* A bomb hidden inside a suitcase exploded at the New Jalpaiguri railway station, 400 miles north of Calcutta, killing 10, including 3 soldiers, and wounding 80 others. The United Liberation Front of Assam, with the backing of Pakistan's Inter-Service Intelligence (according to the U.S. Department of State), claimed credit. 99062201

June 24, 1999. *Africa.* The United States announced the three-day closure of its embassies in Gambia, Liberia, Togo, Madagascar, Namibia, and Senegal because of surveillance by suspicious individuals who could be plotting attacks against American citizens. The United Kingdom closed its embassies in the same countries (except for Liberia and Togo, where the British are not in residence). The media had reported that U.S. officials believed Osama bin Laden was in the final stages of plotting a terrorist attack. The United States reopened all but the Madagascar embassy on June 28.

June 25, 1999. *Russia.* A powerful radio-controlled bomb was found on the road between Makhachkala and Buynaksk in Dagestan, near breakaway Chechnya, where Prime Minister Sergei Stepashin was visiting. He had no plans to travel by car and used a helicopter between the two cities. The bomb was found 15 minutes after journalists covering his visit drove along the road.

June 25, 1999. *United States.* The three-judge panel of the District of Columbia Circuit Court of the U.S. Court of Appeals rejected a claim by the People's Mojahedin Organization of Iran and the Liberation Tigers of Tamil Eelam of Sri Lanka that the 1996 Antiterrorism and Effective Death Penalty Act was unconstitutional and that Secretary of State Madeleine Albright's deeming them terrorist groups in October 1997 was based upon largely secret information to which they had had no notice or opportunity to respond. The court said the foreign organizations had no U.S. presence and thus no constitutional rights.

June 27, 1999. *Germany.* A bomb hidden in a flowerpot exploded outside a restaurant in Merseburg, injuring 16, six of them seriously.

June 27, 1999. *Nigeria.* Five heavily armed youths stormed a Royal Dutch Shell oil platform in Port Harcourt, kidnapping an American, a Nigerian, and an Australian, and causing damage. The gunmen hijacked a helicopter and forced the hostages to fly them to a village near Warri. On July 16, the Australian government reported that the youths had released the hostages unharmed for an undisclosed ransom. The Enough Is Enough in the Niger River group claimed credit. 99062701

June 29, 1999. *Indonesia/East Timor.* More than 100 anti-independence militiamen surrounded a newly opened UN Assistance Mission in East Timor (UNAMET) outpost in Maliana near the West Timor border in the morning, showering the building with stones and injuring one South African diplomat and 12 Timorese who had run inside the UN building seeking refuge from the attack. UNAMET was in East Timor to oversee preparations for a referendum on independence. 99062901

June 29, 1999. *Nigeria.* Armed militants kidnapped two Indian nationals who were driving through Lagos. The hostages were released unharmed on July 14. 99062902

June 29, 1999. *Colombia.* Revolutionary Armed Forces of Colombia (FARC) rebels kidnapped an American from his home in Antioquia Department and demanded a $60,000 ransom. FARC released the hostage on July 26; no ransom was paid. 99062903

June 30, 1999. *Indonesia/East Timor.* Some 15 armed paramilitary terrorists stormed into a UNAMET mission in Viqueque, about 55 miles southeast of Dili, the capital, and threatened staff members. Seven of the 14 UN diplomats were evacuated from the town. The militias were backed by the Indonesian army, which opposed independence. The militias accused the UN and foreign journalists of being biased in favor of independence and threatened attacks on foreigners. 99063001

June 30, 1999. *Angola.* The local press reported that the National Union for the Total Independence of Angola (UNITA) shot down an Angolan-owned plane with five Russian crewmen aboard near Capenda-Camulemba. One crew member died when the plane crashed in UNITA-held territory. UNITA captured the other four crewmen. No demands were made for their release. 99063002

June 30, 1999. *Burundi.* Hutu rebels were suspected of firing on a World Food Program vehicle near Bujumbura, injuring one person. 99063003

July 1, 1999. *Nigeria.* Armed Oboro youths kidnapped an American, a Briton, and a Nigerian near Aleibiri and demanded $80,000 for their release. On July 12, the youths released the hostages unharmed; no ransom was paid. 99070101

July 3, 1999. *Germany.* A firebomb was thrown into a prayer room of a Turkish mosque in Singen, near the Swiss border, causing $2,600 in damage. Two offices were firebombed in western Germany. No injuries were reported. The attacks came after a Turkish court sentenced to death Abdullah Ocalan, leader of the Kurdistan Workers Party (PKK). 99070301-03

July 4, 1999. *Turkey.* A bomb exploded in a crowded Istanbul park, killing 1 person and injuring 25. Police blamed Kurdish rebels.

July 4, 1999. *Indonesia.* Armed militants ambushed a UN convoy, kidnapping an Australian and 15 others. A driver and two other people were wounded. The Besi Merah Putih Militia was suspected. 99070401

July 5, 1999. *Turkey.* A Kurdish suicide bomber set off bombs strapped to her body, killing herself and injuring 14 people near an Adana police station.

July 6, 1999. *Angola.* The local press reported that the National Union for the Total Independence of Angola (UNITA) ambushed a German humanitarian convoy, killing 15, injuring 25 others, and causing major damage. The convoy was transporting goods for Catholic Relief Service. 99070601

July 9, 1999. *Georgia.* A bomb exploded in the UN Observer Mission in Sukhumi, causing minor damage. Authorities safely defused a second bomb nearby. No one claimed credit. 99070901

July 10, 1999. *Ireland.* Irish police arrested a man in his mid-50s at his Dublin home after a month-long investigation by British and Irish police into a plot to dump weed killer into fire hydrants and poison the U.K. water supply. He planned to kill one million people unless British troops were pulled out of Northern Ireland. 99071001

July 14, 1999. *Greece.* An Albanian hijacked a bus near Florina in northern Greece, holding five hostages for 30 hours as he demanded guns, a $780,000 ransom, and safe passage to Albania. He was killed by snipers as Greek special police forces stormed the bus. 99071401

July 14, 1999. *Peru.* Security forces captured Oscar Ramirez Durand (alias Comrade Feliciano), 46, the leader of the Shining Path's Red Shining Path faction since 1992. He was masquerading as a farmer. He and three female and two male bodyguards surrendered peacefully to 20 Peruvian soldiers who had surrounded him near Jauja, 185 miles east of Lima. Only 200 more guerrillas remained at large. President Alberto Fujimori said Ramirez would be tried by a military court. Military strategist Ramirez had tried to reorganize the Shining Path after the capture of Abimael Guzman. He had visited Colombia to study the operations of the Revolutionary Armed Forces of Colombia (FARC).

Following an earlier skirmish between the 2,000 troops in the region and the guerrillas, a starving female rebel showed up at a town store and revealed Ramirez's location. Surveillance flights and intelligence data pinpointed his location and led to his arrest.

Ramirez was found guilty of treason in a closed military trial and sentenced to life in prison on August 30, 1999, according to the Supreme Military Justice Council.

July 14, 1999. *Pakistan.* Abdul Ahad Karzai, 77, former Afghan Populzai tribal leader and deputy speaker of its House of Representatives, was shot to death outside a Quetta mosque by two gunmen who escaped on a motorcycle. He had lived on and off in Laurel, Maryland, since 1983. The U.S. State Department said he was a "major voice for moderation among the Pushtun tribes" who had "played a significant role in the fight against the Soviet occupation of his country." He was a former diplomat and senator allied with former Afghan King Zahir Shah. He often mediated in tribal disputes. He had arrived in Pakistan a few days before the shooting. 99071402

July 16, 1999. *Yemen.* Tribesmen in Omran kidnapped four Belgian tourists, who were released unharmed on July 18. No group claimed credit. 99071601

July 17, 1999. *Moldova.* Turkey arrested Cevat Soysal, a leader of the rebel Kurdistan Workers Party (PKK), which claimed that Soysal was handed over to Turkish authorities by Moldova. PKK leader Abdullah Ocalan claimed that Soysal was in charge of training rebels abroad. Germany had granted political asylum to Soysal. He was flown to Ankara to face charges of organizing separatist activity. He appeared in a Turkish court on July 23.

July 20, 1999. *Mozambique.* The United States announced it would close its embassy in Maputo because of an unspecified threat. 99072001

July 20, 1999. *Nigeria.* Youths stormed a Royal Dutch Shell oil rig in Osoko, detaining 7 Britons and 57 Nigerians. No one was injured. On July 22, the youths released the hostages unharmed. 99072002

July 21, 1999. *Angola.* The Angolan military claimed that National Union for the Total Independence of Angola (UNITA) militants fired mortars and long-range artillery at World Food Program and International Committee of the Red Cross aircraft parked at Huambo Airport. No one was injured; no damage was reported. 99072101

July 23, 1999. *Japan.* Pilot Naoyuki Nagashima, 51, employed by All Nippon Airways for 29 years, was stabbed to death by a hijacker who attempted to divert his Boeing 747 jumbo jet carrying 517 passengers and crew on a domestic flight from Tokyo to Sapporo. The hijacker wanted to go to Yokota Air Base—a U.S. airbase north of Tok-yo—and to Oshima island off the Tokyo coast. He also wanted to fly under the Rainbow Bridge that crosses Tokyo Bay. The hijacker, armed with an eight-inch knife, forced his way into the cockpit by threatening a stewardess at 11:23 A.M. The hijacker tried to tape the pilot's mouth shut. After stabbing the pilot in the neck, he briefly sat in the copilot's seat and took over the plane's controls. He was overpowered by the copilot and six passengers as the plane rapidly descended to an altitude of 1,000 feet near Yokota Air Base. The plane safely returned to Haneda Airport near Tokyo. An off-duty All Nippon Airways pilot traveling as a passenger took control of the plane during the struggle and stopped the dive; the copilot landed the plane. No passengers were injured.

The hijacker was a 28-year-old Tokyo resident who said he liked flight simulation games and wanted to fly a real airplane. Police said he might have psychiatric problems. 999072301

July 23, 1999. *Colombia.* A U.S. Army reconnaissance plane on an anti-narcotics mission was reported missing and feared down at 4:30 A.M., three hours after it took off from a Colombian airbase. Five Americans and two Colombians were on the four-engine, propeller-driven De Havilland RC-7, on a mission to photograph coca cultivation and scout for cocaine-producing laboratories. The area was controlled by Revolutionary Armed Forces of Colombia (FARC) guerrillas. The Americans included two captains, a warrant officer, and two enlisted men from Fort Bliss, Texas. Peasants reported hearing the sound of a low-flying plane followed by an explosion in Betano in the mountainous section of Putumayo Province, near the border with Ecuador, at 4:00 A.M. The plane had taken off at 1:30 A.M. from Apiay Air Base on an eight-hour mission.

U.S. and Colombian authorities conducted an intensive aerial search. It was difficult to do ground searches because of the armed guerrillas and drug traffickers in the region. By July 28, the search teams had reached the wreckage of the plane, which apparently had crashed into the mountain in inclement weather. Visibility was less than five feet due to dense clouds and fog. Later that day, they recovered the bodies of four U.S. soldiers, including one woman. On July 31, the U.S. Army identified the Fort Bliss-based soldiers as Captain Jose A. Santiago, Captain Jennifer J. Odom, Chief Warrant Officer Thomas G. Moore, Private First Class T. Bruce Cluff, and Private First Class Ray E. Krueger. All belonged to the 204th Military Intelligence Battalion. They apparently had used an obsolete map to navigate. The Patascoy Range of the Andes Mountains did not appear on the map; it was simply labeled "incomplete data."

July 23, 1999. *Germany.* An unidentified individual threw a bomb into a Turkish travel agency in Munich, injuring two people and causing minor damage. Authorities suspected that the attack was connected to the conviction of Abdullah Ocalan, leader of the Kurdistan Workers Party (PKK). 99072302

July 26, 1999. *United States.* The Clinton administration announced it would permit U.S. farmers to compete for $2 billion in sales to Iran, Libya, and Sudan, thereby exempting sales of food, medicine, and medical equipment from U.S. economic sanctions. The agricultural products were limited to items ultimately consumed by people or animals, which excludes cotton and tobacco.

July 27, 1999. *Pakistan.* A bomb exploded on a passenger bus, killing 8 and wounding 40. No one claimed credit.

July 28, 1999. *Yemen.* Armed tribesmen kidnapped a Canadian working on the U.S.-owned Hunt Oil pipeline in Shabwah Governorate. He was freed unharmed the next day. 99072801

July 29, 1999. *Sri Lanka.* A suicide bomber jumped onto a car traveling through an intersection, detonated explosives strapped to his body, and killed Neelan Tiruchelvam, a member of the moderate Tamil United Liberation Front Party and head of a research center studying ethnic tensions. The Liberation Tigers of Tamil Eelam (LTTE) was blamed.

July 29, 1999. *Germany.* Roderick W., 32, a U.S. citizen ordered off a flight from Hamburg to London, grabbed an airport police officer's gun and tried to shoot the officer and himself. The gun jammed. He was taken into custody pending charges. He had become enraged when he learned that his plane would land at Heathrow instead of Gatwick. The pilot ordered him off the plane, which was still at the gate.

July 29, 1999. *United States.* The U.S. Department of Justice tightened security as the first anniversary of the Kenya and Tanzania embassy bombings neared. The FBI had stopped public tours the week before.

July 29, 1999. *Madagascar.* Security officials at a roadblock guarding the U.S. Embassy in Antananarivo found traces of plastic explosives in a stopped vehicle. The vehicle was driven away under police escort.

July 29, 1999. *United States.* State Department officials said they would wear blue ribbons to commemorate colleagues who died a year earlier in the Africa bombings.

July 30, 1999. *Colombia.* At 3:15 P.M., a truck bomb exploded at the Medellin office of the army's anti-kidnapping squad, killing 10 and injuring 38. Among the dead were a female passerby, two officials from the federal prosecutor's office, and an agent from the state security police. The bomb razed the GAULA offices. The truck was packed with at least 220 pounds of explosives. The bomb exploded while government peace envoy Victor Ricardo was meeting Revolutionary Armed Forces of Colombia (FARC) leaders in the south.

July 30, 1999. *Venezuela.* Authorities believed that a twin-engine Avior Airlines plane missing with 16 people aboard was probably hijacked, possibly by Colombian drug traffickers. It disappeared from radar on a flight between Barinas and Guasdualito, near the Colombian border.

The plane's two-man crew flew the aircraft to Guasdualito, Venezuela. The Revolutionary Armed Forces of Colombia (FARC) said one of its units discovered the downed plane near the border on July 31. It vowed to free the passengers, but insisted it had not hijacked the plane. FARC blamed Venezuelan dissidents opposed to President Hugo Chavez. It claimed the hijackers had abandoned the plane in the jungle. Venezuelan and Colombian officials rejected the claim. Eight of the passengers were returned to Venezuela on August 9 after being held by FARC guerrillas in a camp just inside Colombia. No ransom was paid. 99073001

August 1999. *Nigeria.* In early August, gunmen took several British oil engineers captive and later released them. 99089901

August 1999. *United States.* Four people died and 27 became ill in an outbreak of West Nile fever in New York. In January 2000, a U.S. government investigation team announced it had turned up no evidence that it was a terrorist attack. The tabloid *Daily Mail* of London published a quotation from a book by Iraqi defector Mikhael Ramadan, stating that Iraq's Saddam Hussein was developing a strain of the virus as a biological weapon.

August 1999. *France.* On September 13, 2000, a court sentenced Jose Bove, a sheep farmer and political activist, to three months in prison for the $100,000 ransacking of a McDonald's restaurant in Millau. He was protesting genetically altered foods and encroaching U.S. economic and cultural domination. He and eight of his nine codefendants were sentenced after the prosecutor requested a lighter sentence—ten months in prison for Bove, with nine months suspended, and suspended sentences for the others. Five defendants were ordered to pay fines of $263 each. Three others received two-month suspended sentences. Another was acquitted. The group was protesting

a U.S. government move to place sanctions against imported French foie gras and Roquefort cheese—a product of Bove's sheep farm. France and other European countries refused to permit the import of U.S. hormone-treated beef. Bove had become a local hero and had been at the violent protests in Seattle against the World Trade Organization. His parents studied at the University of California at Berkeley.

August 3, 1999. *United States.* The FBI delayed the takeoff of a Delta Air Lines flight from Atlanta to Istanbul, questioning six people and detaining one who held an expired visa. Hakan Caglar, 35, had been the subject of a tip saying he was a "potential threat to national security." He had been in the United States since March 7; his visa expired on June 6. He was released on August 5 without any criminal charges. FBI spokesman Tom Bush said, "We have not been able to connect him to any terroristic group."

August 4, 1999. *Sierra Leone.* Former soldiers and a rebel faction kidnapped 34 UN employees, aid workers, journalists, and West African peacekeepers during a meeting near Occra Hills outside Freetown. The hostages included an American, five British soldiers, a Canadian, a Ghanaian, a Russian military officer, a Kyrgyzstani officer, a Zambian officer, a Malaysian officer, a local bishop, 2 UNICEF officials, 2 local journalists, and 16 Sierra Leoneans. No one was injured in the attack. UN officials had arranged the handover of 150 women and children captured during the civil war. After freeing some of the hostages, the gunmen aimed their machine guns at the remaining hostages, demanding supplies and a meeting with UN officials. They demanded the release of imprisoned rebel leader John Paul Karoma. They freed Roman Catholic Bishop Giorgio Biguzzi and Jacqueline Chenard, spokesman for the UN military observer mission, but forced the others to march into the forest. A Reuters reporter and a civilian UN worker were freed the next day with letters from the kidnappers to the government of President Ahmad Tejan Kabbah, the UN observer mission, and US officials. (Other reports claim the rebels freed an American and a local journalist on August 5.) On August 6, Foday Sankoh, Sierra Leone's rebel leader, ordered the faction to free the hostages. Government officials and British negotiators attempted to obtain the hostages' release.

On August 8, the rebels freed 17 people, including 7 UN military observers, 6 local drivers, 2 members of the West African peace force, 2 journalists, 1 Ghanaian aid worker, and 1 Sierra Leonean official. The rebels had planned to free all the hostages, but heavy rains and poor communications delayed the release. On August 7, Idrissa Kamara, a former junta official, walked into the forest to help mediate. He was captured by his former colleagues, but did obtain the August 9 release of four hostages, including three British soldiers, and a promise of the release of the rest.

The rest of the hostages were freed on August 10 after the rebels were told that they would not be prosecuted. The rebels released the hostages along with 200 civilians taken prisoner during the country's eight-year civil war. 99080401

August 6, 1999. *Kyrgyzstan.* Tajikistani rebels kidnapped four Kyrgyzstani government officials in the Batken District. On August 13, the rebels freed the hostages unharmed for an undisclosed ransom. 99080601

August 9, 1999. *Yemen.* Eight Britons and two Algerians accused of having links to Islamic radicals were convicted of forming an armed gang to plot terrorist acts. Four of the Britons were convicted of plotting to bomb the British Consulate, an Anglican church, and a Swiss-owned hotel, all in Yemen. Seven of them were jailed for three to seven years. Three Britons were released for time served. Britain said there was insufficient evidence against the men. The defendants were linked to Islamic radicals of the Aden-Abyan Army, who kidnapped 16 Westerners in December 1998, 4 of whom died in a shootout during a failed rescue attempt. Two leaders of that group received death sentences. 99080901-03

August 10, 1999. *Israel.* A Palestinian man drove his car into a group of Israeli soldiers at a bus stop, then drove back several minutes later to drive into survivors, injuring 12 Israelis. Soldiers and police at the scene shot and killed the driver at the Nachshon Junction, 30 miles west of Jerusalem. Newly installed Prime Minister Ehud Barak called him a criminal, but did not accuse Yasir Arafat's Palestinian Authority of complicity. Peace talks therefore continued.

August 10, 1999. *Nigeria.* Armed youths kidnapped three Britons from a U.S.-operated oil platform in the Niger-Delta region. No one was injured and no group claimed credit. The youths released the hostages unharmed on August 11. No ransom was paid. 99081001

August 10, 1999. *Nigeria.* In a separate incident, unidentified youths kidnapped two British citizens working for the British-owned Niger-Benue Transport Company in the Niger-Delta region. No one claimed credit; no demands were made. The hostages were freed on August 11. 99081002

August 11, 1999. *Liberia.* An armed gang kidnapped one Liberian and six European relief workers—four Britons, one Italian, and one Norwegian—during the morning in Kolahun near the border of Sierra Leone and Guinea, 145 miles north of Monrovia. Three of the hostages worked for the medical charity Merlin and were helping to rebuild hospitals. Another two worked for Doctors Without Borders. The hostages were seized when armed men entered their compound in Lofa County, where President Charles Taylor had declared a state of emergency. The rebels made no demands. No one claimed credit.

On August 13, rebels released the seven aid workers; another 90 UN and other foreign workers fled into Guinea to avoid the fighting. 99081101

August 13, 1999. *Senegal.* Suspected rebels kidnapped ten civilians and soldiers in Casamance Province.

August 14, 1999. *Pakistan.* A bomb exploded in a van in Dina, killing 6 and wounding 14.

August 15, 1999. *Iran.* Kidnappers seized three Spaniards, one Italian, and one Iranian from a hotel dining room in central Iran. This was the third mysterious attack on foreigners in Iran. They were released unharmed on August 31. The Iranian government said the kidnappers were drug smugglers from an influential tribe. No one claimed credit. 99081501

August 15, 1999. *Algeria.* The Armed Islamic Group was believed responsible for killing at least 29 people and injuring 3 others near Beni Ounif, near the western border with Morocco. The death toll was expected to rise, perhaps reaching 40.

August 16, 1999. *Pakistan.* The Jamiat-ul-Ulema threatened to hit U.S. targets if Washington attacked Afghanistan's Taliban militia or its guest, Osama bin Laden. 99081601

August 16, 1999. *Russia.* Unidentified individuals kidnapped two Poles and two Russians in Dagestan and demanded a $50,000 ransom. On January 7, 2000, the Chechen Parliament reported the hostages were released unharmed in December. 99081601

August 20, 1999. *Algeria.* Five rebels dressed in army uniforms stormed an isolated house and slashed the throats of 14 children, most of them under age 10, attending a traditional circumcision party during the evening. The terrorists also bombed a nearby building, seriously wounding five other people. They then fled near the town of Ouzera in Medea Province, 75 miles south of Algiers. Medea is the stronghold of the Armed Islamic Group.

August 21, 1999. *Ethiopia.* Suspected al-Ittihaad al-Islami operatives set off a mine beneath a train carrying 400 Djiboutians near Dire Dawa. The explosion severely wounded two Ethiopian conductors, destroyed a locomotive, and caused extensive damage to the rail line, shutting it down for four days. No one claimed credit. 99082101

August 22, 1999. *Kyrgyzstan.* Uzbek gunmen kidnapped four Japanese geologists, their interpreter, and eight Kyrgyz soldiers in Bishkek. On October 13, four of the soldiers were freed unharmed. Another two Kyrgyz hostages were released on October 18. On October 25, the remaining hostages were released unharmed. No ransom was paid. 99082201

August 22, 1999. *Yemen.* Armed tribesmen in Marib Governorate kidnapped a French diplomat and his wife when their driver stopped for late afternoon prayers. On September 2, the hostages were freed unharmed. No one claimed credit. 99082202

August 23, 1999. *Venezuela.* A small bomb exploded outside the Colombian Consulate in Caracas, causing minor damage, but no injuries. Security officials defused a second bomb at the consulate. Venezuelan police safely defused another bomb found on the first floor of Credival Tower, the building housing the Colombian Embassy. The Tupamaro Revolutionary Movement claimed credit. 99082301-03

August 25, 1999. *Morocco.* A Royal Air Maroc 737-400 flying 79 passengers and 9 crew from Casablanca, Morocco, to Tunis, Tunisia, was hijacked by individuals who demanded fuel and passage to Frankfurt, Germany. The plane landed at Barcelona's El Prat Airport. At least one assailant surrendered at dawn, releasing the hostages, who boarded two waiting buses. 99082501

August 27, 1999. *Russia.* Unidentified individuals in Volograd kidnapped the general director of the Coca-Cola Volograd Company and demanded a $50,000 ransom. The Filipino hostage escaped later that day. No one claimed credit. 99082701

August 28, 1999. *Colombia.* The Revolutionary Armed Forces of Colombia (FARC) and the

National Liberation Army (ELN) were suspected of abducting a Scottish oil engineer working for the U.S./U.K.-owned British Petroleum Amoco Corporation near Yopal city. No one claimed credit or made demands. 99082801

August 29, 1999. *Kyrgyzstan.* President Askar Akayev said he would take all measures against guerrillas holding 16 hostages, including 4 Japanese geologists, in the southern mountains. On October 18, following talks with officials, the Islamic militants freed two hostages—Kyrgyz Interior Troops commander General Anarbek Shamkeyev and his aide—but continued to hold seven others, including the four Japanese geologists and their interpreter. The kidnappers had invaded Kyrgyzstan from neighboring Tajikistan. 99082901

August 30, 1999. *East Timor.* A UN employee was killed by pro-Indonesian government militias. Two other UN employees were missing and presumed dead. 99083001

August 30, 1999. *Jordan.* Police raided and closed several Hamas offices in Amman, arrested a dozen activists, and issued arrest warrants for four senior Hamas figures—Khaled Meshal, head of the Hamas political bureau who was the target of a failed Israeli assassination attempt in 1997; spokesman Ibrahim Ghosheh; Mousa Abu Marzook, a top leader who had been deported by the United States; and Mohammed Nazal, the group's official representative in Jordan.

On September 22, Jordan arrested Jordanian citizens Khaled Meshal and Ibrahim Ghosheh as they arrived at Amman's airport on a flight from Iran. Police also detained four bodyguards of Meshal. Meshal and Ghosheh were charged with affiliation with an illegal organization, which carries a one-year prison term. Mousa Abu Marzook, who held a Yemeni passport and a Palestinian travel document, was deported. He returned to Iran.

August 30, 1999. *India.* Muslim separatists fired on a taxi, killing four police officers and their driver in Hanjiweera.

August 31, 1999. *Russia.* During the night, a bomb containing five to ten ounces of TNT exploded in a children's amusement arcade at Manezh Square, an underground shopping mall adjacent to the Kremlin, spraying glass shards and injuring 29 people, 5 of them seriously. Four children were among the injured. Moscow Mayor Yuri Lazhkov said the "act of terrorism" had an unclear motive.

August 31, 1999. *Colombia.* The Revolutionary Armed Forces of Colombia (FARC) seized the partly U.S.-owned Anchiclaya hydroelectric plant near Buenaventura in western Colombia. They took over without firing a shot and caused no injuries. FARC released 23 hostages on September 3 and another 58 hostages on September 4. They still held 87 workers and threatened to shut down the facility if the region's electricity rates were not reduced by 30 percent. (The State Department's annual terrorism review reported that FARC took 168 hostages and released 58 on September 4 and the rest on September 5. The report also said the Pacific Energy Enterprise power plant was operated jointly by American, Colombian, and Venezuelan firms.) 99083101

September 1999. *Somalia.* Two doctors working on aid projects in southern Somalia were killed. One was a representative of the World Health Organization in the port of Kismayu; the other was a member of a Dutch aid group.

In the middle of the month, Ayub Sheikh Yerow, a senior UNICEF official, was killed by gunmen in an ambush on the road between Jowhar and Afgoi in central Somalia, 45 miles from Mogadishu. UN agencies suspended all activities in southern Somalia for five days. 99099901-03

September 1, 1999. *East Timor.* Pro-Indonesian militias fired automatic rifles and pistols and used machetes in an attack on a Dili neighborhood near the UN headquarters, shooting, burning houses, and sending more than 200 residents, including three dozen foreign journalists, scrambling over the walls of the UN compound. A television crew filmed a man being hacked to death by a half dozen machete-wielding militiamen. An Australian reporter was threatened with a rifle and escaped by jumping into a pond and hiding underwater until he was rescued by a motorcycle policeman. *Washington Post* reporter Keith Richburg was hit on the back with a machete, but ran and hid inside a parked van before climbing the UN wall.

The attacks came two days after a UN-sponsored referendum on East Timorese independence. 99090101-02

September 1, 1999. *India.* Hindu zealots shot eight arrows into the stomach, lungs, and right eye of Rev. Arul Doss, 35, a Roman Catholic diocesan priest. He had been sleeping in a mud hut used for prayer services in Jamubani, a village 12 miles from Labedepur, Orissa State. A group of men wearing loincloths broke in, brandishing torches and *lathis* (heavy sticks). They beat other clerics, including Kate Singh Khuntia, 27, a catechism teacher who was sleeping in the same hut.

Christians suspected the national fundamentalist Hindu youth group Bajrang Dal, which had been upset by Christian conversions among impoverished tribal people known as *adivasis*.

The Indian government launched a manhunt for Dara Singh, a Hindu vigilante also accused of the attack on Australian Rev. Staines on January 23, 1999.

September 2, 1999. *East Timor.* Militias fired on people in the provincial capital of Dili, killing three more UN workers, threatening journalists, and causing Timorese and foreigners to flee. The Indonesian military reversed its earlier statements and said it would welcome an international peacekeeping force if a majority voted for independence in the earlier referendum. Two local UN workers were killed in Maliana, west of Dili, and another in Atsabe. Five other local UN workers were missing and feared dead. Some 33 foreign UN workers took shelter at a local police station. Foreign news organizations chartered planes after reporters were threatened and a BBC reporter was beaten and kicked. Six militiamen charged into the Tur-

ismo Hotel, where many foreign journalists stay. One of them, waving a pistol, threatened to return and kill the foreign reporters that night. A Canadian woman was shoved and kicked during the incident. Members of the Aitarak (Thorn) militia were also seen at Dili's airport. 99090201-03

September 4, 1999. *East Timor.* Following the announcement that 78.5 percent of the electorate had voted for independence, the militias stepped up violence. They stormed the Portuguese Consulate. Others in Liquica shot in the stomach a U.S. civilian who was working as an unarmed UN policeman. He was evacuated in stable condition by medical plane to Darwin, Australia. Still others attacked the downtown Mahkota Hotel in Dili, where many UN staff members and foreign journalists stay. They fired shots at the hotel's front doors while a man with a machete smashed in the front glass window. Indonesian police with automatic weapons stood by; some were seen putting their arms around militiamen and gently trying to move them away. By nighttime, the police were not in the area.

A UN convoy traveling from Liquica to Dili was fired on at three checkpoints by national police who had manned roadblocks alongside militia members.

On May 4, 2001, an Indonesian court found three East Timorese militiamen guilty in the murder of three UN High Commissioner for Refugees aid workers from the United States, Croatia, and Ethiopia. The victims were stabbed and stoned to death in Atambua, in western Timor. Their bodies were dragged into the street and set on fire. Carlos Caceres, 33, was a native of San Juan, Puerto Rico; his family resided in Florida. The court sentenced the trio to 16 to 20 months in prison, leading to protests by UN, U.S., and other foreign diplomats who wanted tougher punishments. The court in April had reduced the charges from manslaughter to "mob violence resulting in death," which had only a three-year maximum term (manslaughter carried a 20-year maximum). The defendants were proud of what they did. Julius Maisama, who received a 20-month sentence, said, "I accept the sentence with pride because I did what I did to defend [Indonesia's] red-and-white flag." Jose Francisco and Joao Alvis da Cruz received 16-month sentences. Three others received 10- to 15-month terms for "damaging property and committing acts of violence in a public place." Suhardi Sumomulyono, defense attorney, said, "My clients made a mistake because three people got killed. But it was a mob attack and they were not the only ones responsible." 99090401-04

September 4, 1999. *Russia.* A car bomb exploded outside an apartment building for Russian military families in Dagestan, killing 64 people and injuring 100. Chechen rebels were blamed.

September 5, 1999. *East Timor.* The campaign continued, apparently with the participation of Indonesian military and police units. The Mahkota Hotel was set ablaze and the nearby Turismo Hotel was also attacked, forcing journalists to leave. The UN compound remained under siege. 99090501-03

September 5, 1999. *Israel.* Within 24 hours of the signing of an Israeli–Palestinian peace agreement, two car bombs exploded prematurely in the northern Israeli cities of Haifa and Tiberias, killing three terrorists planning to detonate the bombs in densely populated neighborhoods and critically injuring an Israeli woman pedestrian in Tiberias. Hamas was suspected.

The bomb in Tiberias went off at 5:10 P.M. in an Audi ten yards from a gas station and less than a mile from the center of town. The driver and his passenger were killed instantly. The woman suffered massive head and facial injuries. Three others were treated for minor injuries.

At 5:30 P.M., a bomb exploded in Haifa in a Fiat parked in a lot within blocks of the central bus station, killing the driver.

The next day, police arrested five Israeli Arabs.

September 6, 1999. *East Timor.* Militias fired into the International Red Cross compound, which had become a safe haven for 2,000 refugees. The terrorists separated the East Timorese from the foreigners at the compound, then marched the East Timorese away. The 11 Red Cross foreign staff members and 8 other foreign aid workers were turned over to the police and taken to the airport to leave.

Other terrorists shot at the Australian ambassador's car and burned down the home of the city's Roman Catholic archbishop, Carlos Belo, winner of the 1996 Nobel Peace Prize. 99090601-02

September 6, 1999. *Yemen.* Armed tribesmen kidnapped three Sudanese teachers in the Marib region, but freed them unharmed on September 17. 99090603

September 8, 1999. *Nigeria.* Gunmen kidnapped an Italian in Bayelsa State, but released the hostage unharmed on September 15. No one claimed credit, no demands were made, and no ransom was paid. Ijaw youths were suspected. 99090801

September 9, 1999. *Russia.* An explosion destroyed a Moscow apartment building at 19 Guryanov Street, killing 94 and injuring 150. Dozens more were believed buried under the rubble. Russian authorities said a bomb with more than 440 pounds of explosives was planted in a first-floor store. An anonymous caller told Interfax that the blast was in retaliation for Russia's recent bombing of Chechen villages. Police said they had identified suspects who had planted the hexogen bomb, an explosive used only in military bombs and shells. A Chechen warlord denied that his Islamic militants were involved.

September 11, 1999. *Ecuador.* A group of 25 to 30 Revolutionary Armed Forces of Colombia (FARC) rebels were believed to be responsible for kidnapping 12 foreigners, including an American, near the Colombian border. Leonard Carter—a U.S. citizen and United Pipeline Systems oil worker— was taken hostage along with one Belgian, three Spaniards, and seven Canadians. The company was an Alberta-based contracting firm. The Canadians and American worked for the firm; the rest were tourists. An Ecuadoran soldier was killed during a gun battle when he tried to stop the kidnappers at a roadblock as they headed north toward Colombia. Ecuadoran police rescued a Canadian hostage later that day. The Ecuadoran Army intensified its search for the hostages on September 13. Helicopter, river, and foot patrols looked throughout the Sucumbios Province.

A month later, a Canadian woman and several Spaniards were released.

On December 19, the rest of the Canadians and the American were freed. They were found in good health near Lagos Agrio, 200 miles northeast of Quito. The freed hostages arrived at Quito Airport on December 20 after 99 days of captivity. Their ransom was paid by City Investing, the Ecuadoran unit of Alberta Energy Company, which had contracted with United Pipeline. Some reports set the ransom as $3.5 million. (The State Department's annual terrorism report indicated that no demands were paid and that FARC officials had denied involvement.) 99091101

September 13, 1999. *Russia.* A bomb went off at 5:00 A.M. in an eight-story Moscow apartment building at 6 Kashirskoye Highway, killing at least 93 people, including 6 children, and injuring 5. The blast was four miles from the site of the September 9 bombing. Authorities announced on September 15 that they had located a truck that might have brought the explosives to Moscow from southern Russia. The driver was missing. The driver of a smaller truck used to distribute the explosives confessed his involvement. Police detained 27 people.

A caller from the Dagestan Liberation Army told Tass that the bombings were "acts of retribution for the terrorist actions of the Russian air force against civilians in Dagestan and Chechnya." Police claimed the Chechens were using individuals with Slavic features, rather than ethnic Chechens, to plant the bombs. These agents were paid $50,000 for each explosion.

The bombers used the identity of Mukhit Laipanov, a man who died several years before, to lease space in both Moscow buildings.

On December 30, 1999, Moscow police reported the arrest of eight people for the bombings of four apartment buildings in Moscow and elsewhere in Russia that killed 300.

Investigators reported on March 16, 2000, that they had identified the explosives, detonators, routes, and at least 6 people who carried out the apartment bombings in Moscow and other cities on September 8 and 13 that killed almost 300 and sparked the Russian military offensive against Chechnya. One person, a driver who brought explosives to Moscow from the northern Caucasus, had been arrested. Investigators found explosives and Casio watches in Chechen villages that were similar to those used in the blasts. In March, they found Arabic literature on mining and demolition and instructions on the use of Casio watches in Duba-Yurt. They found a bomb factory in Urus-Martan that had traces of explosives similar to those used in the bombings. Among those materials were ammonium nitrate and aluminum powder. Nine people were placed on the Russian most-wanted list for the bombings; one of them was the driver.

On May 20, 2000, police in Makhachkala arrested Isa Zainutdinov, 62, a Dagestani resident, on suspicion of being a "major perpetrator" of the bomb attack on an apartment building in Buynaksk in September 1999 that killed 64 people. The suspect admitted he drove a truckload of explosives to the apartment block, but claimed he was unaware of its intended use.

September 15, 1999. *Colombia.* Doctors Without Borders evacuated 11 foreign doctors and nurses from the country and suspended several health projects after receiving threatening phone calls. 99091501

September 16, 1999. *Algeria.* Algerian voters approved by 98 percent an amnesty plan designed to end Muslim insurgent attacks.

September 16, 1999. *Russia.* A GAZ-53 truck bomb exploded at a nine-story apartment building at 5:57 A.M. in Volgodonsk, 600 miles southeast of Moscow, killing 17 and injuring 115.

A bomb went off in a St. Petersburg apartment building, killing two and injuring four.

September 21, 1999. *East Timor.* A shot was fired at an Irish journalist riding a motorbike in the center of Dili. She heard a gunshot and felt the bullet pass by her head. 99092101

September 21, 1999. *East Timor.* Two journalists were attacked and spent the night hiding in the bush. The journalists were rescued by British, Australian, and Indonesian troops. Their driver and a translator were missing as of September 22. 99092102

September 21, 1999. *East Timor.* Sander Thoenes, 30, a Dutch journalist working for the British *Financial Times*, was shot to death. His body was found the next morning behind an abandoned house after Florindo Araujo, a Timorese driver, said six men in Indonesian police uniforms fired at them in a suburb of Dili, the capital. 99092103

September 29, 1999. *Nicaragua.* The Andres Castro United Front (FUAC) kidnapped a Canadian and a Nicaraguan military officer in Bonanza Municipality. The rebels demanded $1 million and a renegotiation of agreements made between the FUAC and the Nicaraguan government in 1997. 99092901

October 1, 1999. *Thailand.* Five armed Vigorous Burmese Student Warriors took over the Burmese Embassy in Bangkok and seized 89 hostages, including 3 Frenchmen, 2 Malaysians, 3 Canadians, 1 German, 1 American, 1 Singaporean, 1 Japanese, and at least 5 Thais, in addition to the Burmese diplomats. They demanded the release of all political prisoners in Burma, a dialogue between the country's pro-democracy leader Aung San Suu Kyi and the military, and the convening of an elected parliament.

On October 2, they freed their hostages and left the compound in two minivans, which drove them to a waiting police helicopter at a nearby school. The helicopter flew them to the border, where the five gunmen fled, apparently to sanctuary with the Karen National Union, a border-based rebel group in Burma.

Burma closed its border with Thailand the next day. 99100101

October 2, 1999. *Ukraine.* Leftist presidential candidate Natalya Vitrenko was injured when homemade bombs were thrown at her during a campaign rally. Another 16 people suffered superficial injuries. Police detained two people.

October 7, 1999. *Algeria.* Muslim rebels slashed the throats of eight members of the same family and kidnapped a teenage girl in Douira, 25 miles west of Algiers.

October 8, 1999. *Germany.* German police arrested five young men believed to have attacked five U.S. Army musicians in Prenzlau after giving a Nazi salute. Eberswalde police said all of the detainees, aged 21 to 25, had confessed. 99100801

October 8, 1999. *Nigeria.* Armed youths attacked a U.S. oil company compound housing employees from the United States, United Kingdom, and Nigeria, injuring four Americans and four Nigerians and causing massive damage to the compound. The youths demanded that the oil facility replace its existing Nigerian staff with local workers. On October 11, the attackers left the compound without further incident. 99100801

October 10, 1999. *South Africa.* Authorities were investigating whether a Muslim terrorist network had been established, following the arrest of Khalen Khamis Mohamed, who was extradited to the United States on charges of involvement in the bombing of the U.S. Embassy in Tanzania in August 1998. Another suspect in Cape Town's Planet Hollywood bombing was a Zimbabwean who was staying in the same area as Mohamed. Both had married Kenyans; some others had married South Africans.

October 11, 1999. *Pakistan.* Rawalpindi's *Nawa-i-Waqt* reported in Urdu that Osama bin Laden had told an international news service that al-Qaeda supported holy war, but not terrorism.

October 11, 1999. *Yugoslavia.* A Bulgarian man working for the UN civilian mission in Kosovo was shot to death in Pristina near the Grand Hotel after his first day on the job. He was on his way to dinner. He was believed to be the first UN staffer killed since the UN took over the administration of Kosovo in June. He was in civilian clothes. The gunman escaped on foot, apparently after shooting the Bulgarian, who had been talking to an ethnic Albanian woman. 99101101

October 12, 1999. *South Africa.* The Pretoria High Court dismissed charges against Dr. Wouter Basson (alias Dr. Death) regarding more than 200 deaths abroad by poison. He was accused of running the apartheid regime's chemical and biological weapons program.

October 12, 1999. *Israel.* Israel announced it would permit Nayef Hawatmeh, leader of the Democratic Front for the Liberation of Palestine, into Palestinian self-rule areas now that he had expressed support for the peace process.

October 12, 1999. *Burundi.* Eight members of a UN convoy arriving in a refugee camp in the south discovered that uniformed men were imposters affiliated with suspected Rwandan Hutu rebels. The terrorists lined up the UN workers against a wall, stole their valuables, and let the foreigners walk away. However, one terrorist asked, "Why should these people be allowed to live?" He then shot to death Luis Manuel Zuniga, 53, a Chilean who ran UNICEF operations in Burundi. He then killed Saskia Von Jeijenfeldt, 34, a Dutch woman whose glasses had been stolen and then returned. She was a logistics specialist for the World Food Program. A UN security officer interceded and in the ensuing gun battle, four local military officers and six Burundians died. The six other UN workers survived, although one Belgian and one Burundian working for the UN, along with four other Burundians, were wounded. No one claimed credit. 99101201

October 13, 1999. *Chile.* Iain Hardy, the U.K. honorary consul in Valparaiso, resigned after death threats tied to the arrest of General Augusto Pinochet in London. 99101301

October 13, 1999. *Georgia.* Masked gunmen seized six UN military observers—from Germany, the Czech Republic, Greece, Switzerland, Sweden, and Uruguay—and their Georgian translator as they were delivering aid in the breakaway territory of Abkhazia. State Security Minister Vakhtang Kutateladze said the kidnappers wanted a $200,000 ransom. (The State Department reported it was a $250,000 ransom demand.) Negotiators were in radio contact with the kidnappers. The next day, four of the UN workers were freed. Jorgen Oberg, a Swede, and Georgios Kapranos, a Greek, were released the following day along with the translator in the remote Kodori Gorge. Oberg said he was well treated and was unaware of a ransom payment. 99101302

October 15, 1999. *Sierra Leone.* Unidentified individuals kidnapped three clergymen—two Italians and one Sierra Leonean. No one claimed credit and no demands were made. Armed Forces Revolutionary Council (AFRC) rebels were suspected. 99101501

October 19, 1999. *Turkey.* A man hijacked an EgyptAir plane flying 6 crew and 48 passengers from Istanbul to Cairo and diverted it to the Hamburg airport, where he surrendered to German police shortly after landing. No one was injured. His motives and nationality were not disclosed. 99101901

October 21, 1999. *India.* Kashmiri militants kidnapped and beheaded a father and daughter suspected of spying for the Indian Army in Kupwara.

October 26, 1999. *Colombia.* Henry Romero, 42, a Colombian freelance photographer who often worked for Reuters, was kidnapped in mountains close to Cali by the National Liberation Army (ELN). The group said he would be tried for revealing the identity of one of their regional commanders in a photograph. 99102601

October 26, 1999. *Yemen.* Marta R. Colburn, a teacher from Portland, Oregon, and her visiting parents, Don and Gladys Colburn, were kidnapped in the Shamar area by gunmen as they returned to Sanaa from a trip to the southern part of the country. She worked for the American Institute for Yemeni Studies in Sanaa. Yemeni tribesmen demanded the release of 25 suspects detained in an attack on an oil pipeline. The tribesmen negotiated with authorities for two days, but released the hostages on October 28. Yemen said it would set up special courts to deal with the kidnapping of foreigners and acts of sabotage. The State Department had issued a travel warning on October 21, saying that "the level of risk for foreigners in Yemen is very high." 99102602

October 27, 1999. *United States.* Several scientists in Cambridge, Massachusetts, received letters booby-trapped with razor blades. The letters were allegedly sent by animal rights activists. Eighty scientists throughout the United States who worked with primates were targeted in a communiqué posted on the Internet.

October 27, 1999. *Armenia.* Five gunmen firing automatic weapons seized the Armenian Parliament, killed the prime minister and six others, and took at least 50 hostages (some reports said 200). They shot to death Prime Minister Vazgen Sarkisian, 40, Speaker Karen Demirchian, Deputy Speaker Yuri Bakhshian, Energy Minister Leonard Petrosian, Deputy Speaker Ruben Miroian, Parliament member Genrikh Abramian, and senior economic official Mikhail Kotanian. Ten other lawmakers were wounded. The terrorists demanded to see President Robert Kocharian.

They released three hostages ten hours into the siege: two parliamentary deputies and Agriculture Minister Gagig Shakhbazian, all of whom suffered heart attacks.

A reporter who was in the chamber during the attack said, "They said it was a coup and called on the journalists to inform people about it. They said they were going to punish the authorities for what they did to the nation." Former journalist and extreme nationalist Nairi Unanian, 34, the group's leader, told a local television station in a telephone interview, "This is a patriotic action. This shake-up is needed for the nation to regain its senses." He said the gunmen had only intended to kill Sarkisian, who he claimed had failed to serve the nation. "The country is in a catastrophic situation, people are hungry, and the government doesn't offer any way out." Unanian had walked up to Sarkisian and said, "Enough of drinking our blood." When Sarkisian replied, "Everything is being done for you and the future of your children," Unanian opened fire. The other gunmen included Unanian's younger brother, Karen, and their uncle, Vram. Unanian had been a member of the Armenian Revolutionary Federation (Dashnak), but had been expelled several years earlier. Dashnak officials denied involvement in the attack.

Television cameraman Gagik Saratikian was permitted inside the chamber after the attack. The gunmen calmly directed him to film scenes in the wrecked hall.

Hundreds of police and soldiers, along with two armored personnel carriers, surrounded the building.

The attack came hours after Deputy Secretary of State Strobe Talbott left Yerevan following talks with Kocharian.

The attackers surrendered the next morning after releasing their hostages following 16 hours of negotiations. President Kocharian promised they would get a fair trial and that force would not be used against them. Before leaving, they recorded a statement that was broadcast on national television. The Defense Ministry called on Kocharian to dismiss the country's chief prosecutor and the national security and interior ministers, blaming them for lax security.

Funeral services were held on October 30; 20,000 people packed Yerevan's Freedom Square.

On November 5, lawmaker Musheg Movsesian was detained. On November 10, he was charged with helping to organize the attack. He was brought to Parliament under heavy police guard and taken away in handcuffs after the other deputies voted to revoke his parliamentary immunity.

On January 8, 2000, Arutun Arutunian, deputy director of Armenian national television, was charged with helping to organize the attack. He was charged two days after he was detained.

October 30, 1999. *Nigeria.* Armed youths seized a helicopter near Warri and kidnapped three Britons. They forced the hostages, pilots for Royal Dutch Shell, to fly to an undisclosed location. Negotiations for the hostages' release were initiated, although no other demands were made. 99103001

November 1, 1999. *Nigeria.* Armed youths seized an American vessel near Bonny Island and kidnapped an American, a Pole, and 12 Nigerians. No one was injured in the attack, although the ship sustained minor damage. The attackers freed the hostages unharmed on November 3. No one claimed credit. 99110101

November 3, 1999. *Panama.* Revolutionary Armed Forces of Colombia (FARC) rebels were suspected of hijacking two Panamanian helicopters carrying four Colombians, two Ecuadorans, and two Panamanian pilots near Colon. No one was injured in the attack. The guerrillas freed the hostages unharmed later that day, but kept the helicopters. 99110301

November 5, 1999. *United States.* James Kenneth Gluck, 53, of Tampa, Florida, was arrested by the FBI for threatening Colorado judges. Police found materials to make ricin. He had sent a ten-page note to a Colorado Court of Appeals judge in which he threatened to wage biological warfare on Colorado's Jefferson County justice center. He mentioned one judge by name and referred to the possible use of ricin.

November 7, 1999. *Greece.* A bomb exploded outside a Levi's jeans store in Athens. A previously unknown Anti-Capitalist Action group issued a deliberately misleading warning message moments before the bomb went off.

Police blamed the Red Line for shooting at the Hellenic-American union in the center of Athens.

No injuries were reported in either incident. They were apparently protests against an upcoming visit by U.S. President Bill Clinton on November 13–15. The attacks were the fourth and fifth in four days. 99110701-02

November 7, 1999. *Israel.* Three pipe time bombs exploded simultaneously at 10:30 A.M. at an intersection in Netanya, injuring 33. Police blamed Islamic militants and arrested two Palestinians on suspicion of planting the bombs, which were packed with nails and planted in a trash can. Authorities destroyed a fourth bomb in the vicinity. During the weekend, Hamas had warned it would escalate attacks, but it did not claim credit for these attacks.

November 8, 1999. *Nigeria.* Fourteen youths armed with machetes boarded a Belize-owned vessel near Escravos in Delta State, kidnapping an American and a Nigerian. The two were freed unharmed on November 12; no ransom was paid. 99110801

November 9, 1999. *Colombia.* A 14-pound bomb exploded under an electricity pole in Bogota, injuring nine people, including three investigators for the Attorney General's Office.

November 10, 1999. *Colombia.* The Revolutionary Armed Forces of Colombia (FARC) kidnapped a Briton working for the International

Committee of the Red Cross (ICRC). He was freed unharmed on November 14 following a meeting between FARC and ICRC officials; no ransom was paid. 99111001

November 11, 1999. *Colombia.* A car bomb exploded in a rich neighborhood in northern Bogota, killing 6 and injuring 40. Drug traffickers were suspected of packing the 175 pounds of explosives in a red Mazda pickup and setting it off by remote control. The Supreme Court had recently approved the extradition of drug traffickers to the United States. First on the list was Colombian trafficker Jaime Orlando Lara (alias the King of Heroin) and Venezuelan trafficker Fernando Jose Flores. Six hours after the blast, President Andres Pastrana signed extradition orders for the duo and for Cuban citizen Sergio Braulio Gonzalez.

November 12, 1999. *Pakistan.* Seven rockets were launched by remote control from three empty vehicles at the U.S. Embassy, World Bank building, and the Saudi-Pak tower, which houses UN offices in Islamabad. Several people were injured, including a Pakistani guard at the American Cultural Center. The rockets fell short of the targets and caused little damage. A car with a UN license plate caught fire. No one claimed credit, and local police had no suspects, although some speculated that Osama bin Laden's agents were behind the attacks. The Taliban in Afghanistan had recently refused to extradite bin Laden, and two days after this decision, the UN had imposed economic and travel sanctions on Afghanistan as a result. Pakistani officials suggested that the attacks were the work of Lashkar, a Pakistan-based Islamic guerrilla group that held a three-day annual meeting near Lahore the previous week. They had vowed a holy war against the West. 99111201-03

November 12, 1999. *Albania.* Police working with American officials arrested Abdul Saleh-U, an Egyptian believed to be associated with Osama bin Laden. (Saleh-U was also identified as Jordanian 'Abd al-Latif Salih, 42, who had obtained

Albanian citizenship.) He was expelled to an undisclosed location. He was also believed to be a member of the Muslim Brotherhood that advocated turning Egypt into a strict Muslim state. He had arrived in Albania in the early 1990s and was a key figure in channeling aid from Islamic states to build mosques and hospitals. He also invested heavily in the construction industry. Reuters reported that a source indicated that there was "evidence that he was connected to other Egyptian nationals extradited from Albania last year and to an Albanian involved in planning an attack on the U.S. Embassy." Maks Ciciku, an Albanian engineer who headed a private security firm, was detained in January on suspicion of spying on U.S. Ambassador Marisa Lino and preparing an attack on the U.S. Embassy. 99111204

November 12, 1999. *India.* A bomb exploded on the Punjab Express bound for New Delhi, killing 13 and injuring 50. Muslim separatists were blamed.

November 22, 1999. *Worldwide.* The UN and United States reportedly had tightened security arrangements at their facilities after the UN's security coordinator, Benon Sevan of Cyprus, released an internal memo indicating that there were "reliable reports" that Osama bin Laden's supporters could attack U.S. or UN targets in Pakistan, Afghanistan, Uzbekistan, Tajikistan, Kazakhstan, or Turkmenistan in retaliation for the sanctions imposed against Afghanistan on November 14.

November 23, 1999. *Jordan.* Police shot and wounded in the hand Nabil Hassan, 20, a man who fired a toy gun at security guards outside the Israeli Embassy in Amman. He was overpowered and arrested.

November 28, 1999. *Spain.* The Basque Nation and Liberty (ETA) announced it was ending its 14-month cease-fire because of the "repressive attacks" by Spain and France and the failure of nationalists to create a Basque state. The next day, the government urged political parties to isolate

ETA. Industry Minister Josep Pique said that there would be no new talks with ETA.

November 29, 1999. *United States.* Immigration and Naturalization Service (INS) officials withdrew their request to Attorney General Janet Reno that she overturn a judge's order to release Nasser K. Ahmed, 39, an Egyptian accused by the FBI of being a terrorist. He was released after spending three and a half years in a New York jail. He was incarcerated based on classified evidence linking him to Sheik Omar Abdel Rahman, who led the conspiracy to bomb the UN. He had served as Abdel Rahman's interpreter. The INS still intended to move to deny his asylum request and have him deported.

November 30, 1999. *Cambodia.* The U.S. Embassy sent most of its staff home and drew down operations following reports that a group linked to Osama bin Laden had arrived in the Philippines several weeks before and had been heard during phone conversations plotting attacks on U.S. installations in Cambodia. 99113001

December 7, 1999. *Sierra Leone.* Former rebels of the Revolutionary United Front (RUF) kidnapped two Doctors Without Borders volunteers—a German and a Belgian. No injuries were reported. The logistics specialist and doctor had been working to open a health project when they were grabbed near Buedu in the eastern Kailahun region, according to a fax sent to Abidjan by the rebels. The two were freed unharmed on December 16. No ransom was paid. 99120701

December 9, 1999. *Venezuela.* A Colombian paramilitary squad reportedly planned to assassinate Venezuelan President Hugo Chavez in San Cristobal, a Venezuelan border town. Days earlier, Cuban President Fidel Castro called a news conference in Havana to denounce a similar plot against Chavez, this one by Cuban exiles in Miami.

December 11, 1999. *Worldwide.* The U.S. Department of State issued a warning for all Americans traveling or living abroad, advising them to take extra security precautions through the first week in January because of intelligence information that terrorists were planning to attack Americans. The warning "indicates the attacks could be planned for locations . . . where large gatherings and celebrations will be taking place." This was the fifth warning since early October. Filipino officials said local groups with ties to Osama bin Laden were being monitored.

December 13, 1999. *Jordan.* Jordanian officials announced the arrest of 13 suspected terrorists who were plotting attacks against Israelis, Americans, and other Christian tourists. They included 11 Jordanians, 1 Iraqi, and 1 Algerian who belonged to a cell organized by Osama bin Laden. Bin Laden's network in Afghanistan trained them in explosives, then smuggled them into Jordan with fake Jordanian and other Arab passports. U.S. officials denied involvement in the arrests. The Jordanian media linked the group to a Jordanian living in exile in the United Kingdom who had been charged in absentia in connection with bombings in Jordan earlier in the 1990s. Other reports tied the detainees to the local Mohammed's Army, which was active in Jordan in the 1990s.

On February 16, 2000, a military prosecutor in Amman indicted 28 suspected terrorists linked to Osama bin Laden. Thirteen of the group were arrested on December 13. The 11 Jordanians, 1 Iraqi, and 1 Algerian were charged with 11 counts of plotting terrorist attacks in Jordan, including "plotting to destabilize public security, possession of explosives and weapons, falsification of passports and official stamps." A 14th suspect, Khalil Deek, a Jordanian with U.S. citizenship, was extradited to Amman from Pakistan. He faced separate charges in another case and was incarcerated in Kafkafa Security Prison in the northern hills. The FBI said a CD-ROM seized from his home contained bomb-making instructions. Deek told *Newsweek* that he had a joint bank account with Abu Zubaydah (variant Mohammed Abu Zubayda; alias Zayn al-Abidin Muhammad

Husayn; variant Mohammed Hussein Zein-al-Abideen), bin Laden's chief executive officer, and gave to Abu Hosher, one of those arrested in Jordan, a copy of *Encyclopedia Jihad*, a military training manual with bomb specifications and advice for insurgents. But he claimed he was framed by the Pakistani police in a sting operation.

The others remained at large. A justice official said they would face a public trial and death sentences. The trial was set to begin in late March at the State Security Court.

On February 29, 2000, the Associated Press reported that officials believed that Abu Zubaydah was a key member of the plot and among the 14 suspects still at large. Jordanian officials said plots in the United States and Jordan were linked. Abu Zubaydah was born in 1973 and went to Afghanistan as a teen, where he met bin Laden. Abu Zubaydah, a Gaza Strip resident believed to be a member of bin Laden's inner circle, fled to Afghanistan after directing the plot from Pakistan. He was believed to be in contact with the Algerians charged in a separate attempt to bomb targets in the United States. Some officials believed he was communications chief and coordinator of bin Laden's international terrorist operations outside Afghanistan. He also served as gatekeeper for bin Laden's training camps in Afghanistan. Abu Zubaydah held a $3,000 joint bank account with Khalil Deek, a suspect in the Jordan plot, and was in close contact with Jordanians Khader Abu Ghoser and his assistant, Raed Hijazi. Abu Ghoser (variants Hosher and Ghosher) was among those detained; Hijazi was still at large, possibly in Afghanistan. Abu Ghoser was an Afghan War veteran who joined Muhammad's Army, a radical Islamic group that mounted terrorist attacks in Jordan in the 1980s. After his release from prison in Jordan in 1993, he moved to Yemen where he contacted Egypt's Islamic Jihad, which is aided by bin Laden. Hijazi traveled on a U.S. passport and had worked as a taxi driver in Boston.

On March 28, 2000, Jordan indicted 28 Arabs linked to bin Laden on charges stemming from a conspiracy to attack Americans and Israelis during New Year's celebrations at Mount Nebo, where tradition says Moses saw the Promised Land, and at a settlement on the Jordan River where Jesus was baptized. Thirteen defendants, including Jordanians, Palestinians, and a Yemeni, had not been found, and were suspected to be in Pakistan, Afghanistan, Britain, Lebanon, and Syria, according to Attorney General Maamoun Khassawneh. Jordanian officials had requested extradition of some of the suspects. The trial was to begin in the State Security Court in mid-April. The group faced the death penalty. The trial began on April 20, 2000.

On September 18, 2000, the military court sentenced six men to death for the plot, but acquitted them of charges that they were linked to bin Laden. Another six were acquitted of all counts. Sixteen others received prison sentences ranging from seven and a half years to life in prison for crimes including counterfeiting and weapons violations to conspiracy to commit a terrorist act. Four of those facing death were tried in absentia; they included Munir Moqda, a prominent Palestinian guerrilla leader based in Lebanon, and Khodor Abu Hoshar, who fought with Muslim guerrillas against the Soviet Union in Afghanistan in the 1980s. Abu Hoshar had been arrested several times since returning to Jordan in 1989. Moqda was hiding in Lebanon's Ain Helweh refugee camp. The chief prosecutor was Mahmoud Obeidat.

Meanwhile, on the same day that the Jordanians shared the terrorist training manual with U.S. intelligence, the press reported on it. The 1,000-page Arabic-language *Encyclopedia* manual discussed how to recruit followers, conduct terrorist operations, and assemble bombs.

On October 1, Raed Hijazi was arrested in Damascus, Syria, and extradited to Jordan, where he was to face trial in a military court in January 2001. Hijazi, a Jordanian of Palestinian origin who was also a U.S. citizen, was one of those sentenced to death in absentia on September 18 by the State Security Court for possession of arms and explosives and conspiracy to carry out attacks against the United States and Israel. He had the right to a retrial once apprehended. He confessed to planning the attacks on December 9, 2000, and to receiving bomb-making training in guerrilla camps in Afghanistan run by bin Laden. 99121301

December 14, 1999. *Pakistan.* In connection with the Jordanian arrest, Pakistan arrested a Palestinian at his home in Peshawar. Khalil Deek, who carried a U.S. passport, was extradited to Jordan two days later. 99121401

December 15, 1999. *United States.* Washington State Police arrested Ahmed Ressam, 32, an Algerian attempting to enter Port Angeles, Washington, when he arrived by ferry from Canada. In his rental car were two 22-ounce bottles of nitroglycerin, more than 100 pounds of urea, and homemade timers. The detonating device consisted of circuit boards linked to a Casio watch and a nine-volt battery, similar to ones used by bin Laden associates.

Ressam attempted to flee after being questioned and Customs Inspector Diana M. Dean asked him to step out of his Chrysler 300, the last car off the ferry. Inspector Carmon Clem removed the trunk floorboard and discovered suspicious packages. Customs agents found 118 pounds of a fine white powder used to manufacture explosives, 14 pounds of a sulfate, 2 jars of nitroglycerin, and 4 small, black boxes believed to be detonators. Senior Inspector Mark Johnson patted down Ressam, looking for weapons, and felt something in a jacket pocket. Ressam slipped out of his jacket and started running. He was caught six blocks away from the ferry port. He was carrying a false Canadian passport and driver's license under two different names.

Witnesses said they saw a possible accomplice walk off the Coho ferry as Ressam was being arrested.

On December 22, Ressam appeared before U.S. Magistrate David Wilson in a Seattle federal court and was charged with knowingly transporting explosives across the Canadian border, having false identification papers, and making false statements to U.S. Customs Service officials. He was represented by court-appointed attorney Tom Hillier, who pleaded not guilty for his client.

Ressam speaks French and Arabic. He had planned to stay at the Best Western hotel in Seattle, close to a variety of holiday events. He had a reservation on an American Airlines flight from Seattle to New York via Chicago and a ticket for a connecting British Airways flight to London. The Seattle hotel had a reservation made on December 14 for Benni Norris, the name on the fake passport. A van parked near his apartment was registered to Benni Antoine Norris. The individual who called a Best Western national 800 number left a credit card number and a contact telephone number in Quebec.

Ressam had been denied refugee status in Canada because of his links to the Algerian Armed Islamic Group (GIA). He had earlier been arrested in Canada and had served a brief sentence for stealing computers and car phones.

Ressam arrived in Canada on February 20, 1994, requesting refugee status. He claimed the Algerian police had arrested him in 1992 on charges of selling guns to the rebels. He said he was held in prison for 15 months and tortured until he signed a false confession. Upon release, he fled to Morocco, Spain, and France, before arriving in Canada. His French passport was for Tehar Medjadi, but he soon admitted that the document and his Catholic birth certificate were fakes. In 1995, he failed to show up for a hearing and was detained, but the court let him go free. On February 8, 1998, an arrest warrant was issued in the theft of a computer from a parked car, a charge for which he served two weeks in jail. Around that time, a deportation order was issued on the basis of three outstanding criminal arrest warrants, two involving thefts from cars and one for breaking and entering. In May 1998, a nationwide immigration arrest warrant was issued, but Canadian officials were unable to find him.

Ressam was held without bail pending his trial, scheduled for February 22. He could be sentenced to 40 years in prison if convicted of the five counts in the indictment, which did not contain conspiracy charges.

The Canadian *Globe and Mail* claimed that U.S. counterintelligence agents had alerted the Mounties about Ressam in Vancouver. The Mounties had had him under surveillance for three weeks at the 2400 Motel in Vancouver, British Columbia.

A spokesman for the Montreal police said Ressam lived for a time with Karim Said Atmani, who was extradited by Canada to France on charges that he participated in the 1995 Paris subway bombing that killed 4 and injured 86. Montreal police announced they had arrested 11 men, mostly Algerians, during the past four months for thefts during the previous two years that obtained 5,000 items, such as computers, cell phones, passports, and credit cards. Some of these men were believed to be aiding Islamic radicals.

French officials said Ressam was linked to Fateh Kamel, an Algerian veteran of the Afghan War with ties to the 1996 bombers in Paris. The bombers left one bystander and several Islamic radicals dead. French officials sent a team to Canada in October 1999 to interview Ressam and Atmani, but neither could be located.

On December 18, the U.S. Customs Service put all 301 ports of entry on high alert. U.S. authorities searched for an accomplice who was with Ressam for three weeks at the 2400 Motel in Vancouver. Ressam paid cash for the $325 per week suite of two rooms, kitchen, and bath. Mounties raided Ressam's apartment house at 1250 Fort Street in Montreal's East End. After breaking in through a window, the police found a .357 Magnum pistol and instructions for making bombs.

Police were searching for Ressam's three possible accomplices. Two might have been the man he shared a motel room with in Vancouver; the third might have been on the ferry.

On December 19, Montreal police found an orange 1989 General Motors van registered to Benni Norris, the alias on Ressam's passport. A bomb squad searched the van and a house.

Montreal police suggested that Ressam had ties with Mourad Gherabli, 40, an Algerian believed to be part of a ring of thieves who had stolen cell phones and computers and used them to finance Islamic terrorist groups around the world. Gherabli denied the charges, observing, "I like girls. I like cocaine. I have a big, big problem with the poker machines. So I steal. But I'm not a terrorist. I don't have enough money to send to anyone." Police believed the theft money moved from Canada to Algeria via France, Belgium, Italy, Kosovo, and Pakistan.

On December 20, U.S. Customs Commissioner Raymond W. Kelly presented Exceptional Service Medals to Inspector Diana M. Dean, Senior Inspector Mark Johnson, and Inspector Carmon D. Clem. A fourth inspector who helped in the arrest, Mike Chapman, was unable to attend.

Ressam reportedly had been seen in training camps used in the 1980s by Islamic militants fighting the Russians in Afghanistan. Ressam had told Canadian immigration officials that he had been wrongly accused in Algeria of being an Islamic radical.

Police were searching for a Ressam associate, Abdelmajed Dahoumane, 32, as of December 17. On December 25, the FBI interviewed Horizon Air ticket agents; one of them had sold a ticket to a man meeting his description. He had a French passport and paid in Canadian currency for a ticket from Bellingham, 90 miles north of Seattle, to Seattle, with a connecting flight to Las Vegas. Canadian police had issued an arrest warrant accusing him of illegally possessing explosives with the intent to cause damage or injury. He had stayed with Ressam in the Vancouver hotel room, which reeked of a rotten egg smell, consistent with the theory that they had been making nitroglycerin.

Ressam reportedly had received terrorist training in Afghanistan and Pakistan and had fought in Muslim military units in Bosnia against Croatian and Serbian militias. French sources said he was suspected of involvement in the 1996 bombing of the Paris subway that killed 4 and injured 91, as well as holdups near Lille.

On December 28, Seattle Mayor Paul Schell announced the cancellation of Seattle's millennium party at the Space Needle because of fears of a terrorist attack.

Authorities announced on December 29 that Ressam was not carrying nitroglycerin, but the more deadly cyclotrimethylene trinitramine (RDX), one of the world's most powerful explosives, often used by military services for demolitions. It can be combined with PETN to form Semtex, a plastic explosive.

Ressam's attorneys asked for a change of venue on January 22, 2000, claiming that media coverage had harmed his chances for a fair trial. They requested a move to San Francisco or Los Angeles. Assistant U.S. Attorney Harold Malkin opposed the change.

Ressam was arraigned on January 27, 2000, in federal court in Seattle on four new counts that superseded the original indictment. U.S. District Judge John Coughenour moved the trial date from February 28 to July 10. Ressam was represented by Public Defender Thomas Hillier.

In February 2000, prosecutors making a case against Ahmed Ressam said the Algerian might have burned himself while handling explosives in his apartment in Canada. Tests indicated that holes and burn marks in tennis shoes and pants seized from the apartment were made by substances used in the making of EGDN explosive, a nitroglycerin equivalent. Traces of EGDN and RDX plastic explosives were also found on the items. He had pleaded innocent to nine counts of a federal grand jury indictment. Federal officials moved for blood and saliva samples so that they could conduct DNA tests.

On March 3, 2000, Judge Coughenour ordered Ressam's trial to be moved to Los Angeles. Public Defender Hillier had argued that Ressam could not get a fair trial in Seattle because his arrest had led to the cancellation of the city's millennium celebration and the community still feared terrorist attacks. There was also concern about the security of the elderly courthouse.

On March 18, prosecutors were reportedly rewriting their indictment to add charges against Abdel Ghani Meskini, 31, of New York, who was believed to have aided Ressam's smuggling operation. Meskini pleaded not guilty in January 2000 to charges of providing and concealing support for

Ressam. Meskini was arrested in Brooklyn in December 1999. Ressam had Meskini's phone number in his pocket when he was arrested. Meskini testified on September 20, 2000, that he had voluntarily made incriminating statements to the FBI after being informed of his rights.

Meanwhile, alleged Algerian accomplice Mokhtar Haouari, 31, remained in Montreal as the United States sought his extradition for a trial in New York. Another hearing was scheduled for April 6. An indictment against Haouari and Meskini accused them of conspiring since October 1997 to support members and associates of a terrorist group. Haouari allegedly provided forged identity documents while Meskini went to Seattle to help Ressam. Haouari was extradited to the United States from Canada, where he had been held since January 10. On August 14, 2000, in a federal court in Manhattan, Haouari pleaded not guilty to charges of providing support to terrorists. The six-count indictment charged that Haouari and Meskini provided and concealed material support to terrorists, transferred fraudulent identification documents, and trafficked in and used fraudulent bank and charge cards.

Haouari was born in Arzew, Algeria, and arrived in Toronto in 1993. When entering Canada, he used a French passport with a different name and claimed refugee status, which was denied. He was convicted in Canada in 1997 of dealing in stolen and counterfeit credit cards. Authorities intercepted a December 25 phone call between Meskini and an individual in Algeria. Meskini claimed that he and Haouari knew Ressam, that Ressam was part of a well-organized group, and that Haouari was part of the same network. On October 26, 2000, a federal judge set an April 17, 2001, trial date for Haouari and Meskini.

On December 7, 2000, Ressam accomplice Abdelmajid Dahoumane, who was indicted in Seattle in January 2000 on charges of conspiracy to bring explosives into the United States, was arrested in Algeria. He apparently accompanied Ressam on the ferry to the United States, but eluded capture. In Algeria, he was detained for a few months for questioning about his role in massacres carried out by the Armed Islamic Group (GIA). The United States had offered $5 million for information leading to his arrest. Dahoumane received training in Afghan camps funded by bin Laden. He faced 25 years in prison if convicted of conspiracy "to destroy or damage structures" and of the one count of reckless disregard for the safety of human life in placing explosives aboard the Port Angeles ferry. Dahoumane was believed to have lived in Montreal for two years. Police raided his apartment, but found no explosives. Algerian authorities rearrested Dahoumane on March 27, 2001, when he returned from Afghanistan where he received training in the use of weapons and explosives.

In mid-January 2001, federal prosecutors alleged in court documents that Canadian police found a map with circles drawn around airports in Los Angeles, Long Beach, and Ontario, California, in Ressam's Montreal home. The filing noted that "it is quite possible a reasonable person would conclude that one or more of these airports may have been an ultimate target of this conspiracy." Ressam also had a French guidebook to California when arrested.

On March 7, 2001, Meskini pleaded guilty in a Manhattan court to charges that he aided the effort to smuggle explosives into the United States and agreed to testify against other suspects. He faced 105 years in prison, although prosecutors said they would seek a lighter sentence and consider putting him in a witness protection program.

Ressam's jury was seated on March 12, 2001, in Los Angeles. Opening arguments began the next day, with Assistant U.S. Attorney Steven Gonzalez saying it was the trial of a lone bomb courier, not of bin Laden's group. Federal Public Defender Jo Ann Oliver said her client was duped by Dahoumane and others. The government noted that Ressam, born in Algeria in 1967, was arrested and jailed for 15 months for arms trafficking with terrorists. He went to France and Canada on forged and altered passports, requesting refugee status (later denied) in Montreal, where he was charged with theft. In March 1998, after buying a round-trip ticket to Karachi, Pak-

istan, he attended a training camp for Islamic fundamentalists in Afghanistan. FBI specialist James Rettberg testified that Ressam's fingerprints were found on four timing devices found in the back of his car. Ressam's case went to a jury on April 5. He was convicted on April 6 and faced 130 years in prison; sentencing was scheduled for June in Seattle. The jury found him guilty on nine criminal counts, including terrorism and assorted charges involving transporting explosives, smuggling, and using false papers. Defense attorney Michael Filopovic said he would appeal. The same day, Ressam was convicted in absentia by a Paris court for belonging to a terrorist group of Islamic militants; he was sentenced to five years.

On May 20, 2001, the *Washington Post* ran a detailed interview with Meskini, who claimed to be unaware of Ressam's activities. He said he had only been told to meet someone named "Reda," whom Meskini now believed was Ressam.

On May 26, the *Seattle Times* reported that Ressam was cooperating in hopes of obtaining a lighter sentence. He offered to testify in the July trial of Mokhtar Haouari in New York. The *Washington Post* reported on May 30 that Ressam confessed that he intended to set off a huge bomb at the Los Angeles International Airport.

On July 3, Ressam told a federal jury in U.S. District Court in lower Manhattan (the court that was hearing Haouari's case) that his group planned to bomb Los Angeles International Airport on New Year's Eve 2000. He said he trained in weapons (explosives, rocket launchers, urban warfare, assassination, and sabotage against airports, power plants, and large corporations) in Afghanistan beginning in March 1998. He claimed to be following a *fatwah* to kill Americans. Although he had circled three targets on his map, he only planned the one bombing. He planned to leave at the airport a suitcase filled with explosives made from fertilizer and nitric acid. Ressam still faced 27 to 130 years in prison.

Ressam said on July 6 that he thought the bombings of the U.S. embassies in Kenya and Tanzania were "a good thing," but he was disappointed that they did not take place within the

United States. The next day, he testified that when he was training in Afghanistan, his instructors deemed the 1995 assassination attempt against Egyptian President Hosni Mubarak a failure and the 1983 bombing of the U.S. Marine Corps barracks in Lebanon a success. He said he was given $12,000 by the leader of the fundamentalist Islamic camp to set up a terrorist cell in Montreal. He used $7,000 on hotel rooms, plane tickets, chemicals, and bomb-making instruments before attempting to enter the United States. He said he was reluctant to name his fellow Montreal conspirators because "they knew where my family lived, where my relatives lived. They might go after them and hurt them."

On July 13, 2001, a federal jury of nine women and three men, after deliberating for two days, convicted Haouari of participating in the plot by supplying a fake Canadian driver's license and $3,000 to Ressam. He faced 50 years in prison for conspiracy to commit fraud and providing material support for a terrorist act. The jury rejected a count of "aiding and abetting" the plot because they were not convinced that he knew that Ressam was targeting Los Angeles International Airport. On November 5, 2001, his sentencing was postponed until December 17.

On July 15, 2001, Abu Doha, 37, an Algerian living in London, was arrested and charged by the U.S. Attorney's Office in New York with being the mastermind of the Los Angeles International Airport bomb plot. Extradition efforts were underway. He faced life in prison. On August 28, 2001, a Manhattan federal grand jury indicted Doha on eight counts, including conspiracy to commit terrorist acts and provide material support to terrorists, stemming from charges of serving as the link between Osama bin Laden and Ressam. He was charged with helping trainees from one camp in their attempt to bomb "an airport or other large facility" in the United States. In the trial of Haouari, Ressam had identified Doha as a participant. The indictment said Doha spoke to Ressam at the Khalden terrorist training camp in Afghanistan about a bombing in the United States. Doha offered Ressam "money or means of

travel to Algeria" after completion of such a bombing. The agreement was sealed in a November 8, 1999, phone conversation. Doha also trained and supported young terrorists by raising money and running a camp in Afghanistan "dedicated exclusively to training Algerian nationals in *jihad* operations."

On November 15, 2001, U.S. authorities served an extradition warrant on Samir Ait Mohamed, 32, an Algerian accused of helping Ressam. He had been in Canadian custody in Vancouver since July 28 for immigration violations. Charges against Mohamed had been sealed in October. A criminal complaint was made public on November 16, accusing him of trying to get two hand grenades and a machine gun with a suppressor so Ressam could raise money for a Los Angeles attack via bank robberies. Mohamed was also accused of working with Mokhtar Haouari to obtain "a credit card in an alias for Ressam's use in connection with his planned terrorist operation and *jihad* work." Court papers said Mohamed provided Ressam with a 9-mm semiautomatic pistol with a suppressor, knowing Ressam intended to conduct a terrorist attack in the United States. Ressam used the gun in an August 1999 holdup attempt at a Montreal currency exchange. Mohamed was charged with two counts of conspiracy to commit international terrorism. He faced a life sentence. On November 29, the FBI released a document in Canada that said Mohamed aimed to get "genuine" Canadian passports to permit a "team of terrorists" to enter the United States. Mohamed was to have obtained the passports from "an individual working inside" the passport agency. In 1999, Mohamed sent four passports to Germany. The recipients had all trained with Ressam at a camp in Afghanistan. Mohamed used a fake French passport in 1991 to move from Algeria to Germany, where he requested asylum. Mohammed was indicted on December 12, 2001 in New York on charges of getting weapons for Ressam. 99121501

December 18, 1999. *Sri Lanka.* A teen assassin set off explosives strapped to her body, slightly injuring the face and seriously injuring an eye of Sri

Lankan President Chandrika Bandaranaike Kumaratunga, 54, as she was about to get into her car at an election rally at Colombo's town hall. (Both of President Kumaratunga's parents served as prime ministers of Sri Lanka.)

The bomb went off as the president's guards dragged away the suicide bomber, whose actions killed 23 people, including a top police officer in charge of the president's security, and injured 110 others. The killer had dressed in a sari and had tried to embrace the president. (Some reports said the killer was a man dressed as a woman.)

Minutes later, another suicide bomber set off an explosive at an election rally of the opposition United National Party in Jaela, nine miles north of Colombo, killing 7 and injuring 40. Presidential rival Ranil Wickremesighe was not at the rally.

The separatist Tamil Tigers were suspected; 15 people were arrested. On January 3, 2000, the government publicly accused the Tamil rebels of the attack.

December 18, 1999. *Pakistan.* A bomb exploded in a marketplace, killing 10, injuring 17, and causing major damage.

December 19, 1999. *United States.* At 8:00 P.M., Vermont police arrested an Algerian with a fake French passport and a Canadian woman who was with him. Dogs found traces of possible explosives in their car. Bouabide Chamchi, 20, and Lucia Garofalo, 35, of Montreal, attempted to cross illegally into Beecher Falls, Vermont, during the night. Asked why they were making the trip, Garofalo said she was looking for a restaurant in East Hereford, Quebec, which is immediately across the border. Chamchi did not have the identification document required for an Algerian in the United States and carried a false French passport in the name of Boudjemaa Ben Ali in the jacket found in their car. He claimed he had never seen it before. Bomb-sniffing dogs—one certified to detect plastic explosives and one to detect black powder explosives—both alerted in the right-rear area of the car's quarter panel, as well as the portion of the trunk that adjoined the right-rear quar-

ter panel. Canadian criminal records indicated that there was an outstanding warrant for Chamchi for an assault charge on August 18 in Quebec. The duo faced sentences of five years in prison.

During the preceding two weeks, Garofalo had driven another Algerian passenger across the border and unsuccessfully tried to drive a Pakistani-born man across under suspicious circumstances. On December 6, she entered the United States at the Pittsburg, New Hampshire, port of entry. She was questioned over a video camera rather than in a face-to-face meeting. She drove a new Chrysler Neon and had two passengers whom she told U.S. inspectors were Canadians. Inspectors did not ask them for identification. On December 12, she crossed back into Canada at Stanstead, Quebec. Canadian customs officials identified her passengers as her son and Mustafa Roubici, an Algerian who had no identification. She said she had entered the United States with the duo on December 6, suggesting that she had lied about their Canadian citizenship. On December 15, she showed up at the Pittsburg, New Hampshire, port at 2:35 A.M. in the Neon. Her companion said he was Ahmed Saheen and claimed to be a Canadian born in Pakistan. A check of the trunk revealed a large amount of baggage. They were refused entry because Saheen lacked a visa. They were told to go to a port of entry with inspectors present; they apparently did not.

They were charged in U.S. District Court in Burlington on December 21 with conspiring to misuse a false French passport and various immigration offenses. She was charged with smuggling an alien into the United States.

On December 23, federal prosecutors claimed that she had connections to a militant Algerian Islamic group. She was carrying a cell phone registered to Brahim Mahdi, 34, an Algerian man believed to be connected to the Algerian Islamic League and driving a car co-registered in his name. The phone account had been opened on July 29 by Mahdi and transferred to her four days later. A phone number connected with Garofalo was called several times in January 1992 from a phone associated with a person under investigation for the theft and sale of dynamite stolen in Ontario.

The Neon was registered to Mahdi and Sabastiana Garofalo. Mahdi denied any connection to terrorism and said in Montreal that he had never heard of the Algerian Islamic League.

The organization was founded and directed by Mourad Dhina, an alleged Algerian international arms dealer who lived in Switzerland and was connected to groups sponsoring terrorist acts in Europe and Algeria. A nuclear engineer who trained at the Massachusetts Institute of Technology, Dhina said he founded the league as a cultural organization, but that it had ceased to exist five or six years before. He denied knowing the duo.

U.S. Magistrate Judge Jerome Niedermeier ordered Chamchi and Garofalo held without bail. The prosecutor was U.S. Attorney Charles R. Tetzlaff; Garofalo was represented by Maryanne Kampmann.

Garofalo's husband, Yasim Rachek, an Algerian, was deported from Canada in 1993 after attempting to enter the country illegally using a false French passport. He now lived in Italy. She was born in Canada, lived on welfare, and claimed to have $8 in her checking account. Prosecutors reported that "she travels all over the world and has taken vacations in Europe, Africa, and the Middle East. Garofalo claims that this travel and her other living expenses are paid for by a wealthy mother." She also had Libyan relatives.

Chamchi entered Canada as a stowaway on a ship in June 1997. He claimed to be employed full-time, but could not remember the name of his employing company.

On December 30, a federal magistrate in Vermont ruled that Garofalo should be held without bail after the Justice Department disclosed that she had close ties with the Algerian Armed Islamic Group (GIA). On January 6, 2000, a federal grand jury in Burlington, Vermont, indicted Garofalo and Chamchi. The two were charged with alien smuggling and misuse of a passport, but not with terrorist-related crimes. Judge Niedermeier agreed to reconsider his refusal to grant bail to Garofalo; Chamchi would remain in custody until his trial

on February 14, 2000. Garofalo was also indicted for having illegally driven three foreign nationals—Mustafa Roubici, John Doe (alias Ahmed Saeen), and Chamchi—into the United States between December 6 and 19.

On January 12, 2000, prosecutors noted that phone records demonstrated ties between Garofalo, Abdel Ghani, and Ahmed Ressam. Judge Niedermeier agreed to continue holding Garofalo without bail until her February 14 trial. She had made a cell phone call to a cell phone in Queens registered to Raja Aslam, a taxi driver from Pakistan whose cell phone was used to make 23 calls to Ghani's alias.

On February 15, 2000, Garofalo pleaded guilty to two immigration charges of attempting to transport an alien into the United States and conspiracy to transport aliens. Although she was linked to a group of Algerians suspected of planning bomb attacks in the United States, she was released from federal prison in Vermont after prosecutors determined that she knew nothing about any terrorist plot. She was turned over to U.S. immigration officials. Her attorney, Maryanne Kampmann, said she could return to Montreal—which she did—and come back to the United States for sentencing on May 8. She faced a maximum of ten years in jail, although her attorney expected that she would serve 6 to 12 months based upon her plea agreement. U.S. District Judge William Sessions approved her release without bail or bond. As of February 16, charges were still pending against Chamchi. On May 18, 2000, Garofalo was sentenced to the 58 days she had already served for immigration violations. The previous day, in a commencement speech at the Coast Guard Academy, President Clinton had said for the first time that bin Laden was behind the plots to attack the United States. 99121901

December 19, 1999. *Pakistan.* Authorities announced the arrest of 80 people who might be considering terrorist attacks against Americans. The arrests occurred in nighttime raids in northwestern Peshawar and in Islamabad. Most of the detainees were Afghans.

December 20, 1999. *Cambodia.* The U.S. Embassy suspended most of its operations and announced it would maintain a skeleton staff until after the Christmas holidays. A spokesman said, "We have credible evidence indicating there is a terrorist threat to U.S. diplomatic installations."

December 20, 1999. *Colombia.* The Revolutionary Armed Forces of Colombia (FARC) and the government agreed to a 22-day holiday cease-fire, the first truce in more than a decade. The truce began at midnight December 19 and was to end on January 10. It followed ten days of fighting, during which more than 230 guerrillas and soldiers were killed, including 9 soldiers and 3 rebels just hours before the truce began.

December 20, 1999. *United States.* Washington, D.C., police announced they had been searching for a blue 1989 Mitsubishi van that might contain explosives. Two Middle Eastern-looking men were reportedly in the truck, which was believed to have left the area. The duo had bought the van in northeast Washington and said they were not concerned about transferring the Texas plates since they would not need the van long. They had told an Exxon gas station attendant to stay away. Police remained on high alert.

On December 24, New York City police found a vehicle that might have been the van in question. It contained no explosives; the occupants were not arrested.

December 20, 1999. *Spain.* On November 8, 2001, Spanish National Police chief Juan Cotino said Basque Nation and Liberty (ETA) terrorists had planned to bomb the Picasso Tower, one of Madrid's tallest skyscrapers. In December 1999, police had found that two vans headed for Madrid were loaded with explosives. Two suspects in a November 6, 2001, bombing told police of the planned "Christmas massacre" at the 44-story glass-and-steel tower in which 5,000 people work. The tower was designed by World Trade Center architect Minoru Yamasaki. Police had stopped one van; questioning led them to a second, aban-

doned van in a hotel parking lot in northeastern Spain.

December 21, 1999. *Ecuador.* The U.S. Embassy in Quito was closed because of concern that it might be targeted by terrorists.

December 22, 1999. *India.* A Muslim separatist was believed to be responsible for throwing a grenade into a crowd in Anatnag, injuring a dozen people.

December 23, 1999. *United States.* The FBI warned that mail bombs might have been sent to the United States from Frankfurt, Germany.

December 23, 1999. *Colombia.* Popular Liberation Army rebels kidnapped an American in the Santander Mountain region. After deciding that the hostage had no ties to the U.S. government, they freed the victim unharmed on January 13, 2000. No ransom was paid. 99122301

December 23–27, 1999. *Japan.* Three small fires were set in trains and two homemade bombs went off at rail stations in Tokyo. The bombs apparently were packed in small Styrofoam balls with timing devices. Police believed the arson attacks were the responsibility of opponents of construction of a second runway at Narita Airport.

On December 24, a small bomb exploded in a bin at a train depot, after it had been swept up with the trash from the Shinkansen train. No injuries were reported.

On December 26, three fires broke out under seats on trains serving Narita Airport. No injuries were reported.

During the morning of December 27, a locker attendant at Urawa Station, north of Tokyo, found a bomb. The bomb exploded as he moved it, injuring two of his fingers.

December 24, 1999. *Algeria.* Islamic militants fired on vehicles at a roadblock, killing at least 28 people near Khemis Miliana, 50 miles west of Algiers.

December 24, 1999. *South Africa.* A bomb exploded outside a Cape Town Manos restaurant, killing two people and injuring seven police officers who were responding to a telephoned bomb threat. No one claimed credit, and the motive was unclear.

December 24, 1999. *Nepal.* Indian Airlines flight 814, an Airbus A300 carrying 189 passengers and 11 crew, was hijacked by 5 men armed with guns, knives, and hand grenades 35 minutes after its 4:55 P.M. takeoff from Katmandu, just as it entered Indian airspace en route to New Delhi. The hijackers claimed to have killed four people, although the pilot said he did not hear any gunfire. The terrorists wore turbans and were initially, and incorrectly, identified as Sikhs.

The hijackers were denied permission to land at Lahore, Pakistan, but touched down in Amritsar, India, for 40 minutes for refueling. Local authorities refused refueling. The pilot took off again. The plane returned to Lahore and made an emergency landing with one minute of fuel remaining. The Pakistani government provided food and fuel. The plane then was denied permission to land in Kabul, Afghanistan, due to lack of landing lights. Authorities in Muscat, Oman, also refused landing permission. It set down at Al Minhad Air Base, 18 miles southeast of Dubai, United Arab Emirates, where 25 hostages were released along with the body of a passenger who had been stabbed to death. He had disobeyed the hijackers' orders to keep his head between his legs and his eyes closed. Three ambulances, three police buses, and a coroner's van rushed to the remote desert base. One freed passenger said they were blindfolded by the hijackers, who warned, "Don't move, otherwise we will shoot you." Several of the passengers had been injured.

The plane then flew to Kandahar, Afghanistan, where it was permitted to land for refueling. The hijackers requested political asylum, but the Taliban refused and demanded that the UN handle negotiations. The hijackers demanded the release of a Pakistani-born Kashmiri militant, Maulana Masood Azhar (variant Masud Azhar), 45, who

had traveled to India in 1992 to help the militants. He was arrested in 1994 and was held in a high-security jail near Jammu in Kot Balwal. Terrorists had conducted three other attacks to attempt to obtain his release. In one, several Western tourists who were hiking were kidnapped. One was killed; the other three have never been found and are presumed dead. India noted that despite press accounts, Azhar was not a religious leader. The press said he was a Muslim cleric and ideologue of the Harkat ul-Ansar terrorist group, believed to have terrorist training camps in Afghanistan.

The hijackers also demanded the release of 35 other militants jailed in Kashmir. They threatened to kill the 161 passengers and crew if negotiations did not begin. Authorities believed one of the hijackers was Maulana's brother, Ibrahim Azhar. The Azhar brothers' father said that Ibrahim was in Saudi Arabia on a *hajj*. One freed passenger said the hijackers included three Kashmiris, one Afghan, and one Nepali.

The dead hostage was Rupin (variant Rippan) Katyal, 25, who was returning with his wife from their honeymoon. They were married on December 3.

Indian officials said the government would not give in to terrorism.

On December 27, Erick de Mul, UN coordinator for Afghanistan, flew from Pakistan to negotiate with the terrorists. He spoke with them by radio for more than an hour and obtained the release of a diabetic Indian passenger, Anil Khurana, whose brother remained on board. The terrorists refused to release the widow of the murdered passenger so that she could attend the funeral. Mohammed Khiber, a Taliban civil aviation authority, reported that the plane's air was "very bad . . . it smells like people have been sick." The terrorists kept the plane's window shades drawn and the engine running. The Taliban demanded that the UN handle negotiations, but the UN did not want to offend India and awaited an Indian request for mediation. Meanwhile, Pakistan and India traded accusations, each saying the other had set up the hijacking to make it look bad. India claimed the terrorists had arrived in Nepal on a flight from Pakistan and were permitted on the Indian plane without proper security checks.

The Taliban said the plane was leaking oil and could have other mechanical problems.

Russia called for a special session of the UN Security Council to discuss the hijacking.

On December 27, the hijackers suspended a deadline after India sent a 7-person negotiating team (some reports said 52 people were in the delegation) that made radio contact with the hijackers. However, the terrorists threatened to kill everyone on the plane if talks broke down. The Taliban said it would rush the plane if passengers were killed. Some reports indicated that the passengers had been forced to keep their eyes covered the entire time. Two doctors on board were given Red Cross supplies to treat fellow passengers for minor ailments and stress. Relatives of the hostages staged sit-ins and demonstrations to pressure the Indian government to obtain the release of their family members. Harkat ul-Mujahedeen militants in Kashmir attacked police facilities.

A fax sent to Pakistani media indicated that Osama bin Laden's group denied involvement, saying that India had staged the hijacking.

The passengers included 150 Indians, 8 Nepalese, 1 Canadian, 1 American woman, 4 Swiss, 4 Spaniards, 1 Belgian, 1 Japanese, 1 Australian, 2 French citizens, and 1 Italian. Four passengers were not listed by nationality. The Belgian was blindfolded and a gun was put in his mouth. The American was Jeanne Moore, 53, a special education teacher from Bakersfield, California, on a private trip to India. The hijackers demanded that the women wear veils.

On December 28, the hijackers upped the ante to a $200 million ransom and the release of 35 more Kashmiri prisoners. However, they also permitted the plane's doors to be opened, letting in fresh air for the first time. Toilets were cleaned, a chute was opened to allow supplies to be brought on board, and two Indian doctors and an engineer were allowed to board the aircraft. Several passengers were said to be cancer patients and diabetics. The engineer worked on repairing the plane's power supply. Afghan officials provided genera-

tors to restore light and climate control in the cabin. The terrorists, however, rejected government requests to release the women and children. They also demanded (but later dropped this demand) the return of the remains of a terrorist who died in a shootout during a prison break in 1999.

On December 30, Taliban officials said they were optimistic after three days of negotiations, but Indian authorities denied that they had agreed to free any of the detainees. The day before, the hijackers had dropped the ransom demand and the demand for the exhumation and return of the dead terrorist. Islamic leaders had claimed that the requests were "un-Islamic." The Taliban gave the hijackers until December 31 to resolve the impasse or leave Afghanistan. Negotiations were conducted by radio, walkie-talkie, and pieces of paper dropped from the plane. The hijackers permitted a cancer patient to leave the plane for medical treatment and then return. Passengers were now being permitted to move about the plane, play cards, and listen to music. Azhar said he did not want to be freed "at the cost of innocent lives."

On December 31, the hijackers freed the hostages in exchange for the release of three of the prisoners, who joined the hijackers. India released Maulana Masood Azhar; Omar Sheikh, a British citizen; and Mushtaq Zargat (also known as Mustaq Ahmad Zarzar), an Indian Kashmiri. Azhar was later identified as the second-ranking member of Harkat ul-Mujahedeen. Zargat was the commander of the militant pro-Pakistan al Umar Mujaheddin. He was arrested in 1991 and charged with murder and other crimes.

Initial press reports indicated that only four hijackers left the plane and that the body of the suspected fifth hijacker was found in the plane, possibly killed by his colleagues. The report was later contradicted by the Indian foreign minister. The group, still armed and wearing ski masks, surrendered to the Taliban, which gave them ten hours to get out of the country. One unarmed Taliban official accompanied them as a hostage to guarantee their safety. The group drove to various consulates in Kandahar to seek asylum. The hijackers were identified by India as Pakistani nationals. Afghanistan and Pakistan said they would not be granted asylum. Only Pakistan, Saudi Arabia, and the United Arab Emirates had diplomatic relations with the Taliban. The Taliban hostage returned unharmed, claiming not to know where the hijackers went. Indian and some Afghan officials later said the hijackers entered Pakistan near Quetta, a two-hour drive from Kandahar. The Taliban later denied making the statement.

Meanwhile, foreign diplomats escorted the freed hostages off the jet 15 minutes later. The hostages immediately boarded two aircraft and flew to New Delhi. They included pilot Devi Sharan, 37, and passengers Rajiv Ahuja, Rajinder Arora, Inder Taneja, R. K. Ghosh, and widow Rachan Ratyal (newlywed of the murdered Rupin Katyal). She did not know that he had died because the women were kept separate from the men. Despite the constant death threats, the hijackers had given hostage Pooja Kataria a shawl on her birthday. American Jeanne Moore was in a wheelchair and said she had pneumonia. On the fifth day, the terrorists had asked her to spell "coffin" for a note they were writing. She said that when the terrorists were not terrorizing, they were telling jokes, giving the passengers a megaphone to tell their own jokes, and encouraging people to pray with them. Sharan and some of the passengers said the hijackers appeared to have acquired more grenades and several rifles while in Kandahar, retrieving them from a cargo hold. Sharan doubted that the plane had been wired with explosives.

The hijackers and freed terrorists apparently escaped across the border into Pakistan, although Pakistan denied that they had arrived and said it would try them if they were found. However, Azhar spoke to 10,000 supporters in front of a central Karachi mosque on January 5, 2000, unimpeded by Pakistani authorities. He called for attacks on U.S. interests, saying, "I have come back, and I will not rest in peace until Kashmir is liberated. . . . This is my duty: to tell you that Muslims should not rest in peace until we have destroyed America and India." He claimed that

the hijackers were Indians who had returned to Kashmir. He claimed that the group traveled together for 25 minutes, driving toward Pakistan. At an isolated spot, they had left the vehicle for another and departed. They told him, "You don't know us. We have never met. We are from India and we respect you and admire you, but we cannot take off our masks. . . . We are returning to India, but we can't travel with you. We will get there another way." Pakistan had permitted him to enter because he did not face any charges there. Freed insurgent Zargat was greeted by Kashmiri militants when he arrived in Muzaffarabad, Kashmir, on January 3, 2000.

The Airbus flew back to New Delhi on January 1, 2000.

Indian Prime Minister Atal Bihari Vajpayee demanded that the international community deem Pakistan a state that supports terrorism and impose sanctions. Indian security adviser Brajesh Mishra said Indian intelligence had intercepted several radio conversations between militant groups in Kashmir that confirmed Pakistani involvement.

On January 6, 2000, India announced that on the fifth day of the hijacking it had arrested four Harkat ul-Mujahedeen accomplices of the hijackers in Bombay. India claimed that the four had provided support for the hijackers for two months before the attack. Two were Pakistanis, one was a Nepali, and one was an Indian. Abdul Latif, the Indian, was recruited by Pakistan's military intelligence service and had trained at guerrilla camps in Pakistan and Afghanistan, according to Home Minister L. K. Advani. Advani claimed that India had intercepted conversations between the hijackers and their Pakistani handlers via an accomplice in Pakistan. The accomplice in turn contacted Latif. Pakistan and the guerrilla group denied involvement. Advani said the foursome had photographs of the hijackers and that when the photos were shown to the freed hostages, they recognized the terrorists. However, the pilot said the hijackers had been masked the entire time and that he could not identify their faces. Advani identified the hijackers as Pakistanis: Ibrahim Athar (alias Chief) from Bahalwalpur; Shahid Akhtar Sayed (alias Doctor), Sunny Ahmed Qazi (alias Burger), and Mistri Zahoor Ibrahim (alias Bhola) from Karachi; and Shaqir (alias Shankar) from Sukkur. The Indians claimed the hijackers had taken three trips on November 1, December 1, and December 17 to Katmandu with their Bombay team to set up the hijacking, traveling by bus, train, and plane. India also noted that 33 of the 36 individuals whose release was demanded were Pakistani nationals.

On January 10, 2000, Bombay pathologist Anita Joshi, a hostage who treated fellow hostages, said she recognized the faces of the hijackers in photos distributed by the Indian government, which also published the hijackers' names and Pakistani home addresses. Joshi said the hijackers spoke in Hindi and Pashto and that they had planned the attack for two years. "They said they saw Hollywood movies and read books on hijacking. They were perfectly trained." The hijackers asked her to treat the two passengers they had stabbed when the plane landed at Amritsar.

On February 4, 2000, Farooq Kashmiri, head of Kashmiri operations of the Harkat ul-Mujahedeen, told reporters his group was not involved in the hijacking and that Islam forbids harming innocent civilians. The group told a reporter that Zahar had severed ties to them while in prison. Western officials were skeptical of the denial. The group had been named Harkat ul-Ansar, but changed the name after being banned by Pakistan.

Early in February 2000, the radical activism by Muslim cleric Maulana Masood Azhar, freed following the Indian Airlines hijacking, led the Pakistani military government to place him in protective custody. The Kashmiri activist had been given a hero's welcome upon his release, speaking at religious meetings throughout the country. He announced that he was forming a new Islamic army of 600,000 men. He called for a *jihad* against India and the United States. Pakistan, attempting to persuade the United States that it was getting tough on terrorists, had enough and urged Azhar to settle down in Punjab with his new bride, whom he married after the hijacking.

The three main Kashmiri rebel groups belonging to the United Jihad Council in Pakistan also condemned his calls for terrorism and a sectarian agenda.

On March 1, 2000, the United Kingdom announced that eight of the hijacked Afghans would be permitted to remain. Asylum appeals by another 32 passengers were rejected. Decisions regarding 37 others were postponed. Criminal charges were pending against 14 more. 99122401

December 24, 1999. *United States.* Bellevue, Washington, police arrested Abdel Hakim Tizegha, 29, and charged him with illegally entering the country and eluding federal officers at the Canadian border. He was scheduled to appear before a federal magistrate on January 5, 2000. Press reports linked him to Ressam and Ghani. Some observers believed he was involved in a splinter group of the Algerian Armed Islamic Group that broke with the GIA over a dispute regarding the targeting of fellow Muslims.

On March 16, 2000, Tizegha pleaded guilty to illegal re-entry and faced up to two years in prison and a $250,000 fine. On June 2, 2000, the *Seattle Times* reported that he would be handed over to immigration authorities for probable deportation. He was sentenced by U.S. District Judge Barbara Rothstein to the time he had served since his arrest.

December 24, 1999. *Zimbabwe.* Mohammed Yesudas, 28, from Durban, South Africa, threatened to blow up a vehicle near the U.S. Embassy in Harare. The Muslim cleric was arrested on January 1, 2000, and charged with threatening to commit acts of terrorism. Police said he went to the embassy and told a security guard he was a commando trained in Afghanistan and planned to set off explosives in a vehicle. 99122402

December 24, 1999. *Colombia.* A bomb exploded outside the Colombo-American Bi-National Center in Cali, causing minor injuries to several people and major damage to the building. The Colombian Patriotic Resistance claimed credit, but police suspected that the National Liberation Army (ELN) had taken part. 99122403

December 27, 1999. *United States.* Seven Jordanians were arrested at the Canadian border near the Blaine, Washington, checkpoint, 100 miles north of Seattle. Although the media initially reported they had terrorist connections, the U.S. Border Patrol soon determined that they were routine border jumpers. In 1998, the Border Patrol caught 2,500 people from 70 countries doing the same thing. The Royal Canadian Mounted Police initially reported that one of the men "had an affiliation with a known terrorist group" and had made "terroristic threats." The FBI clarified that one of the individuals had a criminal record in Philadelphia and that the term probably referred to assault or domestic violence. The FBI said, "We have no reason to believe at this time that these people have any ties to terrorist organizations."

December 27, 1999. *United States.* Jere Wayne Haney, 42, an American Airlines mechanic, was stopped at Dallas-Fort Worth International Airport for a traffic violation. Police found 67 airline serving-size liquor bottles in his car. Police searched his apartment in Grapevine, Texas, and found similar bottles, along with a 50-pound bag of ammonium nitrate (which can be used to form an explosive), a dozen weapons, including 4 assault-style rifles, 62 boxes of ammunition, and white supremacist and anti-government literature that including bomb-making manuals. On December 28, he was charged with possession of bomb-making material. He was released on $5,000 bail. He was removed from his position without pay. He had worked for American since 1991. The FBI was investigating whether he had ties to extremist groups.

December 29, 1999. *Jordan.* Authorities arrested Khalil Ziyad, whom the FBI said was a Florida-based procurement agent for Osama bin Laden. Ziyad obtained computers, satellite telephones, and covert surveillance equipment. Jordan did not publicly reveal the arrest and later released him.

However, *Time* magazine reported that he was cooperating with the FBI and providing information about bin Laden's U.S. operations.

December 30, 1999. *South Africa.* Police seized bomb-making materials and arrested the leader and two members of the vigilante People Against Gangsterism and Drugs (PAGAD) in dawn raids on ten Cape Town homes. During a bombing wave, 2 people were killed and 99 injured.

December 30, 1999. *Lebanon.* A suicide bomber blew up a van near an Israeli Army convoy in southern Lebanon, killing himself and wounding an Israeli soldier and a dozen Lebanese civilians.

Meanwhile, Israel released seven Palestinian security prisoners who lived in East Jerusalem.

December 30, 1999. *United States.* Police in New York and Boston arrested individuals and questioned dozens of others nationwide—including in Washington State, California, New York, Texas, and Massachusetts—in connection with a suspected Algerian Armed Islamic Group (GIA) plan for New Year's Eve terrorist attacks. They noted that the Vermont and Seattle detainees were linked to the GIA. The group had a plan that involved faked passports, aliases, safe houses, and leaving a rented car filled with explosives at a drop-off point in Seattle, where another member of the terrorist group would pick up the vehicle. The FBI said it had not identified any specific U.S. city as the site of the planned attacks.

A joint counterterrorist task force arrested Abdel Ghani Meskini at his Brooklyn apartment. His name and the apartment's phone number were on a scrap of paper found on Ahmed Ressam. Prosecutors said Ghani traveled from New York to Seattle under the alias of Eduardo Rocha and intended to meet up with Ressam. The duo planned to go on to Chicago. Ghani admitted spending time in Afghanistan. A U.S. magistrate ordered him held without bail. He had been under surveillance since his trip to Seattle. Ghani had told a confidential informant that the plot entailed each person involved knowing the tasks of only two others, thereby protecting the group from leaks. Upon returning to New York, he destroyed his plane ticket and a bank statement linking him to Seattle. Ten days before his arrest, FBI agents watched him throw several documents in a trashcan near a Brooklyn supermarket not far from his apartment. FBI agents found a Delta Airlines ticket receipt and itinerary from New York to Seattle, as well as ATM receipts from Seattle. A surveillance camera at a Seattle ATM matched an FBI surveillance photo of Ghani. He appeared before a federal magistrate in New York on December 31. Assistant U.S. Attorney David Kelley called him an illegal alien. Ghani was represented by court-appointed attorney Roland Thau, who asked that the charges be dismissed because the crimes did not occur in the southern district of New York, which comes under the authority of the Manhattan federal court and prosecutors. He did not enter a plea, and bail was postponed. U.S. magistrate Ronald Ellis ruled that the charges could proceed.

Police in Boston arrested five men ranging in age from 26 to 35. They had been sought for questioning as part of an ongoing FBI terrorism investigation and were later arrested on immigration violations.

Rachid Haouari, who was initially detained with Ghani, was arrested on January 12, 2000, on immigration charges.

On January 17, 2000, the Justice Department indicted Abdel Ghani Meskini, 31, and Mokhtar Haouari in U.S. District Court in New York on six counts of conspiracy to provide "material support" to Ressam. They were accused of concealing their support, using false credit and bank cards, and conspiring with others to deal in and use stolen and false identification documents. Since 1997, Haouari had provided members of terrorist groups with false and forged identity documents. Ghani had telephoned Haouari in Montreal. Haouari asked Ghani to travel to Seattle to help Ressam. Ghani did so, using the alias Eduardo Rocha. He used a fake bank card under that name to withdraw money from ATMs in New York and Seattle. Haouari, 31, had been arrested in Mon-

treal on January 10, 2000, by Canadian authorities. He was held in Montreal under a warrant seeking his extradition to the United States. Canadian immigration documents showed Haouari entering Canada in August 1993 on a false passport and seeking refugee status. He claimed his life was in danger from Islamic militants and Algeria's government. Canada turned him down a year later. Quebec Superior Court Judge Jean-Guy Boilard denied Haouari's request for bail.

The *Washington Post* reported on January 20, 2000, that Meskini was cooperating with the authorities in their investigation. He pleaded not guilty to charges in a New York court that he was part of the bomb smuggling efforts.

December 30, 1999. *United States.* A large tower holding a line carrying electricity from Oregon to California was sabotaged and knocked over during the night. Electricity was quickly rerouted; no customers lost power.

December 31, 1999. *France.* In an overnight raid in Pau, police discovered 2,200 pounds of explosives belonging to suspected Basque terrorists. The material contained sodium chlorate and was hidden in a garage near the police station. The Basque Nation and Liberty (ETA) had recently announced the end to its 14-month cease-fire. 99113101

December 31, 1999. *Tajikistan.* At 11:00 P.M., security guards discovered and defused a bomb in central Dushanbe shortly before the beginning of New Year's celebrations. The 17-pound TNT bomb was hidden in trees alongside City Hall, 55 yards from the main square where the party was attended by the prime minister and several cabinet members.

December 31, 1999. *Lebanon.* Militant Sunni Muslims ambushed a Lebanese Army patrol during the night at Dinniyah, opening fire on its vehicles. Four soldiers were killed and another three wounded. The attackers kidnapped a lieutenant colonel and a soldier after the officer reported in to his command and asked for reinforcements.

December 31, 1999. *Colombia.* Three individuals kidnapped a Spanish engineer who worked for a Venezuelan firm from his Santa Ana residence in Barrancabermeja. No one claimed credit, but the attack fit the modus operandi of the National Liberation Army (ELN). 99123102

December 31, 1999. *Worldwide.* On January 6, 2000, U.S. National Security Adviser Sandy Berger announced that authorities in eight countries had arrested suspected terrorists in cooperation with the United States. The FBI announced that it had thwarted 20 threats against power plants and computer networks at the end of the year. A dozen physical incidents involved threats to blow up equipment; six were cyber intrusions. 99123102-09

1999. *Colombia.* Marxist rebels blew up the Cano Limon oil field's 480-mile pipeline at least 77 times during the year. The field, located in northeast Arauca Province, is operated by U.S. multinational Occidental Petroleum Corporation. The pipeline has a capacity of 230,000 barrels per day. It runs to the Caribbean coast oil terminal at Covenas, which was sabotaged on December 26, 1999. Marxist rebels started the year 2000 with another bombing of the pipeline, 40 miles from the oil field. 99999901-77

January 2000. *Niger.* A suspected threat from Algerian terrorists forced organizers to cancel the Niger stage of the Paris–Dakar Road Rally. Race officials bypassed Niger and air-lifted competitors to Libya after receiving information that Islamic extremists based in Niger were planning a terrorist attack. No terrorist attacks occurred on the 11,000-kilometer race through Senegal, Burkina Faso, Mali, Libya, and Egypt. 00019901

January 2000. *France.* A French court sentenced Javier Arizkuren Ruiz (alias Kantauri), a former

Basque Nation and Liberty (ETA) military operations chief, to eight years in prison. In September, a Paris appeals court authorized his extradition to Spain to stand trial for attempting to kill King Juan Carlos in 1995.

January 1, 2000. *Sri Lanka.* Tamil guerrillas attacked a strategic army base in the north. At least 63 people died in the clash, including 50 rebels and 13 soldiers. Another 51 soldiers were wounded in Iyakachchi near the Elephant Pass Base, 175 miles north of Colombo.

January 3, 2000. *Lebanon.* Ahmad Raja Abu Kharub, 30, a Palestinian resident of the country's largest Palestinian refugee camp, fired four rocket-propelled grenades in Beirut. No Russians were hurt, but a Lebanese policeman died in a follow-up firefight. Another seven people were injured. Kharub was shot to death in the hour-long gun battle. He carried a note in his pocket saying that he wanted to be a "martyr for Chechnya." Authorities believed the attack was in retaliation for Russian advances against the Chechen capital of Grozny. Security forces found grenade launchers, ammunition, and a Kalashnikov rifle beside his body. (The State Department's *Patterns of International Terrorism 2000* reported that in January "Asbat al-Ansar launched a grenade attack against the Russian Embassy." This could be referring to the same attack.) 00010301

January 3, 2000. *Namibia.* During the evening, gunmen wearing uniforms fired on a minibus, a rental car carrying a family of French tourists, and two vehicles carrying workers for the Danish aid organization Development Aid from People to People. Three children from one family were killed and their father seriously injured in a remote Rundu–Angola border area. The children were two girls aged 10 and 15 and their 18-year-old brother. The attackers also injured a Scottish citizen and a Namibian, both of whom worked for the aid organization. The attack was one of three that authorities blamed on the National Union for the Total Independence of Angola (UNITA), whose members were looking for money and food. (The other attacks were vehicular attacks that injured two French citizens and two Danish citizens.) UNITA denied the charges, and blamed the Angolan government. The attackers' tracks led from the Caprivi Strip into Angola. 00010302

January 3, 2000. *United States.* Police received 200 pounds of explosives stolen the previous week from a California bomb-squad bunker. They arrested five suspects who were in their late teens and had no apparent links to anti-government organizations.

January 3, 2000. *United States.* The New Woman All Women Health Care Clinic in Birmingham, Alabama, received a fax threat indicating that an anthrax-laced letter had been delivered that day. The list of possible sites included Planned Parenthood clinics in Providence, Rhode Island; Manchester, Connecticut; and Naples, Florida; and a government unemployment office in Immokalee, Florida. Other clinics and offices around the country received similar threats. The Birmingham letter was not contaminated with anthrax; the press did not indicate whether the other letters were contaminated. In January 1998, an off-duty police officer was killed and a nurse severely injured when a bomb went off at the clinic. Eric Robert Rudolph was charged with the bombing, but remained at large.

January 3, 2000. *Worldwide.* Arrested members of Osama bin Laden's al-Qaeda organization told Jordanian authorities that they planned to flatten the Radisson SAS Hotel in Amman "like a pancake" in a coordinated explosives attack on January 3. The members had been arrested in December. They also wanted to attack U.S. tourists at Mount Nebo and at a site on the Jordan River that Christians associate with John the Baptist. Other terrorists affiliated with individuals attempting to enter the United States in mid-December would conduct attacks in the United States. Still others

would bomb the USS *The Sullivans* during a refueling stop in Yemen.

January 4, 2000. *Colombia.* One hundred peasant refugees used sticks to break into the International Committee of the Red Cross (ICRC) headquarters in Bogota, taking 40 officials hostage. They demanded that the government and ICRC find them new homes and grant them health care and education. They had left their homes during the government's war with local rebel groups. The ICRC suspended operations in the country. 00010401

January 4, 2000. *Sri Lanka.* A woman with a bomb strapped to her body set the explosives off near the office of Sri Lankan Prime Minister Sirimavo Bandaranaike, 82, in residential Colombo, killing 12 people and herself. Some 4,500 police arrested more than 700 rebel Tamil Tigers, including the bomber's parents and sister. The government announced that she was a member of the Tamil Tigers' Black Tigers faction. Their women commandos are known as Birds of Freedom. By January 7, at least 1,500 Tamil Tigers had been detained.

Two hours after the bombing, gunmen on motorcycles in a nearby Tamil Tigers neighborhood shot in the head and killed pro-Tamil Tigers politician Kumar Ponnambalam as he drove his car.

January 8, 2000. *Sudan.* Sudan People's Liberation Army (SPLA) rebels attacked a CARE vehicle in Al Wahdah State, killing the CARE office director and his driver and abducting two others, according to the Humanitarian Aid Commission. The SPLA denied responsibility. 00010801

January 9, 2000. *Namibia.* Five suspected National Union for the Total Independence of Angola (UNITA) rebels entered a private residence in western Kavango and killed two Namibians and injured another. No one claimed credit. 00010901

January 10, 2000. *Canada.* Montreal police arrested Mokhtar Haouari, 31, an Algerian, in connection with a New Year's bomb plot. He was tied to Ahmed Ressam, who was arrested in December 1999 and charged with trying to smuggle explosives into the United States from Canada. On April 6, a Canadian judge approved a delay in Haouari's extradition hearing. U.S. authorities suspected him of sending Abdel Ghani Meskini to Seattle, Washington, to help Ressam. Meskini was arrested on December 25, 1999, in the United States. Haouari's lawyer, Joseph Elfassy, denied that Haouari was involved. He said Haouari came to Canada in 1993 with a fake French passport and requested political asylum. He claimed he faced persecution because of his previous association with the Islamic Salvation Front. The request was rejected, but he was permitted to stay in the country temporarily when Canada postponed the expulsion of all Algerians.

January 13, 2000. *Austria.* Financial police in Vienna arrested Nimer Halima, a key associate of Abu Nidal. Abu Nidal reportedly had moved to Egypt from Libya in 1999.

January 13, 2000. *Colombia.* Hugo Carvajal, chief of the Maoist People's Liberation Army (EPL), died from injuries suffered during a gun battle with authorities on New Year's Eve. The group operates in northern Santander Province.

January 14, 2000. *Namibia.* Military officials claimed that National Union for the Total Independence of Angola (UNITA) gunmen attacked a private vehicle near Divundu, killing four and injuring five. 00011401

January 17, 2000. *Pakistan.* A bomb exploded in Karachi, killing 6 and injuring 17. No one claimed credit, but authorities blamed India.

January 17, 2000. *Israel.* A bomb sprayed shrapnel onto elderly people sitting on a Hadera park bench and shoppers on the sidewalk of Rothschild Street, injuring 22. Palestinian rejectionists were suspected.

January 17, 2000. *Yemen.* Yemeni tribesmen kidnapped, released, then re-abducted a French couple after authorities tried to arrest the kidnappers. The French husband and wife and their two Yemeni guides were abducted by members of the al-Shamian tribe, who demanded an increase in government schools and development projects. The two were freed on January 18, but recaptured on the same day. The army tightened its siege around the groups' hideout. The hostages were finally freed unharmed on January 19. 00011701

January 18, 2000. *Angola.* National Union for the Total Independence of Angola (UNITA) defectors told the UN that Jonas Savimbi had ordered a rebel named Gregorio to shoot down two UN planes on December 26, 1998, and January 2, 1999, killing 23 passengers and crew members.

January 21, 2000. *Spain.* Two remotely detonated car bombs exploded in a neighborhood in Madrid, killing army Colonel Pedro Antonio Blanco Garcia, 47, who worked in the economic section of army headquarters in Madrid. One bomb exploded at 8:00 A.M. outside an apartment building in a military family neighborhood. Thirty minutes later, a second car exploded 400 yards away. Basque Nation and Liberty (ETA) was blamed. By afternoon, 3,000 people had arrived to demonstrate against ETA, which had held to a cease-fire since it killed a government party official on June 25, 1998.

January 21, 2000. *Canada.* Police said they were searching in Canada, Ireland, and the United States for Algerian-born Hamid Aich, 34, who shared an apartment in a Vancouver suburb with Abdelmajed Dahoumane, one of the suspects in the millennium bomb plot by Algerian Islamic extremists.

January 21, 2000. *Japan.* Cult followers were suspected of kidnapping the seven-year-old son of

Aum Shin Rikyo leader Shoko Asahara, who was behind the March 1995 sarin gas attack on the Tokyo subways. The kidnappers were believed to have kidnapped Asahara's daughter as well. The media said Aum Shin Rikyo was experiencing infighting. The cult had formally dropped Asahara as its guru three days earlier, apologized to the victims, and changed its name to Aleph. The child and an older member of the cult were found on January 23 staying under false names in a boarding house in the resort town of Hakone, 54 miles southwest of Tokyo.

January 21, 2000. *Namibia.* The local press reported that the National Union for the Total Independence of Angola (UNITA) entered a private residence near Mayara and opened fire, killing three and injuring six. 00012101

January 24, 2000. *Thailand.* On the eve of Thai Army Day, Karen rebels belonging to a Christian breakaway faction called God's Army—led by twin brothers Johnny and Luther Htoo, 12 (that is correct, 12!)—took over a sprawling provincial hospital in Ratchaburi, 75 miles west of Bangkok, and demanded that the hospital treat their wounded. The rebels had infiltrated the facility dressed as medical personnel, then relayed intelligence to the larger strike force. They initially herded all of the doctors and nurses into the emergency room, but later permitted them to attend to patients.

The rebels, wearing face masks and armed with automatic weapons and grenades, held the patients and staff hostage. The rebels demanded that Thailand send medical teams to treat their wounded comrades at their mountain base in Burma. They also wanted refuge on Thai territory. They called for an end to Thai involvement in their insurgency on the Burmese border, including an end to Thai shelling of the border in support of the Burmese military. They placed explosives around the hospital and threatened to blow it up along with the 750 hostages. They released 50 hostages in exchange for food. Thai Interior Minister Sanan Kachornprasart directed the negotiations from Bangkok.

A Thai television cameraman was permitted inside the building.

After a 22-hour standoff, hundreds of Thai commandos launched a predawn raid, killing nine rebels. Several Thai soldiers and police officers were injured. One of the Burmese rebels escaped and was pursued. None of the patients, staff, or visitors was injured. Eight Thai soldiers were injured. At least four patients died from illnesses that went untreated during the siege.

Hostage Decha Yoowong, 32, said, "We were all prepared to die" after the terrorists pulled out hand grenades and reached for the pins during the raid. "They were about to remove the safety pins soon after the commandos broke through the hospital gates. But we persuaded them not to do so."

The group had apparently crossed the border and hijacked a bus, forcing the driver to go 45 miles to Ratchaburi.

The boys' 200 followers believe the twins have mystical powers. The group broke with the Karen National Union, which has fought the Burmese government for 50 years. The group might have ties with the Vigorous Burmese Student Warriors, who had taken over the Burmese Embassy in Bangkok in October, were freed during negotiations, and then disappeared into the jungle.

Thai Army commander General Surayud Chulanond said the Thais would stop shelling the border and would admit unarmed rebels for medical treatment in Thailand.

Thai newspapers later reported that the security forces had killed all ten kidnappers, some execution-style, inside the hospital.

The hospital reopened on January 25.

The twin brothers were reportedly on the run through the jungle after their hideout was overrun by Burmese forces on January 27. The 100 God's Army rebels split into three separate bands headed by the Htoos and adult rebel Su Bia. Other Karen rebels joined in the battle.

On January 31, David Tharckabaw of the Karen National Union said his group would take in God's Army if "they agree to follow our leadership and promise not to do any more foolish acts."

On January 17, 2001, the Thai government

said it would consider giving asylum to the twins, who had surrendered the day before with five boys, two girls, a middle-aged woman, and four young men. Another trio surrendered on January 17. Prime Minister Chuan Leekpai met with the twins at the Suan Phung border patrol police headquarters. The boys admitted they had no mystical powers and said they wanted to give up fighting.

On November 19, 2001, the U.S. Embassy in Bangkok announced that the U.S. Immigration and Naturalization Service was sending a team to interview the duo about possible resettlement for the twins in the United States. 00012401

January 25, 2000. *Yemen.* Kenneth White, an American working for the Dallas-based Halliburton Oil Company, was kidnapped by Fehaid tribesmen in eastern Marib Province and taken to a mountainous area. Police and army troops used helicopters to search for him. He was released unharmed on February 10.
00012501

January 25, 2000. *Angola.* The National Union for the Total Independence of Angola (UNITA) ambushed a vehicle near Soyo, killing a Portuguese national. No one claimed credit.
00012502

January 26, 2000. *Senegal/Mauritania.* After leaving Senegal, Mauritanian citizen Mohambedou Ould Slahi was arrested by the Bureau of Mauritanian Security on suspicion of involvement in the Algerian terrorist bomb plot against the United States. He was reported to be a brother-in-law of Khaled Shanquiti (alias "The Mauritanian"), a lieutenant of Osama bin Laden. Shanquiti was involved in the bombing of the U.S. embassies in Kenya and Tanzania. Slahi had been living in Canada, but left when the Canadians began to investigate him. He was often seen at the Assunna Mosque in Montreal. Slahi had been detained for a few hours at the Dakar, Senegal, airport after arriving from Paris. His name was on an Interpol international watch list. After being questioned,

he was permitted to travel to Nouakchott, Mauritania. Senegal appeared unwilling to hold him without specific charges. Slahi had been in constant communication with a construction company in Khartoum, Sudan, that was owned by bin Laden and that was used as a front for al-Qaeda, bin Laden's group. Slahi worked closely with Mokhtar Haouari, an Algerian charged with involvement in the logistics of the plot. The United States was preparing an extradition request. Authorities were not sure whether he was the mastermind or a messenger in the plot.

On February 1, Mauritania announced it had arrested four Islamic militants suspected of having links to bin Laden. The arrests were part of the inquiry into Slahi's activities. The government did not say who was arrested or when. In early 1999, Mauritanian officials had arrested more than a dozen Muslims for alleged ties to bin Laden, but released them all without charge. Mauritania released the foursome on February 9.

Mauritania freed Slahi on February 20. FBI agents had been permitted to submit questions during his incarceration and interrogation. He did not admit to a role in the bomb plot.

January 27, 2000. *United States.* Immigration and Naturalization Service and Customs Service agents arrested Youssef Karroum, 35, a Moroccan-born Canadian citizen who crossed the Canadian border at Blaine, Washington, near Seattle. Authorities were suspicious about his documentation; he had also been red-flagged by the FBI as a possible associate of Ahmed Ressam, who had been arrested in December while trying to cross into Washington State with bomb-making materials. Bomb-sniffing dogs Leon and Hilda reacted to traces of what might have been nitroglycerin. No bomb was found. Karroum said he was an unemployed electrician. His attorney, Gene Grantham, said he was not held as a suspect in the Algerian terrorist bombing conspiracy case. A U.S. magistrate ordered him held as a material witness the next day. A court appearance was set for February 1. His attorney said on February 3 that he had been cleared of any link to the case.

January 27, 2000. *Spain.* A Citroen car dealership in Iturreta was torched, causing extensive damage to the building and destroying 12 vehicles. The attack had the modus operandi of the Basque Nation and Liberty (ETA). 00012701

January 28, 2000. *Yemen.* Unnamed tribesmen kidnapped another American citizen. 00012801

January 28, 2000. *Pakistan.* A bomb exploded in a mosque in Karachi, killing 4 worshipers and injuring 28. The explosion occurred minutes after a bomb hidden in a motorcycle exploded outside a court building elsewhere in the city, injuring another four. Pakistan blamed Indian intelligence. No one claimed credit.

January 29, 2000. *Colombia.* The Revolutionary Armed Forces of Colombia (FARC) and the National Liberation Army (ELN) were suspected of bombing a section of the Cano–Limon pipeline in Arauquita, causing major damage and suspending oil production for three days. 00012901

February 2000. *Belgium.* Authorities paroled two members of the Cellules Communistes Combattantes after they had served 14 years of their life sentences for involvement in a series of bomb attacks against U.S., NATO, and Belgian interests in 1984 and 1985. One attack killed two firefighters in Brussels.

February 2000. *Paraguay.* Authorities arrested naturalized Paraguayan citizen Ali Khalik Mehri, a Lebanese businessman living in Ciudad del Este. He had financial links to Hizballah and was charged with violating intellectual property rights laws and aiding a criminal enterprise involved in distributing CDs espousing Hizballah's extremist ideals. He also was charged with selling millions of dollars of counterfeit software and sending the proceeds to Hizballah. In a search of his home, police found videos and CDs of suicide bombers calling for others to follow them. He fled the country in June after faulty judicial procedures allowed his release. He was believed to be an al-

Qaeda financier and was a large campaign contributor to members of the ruling Colorado Party.

February 2, 2000. *Yugoslavia.* Gunmen fired an antitank missile at a refugee convoy escorted by KFOR soldiers in Mitrovica, killing two Serbians and injuring five others. No one claimed credit. 00020201

February 3, 2000. *Colombia.* The National Liberation Army (ELN) and Revolutionary Armed Forces of Colombia (FARC) were suspected of bombing the Cano–Limon pipeline, causing major damage, including an oil spill, and again halting production for three days. 00020301

February 6, 2000. *Afghanistan.* An Afghan Ariana Airlines Boeing 727 domestic flight carrying 151 people, including 12 children and 15 crew members (other reports said 179 people), was hijacked 20 minutes after leaving Kabul. The hijackers diverted it to Tashkent, Uzbekistan; Aktyubinsk, Kazakhstan; Moscow, Russia; and finally to London. The plane took off at 12:29 A.M. EST. It arrived at Tashkent at 1:47 A.M., where ten passengers (five women, four men, and one child) were released, the plane was refueled, and hot meals were provided. The plane was permitted to take off when the hijackers threatened to set off explosives. The plane landed again at 7:40 A.M. in Kazakhstan for another refueling and repair to its leaky right fuel tank. More food was brought on board in exchange for a passenger with a heart condition and two close relatives. Negotiations were conducted in English. The pilots were given the choice of flying to Moscow, St. Petersburg, or Kiev, Ukraine. They flew on to Moscow, landing at 1:41 P.M. for another refueling and the release of nine passengers. During the four-hour stopover, food was provided and the toilets were cleaned. The plane finally reached London's Stansted Airport at 9:00 P.M., where it was surrounded by police, military, and safety vehicles. Police established radio contact with the hijackers.

Afghanistan's ruling Taliban claimed that seven or eight Afghan men armed with pistols, rifles, and grenades had taken over the plane as it was winging toward Mazar-e Sharif. Initial reports indicated that the hijackers wanted the release of Ismail Khan, a former Afghan regional governor and now a jailed opposition leader. This report was denied by Taliban Civil Aviation Minister Akhtar Mohammad Mansoor. He urged the British to storm the plane. Another Taliban official in Pakistan said that the hijackers were led by Gul Agha, who was allied with a group seeking the restoration of Afghan King Mohammad Zahir Shah, who had been deposed 30 years earlier. Hamid Gilani, deputy leader of the National Islamic Front of Afghanistan, denied the claim and condemned the hijacking.

On February 7, eight passengers were freed and said they had been treated well.

The four flight crewmen escaped down a rope ladder on February 8, leaving no one on board who could fly the plane. The escapees included the captain, 54, second captain, 50, first officer, 43, and a flight engineer, 54. Another man in his 40s who suffered from asthma was released. A UN High Commissioner for Refugees official arrived at the airport to assist in negotiations.

On February 9, the Taliban claimed that a wedding party of 30 to 40 people on the plane was in cahoots with the hijackers. Several female workers at the Kabul and Mazar airports were arrested by the Taliban, who claimed they had allowed female passengers to smuggle pistols and grenades onto the plane. A male flight attendant released in Tashkent had suggested that the group was involved in an asylum attempt. At least four of the released hostages requested political asylum.

Another 85 hostages, including all of the children, were released at 3:00 A.M. on February 10 following the first face-to-face talks with two of the hijackers in a police car near the parked plane.

Immigration officials in London said the hijackers were seeking assurances that they would not be returned to Afghanistan if they surrendered. Red Cross officials brought in games, books, and soft toys for the hostage children.

The hijackers surrendered on February 10 after 75 hours of negotiations. They never made any

political demands. British officials suspected it was a plot for mass asylum. Police arrested 21 people who were on the plane; there were believed to be only 8 to 10 hijackers. About 90 percent of the hostages expressed interest in staying in London; more than half of the passengers, plus the entire cockpit crew, filed formal petitions for asylum within hours. Tickets for the flight had cost only $20. Many passengers carried more luggage than would be normal for a short domestic trip.

The United Kingdom has a backlog of more than 100,000 asylum applications. Those arriving with no visas often claim asylum and experience a five-year wait for a ruling. Many, including six Iraqis who were convicted of hijacking a Sudanese plane with 197 passengers to the United Kingdom in 1996, receive regular welfare payments. (The Iraqis were jailed, but released by an appellate court. Two of their relatives were granted asylum; the hijackers' asylum request remained open.) Under British law, asylum seekers are entitled to a lawyer, a court hearing, and an appeal if the application is denied. Meanwhile, the United Kingdom sought a country that might be willing to take some of the passengers; Pakistan was offered as a possibility.

The Afghan plane was licensed for domestic trips and was not certified for international travel. British officials were considering hiring a plane from Cambodia to take some of the passengers home. Cambodia had travel agreements with the Taliban.

On February 13, a chartered aircraft carried 73 of the passengers to Kandahar. They were met by representatives of the International Organization for Migration, who escorted them to their home villages. The United Kingdom was still considering 69 asylum requests and was drafting a plan to send some to the United States, India, Pakistan, and other countries with Afghan exile communities.

Nineteen men were arrested in connection with the hijacking and were due to appear in court on February 14. Police said they would face charges of hijacking or air piracy—which carries a life prison sentence—and possession of firearms.

Another man was charged on February 16. The British government announced that the hijacking and its aftermath had so far cost $5.8 million.

In January 2001, nine defendants were tried, but a jury could not agree on a verdict.

On December 5, 2001, a London court convicted nine Afghan men of hijacking, false imprisonment of passengers and crew, possessing grenades, and possessing firearms. A tenth man was acquitted. Sentencing was scheduled for January 18, 2002. The maximum sentence was life in prison, with possibility of parole. The defendants were members of the Young Intellectuals of Afghanistan and had pleaded not guilty. Their leader, Ali Safi, 38, a former university lecturer, had been jailed by the Taliban for playing chess. Of those on the plane, 74, including the accused, had requested asylum. Nineteen applications were granted; the rest were being appealed. 00020601

February 8, 2000. *Colombia.* The National Liberation Army (ELN) was suspected in the bombing of the Canadian-British-Colombian ONCESA consortium oil pipeline near Campo Hermoso, causing extensive damage to the pipeline, an oil spill, and a forest fire. 00020801

February 11, 2000. *United States.* A small pipe bomb exploded at Wall and Water Streets, a few blocks from the New York Stock Exchange, shattering windows and causing a postal worker's ears to ring. Police questioned two disgruntled employees. Police visited the Long Island home of a building engineer who had threatened his bosses after he was put on the midnight shift; he was not arrested. They also questioned a man who was fired from his job in the Barclays Bank building, which was damaged by the explosion. He had been scheduled for an exit interview on the day of the bombing. Four postal workers walked past the bomb and realized it could be dangerous; they ran away shortly before it went off.

February 11, 2000. *Spain.* Four individuals torched a Citroen car dealership in Amorebieta,

destroying the shop. The Basque Nation and Liberty (ETA) was suspected. 00021101

February 13, 2000. *Yugoslavia.* No one claimed credit when gunmen shot and wounded two French KFOR soldiers in Mitrovica. 00021301

February 16, 2000. *Pakistan.* The offer of a $5 million reward for the capture of Osama bin Laden was stamped on the face of Pakistani 100-rupee notes that were distributed around the country. The announcement appeared on both sides of the notes in Pashtu and Dari. Matchboxes with a similar message in Urdu were distributed in Peshawar. These messages attributed a $500,000 offer to the U.S. Consulate in Peshawar.

February 20, 2000. *India.* Some 22 policemen (including an assistant superintendent of police, a sub-inspector and one of his assistants, and three head constables) died when a landmine exploded in Madhya Pradesh State. No group claimed credit, but police suspected the People's War Group, insurgents who attacked landlords and police across forests in Andhra Pradesh, Madhya Pradesh, Orissa, and Maharashtra.

February 22, 2000. *Spain.* The Basque Nation and Liberty (ETA) was blamed for setting off a car bomb that killed a local Socialist politician and his bodyguard in Vitoria, the Basque region's capital. Four days later, more than 60,000 protestors marched in Vitoria to demand an end to ETA's campaign. Another 55,000 marched in Pamplona.

February 25, 2000. *Philippines.* Bombs exploded on a Super Five express ferry at an Ozamis dock. Passengers on board two buses and other vehicles on the ferry jumped into the sea. Fire damaged the ferry and other vehicles. At least 41 people were killed; 36 of them were in the vehicles. Muslim separatists were suspected of setting fire to a Super Five bus in January to avenge a rebel commander's son who died after being hit by one of the firm's buses.

February 26, 2000. *Austria.* Austrian letter bomber Franz Fuchs committed suicide in his prison cell. He had been serving a life sentence for masterminding a series of letter-bomb campaigns in Austria and Germany between 1993 and 1997.

February 27, 2000. *India.* A bomb exploded at a rail station in New Delhi, injuring eight people and causing major damage. Indian authorities suspected Kashmiri militants or Sikhs.

February 29, 2000. *Yugoslavia.* A gunmen shot to death a Russian KFOR soldier on patrol in Srbica. An ethnic Albanian youth was arrested. 00022901

February 29, 2000. *Yugoslavia.* A gunman shot a UN official near Pristina. No one claimed credit. 00022902

March 2000. *Australia.* On August 25, the Auckland, New Zealand *Herald* reported that New Zealand detectives had foiled a plot by Osama bin Laden's followers to bomb a scientific research nuclear reactor in Sydney during the September Summer Olympics. Police raids in March on suspected people-smuggling operatives uncovered evidence of the plot. The paper said no arrests were made, but that the investigation continued. Auckland police raided a house that had been converted into a command center replete with maps of Sydney and notes on police security tactics. The map highlighted entrance points to the reactor. Police believed the organized crime ring had ties to bin Laden and Afghanistan. They determined that the group lacked the means to carry out the attack.

March 2000. *United States.* Peter Bradley, 39, broke into the cockpit of an Alaska Airlines plane and lunged for the controls. On October 20, the prosecutors and defense were working on a plea bargain, having agreed that he was suffering from a rare reaction to encephalitis. Although he had no alcohol or illegal drugs in his system and no history of psychiatric problems or trouble with authorities, Bradley had had headaches for a month. The condition worsened with lack of sleep and the plane's change in air pressure.

March 2000. *Philippines.* The Alex Boncayao Brigade, a breakaway CPP/NPA faction, strafed Shell Oil offices in the central Philippines. The group warned of more attacks against oil companies, including U.S.-owned Caltex, to protest rising oil prices. 00039901

March 2000. *Jordan.* The government expelled eight Libyans it suspected of having terrorist links.

March 1, 2000. *Yemen.* Yamneyatain tribesmen kidnapped Polish Ambassador Krzysztof Suprowicz from his car in the Sanaa suburbs and took him to a remote area 30 miles north of the capital. The Khawlan tribe, which claimed credit, released him unharmed on March 4. 00030301

March 2, 2000. *Israel.* Israeli commandos attacked a Hamas terrorist safe house in Taibeh, killing three Islamic militants. A fourth was taken prisoner; a fifth escaped. They apparently planned to conduct an attack using explosives.

March 3, 2000. *India.* A bomb exploded on a bus in Sirhand, Punjab, killing eight and injuring seven. The government suspected Kashmiri militants or Sikhs.

March 4, 2000. *Canada.* Montreal police arrested an Egyptian refugee, Tarek Adealy Khafagy, on charges of possessing an explosive substance without a lawful excuse and possession of counterfeit money. On March 8, his bail hearing was delayed until March 22 following a report of bomb plots against Israel's embassy in Ottawa and its consulate in Montreal. 00030401

March 4, 2000. *Uganda.* Gunmen kidnapped two Italian missionaries in Kampala, but released them unharmed several hours later. The Lord's Resistance Army was suspected. 00030402

March 7, 2000. *Colombia.* In the largest rebel jail break since May 1998, hundreds of Revolutionary Armed Forces of Colombia (FARC) guerrillas fired homemade missiles, heavily damaging the town of El Bordo, 250 miles southwest of Bogota, and freeing 92 inmates in a local prison. No one was reported harmed during the six-hour battle, which began at 8:00 P.M. The rebels used gas cylinders packed with explosives and threw grenades. At least two dozen buildings in the town were destroyed.

March 10, 2000. *Sri Lanka.* A suicide bomber killed at least 20 other people and wounded 64 on a busy street in Colombo. However, he missed his target of a motorcade of cabinet ministers. Four accomplices killed themselves after hundreds of police and antiterrorist commandos surrounded their apartment hideout. Jackets filled with explosives and two rocket-propelled grenades were found in the area. Tamil separatists were blamed.

March 10, 2000. *Canada.* Montreal police arrested Ayman Bondok, 23, and Kim St. Louis, 31, for possessing illegal explosives. They were charged with threatening Israel in an effort to win the release of Lebanese prisoners. Police believed they were acting on their own, rather than in concert with any terrorist groups. On March 30, Bondok was charged with extortion and possessing explosives. St. Louis was charged with the latter offense, but was released on bail. Police believed Bondok had made a threatening call to the Israeli Consulate. They also suggested that Bondok had provided the tip about the explosives in the apartment of Tarek Adealy Khafagy, who was arrested on March 4. 00031001

March 10, 2000. *El Salvador.* Gunmen kidnapped an American and his Salvadoran nephew from their vehicle near San Antonio Pajonal. They were released unharmed on March 21 for a $34,000 ransom. 00031002

March 14, 2000. *Nigeria.* Armed youths occupied Shell Oil Company buildings in Lagos and held hostage 30 Nigerian employees and 4 guards of the Anglo-Dutch-owned firm. No one claimed credit. The Nigerian Army rescued the hostages unharmed the following day. 00031401

March 20, 2000. *Philippines.* Abu Sayyaf rebels took more than 70 hostages, many of them children from two schools, and demanded that the United States free Ramzi Yousef and Sheik Omar Abdel Rahman. They freed several captives, but also claimed on April 19 to have beheaded two of the hostages. Spokesman Abu Ahmad said that the group would execute more captives for every "negative statement" by Philippine President Joseph Estrada or the police. Ahmad said that negotiators failed to deliver diesel fuel and 85 sacks of rice as promised and that Estrada had made no statement that he would talk to U.S. officials.

The Philippine government sent 500 soldiers to raid an Abu Sayyaf stronghold on April 22 in an effort to free 27 remaining hostages—22 children and 5 adults, including a Roman Catholic priest. Ten rebels and four soldiers died in the clash; another three soldiers were wounded.

The rebels threatened to behead five more male hostages, including a priest, if the government did not withdraw its troops.

On April 26, Philippine troops shelled an Abu Sayyaf encampment in an attempt to rescue the 27 hostages. The next day, a provincial governor offered citizens a $730 bounty for each rebel they killed.

On May 2, the rebels claimed that two foreign hostages died in a clash with government troops. The claim could not be verified immediately.

After the rebels had released 20 hostages, the government attempted to free the others. A priest and three teachers were killed and mutilated on May 3. The terrorist group had initially wanted to negotiate only with Robin Padilla, a Filipino action movie star who converted to Islam while in prison. When he got to the mountain hideout, however, they only wanted to be photographed with him, not negotiate. He ultimately talked them into freeing two hostages before he returned to the Manila movie business.

Fifteen of the hostages were freed, although five were wounded. The rebels, led by Commander Robot, fled with eight remaining hostages.

Two soldiers were killed and six wounded in four separate clashes with the rebels on May 5.

On May 6, military officials found the headless bodies of two Filipino hostages in shallow graves on Basilan Island. The two dead men were believed to be teachers.

On May 7, 13 soldiers and 3 guerrillas died in a gun battle on Basilan Island.

On May 21, soldiers rescued two child hostages who had been held with seven others since March. One soldier and several rebels were injured in the hour-long clash on Basilan.
00032001

March 21, 2000. *India.* Gunmen killed 35 Sikhs in Chadisinghpoora village. Police arrested Muslim militants, who confessed to helping the Lashkar-e-Tayyiba and the Hizbul Mujahedeen.

March 21, 2000. *India.* Militants threw a grenade at police officers, missing their target, but killing 3 civilians and injuring 11 others in Srinagar. The Hizbul Mujahedeen was suspected.

March 29, 2000. *Russia.* Chechen guerrillas ambushed an OMON convoy, an Interior Ministry police unit, killing 32 members of the 41-man unit. Rebels announced the execution of the other OMON members several days after Russian officials refused to exchange them for a Russian army officer accused of raping and killing a teenage Chechen girl. On May 1, Russian forces discovered the bodies of the nine missing OMON members in Chechnya. They had been executed. Eight of them had had their throats slit; one body was mutilated. All had chest and abdominal wounds. Ears had been cut from three of the bodies. The bodies were buried near the hamlet of Dargo, which had often been shelled by the army. Police believed a unit under the command of an Arab Islamic militant, Khattab, was responsible. The area was also the home base of Shamil Basayev, a rebel commander.

March 30, 2000. *Somalia.* Unidentified Somali gunmen fired on a UN aircraft departing Kismaayo. No one claimed credit. No injuries and only minor damage was reported. The UN temporarily suspended humanitarian operations in the area. 00033001

March 30, 2000. *Laos.* Unidentified assailants threw an explosive device at a restaurant, injuring ten tourists from the United Kingdom, Germany, and Denmark. 00033002

April 2000. *Pakistan.* Early in the month, police raided a Peshawar apartment and arrested an Egyptian, Abdul Mohsin, and an Algerian. Mohsin had spent three months in jail in Canada on suspicion of involvement with Osama bin Laden's al-Qaeda group. Police found several forged passports in the apartment. The police had raided the place on a tip that bin Laden's son was living in the apartment with the duo. 00040299

April 2000. *Japan.* Police discovered an Aum Shin Rikyo memo containing the formula for nerve gas. Aum claimed the memo was to help an attorney defend a cult member in a current trial.

April 2000. *France.* The Breton Resistance Army (ARB) claimed credit for a bombing that damaged a McDonald's restaurant at Pornic. 00049901

April 2000. *Colombia.* In October, the Colombian police rescued a five-year-old U.S. citizen who had been held six months by the Revolutionary Armed Forces of Colombia (FARC). 00049902

April 2, 2000. *Pakistan.* Ahmed Abdullah, 32, a Yemeni suspected of having ties to Osama bin Laden, was arrested with two Pakistanis—Bilal, and Muzafar Khan—in Torkham, a border crossing at the foot of the Khyber Pass as they were trying to enter Afghanistan. The Pakistanis were suspected of affiliation with the Harakat ul-Mujahedeen, which sends fighters to Indian Kashmir. Abdullah had a "considerable amount" of money.

The trio had no visas. Abdullah had arrived from Bangladesh two days earlier. 00040201

April 4, 2000. *Pakistan.* Gunmen fired on an Afghan vehicle, killing the governor of the Taliban-held northern Afghan province of Kondoz and his militia commander and wounding his driver and another passenger. No one claimed credit. 00040401

April 7, 2000. *Nigeria.* Gunmen kidnapped 15 British, 15 French, and 10 Korean citizens from residences belonging to the Elf Aquitaine Oil Company in Port Harcourt. They were released unharmed several hours later. Disgruntled landowners were suspected. 00040701

April 12, 2000. *Colombia.* The National Liberation Army (ELN) was suspected of kidnapping a Mexican in Cali and demanding a $5 million ransom. On April 16, police arrested three of the kidnappers and freed the hostage unharmed. 00041201

April 12, 2000. *India.* Militants used a remote-control device to set off a car bomb near an army convoy in Srinagar, killing a bystander. No one claimed credit.

April 13, 2000. *Colombia.* A bomb exploded on the Cano–Limon oil pipeline near La Cadena, causing major damage and suspending oil production for several days. The National Liberation Army (ELN) and Revolutionary Armed Forces of Colombia (FARC) were suspected. 00041301

April 14, 2000. *Nigeria.* Gunmen in Warri kidnapped 19 employees of the Noble Drilling Oil Company, a firm contracted by the Anglo-Dutch-owned Shell Oil Company. Ijaw youths were suspected. 00041401

April 15, 2000. *India.* Gunmen killed 12 and wounded 7, then torched several huts in Tripura. No one claimed credit.

April 19, 2000. *France.* A bomb exploded at a McDonald's in Quevert, Dinan, in the Brittany region, killing a female employee (a 28-year-old relative of the owner) and causing extensive damage to the building. The victim was standing near the back door. Separatists were suspected, and police detained five Bretons on May 2. They included Gael Roblin, spokesman for Emgann (meaning "combat" in Breton), a 200-member group believed to be the political wing of the Breton Revolutionary Army. The group denied responsibility and condemned the bombing. Police ultimately rounded up nine people associated with the Breton Liberation Army (ARB). 00041901

April 20, 2000. *Pakistan.* A bomb exploded near the Jamaat-e-Islami headquarters in Mansuren, injuring two people in a nearby residence. No one claimed credit.

April 23, 2000. *Malaysia.* Six masked Abu Sayyaf gunmen armed with AK-47 assault rifles and an RPG launcher kidnapped 21 people, including 10 foreign scuba divers and tourists, from a restaurant on Sipadan Island, a resort off Malaysia's Borneo coast. They stole the tourists' cash and jewelry. They forced the hostages to swim to two fishing boats offshore and transported them to the southern Philippines. Two Americans, James and Mary Murphy of Rochester, New York, both 51, escaped by claiming that she could not swim, then ran into the woods when the terrorists' attention was diverted. The hostages included nine Malaysians, three Germans, two Frenchmen, two South Africans, two Finns, one Lebanese, and one Filipino who worked at the resort. Local underwater photographer Danny Chin, 48, said that one of the attackers had claimed to be a policeman and stole his cell phone and watch while holding a gun to his head.

Police were not convinced that Abu Sayyaf was involved, noting that the hostage takers spoke Tausug, a Philippine language not commonly used on Basilan Island, the Abu Sayyaf stronghold.

Some suggested they were merely ransom-seeking pirates. An individual who had claimed credit for the attack backed off a few days later.

On April 25, Malaysian police questioned five men in the case. The group consisted of current or former employees of diving resorts on the island.

As of April 26, authorities believed the hostages were being held on a rugged island in the southern Philippines' Sulu archipelago.

On April 27, Philippines President Joseph Estrada rejected the kidnappers' demands for $2.4 million in ransom. Nonetheless, police expected the kidnappers to release two Malaysian hostages soon because they were Muslims. The negotiator for the Philippine government was Nur Misuari, a former Muslim rebel leader. Malaysian Prime Minister Mahathir Mohamad said his government would "do anything to secure the release of the captives."

The media were permitted to meet with the hostages in early May. During a visit by a doctor and several journalists, the hostages, who were being held on Jolo Island, said they were suffering from hunger, thirst, and diarrhea from unclear water. One hostage could not walk and wept in the bamboo hut where she and 20 others were being guarded by 70 heavily armed rebels.

Talks broke off on May 2 after troops and rebels staged a gun battle.

On May 7, government troops fired mortar rounds at the camp where the hostages were being held in outdoor cages in two groups—foreigners and Asians. One German hostage, Renate Wallert, 57, who suffered from high blood pressure, had been allowed to lie in a plastic hammock. One guerrilla was injured, and the hostages were taken deeper into the jungle. The rebels said they would not begin talks until the military withdrew from its Jolo Island encampment. The government rejected the condition. The rebels sent a letter to President Estrada rejecting Nur Misuari as a mediator. He had threatened to quit, saying he could not negotiate without a military withdrawal. The guerrillas said they would negotiate with the ambassadors of the hostages' countries, along with

representatives from Libya, the UN, and the Organization of the Islamic Conference.

On May 17, the rebels upped their demands from $1 million to $2 million for the release of Wallert; government negotiator Robert Aventajado rejected the demand.

On July 10, the Muslim rebels kidnapped a three-person French television crew that sought an interview with the group's leader.

On July 21, National Public Radio reported that the kidnappers had released four Malaysians and seven other people.

On July 27, the rebels released a reporter for a German magazine whom they had held alone in the jungle for 25 days.

On August 2, the *Washington Post* reported that the group had recently released a German woman and six Malaysians after payment of a $4.2 million ransom. Ghalib Andang (also known as Commander Robot) was demanding $1 million for each of the remaining hostages.

On August 7, military chief Angeles Reyes inadvertently disclosed at a cabinet meeting being covered by journalists that the rebels had received $5.5 million in ransom payments.

On August 16, the rebels freed a Filipino woman. Negotiators said minor complications had delayed the planned release of the foreigners, including the three French television reporters. The rebels claimed to have released three Malaysian hostages on August 18 after receiving $1 million more in ransom, apparently from a German woman. There was no independent confirmation of the release.

Negotiations broke down again on August 19. The Muslim kidnappers accused the armed forces of preparing to attack them if all of the hostages were freed. Philippines and Libyan negotiators had held out hope of securing the release of the remaining hostages, but Abu Sayyaf offered to free only two hostages. Former Libyan Ambassador Rajab Azzarouq was among the negotiators.

On August 27, the rebels freed five foreign hostages, including four women, after Libya agreed to pay $1 million in ransom for each. Freed were four tourists—Marie Moarbes, a French-Lebanese citizen; Sonia Wendling of France; Monique Strydom of South Africa; and Renate Wallert of Germany—and Maryse Burgot, who was seized with two other French television journalists when they tried to visit the rebel camp. The rebels still held seven other Westerners and a dozen Filipinos. The freed hostages were flown on a Libyan jet to Tripoli and were to meet with Muammar Qadhafi. Libya denied that it had provided cash, instead claiming it had promised development projects in the Philippines.

The rebels released four European hostages, including German Marc Wallert, on September 9. They still held 2 French journalists, 13 Filipinos, and 1 American. Libya paid $1 million per hostage. One of the freed hostages said the rebels raped some of the female hostages. Earlier in the day, two intermediaries were ambushed three miles from where the hostages were held. A bodyguard was killed and eight others were wounded, as were many civilians.

On September 15, the rebels tentatively agreed to release the French journalists the next day, but the government lost patience when the rebels kidnapped another three people in Malaysia. Negotiations also stalled when the Abu Sayyaf factions clashed over the division of the ransom money already paid. Libya had paid $10 million of the $15 million in ransom.

On September 16, Philippine warplanes and helicopters fired on the hills of Jolo Island, where the hostages were held. At least 3,000 troops and police arrived by amphibious transport to assist in Operation Sultan.

French journalists Roland Madura and Jean-Jacques Le Garrec escaped during the military assault on September 19 as the rebels were crossing a road. The rebels could not pursue them, as the rebels were carrying supplies, weapons, and Wilde Almeda, a Christian evangelist hostage so weak that he was carried through the jungle on a chair. The duo hid in the jungle during the night, then made their way to a military camp after hitchhiking on a military truck. Le Garrec said that Almeda and 11 members of his Jesus Miracle Cru-sade were still in good spirits despite behind held hostage. Televangelist Almeda reportedly had been fasting for 40 days. He and 11 "prayer warriors" had paid $3,000 and 35 sacks of rice to get to the rebel camp in July. They had planned to force the rebels to release the hostages via the power of prayer.

On July 8, 2001, Philippines authorities arrested Nadzmimie Sabtulah (alias Commander Global; alias Al Shariff), the highest-ranking member of the Abu Sayyaf Muslim rebels to be held. In the evening raid, police also nabbed three other rebels in a hideout in General Santos City, 650 miles south of Manila. Sabtulah participated in the mass kidnapping, planning the operation and serving as the group's spokesman. He had also been involved in an attempt to abduct tourists from the Pearl Farm Beach Resort Hotel on Samal Island on May 22, 2001. The government had offered a 5 million peso ($94,000) reward for information leading to his arrest; civilian informants tipped off police to his location. 00042301

April 24, 2000. *Tajikistan.* Armed Afghans broke into a residence in Khatlon Oblast and opened fire, killing one person, injuring another, and kidnapping a third. No one claimed credit. 00042401

April 28, 2000. *India.* A bomb exploded at a police checkpoint in Srinagar, killing a civilian and wounding four police officers and a civilian. No one claimed credit.

April 28, 2000. *India.* Militants threw a grenade at a security patrol in Srinagar, but hit a bus stop instead, injuring two civilians. No one claimed credit.

April 29, 2000. *Germany.* A grenade hidden in a crowded Hamburg disco exploded, hospitalizing nine people, two of them in critical condition. 00042901

May 2000. *Palestinian Authority/Israel.* Palestinian security forces arrested Mohammed Deif (variants Dayf, Dief), 35, the leader of the Izzedine al Qassam Brigades, the armed wing of Hamas. He was charged in Israel with ordering suicide bombings on buses in Jerusalem and Tel Aviv that killed 47 Israelis and wounded 96 in 1996. Israel requested his extradition, which was refused. On December 1, he escaped from a Palestinian jail in the Gaza Strip with the assistance of some of his guards. A Hamas Web site said the guards had been arrested. Israeli security officials said that Yasir Arafat must have ordered his release.

May 2000. *Laos.* A Vientiane morning market was bombed, injuring four Thais. 00059901

May 2000. *Tunisia.* Members of the Algerian Salalfi Group for Call and Combat (GSPC) crossed the border into Tunisia and attacked an outpost, killing three border guards.

May 1, 2000. *Iraq.* Iranian agents were suspected of having fired six rockets on a Baghdad residential quarter during the evening, injuring eight people and damaging several houses.

May 1, 2000. *Sierra Leone.* Members of the Revolutionary United Front (RUF) rebel group captured eight UN military observers and peacekeepers in Makeni. 00050101

May 1, 2000. *Sierra Leone.* Members of the Revolutionary United Front (RUF) surrounded 222 Indian peacekeepers and 11 military observers in the east. The Indians were not forced to give up their weapons and uniforms. The RUF demanded the release of Foday Sankoh and 20 other detained RUF leaders. On June 29, following the intervention of Liberian President Charles Taylor, the RUF released 21 Indian UN peacekeepers to Liberian authorities. The rebels still surrounded 200 Indian UN peacekeeping troops and military observers. The RUF prevented the UN from continuing to send the remaining detainees food and medicine. The detainees sent a distress signal to their headquarters. At 6:00 A.M. on July 15, backed by helicopter gunships, 1,000 UN troops rescued the remaining hostages. The UN forces

met no resistance from the compound in Kailahun. A convoy carrying the soldiers and observers to freedom was later ambushed, wounding two UN soldiers. 00050102

May 2, 2000. *Sierra Leone.* Members of the Revolutionary United Front (RUF) rebel group captured two Russian UN helicopter pilots and three unidentified passengers in the eastern city of Kailahun. Liberian leader Charles Taylor intervened diplomatically with RUF leader Sankoh for their release.

Seven UN military personnel were captured at a rebel roadblock. The incidents occurred as the Nigerian-led West African ECOMOG (Economic Community of West African States Cease-Fire Monitoring Group) intervention force, which had defended the government for eight years of civil war, completed its pullout from the country.

UN officials said they were trying to negotiate the release of the hostages. 00050201-02

May 2, 2000. *Philippines.* The Moro Islamic Liberation Front (MILF) set off several bombs and conducted other attacks that killed 35 people. They took over stretches of a highway near Cotabato, seizing vehicles and more than 100 hostages. One bomb concealed in a plastic bag exploded at the fishing port of General Santos City, killing 2 and seriously injuring 20. Simultaneously, a bomb exploded inside a taxi in front of the city hall, killing a woman. A bomb outside another city office killed one and injured ten. Guerrillas fired RPGs at the Cotabato airport and an adjacent military camp. Philippine Airlines suspended flights to Cotabato and General Santos, where most businesses closed. The 100 hostages escaped on the morning of May 5 after the rebels withdrew from the area.

May 3, 2000. *Algeria.* When a bus driver refused to stop at a fake roadblock, the Salalfi Group for Call and Combat (GSPC) sprayed the bus with bullets, killing 19 and injuring 26.

May 3, 2000. *Angola.* The National Union for the Total Independence of Angola (UNITA) was suspected of attacking a World Food Program humanitarian convoy in Luanda, killing one person, wounding another, and setting the trucks on fire. 00050301

May 4, 2000. *Lebanon/Israel.* Hizballah Shi'ite Muslim guerrillas fired dozens of Katyusha rockets across the Lebanese border into Kiryat Shemona and other locales in northern Israel at 6:00 P.M., shattering windows, setting cars on fire, and sending terrified civilians into underground shelters. Israel retaliated the next day with air strikes on Lebanese power stations, a guerrilla stronghold, and the Beirut–Damascus highway. Hizballah said it was retaliating for an artillery attack by the Israeli-backed South Lebanon Army that had killed two women. 00050401

May 4, 2000. *Sierra Leone.* Rebels continued to take UN Mission in Sierra Leone (UNAMSIL) officials hostage, bringing the total to more than 90, including a British officer and Indian and Kenyan peacekeepers. At least four UN Kenyan peacekeepers were missing and presumed killed in clashes (down from earlier reports of seven dead Kenyans); eight other Kenyans were wounded. Revolutionary United Front (RUF) leader Foday Sankoh had promised to free the hostages, although the clashes continued. By May 5, the RUF had more than 300 UN hostages, 13 UN armored vehicles, and hundreds of UN weapons and uniforms. By May 7, the number of dead UN soldiers was down to one peacekeeper confirmed dead and one peacekeeper missing.

Later that day, the RUF captured 208 Zambian peacekeepers traveling to Makeni to reinforce Kenyan peacekeepers who were under attack. The RUF also seized 24 UN workers elsewhere.

On May 11, the RUF released a Nepalese and an Indian UN peacekeeper. Three Britons and a New Zealand UN peacekeeper also escaped.

On May 14, the RUF sent 157 UN peacekeepers to Liberia. UN officials said 11 military observers and 7 soldiers were released in Sierra Leone.

On May 16, 79 Zambians and 14 Kenyans working for the UN were freed in neighboring Liberia, then flown to Freetown, Sierra Leone. More than 40 UN troops remained in Foya, Liberia. The freed hostages were formally handed over to UN representative Oluyemi Adeniji by Liberian President Charles Taylor, who was serving as an intermediary with his ally Foday Sankoh. One of the peacekeepers was on crutches; some suffered from dehydration. None of them apparently had been shot or injured in combat or during their detention. Following talks with the Rev. Jesse Jackson, Taylor urged the rebels to free the rest of the hostages on May 19. The UN revised its estimate of hostages from 270 to 334; several dozen who supposedly were freed had yet to be returned. The UN believed that 30 hostages were wounded, including a Kenyan with a serious leg fracture.

On May 21, the RUF freed 54 more UN peacekeepers (42 Zambians, 10 Kenyans, 1 Malaysian, and 1 Norwegian), allowing them to be flown in two helicopters to Liberia. Three soldiers had suffered fractures or other injuries and were carried on stretchers to a Monrovia hospital. Some of the soldiers said the rebels were moving other hostages toward the Liberian border for a helicopter pickup. Among the released Kenyan peacekeepers were Mohamed Abdi, Gideon Ongwae, and Cyrus Gitahi, along with Malaysian Army Major Ganase Jaganathan, 42. One freed Zambian soldier said the rebels told the hostages they would not be killed because they worked for the UN, but if they had been with ECOMOG (the Nigerian-led West African peacekeeping team), they would have been killed immediately.

Liberian President Taylor said the fighting on May 23 between government troops and the rebels made the negotiations more complex.

On May 26, the RUF freed 180 more hostages, most of them Zambians. Some 46 of the soldiers were flown to Monrovia. Meanwhile, UN peacekeepers said several decomposed bodies discovered earlier in the week in Rogberi Junction, 50 miles east of Freetown, were probably one Nigerian and four Zambian UN soldiers who had been missing since rebel attacks began in the region earlier in the month. The bodies retained remnants of UN uniforms.

On May 27, the RUF freed 300 children, aged 7 to 18, who had been abducted to fight the government.

Following talks with the Rev. Jackson, Taylor persuaded the rebels to release the last 85 UN hostages on May 28. 00050402

May 6, 2000. *Philippines.* The Moro Islamic Liberation Front (MILF) set off bombs on two buses, killing 6 and wounding 35 on Mindanao Island. The group had declared a unilateral cease-fire the previous day.

May 6, 2000. *United Kingdom.* The Irish Republican Army (IRA) promised for the first time that it would "put IRA arms beyond use" and allow independent observers to make regular inspections of some of its hidden arsenals, thereby moving the peace process forward. The gesture was part of a complex peace plan set forth by the British and Irish prime ministers.

May 6, 2000. *Sierra Leone.* A UN spokesman in Sierra Leone claimed that a UN helicopter gunship fired on Revolutionary United Front (RUF) rebels on the ground, but failed to stop an advance on the capital. The RUF rebels were driving stolen UN vehicles. A senior UN official in New York challenged the field reports of clashes with the RUF, which had gained notoriety for hacking off the limbs of civilians during the insurrection.

May 8, 2000. *Sierra Leone.* Revolutionary United Front (RUF) rebels shot down a UN helicopter delivering food and evacuated the wounded in the Makeni area. Meanwhile, RUF leader Foday Sankoh disappeared from his house while his bodyguards shot down unarmed demonstrators. Progovernment troops captured him near his home on May 17. He was wounded in the left leg, and his bodyguard was killed. 00050801

May 9, 2000. *Sierra Leone.* Revolutionary United Front (RUF) rebels kidnapped two British aid workers. They were released a month later. 00050901

May 13, 2000. *Philippines.* Moro Islamic Liberation Front (MILF) guerrillas were blamed—but denied credit—for the kidnapping of 65 people in a raid on a village in the south.

May 14, 2000. *Colombia.* Gunmen kidnapped an Australian missionary and three Colombians in Canito. The Colombian hostages were freed unharmed several hours later. No one claimed credit. 00051401

May 14, 2000. *Iran.* The Mujahedin-e Khalq set off a bomb in the Kermanshah cultural and sports center, injuring two civilians.

May 24, 2000. *Sierra Leone.* During an ambush by Revolutionary United Front (RUF) rebels near Rogberi Junction, Associated Press Television News producer and cameraman Miguel Gil Moreno de Mora, 32, of Barcelona, and Reuters correspondent Kurt Schork, 53, of Washington, D.C., were killed, as were four government soldiers. South African Reuters cameraman Mark Chisholm and Greek photographer Yannis Behrakis sustained minor injuries. Schork grew up in Rockville, Maryland, and attended Jamestown College in North Dakota. He was a Rhodes Scholar at Oxford University while President Clinton was studying there. Schork went on to cover wars in Sri Lanka, Kurdistan, Afghanistan, Bosnia, Chechnya, Kosovo, and East Timor. 00052401

May 24, 2000. *Angola.* Suspected Front for the Liberation of the Cabinda Enclave (FLEC) rebels kidnapped three Portuguese construction company workers and one Angolan in Cabinda. No one claimed credit. 00052402

May 25, 2000. *Philippines.* Augusto, a disturbed man holding a hand grenade and a gun, hijacked a Philippine Airlines domestic flight carrying 278 passengers from Davao City to Manila. He was wearing a ski mask and swimming goggles. He demanded that the plane return to Davao, but the pilots said the plane was low on fuel. He parachuted out of the plane near Manila after robbing the passengers; no one was injured. Police searched a forested hilly area outside Manila. Passengers described the man as hysterical; he told pilot Butch Generoso that he had family problems. He made flight attendants collect about $25,000 from the passengers, but then demanded more. After the second collection, he screamed at the pilot to open the nearest exit, which the pilot refused to do. Once the plane had descended to 6,000 feet, the pilot depressurized the plane. The hijacker demanded a baseball hat and money belt, then, wearing a homemade parachute, tried to jump from an exit on the right rear side of the plane. The wind was too strong to make the jump, but a flight attendant pushed him out. He pulled the pin from the grenade, but mistakenly threw the pin back into the cabin. He died upon impact with the ground, according to *The Darwin Awards*. 00052501

May 27, 2000. *Indonesia.* Members of the Free Aceh Movement occupied a Mobil Oil production plant, ordering the workers and all Indonesian nationals to shut down production. They held six hostages for several hours before releasing them unharmed and allowing production to resume. They demanded $500,000 to restore operations. 00052701

May 31, 2000. *Russia.* Chechen rebels killed Sergei Zveryev, the Russian government's second-highest official in Chechnya, by setting off a remotely detonated bomb under his vehicle in Grozny. Grozny Mayor Supyan Makhchayev was injured and his assistant was killed. Chechen rebels conducted several other attacks during the week.

June 1, 2000. *Georgia.* Five UN military observers were kidnapped in the breakaway Abkhazia region's mountain village of Lata, in the Kodori Valley conflict zone. The hostages included two British bomb disposal experts, a local interpreter,

and two officers of unknown nationality. (Other reports said they were two Danish UN military observers, a British government employee, and two Abkhazian citizens.) The group demanded a $500,000 ransom. One of the Abkhazian hostages was freed on June 3 and reported that the other four were being treated well. The remaining hostages were released unharmed on June 5. 00060101

June 2, 2000. *Philippines.* Abu Sayyaf Muslim rebels holding 21 hostages on Jolo Island captured German journalists in Bandang village near Jolo Town. They released them after payment of a $25,000 ransom. The journalists were kidnapped along with a Philippines coordinator and two other people. Three journalists were from Germany's ZDF television service, two from Sat. 1, two from RTL television, and one from *Der Spiegel* news magazine. The Germans had planned to visit the rebel camp to interview the hostages, who had been held since April. 00060201

June 2, 2000. *Namibia.* The National Union for the Total Independence of Angola (UNITA) was suspected of kidnapping a woman from her Mut'jiku residence, although no one claimed credit. 00060202

June 2, 2000. *Namibia.* The National Union for the Total Independence of Angola (UNITA) was suspected of kidnapping a man in Rundu. 00060203

June 4, 2000. *Philippines.* A bomb exploded in the morning outside a public toilet near the arrival area of Manila International Airport. No injuries were reported, but the blast cratered the sidewalk and showered the area with broken glass and debris. Two men who sped away in a car were arrested. Police said there were no signs of shrapnel. Police blamed Muslim rebels for a series of bombings.

June 5, 2000. *Mexico.* Carlos Ibarra Perez, 60, spokesman for the Citizen Defense Committee activist group, offered a $10,000 bounty for killing a U.S. Border Patrol agent. He claimed that too many illegal immigrants were being slain by federal agents and private landowners while sneaking into the United States. Two weeks earlier, a Border Patrol agent in Brownsville, Texas, shot to death an illegal immigrant in a struggle on the banks of the Rio Grande. 00060501

June 6, 2000. *Sierra Leone.* The Revolutionary United Front (RUF) kidnapped 21 Indian UN peacekeepers in Freetown. No one claimed credit. 00060601

June 7, 2000. *Russia.* A pair of suicide bombers—a man and a woman—blew up an explosives-laden truck outside a military facility in Alkhan-Yurt, seven miles southwest of Grozny, the Chechen capital. Two soldiers died; five were wounded. The truck had run a military checkpoint and stopped outside a school where Interior Ministry troops were stationed. Shortly after the truck exploded, Chechen snipers near the school directed small-arms fire at Russian troops. Helicopter gunships arrived and the snipers disappeared.

June 7, 2000. *Sri Lanka.* A suicide bomber killed Industrial Development Minister C. V. Goonerathne and 21 others as he walked among supporters in his parliamentary district in Ratmalana, an industrial suburb of Colombo, during the first celebration of War Heroes Day. Police detained 15 suspects in the bombing, which disrupted a fundraiser for the families of slain soldiers. The minister's wife was among the 7 people seriously injured; another 53 were hospitalized. The bomber had jumped out of a taxi and greeted the minister before setting off the bomb. The Liberation Tigers of Tamil Eelam (LTTE) or their suicide unit, the Black Tigers, were suspected.

June 8, 2000. *Greece.* Two November 17 gunmen on motorcycles fired into the car of Brigadier Stephen Saunders, 53, the British defense attaché, on Kifissias Avenue, a main northern Athens street, killing him. Saunders was driving an embassy car along the busy street at 8:00 A.M. when he died in a hail of .45-caliber bullets from a gun used in previous November 17 attacks.

On June 5, the U.S. National Commission on Terrorism had informed Congress that Greece "has been disturbingly passive in response to terrorist activities," observing that "since 1975, there have been 146 attacks against American interests in Greece. Only one case has been solved, and there is no indication of any meaningful investigation into the remaining cases." On June 12, the Greek government announced it would propose to the United Kingdom a European Union initiative to combat terrorism, claiming that the shooting made a case for joint action. Foreign Ministry spokesman Panos Beglitis said a similar agreement for cooperation with the United States had been drafted.

The same month, Greek Foreign Minister George Papandreou had returned from London, where he had requested—unsuccessfully—the return of the ancient marble sculptures that Lord Elgin removed from the Parthenon 200 years ago. The sculptures are now in the British Museum. Some observers believed the attack was in reaction to the British refusal. In a letter sent to the Athens newspaper *Eleftherotypia*, November 17 claimed that Saunders was a coordinator of North Atlantic Treaty Organization (NATO) bombing of Yugoslavia and that the murder was revenge against NATO's military action in 1999 against Serbia. The group also claimed credit for attacks in 1999 on the German and Dutch ambassadors' residences, on three Western banks, and on offices of the governing PASOK party. In a follow-up communiqué in December, the group defended itself against mounting public criticism by trying to appeal to populist, pro-Serb sentiments and also by urging Greeks not to cooperate with the government's counterterrorism efforts.

According to the State Department's *Patterns of International Terrorism 2000*, "The police sought to involve the public in the Saunders investigation and encouraged witnesses to come forward. Minister of Public Order (MPO) Khriskhoidhis led the government's efforts, which included increasing the reward for information on terrorist attacks to $2.5 million. The police also opened toll-free hotlines to enable informants to pass tips anonymously. Although failure to cordon off the Saunders crime scene initially hampered the investigation, the Greek police subsequently worked effectively with British investigators to pursue a small number of useful leads. At year's end, the British Defense Attaché's murder remained unsolved." 00060801

June 11, 2000. *Yemen.* Gunmen kidnapped Norwegian diplomat Gudbrand Stuve, 44, and his son. The duo died in the crossfire when Yemeni security forces stopped the kidnappers' car at a police roadblock in Sanaa. (One report said the son escaped unharmed.) The three remaining kidnappers escaped. No one claimed credit. 00061101

June 11, 2000. *Germany.* Alberto Adriano, 39, a 20-year resident of Germany and Mozambican father of three, was attacked by three skinheads because of the color of his skin. He was walking through a deserted park after midnight when he was set up by the drunken extremists and kicked violently. Upon arrest, the trio described the victim as a "foreign pig." He died two days later of massive head injuries. On August 30, a state court in Halle sentenced Enrico Hilprecht, 24, to life in prison and Christian Richter and Frank Miethbauer, his 16-year-old skinhead accomplices, to nine years each for the murder. All had expressed regret. The younger two were given sentences that were one year less than the maximum permitted for juveniles. 00061102

June 12, 2000. *Japan.* Envelopes containing radioactive, but not harmful, thorium powder were sent to Prime Minister Yoshiro Mori's residence and several government agencies.

June 16, 2000. *Yemen.* Yemeni tribesmen kidnapped an Italian archaeologist in the Marib region. He was released unharmed on July 20. 00061601

June 18, 2000. *Nigeria.* Local militants took hostage 22 Nigerians and 2 foreign workers at a Chevron Corporation facility in the oil-producing Niger Delta region. The foreigners and four Nigerians were freed that day. All were employees of contractors working on an oil pipeline right-of-way in the Benin River near the southern Escravos export terminal. 00601801

June 26, 2000. *Yugoslavia.* A bomb exploded outside a Prizren shop below a UN police officer's residence, slightly injuring him and destroying the shop. No one claimed credit. 00062601

June 27, 2000. *Colombia.* The National Liberation Army (ELN) kidnapped a five-year-old American and his Colombian mother and demanded an undisclosed ransom. 00062701

June 28, 2000. *Iraq.* Fowad Hussein Haydar, 38, broke through an Iraqi security detail and ran into the headquarters of the UN Food and Agricultural Organization (FAO) at 8:30 A.M. He trained two machine guns at 50 hostages and killed 2 FAO workers, identified as Yusuf Abdilleh of Somalia and Marewan Mohammed Hassan of Iraq. He injured seven other people, including two Iraqi workers who were shot in the stomach and a Somali who fractured a pelvis while trying to escape through a window. Four Iraqi security guards were also injured. Haydar claimed to have explosives strapped to his body and demanded compensation for Iraqi victims of UN sanctions, the resumption of flights between Baghdad and Amman, Jordan, an end to U.S.–U.K. air strikes against Iraq, and the building of a statue outside UN headquarters in memory of Iraqi children who died because of the sanctions. He threatened to blow up the building. He surrendered to police after two and a half hours. He denied killing the people and blamed the Iraqi police. He had earlier tried to enter the UN main Baghdad headquarters at the Canal Hotel, but was turned away by Iraqi guards. He decided to go after an easier target—the FAO office. 00062801

June 29, 2000. *Jordan.* Following its announcement that it could be a terrorist target, the U.S. Embassy announced the cancellation of its July 4 reception.

June 30, 2000. *Sierra Leone.* The Revolutionary United Front (RUF) was believed to be behind the ambush of 20 Jordanian peacekeepers in a UN convoy traveling between Kenema and Freetown. One Jordanian soldier was killed and four injured some 80 miles from Freetown.

June 30, 2000. *Ireland/United Kingdom.* A bomb exploded on the Dublin–Belfast rail line. A dissident group phoned using a codeword. 00063001

July 2000. *Laos.* The Vientiane central post office was bombed. Two foreign tourists narrowly escaped injury. 00079901

July 1, 2000. *Sierra Leone.* Gunmen fired on Jordanian UN peacekeepers at a checkpoint at Rokel, 15 miles east of Freetown. There were an undisclosed number of casualties. 00070101

July 2, 2000. *Malaysia.* Gunmen from al-Maunah (The Brotherhood of Inner Power), an Islamic cult, raided two military armories in Sauk, stealing more than 100 assault rifles, grenade launchers, and machine guns. They took four hostages, killing two of them after some of the gunmen were injured in a standoff with police. The group's Web site said it had followers in several countries, who use mystical means to throw enemies backward or tie them up without touching them. The terrorists surrendered after four days. Police recovered the weapons.

July 2, 2000. *Philippines.* Abu Sayyaf Group rebels kidnapped a German journalist working for *Der Spiegel* magazine. He was released unharmed on July 27. 00070201

July 2–3, 2000. *Russia.* Five truck bombs were sent against Russian targets during the late evening and early morning. In one, at 5:00 A.M., a suicide truck bomber rammed a gate in Argun, six miles east of Grozny, outside a two-story dormitory housing Russian anti-riot police, killing 37 Russian soldiers. At least 100 were injured. Police had fired at the truck as it approached the building. The bomb dug a crater 16 feet deep and 32 feet wide and destroyed two buildings. Russian authorities believed the truck contained 1,100 pounds of explosives.

Another 11 civilians and 6 rebels were killed in the attacks. Another four Russian soldiers were missing in the rubble. Most of the other truck bombs were stopped at checkpoints, but exploded with some casualties, including the drivers. Russian troops stopped one of three trucks headed for Gudermes at a bridge, where a firefight broke out. The truck blew up, killing a Chechen policeman and the driver. Another truck was prevented from arriving at the barracks of Interior Ministry troops north of Gudermes. Russian troops fired, killing the driver. The truck exploded, killing a soldier. A third truck rammed the gates of an Interior Ministry battalion. Gunfire broke out. An explosion killed three people plus the driver. The final truck bomb was in Urus Martan, 12 miles southwest of Grozny. The driver tried to break through a cordon to a commandant's building during the evening. Two soldiers in a concrete shelter, along with the driver, were killed in the blast.

July 4, 2000. *Indonesia.* A bomb exploded in the attorney general's six-story office complex in Jakarta. The next day, police removed two more bombs from a cardboard box hanging from a bathroom ceiling in the building.

July 5, 2000. *Jordan.* Three Syrian men tried to hijack a Royal Jordanian flight to Syria. Fifteen passengers were wounded when a hijacker threw a small bomb at security officials who were trying to prevent him from getting into the cockpit; he was killed by guards. The two other hijackers were captured, and the plane returned safely to Amman. Three passengers were in stable condition with shrapnel wounds. 00070501

July 9, 2000. *Russia.* A bomb exploded at an outdoor food market in Vladikavkaz, the regional capital of North Ossetia, killing at least 5 and wounding 16. In March 1999, a bomb at the same location killed more than 50. That bombing was blamed on Chechen separatists.

Another bomb exploded in a department store in Rostov, killing two and wounding two.

July 9, 2000. *Philippines.* Government troops captured Camp Abubakar, the headquarters of the Moro Islamic Liberation Front (MILF) in southern Maguindanao Province. Troops found 30 dead guerrillas in bunkers, trenches, abandoned huts, and the headquarters building of Salamat Hashim, MILF chairman, who was believed to be in Egypt. During the gun battle, 8 soldiers died and 37 were wounded. A rebel spokesman said the government controlled only 10 percent of the camp.

July 9, 2000. *Democratic Republic of the Congo.* Unknown individuals killed eight people in two attacks near Sake near the rebel-held area that borders Burundi.

Rwandan Interahmwe militia attacked a refugee camp near the Rwandan border, killing 30 and kidnapping 4. 00070901

July 10, 2000. *Democratic Republic of the Congo.* Unidentified attackers killed 21 people, including women and at least 2 children, and wounded 19 at Sake, a small village west of the border town of Goma.

July 10, 2000. *Afghanistan.* A bomb exploded at the Pakistani Embassy, causing major damage but no injuries. No one claimed credit. 00071001

July 13, 2000. *India.* Armed militants killed three Buddhist monks in Leh, Kashmir. No one claimed credit.

July 14, 2000. *India.* Gunmen attacked two German hikers in the Himalaya Mountains, killing one and injuring the other. No one claimed credit. 00071401

July 15, 2000. *Sierra Leone.* The Revolutionary United Front (RUF) attacked UNAMSIL troops near Kailahun, killing an Indian soldier and wounding another Indian soldier. 00071501

July 16, 2000. *Sierra Leone.* The Revolutionary United Front (RUF) was suspected of killing a Nigerian UNAMSIL soldier in Rogberi. 00071601

July 16, 2000. *Germany.* Arsonists torched a refugee shelter housing Albanian Kosovars in Ludwigshafen, injuring three children and causing minor damage. No one claimed credit. 00071601

July 16, 2000. *Tajikistan.* A small bomb planted on a vehicle belonging to the European Community Humanitarian Organization (ECHO) exploded in Dushanbe, injuring several children. 00071602

July 18, 2000. *Angola.* The National Union for the Total Independence of Angola (UNITA) kidnapped 14 clergy members from the Dunge Catholic Mission in Benguela. Two people were killed and several escaped during the attack. On July 26, all remaining hostages were freed unharmed. 00071801

July 19, 2000. *United Kingdom.* A bomb was discovered and safely defused in the Ealing Broadway Underground Station in West London after receipt of a telephoned warning that included a codeword used by the Irish dissident group in the June 30 Dublin–Belfast rail line bombing. Police closed the station and Westminster and Victoria stations in Central London after receiving bomb threats by phone from Dublin. The threats disrupted the celebration of the 100th birthday of Queen Elizabeth the Queen Mother. 00071901-03

July 20, 2000. *Angola.* The National Union for the Total Independence of Angola (UNITA) was suspected in the kidnapping of four Namibian citizens from their Kavango residence. The gunmen shot and killed two of the hostages. A third hostage was injured, but escaped with a child. 00072001

July 21, 2000. *United States.* An FBI affidavit charged 18 people with smuggling cigarettes out of North Carolina to raise money for Hizballah in Lebanon. FBI agents arrested most of the suspects in raids on houses and businesses in the Charlotte area. The FBI did not disclose how much money was raised. The 18 suspects were indicted on federal charges including immigration violations, weapons offenses, money laundering, and cigarette trafficking. Three suspects were believed to have provided Hizballah with material support or resources, such as night-vision devices, global positioning systems, digital photo equipment, and computers. Mohamad Youssef Hammoud, identified as the ringleader, was believed to have received Hizballah-sponsored military training. None was accused of participation in terrorist attacks. The group bought cigarettes in North Carolina, which has 5 cents per pack taxes, and sold them in Michigan, which has 75 cents per pack taxes. The profits had been smuggled to Hizballah since 1996. One detainee, Ali Hussein Darwiche, had transported more than $1 million to Lebanon, according to an FBI informant. Another $360,000 in cashier's checks were traced to Lebanon.

On July 26, a federal magistrate in Charlotte ordered eight of the suspects jailed without bond. Eight had been released on bail earlier in the week. The other two were to remain in prison until federal marshals could put them under 24-hour house arrest. The FBI relied upon the "material support" clause of a federal statute. This was only the second time the clause had been used.

Among those arrested was Angela Tsioumas.

The FBI affidavit indicated that the Canadian Security Intelligence Service provided information that detainee M. Harb flew from Charlotte to Seattle in 1994 to deliver a series of forged checks to Mohammad Hassan Dbouk, who used them to buy night-vision goggles and other items for Hizballah. Harb also provided money for computers and cameras. Also jailed was Ahmed Ali Harari, who was alleged to have stored an arsenal with his brothers.

Charlotte's Arab American community claimed that the authorities misunderstood the detainees, who were merely sending money to their family members and were not assisting terrorists.

On August 11, 17 of the 18 defendants pleaded not guilty to charges of conspiracy to launder money, conspiracy to traffic in contraband cigarettes, and breaking federal immigration and naturalization laws. Fatme Mohamad Harb, 20, was being detained by the Immigration and Naturalization Service and was to be arraigned later.

July 24, 2000. *East Timor.* During a morning gun battle between anti-independence rebels and UN troops, Private Leonard Manning, 24, from the Royal New Zealand Infantry Regiment, was fatally shot in the head. He was part of a team that was tracking men who had crossed the border from Indonesian-ruled western Timor. His body was recovered in the afternoon. 00072401

July 24, 2000. *India.* The Hizb ul-Mujaheddin, one of Kashmir's main Muslim rebel groups, declared a three-month truce and called for talks with the government.

July 26, 2000. *Somalia.* Twenty heavily armed militiamen broke into an aid agency compound in Mogadishu and kidnapped a French woman and British man who worked for the French agency Action Against Hunger. 00072601

July 27, 2000. *Germany.* A shrapnel bomb wounded nine immigrants, including six Jews, from the Ukraine, Azerbaijan, and Russia, when it exploded in a commuter rail station. The victims were returning to Solingen from their daily German language lessons in Duesseldorf. A 26-year-old pregnant woman lost her unborn child when shrapnel pierced her stomach. Her husband sustained severe abdominal wounds. Interior Minister Otto Schily suggested the perpetrators were right-wing racists. Authorities offered a $5,000 reward for information about the bombers. 00072701

July 27, 2000. *United States.* At 10:26 P.M., Aaron Amartei Commey ran past security checkpoints at Terminal 4 and took hostage two pilots on a National Airlines plane in New York's John F. Kennedy Airport. As he got past the checkpoint, he pointed a gun at the screeners. One of them pushed an emergency button to summon armed officers. Commey had been planning for months to take over a plane. He chose Terminal 4—normally used for international flights, but used for domestic flights during construction—because the checkpoint and boarding gate are only 40 feet from each other. The 143 passengers and the rest of the crew escaped while he was in the cockpit threatening the pilots with a handgun and knife. Many of the passengers used an emergency chute deployed by the flight attendants. The deployment also immobilized the plane. Flight 19 was scheduled to go to Las Vegas and Los Angeles, but Commey demanded to be taken to Miami, Buenos Aires, and Antarctica. He surrendered at 3:38 A.M. after five hours. No one was injured. He was charged with one count of air piracy and ordered held for psychiatric evaluation. He told authorities that he arrived at the Port Authority bus terminal in Manhattan on July 26. The FBI recovered a bag containing a shotgun and two knives from his bus terminal locker. He claimed that he had been arrested while attempting to transport weapons in Argentina two years earlier. In Brooklyn, Commey's father said he had not seen his son in four years and believed that he was mentally ill. Commey grew up in the Bronx, but had moved to Milwaukee with his mother and brother years before. A National Airlines spokesman said the flight had been chosen randomly; Commey had believed it was an international flight. 00072702

July 27, 2000. *Colombia.* Suspected Guevarist Revolutionary Army (ARG; suspected to be an ELN faction) gunmen kidnapped a French aid worker affiliated with Doctors Without Borders. 00072701

July 29, 2000. *Namibia.* The National Union for the Total Independence of Angola (UNITA) was suspected of crossing into Namibia and kidnapping five Namibian men in Nginga. No one claimed credit. 00072901

July 30, 2000. *Sierra Leone.* Revolutionary United Front (RUF) militants were suspected of firing on Jordanian UNAMSIL troops in Masiaka, killing one soldier and wounding three others. No one claimed credit. 00073001

July 31, 2000. *Nigeria.* Armed youths stormed two oil drilling rigs, taking 165 hostages—145 Nigerians, 7 Americans, 5 Britons, and 8 Australian and Lebanese nationals. All were employed by service contractors of Shell Oil. No one claimed credit. The attackers were believed to be ethnic Ijaw. All hostages were freed unharmed on August 4. 00073101

July 31, 2000. *Sierra Leone.* Revolutionary United Front (RUF) militants ambushed a UNAMSIL patrol in Freetown, killing a Nigerian soldier. 00073101

August 2000. *Ukraine.* Security agents foiled an assassination plot against Russian President Vladimir Putin during his visit. They detained and expelled several suspects, including Chechens. 00089901

August 2000. *Bangladesh.* Local authorities uncovered a bomb plot to assassinate Prime Minister Sheikh Hasina at a public rally. Police believed that Islamic terrorists trained in Afghanistan planted the bomb. 00089902

August 2000. *Saudi Arabia.* A lone gunman opened fire on British and U.S. citizens near Khamis Mushayt early in the month. 00089903

August 1, 2000. *India.* Separatist guerrillas were believed responsible for two attacks in Jammu and Kashmir State that left 48 people dead. Terrorists attacked a marketplace in Pahalgam, south of Srinagar, along a trail crowded with Hindu pilgrims, firing guns and throwing grenades. Hours later, gunmen shot and killed 18 workers mostly from the state of Bihar in the Mir Bazaar area of Anantnag District.

August 1, 2000. *Indonesia.* A car bomb exploded outside the Jakarta home of Philippines Ambassador Leonides Caday as he was entering his driveway in a chauffeur-driven Mercedes sedan. Two Indonesians were killed and 22 others injured, including Caday, who sustained serious injuries to his head, hands, and legs. He was pulled from the car by passersby and taken to the local hospital. He was placed in intensive care following surgery. His residence was partially destroyed. Among the 18 bystanders injured were 1 Filipino and 2 Bulgarians. The bomb damaged several homes nearby. One of the individuals killed was a street vendor who had a stall in front of the ambassador's residence. The bomb was hidden in a van parked in front of the residence. Indonesian President Abdurrahman Wahid said the incident was a foreign effort to discredit the Philippines government. The Moro Islamic Liberation Front (MILF) denied responsibility. 00080101

August 2, 2000. *India.* Lashkar-e-Tayyiba gunmen killed 30 and injured 47 when they threw a grenade and fired on a Rajwas community kitchen.

August 4, 2000. *Georgia.* Ethnic Kists kidnapped two Red Cross workers and their driver in the Pankisi Gorge. All hostages were freed unharmed on August 13 on the condition that the kidnappers would not face criminal charges. 00080401

August 4, 2000. *Namibia.* The National Union for the Total Independence of Angola (UNITA) was suspected of shooting to death a Namibia rebel inside her Mwitjiku residence. No one claimed credit. 00080402

August 5, 2000. *Afghanistan.* Gunmen shot and killed a dozen people, including seven Afghans

working for the UN's Organization for Mine Clearance and Afghan Rehabilitation, near Kotal-e-Subzak on the road between Badghis Province and Herat. The gunmen then set their bodies on fire. The other five victims were local residents who had apparently hitched a ride with the aid workers. 00080501

August 7, 2000. *Spain.* Shortly before 11:00 P.M., four suspected Basque Nation and Liberty (ETA) members, including a woman, died when their car exploded in Bilbao near three newspaper offices. Police believed they were on their way to a bombing. ETA supporters marched in San Sebastian in commemoration of their deaths. One of the terrorists was believed to have been a top ETA commander wanted for the 1997 killing of town councilman Miguel Angel Blanco.

August 8, 2000. *Spain.* Basque Nation and Liberty (ETA) was blamed for setting off two car bombs in Madrid and in northern Spain, killing a businessman, Jose Maria Korta, and injuring 11 others.

August 8, 2000. *Russia.* A pound of dynamite exploded at 6:00 P.M. near a shoe shop in downtown Moscow's Pushkin Square pedestrian underpass, killing at least 8 people (3 others later died of their wounds) and hospitalizing 85, including 2 Russians holding U.S. passports. The bomb was not encased in metal nor armed with projectiles. Some Russian officials blamed Chechen terrorists, although no one claimed credit. Two young men dressed in black were the prime suspects. Another investigator said it might have been a suicide bombing because a man who lost two legs was closest to the blast. Police defused a second bomb. Police also discovered explosives and fuses in storage at a rail station; these materials had not been prepared for detonation. Two people, one a Chechen, were detained, but police doubted that they were involved.

Police later released composite portraits of three suspects—two dark-haired men and a blond man. A victim said he saw two men leave a bag and a briefcase in front of the shop shortly before the explosion. The men said they were going to exchange dollars for rubles and would return to make a purchase. Five minutes later, the bomb went off. 00080801

August 8, 2000. *Angola.* The National Union for the Total Independence of Angola (UNITA) was suspected in an attack on a diamond mine in Lund Norte Province, killing eight South African security officers. No one took credit. (Other sources said two similar attacks took place on August 18 and 19, resulting in the deaths of nine South Africans and the taking of seven Angolan hostages.) 00080802

August 9, 2000. *Colombia.* The National Liberation Army (ELN) kidnapped 26 biological researchers, including an American. The researchers were affiliated with the National University of Bogota's scientific expedition to study the local biodiversity of the grassy highlands of western Colombia in Antioquia Province. ELN commander Nicolas Rodriguez said his group was investigating the scientists' reasons for being in the area. The leftists released the scientists on August 12. The American was identified as John Douglas Lynch, who had recently retired from the faculty of the University of Nebraska at Lincoln, where he was a professor of biological sciences for nearly 30 years. 00080901

August 9, 2000. *Spain.* Two Basque Nation and Liberty (ETA) gunmen shot to death Army Second Lieutenant Francisco Casanova, 36 (or 46), father of two, firing three shots into the back of his head as he sat in a car in his garage in Pamplona. Thousands of marchers protested the wave of attacks.

August 9, 2000. *Angola.* The National Union for the Total Independence of Angola (UNITA) was suspected of shooting to death a South African and abducting seven Angolan workers in a raid on a diamond mine in the northeast. No one claimed credit. 00080901

August 10, 2000. *India.* A car bomb exploded in the main Lal Chowk shopping district in Srinagar, Kashmir, ten minutes after a grenade explosion drew people to the scene, killing 10 officers and a photojournalist and injuring 25. The explosion destroyed or damaged several vehicles and a dozen shops. Hizb ul-Mujaheddin set off the bomb two days after it called off a truce and peace talks with the government.

August 10, 2000. *East Timor.* Militia groups with ties to the Indonesian military attacked UN forces near Suai in the southwest, killing a Nepalese peacekeeper and injuring three other peacekeepers and a civilian. 00081001

August 10, 2000. *United Kingdom.* Federal prosecutors announced the arrest in London of two Kazakh men who had attempted to extort money via the Internet from Bloomberg, a global financial information service based in New York. Oleg Zezov, 27, who used the e-mail alias Alex, was charged with infiltrating Bloomberg's internal computer system and taking information about the firm and its founder, Michael Bloomberg. Over a period of weeks, Zezov had demanded $200,000 in exchange for the information. He ordered Bloomberg to deposit the money in an offshore account, which Bloomberg opened at Deutsche Bank in London. Although Bloomberg deposited money in it, the account was structured so that only a small amount could be withdrawn. Zezov and Michael Bloomberg agreed to meet. Zezov wrote Bloomberg that he was "not a criminal," but "intended to help you understand some drawbacks of your system." Zezov claimed to have "written a report containing copies of confidential information of your firm and your clients," which would be released if the money was not unblocked. "I have all evidences that the Bloomberg system threatens business of its clients. I am honest and well-intentioned person as far as you could see. But I can't give up my principles and in any case will get my money for done job [*sic*]." However, Bloomberg contacted the FBI, which brought in Scotland Yard and the Kazakh Special Services for an international sting. Zezov and Bloomberg met in a London hotel on August 10. Zezov was accompanied by Igor Yarimaka, 37, who claimed to be a former Kazakh prosecutor who would help him negotiate. Bloomberg was accompanied by two undercover Scotland Yard agents, one claiming to be a company executive and the other a translator. Following the meeting, the two Kazakhs were arrested and charged with extortion and computer hacking. Police were seeking a third suspect, Elena Gorokhova. Zezov and Gorokhova were employed by Kazkommerts Securities, based in Almaty, Kazakhstan. They were involved in their firm's contract with Bloomberg for financial information. The two Kazakh men were set to be extradited to the United States from London. They faced more than 20 years in prison if convicted.

August 11, 2000. *United States.* Jonathan Burton, 19, of Las Vegas, attempted to break into the cockpit 20 minutes before Southwest Airlines Flight 1763 was due to land. He hit other passengers and pounded on the locked cockpit door. He was killed by eight passengers who held him down until the flight landed in Salt Lake City. Burton died after being removed from the plane. An autopsy concluded that he did not have a heart attack, but rather died of suffocation. The U.S. Attorney's Office in Salt Lake City said the death was a legitimate act of self-defense by the passengers and that it would not file charges. Some of the 120 passengers told the police that Burton may have been provoked by the flight crew.

August 11, 2000. *Colombia.* The National Liberation Army (ELN) was suspected in the kidnapping of 27 tourists in Antioquia. An American professor and a German student were among the hostages. All hostages were freed unharmed on August 12. 00081101

August 11, 2000. *Colombia.* The Revolutionary Armed Forces of Colombia (FARC) kidnapped

and then killed a Colombian and an Irish citizen in Tolima. 00081102

August 12, 2000. *India.* A grenade exploded near a historic mosque in Srinagar, injuring two Hungarians and two Indians. No one claimed credit. 00081201

August 12, 2000. *Kyrgyzstan.* Islamic Movement of Uzbekistan (IMU) rebels took four U.S. mountain climbers and a Kyrgyzstani soldier hostage in the Kara-Su Valley. The rebels killed the soldier, but the four Americans escaped on August 18. IMU militants also took hostage six German, three Russian, one Ukrainian, and two Uzbek mountaineers, but later freed them. 00081202

August 13, 2000. *India.* In several guerrilla attacks throughout Kashmir, 26 people were killed and 49 injured. Six soldiers died and 45 were wounded when Hizb ul-Mujaheddin landmines exploded under buses carrying troops along a mountainous highway from Jammu to Srinagar. Meanwhile, a bomb exploded near Dal Lake, a tourist attraction in Srinagar, injuring four civilians. Five soldiers died in gun battles with guerrillas in southern Kashmir.

August 14, 2000. *United States.* The Secret Service announced the arrest of Lawrence David Meyers, 56, a self-employed publisher, at his Santa Monica, California, apartment. He was believed to have phoned in bomb threats to the Democratic National Convention and a newspaper. He claimed he had placed bombs at Staples Center and the *Record-Gazette* newspaper in Banning, California. No bombs were found. Meyers claimed membership in the American Revolutionary Party. He was arraigned in federal court on August 18 on two felony counts of maliciously making a telephone threat to damage or destroy property by explosives. Assistant U.S. Attorney Shannon P. Wright asked that he be held without bail. U.S. Magistrate Judge Carla Woehrle permitted Meyers to be freed on $100,000 bond provided he wear an electronic monitoring device until his September 11 hearing.

August 16, 2000. *Brazil.* Eight gunmen stole nearly $3 million in cash from an armored car, then hijacked a plane with 72 people aboard. They forced it to land on a rural airstrip before escaping in a pickup truck. 00081601

August 16, 2000. *Greece.* The Mavro Asteri (Black Star) phoned a local newspaper to take credit for torching a car belonging to an Italian Embassy official. No one was injured.
00081602

August 17, 2000. *Latvia.* At 5:30 P.M., two bombs exploded in the five-story Centers shopping center in Riga's medieval old town, injuring 21 people, 3 seriously. The bombs were hidden in a checked baggage area. Victims sustained serious burns, broken limbs, and facial cuts. Chief of Police Valdis Pumpers was among the injured. No warnings were given, and no motive was known.

August 18, 2000. *Kyrgyzstan.* Government troops freed four U.S. mountaineers held hostage by Islamic rebels believed to be members of the Islamic Movement of Uzbekistan (IMU), which opposed Uzbek President Islam Karimov.
00081801

August 18, 2000. *Angola.* The National Union for the Total Independence of Angola (UNITA) was suspected of attacking a diamond mine in the northeast, taking hostage seven Angolans.

August 25, 2000. *Turkey.* Police arrested seven suspected Revolutionary People's Liberation Army-Front urban guerrillas who were planning a bombing of Adana's Incirlik Air Base, which hosts U.S. and U.K. air patrols over Iran. The suspects were also planning bombings to protest transfers of prisoners to the new "F-type" jails, where inmates are kept in cells like large dorms, where the leftist terrorists recruit. 00082501

August 25, 2000. *Sierra Leone.* Rebel soldiers seized 11 British troops and 1 Sierra Leonean soldier in the Masiaka-Forodugu area, 60 miles east of Freetown. The rebels demanded food, medicine, and the release of one of their leaders from prison, and suggested that the government step down so that the West Side Boys and another faction could run for office. The West Side Boys groups former army soldiers who claim allegiance to the military junta that ran the country from 1997 to 1998. The rebels freed five British soldiers on August 30. Negotiations soon broke down over the rebels' "extravagant" demands, including scholarships to study abroad, release of their Commander Bomb Blast, and amnesty for the kidnappers.

In a 6:30 A.M. raid on September 10, elite British troops attacked the rebel base in Forodugu, located in the Occra Hills on the banks of Rokel Creek, 30 miles east of the capital. After a gun battle, the raiders rescued the remaining six British soldiers and Sierra Leonean officer. The hostages were helicoptered in five UH-1H Hueys to the HMS *Sir Percival*, anchored just off Freetown. One British paratrooper died; a dozen were wounded, one seriously. The rescuers killed 25 militia members, including 3 women, and captured 18 to 25, including their leader, Brigadier Foday Kallay. 00082502

August 27, 2000. *Indonesia.* A grenade exploded at the Malaysian Embassy. No injuries were reported. Police arrested 34 people suspected of involvement in this bombing and in the attack on the Jakarta stock exchange. Lack of evidence forced the release of all suspects in mid-October. Police claimed that the Free Aceh Movement (GAM), which seeks an independent state in northern Sumatra, conducted both attacks and planned another against the U.S. Embassy to "create chaos" in Jakarta. 00082701

August 29, 2000. *Philippines.* Abu Sayyaf rebels in Jolo kidnapped Jeffrey Craig Edwards Schilling, 24, an American from Oakland, California. He was trying to visit a rebel camp despite warnings.

He had arrived in the country on March 8 and was living in Zamboanga with his Muslim Filipino girlfriend, Ivi Osani, who was related to an Abu Sayyaf member. The couple had been invited to visit the rebel camp, according to her mother. The terrorists threatened to behead him if a $10 million ransom was not paid and three Islamic terrorists imprisoned in the United States for the 1993 bombing of the World Trade Center were not released. He was reported to be seriously ill, needing regular doses of prescription medicine. The rebels said that the graduate of the University of California at Berkeley was a CIA agent because he had introduced himself as a Muslim convert, but knew little about the faith.

The faction that held him had kidnapped 50 schoolchildren and teachers in March on Basilan Island; the group had beheaded two of the teachers after the United States rejected similar demands.

The Philippines government said it would review its approach to a hostage crisis that had dragged on since April.

Rebel spokesman Abu Sabaya said the guerrillas were willing to begin negotiations with the United States on August 31, but also wanted representatives of North Korea, China, Iraq, Saudi Arabia, and Libya present. The U.S. Embassy said, "We will not pay ransom, change policies, release prisoners, or make any concessions that reward terrorists."

Schilling reportedly was on a hunger strike on September 2. He had voluntarily entered the camp, but had angered the rebels by arguing about religious issues and was taken hostage. Ten to 15 men were guarding him in a bamboo hut when a reporter was permitted to see him. His hands were tied with electrical wire. He had damaged the door to the hut while shouting that he needed cleaning solution for his contact lenses. He had also argued with the rebels regarding the age at which Muslim boys could use weapons and whether tribal distinctions should be retained after the creation of a Muslim Philippine state.

The Red Cross instructed its staff not to deliver food to the rebel camp because of the danger of abduction.

On September 5, the rebels refused to exchange Schilling for a suspected guerrilla. Schilling's legs were bound because he had tried to escape. Police had arrested a 73-year-old man on September 4. He was suspected of taking part in Abu Sayyaf kidnappings on Basilan Island. Spokesman Abu Sabaya said he was his grandfather, but refused to trade Schilling for him "for even ten, even one hundred of my grandfathers."

The Philippines government launched a massive offensive against the rebels, with 5,000 troops in pursuit on September 16. The troops quickly overran two major Abu Sayyaf camps and smaller hideouts, but failed to free any of the 19 foreign and Filipino hostages on September 17. The government said 4 civilians were killed, along with 6 rebels; another 20 rebels were arrested. Four soldiers were wounded in six clashes.

Troops claimed that they spotted some of the 19 hostages on September 18.

A government spokesman said on September 21 that Schilling was being held with Roland Ullah, a Filipino diving instructor, in southern Jolo Island. DxRZ radio station broadcast a message from Schilling in which he called for negotiations to secure his release. He claimed the military assault was principally killing civilians. "I am appealing to the negotiators to talk to the U.S. government, have the operation immediately ceased and negotiations continue. The majority will be affected . . . will be civilians and what this will do is this will create further support for Abu Sayyaf. Therefore the operation will fail even if all members are killed . . . there will be resistance and hostility to the government because of the actions toward the civilians." Schilling and the rebels had earlier called the station.

The military negotiated for Schilling's release on September 23, but was rebuffed. Residents of the island town of Luuk said Schilling's ankles and wrists were tied with ropes. His arms and legs had cuts, apparently from his jungle trek. Rebels kicked him from behind as they walked. Military operations resumed, leading to the death of a soldier and the wounding of senior rebel leader Radulan Sahiron.

Some 2,000 government troops backed by attack helicopters and artillery chased Schilling's 500 kidnappers on September 25. On September 26, the rebels claimed they had escaped Jolo with Schilling. The government announced on September 28 that 111 guerrillas and 7 soldiers had been killed in the operation. Two soldiers were killed on September 28 in an area where the rebels were believed to be holding Schilling.

Troops freed the 12 Filipino evangelists of the Jesus Miracle Crusade on October 2, 2000. One evangelist, Fernando Solon, had escaped his captors after asking to take a bath on September 30 and noticing that the rebels did not follow him. He hid in a mangrove swamp that night, then found the soldiers. The troops flew him in a military helicopter to identify the location of the rebel camp. The rebels fled after a brief firefight. Among those freed was Wilde Almeda.

On October 15, Philippines troops arrested 36 people believed to be members or supporters of the kidnappers.

On April 5, 2001, the rebels announced they had postponed beheading Schilling in response to an appeal from his mother and wife to free him; they would allow a chance for talks.

On April 12, Philippines marine and police commandos raided the jungle hideout and freed Schilling, killing and wounding some of the rebels in fighting that continued for several hours. 00082901

August 29, 2000. *South Africa.* A bomb went off near the U.S. Consulate in Cape Town, injuring several people and destroying a car. 00082902

September 6, 2000. *Western Timor.* Thousands of militiamen and their supporters attacked a UN office in Atambua in the western Timor border area, killing Samson Areghaegn of Ethiopia, Carlos Caseras of Puerto Rico, and Pero Simundza of Croatia. Four UN helicopters dispatched from East Timor evacuated 54 other UN employees, some of whom were injured. Several foreign UN workers escaped; three were injured, one seriously. The seriously injured worker was a Brazilian

woman who had been hacked by an ax. Indonesian forces reportedly stood by and watched the UN offices being burned and UN workers being beaten. One witness said that after the militiamen beat the victims to death inside the building, they pulled them outside, put them on a woodpile, doused them with gasoline, and set them on fire. The militias were upset over the death of Olivio Mendoza Moruk, 45, who was found dead on September 5. 00090601

September 7, 2000. *Guinea.* The Revolutionary United Front (RUF) of Sierra Leone kidnapped three Catholic missionaries—a U.S. citizen and two Italian priests—in Pamlap. The two Italians escaped in early December. 00090701

September 10, 2000. *Spain.* Basque Nation and Liberty (ETA) claimed credit for setting off a bomb at 11:00 A.M. in the empty Txitxarro disco in Deba, 15 miles west of San Sebastian. No one was hurt, but extensive damage was reported to the building's roof. A caller warned of an imminent explosion. He said two people who were cleaning inside had been left handcuffed to a tree along a road. Soon after, a hunter found a man and a woman tied to a tree. The duo confirmed that no one else was inside. Deba Mayor Jesus Maria Aguirrezabala said the target was the disco's owner, Narciso Korta, a brother of a businessmen killed in an ETA car bombing in August.

September 11, 2000. *Malaysia.* Gunmen kidnapped three Malaysians from a diving resort off Kota Kinabalu on the east coast. Diplomats and police suggested the attack was similar to those by the Philippine Abu Sayyaf rebels. The hostages were rescued in a mangrove forest in a clash between their 30 captors and military troops on October 25. 00091101

September 12, 2000. *South Africa.* A bomb strapped to a tree between a mosque and a community center exploded outside an evening political rally in Cape Town. Gerald Morkel, Western Cape provincial premier, was scheduled to appear.

Twenty bombings had occurred in the Cape Town area in two years. Seven people were injured, including a police officer and a young girl. Morkel was unhurt in the blast that was blamed on the Muslim People Against Gangsterism and Drugs (PAGAD). PAGAD members denied involvement in the bombings. A local judge presiding over several terrorism cases apparently involving PAGAD had been assassinated the previous week.

September 13, 2000. *Spain.* In a series of dawn raids in Madrid, the Basque country, and neighboring Navarre region, some 300 police arrested 19 people believed to be leaders of Basque Nation and Liberty (ETA). They were accused of membership in EKIN, ETA's clandestine strategy unit, and would be charged with membership in an armed group. ETA had been linked to 12 killings in the year 2000 since calling off a 14-month cease-fire in December 1999.

September 13, 2000. *Indonesia.* A car bomb exploded in a garage under the Jakarta Stock Exchange, killing at least 15, injuring 30, some seriously, and damaging 400 cars. Ten victims died of asphyxiation and burns; five died from injuries from flying debris. The bomb went off 30 minutes before thousands of workers would have headed home. Five people were held for questioning. No one claimed credit. Many believed that the bombers were aiming at dissuading foreign investors. Many of the dead and injured were believed to be hired drivers who remained with the cars. On September 15, President Abdurrahman Wahid ordered police to arrest Tommy Suharto (also known as Hutomo Mandala Putra), 38, the youngest son of former President Suharto, in connection with the recent bombing campaign. Wahid also suspected Habib Alwi Baaqil, leader of a pro-Suharto Muslim group, who claimed innocence. Two days later, Wahid ordered Tommy Suharto's bodyguards to be disarmed. Police questioned whether they had enough evidence to warrant an arrest. On September 17, Wahid replaced national Police Chief General Rusihardjo. Later in the month,

courts dismissed the case against the elderly Suharto because he was medically unable to stand trial, but Wahid attempted to resurrect the charges.

On September 25, Indonesian police arrested two members of the armed forces after a shootout. Police General Bimantoro claimed that the duo had acted as individuals and that the military was not behind the series of bombings.

September 13, 2000. *Colombia.* The National Liberation Army (ELN) set up a fake roadblock in Antioquia and kidnapped two Russian civil engineers. They were freed on September 21. 00091301

September 14, 2000. *United States.* The FBI announced it was working with the New York City police investigation into the possible poisoning of bottled water with lye and ammonia. Three people, including an 18-month-old, had become ill.

September 15, 2000. *France.* Police detained Ignacio Gracia Arregui, 45, and his girlfriend, in a raid on Basque Nation and Liberty (ETA) in Bidart in the southwest. He was believed to be the leader of ETA's military wing and allegedly ordered the failed 1995 assassination attempt of King Juan Carlos of Spain. 00091501

September 15, 2000. *Colombia.* Unknown gunmen kidnapped three Italians in Medellin. 00091502

September 16, 2000. *Spain.* Police with helicopters and sniffer dogs found eight grenades in woods near Hernani just before a visit by King Juan Carlos, Prime Minister Jose Maria Aznar, and German Chancellor Gerhard Schroeder. Authorities blamed Basque Nation and Liberty (ETA), which had warned that only the German was welcome in the town. The grenades were in launching tubes in a pit 600 yards from the open-air museum of sculptor Eduardo Chillida, which was inaugurated by the king and visited by the others and more than a dozen Spanish politicians. 00091601

September 17, 2000. *Colombia.* The National Liberation Army (ELN) was believed to be responsible for kidnapping 80 people from two restaurants and Colombian citizen Eduardo de Lima, his wife Elena, and two other family members from their farm in Cali. De Lima's brother owned the De Lima Insurance Company, one of the region's largest. De Lima's wife was a U.S. citizen from Timonium, Maryland, who had lived in Colombia for 34 years. Some 50 armed men, many wearing military-style uniforms and bulletproof vests, stormed into the Cabana Restaurant and the Embajada de Ginebra restaurant, ten miles outside Cali. No immediate demands were made.

The next day, gunmen released 25 captives, including Elena de Lima, who said she was freed to deliver ransom demands for her husband's sister and nephew to a wealthy brother-in-law. Eduardo had been released earlier. 00091701

September 17, 2000. *Guinea.* Sapeu Laurence Dejya, 37, an Ivorian based in the UN relief agency's office in Abidjan, Ivory Coast, was kidnapped by suspected Sierra Leonean Revolutionary United Front (RUF) rebels in an attack in which a UN colleague, Mensah Kpognon, the Togolese head of the UN refugee operation in Macenta, Guinea, was killed. She had disappeared after delivering supplies to a UN base for refugees in Macenta. After escaping, Dejya and five refugees walked in the jungle for days before reaching Liberia's northern district of Zorzor, where they were rescued by Liberian troops who took her to Monrovia, Liberia, on September 28. Liberian Information Minister Joe Mulbah blamed Guinea dissidents. The UN High Commissioner for Refugees withdrew all of its field personnel in Guinea to Conakry following the attack. 00091702

September 18, 2000. *Serbia.* North Atlantic Treaty Organization (NATO) troops arrested three Serbs at midnight in Kosovo and charged them with planning to bomb international organizations on orders from the Yugoslav government. Troops found three pounds of explosives, various types of detonators, wiring equipment, two grenades, and four firearms at two houses and the Cemetery Bar in Gracanica, an ethnic Serb enclave politically controlled by members of Yugoslav President Slobodan Milosevic's ruling party. Investigators uncovered a list of potential targets, including "prominent facilities" associated with international organizations. NATO had earlier raided arms caches believed to belong to the officially disbanded Kosovo Liberation Army, an ethnic Albanian rebel force.

September 19, 2000. *Pakistan.* A bomb hidden in a truckload of grapes exploded in Islamabad in the morning, killing 16 and wounding more than 80. No one claimed credit. Workers were unloading crates from the truck when the bomb went off. Police detained seven truck drivers for questioning and later arrested three men in the Kurram Agency, which borders Afghanistan where the truck began its trip.

September 20, 2000. *United Kingdom.* A small missile was fired at the headquarters of MI-6 (overseas intelligence) in Central London during the night. The missile hit the eighth floor, causing minimal damage (to a window and two wall panels). Irish Republican Army (IRA) dissident groups were suspected. Witnesses said they heard two explosions. The next day, police found part of a rocket-propelled grenade launcher in a nearby park.

September 21, 2000. *Indonesia.* Police arrested 25 people planning to blow up the U.S. Embassy in Jakarta. Most of them were from the separatist province of Aceh. The first man, Iwan Setiawan, was arrested at a traffic light on September 21 and found to be carrying a hand grenade. The detainee admitted involvement in the explosion at the Malaysian Embassy and the September 13 bombing of the stock exchange. He said the next targets were to be the U.S. Embassy and a nearby Sarinah department store. The other two dozen people were picked up on September 24. Senior Superintendent of Police Saleh Saaf said the detainees were not linked to the military or police. The Free

Aceh Movement denied involvement in the bombings. 00092101

September 21, 2000. *Russia.* Iskandar Khatloni, 45, a Moscow-based correspondent for the U.S.-funded Radio Liberty's Tajik division, died from head wounds sustained on a Moscow street. He was found unconscious on the street and died several hours later. Radio Free Europe and Radio Liberty said he had been attacked, but did not offer a motive. He was working on stories about human rights abuses. He had published four volumes of poetry. He joined Radio Liberty in 1996, having earlier worked for the BBC.

September 27, 2000. *Gaza Strip.* Two Israeli soldiers were wounded, one seriously, when two roadside bombs exploded near a convoy of Jewish settlers at Netzarim Junction. The convoy was accompanied by Israeli military vehicles. It was heading toward Netzarim, south of Gaza City, when the bombs exploded and the vehicles were fired upon.

September 29, 2000. *Colombia.* The Revolutionary Armed Forces of Colombia (FARC), in a statement on the Internet, warned U.S. soldiers based in Colombia that they would be considered a "military target" if they took a front-line combat role against them. Senior rebel commander Andres Paris said, "All Colombian or foreign military personnel in combat zones will be a military target of the FARC . . . . At the moment, FARC guerrillas do not wish to reveal if there are concrete plans to attack U.S. military bases in the country." He observed that the U.S. soldiers were "very close to regions where guerrillas recently staged intense combat that caused government forces important casualties." 00092901

October 2000. *Azerbaijan.* The Supreme Court in Baku found 13 members of Jayshullah, a local terrorist group that may have planned to attack the U.S. Embassy, guilty of committing terrorist actions. The court sentenced them to prison terms ranging from eight years to life.

October 2000. *Italy.* Authorities in Naples issued arrest warrants for 11 members of Al-Takfir w'al Hijra, a North African Muslim extremist group. Seven were apprehended in Naples, France, and Algeria, but four eluded arrest. Officials noted that members of the group, also active in Milan and other cities, engaged primarily in forging travel documents and raising funds from expatriate Muslims.

October 2000. *Paraguay.* Counter-narcotics police arrested an individual believed to be representing the Revolutionary Armed Forces of Colombia (FARC) for involvement in a guns-for-cocaine ring between Paraguay and FARC.

October 1, 2000. *Tajikistan.* Unidentified militants set off two bombs in a Christian church in Dushanbe, killing 7 and injuring 70. The church was founded by Korean-born U.S. citizens. Most of those killed and wounded were Korean. No one claimed credit. 00100101

October 2, 2000. *Germany.* A Duesseldorf synagogue was firebombed. Police arrested two Arabs on December 7—a 20-year-old German citizen of Moroccan origin and a Palestinian who was born in Jordan and had lived in Germany for several years. The duo attacked out of anger at the violence in the West Bank and Gaza Strip.

October 2, 2000. *Uganda.* Lord's Resistance Army (LRA) rebels shot and killed an Italian priest as he drove to church in Kitgum. 00100201

October 2, 2000. *Sri Lanka.* A suicide bomber was suspected of setting off an explosion that killed at least 19, including ruling party candidate Mohommed Bayatullah and 2 policemen, and injured 40, including 7 police officers, at an election rally in Muttur, 150 miles east of Colombo.

Hours earlier, a deputy minister in the government missed injury in a roadside bombing that killed one person.

The Tamil Tigers were suspected of both attacks.

October 4, 2000. *Middle East.* As hopes for a negotiated peace settlement broke down in the midst of increasing rioting in the area, the State Department announced the closure of all U.S. embassies and consulates for three to four days.

October 12, 2000. *West Bank.* During the previous two weeks of violence, nearly 100 people, mostly Palestinians, were killed in rioting. The most publicized act, however, was when Palestinians stormed a Palestinian police precinct and killed two Israeli reserve soldiers.

Vadim Nourjits, 33, had set out at 7:00 A.M. from his parents' house to meet up with fellow reservist Yossef Avrahami, 38. They had been ordered to go to Bet El, an army base near Ramallah. They apparently got lost, took a wrong turn, and were spotted by rioters, who believed them to be operatives from an Israeli plainclothes anti-fugitive unit, even though they were partially uniformed. They were picked up by the Palestinian police, who took them to the Ramallah police station. The rioters broke into the station and shot Avrahami in the head. Avrahami was turned over to Israeli officials, but died soon after. Nourjits was beaten and burned almost beyond recognition. International newspapers ran a photo of his body being thrown from the window of the police station. In another photo, one of his attackers waved his blood-stained hands to the mob outside. Nourjits's body was beaten with a metal screen and stomped on. The corpse was tied to a car and driven through the streets to the center of town, where it was set on fire. Nourjits had married a week earlier.

Israel claimed that Yasir Arafat had ordered the release from Palestinian jails of dozens of members of Hamas and Islamic Jihad. One of them, Mohammed Deif (variants Dayf, Dief), a Hamas leader, was accused of planning and commanding several bloody bombings. A Palestinian official said they had escaped.

Israel retaliated with a helicopter gunship rocket barrage against Palestinian Authority sites in Ramallah, Bayt Lahia, and Gaza City, where Arafat had his principal headquarters.

Two days later, Arafat agreed to an emergency summit with Israeli Prime Minister Ehud Barak, U.S. President Bill Clinton, UN Secretary General Kofi Annan, Egyptian President Hosni Mubarak, and King Abdullah of Jordan.

On October 26, the Israeli Army announced the arrest of a 20-year-old Palestinian suspected of participating in the killing of the two reservists. Other suspects were still being interrogated. The suspect was photographed holding up a hand covered in blood. By July 6, 2001, at least 15 Palestinians, including one named Salha, were arrested in the case. Palestinians were arguing that Salha, a karate brown belt, was held in a case of mistaken identity. Israel arrested Salha on June 14 and said he had confessed under interrogation to being the man in the photo. His family said he was in the crowd at the time of the lynching, but was not the photographed man.

On July 16, 2001, Israel arrested another suspect in the mob killing.

October 12, 2000. *Yemen.* A 20-foot boat laden with explosives came alongside the 8,600-ton USS *Cole*, DDG 67, and detonated, ripping a 40-by-40-foot hole in the hull's half-inch-thick armored steel plates near the engine rooms and adjacent eating and living quarters. At least 17 American sailors were killed by the blast; another 44 were injured. Until the bodies of ten missing crewmen were found, the Pentagon would not formally declare them dead. No Yemenis were killed in the Aden port blast. Thirty-four injured men and five injured women were flown to Ramstein Air Force Base in Germany; three had serious injuries. By the next day, five sailors with minor injuries had returned to the *Cole*. One sailor had a punctured lung; another suffered burns on her face and hands; three others had compound fractures and were scheduled for surgery.

The small harbor workboat had been involved with the refueling of the 505-foot Arleigh Burke-class guided-missile destroyer. After delivering a mooring line to a buoy, the boat returned to the ship, then exploded just after noon. The two men seen on board the boat were believed to be on a suicide mission. The blast warped hatchways at the top of the ship.

Suspects in the bombing included the Palestinian Islamic Jihad, Hamas, Hizballah, the bin Laden organization, Iraq, the Egyptian Islamic Jihad, Libyan opposition groups, the Algerian Armed Islamic Group, and the Yemeni terrorist organization Islamic Army of Aden (also known as Aden-Abyan Islamic Army). Abyan is a southern province. Sheik Omar Bakri Muhammad, a Syrian-born cleric living in the United Kingdom, said the Yemeni group had claimed credit.

Some observers believed Yemeni authorities might have been involved with the terrorists, as the attackers apparently knew the precise timing of the four-hour refueling mission.

The dead were identified as:

- Kenneth E. Clodfelter, 21, Mechanicsville, Virginia
- Richard Costelow, 35, Morrisville, Pennsylvania
- Lakeina M. Francis, 19, Woodleaf, North Carolina
- Timothy L. Gauna, 21, Rice, Texas
- Cherone Louis Gunn, 22, Rex, Georgia
- James Rodrick McDaniels, 19, Norfolk, Virginia
- Marc Ian Nieto, 24, Fond du Lac, Wisconsin
- Ronald S. Owens, 24, Vero Beach, Florida
- Lakiba Nicole Palmer, 22, San Diego, California
- Joshua Parletta, 19, Level, Maryland
- Patrick Roy, 19, Keedysville, Maryland
- Kevin Shawn Rux, 30, Portland, North Dakota
- Ronchester Santiago, 22, Kingsville, Texas
- Timothy L. Saunders, 32, Rinngold, Virginia
- Gary Graham Swenchonis, Jr., 26, Rockport, Texas
- Andrew Triplett, 31, Macon, Mississippi
- Craig Wibberley, 19, Williamsport, Maryland

Only one of the dead was an officer.

The injured included Petty Officer Johann Gokool, 21, a Trinidad native; and Andrew Nemeth, 19, of Amherst, Ohio.

State Department and Defense Department officials questioned each other's judgment regarding the visit. Some noted that U.S. warships had made 12 other visits to the Aden port in the past 15 months without incident.

The United States was concerned about anti-Israeli and anti-American sentiments throughout Yemen, including those recently expressed by members of the government, but nonetheless sent more than 160 investigators, including Marines from a Fleet Anti-Terrorism Security Team, a Federal Emergency Security Team, FBI lab experts, the Naval Criminal Investigative Service, and the State Department.

By October 14, Yemeni officials had begun to detain suspects for questioning.

Yemeni President Ali Abdallah Salih later told CNN that some detainees belonged to the Egyptian al-Jihad, whose leader, Ayman Zawahiri, was with bin Laden in Afghanistan. Salih said a 12-year-old boy told investigators that a bearded man with glasses gave him 2,000 rials ($12) and asked him to watch a four-wheel-drive vehicle parked near the port on the day of the attack. The man took a rubber boat off the top of the car and headed into the harbor, never to return. The car led investigators to a modest house in the Madinet al-Shaab (variant ash-Shaab) suburb of Aden.

On October 16, Yemeni investigators discovered bomb-making material in an apartment used by individuals believed to have been involved. Yemeni security officers said they were non-Yemeni Arabs; others said they were Saudis who stayed for six weeks in a house near Aden's power station. Another house, close to the Aden refinery and oil storage facilities in the al-Baraiqa neighborhood had been discovered by October 21. The suspects apparently had briefly left and then re-entered Yemen before the bombing. They had parked a fiberglass boat in the driveway; the boat was now missing. Police tracked the car to a house in al-Baraiqa, or Little Aden, west of Aden, on Zahra (Flower Street).

The U.S. Navy revised its theory of the bombing on October 20, saying the destroyer had been moored for two hours and was already refueling when the bomb boat came alongside. The boat blended in with harbor workboats and was not suspected by the gun crews on the ship.

By October 24, the investigators were looking at three safe houses that served as the terrorists' quarters in al-Baraiqa, a workshop in Madinet al-Shaab, and a lookout perch in the Tawahi neighborhood. A lease for the lookout apartment was signed by Abdullah Ahmed Khaled al-Musawah. Binoculars and Islamic publications were found in the apartment. The same name was found on a fake ID card in personal documents seized in the safe houses. Yemeni investigators detained employees of the Lajeh civil registration office in the northern farming region. Investigators looked at a possible Saudi connection—one of the individuals had a Saudi accent. Others looked at the mountainous province of Hadramaut (variant Hadramut) as one suspect used a name common to the area. The press also indicated that the terrorists' will dedicated the attack to the al-Aqsa Mosque in Jerusalem. Authorities questioned more than 100 people, including port workers, government employees, neighbors, acquaintances of the suspects, and employees of the Mansoob Ship Supply and Trading Company, a local firm that supplied the Cole.

On October 25, Yemeni President Salih told a television interviewer that the bombing was carried out by Muslims who had fought against the Soviet Union in Afghanistan and then moved to Yemen. Egyptian Islamic Jihad terrorists affiliated with bin Laden remained the key suspects; a witness identified one of the bombers as an Egyptian. Yemeni authorities arrested Islamic activists originally from Egypt, Algeria, and elsewhere, as well as local Yemenis. A local carpenter confessed he had worked with two suspects in modifying a small boat to hold explosives and helped them to load the explosives on board. He had rented the suspects the building where they prepared the boat. A

Somali woman who owned a car used by the suspects to haul the boat was questioned. Yemeni investigators believed the terrorists had given her money to buy the car.

The Taliban in Afghanistan said bin Laden was not responsible. Bin Laden welcomed the attack.

On October 29, the navy tugboat USNS *Catawba* towed the *Cole* to the Norwegian transport ship *Blue Marlin*, which carried the *Cole* back to the United States.

Yemen arrested four men living in Aden on November 5 to 6 after tracing them via phone records that showed they had been in contact with the suspected bombers. Officials in Lahej had provided the bombing suspects with government cars for use in Aden. The bombers knew the officials from their time together in Afghanistan in the 1980s.

President Clinton asked Yemen's president for FBI access to the detainees. Meanwhile, the FBI was attempting to track the source of the C-4 plastic explosive.

On November 11, Yemeni investigators said that at least three plots against U.S. targets in Yemen had failed in the past year. Yemeni officials said a detainee claimed that terrorists had planned to bomb the U.S. destroyer USS *The Sullivans* during refueling in Aden on January 3, 2000. The explosives-laden small boat sank from the weight of the explosives.

The *Washington Post* reported on November 13 that the sentries on the *Cole* did not have ammunition in their guns and were not authorized to shoot first without permission of an officer. The *Post* also suggested that the *Cole* could have been boarded and surveilled by Islamic militants (and possibly one of the bombers) disguised as Egyptian souvenir vendors as it passed through the Suez Canal. The FBI was looking into whether the Yemeni pilot who guided the *Cole* into port was agitated. Yemeni harbor workers apparently had also acted suspiciously. They had refueled the ship very quickly and then run into a cement hut shortly before the explosion.

Although the Yemenis did not want the FBI to interrogate Yemeni citizens directly, they arranged for the FBI agents to watch the interrogations via television monitor and one-way mirrors. They signed an agreement to cooperate with the FBI on November 29.

On November 16, Yemeni Prime Minister Abdel-Karim Ali Iryani said that the two Yemeni bombers were veterans of the Afghan War. One was a Yemeni born in the eastern province of Hadramaut. (Osama bin Laden had Yemeni citizenship because of his father's birth in the Hadramaut region.)

On November 19, Yemeni authorities said that they had detained "less than 10" suspected accomplices out of the more than 50 people still held for questioning. One source claimed that the Yemenis had detained six men who were key accomplices, including a main plotter. The bombers had moved in and out of Yemen since the Afghan War. The attack planned for January failed when TNT packed into the hull of a small boat absorbed seawater and became much heavier, causing it to sink after launch. An explosives expert reconfigured the charge using lightweight C-4 plastique. The Yemen *Observer* reported that the fiberglass boat was brought in from another country. Authorities retrieved red rope used to tether the skiff to a trailer and a pair of glasses matching those used by a bomber for his fake ID.

On November 21, U.S. officials said the bombing appeared to be linked to the bombings of the U.S. embassies in Africa in 1998. A composite sketch of one of the bombers appeared to match that of a man wanted for questioning in the Africa bombings.

On November 25, Yemeni Prime Minister Iryani said that "investigations into the USS *Cole* blast have revealed that the two men who carried out the operation were Saudis of Yemeni origin. . . . Investigators also found that Osama bin Laden, who is also of Yemeni origin, was also involved in the attack on the destroyer, even if indirectly. But the investigation has not found evidence of this yet."

The following day, the Associated Press cited a source near the investigation as indicating that two suspects would be charged with carrying out the

bombing, threatening state security, forming an armed gang, and possessing explosives. Death by firing squad in public was a possibility.

The State Department announced on December 7 that it supported Yemen's decision to prosecute three—and possibly six—Yemeni suspects in January, following the end of the holy month of Ramadan. One of them, Fhad al-Quoso, reportedly told investigators that an associate of bin Laden had given him more than $5,000 to finance the planning and videotaping of the USS *Cole* suicide bombing. ABC News reported that suspect Jamal al-Badawi admitted he was trained in bin Laden's camps in Afghanistan and was sent with bin Laden's forces to fight in Bosnia's civil war. He was believed to have obtained the boat. The defendants could face lengthy prison terms or execution. Yemen had also identified Muhammad Omar al-Harazi, a Saudi born in Yemen, as a planner of the attack and a member of al-Qaeda, bin Laden's organization. He might also have played a role in the truck bombings in Tanzania and Kenya in 1998.

An interview with Yemeni President Salih was published in the *Washington Post* on December 10. In it, he suggested that bin Laden, the Israelis, regional and national intelligence agencies, or others could have been behind the blast. He noted that extradition is constitutionally prohibited.

On December 13, the USS *Cole* arrived home in Pascagoula, Mississippi, on board the *Blue Marlin*. It returned to the Litton Ingalls Shipbuilding facility where it was built in 1995. The *Cole* would be given a temporary 40-ton patch, unloaded, and taken to a nearby naval station for cleanup and weapons removal. In January, it would go to a Litton dry dock for $240 million in repairs.

On January 2, 2001, a Pentagon inquiry report concluded that the military needed to better anticipate terrorist attacks and protect ships, aircraft, and troops in transit, and called for U.S. intelligence to devote more resources to acquiring human reporting on terrorist plans. The report was scheduled for release the following week. Follow-up Pentagon reports recommended against punishing any individual military personnel and held the entire chain of command responsible.

In late January, the Yemenis agreed to postpone a planned trial of suspects to give the FBI more time to conduct interrogations on Yemeni soil. FBI agents were at last permitted to question witnesses and suspects directly.

On January 30, 2001, ABC News reported that Mohamed Rashed Daoud Owhali, a defendant in the bombings of U.S. embassies in Africa, allegedly had told the FBI in 1998 about a plan for a rocket attack on a U.S. warship in Yemen. The *Washington Post* reported that the FBI sent a message to the Pentagon regarding the plan on August 25, 1998.

On February 17, Yemen detained two more suspects when they returned from Afghanistan.

Osama bin Laden applauded the attack on February 26, saying the *Cole* was a ship of injustice that sailed "to its doom." His comments were made at a family celebration in Afghanistan and broadcast on Qatar's satellite channel *al-Jazeerah*. He recited a poem to celebrate the January marriage of his son, Mohammed, in Kandahar, saying, "In Aden, the young man stood up for holy war and destroyed a destroyer feared by the powerful." He said the *Cole* sailed on a course of "false arrogance, self-conceit, and strength."

On March 31, Yemeni police announced the arrests of several more suspects believed to be Islamic militants. The main suspect apparently had fled to Afghanistan. Ali Mohammed Omar Kurdi was arrested; his house was searched the previous day.

Yemen arrested 5 suspects with ties to Islamic terrorist cells on April 14 to 15, 2001, bringing the total in custody to 28. Two jailed suspects had informed security officials about terrorist cells operating in the country. The cells had two or three members each and were directed by leaders of Yemen's Islamic Jihad (YIJ) who were based in several countries outside Yemen, including Afghanistan. The cells assisted non-Yemeni Arabs with ties to YIJ by providing forged Yemeni passports, safe houses, and information on Yemeni security.

John Clodfelter, father of Kenneth Clodfelter, who was killed in the explosion, began a campaign to issue a Virginia commemorative license plate honoring the victims. (See www.remembertheCole.homestead.com for further information.)

A 100-minute videotape made by Al-Sahab (The Clouds) Productions and circulated in Kuwait City by Muslim militants showed Osama bin Laden for several minutes and suggested that his followers bombed the *Cole*. Bin Laden recites a poem that includes the lines, "And in Aden, they charged and destroyed a destroyer that fearsome people fear, one that evokes horror when it docks and when it sails." His followers training at the Farouq camp in Afghanistan sing a song that includes, "We thank God for granting us victory the day we destroyed *Cole* in the sea."

On June 18, 2001, Yemeni authorities arrested nine people affiliated with the Islamic Army of Aden who were plotting to attack FBI investigators in the *Cole* case. The FBI had ordered all U.S. investigators out of Yemen on June 15. The men were found with hand grenades, small arms, and documents, including a map of the U.S. Embassy in Sanaa. FBI investigators returned to Yemen in late August 2001.

On October 26, 2001, Jamil Qasim Saeed Mohammed, 27, a Yemeni microbiology student and active member of al-Qaeda, was handed over to U.S. authorities by Pakistani intelligence, according to Pakistani government sources. Pakistan bypassed the usual extradition and deportation procedures. 00101201

October 12, 2000. *Bosnia.* Janko Janjic, 43, a Serbian war crimes suspect, set off a hand grenade as North Atlantic Treaty Organization (NATO) peacekeeping troops tried to arrest him in Foca, 25 miles southeast of Sarajevo. The blast killed him and wounded four German soldiers, none critically. He was the third suspected war criminal to die while resisting arrest. Janjic had been a car mechanic before the war. He was one of four Bosnian Serb sub-commanders indicted for the torture, rape, and enslavement of women and girls in Foca in the summer of 1992. His three colleagues went on trial in The Hague, Netherlands, in March. 00101202

October 12, 2000. *Ecuador.* Five Americans were kidnapped from oil camps in the El Coca region, 150 miles east of Quito by heavily armed men wearing fatigues. The oil field was operated by the Spanish-Argentine firm Repsol-YPF SA, on the shores of the Napo River, 120 miles east of Quito.

The government blamed left-wing Revolutionary Armed Forces of Colombia (FARC) terrorists (who denied responsibility); others said it was a criminal case. Observers believed the same gang kidnapped a dozen Canadian oil workers in 1999. They were released three months later for $3 million.

The hostages were David Bradley of Casper, Wyoming, an oil field platform foreman for Helmerich and Payne; Ronald Clay Sander, 54, of Sunrise Beach, Missouri, a technician working on an oil rig with the same firm based in Tulsa; and Arnold Alford, 41, Steve Derry, 41, and Jason Weber, 29, all employees of the Oregon-based Erickson Air-Crane Company and residents of Gold Hill, Oregon. Also kidnapped were a Chilean; an Argentine; Dennis Corrin of Nelson, New Zealand; and two French helicopter pilots. The gunmen also hijacked the helicopter. The Frenchmen escaped within days of the attack.

Negotiations with the kidnappers, believed to be a criminal gang, stalled over ransom demands.

On January 31, 2001, Sander's body was found in an isolated jungle region of El Condor, 110 miles northeast of Quito. He had five gunshot wounds in the back. A message on a sheet covering his body said, "I am a gringo. For nonpayment of ransom. HP company." Sander had worked for the company for 24 years.

Ecuadoran Vice Admiral Miguel Saona, head of the Joint Chiefs of Staff, told reporters on February 14, 2001, that the kidnappers had agreed to accept a ransom before their deadline for killing another captive. "With relation to the deadline of today or tomorrow to execute a second captive, I have information that yesterday negotiations were restarted. . . . The criminal group said it would not execute anyone else and I understand they have

reached some economic arrangement." He did not know the details.

The kidnappers freed the seven foreign oil workers on March 1 following payment of $13 million sent in by helicopter. A military patrol picked up the hostages at 11:00 A.M. in Santa Rosa, 18 miles south of the Colombian border. The hostages were in fair health and suffering from fatigue. They underwent medical checks near Lago Agrio, the provincial capital, before going to Quito. The Chilean was experiencing heart palpitations.

In press interviews, the hostages said they were chained, ate rats, and constantly feared death while living in enforced silence. Argentinian Juan Rodriguez said the kidnappers "lied to us, told us that our colleague Ron had been moved to Quito." They survived by eating rice and sardines, and kept up their spirits with thoughts of their families. Weber made a calendar with a piece of paper and a pen. The kidnappers gave them a small magnetic chess set. The hostages worked out on a gym made by Alford from ropes strung on trees.

The Americans returned to the United States on March 3.

On June 22, 2001, Colombia announced the arrest of 50 gang members in the kidnappings, including the ringleader, Gerardo Herrera, a former member of the Colombian People's Liberation Army (EPL); seven Ecuadorans were arrested in Ecuador. 00101203

October 12, 2000. *Colombia.* Right-wing paramilitary extremists were believed to be responsible for kidnapping 11 villagers. Seven homes were spray-painted with the letters AUC, the Spanish initials of the United Self-Defense Forces of Colombia, although the group did not claim responsibility. The next day, the seven men and four women were found shot to death along a dirt road outside Barbosa, 18 miles northeast of Medellin. The paramilitaries had accused the victims of collaborating with leftist guerrillas. They had been selected with the help of a female rebel who had been captured by the paramilitaries.

October 13, 2000. *Yemen.* A bomb was thrown over the wall at the U.K. Embassy in Sanaa, causing a huge fireball when it exploded next to a diesel generator. No injuries were reported. The bomb shattered windows of nearby buildings, including that of the Dutch Embassy. The Yemeni government claimed it was an accident involving the generator; others believed it was terrorism. 00101301

October 13, 2000. *Bosnia.* Four German NATO-led Stabilization Force (SFOR) soldiers were injured in Sarajevo when they attempted to arrest a Bosnian who detonated a hand grenade, killing himself and wounding the soldiers and a civilian. 00101301

October 13, 2000. *Indonesia.* A bomb exploded in Lombok, damaging the offices of the PT Newmont Nusa Tenggara Mining Company, which is jointly owned by U.S., Japanese, and Indonesian interests. No one took credit. 00101302

October 13, 2000. *Yemen.* A small bomb exploded in the British Embassy compound. No injuries were reported. 00101303

October 14, 2000. *Saudi Arabia.* Four Saudis and one Ethiopian hijacked Saudi Arabian Airlines Flight 115, a Boeing 777-200 carrying 105 people from Jeddah to London. The hijackers called for the Saudi royal family to leave power and end the monarchy. One claimed, "We are just ordinary people and we are calling for the rights of the Saudi people such as decent education, decent health, and other services." The hijacking apparently was not related to other Middle Eastern violence. The passengers included 40 Britons, 1 American, 15 Saudis—including a member of the royal family—15 Pakistanis, and others from South Africa, Yemen, and Kenya.

The pilot radioed Egyptian air traffic controllers in the afternoon that the plane had been hijacked. He told them the hijackers had threatened to blow up the plane with dynamite unless it was flown to Damascus, Syria. Syria initially refused permission to land, but later relented. The

hijackers, however, ordered the landing aborted and flew on to Baghdad, Iraq.

The plane landed in Baghdad, where authorities arrested the hijackers after three hours of negotiations. The hijackers had threatened to blow up the plane in the air and on the tarmac. The hijackers' sole demand was to speak to a Saudi official. Iraqi authorities showed two Saudi hijackers in their mid-20s to reporters at Saddam International Airport. Iraq announced on October 17 that it would not extradite the duo, but could reconsider the decision if Riyadh changed its anti-Baghdad stance.

The plane returned to Riyadh on October 16. The passengers spent the night there before flying on to London. Among the passengers was Jacky Doyle, who worked for the British Museum. 00101401

October 14, 2000. *South Africa.* Demonstrators, possibly including People Against Gangsterism and Drugs (PAGAD) members, vandalized and threw rocks at a McDonald's restaurant in Cape Town. No one was injured, but significant damage was reported at the restaurant and to customers' vehicles.

October 15, 2000. *Europe/Lebanon.* Israel said that Israeli businessman Elhanan Tennenbaum was kidnapped by Hizballah operatives in Europe, possibly Switzerland. Hizballah spokesman Said Hasan Nasrallah said Tennenbaum was a Mossad colonel who was picked up in Lebanon while trying to recruit one of the group's members. Nasrallah said the hostage flew to Lebanon from Brussels on a forged foreign passport to meet a Hizballah activist via a go-between. Hizballah provided information as bait before setting up the meeting. Hizballah said Tennenbaum was an artillery officer in the Israeli Army who took part in the invasion of Lebanon in 1982 and the siege of Beirut. He denied Israeli claims that the Iranians and Syrians aided in the abduction. 00101501

October 19, 2000. *Colombia.* The shooting down by the Revolutionary Armed Forces of Colombia (FARC) of a U.S.-made UH-60 Black Hawk helicopter, in which 22 people were killed, led to a three-day gun battle in which 54 members of the national police and army died in the mountains of Antioquia. The government had earlier claimed that the helicopter crashed in an accident in which 18 soldiers and 4 crewmen died.

October 19, 2000. *Sri Lanka.* A suicide bomber detonated explosives he was wearing near the Colombo town hall, killing 4 and wounding 23, including 2 Americans and a British citizen. The Liberation Tigers of Tamil Eelam (LTTE) was suspected. 00101901

October 23, 2000. *Middle East.* U.S. military forces at bases in Qatar, Bahrain, the Persian Gulf, and Incirlik, Turkey, were put on Threat Condition Delta, the highest possible state of security alert, after receipt of a terrorist threat. Delta is called if the military believes a specific threat of attack against a specific target is likely. All incoming vehicles are searched; all packages and suitcases are inspected. Journeys outside the post are kept to a minimum. A school in Bahrain attended by American and other foreign students was closed indefinitely. Other targets included the U.S. embassies in Bahrain and Qatar and a U.S. military site in Qatar.

October 26, 2000. *Yemen.* Security was tightened at the Aden Hotel after a warning of a possible truck bomb attack. Dozens of American investigators were staying in the hotel. A Yemeni Army pickup truck with a mounted machine gun was stationed at the entranceway.

October 26, 2000. *Gaza Strip.* A Palestinian on a bicycle set off a bomb at the wall of an Israeli Army post, injuring a soldier. The Islamic Jihad claimed credit, identifying the dead terrorist as Nabil al-Arair.

October 29, 2000. *Peru.* Sixty rebellious army soldiers led by Lieutenant Colonel Ollanta Moises Humala Tasso, head of the artillery division at Tacna, seized a strategic mining town in the south and demanded the resignation of President Alberto Fujimori. Tasso was assisted by his brother, Antauro, a former army major dismissed in 1998. They fled with hostages, including their commanding general, Oscar Bardales, and drove to Toquepala, a copper mining settlement 640 miles southeast of Lima, run by the Mexican-owned Southern Peru Copper Corporation. The move came a day after Fujimori replaced the commanders of the army, air force, and navy. Many military officers believed that Fujimori was attempting to assist his former intelligence chief, Vladimiro Montesinos, to escape capture. Two hours later, Tasso grabbed a microphone at a local church and called on other military units to join the revolt. He sent the 2,000 residents to their homes and cut off roads for eight hours. The soldiers grabbed a bus and provisions from the mining company and escaped with Bardales and four other hostages. They were driving to the distant Santa Rosa Fort, near the Bolivian border. Three truckloads of army loyalists were in pursuit. 00102901

October 30, 2000. *Spain.* The Basque Nation and Liberty (ETA) set off a car bomb during the Madrid morning rush hour, killing a supreme court judge, his driver, and his bodyguard, and wounding more than 60 people on a nearby bus, including the driver, who died nine days later of head injuries. On November 19, ETA claimed credit for 19 attacks since July that killed eight people, but regretted the death of the bus driver.

November 2000. *Paraguay.* Authorities arrested Salah Abdul Karim Yassine, a Palestinian who allegedly threatened to bomb the U.S. and Israeli embassies in Asuncion, and charged him with possession of false documents and entering the country illegally. He was alleged to be obtaining $100,000 in financing while living in Ciudad del Este. He said he was making the threats as a joke. He remained in prison at the end of December 2000.

November 2000. *Kuwait.* The government disrupted a suspected international terrorist cell.

Working with regional counterparts, Kuwaiti security services arrested 13 individuals and recovered a large quantity of explosives and weapons. The cell reportedly was planning to attack Kuwaiti officials and U.S. targets in Kuwait. 00119901

November 2, 2000. *Indonesia.* The U.S. Embassy extended its closure until early the following week because of an unspecified threat and counseled Americans in the country to be cautious.

November 4, 2000. *Greece.* Christos Kendiras, 48, a car mechanic from Galata, hijacked a busload of elderly Japanese tourists on an Athens–Corinth highway after killing his mother-in-law and an estranged friend, Stamatis Taktikos, whom he suspected of having an affair with his wife. He had forced the bus to stop by setting his car on fire. Carrying a pistol, a container filled with gasoline, and a shotgun (some reports said rifle), he ordered the driver to head for Athens. He warned police by cell phone that interference would lead him to shoot the passengers, who included 33 Japanese tourists visiting archaeological sites on the Peloponnesian Peninsula. Two dozen police vehicles and helicopters escorted the bus, and highway traffic was shut down. When a motorcycle policeman got too close, Kendiras fired his pistol, shattering the windshield; glass shards hit the bus driver in the face. Kendiras, who threatened to commit suicide, forced the driver to change direction several times, then said that he wanted to talk to television personality Makis Triandafyllopoulos, who often handles sociopathic matters. He called the television host on his cell phone, saying that he wanted to "get rid" of his 77-year-old mother-in-law because she was scheduled for an expensive heart operation to be covered by state health insurance. He said, "I just want the Greek people to know that I saved them a million and a half drachmas" ($3,800). Kendiras agreed to turn himself over to the police when the bus arrived near the private television studio near Athens. He dropped his weapons and bowed to the hostages, ending the ten-hour crisis. The hostages applauded. The next day, Kendiras committed suicide

when he broke away from four officers and threw himself through a window after his handcuffs were removed so that his fingerprints could be taken.

November 8, 2000. *Japan.* Police arrested Fusako Shigenobu, 55, founder of the Japanese Red Army (JRA), after she had spent more than 25 years underground. She was picked up as she left an Osaka hotel with two companions. She yelled, "I'll fight on," as she arrived in Tokyo under heavy guard. However, on April 14, 2001, a supporter quoted her as saying in a letter to Tokyo followers that "I will disband the Japanese Red Army and launch new fights." She was charged with taking hostages in a 1974 attack on France's embassy in The Hague. Her husband died in a 1974 JRA attack at Lod Airport in Tel Aviv that killed 24 people.

November 9, 2000. *Kuwait.* Police arrested three Kuwaitis on charges of domestic and foreign terrorist attacks. Two days later, the Interior Ministry announced the recovery of 293 pounds of high explosives that the trio and an at-large North African had planned to use in an attack on Camp Doha, a U.S. Army camp 14 miles north of Kuwait City, and on the homes and cars of Western military personnel.

On November 11, the Kuwaitis picked up two more Kuwaiti suspects at an international express mail office after they took delivery of forged passports. Another suspect was detained in Qatar for extradition to Kuwait. 00110901

November 11, 2000. *Russia.* The press reported that four Chechen hijackers seized a Dagestan Airlines (other reports said Ynukovo Airlines) Tu-154 with 58 people on board after it left Makhachkala for Moscow, and demanded that it stop in Baku, Azerbaijan, for refueling before landing in Israel. The hijackers said it was a gesture of support for the Palestinian uprising. The hijackers called the attack Operation al-Aqsa and threatened to blow up the plane. They also demanded a news conference. Israel initially refused landing at the hijackers' first choice of Ben-Gurion International

Airport near Tel Aviv, but later allowed the plane to land at the Uvda military airfield in the southern Negev desert. The plane was accompanied over the Mediterranean by an Israeli Air Force jet. Prime Minister Ehud Barak postponed a trip to Washington to deal with the crisis.

The incident ended on November 12 when Amarchenov Avmerchan, a Dagestani in his late 20s or early 30s with a fake bomb strapped to his body, surrendered soon after landing. He had said nothing about Palestinians. He had disarmed crew members and possibly a security agent who were carrying pistols. The "bomb" was an instrument for measuring blood pressure, covered by a bandage. He said he had been sent by his father to transmit a message "to the world and the emperor of Japan." The videotape and two letters "warned the world about the yellow race taking control of the white race," according to Major General Yom Tov Samia, chief of the Israeli Army's southern command. Israeli authorities denied Avmerchan's demand for a news conference and handed him over to the Russians for extradition to Moscow.

Among the passengers was Apti Bakayev, 11, a leukemia patient wearing a surgical mask. He was on his way to Moscow for treatment, accompanied by his mother, Tamara. 00111101

November 12, 2000. *Greece.* The far-left nationalist Revolutionary Nuclei mounted three nearly simultaneous attacks against a British bank, a U.S. bank, and the studio and home of the Greek sculptor whose statue of General George C. Marshall is displayed at the U.S. Embassy. 00111201-03

November 13, 2000. *Israel.* At 4:30 P.M., Palestinian gunmen driving a Fiat Uno in the West Bank near the Jewish settlement of Ofra fired automatic weapons on an army bus and a private car, killing three Israelis and wounding several others. The driver of the private car was wounded and his female companion was killed. The Uno moved on to a military bus, where the terrorists fired 50 rounds, killing two Israeli soldiers and wounding six. The car disappeared into Ramallah.

Three hours later, an Israeli truck driver was shot to death in a similar drive-by shooting in Gaza.

November 14, 2000. *Yemen.* Armed Gahm tribesmen kidnapped a Swedish employee of a local power station in Sanaa. He was released on November 30. 00111401

November 17, 2000. *Saudi Arabia.* At midday, a powerful bomb hidden under the driver's seat of a car killed Christopher Rodway, 48, a British technician who had worked for eight years as chief engineer in the VIP section of the Military Hospital in Riyadh. His wife Jane was slightly wounded. He was driving near a busy intersection in a popular commercial area of Riyadh. His leg was severed by the blast, and he died from loss of blood.

There was no immediate claim of responsibility. The Arab media had been broadcasting images of the Palestinian uprising against Israel. The bombing came on the eve of a 50-nation energy conference in Riyadh.

On November 19, British nationals were warned to take extra precautions.

On December 13, *al-Watan*, a Saudi paper, reported that Michael Sedlak, an American working for Vinell Corporation, a Fairfax, Virginia-based defense firm that works with the U.S. Army in Riyadh to train the Saudi National Guard, had been arrested on November 28 and questioned about the bombing. Sedlak had been in a low-level position with Vinell for eight years. A U.S. consular officer visited Sedlak on December 9. The State Department reported that "Mr. Sedlak has not been charged, nor has the embassy been informed of any charges against him." Deputy Interior Minister Prince Ahmed ibn Abdulaziz had claimed that the explosions were linked to a personal issue and were not politically motivated. On December 15, the Saudi Press Agency said Sedlak had not been firmly linked to the blast and that he was one of several suspects.

On February 4, 2001, Saudi television showed three men—Alexander Mitchell, a Briton; William Sampson, a Canadian; and Raf Skivens, a Belgian—taking responsibility for the car bombing that killed Rodway and for another that injured five on November 22 in Riyadh. Sampson and Mitchell claimed credit for the Rodway bombing. Mitchell said he was also involved with the other two in the second bombing that injured three Britons and an Irish woman. Mitchell was arrested in December for alcohol-related offenses. He said he carried out the first bombing on instructions. The trio implicated no one else in the remote-controlled bombings. Saudi Arabia's interior minister later said that Islamic law, which calls for the death penalty (beheading) for murder, would apply. By April 25, the Saudi government was saying that the Rodway murder was a gang-style killing over the black market for alcohol.

The Saudi interior minister said on February 18, 2001, that three Americans were being interrogated in connection with the two bombings. State Department officials said the three were arrested in January, possibly on suspicion of alcohol smuggling. 00111701

November 19, 2000. *Jordan.* Israeli Vice Consul Yoram Havivian was shot and wounded slightly by gunmen outside his home in Amman. The Movement for the Struggle of the Jordanian Islamic Resistance Movement (or Movement for the Struggle of the Jordanian Islamic Resistance) and the Ahmad al-Daqamisah Group (or Holy Warriors of Ahmad Daqamseh) claimed credit. Daqamseh, a Jordanian soldier, was serving a life sentence at this time for killing six Israeli school-girls in 1997. Havivian returned to Israel shortly after the attack. By year's end, Jordanian authorities had detained several suspects. 00111901

November 19, 2000. *Namibia.* The National Union for the Total Independence of Angola (UNITA) was suspected of kidnapping seven men and their cattle in Mahane village and moving them to Angola. Three men escaped. 00111902

November 20, 2000. *Israel.* A bomb made from a high-caliber mortar shell blasted shrapnel into a school bus carrying Israeli settler children and their teachers to classes near Kfar Darom settle-ment in Gaza in the morning, killing two adults—a 35-year-old female teacher and a 34-year-old man—and badly wounding ten others, including students. Three children from one family were wounded. A 12-year-old had his leg amputated. His seven- and ten-year-old siblings were each in critical condition with injuries to their legs and arms. The bomb was wrapped with metal and exploded a few yards from the armor-plated bus, opening fist-sized holes in the bus's sides. The Omar al-Mokhtar Wing, the Al-Aqsa Martyrs, and the Palestinian branch of Hizballah all claimed credit. Israel blamed the Palestinian Authority, which denied responsibility.

In retaliation, Israeli helicopter gunships fired 20 antitank missiles at the offices of Yasir Arafat's Palestinian Authority in Gaza City, injuring 20 Palestinians.

November 22, 2000. *Israel.* A car bomb exploded during rush hour in Hadera, blowing a busload of passengers into the air, killing two Israelis, and injuring more than 50 people, among them an Arab father and his one-year-old daughter, pedestrians, and shopkeepers in the commercial district on President Street. The bomb contained home-made explosives and was hidden inside a parked Mitsubishi sedan. It apparently was set off by remote control as the bus pulled alongside at 5:20 P.M. The blast shattered windows five floors up and destroyed shops and cars. At least ten people had moderate to severe injuries. Israel blamed Yasir Arafat.

November 22, 2000. *Saudi Arabia.* A bomb went off in a car, slightly injuring its British passengers—two men and one woman who were working in Saudi Arabia. An American was arrested and questioned about the bombing and the November 17 bombing. 00112201

November 24, 2000. *Cambodia/United States.* The anticommunist Cambodian Freedom Fighters (CFF), an anti-government group based in California, claimed credit for a midnight shootout at a police station and government buildings in

Phnom Penh. Between 3 and 6 attackers and 1 civilian died; another 12 were wounded. The 50 attackers were armed with AK-47 riles and rocket-propelled grenades. A Cambodian court charged the group's leader, Chhun Yasith, in absentia with terrorism and forming an illegal armed group. The court filed the same charges against 49 others and charged two other U.S. citizens in absentia. The U.S. government began an investigation into whether U.S. citizens or residents were involved. U.S. citizens who took part could be liable to prosecution under the Neutrality Act, which prohibits military expeditions against foreign states with which the United States is at peace.

The attack was to be the first phase of Operation Volcano, an attempt to overthrow the Cambodian government by targeting 291 locations. The plan was led by exiles in Long Beach, California.

On June 22, 2001, a Cambodian court sentenced five men, including three Americans of Cambodian descent, to life in prison for conspiracy to commit terrorism and belonging to an illegal armed group. The sentences were in response to the attack, which was designed to overthrow Hun Sen's government. Two of the Americans were tried in absentia. Another 25 people received sentences ranging from 3 to 20 years. Two defendants were acquitted. CFF leader Chhun Yasith, 43, a tax accountant from Long Beach, California, was also convicted of being the mastermind behind the violence. Thong Samien, 60, a Long Beach travel agent, was convicted of handling logistics for the attack. Richard Kiri Kim, 51, of Oregon, was the only American citizen in custody; he was accused of being a key planner of the attack. 00112401

November 27, 2000. *Sri Lanka.* Velupillai Prabhakaran, leader of the Liberation Tigers of Tamil Eelam (LTTE), said he was ready for unconditional peace talks with the government and offered a pre-talks cease-fire. "We propose a process of de-escalation of war leading to cessation of armed hostilities and the creation of a peaceful, cordial environment."

November 27, 2000. *Chile.* A bomb planted in front of the Colombian Embassy exploded, causing some property damage, but no injuries. No one claimed credit. 00112701

November 30, 2000. *Colombia.* Police near Barrancabermeja defused two bombs a few hours before the visit of Senator Paul D. Wellstone and U.S. Ambassador Anne W. Patterson. A man belonging to the National Liberation Army (ELN) was arrested at the scene, although U.S. and Colombian officials said there was no evidence that the U.S. visitors were the targets. The two shrapnel-filled bombs were discovered near the route from the airport. They were rigged to a detonator.

December 2000. *Saudi Arabia.* A Scotsman was blinded in one eye in a bombing in Khobar. 00129901

December 5, 2000. *Jordan.* Shlomo Ratsabi, an Israeli Embassy employee, was shot in the leg when his car was ambushed in Amman at 7:00 P.M. as he, his wife, and their bodyguard drove off from an Amman supermarket. At least two bullets hit the car, which had Jordanian license plates. He was taken to a hospital for treatment of his fractured left ankle and was reported in stable condition. He returned to Israel soon after. The Movement for the Struggle of the Jordanian Islamic Resistance and the Holy Warriors of Ahmad Daqamseh claimed credit. By year's end, Jordanian authorities had detained several suspects. 00120501

December 5, 2000. *Burundi.* Small-arms fire hit a Sabena airliner landing in Bujumbura, injuring a Belgian stewardess and a Tunisian passenger. The plane was on a routine flight from Brussels. No one claimed credit. 00120502

December 6, 2000. *Indonesia.* More than a dozen men, who appeared to be out-of-uniform soldiers, in three vehicles surrounded an aid workers' vehicle and forced Nazaruddin Abdul Gani, 22, and his three fellow passengers—Idriss Yusuf, 27, Ernita binti Wahab, 23, and Bakhtiar, 24—out of their car at gunpoint near Matang Baru in Aceh Province. The group told the soldiers that they were not separatist rebels, but humanitarian aid workers funded by the Danish government helping to counsel torture victims. They showed their written authorization to travel freely in the area. The assailants replied that the group was "trying to give the rebels spirit to fight against us" and threatened to kill every aid worker. The group was taken to a military command post past two army checkpoints, then driven into a forest. Four hours later, Gani's three colleagues and another man were shot execution-style after being stripped, interrogated, and beaten by two assailants, a government informant and an out-of-uniform soldier. Gani escaped seconds before he was to be executed. He speculated that his abductors were plainclothes soldiers. A family that witnessed the abduction was still missing. 00120601

December 8, 2000. *Sudan.* Abbas Baqer Abbas walked up to the al-Sunna al-Mohammediyya Mosque in Garaffa (a suburb of Omdurman, the country's twin capital) during the evening prayers and fired an automatic rifle through its window, killing 20 and wounding 40, including a policeman. Police shot Abbas to death when he refused to surrender. He was a member of a rival militant Islamic group Takfir wal Hijra (Repentance and Flight) from the central region of el-Gezira. He had belonged to the mosque but left over religious differences and had made violent threats against members of his erstwhile group.

December 9, 2000. *Russia.* A car bomb exploded near a mosque in a village in Chechnya, killing 16 civilians and wounding 20.

December 11, 2000. *United States.* The Clinton administration dropped efforts to deport nine Irish Republican Army (IRA) members whose convictions for paramilitary actions should have barred them from entry to the United States. Clinton announced, "While in no way approving or condoning their past criminal acts, I believe that removing the threat of deportation for these individuals will contribute to the peace process in Northern Ireland." Clinton then left for Ireland and Northern Ireland. All nine had finished sentences in the United Kingdom ranging from 3 to 14 years for crimes including murder and attempted murder, bombing, and weapons offenses before they came to the United States. They illegally concealed those convictions to gain entry to the United States.

December 12, 2000. *United States.* American Airlines Flight 8, flying from Honolulu to Dallas, made an emergency landing in Los Angeles at 1:18 A.M. after Paul Gordon, 46, of Texas became claustrophobic and pulled a pocketknife on crew members at 1:00 A.M. He said he did not like the number of people around him, then threatened people. As the jet taxied to the gate, Gordon opened a hatch and stood in the doorway with the two-inch pocketknife in his hand. Police entered the plane and tackled Gordon when he threatened to jump from the doorway. He was held at a local hospital for mental evaluation. No injuries were reported. Upon landing, the plane's 190 passengers were placed on another flight and arrived in Dallas at 6:45 A.M. Gordon faced 20 years to life for interfering with the flight using a lethal weapon.

December 12, 2000. *Ecuador.* A terrorist bomb exploded on the country's only crude oil pipeline, engulfing a passing bus in flame, killing 5 passengers and injuring 19.

December 13, 2000. *Namibia.* The National Union for the Total Independence of Angola (UNITA) was suspected when a landmine placed near a residence in Shighuru exploded, injuring the owner. 00121301

December 16, 2000. *Algeria.* Rebels machine-gunned to death 15 teenage students and a teacher as they slept in their beds at the Lycée Technique boarding school of Media, 55 miles south of

Algiers. Another six boys, aged 17 to 19, were injured as they dived under their beds during the ten-minute raid. Islamic extremists were blamed.

December 17, 2000. *Israel.* A car belonging to the *Washington Post* and another car owned by the *Post*'s Jerusalem correspondent were doused with gasoline and set on fire at the front gate of the paper's Jerusalem bureau during the evening, causing heavy damage, but no injuries. Police said the fires were the work of at least one arsonist. The cars were parked within several feet of a metal plaque identifying the building as the *Post*'s bureau (the bureau is also the correspondent's residence). The *Post* car was marked with "TV" in large block letters using bright orange tape. 00121701

December 18, 2000. *Italy.* A worker at Milan's Duomo Cathedral found a time bomb near a gargoyle on a popular rooftop terrace 15 hours before the bomb was set to explode.

December 22, 2000. *Israel.* A suicide bomber walked into a roadside restaurant near the Jewish settlement of Mehola in the Jordan River Valley. The Palestinian man detonated an explosives belt, injuring three Israeli soldiers, two severely. The attack came on the last Friday of Ramadan.

December 22, 2000. *India.* Two gunmen fired at the Red Fort in New Delhi, killing a soldier and two civilians before escaping. The Pakistan-based Lashkar-e-Tayyiba claimed credit. The group opposes Indian rule of the Himalayan region. The 17th-century fort was built by the Mughal Emperor Shah Jahan. Part of it is open to tourists during the day; the rest is the garrison of a battalion of 1,000 soldiers.

December 22, 2000. *Algeria.* Some 25 Muslim extremists broke into a disco in Berrahal, 250 miles east of Algiers, and slashed the throat of a 23-year-old female pop singer. They dragged off two members of her band. Thirteen people were injured; some were shot and others received cuts as

they jumped through windows to escape the attackers.

Rebels killed another 11 people in other attacks, bringing the Ramadan monthly death toll to more than 240.

December 23, 2000. *Colombia.* The National Liberation Army (ELN) released 42 police officers and soldiers during the afternoon in the remote Catatumbo region near the Venezuelan border. The hostages had been held for two years. A Red Cross helicopter flew them to Bucaramanga, where they were given medical and psychiatric attention. The release followed a fortnight of negotiations in Havana that were attended by ELN leaders, Colombian Peace Commissioner Camilo Gomez, Cuban President Fidel Castro, and President Castro's brother Raul. The ELN did not renounce kidnapping and continued to hold 700 Colombians hostage. Antonio Garcia, the ELN's deputy chief, said this was a "gesture in which we hope to put the peace process on track." The ELN did not seek anything in return and promised to release six other police officers and soldiers soon. Some 2,500 people remained hostages of various rebel groups and other criminals.

December 24, 2000. *Indonesia.* Muslims attacked Christians throughout the country. At least 18 people were killed and 84 injured.

In Jakarta, bombs went off at five Catholic and Protestant churches within an hour and a radius of one mile. Three people were killed. An unexploded bomb was found near the city cathedral as Christians were arriving for midnight mass.

Four bombs went off outside a church in Menteng. Other churches were evacuated after receiving threats.

A man died when a bomb went off at a bus stop outside a church and an adjacent Christian school in eastern Jakarta.

In Pekanbaru on Sumatra Island, a bomb went off when policemen tried to disarm it. A civilian also died.

Bombs went off outside churches in Medan on Sumatra.

A bomb went off at a Christian-owned house in Bandung on Java, killing two.

On Batam Island, three bombs injured 22 people.

Three churches were bombed in Mojokerto in East Java.

Three churches were bombed in Mataram on the tourist island of Lombok.

On January 6, 2001, bombing suspect Dedi Mulyadi said that he and two accomplices learned bombing techniques at an Afghan camp in the early 1990s.

December 25, 2000. *Senegal.* A landmine killed five civilians in the tourist province of Casamance. The government and separatist rebels had begun peace talks nine days earlier.

December 25, 2000. *Sri Lanka.* The Liberation Tigers of Tamil Eelam (LTTE) promised to abide by their month-long cease-fire even though the government had rejected it. The Tamil rebels called for international pressure to get Colombo to negotiate. The government had begun a new offensive on December 22 that led to 167 deaths. However, soldiers abided by a 24-hour Christmas truce.

December 25, 2000. *India.* A Jamiat ul-Mujaheddin car bomb killed 8, including 4 Indian soldiers, and wounded 20, including 7 soldiers, near Srinagar.

December 25, 2000. *Pakistan.* More than 40 were wounded in three bomb blasts in various cities.

December 25, 2000. *Greece.* A bomb exploded at a Citibank ATM in Athens, causing major damage to the exterior ATM and the bank interior. The Anarchists Attack Team said it was showing support for the dead prisoners in Turkey. 00122501

December 28, 2000. *Philippines.* Police arrested a member of Abu Sayyaf who was armed with several grenades and sketches of potential targets in Manila.

December 29, 2000. *Pakistan.* A bomb exploded in a Karachi market, killing a child and injuring ten.

December 29, 2000. *Belarus.* Firebombs were thrown at a synagogue in Minsk, but a security guard put out the flames.

December 29, 2000. *Burundi.* Rebels killed 21 people, including a British woman, by firing on a tourist bus and two other vehicles on the country's main road; they then executed the bus passengers. 00122901

December 29, 2000. *Colombia.* Gunmen ambushed the vehicle of Representative Diego Turbay, 40 (or 47), on a jungle road in Caqueta State in southern Colombia. After forcing the group to get out of the vehicle, the gunmen punctured the tires. The attackers forced the passengers to lie on the road, then shot in the head Turbay, his mother, his brother-in-law, and four others. The media reported that one of the victims was a Colombian journalist traveling with the party.

Turbay, a member of the opposition Liberal Party, was president of the peace committee of the Chamber of Representatives and a relative of former President Julio Cesar Turbay Ayala, who led Colombia from 1978 to 1982. Turbay was traveling to the inauguration of a mayor when his armored car was stopped at a crossroads between the city of Florencia and the jungle safe haven of the Revolutionary Armed Forces of Colombia (FARC).

President Andres Pastrana said there was evidence of FARC complicity, putting the peace process at risk. FARC had suspended negotiations in November. Right-wing paramilitary groups also operated in the area and had tried earlier in the month to assassinate a labor leader who was working with the government on a peace deal with another leftist rebel group.